CHURCHILL AND DE GAULLE

CHURCHILL
AND
DE GAULLE

FRANÇOIS KERSAUDY

ATHENEUM

New York

1982

Library of Congress Cataloging in Publication Data

Kersaudy, François, ———
    Churchill and De Gaulle.

    Bibliography: p.
    Includes index.
    1. World War, 1939-1945—Diplomatic history.
2. Churchill, Winston, Sir, 1874-1965. 3. Gaulle,
Charles de, 1890-1970. 4. Great Britain—Foreign
relations—France. 5. France—Foreign relations—
Great Britain. 6. Prime ministers—Great Britain—
Biography. 7. France—Presidents—Biography.
I. Title.
D750.K47   1982   940.53′22′41   81-69154
ISBN 0-689-11265-3   AACR2

To the Warden, the former Warden,
the Fellows and students of
Keble College, Oxford

Contents

Illustrations

Acknowledgements

Curious though it may seem, no book has ever been written on the relations between Winston Churchill and Charles de Gaulle. The present book would not have been written either but for the extremely generous moral and material support afforded during the last three years by the Franco-British Council and by some of its leading members on both sides of the Channel, first and foremost Messrs G. M. E. Paulson and James Hadley in Britain, Geoffrey de Courcel and Philippe Daudy in France. I am also much indebted to the Franco-American Commission, the North Atlantic Treaty Organization, the Fulbright Foundation and the British Academy for sponsoring my numerous research trips to the United States, Britain, Norway and the Netherlands.

Many eye-witnesses of the events described in this book have helped me with their recollections, and I owe a particular debt of gratitude to the late Earl Mountbatten of Burma, to Lady Diana Cooper, Sir John Colville, General Billotte, and Messrs René Massigli, Maurice Dejean, Gaston Palewski, Jacques Vendroux and Pierre Olivier Lapie. I should also like to thank Brigadier Douglas Henchley and Dr Malcolm Parks of Keble College, Oxford, for their wise and competent advice, Colonel Aylmer for some precious help in tracking down information on Middle East Affairs and on a certain flight from Bordeaux to London, and Mr Archibald Maclachlan for expert information on the finer points of Scottish terminology. For some invaluable technical assistance during the last three years, I am much indebted to Professor Ole Kristian Grimnes and to his whole family, as well as to Doctor Cesar H. Nuevo of Trinity College, Oxford, and Professors Peter and Natacha Squire of Cambridge University.

Grateful acknowledgement is made to Her Majesty's Stationery Office for permission to reproduce extracts from documents in the

Public Record Office. Other acknowledgements for permission to quote from printed material are made as they occur.

I wish to express my gratitude to the keepers and employees of the twenty archives mentioned on page 466 for their competent assistance and unfailing courtesy. This gratitude extends to the Institut Charles de Gaulle, which has been extremely helpful at all times, to the *Service d'Informations et de Relations Publiques des Armées*, and to the administration and personnel of that extraordinarily precious French library that is forever tottering on the brink of bankruptcy; many readers will have recognized the *Bibliothèque de Documentation Internationale Contemporaine* in Nanterre.

Grateful acknowledgment is made to Cassell and Co. and Houghton-Mifflin for permission to quote from W. S. Churchill, *The Second World War*, vol. 1 to 6, and A. Eden, *The Reckoning*, vol. 3; to Cassell and Co. for permission to quote from *The Diaries of Sir Alexander Cadogan,* edited by David Dilks; to Granada Publishers Ltd for permission to quote from Duff Cooper, *Old men Forget*; to Eyre-Methuen for permission to quote from E. L. Spears, *Two Men Who Saved France*; to Leo Cooper Ltd for permission to quote from E. L. Spears, *Fulfilment of a Mission*; to Cassell and Co. and McClelland and Stewart Ltd, Toronto, for permission to quote from W. S. Churchill, *Complete Speeches*, vol. 4 to 7; to W. Heinemann for permission to quote from M. Gilbert, *Winston Churchill*, vol. 3 to 5.

Last but not least, I am deeply grateful to Mr John Grigg and to Mr Richard Ollard of William Collins and Co., both of whom contributed countless highly relevant remarks and suggestions. It goes without saying that all remaining defects and errors are my sole responsibility; any reader who could point out such errors or contribute additional information on the subject is assured in advance of the author's gratitude.

F. KERSAUDY

Introduction

It was an uncommon man who became His Majesty's First Lord of the Admiralty in October 1911; his illustrious ancestry and his father's short but brilliant political career were well known in Britain at the time, as was the fact that he had fought with great distinction as a young officer in India, the Sudan and South Africa, that he was a brilliant speaker and a talented writer, and that he had already spent an eventful decade in politics as Conservative, then Liberal Member of Parliament, Colonial Under-Secretary, President of the Board of Trade and Home Secretary. But those who knew Winston Spencer Churchill and had worked with him during these early years were aware that he combined, to a high degree, rare and valuable qualities: boundless drive and energy, a high degree of moral and physical courage, an outstanding memory coupled with amazing inventiveness, a genuine devotion to King and Country, and finally a fascination with momentous events, together with the ardent desire to play a role in them. By 1911, with the growth of tension in Europe, it was clear that such events were impending, and that the new First Lord of the Admiralty would indeed have a role to play in them.

Once in Whitehall, Winston Churchill lost no time in preparing the navy for the approaching European conflict. Although he continued to hope until the last moment that war could be averted, he acted with characteristic forcefulness and obvious relish once he recognized it to be inevitable. By 28 July 1914, without awaiting the Cabinet's decision, he ordered the First Fleet to take its war stations in the North Sea. Five days later, Britain was at war, and the members of His Majesty's government were astonished at the impulsiveness and imagination displayed by Churchill in discharging his duties – and those of others as well. In fact, he was to keep on fighting until the very end of the war, and even on into peace. By October 1914, the First Lord of the Admiralty had already taken charge of the air defence of Britain, sent three squadrons of the naval air service, armoured cars and an artillery battalion to France, crossed the Channel half a dozen times to inspect fortifications and boost the morale of the troops, and even landed in besieged Antwerp, from where he sent the Prime Minister a telegram offering to resign his office and take command of the forces assigned to the defence of the Belgian port.

Back in London, Winston Churchill redoubled his efforts to infuse an offensive spirit into the general strategy; any plan, action, device or invention that could lead to success in the field was immediately seized upon and pushed through with the utmost vigour by the First Lord, for whom the defeat of the Germans had become the one and only preoccupation. In November 1914, he was supervising air raids by naval aviators on the Zeppelin sheds of Friedrichshafen; a few weeks earlier, he had asked for the construction of 'trench spawning cars', which by January 1915 had become 'steam tractors with small armoured shelters and equipped with caterpillars'[1]; these early tanks were soon to be developed at the Admiralty under his personal supervision. In the meantime, Churchill had also pressed for an attack on the German island of Borkum, a plan which he soon cast aside in favour of an even more daring project: the forcing of the Dardanelles, in which he saw the long-sought means of shortening a war that had bogged down in the mud and trenches of northern France. But the naval attacks in the narrows of the Dardanelles, then the landing operations on the Gallipoli peninsula failed one after the other, largely as a result of insufficient means and a lack of drive on the spot. Winston Churchill was blamed for this failure and forced to resign from the Admiralty.

Given a sinecure, the Chancellorship of the Duchy of Lancaster, Churchill had nothing else to do after May 1915 than to appoint county magistrates; yet he could not be kept away from the prosecution of the war, and he was soon bombarding the Prime Minister, the War Office and his successor at the Admiralty with an endless stream of memoranda which called for the reinforcement of the eastern front, renewed attacks at the Dardanelles, the accelerated development of tanks, the formation of an independent air department, and even 'an immediate advance against Turkey and Bulgaria by an Anglo-French force reinforced by 150,000 Russians, armed by Britain with Japanese rifles'.[2]

When he learned that the Cabinet was about to abandon the

Dardanelles, Churchill resigned from the Duchy of Lancaster, and by November 1915, we find him at the front in France as a major with the Grenadier Guards. He was to stay six months in the muddy and shell-torn trenches of Flanders, and all those who were there with him seem to agree that Winston Churchill was fascinated by war and utterly unafraid of danger.[3] But by the spring of 1916, Major Churchill was back in the House of Commons to attack the government on their wasteful and irresolute war policy. Yet he had no support from political parties, no following in Parliament, and he was viciously attacked by the press. Hence fourteen more months were to pass before he was appointed Minister of Munitions in the Lloyd George government; there, his impressive capacities were again put to use. Not content with boosting the production of munitions and war equipment to unprecedented heights, organizing the mass production of tanks, constantly visiting the French battlefields and sending letters of guidance to Lloyd George, the new Minister of Munitions was once again devising bold strategic plans to capture the initiative and win the war.* There is no evidence that Churchill's numerous and occasionally misguided strategic schemes were taken at all seriously by his Cabinet colleagues, but his boundless energy and drive were clearly an asset to the Lloyd George government until the very end of the war.

After the return to peace, Churchill became Secretary of State for War and Air, and, from this post, he directed Britain's intervention against the Russian Bolsheviks. After having served three years as Colonial Secretary, Churchill rejoined the Conservative ranks in 1924, and became a somewhat less than successful Chancellor of the Exchequer. After 1929, however, he found himself in opposition to his party over the India Bill, and in 1931 he resigned from the Conservative Shadow Cabinet. From then on, and until the end of the thirties, Churchill was to be a solitary figure on the British political scene. However, the turn of events in Europe soon provided him with a cause to defend – a cause that appealed strongly to his vast imagination and intense patriotism: it was no less than the preservation of England, and indeed of Western civilization, from the dark and mortal peril of German Nazism.

Much sooner than most of his compatriots, Churchill had realized

---

*Among these was yet another scheme for the capture of the Frisian islands of Borkum and Sylt.

the dangers of the disarmament policy pursued by Ramsay
MacDonald's Labour government at a time when totalitarian
ideologies were progressing all over Europe. Ramsay MacDonald
having announced in the Commons on 29 June 1931 that he would
seek an 'all round' reduction of armaments in Europe, and then
make 'still further reductions', Winston Churchill immediately
replied that Britain had so disarmed already that she was now
'extremely vulnerable', with an army 'cut to the bone' which was no
more than 'a glorified police force', and an air force only an eighth as
strong as that of France.[4]

Churchill's attacks on MacDonald's pacifist policies naturally
became more virulent as Hitler rose to power and the danger to
Europe increased correspondingly. He declared on 23 March 1933
that MacDonald's four years of control over British foreign policy
had brought England nearer to war and made her 'weaker, poorer
and more defenceless'; as for the Disarmament Conference in
Geneva, Churchill asserted that it had become 'a solemn and
prolonged farce'.[5] The same year, answering Sir John Simon's call
for 'international agreement on disarmament', Churchill warned
that Britain had already disarmed 'to the verge of risk – nay, well
into the gulf of risk'.[6] In July 1934, he commented sarcastically:
'There has been during these recent years a steady deterioration in
the relations between different countries, a steady growth of ill-will,
a steady, indeed a rapid increase in armaments that has gone on . . .
in spite of the endless flow of oratory, of perorations, of well
meaning sentiments, of banquets that has marked this epoch.'[7]

From then on, Churchill was to call ceaselessly on the government
to strengthen Britain's defences, to double and redouble the air
force, set up a ministry of defence and a ministry of supply,
reorganize the industry for conversion to war purposes, modernize
the fleet, strengthen British alliances on the Continent and support
the League of Nations. In countless speeches and articles, he
denounced the purges and racial persecutions in Germany, the
beginning of German rearmament, the remilitarization of the
Rhineland, the annexation of Austria, the invasion of Czechoslovakia and the threat to Poland. In even more numerous articles and
speeches, he showed that Germany was rearming at breakneck
speed, and he warned in 1934 that the German air force was already
two thirds as strong as the British air force, in 1935 that parity had
been reached, in 1936 that the German air force was 50 per cent

stronger, and in 1938 that it was twice as strong. With a powerful blend of eloquence, persuasion, irony and sarcasm, Churchill relentlessly took the government to task for the slowness of its rearmament effort, and repeatedly appealed to Parliament and public opinion. At a debate on defence in November 1936, he declared in the House of Commons:

> The First Lord of the Admiralty in his speech the other night . . . said, 'We are always reviewing the position.' Everything, he assured us, is entirely fluid. I am sure that that is true. Anyone can see what the position is. The government simply cannot make up their mind, or they cannot get the Prime Minister to make up his mind. So they go on in strange paradox, decided only to be undecided, resolved to be irresolute, adamant for drift, solid for fluidity, all powerful to be impotent. So we go on preparing more months and years – precious, perhaps vital, to the greatness of Britain – for the locusts to eat.[8]

But it was all in vain; Ramsay MacDonald was strongly influenced by pacifist sentiment, Stanley Baldwin feared that rearmament would weaken the Conservative Party's electoral position, and Neville Chamberlain was convinced that he could avoid war by reaching an agreement with the dictators. Thus, the three successive Prime Ministers managed to weather all attacks by denying past mistakes and present negligence, dismissing Churchill's armament figures as distorted, his warnings as alarmist, his exhortations as sabre-rattling, his speeches as hollow eloquence and his personality as brilliant but erratic. As a result, Churchill was effectively kept out of government, while remaining in Parliament a solitary figure whose eloquent diatribes were followed with a mixture of admiration, amusement and indifference by his fellow MPs and by a public opinion that still failed to realize the gravity of the hour. As Philip Guedalla later noted: 'Mr Churchill's recurring intimations of the wrath to come were as familiar as the voice of the Muezzin announcing the hour of prayer.'[9]

However trying these ten years of political wilderness must have been for Churchill – and in Major Morton's words, 'He was exactly like a child whose toy is broken'[10] – it is a fact that Churchill's wilderness was more inhabited than most. For one thing, he was driven on by the conviction that he was correctly analysing the present and anticipating the future. As early as 1921, after all, he had warned against 'the frightful rancour and fear and hatred which exist between France and Germany at the present time and which, if left unchecked, will most certainly in a generation or so bring about a renewal of the struggle of which we have just witnessed the conclusion'.[11] And eleven years later, in 1932: 'All these bands of sturdy Teutonic youths, marching through the streets and roads of Germany, with the light of desire in their eyes to suffer for their Fatherland, are not looking for status. They are looking for weapons, and, when they have the weapons, believe me they will then ask for the return of lost territories and lost colonies, and when that demand is made it cannot fail to shake and possibly shatter to their foundations every one of the countries I have mentioned, and some other countries I have not mentioned.'[12]

Churchill was convinced that he understood Hitler's ultimate ambitions, and just as in 1915, he had no doubt that he could mobilize and lead the forces of the nation more successfully through the impending conflict than any other man in England. Indeed, he was not alone in this conviction, and as time went by, more and more individuals began to contact this apparently solitary figure. The first among them was probably Major Desmond Morton, whom Churchill had known during the First World War. In the thirties, Major Morton was working at the Industrial Intelligence Centre, an organ set up to keep a close watch on German industrial development, and he began to supply Churchill with facts and figures on German rearmament which Churchill used to good effect when denouncing the slowness of British rearmament.[13] By 1935, more men were coming forth and volunteering information; among them was Ralph Wigram, who was to supply Churchill with all the data on German aeroplane production available at the Foreign Office – data which the government itself refused to take seriously. A few months later, the First Sea Lord, Admiral Chatfield, wrote to Churchill the first of many letters on the navy's needs and problems: 'We have years of arrears to overtake,' Chatfield wrote, 'anti-aircraft guns and anti-aircraft ships cannot be immediately produced by voting money and for the next three or four years we are bound to be undergoing horrible risks . . .'[14] In May 1936, the director of an RAF training school, Squadron Leader Tore Anderson, also began to provide Churchill with charts and information on the grave insufficiencies of personnel, training and equipment in the Royal Air Force. Only a few months later, it was Brigadier Hobart, inspector of the Royal Tank Corps, who asked to speak to Churchill on important and confidential matters.

Other officers informed Churchill more openly, seeking to enlist his support and make use of his capacities; among them was the new Secretary of State for Air, Sir Philip Cunliffe-Lister, who asked Stanley Baldwin in July 1935 if Churchill could join the air defence research sub-committee.[15] Baldwin agreed, and Churchill was associated with the committee's work, which brought him much useful information on air defence – and on the dilatory way such committees worked. During the following years, other high officials sought to placate him by demonstrating that the rearmament was proceeding satisfactorily; the Chief of the Imperial General Staff thus sent Churchill a memorandum on the tank programme, the Minister for the Co-ordination of Defence invited him to visit the Austin Shadow factory, and the Secretary of State for Air offered to show him the new radar station.[16] Churchill was always interested, but saw many flaws; he complained that no medium tank was in production, and that the factories and radar stations were not properly protected from the threat of bombing. In the process, however, he certainly amassed a vast amount of knowledge on his country's resources and defences.

The third reason why Churchill was not exactly a solitary figure in his wilderness is that his opponents, and even the successive Prime Ministers who effectively kept him away from government, knew his worth and acted accordingly. Thus, in 1929, Major Desmond Morton, whom Churchill had asked for secret information, went to see Ramsay MacDonald and asked him what he should do. 'Tell him whatever he wants to know, keep him informed,' the Prime Minister had replied. He put this permission in writing, and all through the years, it was endorsed by his successors Baldwin and Chamberlain.[17] Considering that the information in question was often used by Churchill to denounce the flaws in their administration, it must have cost them dearly; yet the permission was never rescinded, and for a simple reason: all three Prime Ministers knew the man, and his value in the event of war. In November 1935, Stanley Baldwin wrote to a friend: 'If there is going to be a war – and no one can say that there is not – we must keep him fresh to be our war Prime Minister.'[18] Even Chamberlain, who referred to Churchill as 'a d——d uncomfortable bedfellow'[19] and accordingly did his level best to keep him away from government, had no doubt that war would bring Churchill back to the fore; 'The nearer we get to war,' he wrote in the summer of 1939, 'the more his chances improve, and vice versa.'[20]

The only hitch was that until very late in the day – almost too late in fact – Chamberlain believed that war could be avoided. He even told his friends that 'Winston Churchill's nomination to the Cabinet would be a message of open warfare to Berlin'.[21] And so it was that by the summer of 1939, Winston Churchill, now 65, was left to gaze with alarm and fascination at the direct and mortal peril that threatened the peace of Europe. In the course of thirty-five years, he had acquired a more varied experience of government than any Prime Minister in British history. For ten years, unsupported by any political party, he had tried to save his country from the very situation that was now developing. For thirty years, he had known the exact state of Britain's defences, and he remained convinced that he had the energy, the drive and the imagination to galvanize them. But he was still out of office.

In October 1912, a 22-year-old second-lieutenant graduated from the French military academy of Saint-Cyr. According to one of his instructors, he was 'average in everything, except height'.[22] This was at best an unperceptive comment, for there was nothing average about Charles-André-Joseph-Marie de Gaulle. Both his fellow graduates and his less prejudiced instructors had noted with amazement that the aloof and towering young man had a vast historical culture, a phenomenal memory, and a passion for the military career. In addition, his father, the austere and erudite Henri de Gaulle, had bequeathed him 'a certain idea of France' which was a blend of respect, awe and devotion to the past glories and the present interests of the French motherland. 'I did not doubt,' Charles de Gaulle later wrote, 'that France would have to go through gigantic trials, that the interest of life consisted in one day rendering her some signal service and that I would have the occasion to do so.'[23]

In 1913, Second-Lieutenant de Gaulle joined the 33rd Infantry Regiment stationed at Arras and commanded by Colonel Philippe Pétain, then an obscure officer with somewhat heretic views on strategy.* When the First World War broke out on 2 August 1914,

---

*In France, before the First World War, the reigning military doctrine considered the offensive role of the infantry as the main and almost the only factor in military strategy. Colonel Pétain, on the other hand, emphasized the vital role of prepared positions and massive artillery cover in any strategic initiative.

de Gaulle had been promoted to the rank of lieutenant and was serving with the 1st Battalion of the 33rd Infantry Regiment.

On the bloody battlefields of the Meuse, in the dismal trenches of the Champagne front, among the flattened ruins of Verdun, Lieutenant, then Captain de Gaulle fought with exceptional bravery and was wounded three times. The third time, at Douaumont on 2 March 1916, he was severely injured while leading his company in a bayonet charge, and was reported killed in action. The now illustrious General Pétain thereupon awarded him a posthumous cross of the *Légion d'Honneur*, together with a glowing citation.* But Captain de Gaulle was not dead; he had been captured by the enemy, and ended the war a prisoner in Germany.

During his imprisonment at Friedberg, then at Ingolstadt, de Gaulle did not remain inactive; in between his many unsuccessful attempts to escape, he followed the progress of the war with great attention, and lectured extensively to his fellow prisoners on military strategy and the latest developments in the war. One of these particularly aroused his interest: the advent and initial employment of the tank, on which de Gaulle seems to have meditated for a long time during his months of enforced leisure.**

The armistice of November 1918 put an end to the young captain's involuntary exile. In May 1919, he went to Poland where he fought with the Polish army against the Soviets, then became a lecturer in infantry tactics at the Rembertow officer school near Warsaw. By the end of 1921, however, he was called back to France by the Ministry of War to serve as assistant lecturer in military history at the Saint-Cyr Military Academy. In 1922, de Gaulle also became a student at the prestigious *Ecole supérieure de Guerre* in Paris, where he was to prove a brilliant but controversial figure; for the teaching of the school was exclusively inspired by the lessons of the First World War: a battle ought to be fought on prepared positions, with massive artillery support and an almost exclusively defensive strategy. De Gaulle, on the other hand, made no secret of

*'Captain de Gaulle, company commander, reputed for his high intellectual and moral character; as his battalion, undergoing a frightful bombardment, was decimated and the enemies had surrounded the company, led his men in a furious charge and fierce hand to hand fighting, the only solution he considered compatible with his sentiment of military honour. A peerless officer in all respects.'[24]

**Among the other prisoners there at the time was the future Soviet army Marshal Tukhachevsky, and Major Catroux, whom we shall meet more than once during this narrative.

the fact that he rejected the concept of prepared positions and had no faith in defensive strategy – which made him less than popular with the traditionally minded officers of the *Ecole de Guerre*. As a result, and even though he graduated with high marks in 1924, de Gaulle was sent far from Paris, to the General Staff of the Rhine army.

But the unconventional young captain had a powerful and illustrious protector: Marshal Philippe Pétain, the victor of Verdun and saviour of the French army. Ever since 1913, Pétain greatly admired the uncommon capacities of Charles de Gaulle, whose present struggle against the outdated military concepts of the *Ecole de Guerre* no doubt reminded him of his own solitary crusade against the perilous military doctrines of the pre-war period. In fact, during the next few years, the ill-will of Captain de Gaulle's superiors was largely offset by the support of the all-powerful Marshal.

For a start, de Gaulle was recalled from Mayence in the autumn of 1925, and appointed to the Cabinet of the Vice-President of the *Conseil Supérieur de la Guerre* – who was none other than Pétain himself.* The post was hardly a sinecure, but it gave de Gaulle a privileged position very near the centre of French military decision-making. Later on, after a period of command with the 19th Battalion of *Chasseurs* at Trier, and a two-year tour of duty in the Levant, Major de Gaulle was detailed to the secretariat of the *Conseil Supérieur de la Défense Nationale*, an organ created on the initiative of Marshal Pétain. He was to remain there for six years, and he later wrote in his memoirs:

> From 1932 to 1937, under fourteen governments, I found myself involved, in a planning capacity, in the whole range of political, technical and administrative activity concerning the country's defence. I was, in particular, to acquaint myself with the plans for security and for limitation of armaments presented by André Tardieu and Paul-Boncour at Geneva; to supply the Doumergue Cabinet with the elements for its decisions when it chose to adopt a different course after the Führer's accession to power; to weave the Penelope-web of the bill for the wartime organization of the country; and to go into the measures involved by the mobilization of the civil departments, of industry and of public services. The work I had to do, the deliberations which I witnessed, the contacts I had to establish, showed me the extent of our resources, but also the infirmity of the state.[25]

*Pétain was also Inspector General of the Army, and Chief of all French forces in the event of war.

From this privileged vantage-point, Lieutenant-Colonel de Gaulle was indeed to see a lot, and he was dissatisfied with what he saw: an almost total paralysis at government level, resulting from constitutional weakness and parliamentary intrigue; a heavy, bureaucratic, obsolescent military machine, whose doctrines, training and armament had varied very little since 1870, and not at all since 1918; and a General Staff that had complete faith in the power of the defensive and the strength of its fortifications. All this at a time when Hitler had assumed power in Germany, was making no secret of his determination to smash the Treaty of Versailles, and had accordingly embarked on a gigantic rearmament effort. It was therefore obvious that France was in a mortal peril unless she took the necessary steps to restore the balance in her favour. But how? After a long period of meditation and observation, de Gaulle eventually came up with a detailed answer; it was summarized in a short book published in May 1934, and entitled *Vers l'Armée de Métier*.[26]*

This was a remarkable book by any standards. Written in a very pure and classical style, it began by evoking the extreme vulnerability of France's north-eastern borders, which throughout the ages had allowed every invader to reach the heart of France by the shortest and most direct route: 'This breach in the rampart,' de Gaulle wrote, 'is the age-old weakness of the country . . . In this fatal passageway, we recently buried one-third of our young men . . . Is this poorly protected nation at least on her guard? Twenty centuries answer, No!'[27] The twentieth was no exception: fortifications alone could not ensure the protection of the nation, the system of mass recruitment in times of emergency was unsuited to modern times, and the duration of active service had steadily declined, from three years to one year in less than a decade. Crowning all this was the weakness of the institutions and the national tendency of Frenchmen to quarrel and divide. What, then, was the remedy?

'A professional army,' de Gaulle answered, 'an army of 100,000 men, young, skilled, devoted to their task' – and a fascinating task it was: to restore mobility and manoeuvrability to the French army, which had lost it in the trenches of the First World War. The instrument: six divisions of a new type, armoured, tracked, and fully mobile; each one with three brigades: a tank brigade to conquer the ground, a motorized infantry brigade to occupy it, an artillery brigade to support the two others. Each tank brigade would include five hundred heavy and medium tanks, together with a few light units for reconnaissance purposes. Altogether an élite formation, manned by professionals, with great mobility, devastating fire-power, and the ability to pierce any front in a surprise onslaught. Here then was the sword that could defend this vulnerable nation in time of conflict; France ought to grasp it without delay.*

Lieutenant-Colonel de Gaulle spared no effort to gain acceptance for his views. In this, he received much help from a few close friends, particularly Lieutenant-Colonel Emile Mayer, Colonel Lucien Nachin and a barrister named Jean Auburtin. He also gained a few allies among the deputies of the Left – including Marcel Déat, Philippe Serre, Léo Lagrange – and some support on the Right as well. He was helped by several newspapers, including from Right to Left *l'Echo de Paris, le Temps,* and *l'Ordre.* He also secured the active co-operation of Paul Reynaud, a highly influential politician and ex-Minister of Finance, who promised to defend his project in Parliament. Finally, this was a time when Marshal Pétain was Minister of War. With all this help, there was ground to believe that reason would prevail in the end.

It did not; Marshal Pétain was by then 78 years old, and no longer accessible to new ideas; besides, his sympathy for de Gaulle had cooled noticeably, and their relations were to worsen before long.* Paul Reynaud effectively defended de Gaulle's plan in the Chamber, and on 15 March 1935, he even introduced an amendment to the defence bill which provided for the creation of an armoured corps. But the Left rejected the professional army as the possible instrument of a Right-wing coup-d'état, the Right feared that it would be used by the extreme Left to crush the bourgeoisie, and the Centre considered that France could not afford the additional expense involved. As a result, the amendment was rejected out of hand and quickly forgotten.

But the most formidable obstacle to the acceptance of de Gaulle's

*There was nothing really new or revolutionary in de Gaulle's proposal; Colonel Estienne had made a very similar one in 1914, calling for the construction of 400 armoured vehicles at a time when the tank had not yet been developed. After the war, Generals Estienne and Doumenc in France, General Fuller and Captain Liddell Hart in Britain had perfected the doctrine of armoured warfare, and de Gaulle drew his inspiration from their work. So did the Germans.
**In 1938, when de Gaulle published *La France et son Armée*, the book was dedicated to the Marshal, but not in the terms Pétain would have wanted. A bitter quarrel ensued, and Pétain had not forgiven de Gaulle by 1940.

ideas was naturally the steadfast opposition of the French General Staff, which was mostly composed of aged men still reasoning along the lines of First World War strategy – complete with continuous fronts, trenches and cautious infantry progressions under massive artillery cover; such men had no use for de Gaulle's project: it would split the army in two, affect the morale of the infantry, take resources away from static defences, and perhaps worst of all, it would compromise their own careers. As for tanks, the French army had more than enough of them, and they were used as they ought to be used: spread out among the infantry formations in order to offer protection and support to the slowly-advancing infantrymen, just as in 1918. Such were the views held by General Weygand, Pétain's successor at the head of the French army, by Weygand's successor, General Gamelin, and by France's successive war ministers. De Gaulle's ideas were therefore rejected by the high military circles, and had very little impact on French public opinion. In fact, no more than seven hundred copies of *Vers l'Armée de Métier* were sold in France. In Germany, however, the book sold much better.

With amazing perseverance, de Gaulle nevertheless continued to defend his ideas and warn his compatriots during the years that followed. Parliament, the press, the radio, the parties, all were used in an effort to enlighten the public and persuade the authorities before it was too late. By the end of 1935, Germany had one armoured division and had announced her intention of building more. By the beginning of the next year, Hitler had reoccupied the Rhineland with no reaction from France or Britain. Soon, there were three armoured divisions in Germany, the Wehrmacht and the Luftwaffe were expanding at breakneck speed, Austria was annexed in the spring of 1938, and Czechoslovakia was directly threatened. Still there was no decision in France to modernize the army behind the illusory and incomplete shield of the Maginot Line. Shortly after Munich, however, it was decided to create two tank divisions. But they only included light tanks, there were to be only four battalions of them, and their assembly was to be deferred pending further study. The air force was similarly neglected, and General Bergeret, Assistant Chief of the Air Staff, was heard to say at the time: 'I'll be hanged if we are able to wage war at all before 1942.'[28]

De Gaulle was promoted to the rank of colonel at the end of 1937, and sent to command the 507th Tank Regiment stationed near Metz. From there, he continued to correspond with the proponents of his project, including Paul Reynaud, and to view the international situation with increasing dismay. His views on the future were at times strangely prophetic, as evidenced by the following statement he made to his brother-in-law, Jacques Vendroux, in July 1937:

> France will be unable to defend herself, all the more so as she will have to bear the brunt of the initial onslaught; the British are not ready; we are not at all assured of Russian support. As for the Americans . . . they will remain spectators at the start, albeit sympathetic ones. Our territory will be invaded once again; Paris can be reached within a few days. After that, we will have to start out from Britanny, or from the mountain regions, if not from Algeria, and fight for months before winning the final battle with the support of our allies. But how much blood will have been shed in the meantime![29]

Year after year, de Gaulle had seen the enemy apply the very theories he was advocating, and his countrymen reject them on trivial grounds. Yet in spite of countless disappointments, he continued to call for a complete change in strategic outlook, and to steel himself for the impending struggle. In fact, Colonel de Gaulle never seems to have doubted that he would be called to play an important part in that struggle, and many of those who met him shared this impression. Thus, as early as 1927, General Matter, Director of the Infantry, described de Gaulle as 'a future Supreme Commander of the French army'.[30] De Gaulle's superiors, even those who opposed him the most fiercely, like Weygand, Gamelin or Daladier, were not unaware either of his exceptional talents; and then there was Captain Chauvin, who had told de Gaulle in 1924: 'My dear chap . . . I have the curious feeling that you are heading for a very great destiny.' To which de Gaulle had replied simply: 'Yes, me too.'[31]

Indeed, then as later, de Gaulle was never one to underestimate his own capacities: 'I did not doubt . . . that the interest of life consisted in one day rendering France some signal service, and that I would have the occasion to do so.'[32] But by the summer of 1939, at the head of a regiment of light tanks soon to be broken up among several infantry formations, there seemed to be precious little Colonel de Gaulle could do for his country.

CHAPTER 1

Francophilia and Anglophobia

A large part of the following narrative would be unintelligible if it were not known that Winston Churchill had a special relationship with France. Indeed, Churchill was another man with 'a certain idea of France'. He seems to have developed a strong and lasting attachment to that country rather early in life, perhaps even at the time when he was wheeled by his nurse down the 'Shams Elizzie', as he then called them.[1] At any rate, Churchill never forgot the summer of 1883 when, aged nine, he drove with his father through the Place de la Concorde. Sixty-three years later, he was to evoke this episode: 'Being an observant child I noticed that one of the monuments was covered with rags and crepe and I at once asked him why. He replied, "These are monuments of the Provinces of France. Two of them, Alsace and Lorraine, have been taken from France by the Germans in the last war. The French are very unhappy about it and hope some day to get them back." I remember quite distinctly thinking to myself, "I hope they will get them back."'[2]

As a young man in his early thirties, Winston Churchill had hardly improved his command of the language: his French remained somewhat primitive, and always owed a lot to personal initiative; but Churchill knew the history of France as well as any Frenchman, and even better than most. With his intensely sentimental and romantic mind, he greatly admired 'France's contribution to human freedom and wisdom'; the heroes of French history he admired even more, first and foremost Joan of Arc and Napoleon. But he was to have a closer contact with France that proved decisive: in 1907, as a young minister of the Crown, Churchill attended the manoeuvres of the French army. He had attended many manoeuvres in England and Germany before, he was to see many more later on; but these particular French manoeuvres seem to have fascinated him. To be sure, he met on this occasion many distinguished French officers who were later to become famous, and this was a time when the *Entente Cordiale* reigned supreme; but there was obviously something else, a psychological effect, which Churchill himself once sought to define: 'In those days the soldiers wore blue tunics and red trousers and many of the movements were still in close order. When I saw, at the climax of these manoeuvres, the great masses of French infantry storming the position, while the bands played the 'Marseillaise', I felt that by those valiant bayonets the rights of man had been gained and that by them these rights and also the liberties of Europe would be faithfully guarded.'[3] Until the end of his life, Winston Churchill was to refer countless times to this important occasion; 'Ever since 1907,' he wrote in June 1944, 'I have in good times and bad times been a true friend of France.'[4]

Indeed, at the time of the Agadir crisis in 1911, France had no stauncher ally within the British government than Churchill himself. At the Admiralty just before the war, he was also a strong proponent of closer Anglo-French relations. However, it was unquestionably the First World War that forever anchored France to Churchill's heart. The endurance and bravery of the French infantryman, the glorious and bloody victories at the Marne and Verdun, the comradeship in arms between the French and the British on countless battlefields, which he saw at first hand during his six months as an officer in the trenches of France, all touched Churchill's sentimental mind and fired his romantic imagination. In addition, he was to rub shoulders with several leading French personalities during that war; one of these was General Foch, the Supreme Commander of the Allied Armies in 1918, whom Churchill later described thus: 'His postures, his captivating manner, his vigorous and often pantomimic gestures – comical if they had not been fully expressive – the energy of his ideas when his interest was aroused, made a vivid impression upon me. He was fighting all the time, whether he had armies to launch or only thoughts . . . Calm he certainly was not. He was vehement, passionate, persuasive, but clairvoyant, and above all, indomitable.'[5]

For Churchill, Foch represented one aspect of France: 'the France whose grace and culture, whose etiquette and ceremonial have bestowed its gifts around the world. There was the France of chivalry, the France of Versailles, and above all, the France of Joan of Arc.'[6] But for Winston Churchill, France was also symbolized by Clemenceau, the Tiger, for whom he had even greater admiration:

'As much as any single human being, miraculously magnified, can ever be a nation, he was France. Fancy paints nations in symbolic animals – the British Lion, the American Eagle, the Russian double-headed ditto, the Gallic Cock. But the old Tiger, with his quaint, stylish cap, his white moustache and burning eye, would make a truer mascot for France than any barnyard fowl. He was an apparition of the French Revolution at its sublime moment.'[7]

With these men, and with a few others, such as General Georges, Churchill established privileged relations during his numerous visits to France, as First Lord of the Admiralty in 1915, as a major in 1916, or as Minister of Munitions in 1917. He continued to visit them long after the war; and when, in 1940, Churchill evoked France, the images of Foch and Clemenceau were never far from his mind.

In the inter-war years, France could not have found in Britain a more forceful and vocal champion than Winston Churchill. With his innate sense of fairness, he believed that France, 'poor, mutilated, impoverished France,' was fully entitled to the peace and security for which she had sacrificed almost two million men, and that after the Treaty of Versailles, she had been badly let down by Britain and America. In July 1921, he was saying to the imperial Prime Ministers:

> Our duty towards France . . . is rather an obvious one because she gave up her claims – very illegitimate claims as we thought, but she waived them – to make a strong strategic position along the Rhine which her Marshals advised her to do . . . We said to her, if you give up the strategic position, England and America will be with you in the hour of need . . . but it is a fact that the treaty is naturally invalidated by America not having made good and France got neither Britain nor America, nor did she get her strategic frontier on the Rhine. The result of that is undoubtedly to have created a deep fear in the heart of France, and a fear which anyone can understand who looks at the population of the two countries . . . If at any time the means arises of reducing that fear . . . I think we ought to consider it very carefully indeed.[8]

Churchill would have liked to reduce that fear by means of a treaty binding Britain to protect France against unprovoked aggression. For eighteen years, in and out of government, he was to press for such a treaty. And during the whole inter-war period, in the government or outside it, at the House of Commons or the Conservative Club, in his public speeches or his private letters Churchill sought to bring about a greater measure of co-operation and understanding between England and France. On 4 May 1923, during the French occupation of the Ruhr, which was very unpopular in England, he declared: 'We must not allow any particular phase of French policy to estrange us from the great French nation. We must not turn our backs on our friends or our past.'[9] As Chancellor of the Exchequer, Churchill went to negotiate the amount of France's debt to Britain, a debt incurred during the war. Churchill presented very moderate terms to the French, who were much gratified. He was to explain his position on the matter at a Conservative Club dinner in Birmingham on 16 September 1925: 'We have not sought to be judged upon this question by our ability to extract the uttermost farthing. We think it our duty to consider not only the capacity of our debtors to pay, but the circumstances in which these debts were incurred.'[10]

Until 1931, Churchill's great idea was to bring about a reconciliation among France, Germany and Britain, which he considered as the only real security against the renewal of war. In 1931, he was still saying: 'We must use of our influence to modify the age-long antagonisms . . . between Germany and France.'[11] But with the rise of Hitler and the efforts of the British Labour Party to promote disarmament – particularly at the expense of France – Churchill increasingly stressed another point: 'It is not in the immediate interest of European peace that the French army should be seriously weakened. It is not in British interests to antagonize France.'[12] Two years later on 14 March 1933, he was still saying in the House of Commons: 'In the present temper of Europe, can you ever expect that France would halve the air force and then reduce the residue by one third? Would you advise her to do so? If she took your advice and did it, and then trouble occurred, would you commit this country to stand by her side and make good the injury? . . . I read in the newspapers today that the Prime Minister has been giving an ultimatum or making a strong appeal to France to disarm. Whether you deal with the army or the air, you are taking an altogether undue responsibility at a time like this in tendering such advice to a friendly nation.'[13] And the next year again: 'I urge the very greatest caution upon His Majesty's government at the present time in pressing the French government to weaken their strength relatively to Germany. I am sure on the other hand, that France, which is the most pacific nation in Europe at the present time . . . would never . . . commit an overt act against Germany without the sanction of the treaty, and, least of all, in opposition to the country with which she is in such amicable relations – Great Britain.'[14]

For five more years, Winston Churchill continued to harp on this theme. The French were 'peace-loving', 'pacifist to the core', 'liberal', 'democratic', and besides, he repeated, 'England's safety was bound up with that of France.'[15] The latter argument explains why Winston Churchill could easily reconcile his love for France with his own deep patriotism. For he had perceived very early in his career that England could not be secure without a strong France. As early as August 1911, at the time of the Agadir crisis, he had written to Lloyd George from the Home Office: 'It is not for Morocco, nor indeed for Belgium, that I would take part in this terrible business. One cause alone could justify our participation – to prevent France from being trampled down and looted by the Prussian Junkers – a disaster ruinous to the world and swiftly fatal to our country.'[16]

Now, in the thirties, as the pace of British rearmament and the strength of British defences lagged increasingly behind that of Germany, Churchill could only see salvation in a close, indeed an intimate co-operation between England and France; in pursuance of this ideal, he displayed the most remarkable eloquence: 'France and Britain have found their way to freedom by very different roads,' he declared on 18 November 1936, 'but here we are and here we stand. While we stand together we will be very dangerous to molest and very hard to destroy. Those who embody the tradition and revive the force of Nelson's fleet and Napoleon's armies will not in combination be found a helpless prey. But if to these martial virtues they add the sovereign conceptions of justice and freedom, then indeed they will be unconquerable.'[17]

In March 1938 Churchill was still pursuing the same theme with renewed vigour:

> Great Britain and France have to stand together for mutual protection. Here, then, is the great security for the two countries. Proclaim it. Do not conceal it . . . Treat the defensive problems of the two countries as if they were one. Then you will have a great deterrent against unprovoked aggression, and if the deterrent fails to deter, you will have a highly organized method of coping with the aggressor . . . Having gone so far, there is no safe halting place short of an open defensive alliance with France, not with loose obligations, but with defined obligations on both sides and complete inter-staff arrangements.[18]

And in the *Daily Telegraph*, three weeks later he wrote: 'If France broke, everything would break, and the Nazi domination of Europe, and potentially of a large part of the world, would seem to be inevitable.'[19]

By August 1938, the British government had at last given assurances in the House of Commons that thorough staff arrangements for combined defensive action would be made with the French Republic – but six months later Churchill expressed his dissatisfaction with the way these assurances were being implemented: 'No doubt many conversations have taken place, but when I was in France a little while ago, it seemed to me, from what I heard, that they had hitherto moved far too slowly . . . No one, once the honour of the country is engaged, would tolerate for a moment the insulting idea that one ally should do the paying and the other most of the dying.'[20]

By the spring of 1939, slowly, tardily, month by month, an alliance based upon the closest military, naval and air co-operation had at last been set up between France and Britain. No one was more satisfied than Winston Churchill: in the House on 24 March 1939 he summed up his position on the matter with perfect frankness: 'Some people talk sometimes as if it is very fine and generous of us to go to the help of France. But I can assure you that in the pass to which things have come, we stand at least as much in need of the aid of France as the French do of the aid of Britain.'[21]

One of the most interesting features in Churchill's relationship with France was perhaps his unshakeable faith in the strength of the French army. In fact, he continued to believe in the 'unquestionable French military superiority' long after it had ceased to be unquestionable. After all, this was the army that had won the war in 1918; it was the army of Foch and Clemenceau; it was now commanded by General Gamelin, an excellent soldier, who was also Churchill's friend – and besides there was now the famous Maginot Line, which seemed absolutely invulnerable. In Churchill's blind faith, there may also have been a measure of wishful thinking: the security of Europe, and that of Great Britain, rested upon the French army. Therefore, this army had to be the best, and it surely was. Churchill's faith was reinforced by his visits to France; in September 1936, he attended the French army manoeuvres and was quite pleased with what he saw. On 13 September he wrote to his wife: 'I drove about all day with General Gamelin the Generalissimo, who was communicative on serious topics. There was nothing to see, as all the troops were hidden in holes or under bushes. But to anyone with military knowledge it was most instructive. The officers of the French army are impressive by their gravity and competence. One feels the strength of the nation resides in its army.'[22] Sir Basil Liddell-Hart, who met Winston Churchill that same year, noted in his diary: 'Winston took up his familiar theme that the French army was the only safeguard of Europe. He thought its value was much higher than the British General Staff would allow. Under-rating the French had always been their attitude.'[23]

In 1938, the French army was still for Churchill 'the finest in Europe'.[24] 'This,' his friend Major Morton later recalled,

> was an obsession with the man. I recall how before the war I gave him, with permission, full information about the utterly rotten state of the equipment . . . of the French army and air force, and pointed out the certain consequences of this, he just would have none of it. We had many an argument. My prophecy in the winter of 1938/39 supported by fact and calculations . . . that if attacked by the weight of German arms as they then stood, France would be overrun in less than a month, nearly made him froth with rage. And yet he accepted the conclusions drawn through similar facts and calculations, based on industry, economics and world trade, in regard to every other country in the world. 'The unshakeable glory of France' was an obsession.[25]

Sir Henry Channon also noted in his diaries what Winston's cousin had to say on the matter: 'Charlie Londonderry went on to tell us how his political prospects were blighted by an unfortunate dinner party at Emerald's before the war, when he argued with Winston, and said that France was unreliable and rotten and could not be depended upon. Winston lost his temper, being a fanatical Francophile; and could not forgive Londonderry then, and certainly not later.'[26]

During the inter-war years, Churchill entertained privileged relations with senior French politicians, including Edouard Herriot, Paul Reynaud, Pierre Etienne Flandin, Paul Boncour and Daladier. He had even more sympathy for the socialist leader Leon Blum, and was also a friend of Georges Mandel. With all these personalities he corresponded regularly, and Flandin, Blum and Daladier, when they were Prime Ministers, even gave him regular information on French and German military strength. He also visited them regularly, and one of these visits in March 1938 is described by Sir

Eric Phipps in a report to Lord Halifax: 'Winston Churchill's stay here has continued in an increasingly kaleidoscopic manner. Almost every facet of French political life has been presented to him at and between meals.' And he added: 'His French is most strange and at times quite incomprehensible. For instance, to Blum and Boncour the other night he shouted a literal translation of "We must make good", by "nous devons faire bonne (not even 'bon')". This clearly stumped Boncour, who may even have attributed some improper meaning to it.'[27]

Though Winston Churchill made it a point never to intervene in French politics, he was not adverse to playing the role of a counsellor at times. On 27 March 1938, for instance, he did his best to dissuade Flandin from bringing down the Popular Front government and instituting government by decree.[28] In September of that year, during the Czechoslovak crisis, when Mandel and Reynaud had resigned from the Daladier government to protest against their country's policy in the matter, Churchill flew to Paris expressly to urge them to withdraw their resignations. To be sure, these visits were not appreciated by all in France; thus on 2 October, shortly after Churchill's trip to Paris, Sir Maurice Hankey wrote in his diary: 'Winston Churchill's sudden visit to France by aeroplane, accompanied by General Spears, and his visit only to the members of the French government like Mandel, who is opposed to the policy of peace, was most improper – Bonnet, the French Foreign Minister, has complained about it, asking what we would say if our prominent French statesmen did the same: he has also protested against being rung up by Churchill and Spears from London for information.'[29]

Churchill's investigations and his role as a counsellor extended to military matters, and there is no doubt that he detected some flaws in the French military apparatus. Thus, he asked Blum in 1937:

'Are you satisfied with your air force?'

'Why, yes,' Blum answered, 'I believe it is all right.'

'This is not what I am told,' Churchill then said. 'I believe that your planes are inferior to the planes that are now being produced in Germany. You should look into this matter carefully.'[30]

Churchill was again in Paris at the end of March 1938. This time, he told Blum, 'The German Field Howitzer is believed to be superior in range and . . . in striking power to the 75 even when relined.'[31] At the time, Churchill also conferred with Paul Reynaud, who tried to persuade him of the efficiency of armoured divisions. This is when

Churchill first heard of Colonel de Gaulle and his theories on armoured divisions. 'It seemed,' Churchill recalled later, 'that a Colonel de Gaulle had written a much criticized book about the offensive power of modern armoured vehicles.'[32] But Churchill had not followed the latest developments in tank warfare, and he still expected the future war to resemble the last, complete with trenches which, he said, 'were certain to be encountered at an early stage in a European war'.[33] Besides, his friends Generals Gamelin, Georges, and Giraud did not take de Gaulle's writings seriously, and Churchill trusted his friends. Hence he did not appreciate the importance of de Gaulle's theories, and expressed no desire to meet him.

During the spring and summer of 1939, Winston Churchill, though a bit preoccupied by the vulnerability of the Maginot Line's 'shoulder' opposite the Ardennes,[34] still had the greatest confidence in the French army. In May of that year, he called it 'the finest, though not the largest, army in existence at the present time'.[35] In June he assured the American columnist Walter Lippmann that the German army couldn't pierce the French carapace.[36] Churchill was to retain his absolute confidence in the superiority of France's army, in the ability of her leaders, and in the valour of her sons until May 1940. After that, events seemed to prove him wrong; but events themselves would prove no match for Churchill's convictions.

Charles de Gaulle's attitude towards England was in no way comparable to Churchill's relationship with France. Charles's father, Henri de Gaulle, was not exactly an Anglophile; for him, as for many of his contemporaries, the words 'Perfidious Albion' were not devoid of meaning. 'Perfidious?' he used to say, 'the adjective hardly seems strong enough.'[37] Charles de Gaulle, who had been educated by his father more than by anyone else, was probably influenced by this attitude – and the fact that he had an Irish grandmother cannot have improved matters. Furthermore, Charles de Gaulle's immense interest in France and French history all too often showed him England as the enemy of France, with England's triumphs usually coinciding with France's disasters. In his memoirs, he was to write, 'Nothing saddened me more profoundly than our weaknesses and our mistakes,'[38] and the first instance he quoted was Fashoda – an incident long forgotten in Britain, but which deeply

marked a whole generation of Frenchmen. For this reason, and a
few others, Anglophobia was an extremely common disease among
the French officers' corps at the beginning of the twentieth century.

Apart from her history, Charles de Gaulle knew little of England.
He had never been there and did not speak English fluently,
although he understood it quite well. De Gaulle had certainly
approved of the *Entente Cordiale*, but unlike Churchill, he was not
much impressed by the comradeship in arms between France and
England during the First World War; after all, he used to say, there
were no Englishmen on the Marne when the victory was won, and
besides, the British had dispersed a bit too hastily during the great
German offensives of 1918.[39]

For the immediate post-war period, de Gaulle certainly shared
Churchill's views: France had been let down by her allies. For this,
de Gaulle blamed Lloyd George[40], Perfidious Albion and the United
States – probably in that order. 'The ill-will of the Anglo-American
powers,' he later wrote, 'taking advantage of the inconsistency of
our regime, led us . . . to renounce the guarantees and reparations
which had been granted us in exchange for control of the Reich and
the Rhine frontier.'[41] At times, he seemed to have an even greater
suspicion of British deviousness. Thus, he later wrote that during the
inter-war years, 'England treated Berlin gently in order that Paris
might have need of her.'[42] In addition, it must be recalled that de
Gaulle had served two years as a staff officer in the Levant – at the
time a hotbed of intrigue and the scene of a discreet but permanent
Franco-British confrontation. It was said in those days that any
French officer serving in the Levant inevitably became anti-British,
and indeed de Gaulle returned from there deeply suspicious of
Britain's policies and intrigues in the Near East.

De Gaulle did believe that Great Britain would help France in
case of need, but only if her own interests dictated it; in 1934, he
wrote in his book *Vers l'Armée de Métier*, 'In return for the
acknowledgement of Britain's maritime supremacy, at the cost of
immense colonial sacrifices, if certain Norman islands are left
unmentioned, and provided we accept a sort of control, we may
count on English neutrality – jealous in prosperity but benevolent in
adversity – and which may even turn into an alliance for mutual
interest.'[43] But meanwhile, 'it was on France alone that the burden
fell of containing the Reich',[44] and the British had even gone so far as
to ask France to disarm, which he considered as another proof of

their deviousness, probably mixed with 'a certain Anglo-Saxon piety'.[45]

During the inter-war years, de Gaulle certainly did not go out of his way to establish contacts with British personalities across the Channel, not even when this would have seemed natural. Thus he did not meet Liddell-Hart or General Fuller, although he greatly admired their writings and drew his inspiration from them. Last but not least, unlike Churchill's continuing admiration for the French army in the thirties, de Gaulle had no illusions at all about the British army; in July 1937, he said to his brother-in-law Jacques Vendroux, 'France will be unable to defend herself, all the more so as she will have to bear the brunt of the initial onslaught; the British are not ready.'[46]

By the end of the thirties, de Gaulle was not really an Anglophobe, at any rate not nearly as Anglophobe as Churchill was Francophile. But it is quite certain that he deeply mistrusted the motives behind British Foreign and Colonial policy. In his conviction that 'a state is the coldest of cold monsters', de Gaulle seems to have kept a place apart for the British state – it was probably even colder than the others. Of course, this state of mind could not be entirely without influence on de Gaulle's attitude during the dramatic events that were to follow.

CHAPTER 2

The Outbreak of the Storm

The invasion of Czechoslovakia on 15 March 1939 finally convinced Neville Chamberlain that Hitler was not a gentleman after all. From then on, the dark spectre of war loomed larger with every new initiative taken in Europe: the British guarantee to Poland, the Danzig crisis, the Russo-German pact, the German build-up on the Polish border. Until the very last moment, however, Chamberlain remained convinced that a war could be averted and that Churchill could be kept out of office. But by that time, British public opinion evidently thought otherwise, and so did the press, which was almost unanimous in demanding Churchill's return. When Hitler finally unleashed his attack on Poland, Chamberlain had no choice: on 3 September, Britain declared war on Germany – and Churchill was appointed First Lord of the Admiralty. Before the day was over, France had also joined the fray.

Having returned to the post he occupied a quarter of a century earlier, Churchill lost no time in assuming command of the war at sea; and just like in 1914, the First Lord had a few pet projects of his own to help bring the war to a speedy conclusion. Foremost among them was 'Catherine', a plan to enter and dominate the Baltic with specially designed armoured and torpedo-proof warships. There was also an outline plan for the interruption of German iron-ore traffic coming down through the Norwegian leads; and of course numerous schemes that had very little to do with sea warfare, ranging from the reconditioning of heavy howitzers and the reorganization of the air force to the development of special trench-digging tanks. By the beginning of November, we find the First Lord of the Admiralty in France for discussions with his opposite number, M. Campinchi, and with his friends Reynaud, Blum, Mandel and Leger. The First Lord also inspected the forward French defences, and the headquarters of the British

Expeditionary Force, which already comprised four divisions stationed on the Franco-Belgian border. From his visit Churchill derived the impression that the French officers were relying exclusively on a defensive strategy, and that the morale of the French soldiers was astonishingly low.

This impression was well-founded: the French politicians and generals, remembering the appalling slaughter of the First World War, had lost all confidence in the offensive capacity of their army; on 6 September, while the bulk of the German army was engaged in Poland, the Commander-in-Chief, General Gamelin, had ordered a cautious advance that brought the French army five miles inside German territory. Twenty German villages were occupied before the 'offensive' was stopped on 12 September and the French troops returned to prepared positions on the French border. There, they confidently awaited the German onslaught, which would no doubt resemble that of Verdun, and could be dealt with much in the same way as in 1916. To be sure, the French High Command was receiving detailed reports on the lightning victory of the German army and air force in Poland; but curiously enough, this had not the slightest effect on General Gamelin's strategic conceptions, which were to remain obstinately defensive and antediluvian throughout the winter and spring of 1940.

The French government and High Command were not adverse to an offensive operation outside France; something that might reinforce the blockade of Germany, interrupt her supplies of raw materials and ruin her economy was certainly worth undertaking, especially if it was not too costly, if it involved the British allies, and carried the war as far as possible from the French borders. As the Soviet Union had signed a pact with Germany and had attacked Finland at the end of November, the French planners envisioned war operations against the Soviets as well as the Germans – with a marked preference for the former. By February 1940, therefore, the French High Command and the Ministry of War were working on plans for operations in northern Finland to help the Finns against the Soviet invaders, as well as landings in Norway to interrupt the flow of iron ore to Germany, an incursion into northern Sweden to occupy the ore mines, naval attacks against German oil supplies passing through the Black Sea, and aerial bombings of the Russian oilfields in the Caucasus. Among all these exotic projects, there was no trace of a plan for war operations against Germany, apart from the simple recipe of First World War vintage: *On s'enterre et on les attend*. This is why, six months after the declaration of war, northern France remained astonishingly calm – and extraordinarily vulnerable.

From his command post on the lower Rhine, Colonel de Gaulle surveyed these developments with increasing dismay. He was now in command of the tank brigade of the 5th French Army – a few dozen light tanks which could only operate in support of the infantry; here again, the lessons of Poland had not been learned. And yet, in January 1940, de Gaulle had sent to 80 of the most important civil and military personalities in the country a memorandum in which he repeated his previous arguments: the enemy would attack with a powerful armoured force, strongly supported from the air, and the French army would be defeated unless it immediately collected all existing tanks in several autonomous armoured divisions that could alone oppose the imminent German offensive. But no one paid any attention to the memorandum, except the few who were powerless to impose it and the many who were determined to oppose it. Colonel de Gaulle even sought to convince a delegation of British Members of Parliament who had come to visit the front; at the end of the manoeuvres, he told them: 'Gentlemen, this war is lost. We must therefore prepare another one, and win it – by using mechanized power.'[1] The British MPs, like their French counterparts, dismissed all this as fantasy.

For Colonel de Gaulle there was, however, a glimmer of hope: on 21 March, the Daladier government was toppled, and two days later Paul Reynaud was invested by a slim majority.* The new President of the Council was planning to appoint de Gaulle as Secretary of the War Committee, but this proved impossible for political reasons,** and de Gaulle, disappointed once again, returned to the front. Before doing so, however, he visited General Gamelin, who informed him that he intended to create two more armoured divisions, and that de Gaulle would be given command of one. This was good news, except for the fact that the 4th Armoured Division would be just as weak as the two existing ones, that it would not be autonomous either, and that it would only begin to exist on 15

*One vote.
**Daladier, who remained Minister of War in the new government, categorically opposed de Gaulle's nomination – and Reynaud needed the support of Daladier's party to remain in office.

May. De Gaulle could only return to his post and hope for the best.

In England, Winston Churchill, in spite of the prestigious post he occupied, had little more success than Colonel de Gaulle in influencing the strategy of his government. His boldest schemes had been rejected out of hand – which in some cases was just as well – and even his sounder plans, like the mining of German waterways or the interruption of the iron ore traffic to Germany, were the object of endless and inconclusive debates in the Cabinet. The First Lord mobilized his boundless energy and formidable rhetoric in support of the latter plan, which he considered as the best means of bringing the war to a speedy conclusion. Hundreds of memoranda were fired at the Prime Minister, and dozens of forceful speeches delivered in Cabinet during the winter. But even at this juncture, Chamberlain continued to hope that peace would return before war really started, and he stubbornly opposed any undertaking that appeared to have a warlike flavour. As a result, 'Wilfred', the plan to mine Norwegian territorial waters, suffered endless delays until it became all but useless. When at last it was carried out, the Germans had taken an initiative of their own which was much bolder and better organized: in a few hours on 9 April, they had occupied all the main Norwegian towns from Oslo to Narvik.

The British hastily improvised an expedition to help the Norwegians and turn the Germans out. But in the campaign that followed, the Allied forces were outnumbered, out-gunned, out-manoeuvred, bombed out, and eventually forced to evacuate southern Norway at the beginning of May. The First Lord's energetic and occasionally misguided interventions during the campaign had certainly added to the confusion, but Britain's lack of military preparedness was by then becoming glaringly evident to civilians and military alike; only years of pacifism and criminal neglect in defence matters could explain such a stunning defeat, and only one man had been in power long enough to bear responsibility for this state of affairs: the Prime Minister. In the Commons on 7 and 8 May, Neville Chamberlain therefore came under fierce attack from all sides of the House, and when the debate ended with a vote, the government majority had dropped to 81; 60 Conservatives had abstained, 30 had voted with the Opposition.

Chamberlain was much shaken by this unmistakable disavowal of his policy. It was clear to him that only a national government regrouping all parties could now carry on with the war – but would the Labour and Liberal leaders agree to serve under him? The answer was almost certainly no; on the afternoon of 9 May, Churchill and Lord Halifax were therefore summoned to Downing Street, and the Prime Minister told them that he intended to resign; he would now have to advise the King on the choice of a successor. Chamberlain would have much preferred to see Halifax succeed him, but he knew that this would pose some problems;* Halifax knew it too, and said so; Churchill said nothing and was appointed by tacit consent. The next day, Chamberlain accordingly saw the King and advised him to appoint Winston Churchill as his next Prime Minister. For Churchill, it would be no sinecure: that very morning, Belgium and Holland had been invaded; the twilight war was over.

Churchill himself described what he felt that evening after the King had formally asked him to form a government: 'As I went to bed at about 3 a.m., I was conscious of a profound sense of relief. At last I had the authority to give directions over the whole scene. I felt as if I were walking with Destiny, and that all my past life had been but a preparation for this hour and this trial.'[2] Not unnaturally, Churchill was also feeling some anxiety; to his private detective, Inspector Thompson, he confided that same evening: 'I hope that it is not too late. I am very much afraid that it is. We can only do our best.'[3]

The situation was indeed a delicate one. Britain was not ready for war, and the greater part of her army, commanded by Lord Gort, was advancing into Belgium with the First French army group to meet the German invasion. By 12 May the Allied armies had reached their assigned positions along the Dyle and the Meuse in the north; they were confronting twenty-two German divisions, including three armoured ones. But the surprise came further south: on 14 May seven Panzer divisions, having crossed the Ardennes and the Meuse, crashed through the French positions at Sedan and Dinant. Supported by dive bombers, followed by motorized infantry, they wreaked havoc in the lines of the French Second and Ninth Armies, which fell back in confusion. On the northern front, the French, Belgian and British divisions, already hard-pressed and badly battered, were now in danger of being cut off from their supply lines by the unexpected breakthrough at Sedan. At 6 a.m. on the morning

*The fact that Halifax was a peer constituted an obstacle – though not necessarily an insuperable one.

of 15 May, Paul Reynaud received a frantic phone call from Daladier: 'Our army is dissolving . . . the battle is lost.'⁴ And an hour and a half later, in London, Churchill was awakened with the news that Reynaud was on the phone. The French Premier had already called the day before to ask for more plane squadrons to assist the French troops; but this time the tone was different; as Churchill later recalled:

> He spoke in English, and evidently under stress. 'We have been defeated.' As I did not immediately respond he said again: 'We are beaten; we have lost the battle.' I said: 'Surely it can't have happened so soon?' But he replied: 'The front is broken near Sedan; they are pouring through in great numbers with tanks and armoured cars' – or words to that effect. I then said: 'All experience shows that the offensive will come to an end after a while. I remember the 21st of March, 1918. After five or six days they have to halt for supplies, and the opportunity for counterattack is presented. I learned all this at the time from the lips of Marshal Foch himself.' Certainly this was what we had always seen in the past and what we ought to have seen now. However, the French Premier came back to the sentence with which he had begun, which proved indeed only too true: 'We are defeated; we have lost the battle.' I said I was willing to come over and talk.⁵

By the evening of the 15th, the German spearhead had advanced sixty miles and reached Montcornet. In the north, the Dutch had capitulated, while in the centre, west of Dinant, the French Ninth Army had all but disintegrated. Churchill, however, relying on his First World War experience, persisted in considering all this as a temporary setback. On the morning of the 16th, Sir Alexander Cadogan noted in his diary: 'Cabinet in morning at which we received blacker and blacker news from France. Finally Dill explained plans for withdrawal in Belgium. This infuriated Winston, who said we couldn't agree to that, which could jeopardize our whole army. Sprang up and said he would go to France – it was ridiculous to think that France would be conquered by 120 tanks. . . . He said he would leave after lunch and asked N.C.* to mind the shop!'⁶ At 3 p.m. that afternoon, Churchill flew to Paris for an urgent meeting of the Supreme War Council; he was accompanied by General Dill and General Ismay.

Landing at Le Bourget, both Churchill and Ismay were immediately struck by the atmosphere of depression that reigned

*Neville Chamberlain.

everywhere. Ismay was even told that the Germans could be in Paris 'in a few days at most'.[7] When the party arrived at the Quai d'Orsay, bonfires were already burning in the gardens; they were being fed with great heaps of archives. Reynaud, Baudouin, Daladier and General Gamelin were all there, and Churchill noted that 'utter dejection was written on every face'.[8] General Ismay, on the other hand, recalled that 'Churchill dominated the proceedings from the moment he entered the room. There was no interpreter, and he spoke throughout in French. His idiom is not always correct, and his vocabulary was not equal to translating all the words which he required with exactitude. But no one could be in any doubt as to his meaning. 'Things seem pretty bad,' was his opening gambit, 'but this is not the first time that we have been in a mess together. We will get out of it all right. What is the situation?'[9] General Gamelin was called upon to reply, and for five minutes he painted a very bleak picture of the military situation: the Germans were advancing at frightening speed towards Amiens and Arras, from which they might either reach the coast or race towards Paris. The armoured columns had opened a large east-west gap which effectively cut the Allied armies in two. This bulge was fifty kilometres wide. The armies in the north would probably have to withdraw, General Gamelin concluded.

'When he had finished his tale of unmitigated woe,' Ismay noted, 'the Prime Minister slapped him heartily on the shoulder (the General winced) and said: "Evidently this battle will be known as the Battle of the Bulge." (On the spur of the moment, "Boolge" was the nearest he could get to this in French.) "Now, my General, when and where are you going to counter-attack – from the north or from the south?" General Gamelin replied dejectedly that he had nothing with which to counter-attack, and that, in any case, he suffered from inferiority of numbers, equipment, method and morale.[10] 'Où est la masse de manoeuvre?' Churchill asked. General Gamelin shook his head dejectedly and answered: 'Il n'y en a aucune.'[11] Churchill was dumbfounded: 'I admit this was one of the greatest surprises I have had in my life. Why had I not known more about it, even though I had been so busy in the Admiralty? Why had the British government, the War Office above all, not known more about it? It was no excuse that the French High Command would not impart their dispositions to us or to Lord Gort except in vague outline. We had a right to know. We ought to have insisted.'[12] Looking out the window, Churchill could still see the French archives being brought out in wheelbarrows and dumped into the flames; a more depressing sight could hardly be imagined. But the Prime Minister lost nothing of his cheerful countenance; the Germans, he said, could not yet have brought much of their strength across the Meuse, they could not have mechanized forces everywhere, a retreat in Belgium was surely inadvisable and a counter-attack certainly called for. General Gamelin replied that this would require mechanized forces, and also fighters to protect the infantry. 'The French,' he said, 'had begun the battle with 650 fighters, and they now had only 150 left.' Over and over again, Gamelin and Reynaud asked for more fighters and Churchill replied that the British had only 39 squadrons for the protection of England. Although the RAF had already sustained heavy losses over France, the British War Cabinet had that morning decided to give four more squadrons, which would arrive in the course of the day. Returning to the German attack in the north, Churchill said that 'the question was whether the vigour of this offensive would diminish.

– M. Daladier said that it would be wrong to think so, and that the power of the attack would increase as the attack continued.

– General Dill said that surely the petrol would run out.

– M. Daladier said that they brought the petrol with them.'[13]

General Gamelin returned constantly to the necessity of air support: if the enemy armoured force could be stopped by air action, attacks from the flank might have a good chance of success. Churchill replied time and again in his improvised French that British fighters were not suited for attacks on armoured vehicles: *Mon général, on ne peut pas arreter les chars avec des avions de chasse. Il faut des canons – Poof! Mais si vous voulez nettoyer le ciel, je demanderai de mon cabinet.*[14] Indeed, the Prime Minister finally decided to ask his Cabinet for ten additional fighter squadrons instead of four. When the conference was over, Churchill returned to the British Embassy, and drafted a telegram for the War Cabinet:

I shall be glad if the Cabinet could meet immediately to consider following. Situation grave in the last degree . . . the question we must face is whether we can give further aid in fighters above four squadrons, for which the French are very grateful, and whether a larger part of our long-range heavy bombers should be employed tomorrow and the following nights upon the German masses crossing the Meuse and flowing into the Bulge. . . . I personally feel that we should send squadrons of fighters demanded (*i.e.*, six more) tomorrow, and, concentrating all available French and British aviation, dominate the air above the Bulge for the next two or three days, not for any local purpose, but to give the last chance to the French army to rally its bravery and strength. It would not be good historically if their requests were denied and their ruin resulted. . . . I must have answer by midnight in order to encourage the French. Telephone to Ismay at embassy in Hindustani.[15]

The telegram was forcefully worded; it carried conviction. By 11.30, the reply came from London: 'Yes.' Churchill thereupon decided to go and announce the good news to Reynaud; it was by now almost midnight. . . . Reynaud was surprised at the intrusion, but delighted at the news. Churchill persuaded him to ask Daladier to come over, which the Premier did after some hesitation; after which the Frenchmen were submitted to one of Churchill's famous late-night pep-talks: 'Mr Churchill,' Baudouin recalled, 'was remarkable for his energy and vehemence as, crowned like a volcano by the smoke of his cigars, he told his French colleagues that even if France were invaded and vanquished England would go on fighting until the United States came to her aid, which she would soon do and in no half-hearted manner. "We will starve Germany out. We will destroy her towns. We will burn her crops and her forests." Until one in the morning he conjured up an apocalyptic vision of the war . . . Mr Churchill made a great impression on Paul Reynaud, and gave him confidence.'[16]

Reynaud was indeed much encouraged. By the next day, he even felt emboldened to make a move he had contemplated for some time; he, Reynaud, would remove Daladier from his post and take personal charge of the Ministry of War. He would also appoint Georges Mandel as Minister of the Interior, call in Marshal Pétain as Vice-President of the Council, and replace General Gamelin as Commander-in-Chief. Replace him with whom? General Weygand was a possible successor. To be sure, he was 73, and no one regarded him as a military genius; but Weygand had been General Foch's Chief-of-Staff during the First World War, and this would no doubt encourage the French troops, who needed it badly. Besides, there was no one else; General Weygand was therefore called back from Syria.

Whether this would be enough to stem the German advance was

of course far from certain; the French army was not only fighting with First World War generals, but also with a First World War army. At Rethel, St Quentin, Charleroi, the German tanks swept everything before them, and the Allied units were in full retreat. And the French tanks? Accompanying the infantry, operating in small units, deprived of radio contact with each other, they launched several fruitless counter-attacks, were badly mauled and soon engulfed in the general retreat. The 1st, 2nd and 3rd Armoured Divisions disappeared in this way. There remained the 4th Division – the one that was not yet formed, but already had a commander: Colonel de Gaulle.

Colonel de Gaulle was summoned to General Headquarters on 15 May and given his instructions: a defensive front was to be established on the Aisne and the Ailette to bar the way to Paris. De Gaulle's division would operate in the Laon region and contain the enemy long enough to allow this defensive position to be set up. Colonel de Gaulle would be entirely on his own, he would be directly under the orders of General Georges, Commander-in-Chief on the north-east front, and he would receive the necessary tanks . . . as soon as possible.

De Gaulle had probably never thought that his theories would be put to the test under such improvised conditions; nevertheless, he established his headquarters near Laon, and on the morning of 17 May, having received three battalions of tanks, he led them in an offensive towards the road junction of Montcornet, north-east of Laon. On the 19th, having received two more tank squadrons – new, untried, with inexperienced crews – he launched a new attack north of Laon towards the Serre. Both operations caught the Germans by surprise, inflicted cruel losses, and were undeniably successful. General Guderian, the German Panzer commander, later wrote, 'On the 19th, a few of de Gaulle's tanks . . . succeeded in penetrating to within a mile of my advance headquarters . . . and I passed a few uncomfortable hours until eventually the threatening visitors moved off in another direction.'[17] That day, in fact, de Gaulle's units turned back towards the south; they were heavily outnumbered and constantly bombed from the air. Besides, the French defences had now been reorganized in the rear, and de Gaulle's improvised tank division was badly needed on another front.

Indeed, the situation on the Somme was now very grave. The German columns, instead of heading south, had turned westwards towards the sea, and were threatening Amiens and Abbeville. The French and British armies were all but trapped in the north, and still the attack on the Bulge from north and south had not materialized. On 19 May, General Gamelin had ordered the northern armies to force their way southwards and attack the Panzer divisions on the Somme . . . but the order was cancelled by General Weygand, who replaced him the next day. On the 21st, Weygand himself gave orders for a north-south attack on the German columns, but by then the Allied front was dissolving in chaos: many French units did not receive the order, others could not carry it out, and Lord Gort was already thinking of a possible withdrawal towards Dunkirk.

In London, Churchill and his Cabinet, receiving confused and contradictory news from the fighting, could only instruct Lord Gort to follow the directives he received from the French, and send advice to Reynaud and Weygand. But Lord Gort was receiving no instructions from the French, and Weygand was taking no advice from the British. In fact, there was a glaring lack of liaison between the French and the British, and Churchill was forever thundering at 'the liaison that did not liaise'. He returned to Paris on 22 May for another meeting of the Supreme War Council; there, he expressed his agreement with General Weygand's plan to re-establish communications between the northern and southern armies, but expressed some concern at the lack of leadership in the north.[18] The commander there, General Billotte, had been killed, and General Blanchard had replaced him; but there was still no satisfactory liaison between Lord Gort and Blanchard.

The offensive against the German flank between Amiens and Arras was slow in materializing: the Germans had already reached Abbeville and had captured Boulogne on the 25th. An Anglo-French force from the north tried to break the encircling line by attacking around Arras, but it was repulsed; meanwhile, twenty French divisions were assembling behind the Somme, under the command of General Frère. De Gaulle's 4th Armoured Division was among them, having covered 180 kilometres from east to west in just five days. On 26 May, it received orders to attack a German bridgehead south of Abbeville. The next day, de Gaulle, now a temporary brigadier, launched his attack on Abbeville with 140 tanks and 6 infantry battalions. Here again, he succeeded in piercing the German lines and capturing 500 prisoners; here again, he was unable to exploit his initial success for lack of reinforcements and air cover. On 30 May, he withdrew southwards and regrouped his division near Beauvais.

By then, the campaign in the north was virtually lost. The German armoured divisions, converging from the west, south and north, inexorably closed in on the Allied armies regrouped in a large bridgehead around Dunkirk. On 28 May, the Belgian army capitulated. The day before, the War Office had informed Lord Gort that his task was 'to evacuate the maximum force possible', and the British were beginning to fight their way towards the sea. General Blanchard's troops, having received no such orders, were slow in following, and five French divisions were trapped around Lille. By 30 May, the badly battered British divisions had all succeeded in reaching the defensive perimeter around Dunkirk, and half the 1st French Army had joined them. A gigantic naval effort was now under way to evacuate the troops from Dunkirk. Churchill himself was back in Paris on 31 May for yet another meeting of the Supreme War Council; at this very grave juncture, when the Allied armies were struggling for survival in the north, he wanted to avoid any misunderstanding between the British and the French: the evacuation, he insisted, should proceed 'bras dessus, bras dessous'.[19]

By the beginning of June, the evacuation of Dunkirk was still in full swing, and the Allied armies further south had regrouped behind the Aisne and the Somme. But what would happen if these lines were broken? Paris would have to be abandoned. And then? There was a plan for evacuation to Tours; another one for making a last stand in Brittany. It was not yet the end; it was certainly the beginning of the end.

CHAPTER 3

Shipwreck

As the first week of June drew to a close, the grim veil of defeat inexorably shrouded the battlefields of northern France. To be sure, Operation Dynamo, the evacuation of Dunkirk, had succeeded beyond all hope: 340,000 allied soldiers had been brought out of France; but nearly all their arms and equipment were left behind. The French army had lost more than one-third of its fighting power, and the rest was entirely disorganized. The British had only two badly battered divisions left in France, they had lost a thousand guns, several thousand lorries, and their air force was outnumbered four to one. On 6 June, a fresh attack by a hundred German divisions had developed on the Somme and the Aisne; further west, Rouen and le Havre were directly threatened. England itself was now highly vulnerable to invasion. The country was defended by only 500 guns, 450 tanks, 29 air squadrons and three infantry divisions. Fourteen divisions were 'under instruction' – armed only with rifles and a few machine-guns.

In London, Winston Churchill was kept constantly informed of the latest developments. All day and well into the night, from his office, from his train, from his bed, he sent a continuous stream of notes and directives to the Chiefs-of-Staff committee and to the various departments: an entirely new army had to be created, and the island was to be turned into a fortress. By ceaseless prodding, by his numerous plans for defensive and even offensive operations, and above all by his formidable speeches, Churchill galvanized the energies of the British people. On 4 June, the day after the completion of the Dunkirk evacuation, he declared in the Commons:

> We shall not flag or fail. We shall go on to the end. We shall fight in France, we shall fight on the seas and oceans, we shall fight with growing

confidence and growing strength in the air. We shall defend our island, whatever the cost may be. We shall fight on the beaches, we shall fight on the landing grounds, we shall fight in the fields and in the streets, we shall fight in the hills. We shall never surrender! And even if, which I do not for a moment believe, this island or a large part of it, were subjugated and starving, then our empire beyond the seas, armed and guarded by the British fleet, would carry on the struggle until in God's good time the New World, with all its power and might, steps forth to the rescue of the old.[1]

But supervising the rebirth of a battered army while fortifying the island and the spirit of its inhabitants was not for Churchill the only imperative. There was also England's duty to the French: 'It would not be good historically if their requests were denied and their ruin resulted,' he had written to the War Cabinet on 16 May,[2] and this idea continued to govern his initiatives; even before the Dunkirk evacuation was completed, he ordered the British Expeditionary Force to be reconstituted out of other units and sent back to France as quickly as possible. He also ordered two additional fighter squadrons to be sent, thereby leaving only 27 fighter squadrons for the defence of England.

And yet Churchill had by then lost his invincible confidence in the French army[3]; in fact, he had even developed grave doubts about its leaders. This realization cost him dearly, for Churchill loved France and hated to be proved wrong. But he had seen the Commander-in-Chief, General Gamelin, whom he much respected and admired, lose all hope of victory only six days after the beginning of the German offensive.[4] A week later, he was forced to conclude that General Billotte 'had been singularly ineffective',[5] and soon he expressed his grave anxieties concerning General Blanchard's 'incomprehensible lack of control'.[6] By the beginning of June, he was also incensed with the conduct of Admiral Abrial, in charge of the evacuation at Dunkirk; he was not impressed either by the performance of General Vuillemin, in command of the French air force, and had been repeatedly struck by the pessimism and lack of co-operative spirit of the new Commander-in-Chief, General Weygand. In old Marshal Pétain, he saw the very picture of defeatism, and even Premier Reynaud's resolve seemed to be flagging, though he was incessantly calling for more British soldiers and airmen. On the morning of 6 June, Winston Churchill phoned General Spears, his liaison officer and personal representative to the

French; 'Was there any real plan?' he asked. 'What would the French do if their line was broken? Was there anything in the Brittany project? Was there an alternative?' And General Spears recalled: 'His confidence in the French command was evidently much shaken . . . he was obviously disappointed, distressed, puzzled and rather angry.'[7] The day before, Churchill had written to the Canadian Prime Minister, Mackenzie King: 'I do not know whether it will be possible to keep France in the war or not.'[8]

In Paris on 5 June, Paul Reynaud, helped by the gravity of the hour, had once again reshuffled his cabinet and this time he removed Daladier from the government. At his divisional HQ near Beauvais, General de Gaulle was now convinced that even if this war were to be lost, another war could be won using the French Empire as a springboard. On the morning of the 6th, he was informed that Paul Reynaud had just appointed him Under-Secretary of State for National Defence and was summoning him to Paris; the General left at once.

That afternoon, at the rue St Dominique in Paris, de Gaulle had a long conversation with Paul Reynaud, during which he outlined his ideas for the continuation of the war: 'While keeping up the fight on European soil as long as possible,' he said, 'we must decide and prepare to continue the struggle in the empire. That implies an adequate policy: the necessary means must be sent to North Africa, leaders qualified to direct the operation must be chosen, close contact with the British must be maintained, whatever grievances we may have against them.'[9] Paul Reynaud agreed, discussed the possibility of holding out in Brittany, then said: 'I ask you to go to London as soon as possible. During the conversations I had with the British government on 26 and 31 May, I may have given the impression that we did not rule out the prospect of an armistice. But now, the British must be convinced that we shall stand firm whatever happens, even overseas if need be. You will see Mr Churchill and tell him that my Cabinet reshuffle and your presence at my side are the signs of our resolve.'[10] De Gaulle was also to try to obtain a firm commitment from London that the RAF would continue to be available for operations in France. He was finally instructed to find out how long it would take for the British units evacuated at Dunkirk to be re-equipped and re-armed, and sent back to the Continent.[11] 'I was happy,' Paul Reynaud later wrote, 'to show the English a general with an aggressive spirit.'[12]

De Gaulle flew to London early on 9 June, accompanied by his aide-de-camp, Geoffrey de Courcel, and the head of the Prime Minister's diplomatic secretariat, Roland de Margerie. Immediately upon arrival, he was driven to 10 Downing Street and there, for the first time, General de Gaulle met Winston Churchill.

The immensely tall and rather aloof general officer Churchill now had in front of him certainly did not resemble the French officers he had known in the past. But the man was not completely unknown to him either; Churchill probably had a vague recollection of the Colonel de Gaulle Paul Reynaud had mentioned to him in March 1938 as 'the author of a much-criticized book about the offensive power of modern armoured vehicles'.[13] Moreover, Churchill certainly knew of de Gaulle's recent exploits in northern France at the head of his tank columns; for the British Prime Minister had taken an anxious interest in every development of the campaign, and the news of a French advance amongst all the sad tales of retreat could not possibly have escaped him. Finally, he had read the article concerning General de Gaulle in *The Times* two days earlier; it included the following description: 'Rather aggressively "right-wing", intensely theoretical, an almost fanatical apostle of the mass employment of armoured vehicles, he is also clear-minded, lucid, and a man of action as well as a man of dreams and abstract ideas.'[14]

There was both action and abstraction in the ideas which de Gaulle presently submitted to the British Prime Minister. He expressed the French government's determination to continue the struggle, from the empire if need be, and it was at once apparent that de Gaulle's determination in that respect was greater than that of his government. Churchill expressed his satisfaction at these words, but added that he no longer believed in the possibility of a victory in France. A Canadian division would still be sent to Normandy, and the 51st Scottish Division would remain in France, together with what was left of the mechanized division still fighting at the front; but the Prime Minister was unable to give even an approximate date for the return to France of the British units that had escaped from Dunkirk.[15] In addition, he categorically refused to send his remaining air squadrons to participate in the Battle of France.

De Gaulle was undoubtedly disappointed with the results of this first interview; for it was all too obvious that the British Prime Minister had lost all faith in the success of French arms. But Churchill himself had certainly made a strong impression upon the

General: 'The impression he gave me,' de Gaulle later wrote, 'confirmed me in my conviction that Great Britain, led by such a fighter, would certainly not flinch. Mr Churchill seemed to me to be equal to the rudest task, provided it also had greatness. The assurance of his judgement, his vast culture, the knowledge he had of most of the subjects, countries and men involved, and finally his passion for the problems of war, found here their full scope. He was above all fitted by his character to act, take risks, play the part out and out and without scruple. In short, I found him well in the saddle as guide and chief. Such were my first impressions.'[16] We know little of the first impression de Gaulle made on Churchill; an extremely favourable one, according to the French Ambassador, Corbin, who had it from 'sources close to the Prime Minister'.[17] This is more than probable: unlike the other French officers Churchill had met in May, de Gaulle was calm, cool, completely unrattled. Moreover he had not even contemplated the prospect of defeat or armistice; he talked only of continuing the struggle with all possible means, in Brittany, in the Massif Central, on the Maginot Line, in the empire if need be.

For all that, de Gaulle, who had just been appointed Under-Secretary for National Defence, was speaking in Paul Reynaud's name, and Churchill knew that the latter had alternate phases of firmness and irresolution; he also knew, from his telephone conversations with General Spears, that defeatism was rapidly spreading among Paul Reynaud's cabinet colleagues; this defeatism was of course much helped by the further deterioration in the military situation – the enemy had now reached the Seine below Paris, and the capital was threatened from three sides. Worse still, on the very next day, 10 June, Mussolini declared war on France. Churchill decided to go to Paris that very afternoon for another meeting of the Supreme War Council. The news that the capital was in danger of falling into German hands could not have deterred him; the news that the French government was evacuating it was more effective. The French GHQ was now in Briare, south-east of Orleans, and Churchill decided to fly there on the afternoon of 11 June, in order to infuse the French leaders with some of his aggressive spirit.

Meanwhile, on the afternoon of 10 June, amid preparations for the evacuation of the capital, Paul Reynaud and General de Gaulle had a stormy interview with the Commander-in-Chief, General

Weygand, who once again advocated capitulation. At midnight, de Gaulle and Reynaud set out for Orleans, which was reached at dawn on the 11th, and there, Paul Reynaud learned to his great surprise from General Weygand that Mr Winston Churchill would be arriving that afternoon in Briare. Both de Gaulle and Reynaud were under the impression that Weygand had invited the British Prime Minister on his own authority, and they were outraged. It was decided then and there that General Weygand should be replaced as Commander-in Chief, and de Gaulle set out to see General Huntziger, considered as a possible successor.[18] De Gaulle would then rejoin Paul Reynaud at Briare, at the 'Chateau du Muguet', where the impromptu conference with the British was to take place.

That afternoon, Churchill, accompanied by Anthony Eden, General Ismay and the Chief of the Imperial General Staff, General John Dill, landed on a small airfield near Briare.

'There were a few Frenchmen about,' Churchill wrote, 'and soon a colonel arrived in a motor car. I displayed the smiling countenance and confident air which are thought suitable when things are very bad, but the Frenchman was dull and unresponsive. I realized immediately how very far things had fallen even since we were in Paris a week before. After an interval we were conducted to the chateau, where we found Mr Reynaud, Marshal Pétain, General Weygand, the Air-General Vuil- lemin, and some others, including the relatively junior General de Gaulle, who had just been appointed Under-Secretary for National Defence. Hard by on the railway was the headquarters train in which some of our party were accommodated. The chateau possessed but one telephone, in the lavatory. It was kept very busy, with long delays and endless shouted repetitions.'[19]

The conference opened at 7 p.m., and Churchill was the first to speak:

He had come to France, he said, to consider with Monsieur Reynaud and his advisers the realities of a situation which must be faced without flinching. The matter for discussion was how best to carry on with the struggle which nothing could prevent the British from pursuing. His own impression was that as soon as the Germans had stabilized themselves on a front in France, they would turn on England. He hoped they would do so for two reasons. It would give France relief and enable the British to take a fuller and more equal share in the struggle, but, above all, it would give our RAF the opportunity of smashing the German air power. He had complete confidence that they would do so.

Every effort was being made in Great Britain to turn out arms and re-equip the armies. At this very moment the British were sending troops to France, and a British infantry division was deployed about Le Mans. A Canadian division and seventy-two guns were landing that night, so that there were now four British divisions in France. Another division would arrive about 20 June. The dispatch of yet a further division would depend on the guns the French could provide. Then there were the troops from Narvik . . . If the French army could hold out till the spring of 1941, the British would have from 20 to 25 divisions to place at the disposal of the French Command, to employ anywhere.[20]

Reynaud thanked him, then asked Weygand to report on the military situation. This he did, and it was a tragic report: the German army was three times stronger than the French, the Germans had reached the last French line of organized defence on the Seine and the Marne, and had even formed several bridgeheads further south; the French troops were exhausted, there was not a single French battalion in reserve, and he could not even guarantee that the line would hold the next day. . . . The French army was fighting admirably well, but it was overwhelmed by superior armament. . . .[21] Churchill had previously asked to hear the opinion of his old friend General Georges, and Weygand presently asked for General Georges to be introduced. The latter only confirmed the account given by General Weygand: the German strength was constantly increasing, the French had very few fighters left, their army had no more reinforcements and was not in a position to oppose another powerful thrust.[22]

The British Prime Minister had the greatest confidence in General Georges, and he was obviously much distressed by this sad description. But Churchill had come to galvanize the French, and this he would do; during the next two hours, he used all the arguments he could muster in favour of a continued resistance, and there were not a few: 'We came near disaster before in the last war, and we survived,' he assured them; 'the German armies must be exhausted by now'[23]; 'Paris, if stubbornly defended, could absorb immense armies'; 'six to eight squadrons from England were taking part in the battle every day'; 'could not bridgeheads be established on the Atlantic? How about guerrilla warfare? Surely some effective means of holding up the German tanks could be devised.'[24] At one point, General Weygand abruptly asked the British Prime Minister what he would do if Germany invaded England. Churchill answered that he had 'not thought that out very carefully, but broadly speaking he would propose to drown as many as possible of them on their way over, and then to '*frapper sur la tête*' anyone who managed to crawl ashore'.[25] At any rate, the fighter force in England would surely cripple the German air force when it came, but 'whatever happened we would fight on and on and on, toujours, all the time, everywhere, partout, pas de grâce, no mercy. Puis la victoire!'[26] 'Churchill,' Eden noted, 'in his eagerness to convey his meaning, broke into French. At the end of one such passage, Reynaud murmured absently, "Traduction".'[27]

That did not matter: it was a commanding performance in any language, and no one could possibly misunderstand the British Prime Minister's meaning. But to Churchill's dismay, Weygand, Pétain, Georges, and even Reynaud raised all sorts of objections: the French army had no reserves, there could be no comparison between the last and the present war, the British squadrons should be based in France in order to be effective, a bridgehead in Brittany would be useless because it had neither fortifications nor resources, and guerrilla warfare 'would mean the destruction of the country'.[28] Nevertheless, Weygand and Reynaud requested that every British fighter squadron should immediately be thrown into the battle, as this was the decisive moment. But Churchill replied, 'This is not the decisive point and this is not the decisive moment. That moment will come when Hitler hurls his Luftwaffe against Great Britain. If we can keep command of the air, and if we can keep the seas open, as we shall certainly keep them open, we will win it all back for you.' Before Churchill left England for the meeting at Briare, Air-Marshal Dowding, Commander-in-Chief, Fighter Command, had given the Cabinet the most solemn warning that if any more fighter squadrons were sent to France, he could not guarantee the security of the British Isles. Twenty-five fighter squadrons had to be maintained at all costs for the defence of Britain, and nothing could make Churchill give up these.

When he left Briare the following morning, Winston Churchill could not have been satisfied with the results of the meeting; he had not succeeded in dispelling the prevailing defeatism, and even General Georges had told him in private that 'it was all but over with the French army', and that 'in his opinion an armistice would soon be inevitable'.[29] Only Paul Reynaud still seemed to show some inclination to fight on. Churchill was also much preoccupied with the fate of the French fleet if France should capitulate, though before leaving, he had extracted from Admiral Darlan a solemn promise never to surrender the fleet. General de Gaulle was also disappointed with the outcome of a conference during which the continuance of the struggle in the empire had not even been mentioned. But the British Prime Minister's masterful performance had filled the General with admiration . . . and left him mildly suspicious; 'Mr Churchill,' he later wrote, 'appeared imperturbable, full of buoyancy, yet he seemed to be confining himself to a cordial reserve towards the French at bay, being already seized – not, perhaps, without an obscure satisfaction – with the terrible and magnificent prospect of an England left alone in her island, with himself to lead her in her struggle towards salvation.'[30]

Churchill had noticed de Gaulle's presence at the start of the conference,[31] and the General must have appeared to the British Prime Minister as Spears described him that day: 'His bearing alone among his compatriots matched the calm, healthy phlegm of the British. A strange-looking man, enormously tall; sitting at the table, he dominated everyone else by his height, as he had done when walking into the room. No chin, a long, drooping, elephantine nose over a closely-cut moustache, a shadow over a small mouth whose thick lips tended to protrude as if in a pout before speaking, a high receding forehead and pointed head surmounted by sparse black hair lying flat and neatly parted. His heavily hooded eyes were very shrewd. When about to speak he oscillated his head slightly like a pendulum, while searching for words.'[32]

De Gaulle had in fact spoken very little during the conference, intervening only on a technical matter. But at the dinner that followed, he had instructions – no doubt from Paul Reynaud – to sit next to Churchill.[33] What was said during the dinner is not known, but it must have contrasted vividly with the defeatist talk Churchill had just heard at the conference; de Gaulle, for one, was in favour of carrying on a guerrilla warfare,[34] and they both agreed that capitulation was out of the question; 'Our conversation,' de Gaulle later wrote, 'fortified my confidence in his strength of purpose. He himself, no doubt, went away with the feeling that de Gaulle, though without means, was no less resolved.'[35]

The General's assumption was correct, for Churchill was to write in his memoirs: 'General de Gaulle . . . was young and energetic and had made a very favourable impression on me. I thought it probable that if the present line collapsed Reynaud would turn to him to take command.'[36] Back in London at noon on the 12th, Churchill wrote to the President of the United States, summing up the situation:

> I spent last night and this morning at the French GQG, where the situation was explained to me in the gravest terms by Generals Weygand and Georges . . . the practical point is what will happen when and if the French front breaks, Paris is taken, and General Weygand reports formally to his government that France can no longer continue what he calls 'co-ordinated war'. The aged Marshal Pétain . . . is I fear ready to lend his name and prestige to a treaty of peace for France. Reynaud on the other hand is for fighting on and he has a young General de Gaulle who believes much can be done . . . it seems to me that there must be many elements in France who will wish to continue the struggle either in France or in the French colonies, or in both. This therefore is the moment for you to strengthen Reynaud the utmost you can, and try to tip the balance in favour of the best and longest possible French resistance.[37]

Churchill obviously hoped to stir Roosevelt into increasing the American commitment to the embattled French. In addition, anything that could bolster French morale seemed to him to be worth trying. Before leaving Briare, he had told Reynaud: 'Should there be a fundamental change in the situation, I must request you, before coming to a final decision which may govern French action in the second phase of the war, to let the British government know at once. They will come over immediately to meet the French government at any convenient place which you choose to indicate to discuss the new circumstances with you.'[38] Churchill was to be taken at his word much sooner than he thought.

On the afternoon of the 12th, Reynaud motored to Cangé, in Touraine, where the Council of Ministers was to be held. It started at 7 p.m., and resulted in a rather confused debate, with General Weygand pressing the government to make an immediate request for an armistice, and Marshal Pétain supporting him. Reynaud, on the contrary, was in favour of leaving France and carrying on the struggle from North Africa; in this, he was supported by what seemed to be a majority in the Cabinet. After all, at the Supreme War Council on 28 March, there had been an agreement that neither Britain nor France would negotiate or conclude an armistice or peace except by mutual agreement. But several ministers still hesitated to commit themselves. Finally, Reynaud proposed to ask

Mr Churchill to return to France the next day in order to lay his views on the matter before the French ministers; this was agreed upon.[39] There followed an even more confused and inconclusive debate on whether the government should now proceed to the 'Breton redoubt' and organize resistance from there. Whereupon the council adjourned.

On the morning of 13 June, Winston Churchill was given Paul Reynaud's message asking him to come to Tours, where the French government had now withdrawn. By 11 a.m., Churchill was flying over to France for the fifth time in his yellow Flamingo aeroplane, escorted by twelve hurricane fighters. With him were Lord Beaverbrook, Lord Halifax, General Ismay, and Sir Alexander Cadogan, the Under-Secretary of State for Foreign Affairs. Though Churchill did not yet know it, this was to be his last visit to France for exactly four years. 'Arrived over Tours,' Churchill later wrote, 'we found the airport had been heavily bombed the night before, but we and all our escort landed smoothly in spite of the craters. Immediately one sensed the increasing degeneration of affairs. No one came to meet us or seemed to expect us. We borrowed a service car from the station commander and motored into the city, making for the Préfecture, where it was said the French government had their headquarters.'[40]

After considerable delay, Paul Reynaud also arrived at the Préfecture and the conference was opened. The only other Frenchman present was Paul Baudouin, the Under-Secretary of State for Foreign Affairs, soon to be joined by Roland de Margerie; General Spears had also joined the British party. Reynaud opened the proceedings, and the British were startled with what they heard: 'General Weygand,' Reynaud said, 'had declared the preceding evening that the situation of the army was desperate, and that an armistice should be asked for at once.' 'The majority of the Cabinet,' he continued, 'had not endorsed this point of view, but if Paris fell, and this seemed inevitable, the question would have to be raised again.'[41] Mr Reynaud then read the communication he had sent to President Roosevelt on 10 June, and he told Churchill that he intended to send a new and pressing message to the President of the United States. 'Our only chance of victory is the prompt entry of the United States into the war; President Roosevelt must realize this and accept the responsibility.' Paul Reynaud went on to say that his government would not continue the struggle unless Roosevelt's reply conveyed a firm assurance of immediate aid. The alternative, he said, was an armistice and peace.[42]

The British listened with amazement, not clearly understanding whether Paul Reynaud was speaking for himself or for his government. They were not helped by the end of Reynaud's speech either, but they were dumbstruck by its implications: 'The government,' Reynaud continued, 'had not lost sight of the fact that a solemn pledge had been entered into that no separate peace would be concluded. But what was the British government's attitude in view of the present situation? France, as General Weygand had said, had been completely sacrificed . . . she had nothing left. This being the plain and terrible truth, it would come as a shock to the French government and people if Britain failed to understand and did not concede that France was physically incapable of carrying on . . . would Great Britain realize the hard facts now facing France?'[43]

Was Paul Reynaud really asking the British to release France from her promise to go on fighting? In view of what he had said the day before at the Cabinet meeting about continuing the fight in North Africa, this appeared to be a bewildering about-face; and yet, no one present at the conference was in any doubt as to the meaning of this question put in hypothetical form. Paul Baudouin's notes show Paul Reynaud as saying in his conclusion: 'It is now materially impossible to carry on the fight. Will Great Britain release France from her promise? That is the first question, and we ought to examine it at once.'[44] Paul Baudouin, a partisan of capitulation, had of course a vested interest in producing this version of Reynaud's words. But all the British personalities present understood the same, though they certainly would have preferred not to; General Ismay noted that Paul Reynaud 'asked that in view of the sacrifices which France had made and the hopelessness of their position, Britain should release her from her promise'.[45] And Sir Alexander Cadogan: 'He (Reynaud) said French army bust and asked us to release him from no separate peace agreement.'[46] Finally, Churchill: 'Reynaud asked us whether, in view of the sacrifices and sufferings of France, we would release her from the obligation about not making a separate peace.'[47]

Churchill's answer to this question is all important for the understanding of what will follow. At the time, this answer must have cost him dearly. He was a great friend of France, and Reynaud had just told him in effect that the interests of the two nations had ceased to coincide; this he could not accept: 'I fully understand,' he began, 'what France has endured and is still suffering. I am deeply moved by the fact, and I do not underestimate her frightful sorrows. In England our turn will come soon, and England is ready. . . . If our army had not been lost in the north, you might perhaps have resisted, for we should then have played an important part in the present defensive battle which opened on 5 June. But we could not be at your side because of reverses suffered owing to our having accepted the strategy of the command in the north.' Then, his tone changed: 'The British people have not yet felt the German lash, but they do not underestimate its force. This in no way deters them; far from being cowed, they are looking forward to thrashing Hitler. They have but one thought, to win the war and destroy Hitlerism.'

'Winston,' General Spears noted,

> was gathering momentum as he went, his eyes flashed, his hands were clenched as if grasping a double-handed sword. The picture he was drawing made him splutter with rage as he contemplated it. . . . 'We must fight, we will fight, and that is why we must ask our friends to fight on.' A short pause, then: 'You must give us time. We ask you to fight on as long as possible, if not in Paris, at least behind Paris, in the provinces, down to the sea, then, if need be, in North Africa. At all costs, time must be gained. The period we are asking you to endure is not limitless. A pledge from the United States would make it quite short . . . And what is the alternative? The alternative is the destruction of France, more certain than if she fights on, for Hitler will abide by no pledges. . . . France must fight on. She still has her fine navy, her great empire. . . .[48] The French army ought to go on fighting, and if, as General Weygand maintains, its formations break up, it should develop and multiply its guerrillas. A guerrilla movement on a big scale will wear out the German army. . . .[49] The war will continue, and can but end in our destruction or our victory.

He stopped, Spears noted, then said, looking hard at Reynaud: 'That is my answer to your question.'[50]

Reynaud then remarked – rather curiously in view of what had just been said – that Churchill had not really answered his question; 'If the French army was beaten, and "a French government" decided to ask for a separate peace, would Britain authorize them to do so?' The British Prime Minister then proceeded to make things even clearer: 'Under no circumstances will Great Britain waste time in reproaches and recriminations. But that is a very different matter from becoming a consenting party to a peace made in contravention of the agreement so recently concluded.' Then he added, probably to soften the blow: 'Before posing ourselves decisive questions, we must appeal to Roosevelt. Let the French government undertake to do this and we will support them by telegram. That is the first thing to do, and it must be done before an answer is given to the extremely grave question put by M. Reynaud.'[51] And Churchill concluded, with tears in his eyes:[52] 'I have already said we would refrain from reproaches and recriminations. The cause of France will always be dear to us, and if we win the war we will one day restore her to all her power and dignity. But that is a very different thing from asking Great Britain to consent to a departure from the solemn undertaking binding the two countries.' He stopped, Spears noted, 'but went on looking at Reynaud with the utmost sternness, awaiting his answer'.[53]

Reynaud thereupon spoke at length of the possibility and the necessity of American intervention. There followed a lengthy exchange of secondary importance, except for the fact that Churchill, to reinforce his argument, gave a stern warning that if France were occupied by Germany, she would not be spared by the English blockade. As for Reynaud, he said not a word about continuing the fight in North Africa.

Churchill then expressed the desire to confer with his colleagues; 'dans le jardin,' he added. So the meeting was suspended, and all the British participants trooped out. It was during this pause that de Gaulle arrived at the Préfecture; the first misunderstanding between him and Churchill was to start then and there.

De Gaulle had spent the day of the 12th at the chateau de Beauvais, working with General Colson on the plan for transportations to North Africa. Late in the evening, he had gone to see Paul Reynaud, just back from the Cabinet meeting at Cangé, and he again raised the question of North Africa; de Gaulle also saw Reynaud on the morning of the 13th, when Reynaud, no doubt under the influence of Baudouin and of his mistress, Madame de Portes, decided to transfer the government to Bordeaux. De Gaulle insisted that Reynaud should at least issue an order telling the Commander-in-Chief to prepare for transportation to North Africa, which Reynaud finally did towards noon. But strangely enough, neither on the evening of the 12th nor the next morning did Paul Reynaud tell de Gaulle that there was to be another conference with Churchill that same afternoon; de Gaulle, however, was to learn of it *in extremis*:

'I was at Beauvais at the beginning of the afternoon,' de Gaulle later recalled, 'when M. de Margerie, Paul Reynaud's Chef du Cabinet Diplomatique, rang me up: "A conference is about to start in a moment at the Préfecture de Tours, between the President du Conseil and Mr Winston Churchill, who has just arrived with several of his ministers. I am warning you in haste as I was warned myself. Although you are not invited, I suggest you should come. Baudouin is at work and I don't like the look of things." Such was M. de Margerie's communication. As I drove towards Tours, I was well aware of all the alarming implications of this unexpected meeting. . . . The courtyard and corridors of the Préfecture were filled with a crowd of Members of Parliament, civil servants and journalists, whom the news had attracted and who formed, as it were, the tumultuous chorus of a tragedy nearing its epilogue. I entered the office occupied by M. Paul Reynaud. Baudouin and de Margerie were with him. The conference was adjourned. Margerie informed me rapidly that the British ministers, after deliberating in the garden, would give their reply to the following question, put to them by the French: "In spite of the agreement of 28 March 1940, which excludes any separate laying down of arms, would England consent to France asking the enemy what would be, for her, the terms of an armistice?"'[54]

When de Gaulle sat down – in Sir Alexander Cadogan's armchair – and saw the British participants filing back into the room, he was already under a misapprehension: for the British ministers were *not* about to give their reply to the question put to them; as we have seen, this reply had already been given, and at length, by Churchill himself. De Gaulle did not know it, and this was the beginning of the misunderstanding. In his memoirs, the General was to describe the conference after its resumption in the following terms:

Mr Churchill sat down, Lord Halifax, Lord Beaverbrook and Sir Alexander Cadogan took their places, as well as General Spears, who accompanied them. There was a moment of crushing silence. The Prime Minister began to speak, in French. In an even, sad voice, rocking his head, with his cigar in his mouth, he began by expressing his commiseration, that of his government and that of his people, for the lot of the French nation. 'We can see plainly,' he said, 'how things are with France. We understand that you feel cornered. Our friendship for you remains intact. In any case, you may rest assured that England will not withdraw from the struggle. We shall fight to the end, no matter how, no matter where, even if you leave us alone.' When he came to the prospect of an armistice between French and Germans, which I expected would provoke an outburst of indignation on his part, he expressed, on the contrary, a compassionate understanding. But suddenly, moving on to the question of the fleet, he became very precise and very rigorous. It was plain that the British government was so afraid of seeing the French fleet handed over to the Germans that it was disposed, while there was still time, to barter its renunciation to the agreement of 28 March against guarantees about the fate of our ships. This was, in fact, the conclusion which emerged from that abominable conference.[55]

For once, the description given by de Gaulle is not at all accurate. On the one hand, he did not register Churchill's first words upon resumption of the conference: 'Nothing in the discussion he had just had with his colleagues had led any of them to change their views. Lord Halifax and Lord Beaverbrook had expressed their approbation of what he had said just now, and it could therefore be assumed that the Cabinet would also agree.'[56] De Gaulle could not know that Churchill was referring here to his previous refusal of a French armistice; of course, the fact that the Prime Minister spoke in a Churchillian mixture of English and schoolboy French, with an unlit cigar in his mouth, probably did not facilitate comprehension either. But the 'compassionate understanding' which Churchill expressed was, as usual, for France and her plight. It was in no way for the prospect of an armistice: we have seen that Churchill would not hear of that. Finally there is the 'but suddenly, moving on to the question of the fleet, he became very precise and very strict'. Churchill in fact did not mention the problem of the French fleet during this conference, and there is obviously a confusion in the General's mind; the question of a barter deal involving the fleet and the 28 March agreement was to arise only several days later, in a very different context.

It is interesting to note that both men's prejudices contributed to the misunderstanding. Churchill's permanent affection and compassion for France was mistaken for agreement with the positions of the French defeatists, and de Gaulle's deeply ingrained suspicion of British policy led him to see a selfish barter where none was contemplated. Four years later, de Gaulle was still telling the Canadian Prime Minister, Mackenzie King: 'It was . . . at that time that I had formed the impression that Britain was ready to let France go if the necessity arose to save herself.'[57]

The conference ended at 5.50 p.m., after Churchill had repeated that President Roosevelt should be approached without delay, and promised to send an appeal himself that same evening. Both parties also agreed to meet again after the President's answer had been received, and Churchill added, 'Hitler cannot win. Let us patiently await his demise.'[58]

There can be no doubt that Churchill was terribly disappointed with Paul Reynaud; the latter was clinging only to the hope of American help, and had not once talked of continuing the war in North Africa, thus making a giant stride towards capitulation. In his disappointment, Churchill seems to have been casting about for an energetic personality, and the image of de Gaulle came to his mind. In the garden of the Préfecture, during the pause, he asked General Spears about de Gaulle; Spears said he was certain that de Gaulle 'was completely staunch'.[59] The idea must then have continued to travel in Churchill's mind, as evidenced by what happened after the conference: 'As we went down the crowded passage into the courtyard,' Churchill later wrote, 'I saw General de Gaulle standing stolid and expressionless at the doorway. Greeting him, I said in a low tone, in French: "l'Homme du destin". He remained impassive.'[60]

De Gaulle's aide-de-camp, Geoffrey de Courcel, who was standing next to the General, did not hear these prophetic words.[61] Did de Gaulle hear them? 'No, I didn't,' the General later answered, and he added: 'You know, Churchill is a romantic type.'[62] After all, Churchill spoke in a low tone, and the distance between the Prime Minister's mouth and the General's ear was not inconsiderable; but being 'a romantic type', Churchill may have had, then and there, the intuition that he had before him the very model of the historic figure, who remains unrattled when others panic, simple, reserved, resolved, 'sans peur et sans reproche'.

De Gaulle, as we have seen, was in a much less romantic frame of mind, and what he heard immediately afterwards in the courtyard appeared to confirm his suspicions. General Spears later recalled:

As I stood in the doorway, de Gaulle appeared. . . . He called me aside and said that Baudouin was putting it about to all and sundry, notably to the journalists, that Churchill had shown complete comprehension of the French situation and would understand if France concluded an armistice and a separate peace. . . . Had Churchill really said that?, de Gaulle asked. . . . I asserted that the Prime Minister could not have made anything approaching such a statement after the conference, for at it he had clearly indicated the contrary. What he had said in French, when the idea was indicated by Reynaud, was 'Je comprends' (I understand) in the sense of 'I understand what you say', not in the sense of 'I agree'. . . .

'Well, that's what Baudouin is saying,' de Gaulle replied. 'He is putting it about that France is now released from her engagement to England. It is unfortunate.'

'I will see if I can catch the Prime Minister before he leaves,' I said and, running out, I found my car and pelted after the English party. At the aerodrome all the planes were revving up against the dismal background of smashed hangars and a bomb-pitted runway. I told Churchill of Baudouin's effort, and got from him the absolute and categorical confirmation that at no time had he given to anyone the least indication of his consenting to the French concluding a separate armistice. 'When I said "Je comprends", that meant I understand. Comprendre means understand in French, doesn't it? 'Well,' said Winston, 'when for once I use exactly the right word in their own language, it is going rather far to assume that I intended it to mean something quite different. Tell them my French is not so bad as that.'[63]

'*Je comprends*'; I understand. Churchill had said this several times during the conference to indicate that he understood Reynaud's words before they were translated. Baudouin seems to have used this double meaning to good effect. As for de Gaulle, he evidently thought that far too much understanding had been shown on that occasion.

By the end of the Tours conference, de Gaulle was bewildered and angry at Reynaud's sudden about-face, and he made no effort to hide it:

I went over to M. Paul Reynaud and asked him, somewhat forcibly, 'Are you really contemplating the prospect of France asking for an armistice?' 'Certainly not!' he told me. 'But we must give the British a jolt in order to get more help out of them.'* I could not, of course, consider this reply as a valid one. After we had parted amidst the confusion of the Préfecture courtyard, I went back to Beauvais, overwhelmed, while the President du Conseil telegraphed to President Roosevelt to entreat him to intervene, letting it be understood that, failing this, all was lost for us. . . . It was obvious to me that all would soon be over. Just as a besieged fortress is very near surrender when its governor talks of one, so France

*Indeed, at the French Cabinet meeting two hours later, Paul Reynaud spoke in favour of continuing the struggle. Much has been written on Paul Reynaud's subtle tactics in those days, when he appeared irresolute to his determined British allies, and inflexibly resolved to his wavering cabinet. Whatever the alleged merits of this ambivalent attitude, it evidently failed to encourage the advocates of resistance, to discourage the advocates of capitulation.

was rapidly heading for an armistice because the head of her government officially contemplated one.[64]

De Gaulle, for one, was contemplating resignation; but Georges Mandel, the Minister of the Interior, asked to see him and dissuaded him from leaving the Cabinet; 'We are only at the beginning of a world war,' he said. 'You will have great duties to fulfil, General! But with the advantage of being, among all of us, an untarnished man. Think only of what has to be done for France, and consider that your present position may one day make things easier for you.'[65] De Gaulle was persuaded and decided to stay on.

By the next day, 14 June, the Germans had entered Paris, and the government was withdrawing further south towards Bordeaux. De Gaulle arrived there by the end of the afternoon, 'after a gloomy journey along a road thronged with processions of refugees'. He immediately went to see Paul Reynaud and told him bluntly:

> During the last three days I have realized the speed with which we are drifting towards capitulation. . . . I gave you my modest help, but this was to make war. I refuse to submit to an armistice. If you stay here, you will be submerged by defeat. We must go to Algiers forthwith. Are you or are you not resolved to do so?
>
> 'Yes!' answered M. Paul Reynaud.
>
> 'In that case, I myself must go to London in order to get the British to assist us in our transportation plans. I shall go tomorrow. Where shall we meet again?' The President of the Council's answer was: 'We will meet again in Algiers.'[66]

De Gaulle left during the night and drove towards Brittany, where he spent most of 15 June, first at Rennes, then at Brest. From Brest, he embarked for England in the destroyer *Milan*. It was a gloomy passage; de Gaulle remained sombre and silent most of the time, though at one point he asked the captain of the *Milan*: 'Would you be ready to fight under the British flag?' to which the French officer answered in the negative. De Gaulle also made this cryptic statement: 'Do you think General de Gaulle's lot is an enviable one these days?'[67]

De Gaulle would probably have been even more sombre had he known that in the meantime, Reynaud, again under the influence of the defeatists in his Cabinet, was sending Churchill a telegram asking the British government's agreement to a French demand for armistice terms, and implying that he, Reynaud, would resign if the British refused.

General de Gaulle arrived in London at dawn on 16 June. Shortly afterwards, in his room at the Hyde Park Hotel, he was visited by two Frenchmen, Jean Monnet and Ambassador Corbin. They first informed him of the telegram sent by Paul Reynaud to the British government, and added, 'We do not yet know what reply the British will give – it is to be sent this morning. But we think they will consent, in return for guarantees regarding the fleet. So we are nearing the last moments. All the more so as there is to be a Cabinet meeting at Bordeaux in the course of the day and, in all probability, this meeting will be decisive.' But Corbin and Monnet also had a proposal to make, and a rather sensational one at that:

It has occurred to us that some unexpected stroke, by introducing an entirely new factor, might change the state of minds and, in any case, strengthen M. Paul Reynaud in his resolve to leave for Algiers. We have therefore worked out with Sir Robert Vansittart, Permanent Under-Secretary at the Foreign Office, a plan which seems striking. It would consist of a proposal for the union of France and England, to be solemnly addressed by the London government to the Bordeaux government. The two countries would decide on the fusion of their administrations, the pooling of their resources and of their losses, in short a complete linking of their respective destinies. Faced with such a proposal, made in such circumstances, our ministers may wish to think again and, at the very least, to postpone surrender. But our project must first be adopted by the British government. You alone can obtain that from Mr Churchill. It is arranged that you will lunch with him. That will be the supreme opportunity – if, of course, you approve of the idea.[68]

De Gaulle examined the text which was put before him; he later wrote in his memoirs:

It was at once clear to me that the very magnitude of the project at any rate made its rapid realization impossible. It was obvious that one could not, even in principle, with a simple exchange of notes, fuse England and France together, with all their institutions, their interests and their empires, even supposing this were desirable . . . but the offer addressed by the British government to ours would imply a manifestation of solidarity which might take on a real significance. Above all, I thought, like M. Corbin and Monnet, that the proposal could provide M. Paul Reynaud, in the supreme crisis in which he was plunged, with an element of comfort, an argument for tenacity to persuade his ministers. I agreed, therefore, to try and get Mr Churchill to adopt it.[68]

During the few hours that remained before his appointed lunch with the British Prime Minister, de Gaulle proceeded to settle the question of transports to North Africa with the relevant British authorities.

Since his return from Tours, Churchill, for whom giving up was obviously a foreign word, had redoubled his efforts to bolster French resistance. Materially, he had given orders for the British reinforcements to keep on landing in France, though the battle was clearly lost by now. General Ismay had objected to this, and added: 'Need we be in too much of a hurry? Could we not unobtrusively delay their departure?' But Churchill would have none of it. 'Certainly not. It would look very bad in history if we were to do any such thing.'[69]

Churchill felt that moral encouragement was also needed. On the evening of the 13th, he drafted a message which the Cabinet then sent to Paul Reynaud. It ended with these words: 'We shall never turn from the conflict until France stands safe and erect in all her grandeur.'[70] In addition, on the 13th, 14th and 15th of June, Churchill sent an uninterrupted flow of telegrams to President Roosevelt, reminding him that the French condition for carrying on the fight had been a promise of active US support, and that failing such support, French resistance on the Continent would almost certainly come to an end.[71]

Whatever the Prime Minister's earnest desire to keep on helping France, his attention was increasingly monopolized by the dangers threatening the British Isles. For England was now being subjected to massive bombings, her defences remained appallingly weak, and there was still the formidable threat of the French fleet falling into German hands if the French government capitulated. Such were Churchill's preoccupations when, on the day before de Gaulle's arrival, he was first told of the grandiose project of a Franco-British Union.

Churchill, as we know, had other preoccupations, and although a Francophile, he was also a realist: the proposal did not seem practicable to him, and Captain Margesson reported that upon hearing of it, the Prime Minister had been 'bored and critical'.[72] Churchill later confirmed this: 'My first reaction was unfavourable. I asked a number of questions of a critical character, and was by no means convinced. However, at the end of our long Cabinet that afternoon the subject was raised. I was somewhat surprised to see the staid, stolid, experienced politicians of all parties engage themselves so passionately in an immense design whose implications and consequences were not in any way thought out.'[73] One of Churchill's secretaries, John Colville, was to write that 'the suggestion was far from Churchill's thoughts: his mind was concentrated on the importance of keeping the French fleet out of German hands if France should capitulate.'

Sir John Colville was with Churchill during the next two days, and his diary for the evening of 15 June reads:

> We arrived at Chequers in time to dine at 9.30. The party consisted of Winston, Duncan and Diana Sandys, Lindemann and myself. It was a dramatic and fantastic evening. Before going into the dining-room, I learned by telephone that the position was deteriorating fast and the request to be allowed to make a separate peace was being put in a more brutal form. I imparted this to Winston who was immediately very depressed. Dinner began lugubriously, the Prime Minister every now and then firing some technical question at Lindemann, who was quietly consuming his vegetarian diet. The Sandys' and I sat silent, because our sporadic efforts at conversation were not well received. However, champagne, brandy and cigars did their work and we soon became talkative, even garrulous. Winston, in order to cheer himself and us up, read aloud the messages he had received from the Dominions and the replies he had sent to them and to Roosevelt. 'The war is bound to become a bloody one for us now,' he said, 'but I hope our people will stand up to bombing and the Huns aren't liking what we are giving them. But what a tragedy that our victory in the last war should have been snatched from us by a lot of softies!' . . . Winston and Duncan Sandys paced up and down the rose garden in the moonlight. . . . I spent much of the time telephoning, searching for Winston among the rose bushes and listening to his comments on the war. I told him that fuller information had been received about the French attitude, which appeared to be slipping. 'Tell them,' he said 'that if they let us have their fleet we shall never forget, but that if they surrender without consulting us, we shall never forgive. We shall blacken their name for a thousand years!' Then, half afraid I might take him seriously, he added: 'Don't, of course, do that just yet.' He was in high spirits, repeating poetry, dilating on the drama of the present situation.[74]

The Prime Minister's lunch with de Gaulle was to take place the next day, 16 June, at Chequers. But that morning, Churchill, having finally been given the exact content of Paul Reynaud's telegram about the request for armistice terms, called a Cabinet meeting for 10.15 to draft a reply, and the lunch with de Gaulle was therefore to take place at the Carlton Club immediately afterwards. The reply that was finally dispatched to Bordeaux was couched in the following terms:

Our agreement forbidding separate negotiations, whether for armistice or peace, was made with the French Republic, and not with any particular French administration or statesman. It therefore involves the honour of France. Nevertheless, *provided, but only provided, that the French fleet is sailed forthwith for British harbours pending negotiations,* His Majesty's government give their full consent to an enquiry by the French government to ascertain the terms of an armistice for France. His Majesty's government, being resolved to continue the war, wholly exclude themselves from all part in the above mentioned enquiry concerning an armistice.[75]

When Churchill finally arrived at the Carlton Club to lunch with de Gaulle, Corbin, Monnet, Eden and Sir John Dill, the Declaration of Franco-British Union was probably the last thing on his mind; we have already seen that he was not favourable to it, and furthermore, according to Sir John Colville, 'there had been no word spoken of Franco-British Union at Chequers and Churchill, who seldom kept anything of importance entirely to himself, had evidently forgotten all about it or dismissed it from his mind as a fantasy'.[76]

Thereupon, Winston Churchill and General de Gaulle met for the fourth time. Their discussion during lunch first centred on Churchill's main preoccupation of the moment, the French fleet, and de Gaulle told him bluntly:

In order to make sure that the enemy will never seize our ships, we would have to remain at war. Well, I must tell you that your attitude at Tours came as an unpleasant surprise to me. You seemed to attach little value to our alliance. Your resignation plays in the hands of those in France who favour capitulation. 'You see that we have no choice,' they say. 'The British themselves are giving us their consent.' No! you must do something quite different to encourage us in the frightful crisis with which we are faced. I then raised with Mr Churchill the proposal for the union of the two peoples. 'Lord Halifax has spoken to me about it,' he told me. 'But it's an enormous piece.' Yes, I answered, and its implementation would involve a great deal of time. But the gesture can be immediate. As things now stand, you must neglect nothing that can support France and maintain our alliance.[77]

Monnet and Corbin were probably right in thinking that de
Gaulle was the only one who could convince Churchill. In fact,
presented in this way, the proposal immediately became much more
attractive to the British Prime Minister; after all, anything that
might keep France fighting alongside England was worth trying, and
Churchill was not the man to balk at a gesture. 'After some discussion,' de Gaulle writes, 'the Prime Minister fell in with my view.'

For the next few hours, de Gaulle and Churchill were to co-
operate closely in a race against time to prevent the French Premier
from resigning, his government from capitulating, and the French
army from surrendering. Churchill at once summoned the British
Cabinet for 3 p.m., and left for Downing Street to preside over the
meeting. De Gaulle went with him, after having phoned Paul
Reynaud to warn him of what was afoot. The conversation was
recorded at the time:

> *De Gaulle*: I have just seen Churchill. There is something stupendous in
> preparation, affecting the entity of the two countries. Churchill proposes
> the establishment of a single Franco-British government, with you,
> perhaps, Monsieur le President, as head of a Franco-British War
> Cabinet.
> *M. Reynaud*: It is the only possible solution for the future. But it must
> be done on a large scale and very quickly, above all very quickly. It is a
> question of minutes. I give you half an hour. It would be splendid.[78]

The Cabinet met at 3 p.m. De Gaulle and Corbin were ushered
into a room adjoining the Cabinet room, and de Gaulle later wrote:
'The meeting of the British Cabinet lasted two hours, during which,
from time to time, one or other of the ministers came out to clear
some point with us French.'[79] Inside the Cabinet room, Churchill
was using all his influence in favour of the project; he recalls: 'The
draft statement was passed round, and everyone read it with deep
attention. All the difficulties were immediately apparent, but in the
end a Declaration of Union seemed to command general assent. I
stated that my first instinct had been against the idea, but that in this
crisis we must not let ourselves be accused of lack of imagination.
Some dramatic announcement was clearly necessary to keep the
French going. The proposal could not be lightly turned aside, and I
was encouraged at finding so great a body of opinion in the War
Cabinet favourable to it.'[80] Meanwhile, Sir John Colville noted: 'De
Gaulle has been strutting about in the Cabinet room, with Corbin
too: the Cabinet meeting turned into a sort of promenade, Winston

beginning a speech in the Cabinet room and finishing it in some other room; and everybody has been slapping de Gaulle on the back and telling him he shall be Commander-in-Chief (Winston muttering: "je l'arrangerai").'[81]

Just before 4 p.m. de Gaulle phoned Reynaud again, and informed the British Cabinet of the result; Churchill later wrote: 'At 3.55 p.m. we were told that the French Council of Ministers would meet at 5 p.m. to decide whether further resistance was possible. Secondly, General de Gaulle had been informed by M. Reynaud on the telephone that if a favourable answer on the proposed proclamation of unity was received by 5 p.m. M. Reynaud felt he could hold the position.[82] This, as well as Churchill's forceful advocacy of the plan, produced its effect, and finally the War Cabinet, after having discussed several amendments, reached the conclusion that 'the draft as amended did not present any insuperable difficulties, and that the right course was to proceed with the proposal, since it gave the resolute elements in France a chance to hold their own'. They also 'authorized a message to be sent by telephone to M. Reynaud informing him of the draft in time for the meeting of the Council of Ministers at 5 p.m., and invited the Prime Minister, Mr Attlee and Sir Archibald Sinclair to meet M. Reynaud at the earliest possible moment to discuss the draft proclamation and related questions'.[83] In the adjoining room, de Gaulle's long wait had come to an end: 'Suddenly,' he wrote,

> they all came in, led by Mr Churchill. 'We are agreed,' they exclaimed. Indeed, apart from a few details, the text they produced was exactly the same as the one we had proposed to them. I immediately telephoned M. Paul Reynaud and dictated the document to him. 'It's very important!' said the Premier. 'I shall use it at the meeting that is about to start.' With a few words I encouraged him as much as I could. Mr Churchill then took the telephone: 'Hallo, Reynaud! de Gaulle is right! Our proposal may have great consequences. Il faut tenir!' Then, after listening to the reply, he said, 'Well, see you tomorrow! At Concarneau.'[84]

At Downing Street, a climate of optimism and mutual sympathy now prevailed. De Gaulle, who did not really believe in the project, had succeeded in persuading Churchill, who did not believe in it either, and together they had persuaded the British Cabinet and the French Premier to adopt it. De Gaulle and Churchill probably felt, with some justification, that they had done their utmost to strengthen Reynaud's hand and enable him to convince his Cabinet colleagues to continue the struggle from the empire; this was no mean achievement. De Gaulle had a last interview with Churchill in the Cabinet room just before leaving for Bordeaux; Jean Monnet was also present, and he asked the Prime Minister once again to send all remaining British fighter squadrons to share in the final Battle of France. But the Prime Minister's answer was again negative:

> I told him that there was no possibility of this being done. Even at this stage he used the usual arguments – 'the decisive battle', 'now or never', 'if France falls, all falls', and so forth. But I could not do anything to oblige him in this field. My two French visitors then got up and moved towards the door, Monnet leading. As they reached it, de Gaulle, who had hitherto scarcely uttered a single word, turned back, and, taking two or three paces towards me, said in English: 'I think you are quite right.' Under an impassive, imperturbable demeanour he seemed to me to have a remarkable capacity for feeling pain. I preserved the impression, in contact with this very tall, phlegmatic man: 'Here is the Constable of France.' He returned that afternoon in a British aeroplane, which I had placed at his disposal, to Bordeaux.[85]

And de Gaulle himself was to write: 'I took leave of the Prime Minister. He lent me an aeroplane in which to fly back to Bordeaux at once. We agreed that the machine should remain at my disposal in case of events which might lead me to return. Mr Churchill himself was going to catch a train in order to board a destroyer for the journey to Concarneau. At 9.30 p.m. I landed at Bordeaux.'[86] At Bordeaux airport, two of de Gaulle's collaborators, Colonel Humbert and J. Auburtin, told him what had just happened at the Cabinet Council: Paul Reynaud had resigned, and Marshal Pétain was being asked to form a government. The Marshal would certainly ask for an armistice. It was all over.*

---

*At the Cabinet meeting in Bordeaux, Paul Reynaud had read the Declaration of Union, and explained its importance. But to his surprise, he met with absolutely no support from members of the Cabinet. Some of them stated that France would then become a British dominion, and the majority appeared to believe that the Declaration was irrelevant. Paul Reynaud was depressed at this, and his suggestion that only the army should lay down arms, while the government continued the war outside France, was likewise violently opposed by Weygand and Pétain. On the other hand, a majority of the Cabinet seemed to be in favour of Mr Chautemp's proposal that Germany should be asked to communicate her armistice terms. Paul Reynaud thereupon said that he could not himself pursue such a policy and that President Lebrun would then have to ask Marshal Pétain to form a government instead of him. The meeting closed at 7 p.m., with the government having in fact resigned. Shortly after 10 p.m. that night, President Lebrun formally asked Marshal Pétain to form a government.

Though de Gaulle had lost all illusions about Paul Reynaud's determination since the meeting at Tours, he genuinely expected that the Declaration of Franco-British Union would enable the French Premier to carry the day that afternoon. The news of Reynaud's demise must therefore have come as a crushing blow; but de Gaulle was not unprepared: on the evening of 13 June, he had already told his friend Jean Auburtin: 'The more I think of it, the more I believe that the only solution lies in the retreat to North Africa . . . at any rate, I will never sign the armistice. It would be contrary to honour and French interests . . . protected by the sea, we will be able to amass a large quantity of equipment supplied by England and America. . . . In one or two years we will have a crushing superiority in material . . . and then from the empire we will reconquer the mainland.'[87] When in London on the 16th de Gaulle had already ordered the French cargo ship *Pasteur*, bound for Bordeaux with cannons and machine-guns from America, to be diverted to a British port.[88] Finally, there was his last conversation with Churchill, with these words about the plane bringing him back to France: 'We agreed that the machine should remain at my disposal in case of events which might lead me to return.'[89] At any rate, upon hearing the news of Reynaud's resignation, de Gaulle did not hesitate: 'My decision,' he wrote, 'was taken at once. I would leave as soon as morning came.'[90]

That evening, de Gaulle went to see Paul Reynaud, whom he found 'with no illusions about the consequences of the Marshal's access to power and, on the other hand, as if relieved from an intolerable burden'.[91] De Gaulle told him of his decision to leave for England, and later in the evening, Paul Reynaud sent him 100,000 francs, drawn from secret funds. De Gaulle then went to the residence of the British Ambassador, Sir Ronald Campbell, and also told him of his intention to leave for London. General Spears, who was there as well, said that he would accompany him, and shortly before midnight, he called Churchill on the phone. Whether or not de Gaulle was afraid of being arrested that night, as Spears was to state, is not known. But Churchill remembers that Spears 'spoke with some anxiety about the safety of General de Gaulle'. He had 'apparently been warned that as things were shaping it might be well for de Gaulle to leave France'; and Churchill adds: 'I readily assented.'[92]

On the following day, the 17th, at 7 a.m., de Gaulle and his ADC,

Lieutenant Geoffrey de Courcel, joined General Spears, and before driving to the airport, de Gaulle stopped at the rue Vital-Carles, where the General Staff and the President of the Council had their headquarters; Jean Mistler, then President of the Commission for Foreign Affairs at the Chamber of Deputies, remembers having seen him there, in the office of General Lafont: 'De Gaulle sat down on the general's desk,' he recalls. 'I can still see him with his arms raised, saying dispassionately, calmly, as if it were obvious: "The Germans have lost the war. They are lost, and France must keep on fighting." '[93]

This was an astonishing thing to say in mid-June 1940. But whatever de Gaulle's thoughts about the future, his decision to leave was an instinctive one. 'The defeated,' he had said a few days earlier, 'are those who accept defeat.'[94] And de Gaulle, thinking of France's honour, Britain's fighting spirit and America's resources, could not accept defeat; this is why, at 10 a.m. on 17 June, he was flying towards England, and an unknown destiny. He had only his faith and his determination to prove that France had not lost the war. But in England, at that time, he also had a powerful ally: the British Prime Minister himself.

Churchill had heard of Reynaud's resignation at 10 p.m. on the evening of the 16th, as he was about to take the train for Southampton. At 11.30, he heard that Pétain was to succeed him, and understood instantly what this meant for France. His trip to France was by then quite useless, but Churchill would not give up; that night, he decided to call Marshal Pétain. At 2 a.m., after long and frustrating delays, the Marshal was finally reached on the telephone. General Hollis was with Churchill that night, and he recalls: 'It was the most violent conversation I ever heard Churchill conduct; he only spoke so roughly because he felt that anger might sway the old Marshal when nothing else would. But, like the journey, it was all in vain.'[95]

By the morning of 17 June, the British Prime Minister was no longer in doubt: England was now on her own. To be sure, Churchill knew no fear; besides, he realized the advantages of Britain's insular position, as well as the might of her fleet and air force. But he could not really admit that France was disappearing from the camp of democracy and from the alliance of free nations, where he had always put her; and how would the British people react? Now, at the time of greatest peril, the British people were to be told that their only ally was gone; a greater blow to British morale could hardly be conceived. These were some of Churchill's thoughts when, at the beginning of the afternoon, de Gaulle and General Spears arrived at Downing Street after an eventful flight. 'Winston,' Spears later wrote, 'was sitting in the garden enjoying the sunshine. He got up to greet his guest, and his smile of welcome was very warm and friendly.'[96]

This was their fifth meeting, and neither of the two men ever forgot it. Churchill's intuition at Tours had proved correct after all. At that moment, he saw in de Gaulle the very picture of undefeated France coming to share England's ordeal; during the next few years, and indeed long after that, the memory of this moment was to bring tears to Churchill's eyes. 'Undefeated France' was precisely what de Gaulle wanted to stand for; and in Churchill, he found a man who understood him from the start: 'This exceptional artist,' he wrote in his memoirs, 'could certainly feel the dramatic character of my mission.'[97] And the General added: 'Washed up from a disastrous shipwreck upon the shores of England, what could I have done without his help? He gave it to me at once. . . .'[98]

Indeed, Churchill was to lend de Gaulle a strong and willing hand. Without it, the General's subsequent efforts would have been utterly vain, and de Gaulle himself later admitted as much.[99] Even when the British Prime Minister ceased to be a friend, even when he almost became an enemy, the General never forgot that by helping de Gaulle in the dark days of June 1940, Winston Churchill had vitally helped the cause of France.

CHAPTER 4

Hoisting the Flag

The dawn of 18 June rose over a day of great uncertainties. France would probably capitulate, but she had not yet done so. England had not yet been attacked, but that was sure to come. Few Frenchmen doubted that England would soon be submerged by the Nazi hordes, and this was a potent argument in favour of capitulation. In fact, few Englishmen believed that England could indefinitely resist the German onslaught either, but this was an added reason for putting up a spirited fight.

General de Gaulle, living his second day of exile in England, did not share these uncertainties. He knew the men of Bordeaux, and had not the slightest doubt that they would capitulate. He had also measured the determination of the British people, and was convinced that they would hold out. That is why on 17 June, he had asked Churchill for permission to use the BBC in order to broadcast an appeal to resistance. The Prime Minister had assented at once; he entirely shared de Gaulle's views on the Bordeaux government, and was not unmindful of the propaganda value of the General's undertaking at a time when France was about to disappear from the Allied camp.

The members of the War Cabinet had not yet grasped the realities of the situation, and they were much less understanding; at their meeting on the morning of 18 June, in Churchill's absence, they agreed that 'it was undesirable that General de Gaulle, as *persona non grata* to the present French government, should broadcast at the present time, so long as it was still possible that the French government would act in a way conformable to the interests of the alliance'.[1] But that afternoon, General Spears visited Churchill and persuaded him that this would not do; with the Prime Minister's backing, he then set out to convince the ministers that they should reverse their decision. Spears was persuasive, Churchill's backing

was decisive, and the minutes of the War Cabinet simply state that
'The members of the War Cabinet were consulted again indi-
vidually, and agreed.'[2]

At 6 p.m. that evening, General de Gaulle broadcast his appeal to
France.* It was a call to arms. It was also an explicit reproach to the
new leaders of France for negotiating with the enemy before the
battle was really lost. It was above all an act of dissidence, and no
one was more aware of this than Charles de Gaulle himself: 'As the
irrevocable words flew out upon their way, I felt within myself a life
coming to an end – the life I had lived within the framework of a
solid France and an indivisible army. At the age of 49 I was entering
upon adventure, like a man thrown by fate outside all terms of
reference.'[3]

For de Gaulle, it must indeed have been an agonizing dilemma.
From a country that was bracing for invasion, a brigadier-general
challenged the authority of a Marshal of France. To the first men
who answered his call, de Gaulle did not conceal the extraordinary
difficulty of his undertaking: 'I have neither funds nor troops. I don't
know where my family is. We are starting from scratch. . . .'[4] From a
flat furnished with a few tables and chairs on the third floor

*This was General de Gaulle's message to the French people:

The leaders who, for many years past, have been at the head of the French armed forces,
have set up a government.

Alleging the defeat of our armies, this government has entered into negotiations with
the enemy with a view to bringing about a cessation of hostilities. It is quite true that we
were, and still are, overwhelmed by enemy mechanized forces, both on the ground and in
the air. It was the tanks, the planes, and the tactics of the Germans, far more than their
numbers that forced our armies to retreat. It was the German tanks, planes and tactics that
took our leaders by surprise and brought them to their present plight.

But has the last word been said? Must we abandon all hope? Is our defeat final? – No!

Speaking in full knowledge of the facts, I ask you to believe me when I say that the cause
of France is not lost. The very factors that brought about our defeat may one day lead us to
victory.

For France is not alone! She is not alone! She is not alone! Behind her is a vast empire,
and she can make common cause with the British Empire, which commands the seas and is
continuing the struggle. Like England, she can draw unreservedly on the immense
industrial resources of the United States.

This war is not limited to our unfortunate country. The outcome of the struggle has not
been decided by the Battle of France. This is a world war. Mistakes have been made, there
have been delays and untold suffering, but the fact remains that there still exists in the
world everything we need to crush our enemies some day. Today we are crushed by the
sheer weight of mechanized force hurled against us, but we can still look to a future in
which even greater mechanized force will bring us victory. Therein lies the destiny of the
world.

I, General de Gaulle, now in London, call on all French officers and men who are at
present on British soil, or may be in the future, with or without their arms; I call on all
engineers and skilled workmen from the armament factories who are at present on British
soil, or may be in the future, to get in touch with me. Whatever happens, the flame of
French resistance must not and shall not die. Tomorrow, I shall broadcast again from
London.

of St Stephen's House, overlooking the Embankment, General de Gaulle set out to rebuild an undefeated France. With him were his ADC, Lieutenant Geoffrey de Courcel, and his Chef de Cabinet, Lieutenant Hettier de Boislambert.

The obstacles were formidable, and would have crushed lesser men. To begin with, Foreign Office opposition prevented General de Gaulle from broadcasting for several days after 19 June.[5]* There were also the waverings and procrastinations of the Vansittart Committee, which was set up to 'examine and co-ordinate all plans for dealing with the continued resistance of France',[6] but in fact co-ordinated very little and decided even less. There were the ravages of defeatism and the intrigues of Bordeaux, which prevented all the French personalities contacted by de Gaulle, including General Weygand, Paul Reynaud, General Noguès, Georges Mandel, General Mittelhauser, André Maurois, Jean Monnet, Marcel Peyrouton, and countless others from joining Free France and reinforcing it with the prestige of their names. There was the scepticism of the British establishment, reluctant to back a movement which comprised none of the traditional French politicians, and also the malevolence of some exiled Frenchmen who denounced de Gaulle's undertaking as a Fascist coup or a Communist plot. There were the enormous difficulties involved in recruiting soldiers, sailors and airmen among the victors of Narvik and the vanquished of Dunkirk, in the face of a determined obstruction by the War Office which at times looked astonishingly

---

*The Foreign Office, and particularly Lord Halifax, feared that supporting de Gaulle too openly might damage Britain's relations with Marshal Pétain. When de Gaulle was again allowed to broadcast, it was on the express condition that the script of his speech be vetted in advance by the Foreign Office. But the latter soon found out that they were dealing with a very difficult customer; de Gaulle was to deliver a major broadcast to France on 26 June at 8.30 p.m., and Lord Gladwyn later recalled:

> Seven o'clock and still no script. My chief, Sir Alexander Cadogan, went off leaving me with strict instructions. Shortly after, it arrived. I found it brilliant, but it did violate several of my rules. Making the minimum changes and even so taking a very considerable risk, I rushed round to the Rubens Hotel, only to be told that the General had not yet finished his dinner. Just before eight he emerged, clearly in a bad temper, and gazing down on me said: '*Qui êtes-vous?*' I explained that I was a mere subordinate, but that owing to the late arrival of the text it had fallen to me to propose certain '*légères modifications*'. '*Donnez-les moi!*' Awful pause. '*Je les trouve ridicules,*' said the General. '*Parfaitement ri-di-cules.*' I felt bound to point out that it was now five past eight, that the delay was not my fault and that, not to put too fine a point on it, if he could not accept the '*modifications*' he would not be able to broadcast. The ultimatum succeeded. . . . '*Eh bien,*' he said, '*j'accepte, c'est ridicule, mais j'accepte.*'[5bis]

like systematic sabotage.[7] There were the anti-Gaullist and anti-British activities of the French Naval Mission in London which, according to MI5, would have warranted the arrest of several of its members, although the Admiralty and the War Cabinet proved curiously powerless to deal with them for a very long time.[8] There was British Intelligence, which took to recruiting agents among Frenchmen who had come from France to join de Gaulle.[9] Finally there was the bombardment of the French Fleet at Mers-el-Kebir, which brought recruiting in Free French ranks to a near standstill at the beginning of July.

Such were the odds confronting General de Gaulle at a time when the French government had finally signed the Armistice, the Germans occupied the greater part of France, and the old Marshal had assumed all powers in the remaining 'Free Zone'. De Gaulle was also faced with personal problems: back in France, his mother was critically ill, and she was to die on 16 July. A fortnight earlier, de Gaulle had learned that he was being summoned to appear before a French military tribunal 'for the crime of refusal to obey orders in presence of the enemy and of inciting members of the armed forces to disobedience'.[10] A Vichy court was soon to judge the General by default . . . and sentence him to death.

In spite of all the injuries wrought by fate, enemies, allies and compatriots, General de Gaulle persevered in his undertaking, for he retained the unshakeable conviction that he was acting in the best interests of his country. 'We alone are betting on France,' he told Christian Fouchet on 19 June. 'One is always right to bet on France.'[11] And by the end of July there were already some results to show for the persistent efforts of General de Gaulle and his men. Having toured the camps at Trentham Park, Aintree, Haydock, St Albans and Harrow Park, where the French soldiers, sailors and airmen were stationed pending re-embarkation, they succeeded in enlisting veterans from Norway and Dunkirk, the greater part of two battalions of the 13th Half-Brigade of the Foreign Legion, two hundred *Chasseurs Alpins*, part of a tank company and some elements from specialized units. These were soon joined by dozens of airmen and hundreds of sailors, including the crews of several submarines and patrol craft, merchant seamen, Frenchmen residing abroad, and individual volunteers who succeeded in escaping from France. In all, some 7000 officers and men had rallied to Free France by the end of July. Among them were officers of great valour, like

Captain Tissier, Lieutenant-Colonel Magrin-Verneret, Captain Koenig, Air Force Captain de Rancourt, Commandant Pijeaud, Capitaine de Corvette d'Argenlieu and Vice-Admiral Muselier. These men were to be the main organizers and commanders of the Free French forces. Very reduced forces they were at the time; besides, their equipment was insufficient and their morale rather low. Yet the War Office and the Admiralty did very little to remedy this state of affairs, having little confidence in these self-styled 'Free French', and completely overlooking their political significance. But Free France in her infancy certainly benefited from the whole-hearted support of General Spears, who worked tirelessly in London to overcome the reluctance of the administration, the prejudices of the Establishment and the ill-will of the military. In the process, he made countless enemies among his compatriots; later on, he was to make many more among the Free French themselves. At the beginning of July, another officer had joined Free France; his name was Captain Dewavrin. Under the pseudonym of 'Passy', he was to set up and command General de Gaulle's ubiquitous and highly efficient intelligence network.

No French politician of note having made his way to England, General de Gaulle remained the solitary leader of a movement set up in defiance of the armistice – and the only representative of unconquered France. This forced him to assume the role of a political as well as a military leader; at the time, Professor Cassin, de Gaulle's legal adviser, enquired about the status of the movement: 'Are we rebuilding the French army as allies (of the British) and trying to maintain French unity?' he asked. 'We are France!' de Gaulle answered simply.[12] In June 1940, there were very few people in official capacity who were prepared to recognize General de Gaulle as representing France; but the Prime Minister of the United Kingdom, Winston Churchill, was one of them.

Ever since 18 June, Churchill's attention had been increasingly absorbed by the gravity of the military situation. Indeed, after the old Marshal had announced to the French people that he was negotiating an end to hostilities, all organized defence in France dissolved rapidly, and Operation 'Ariel', the evacuation to Britain of some 200,000 Allied troops, proceeded with the utmost dispatch. It was now certain that the full might of the Nazi war machine would be turned against Britain – and yet the island was only defended by a few badly disorganized divisions armed with rifles, less than 500 field-guns, 200 tanks and 25 air squadrons. Even the navy was overstretched and woefully short of destroyers. But Churchill's ceaseless efforts to mobilize the island's resources, improvise new ones, inspect all parts of the defence apparatus, set up plans for counter-offensive operations and support the morale of the British people did not entirely divert his attention from French affairs.

The announcement of the Armistice in France on 23 June came as no surprise to Churchill – and yet he denounced it with the utmost vigour: 'The terms of the Armistice just signed in contravention of agreements solemnly made between the Allied governments reduce the Bordeaux government to a state of complete subjection to the enemy and deprive it of all liberty and of all right to represent free French citizens. His Majesty's government therefore now declare that they can no longer regard the Bordeaux government as a government of an independent country.'[13] But Churchill had for some time been looking for means to 'lessen the shock of the impending French surrender',[14] and General de Gaulle was clearly one of them. In fact, de Gaulle had just written him a letter outlining proposals for setting up a Council of Liberation (Comité National Français) and asking the British government to recognize it. In Cabinet that day, Churchill warmly defended the proposal: 'General de Gaulle was a fine fighting soldier, with a good reputation and a strong personality, and might be the right man to set up such a council.'[15] And that evening, the BBC broadcast the following statement: 'His Majesty's government have taken note of the proposal to form a provisional French National Committee fully representing independent French elements determined on the prosecution of the war in fulfilment of the international obligations of France. His Majesty's government declare that they will recognize such provisional French National Committee and will deal with them in all matters concerning the prosecution of the war so long as that committee continues to represent all French elements resolved to fight the common enemy.'[16]

Actually, matters were somewhat more complicated at the time; Churchill – like General de Gaulle himself – was still expecting at this juncture that some prominent French politicians would arrive in England and preside over the movement. To the War Cabinet, Churchill had also said that day: 'Before . . . approving the proposal [for setting up a Council of Liberation] and giving it official recognition, it would be as well to ascertain what French personalities were available to serve on the Council. . . .'[17] However, the next few days, with the sad episode of the *Massilia* and the failure of the Duff Cooper mission,* showed that this was a forlorn hope, and notwithstanding the hostility of the British military, the disapproval of Ambassador Corbin and the objections of Lord Halifax – who wanted to 'go slow in withdrawing recognition from the Pétain government'[18] – Churchill decided to put an end to delays. On the evening of 27 June, he called General de Gaulle to Downing Street, and told him: 'You are alone – well! I shall recognize you alone.'[19] And the following communiqué was published the next morning, 28 June: 'His Majesty's government recognizes General de Gaulle as leader of all Free Frenchmen, wherever they may be, who rally to him in support of the Allied cause.'[20]

This personal recognition was clearly a limited one, and it underlined de Gaulle's failure to set up a national committee; but as it was, it gave a legal basis to de Gaulle's relations with the British government, and all the bilateral agreements concluded thereafter rested on this initial recognition. Coming from the British Prime Minister, it was an act of faith in a solitary man and an abstraction called Free France. Later events proved that it had been a wise move -- and yet Churchill was to regret it more than once during the next five years.

For the time being, however, Churchill had other preoccupations, and one problem haunted him above all others: the fate of the French fleet on the morrow of France's defeat. If such a powerful fleet were to fall into Hitler's hands, Britain and her supply lines would become extraordinarily vulnerable. To be sure, Admiral Darlan, Paul Baudouin and even Marshal Pétain had repeatedly assured the British that this would never be allowed to happen. But then, the British had already been assured that France would never sign a separate peace, that 400 captured German pilots would be turned over to the British army, that Britain would be consulted as soon as armistice terms were received from the Germans – and none

---

*The *Massilia*, an armed auxiliary cruiser, sailed from France on 21 June with twenty-four deputies, one senator and several ex-ministers who wished to continue the fight from Africa. Among them were Mandel, Daladier and Campinchi. The ship arrived at Casablanca on 24 June, but the passengers were arrested and left on board the ship in Casablanca harbour for several weeks. A British mission, led by Mr Duff Cooper and Lord Gort, was sent to Morocco on 26 June, but failed to secure the release of the prisoners, or even to get in touch with them. The passengers of the *Massilia* were subsequently sent back to France.

of these promises had been kept. Besides, the French government was not even a free agent by now, and Article 8 of the Franco-German armistice provided for the demolishing and disarming of French warships *under German or Italian control*. To be sure, this was accompanied by a German declaration that the ships would not be used for Germany's own purposes during the war . . . but whereas relying on the French government's word was already difficult at this juncture, relying on Hitler's word was clearly impossible.

In view of Churchill's immense respect for France and her soldiers, the ensuing decision must have been a heart-rending one. 'A hateful decision,' he later wrote, 'the most unnatural and painful in which I have ever been concerned.'[21] But it was a matter of life and death, and on the afternoon of 3 July, in the port of Mers-el-Kebir near Oran, the French battle-cruisers *Dunkerque* and *Strasbourg*, the battleships *Bretagne* and *Provence*, together with numerous smaller units, were attacked reluctantly but relentlessly by the overwhelming forces of Vice-Admiral Somerville. The *Bretagne* blew up, the *Dunkerque* ran aground, and the *Provence* was beached. Many French sailors perished on that frightful day.*

Churchill was not unduly worried by the reaction of the French government, which had moved to Vichy three days earlier; yet he was clearly preoccupied by de Gaulle's response upon learning of the carnage at Mers-el-Kebir. The General's initial reaction was indeed an extremely violent one,[22] but when General Spears saw him a few hours later, de Gaulle had already recovered his temper: 'His calmness was very striking, the objectivity of his view astonishing. He had evidently done a lot of thinking. What we had done, he said, was no doubt inevitable from our point of view. Yes, it was inevitable, but what he had to decide was whether he could still collaborate with us or whether he would retire from the scene and withdraw to private life in Canada. He had not yet made up his mind but would do so before morning. . . . I then went to tell the Prime Minister of the magnificent dignity displayed by de Gaulle.'[23]

Churchill was evidently much impressed. He was even more impressed when de Gaulle, after much reflection and soul-searching, broadcast the following speech to France on 8 July:

*Simultaneously, all French ships then at Portsmouth and Plymouth were taken under British control, and a French force including a battleship and four cruisers was permanently immobilized at Alexandria. At Dakar, the battleship *Richelieu* was torpedoed and damaged.

In the momentary disintegration of the French armed forces following the capitulation, one incident, which took place on 3 July, was particularly tragic. You will understand that I refer to the frightful shelling at Oran.

I shall speak quite frankly on this subject, for the present drama is one in which the future of each country is at stake, and it is therefore imperative that men of feeling should have the courage to face facts and speak their minds. Let me, then, say here and now that there is not a single Frenchman who did not learn with grief and anger that certain vessels of the French fleet had been sunk by our allies. This grief and anger comes from the innermost depths of our being.

We have no reason to dissemble our feelings and, personally, I am prepared to express them openly. I therefore ask the British to spare us, as well as themselves, any portrayal of this hateful tragedy as a direct naval success. To consider it as such would be both unjust and out of place.

In reality, the ships stationed at Oran were not in a fit state to fight. They were lying at their moorings, and could neither manoeuvre nor disperse. Their destruction was not the outcome of a glorious battle. As a French soldier, I do not hesitate to say this to our British allies, especially as I am second to none in my admiration for their navy. This being said, let me address a word to my compatriots, asking them to consider the whole affair fundamentally from the one point of view that matters in the end, that is to say, the point of view of ultimate victory and the deliverance of our country. By virtue of an agreement contrary to all honour, the government then established in Bordeaux agreed to place our ships at the mercy of the enemy. There cannot be the slightest doubt that, on principle and of necessity, the enemy would have used them either against Britain or against our own empire. I therefore have no hesitation in saying that they are better destroyed.

I prefer to know that even the *Dunkerque* – our dear, magnificent, powerful *Dunkerque* – is stranded off Mers-el-Kebir, rather than to learn one day that she has been manned by Germans and used to shell British ports, or perhaps Algiers, Casablanca, or Dakar. . . .

All serious-minded Englishmen must know that victory could never be achieved if the sympathies of France were enlisted under the banner of the enemy.

No Frenchman worthy of the name can for a moment doubt that a British defeat would seal for ever his country's bondage.

Come what may, even if for a time one of them is bowed under the yoke of the common foe, our two peoples – our two great peoples – are still linked together. Either they will both succumb, or they will triumph side by side.

As for those Frenchmen who are still free to act in accordance with the honour and interests of France, I may say on their behalf that, once and for all, they have taken this inflexible resolve: to fight on to the finish.[24]

For Churchill, this speech was concrete proof that de Gaulle was entirely trustworthy as an ally – which was undoubtedly true – and that he was a great friend of England – which was perhaps a hasty conclusion. But then, as every so often, there was a measure of wishful thinking in the Prime Minister's judgement: France had just broken off diplomatic relations with Britain after Mers-el-Kebir, yet in the person of General de Gaulle, the undaunted leader of all Free French, Britain's privileged ties with France were maintained, and the friendship could live on. This representation was necessary to a great Francophile such as Churchill; it was also indispensable to the morale of the British people, and Churchill, as a propagandist of genius, knew it better than anyone else.

De Gaulle, however, was not exactly publicity-conscious. At first, he even refused to be photographed, and he said to General Spears: 'I do not want to be made a film star by the press.'[25] He also said, only half in jest: 'Churchill will launch me like a new brand of soap.'[26] This was not far off the mark; on 18 July, Richmond Temple, an advertising consultant, was given the task of 'making the name of General de Gaulle thoroughly well-known throughout the world and particularly in Great Britain and the British Empire'.[27]

As far as Great Britain was concerned, this was no longer necessary, for de Gaulle was already a familiar figure; the story of his arrival in England had appeared in the press, together with excerpts of his first broadcast to France and reports of his efforts to set up a Free French fighting force. In fact, the image of this lonely man refusing defeat and coming to join England in her fight had struck a sentimental chord with the British people – as one Frenchman, Robert Mengin, found out to his amazement towards the end of July: 'What's this?' his British acquaintances told him, 'you are not a Gaullist? But then you must be a Pétainist? No? Then you are not on our side? You say you are? But we are backing your wonderful General de Gaulle! Oh, you Frenchmen are so complicated!'[28]

De Gaulle himself was not unaware of the esteem, sympathy and admiration that surrounded him and his movement: 'The generous kindness which the English people everywhere showed towards us was truly unimaginable,' he later wrote. 'Numerous charities were formed to help our volunteers. Countless people came to offer their services, their time and their money. Every time I appeared in public, it was in the midst of the most comforting demonstrations. When the London papers announced that Vichy was condemning me to death and confiscating my property, many jewels were left at Carlton Gardens anonymously, and dozens of unknown widows sent their wedding rings in order that the gold might help General de Gaulle in his undertaking.'[29]

The example was set from above; King George VI, together with every member of his family, lost no opportunity of showing support for the Free French and their leader. On 24 August, the King personally visited the renascent French army; and four days earlier, Winston Churchill had delivered an admirable speech in Commons: 'We have profound sympathy with the French people. Our old comradeship with France is not at an end. In General de Gaulle and his gallant band – (Hear, Hear) – that comradeship takes an effective form – (Hear, Hear). These Free Frenchmen have been condemned to death by Vichy, but the day will come, as surely as the sun will rise tomorrow, when their names will be held in honour, and their names will be graven in stones in the streets and villages of a France restored in a liberated Europe to its full freedom and its ancient fame.'[30]

But Churchill's action in favour of the General was not limited to verbal support in Parliament. If de Gaulle was able to recruit his men and collect some equipment, it was almost entirely due to the Prime Minister's ceaseless prodding of his highly reluctant generals and admirals. During the summer, Churchill was kept constantly informed of everything that concerned France in general, and Free France in particular – after which he would swoop down ruthlessly on the unfortunate official of the Ministry of Supply who seemed to show insufficient zeal in meeting de Gaulle's requests, or on the War Office department that appeared guilty of obstruction in Free French affairs. Even in the absence of such instances, there was always some scope for the Prime Minister's intervention: 'I could not reconcile myself,' he wrote to the Foreign Secretary, 'to leaving a large number of influential Frenchmen who are the adherents of the Pétain government free to run an active and effective propaganda in our Service circles and in French circles in this country, against the whole policy of aiding General de Gaulle, to which we are publicly and earnestly committed.'[31] And to General Ismay on 12 July:

Will you bring the following notice to the attention of the Chiefs-of-Staff: It is the settled policy of His Majesty's government to make good strong French contingents for land, sea, and air service, to encourage these men to volunteer to fight on with us, to look after them well, to indulge their sentiments about the French flag, etc., and to have them as representatives of a France which is continuing the war. It is the duty of the Chiefs-of-Staff to carry this policy out effectively. . . . I hope I may receive assurances that this policy is being whole-heartedly pursued. I found the conditions at Olympia very bad, and there is no doubt that the French soldiers were discouraged by some officers from volunteering. An opportunity of assisting the French would be to make a great success of their function of 14 July, when they are going to lay a wreath on the Foch statue.[32]

And to the Minister of Information at the beginning of August: 'It is important to keep General de Gaulle active in French on the broadcast, and to relay by every possible means our French propaganda to Africa. I am told the Belgians will help from the Congo.'[33] To the War Cabinet on 5 August he declared: 'It has been one of our principal objects, since the defection of the Bordeaux government, to establish the rule of a French government friendly to His Majesty's government and hostile to Germany in as many parts as possible of the French Empire. General de Gaulle with the Free French forces now in the UK has the same object, and it is right that we should give them every encouragement in carrying it out.'[34] To the Secretary of State for War during the same period: 'It . . . becomes of the utmost consequence and urgency to complete the equipment of his (de Gaulle's) three battalions, company of tanks, headquarters, etc. . . . Evidently action is being taken already, but I shall be much obliged if you will accelerate this action by every means in your power, and also if you will let me know in what way the situation has improved since Major Morton's minute of yesterday.'[35] And to Hugh Dalton at the Ministry of Economic Warfare, on 18 August: 'Ensure that General de Gaulle is consulted in regard to the subject matter of any leaflet which may in future be dropped over France or French colonies.'[36] To General Ismay at the end of August: 'If French India wish for trade they should be made to signify association with General de Gaulle. Otherwise no trade! This is not a matter upon which to be easy-going. Secretary of State for India to be informed.'[37] The exasperation of the recipients of these meddlesome instructions can easily be imagined. Yet there was nothing to be done: General de Gaulle was a friend of the Prime Minister's, nay, he was England's friend, and one could never do too much for him.

There was another instance when Churchill's intervention proved decisive – and it was a matter of capital importance to the Free French movement. Immediately after de Gaulle had been recognized by His Majesty's government as leader of all Free Frenchmen, Franco-British negotiations had started in earnest on the text of an agreement concerning the organization, employment and conditions of service of the French volunteer movement. Very difficult negotiations they proved to be, as General de Gaulle's peculiar diplomatic status was unique and without precedent, his claim to speak for France highly disconcerting to the Foreign Office, and his demands far from modest. 'The arguments over the text of the agreement between His Majesty's government and de Gaulle,' General Spears recalled, 'was conducted with exasperating acerbity on the latter's behalf by his tiresome bearded legal adviser, Professor Cassin, until even the best disposed of Foreign Office officials grew weary of trying to meet what appeared to be the manifestation of the overwrought nerves of our guests.'[38]

There were to be three rounds of negotiations, six different drafts, and the proceedings dragged on for one whole month. But by the end of July, all the main points had been cleared: General de Gaulle's force of volunteers, 'which included naval, land and air units and scientific and technical personnel, would be organized and employed against the common enemies'. It would 'as far as possible, retain the character of a French force in respect of its personnel, particularly as regards discipline, language, promotion and duties'. In addition, 'His Majesty's government would as soon as practicable, supply the French force with the additional equipment which may be essential to equip its units on a scale equivalent to that of British units of the same type'. De Gaulle himself 'declared that he accepted the general direction of the British High Command', but it was also stated that he was 'in supreme command of the French force', and that this force 'will never be required to take up arms against France'. Agreement had also been reached on the all important financial clause: 'Any expenditure incurred for the purpose of the constitution and maintenance of the French force under the provisions of this agreement will be met, in the first instance, by the appropriate departments of His Majesty's government in the United Kingdom.' But of course, France could accept no charity: 'The sums required will be regarded as advances and specially recorded; all questions relating to the ultimate settlement of these advances, including any credits which may be set off by agreement, will be a matter for subsequent arrangement.'[39]

Yet the conclusion of this all-important agreement was held up by a persistent difficulty: after the defeat of France, the British army, navy and air force had recruited numerous French soldiers, sailors and airmen, as well as officers and specialists from all three services. The British ministers concerned were quite satisfied with that arrangement, and they absolutely refused to give General de Gaulle any authority or right of control over the men already recruited – or those who would be recruited in the future. A deadlock having been reached, the matter was submitted to the Prime Minister's arbitration, and Churchill decided against his own service ministers! As a matter of principle, it was desirable that 'new recruits should join their own national forces'.[40] General de Gaulle was also to be supplied with detailed lists of all Frenchmen having joined the British armed forces since 15 June, and could make representations to the British government in individual cases. The definitive text was finally signed on 7 August at Downing Street, instead of the Foreign Office. Not surprisingly, the principal memorandum, together with the additional letters exchanged thereafter, became known as the 'Churchill-de Gaulle agreement'.* 'The August 7th agreement,' de Gaulle later wrote, 'had a considerable importance for Free France, not only because it got us out of immediate material difficulties, but also because the British authorities, having now an official basis for their relations with us, no longer hesitated to make things easier for

*The letters exchanged were of some importance and clearly reflected de Gaulle's suspicions of British policy: 'Bearing in mind, on the one hand, the hypothesis that the fortunes of war might bring England to a compromise peace and considering, on the other, that the British might perhaps be tempted by this or that overseas possession of ours, I insisted that Great Britain should guarantee the re-establishment of the frontiers of metropolitan France and of the French Empire.'[42] In a letter of 7 August, Churchill wrote: 'It is the determination of His Majesty's government, when victory has been gained by the Allied arms, to secure the full restoration of the independence and greatness of France.' In another letter, he pointed out that: 'The British government interprets the expression "full restoration of the independence and greatness of France" as having no precise relation to territorial frontiers.' And he added: 'We have not been able to guarantee such frontiers in respect of any nation now acting with us, but, of course, we shall do our best.' De Gaulle's suspicions were immediately aroused, and he answered somewhat harshly: 'I take note, Mr Prime Minister, that this is the meaning which the British government gives to the expressions quoted above. I hope that events will one day enable the British government to consider these questions with less reserve.'[43]

us. Above all, the whole world knew that a new beginning of Franco-British solidarity had been made in spite of everything.'[41]

During July and early August, while the German landing was still expected and the battle of Britain raged over the Channel and the southern ports, the Prime Minister and the Free French leader met more than once to exchange their views on the course of the war. In fact, de Gaulle was by then a regular visitor to Chequers, where Churchill liked to invite his friends. In this relaxed atmosphere, Churchill would hold his guests for a week-end under the spell of his persuasive charm and commanding personality. It is a fact that the Prime Minister's remarkable grasp of history and his unflinching resolve never failed to impress General de Gaulle on these occasions. Yet to Churchill's surprise, de Gaulle never came to Chequers as a private person; he always took France with him, and was in no way easier to deal with at Chequers than at Downing Street. For all that, the two men had long and fruitful discussions during these private meetings, and they evidently gained in the process a fair measure of insight into each other's personality and objectives. De Gaulle himself recalled one such occasion at the beginning of August, when the battle of Britain was once again the topic of their conversation:

> I can still see him raising his fists towards the sky as he cried: 'So they won't come!' 'Are you in such a hurry,' I told him, 'to see your towns devastated?' 'You see,' he replied, 'the bombing of Oxford, Coventry, Canterbury, will cause such a wave of indignation in the United States that they'll come into the war!' I expressed some doubt about that, reminding him that two months earlier the distress of France had not caused America to abandon her neutrality. 'That's because France was collapsing!' the Prime Minister said. 'Sooner or later the Americans will come, but on condition that we here do not flinch. That's why I only think of the fighter force.' He added: 'You see that I was right to refuse it to you at the end of the battle of France. If it was destroyed today, all would be lost for you, as well as for us.' 'But,' I replied, 'the intervention of your fighters, if on the contrary that had happened, might perhaps have given new life to the alliance and decided France to continue the war in the Mediterranean. In that case the British would have been less threatened and the Americans more tempted to engage themselves in Europe and in Africa.' Mr Churchill and I agreed modestly in drawing from the events which had crushed the West this commonplace but final conclusion: when all is said and done, Great Britain is an island; France the cape of a continent; America, another world.[44]

It must not be imagined, however, that the British Prime Minister
and the leader of Free France spent the better part of their time
together evoking past opportunities and reaching commonplace
conclusions. By then, in fact, they were earnestly examining a plan
of operation code-named 'Scipio', and later renamed 'Menace' – a
plan that was to have considerable importance and awesome
implications.

Ever since General de Gaulle had formed the embryo of a new
army – and of a new France – his main preoccupation had been to
bring them both into the war. In this respect, it immediately
appeared to him that Africa would be the most promising theatre of
operations. After all, the French possessions in Africa were also a
part of France; they had to be defended against the Germans – and
against Vichy. They also had to be defended against the British who
might otherwise 'be tempted to make sure of them for their own
fighting needs and for their own account'.[45] Furthermore, these
African territories would make a very good base for Free France,
which would then evolve from an exile movement in Britain to an
independent and sovereign administration on national soil. Finally,
it was obvious that Africa would be a springboard of the first order
for the reconquest of Europe.

General de Gaulle had at first contemplated an action in North
Africa, but by late July, the climate there was unfavourable to Free
France – especially after the operation at Mers-el-Kebir. Conditions
in Equatorial Africa were much more favourable, and de Gaulle,
with the help of the British Minister for Colonies, Lord Lloyd, made
detailed plans for the takeover of Chad, Cameroons and the Congo.
Several key men like Pleven, Parant, Hettier de Boislambert,
Captain de Hauteclocque* and Colonel de Larminat were to lead
the operation, which was planned for the latter part of August. But
West Africa, with its great naval base at Dakar, remained the largest
and strategically most important block to be dealt with. By the end
of July, the Free French leader, with the help of General Spears and
Major Morton, had devised a plan for the peaceful rallying of the
West African block and its all-important naval base. 'My initial
plan,' de Gaulle wrote,

> ruled out direct attack. The idea was to land at a great distance from the
> base a resolute column which would progress towards the objective,

*The future Général Leclerc

progressively rallying the territories through which it passed and the elements which it encountered. One could thus hope that the forces of Free France, growing by contagion, would reach Dakar by land. Konakry was the place where I planned to land the troops. From there one could make use of a continuous railway and road for the march on the capital of West Africa. But, to prevent the Dakar naval squadron from annihilating the expedition, the latter had to be covered from the sea – and this cover was to be requested from the British fleet. I had revealed my project to Mr Churchill in late July.[46]

The Prime Minister was fully aware of the cardinal importance of Dakar to the British war effort. Should the base fall into German hands, British sea communications in the South Atlantic would be in mortal danger, as German submarines and surface raiders would then be able to strike at Britain's maritime links with the Middle East, India and Australia around the Cape of Good Hope. In addition, all British colonies in West Africa would be directly threatened. On the other hand, if the British were able to seize Dakar, this might have a decisive effect on the battle of the Atlantic and provide a safe haven for Allied convoys to and from the Middle East. Finally, Churchill had yet another reason to be interested in Dakar; ever since the evacuation at Dunkirk, he had been trying to mount an offensive operation against the Germans somewhere along the occupied coastline of Europe. This had not proved feasible, and yet Churchill deemed an offensive operation indispensable to British morale. Actually, his attention had already been called to Dakar at the beginning of July, when the British Consul-General there had reported that 'a show of force should be made by the British fleet if possible by 10 July', and that 'arrival in force in the near future might have the desired effect without much bloodshed'.[47] Churchill had taken up the idea with enthusiasm, but it was soon rejected by the Service Chiefs as 'not practicable from the military point of view'.[48] Then came a fresh plan for the seizure of Dakar, this time from General de Gaulle.

The proposal came just in time. It seemed to vindicate Churchill's views, and the latter lost no time in submitting it to the Chiefs-of-Staff and to the War Cabinet. He made it clear to both of them that the plan, code-named 'Scipio', had his approval, and that 'he didn't want a lot of military objections put up by the Chiefs-of-Staff'.[49] Objections came nevertheless, and not only from the Chiefs-of-Staff. After a conference with de Gaulle, Spears and Morton, the First Sea

Lord reported that the operation would require a heavy commitment on the part of the Royal Navy, and for an extended period of
time. Churchill had much respect for Admiral Dudley Pound's
judgement, but no one could accuse the Prime Minister of lacking
imagination in strategic matters – and on 6 August, de Gaulle was
called to Downing Street.

'As usual,' the General later recalled,

> I found him in that large room in Downing Street which is used by
> tradition both as the Prime Minister's office and as the conference room
> of His Majesty's government. On the enormous table which fills the
> room, he had had some maps laid out, before which he paced up and
> down, talking with animation. 'We must gain control of Dakar
> together,' he said to me. 'It is capital for you. For if the operation
> succeeds, large French forces will be brought back into the war. It is very
> important for us. For being able to use Dakar as a base would help us
> considerably in the hard battle of the Atlantic. That is why, having
> conferred with the Admiralty and the Chiefs-of-Staff, I can tell you that
> we are ready to co-operate with you in the expedition. We are planning
> to assign a considerable naval squadron to it. But we would not be able
> to leave this squadron on the African coast for long. The necessity of
> bringing it back to help in covering England as well as in our operations
> in the Mediterranean demands that we should act very quickly.
> Therefore we cannot agree with your plans for landing at Konakry and
> progressing slowly across the bush – which would oblige us to keep our
> ships in these parts for months. I have something else to propose to you.'
> Then Mr Churchill, with vivid and colourful rhetoric, proceeded to
> conjure up the following scene: 'Dakar wakes up one morning, sad and
> uncertain. But behold, by the light of the rising sun, its inhabitants catch
> sight of a sea covered with ships in the distance. An immense fleet! A
> hundred war or transport vessels! They approach slowly, radioing
> messages of friendship to the town, to the navy, to the garrison. Some of
> them are flying the tricolour. The others are sailing under the British,
> Dutch, Polish, and Belgian colours. From this Allied squadron comes
> forth an inoffensive little ship bearing the white flag of truce. It enters the
> port and sets ashore the envoys of General de Gaulle. These are led to
> the Governor. He is to be convinced that, if he lets you land, the Allied
> fleet will retire, and there will only remain for you and him to settle the
> terms of his co-operation. On the contrary, if he wants to fight he is very
> likely to be crushed.' And Mr Churchill, brimming over with conviction,
> described and mimed, one by one, the scenes of the future, as they sprang
> up from his wishes and his imagination. 'During this conversation
> between the Governor and your representatives, Free French and

British aircraft are flying peacefully over the town, dropping friendly leaflets. The military and the civilians, among whom your agents are at work, are discussing passionately among themselves the advantages offered by an arrangement with you and the drawbacks presented, on the contrary, by a large-scale battle against those who, after all, are the allies of France. The Governor feels that, if he resists, the ground will give way under his feet. You will see that he will pursue the talks until they reach a satisfactory conclusion. In the meantime, perhaps he will wish to fire a few shots "for honour's sake". But he will go no further. And that evening he will dine with you and drink to final victory.'*

Laying aside the seductive ornaments with which Mr Churchill had adorned his exposition, I had to recognize, on reflection, that it was based on hard facts. Since the British could not divert important forces to the Equator for long, I could only envisage a direct operation for the seizure of Dakar. But short of a full-scale attack, this operation was bound to involve some mixture of persuasion and intimidation. At the same time, I deemed it probable that the British Admiralty would be led, one day or another, with or without the Free French, to settle the question of Dakar, as the existence there of a great Atlantic base and the presence of the *Richelieu* could not fail to arouse both its interest and its anxiety. I concluded that if we were present, the operation might take the character of a rallying – though perhaps a forced one – to Free France. If, on the contrary, we held back, the English would want sooner or later to operate on their own account. . . . After a short delay, I went back to see Mr Churchill and told him that I accepted his suggestion.[50]

De Gaulle and Churchill now had a common plan; it was based on a mixture of persuasion and intimidation', and the Chiefs-of-Staff accepted it on 7 August – admittedly without great enthusiasm. The British services thereupon set to work in earnest planning the operation in detail. From the very beginning, Churchill interfered in this planning with great energy and relish. On 8 August, he wrote to the Chiefs-of-Staff committee:

It would seem extremely important to British interests that General de Gaulle should take Dakar at the earliest moment. If his emissaries report

*In this connection, the following judgement on Churchill by Neville Chamberlain in 1928 seems worthy of note: 'In the consideration of affairs his decisions are never founded on exact knowledge, nor on careful or prolonged consideration of the pros and cons. He seeks instinctively for the large and preferably the novel idea such as is capable of representation by the broadest brush. Whether the idea is practicable or impracticable, good or bad, provided he can see himself recommending it plausibly and successfully to an enthusiastic audience, it commends itself to him. . . . So quickly does his mind work in building up a case that it frequently carries him off his own feet.'[49]

that it can be taken peaceably so much the better. If their report is adverse an adequate Polish and British force should be provided and full naval protection given. The operation, once begun, must be carried through. De Gaulle should be used to impart a French character to it, and of course, once successful, his administration will rule. But we must drive him on and provide the needful balance of force.

The Chiefs-of-Staff should make a plan for achieving the capture of Dakar. For this purpose they should consider available: (a) de Gaulle's force and any French warships which can be collected; (b) ample British naval force, both to dominate French warships in the neighbourhood and to cover the landing: (c) a brigade of Poles properly equipped; (d) the Royal Marine brigade which was being held available for the Atlantic islands, but might well help to put de Gaulle ashore first, or alternatively commandos from Sir Roger Keyes' forces; (e) proper air support, either by carrier or by machines working from a British West African colony.

Let a plan be prepared forthwith, and let the dates be arranged in relation to the Mediterranean operation.

It is not intended, after Dakar is taken, that we shall hold it with British forces. General de Gaulle's administration would be set up, and would have to maintain itself, British assistance being limited to supplies on a moderate scale, and of course preventing any sea-borne expedition from Germanized France. Should de Gaulle be unable to maintain himself permanently against air attack or air-borne troops, we will take him off again after destroying all harbour facilities. We should of course in any case take over *Richelieu* under the French flag and have her repaired. . . .

In working out the above plan time is vital. We have lost too much already. British ships are to be used as transports whenever convenient, and merely hoist French colours. No question of Orders-in-Council or legislation to transfer British transports to the French flag need be considered.

The risk of a French declaration of war and whether it should be courted is reserved for the Cabinet.[51]

The minute was labelled ACTION THIS DAY, and by 10 August, the Joint Planning sub-committee had already produced an outline plan, which was approved by the Chiefs-of-Staff. Shortly thereafter, Vice-Admiral John Cunningham and Major-General Irwin were appointed as commanders of the expedition. Churchill invited them to Chequers on 12 August, gave them the full treatment, and even drafted their instructions himself. Churchill's interventions were of course resented by the Chiefs-of-Staff – and even more by the Joint

Planners. As Marshal of the Royal Air Force Sir John Slessor, who was then Director of Plans, later wrote: 'The JP were very opposed to "Menace" from the beginning, but WSC [Churchill] put very severe (and I think improper) pressure on us – even to the extent of coming in to us in committee and bullying us. Actually, tempers got rather frayed – we made him angry by saying we thought it was an operation which could only succeed with the hearty co-operation of the enemy, which we did not think was a sound basis for planning!'[52]

Apart from the high degree of scepticism displayed by the Joint Planners, other problems dogged operation 'Menace' at this early stage, as General de Gaulle and General Spears soon found out. The latter was to note: 'Once the general lines of the operation and its dates had been settled at meetings which de Gaulle and I attended with the joint commanders, Admiral Cunningham and General Irwin, neither I nor de Gaulle were kept in the picture beyond receiving the information necessary to enable de Gaulle to issue the necessary movement orders to his troops. Everything was in the hands of the planners.'[53]

To make things worse, the British forces earmarked for the operation were gradually whittled down as planning progressed. In the end, the formidable armada of a hundred ships envisioned by Churchill was reduced to two old battleships, four cruisers, an aircraft carrier, a few destroyers and three transport ships carrying two battalions of Marines. De Gaulle himself could only assemble three sloops, two armed trawlers, four cargo boats and two Dutch liners. They would carry some two thousand men, including a battalion of the Foreign Legion. The Polish brigade, on which both Churchill and de Gaulle were counting, had disappeared from the plan at an early stage for no apparent reason.

There was also much uncertainty as to the target date for the operation. 'We had hoped to strike on 8 September,' Churchill wrote,

> but now it appeared that the main force must first go to Freetown to refuel and make their final poise. The plan was based upon the French troopships reaching Dakar in sixteen days at twelve knots. It was found however that the ships carrying the mechanical transport could only make eight to nine knots, and this discovery was reported only at a stage of loading when the time lost in re-loading into faster ships offered no gain. In all ten days' delay from the original date became inevitable: five days for the miscalculation of the speed of the ships, three days for

unforeseen loading troubles, two days for the refuelling at Freetown. We must now be content with 18 September.[54]

In fact, despite the Prime Minister's ceaseless prodding, the target date was again postponed to 19 September – and there were to be further delays after the expedition finally sailed.

There were many other shortcomings – some of them astonishingly reminiscent of the worst muddles of the Norwegian campaign. To begin with, everyone, including de Gaulle and Churchill, agreed that the operation should be an entirely peaceful one. Churchill had in fact told the Chiefs-of-Staff that 'the whole place must be given the air of a fair, a *kermesse*'.[55] But although information on the political conditions in Dakar was very incomplete, all data available on the attitude of Governor-General Boisson, a Vichyite, gave reason to expect that Dakar would not surrender without a fight; yet should an armed attack become necessary after the failure of negotiations, the attackers would have lost all the benefit of surprise by the time they ran the gauntlet of Dakar's defences. There was also an astonishing lack of information on the strength of these defences, including the number of batteries, their calibre, their positions, and the topographical characteristics of the main landing beaches around Dakar. As for any information on the surf conditions at these landing places, Rear-Admiral Maund recalls that it 'was in the nature of "it may be rough and it may not"'.[56] To make things worse, the information about Dakar given to the commanders of the expedition had been collected before the war – before the First World War, that is. More up-to-date information about troop strength in Dakar had reached the War Office in June 1940, but it remained buried there and was not used.[57] As a result, both coastal defences and troop strength at Dakar were grossly underestimated by the planners.

To all this must be added a certain weakness at the organizational level; radio communication between the Allied ships participating in the expedition was deficient, the signals staff lacked training, the force commanders did not know their men, the men had no adequate training for landing operations, and several important pieces of equipment were eventually left behind. Just before the expedition was due to sail, there were also a number of embarrassing security leaks: the Free French officers toasted '*à Dakar*' in several restaurants in London and Liverpool.[58] One particular French officer also proved alarmingly talkative in his relations with the fair sex.[59] Yet the French were far from being the only offenders; the collection of intelligence by British officers at travel agencies in London had proceeded with an appalling lack of discretion, the precise destination of the expedition was common talk among the dockers of Liverpool,[60] and on two occasions, first at the Clyde, then at Euston station, a case earmarked for embarkation was handled clumsily and burst open, scattering hundreds of tricolour leaflets inscribed: 'AUX HABITANTS DE DAKAR' and 'FRANÇAIS DE DAKAR! JOIGNEZ-VOUS A NOUS POUR DELIVRER LA FRANCE.'[61]

Undaunted by all these blunderings, de Gaulle was still confident that the operation would succeed. The rallying of Chad to Free France on 26 August, that of Cameroons on the 27th and of the Congo on the 28th had of course greatly encouraged the General and his followers. On 30 August, de Gaulle lunched with the Prime Minister at Downing Street, and the atmosphere was resolutely optimistic. The next day, the expedition finally sailed from Liverpool, with de Gaulle, General Spears and Captain d'Argenlieu on board the Dutch liner *Westernland*. Before leaving, de Gaulle had left a letter for General Catroux, who had rallied to Free France and was to arrive in London shortly thereafter. The letter is indicative of the Free French leader's state of mind at the time: 'When you receive this letter, I shall have left for Dakar with troops, ships, aircraft and ... the support of the British. I have full confidence in final victory. The English have gone all out for it and, luckily for them and for us, Mr Winston Churchill is integrally "the man for this war". The game is between Hitler and him.'[62]

But once the expedition had sailed, just about everything went wrong. The Allied ships only arrived at Freetown on 17 September, and in the meantime, it was learned that a squadron of Vichy ships from Toulon with three large modern cruisers and three light cruisers had passed the Straits of Gibraltar on 11 September, without being stopped by the British fleet. This squadron had successfully evaded interception on its way down the African coast, and anchored at Dakar on 14 September. Yet by the 19th, the six cruisers, reinforced by a seventh one, the *Primauguet*, left Dakar and steamed southwards. Their mission was evidently to bring the Congo and the Cameroons back under Vichy allegiance. This time, however, they were intercepted by Admiral Cunningham's fleet, and were forced to turn back. For the newly rallied colonies of Equatorial Africa, it had been a narrow escape; but for the Allied expedition, it was a very hard blow. Of the seven cruisers that turned back, five returned to Dakar, thus reinforcing the base with reliable officers, personnel, and navy gunners for the shore batteries.

Churchill understood the danger at once upon having been informed of the Vichy cruisers' arrival at Dakar on the 14th. 'I had no doubt whatever,' he later wrote, 'that the enterprise should be abandoned.' On 16 September, the War Cabinet adopted Churchill's advice, and dispatched the following orders to the chiefs of the expedition: 'His Majesty's government have decided that presence of French cruisers at Dakar renders the execution of Dakar operation impracticable. . . . Best plan appears to be for General de Gaulle's force to land at Duala with the object of consolidating the Cameroons, Equatorial Africa and Chad, and extending influence of de Gaulle to Libreville. The British portion of the force would remain for the present at Freetown. Unless General de Gaulle has any strong objections to the latter course it should be put into operation forthwith.'[63]

But de Gaulle had strong objections, and so did the force commanders. They all wanted to go ahead wih the operation, and asked for permission to do so. Churchill was much impressed by their determination, and permission was finally granted by the War Cabinet at noon on 18 September. Yet when the Anglo-French forces finally appeared in front of Dakar on the morning of 23 September, the inhabitants of the town were not treated to the delectable vision contemplated by Winston Churchill a month and a half earlier; indeed, a very thick fog covered everything, and the armada remained absolutely invisible from the shore. Yet the plan was carried out. At 6 a.m. de Gaulle broadcast an appeal to the sailors, soldiers and inhabitants of Dakar. Shortly thereafter, two small French planes left the aircraft carrier *Ark Royal* and landed on Dakar airfield. Other French and British planes flew over the city dropping friendly tracts and tricolour streamers. There was no immediate reaction from the town, and de Gaulle began to hope that all would go well.

Suddenly the anti-aircraft guns of the fortress opened up on the French and British planes, and the cannons of the *Richelieu* soon joined in. The three Free French officers who had landed on Dakar airfield were almost immediately arrested. In the meantime, two launches with Free French emissaries led by Captain d'Argenlieu had entered the harbour flying the tricolour and the white flag; but upon landing, the emissaries were threatened with arrest, and they were forced to leave the harbour under heavy machine-gun fire. Thereupon, the shore batteries and the cannons of the *Richelieu* opened a heavy fire on the Anglo-French ships, and the cruiser *Cumberland* was seriously damaged. The fire was returned and a long cannonade ensued.

That afternoon, it was decided to attempt a landing at the near-by port of Rufisque, but the heavy fog reigned supreme, the advance landing party encountered heavy resistance, and the attempt was finally called off. The exchange of cannon fire was to continue intermittently during the next two days, with losses on both sides but no definite results. Communications between Free French and British ships proved more and more difficult, owing to unreliable equipment. By the evening of the 25th, with Dakar no nearer surrender and the British cruiser *Resolution* heavily damaged, de Gaulle and Admiral Cunningham decided that the undertaking should be abandoned, and the Anglo-French expedition turned back towards Freetown.

De Gaulle's state of mind during the next few days can easily be imagined. Failure left a bitter taste, and the Free French leader came very near to giving up the struggle there and then. 'He . . . is so hypnotized by the fear of being accused of attacking Frenchmen that it is entirely vitiating his judgement,' General Spears wrote in his diary on the 25th.[64] In fact, de Gaulle contemplated several courses of action during the next few days – and suicide seems to have been one of them.[65] Another recurring thought was to take his troops to Egypt to fight the Italians and 'efface the impression of Dakar'.[66] On 1 October, Spears also noted, 'He [De Gaulle] is very concerned to hear of impression Dakar has made and fears for Winston.'[67]

The impression created by the failure of the expedition was indeed a disastrous one. Not surprisingly, Vichy and German propaganda sought to make the most of the event. But the British press was just as outspoken in its criticism: until the end of September, the *Daily Mail*, the *Daily Herald*, the *Manchester Guardian*, the *New Statesman*, the *Daily Telegraph*, *The Times*, the *Observer and* the *Daily Mirror* fired a series of ferocious broadsides at the government, at General de Gaulle and at all those responsible for the expedition.

The *Daily Mirror,* for instance, spoke of 'gross miscalculation, muddled dash, hasty withdrawal, wishful thinking and half-measures', and it added: 'Dakar has claims to rank with the lowest depths of imbecility to which we have yet sunk.'[68] Most of this grossly unfair criticism was of course taken up with great relish by a large part of the American press, and found its way around the world.

In spite of all that, de Gaulle had no reason to fear for Churchill's position – or for his own. The Prime Minister was as pugnacious as ever, and less inclined than ever to abandon a friend in adversity. 'We were no more anxious than was General de Gaulle,' he told the House on 8 October, 'to get involved in a lengthy or sanguinary conflict with the Vichy French. That General de Gaulle was right in believing that the majority of Frenchmen in Dakar was favourable to the Free French movement, I have no doubt; indeed, I think his judgement has been found extremely sure-footed, and our opinion of him has been enhanced by everything we have seen of his conduct in circumstances of peculiar and perplexing difficulty. His Majesty's government have no intention whatever of abandoning the cause of General de Gaulle until it is merged, as merged it will be, in the larger cause of France.' Having then explained the main reasons for the failure of the expedition, Churchill concluded with a ferocious counter-attack on his detractors: 'Criticism which is well meant and well informed and searching is often helpful, but there is a tone in certain organs of the press, happily not numerous, a tone not only upon the Dakar episode but in other and more important issues, that is so vicious and malignant that it would be almost indecent if applied to the enemy.'[69]

Though not entirely convinced by Churchill's explanations, the press was somewhat hushed by the Prime Minister's energetic intervention and caustic comments. Criticism of General de Gaulle disappeared, attacks on the government tapered off, and interest switched to other aspects of the war. Back in Africa, General de Gaulle was much heartened by the Prime Minister's gallant defence of Free France and her leader. By then, he had recovered all his fighting spirit and was preparing to leave for a tour of inspection of Free French territories in Equatorial Africa. Together with Colonel Leclerc, he was also preparing a lightning operation for the take-over of Libreville and the whole of Gabon – an operation that was to be crowned with success a month later.

For all that, the failure of de Gaulle and Churchill's first common venture was to prove most damaging to the cause of Free France. It dashed all hopes of an early rallying of West and North Africa. It discouraged many Frenchmen from joining de Gaulle, and comforted many more in their hostility to his cause. In England, it led many people to believe that the Free French were untrustworthy – which was unfair – and that their indiscretions before the start of the expedition had compromised the whole operation – which was untrue.* Yet many people in the War Office and Admiralty were to use this as a pretext for excluding the Free French from the planning of future operations. More damaging still were the repercussions in the United States: President Roosevelt, who had shown much enthusiasm for the undertaking before it started,[70] was unfavourably impressed by its failure, and thereby comforted in his low esteem for General de Gaulle,[71] whom he already considered as a puppet of the British. Later in the war, he was also to use Dakar as an excuse for excluding the Free French from Allied operations in Africa . . . and elsewhere.

---

*Vichy had in fact received no advance information on the planned expedition. As we have seen, the Vichy cruiser squadron whose arrival compromised the operation had sailed from Toulon to reconquer Cameroon and the Congo, not to defend Dakar.

CHAPTER 5

Partnership

Churchill was most distressed at the failure of the Dakar operation. Yet, as he had told the honourable Members of Parliament, this failure had by no means diminished his confidence in General de Gaulle. Indeed, he had been much impressed by the General's determination to go ahead with the operation against formidable odds. Besides, unlike many irresponsible critics of the operation, Churchill knew the real reason for the failure of the expedition: an extraordinary breakdown in communications at the Admiralty, allowing the Vichy cruiser squadron to leave the Mediterranean unhindered and arrive at Dakar. As for the often repeated argument that de Gaulle had imposed the Dakar plan on Churchill, it was nothing but ill-informed chatter, and no one knew it better than the Prime Minister himself. The Dakar fiasco may have had many ill effects, but a deterioration in the relations between de Gaulle and Churchill was certainly not one of them.

For all his efforts to increase de Gaulle's influence, authority and power, Churchill was not entirely taken in by the fiction he had so decisively helped to create. Whatever de Gaulle's courage and stature, it was obvious that he and his movement could not claim to be an alternative French government – nor could they speak for the whole of France; and yet Churchill could not resign himself to losing all contact with this unfortunate country and its captive government. For this, there were some highly pragmatic reasons: the Vichy government still controlled the French fleet and the greater part of the empire; there was also another reason, as evidenced by the following letter written by Churchill to Lord Halifax on 25 July: 'I want to promote a kind of collusive conspiracy in the Vichy government whereby certain members of that government, perhaps with the consent of those who remain, will levant to North Africa in order to make a better bargain for France from the North African shore and from a position of independence. For this purpose I would use both food and other inducements, as well as the obvious arguments.'[1]

But as always with Churchill, pragmatism was mixed with sentiment – especially where France was concerned. Hugh Dalton, who met him at Downing Street on 3 September, wrote in his diary: 'He is very vexed at the difficulties of communication with France. He says: "I can't even find an American who would take a letter from me to General Georges. It would be quite a short letter. I should simply say, as Thiers said: 'On pensez toujours! On parlez jamais! . . .' He would understand that. I should need to say no more." '[2]

In spite of the Prime Minister's rather shaky French grammar, General Georges probably would have understood the allusion; but he was too old to participate in the collusive conspiracy which Churchill had in mind. As for the inducement of food to bring about an increased Vichy resistance in North Africa, it certainly prompted a long dialogue between the Vichy Foreign Minister Paul Baudouin and the Foreign Office, with the British Embassy at Madrid serving as a go-between. But no really positive proposal was made by Vichy in exchange for a relaxation of the British blockade, and for all his sentimentalism, Churchill was not the man to give something for nothing.

General Catroux, who arrived from Indochina on 17 September to join the Free French movement, was to have a privileged insight into the Prime Minister's astonishing blend of sentimentalism and pragmatism. According to Catroux, Churchill talked of de Gaulle 'in the warmest and most grateful terms, he praised his force of character and his sense of honour. He told me that he would never forget that he (de Gaulle) had been faithful to Great Britain at the most critical hour and that he had never varied, even after the ordeal of Mers-el-Kebir.' But Churchill had also told Catroux that day: 'All in all, I believe it is in London that your presence would be the most useful at the present time. The Free French movement needs to be led, and I believe you ought to assume its leadership.'[3]

These words can be interpreted in several ways. Lord Lloyd, with whom Catroux talked immediately afterwards, told him that the Prime Minister was concerned with the failure of the Free French movement to command the allegiance of more than a handful of Frenchmen, and thought that Catroux, being better known and more familiar with international circles, might have more success in this respect.[4] This was Lloyd's interpretation, and it was probably more a reflection of his own ideas. General de Gaulle, to whom Catroux naturally reported the conversation, deduced that the Prime Minister was merely out to 'divide and rule'.[5] The real explanation seems to be that the Free French movement being torn by intrigue and inner strife at the time, Churchill thought that Catroux could put an end to the squabbles pending de Gaulle's return. After all, Churchill's precise words had been: 'I believe it is in London that your presence would be the most useful *at the present time*.'[6] Some people might still object that Churchill was meddling in affairs that were not his concern – but then Churchill was forever meddling in affairs that were not his concern.

In Madrid, meanwhile, informal contacts were being maintained between the Vichy French and the British Embassy. On 13 September, the British Ambassador, Sir Samuel Hoare, transmitted a message from Baudouin proposing 'a colonial *modus vivendi*'.[7] A fortnight later, the embassy in Madrid relayed yet another message from the same source. It said that:

> If the French government was not to be driven entirely into German hands, Great Britain must let supplies pass from French colonies to unoccupied France. If these supplies were allowed, the French government would be prepared to arrange any necessary supervision and would give a guarantee that neither the supplies nor their equivalent in France would be seized by the Germans. If the Germans made an attempt to seize them, the French government would be transferred to Morocco and France would be once again allied with the United Kingdom against Germany.[8]

This time, the British government began to show some interest, and they replied that they would be prepared to study the Vichy proposals; but they added:

> It should be made clear that His Majesty's government attach the utmost importance to their blockade weapon, which they must continue to employ to the full against the enemy. They would only contemplate any relaxation if absolutely satisfied that the French government are able and willing, as regards their overseas territories, to act independently of German or Italian dictation and are moreover ready to adopt a more co-operative attitude than they have hitherto shown in their dealings with His Majesty's government.[9]

It must not be imagined that this indirect dialogue with Vichy was conducted without de Gaulle's knowledge. The Free French leader, then in Lagos, was kept fully informed by Churchill of the above exchange, and he even asked the Governor of Nigeria on 3 October to transmit the following comments to the Prime Minister:

1. De Gaulle has noted with greatest interest that, for the first time in an official communication, the Vichy government has envisaged such circumstances in which official France would resume war on the side of Great Britain.

2. In view of the *fait accompli* and the policy followed by the government of Vichy, such a step must be considered as a sign of political disarray bordering upon despair, rather than a frank admission of an immeasurable national and international error.

3. In any case, it is necessary to emphasize the following point: Even if the Vichy government moved one day, either in whole or in part, to North Africa and proclaimed their will to take up the fight again, they could have neither authority nor effectiveness enough for waging war.

4. Whatever arrangements the British government could be prevailed upon to agree to with the Vichy government as regards the economic relations between unoccupied France and the French Empire, there is no doubt that these arrangements would entail a strengthening, at any rate temporarily, of the influence of Vichy on the colonies, which at the moment is dwindling. It would probably be preferable to suggest to the Vichy government that direct supplies should be made through assistance organizations in the United States, provided that adequate control should be established. In this case and in accordance with a previous suggestion made by General de Gaulle, it would be advisable that the supply arrangements should be considered as having been agreed to at the request of General de Gaulle.[10]

Vichy's reply was not satisfactory from the British point of view, as it gave not the slightest hint of a change in policy – though it reaffirmed the French government's determination to retain control of their empire and fleet. Thereupon, the British ambassador was instructed to convey orally to his French colleague that 'although disappointed with tenor of reply His Majesty's government are still prepared to continue discussion on lines indicated in their last communication . . . they would be glad to examine any concrete French proposals'.[11] Lord Halifax informed de Gaulle of this exchange and added:

We are disagreeably impressed though not surprised with the Vichy
government's reply, but as they apparently do not wish to break with us,
we should be glad to extract what we can from this situation. We think it
well to pursue this exchange of views with the Vichy government in the
hope that they will find it in their interest to reach an accommodation
with us. We realize that they are under the German heel and they cannot
be regarded as free agents in anything that they do.[12]

This was precisely what worried Churchill. Rumours were
reaching him from various quarters that the Vichy government were
preparing to put their fleet and empire at the disposal of Germany.
Churchill accordingly wrote on 20 October to President Roosevelt:
'If the French fleet at Toulon were turned over to Germany, it would
be a very heavy blow. It would certainly be a wise precaution,
Mr President, if you would speak in the strongest terms to the
French Ambassador, emphasizing the disapprobation with which the
United States would view such a betrayal of the cause of democracy
and freedom. They will pay great heed in Vichy to such a
warning.'[13]

Churchill also wrote to Pétain and told him: 'We cannot
understand why no French leaders secede to Africa and make
common cause with us there.' Yet by the evening of 20 October, the
Prime Minister was still not satisfied that everything had been done
to dissuade the old Marshal from sliding further down the slippery
slope of collaboration. And what would the French people say?
Churchill continued to brood, and General Ismay, who was with
him that evening, recalls what followed:

We were alone in the Hawtrey Room at Chequers, and the clock had just
chimed midnight. Mr Churchill looked tired out and I had visions of an
early bed. But suddenly he jumped up, exclaiming, 'I believe that I can
do it'. Bells were rung; secretaries appeared; and he proceeded to dictate
his first broadcast to France. He had no notes; but slowly and steadily,
for a space of some two hours, the words poured forth. The result would
have been a tour de force by any standards at any time; but, in those
circumstances, it was a most remarkable triumph of mind over matter.[14]

Somewhat more modestly, Churchill later wrote: 'I took great
pains to prepare this short address, as it had to be given in French. I
was not satisfied with the literal translation at first provided, which
did not give the spirit of what I could say in English and could feel in
French, but M. Dejean, one of the Free French staff in London,
made a far better rendering, which I rehearsed several times and

delivered from the basement of the annexe, amid the crashes of an air raid.'[15]

The result was indeed an impressive one. On the evening of 21 October, the French people tuning in to the BBC were amazed to hear the following address, delivered in French with unmistakably Churchillian accents:

Frenchmen! For more than thirty years in peace and war I have marched with you, and I am marching still along the same road. Tonight I speak to you at your firesides wherever you may be, or whatever your fortunes are: I repeat the prayer around the louis d'or, '*Dieu protège la France.*' Here at home in England, under the fire of the Boche, we do not forget the ties and links that unite us to France, and we are persevering steadfastly and in good heart in the cause of European freedom and fair dealing for the common people of all countries, for which, with you, we drew the sword. When good people get into trouble because they are attacked and heavily smitten by the vile and wicked, they must be very careful not to get at loggerheads with one another. The common enemy is always trying to bring this about, and, of course, in bad luck a lot of things happen which play into the enemy's hands. We must just make the best of things as they come along.

Here in London, which Herr Hitler says he will reduce to ashes, and which his aeroplanes are now bombarding, our people are bearing up unflinchingly. Our air force has more than held its own. We are waiting for the long-promised invasion. So are the fishes. But, of course, this for us is only the beginning. Now in 1940, in spite of occasional losses, we have, as ever, command of the seas. In 1941 we shall have command of the air. Remember what that means. Herr Hitler with his tanks and other mechanical weapons, and also by Fifth Column intrigue with traitors, has managed to subjugate for the time being most of the finest races in Europe, and his little Italian accomplice is trotting along hopefully and hungrily, but rather warily and very timidly, at his side. They both wish to carve up France and her empire as if it were a fowl; to one a leg, to another a wing or perhaps part of the breast. Not only the French Empire will be devoured by these two ugly customers, but Alsace-Lorraine will go once again under the German yoke, and Nice, Savoy and Corsica – Napoleon's Corsica – will be torn from the fair realm of France. But Herr Hitler is not thinking only of stealing other people's territories, or flinging gobbets of them to his little confederate. I tell you truly what you must believe when I say this evil man, this monstrous abortion of hatred and defeat, is resolved on nothing less than the complete wiping out of the French nation, and the disintegration of its whole life and future. . . . You will excuse my speaking frankly because this is not a time to mince words. It is not defeat that France will now be made to suffer at German hands, but the doom of complete obliteration. Army, navy, air force, religion, law, language, culture, institutions, literature, history, tradition – all are to be effaced by the brute strength of a triumphant army and the scientific low cunning of a ruthless police force.

Frenchmen – re-arm your spirits before it is too late. . . . Never will I believe that the soul of France is dead. Never will I believe that her place amongst the greatest nations of the world has been lost for ever! . . .

Remember we shall never stop, never weary, and never give in, and that our whole people and empire have vowed themselves to the task of cleansing Europe from the Nazi pestilence and saving the world from the new Dark Ages. Do not imagine, as the German-controlled wireless tells you, that we English seek to take your ships and colonies. We seek to beat the life and soul out of Hitler and Hitlerism. That alone, that all the time, that to the end. We do not covet anything from any nation except their respect. Those French who are in the French Empire, and those who are in so-called unoccupied France, may see their way from time to time to useful action. I will not go into details. Hostile ears are listening. As for those to whom English hearts go out in full, because they see them under the sharp discipline, oppression, and spying of the Hun – as to those Frenchmen in the occupied regions – to them I say, when they think of the future let them remember the words which Thiers, that great Frenchman, uttered after 1870 about the future of France and what was to come: 'Think of it always: speak of it never.'

Good-night, then: sleep to gather strength for the morning. For the morning will come. Brightly will it shine on the brave and true, kindly upon all who suffer for the cause, glorious upon the tombs of heroes. Thus will shine the dawn. *Vive la France!* Long live also the forward march of the common people in all lands towards their just and true inheritance, and towards the broader and fuller age.[16]

The many Frenchmen who heard this broadcast never forgot it, as they were to make abundantly clear four years later. As far as Pétain was concerned, Churchill had no real cause for anxiety: in spite of a somewhat altered lucidity, the old Marshal had not entirely lost sight of French interests. In fact, he was hoping to secure for France the most favourable conditions by playing a complicated game between Britain and Germany – as Hitler himself was to find out when he met the Marshal three days later. Another man, Professor Louis Rougier, also gained some insight into Pétain's strategy when he visited him on 20 September. He had come to ask for permission to go to England, in order to try and secure a relaxation of the

British blockade. Somewhat unexpectedly, at least to those who did not know him, the old Marshal answered that it was an excellent idea, and gave Rougier the necessary authorizations.

Professor Rougier arrived in London on 22 October. Two days later, he was received by the Prime Minister. The latter was still much preoccupied by the difficulty of communicating with France, the lack of response to his calls for resistance in North Africa, and the rumours about an imminent agreement between Vichy and Germany. He thus received Rougier with some warmth, and both men discussed the possibility of an understanding whereby Vichy would refrain from attacking colonies that had rallied to de Gaulle, and the British would likewise abstain from attacks against colonies under Vichy obedience. This was in fact the 'colonial status-quo' that had already been mentioned in the notes coming from Madrid. Yet Churchill warned that if a colony were to rally spontaneously to the Free French, 'we could not disavow General de Gaulle'. The Prime Minister further hinted that he 'should certainly consider relaxing the blockade' between France and North Africa 'if the French would resist German threats and blandishments and would organize a sphere of resistance in North Africa'.[17] But in France, meanwhile, Pétain had met Hitler at Montoire, and a fresh spate of alarming rumours about the results of this meeting presently began to reach England.

Early on 25 October, a report arrived from Madrid that Laval and Admiral Darlan had been pressing for an agreement whereby the French fleet and bases would be transferred to the Germans. Chuchill thereupon declared in Cabinet: 'If the fleet and naval bases were transferred to Germany, our navy would be faced with the most serious problems, and the situation would become an anxious one.'[18] Churchill also asked King George VI and President Roosevelt to send messages to Pétain requesting the latter to resist German demands. The evening before, he had gone one step further, and sent the following minute to the Chiefs-of-Staff:

> I see rumours in the papers that they may cede the use of their bases or some of them to Germany and Italy. If anything like this were to come from Vichy, immediate action would have to be taken. Let the Joint Planning Committee set to work at once upon a plan to capture Dakar as an important and purely British operation. . . . I should think myself that a landing by fifty or sixty tanks out of range of the guns of the fortress would very quickly bring about a decision. It must be recognized

as quite intolerable that Dakar should become a strong German U-boat base. Time is very precious, and the sooner a plan is made the better. We can go into ways and means after.[19]

This was yet another of the Prime Minister's exercises in theoretical strategy. But it was not his only instinctive reaction to the rumours appearing in the press at that time. Another disquieting piece of news, relayed from Berne, appeared in the London press on the evening of 25 October: it was to the effect that a separate peace treaty had been signed between Pétain and Hitler at Montoire. When Professor Rougier came to Downing Street the following day for a second interview with the Prime Minister, he found him in a state of barely controlled fury. 'I will send the Royal Air Force to bomb Vichy,' Churchill shouted, 'I will broadcast to the people of France to tell them of my resolve to pursue their government of traitors wherever they may go.'[20]

M. Rougier, who was less impulsive – or knew the Marshal better – succeeded in convincing the Prime Minister that the news relayed from Berne was quite probably a German-inspired provocation. Thereupon, Churchill calmed down and the discussions were resumed. The results of these discussions were to be consigned in a protocol written two days later, and corrected by Churchill himself. According to this document, Vichy would not seek to reconquer the colonies that had rallied to General de Gaulle, it would never surrender the forts of Provence, the bases of French North Africa, Morocco or West Africa to the Axis. It would scuttle the units of the French fleet rather than let them fall into the hands of the Germans or the Italians. Britain, on the other hand, would not try to conquer any French colony that remained under Vichy obedience, the BBC would abstain from any verbal attacks on Marshal Pétain, and British authorities would relax the blockade 'if France were to assist, either passively or actively, in a British victory'.[21]

This document reflected an exchange of views on the terms of a possible agreement. It was by no means a treaty or a binding agreement, and in fact it was never ratified. Yet it certainly reflected Pétain's preoccupation at this juncture: to keep an even balance between Germany and Britain until further notice, and obtain an attenuation of the British blockade in the meantime. But it was an even better reflection of Churchill's own objectives. The protocol mentioned that 'if the French government were to surrender any air or naval bases to the totalitarian powers, Great Britain could no longer give any guarantees as to the future of France and of her empire'. To this, Churchill added in his own hand: 'In such case, Great Britain would do everything in her power to strike at a government which had been guilty of so base a betrayal.' So much for the defensive. But Churchill also added on top of the document: 'If General Weygand will raise the standard in North Africa, he can count on the renewal of the whole-hearted collaboration of the governments and peoples of the British Empire, and on a share of the assistance afforded by the US.'[22]

In the autumn of 1940, the Foreign Office – and of course Professor Rougier – took this document very seriously indeed. For Churchill, however, it could only serve two purposes: to prevent Vichy from joining the Axis camp, and to encourage secession in North Africa. The latter was very much on his mind, as evidenced by the message in French which he wrote to General Weygand immediately afterwards, inviting him to *'brandir l'étendard de la rebellion'* in North Africa, and asking him to send an officer to Tangier and thence to Gibraltar in order to tell the British what kind of equipment he would need to resume the fight against the Axis. As could be expected, Weygand flatly refused.[23]

The Foreign Office insisted on keeping de Gaulle in ignorance of the conversations held with Professor Rougier. But it did inform him of the gist of all conversations with Vichy via Madrid, of the offer made to Weygand and of Vichy's dealings with Hitler, about which the Foreign Office still knew very little. On 31 October, Halifax wrote to de Gaulle:

> We still do not know what has been conceded by the Vichy government in their negotiations with Hitler. . . . The position remains obscure but there seems indeed some chance that no irrevocable decisions have yet been taken by the Vichy government. . . . Wishing to avoid any provocative action which might turn the scale against us particularly with regard to crucial question of the fleet and naval and air bases, we shall avoid any public condemnation of Vichy government on the assumption that their betrayal was minimal.[24]

De Gaulle, who had set up an Empire Defence Council on 27 October and was preparing to give the go-ahead for Free French operations in Gabon, was beginning to see some danger to his movement in the continued British talks with Vichy. On 2 November, he wrote to the Prime Minister:

General de Gaulle and the French Empire Defence Council understand the reasons which might at present lead the British government outwardly to conciliate the Vichy government as long as it is proved that the Vichy government has not made to Germany and Italy fresh concessions of a nature that would unfavourably influence the military situation of the British Empire. . . .

Nonetheless, General de Gaulle and the French Empire Defence Council believe it their duty to point out to the British government that their policy and attitude towards Vichy, being inspired by specifically French considerations, differ somewhat appreciably from the present policy and attitude of the British government.

The mere fact that the Vichy government exists under the present conditions represents in the eyes of the Free French an injury to the honour and interests of France for which there is no possible justification. . . . The acceptance of collaboration with the enemy, officially proclaimed by Vichy, constitutes, whatever form this collaboration is to take in practice, a fresh and intolerable abasement which renders any kind of conciliation towards those guilty of it out of the question. . . .

General de Gaulle and the Empire Defence Council raise no objection to the British government sending messages of encouragement to certain French authorities hitherto docile to Vichy, but who, it is not unreasonable to think, may try one day to free themselves from it, as for example Generals Nogues and Weygand. . . . In any case, if such a reversal by these authorities were to take place and involve their making contact with the British government and asking this government for support, General de Gaulle and the Empire Defence Council consider that no agreement ought to be concluded without their direct participation and formal consent. . . .[25]

Churchill was by now in a difficult situation. He still did not know where he stood with Vichy, and in fact, he had just told the French Foreign Secretary, 'It would be better from our point of view if Pétain had either definitely accepted the most humiliating terms from Germany – in which case the French people would have probably thrown out the government – or alternatively if he had definitely rejected Hitler's terms. As it was, thanks to Laval's machinations, we ourselves were getting the worst of both worlds.'[26] On the other hand, de Gaulle was anxious to press on with operations in Africa, yet as Churchill said, 'We, however, were reluctant to take part in them until we knew more clearly how we stood with Vichy.'[27] By the beginning of November there was as much uncertainty as ever on that account. Vichy was reportedly trying to bring two French battleships, the *Richelieu* and the *Jean Bart*, from Africa to the Mediterranean, a threatening move which Churchill at once took steps to prevent. Besides, Laval and Darlan were reported to be pressing for a French declaration of war on Great Britain, whereupon Churchill asked President Roosevelt to send yet another intimidating note to Marshal Pétain.

As a matter of fact, the British were really 'getting the worst of both worlds', for quite apart from de Gaulle's letter of 2 November, the General's 'Brazzaville Manifesto', setting up the Empire Defence Council, had taken them entirely by surprise. The Foreign Office was shocked by the wording of the declaration* (which looked at times like a declaration of war on Vichy) and asked the British press not to feature it. Immediately afterwards came the news that General de Gaulle had handed a note to the United States Consul in Leopoldville for transmission to the President. After announcing the creation of the Empire Defence Council, the General stated that he had enough forces to ensure the protection of the Antilles, French Guiana and Saint Pierre et Miquelon in co-operation with the American fleet, and that the Empire Defence Council would assume responsibility for the administration of these territories should the Americans decide to occupy them. De Gaulle went on to say that the Empire Defence Council was ready to

*This was the Manifesto issued at Brazzaville by General de Gaulle on 27 October:

France is passing through the most terrible crisis in her history. Her frontiers, her empire, her independence and her very soul are threatened with destruction.

Yielding to an inexcusable panic, some job lot authorities have accepted and are submitting to the law of the enemy. Nevertheless, innumerable proofs show that the people and the empire do not accept the horrible servitude. Millions of French people or of French subjects have decided to continue the war until liberation. Millions and millions more are only waiting to do so till they have found leaders worthy of the name.

But there is no longer a truly French government. In point of fact, the body that has its seat at Vichy and claims to bear that name is unconstitutional and in subjection to the invader. In its state of servitude, this body can only be, and is in fact only, an instrument used by the enemies of France against the honour and interests of the country. It is necessary therefore for a new authority to assume the burden of directing the French war effort. Events are imposing this sacred duty upon me. I shall not fail in it. . . .

To assist me in my task, I am setting up as from today's date an Empire Defence Council. This council, composed of men who are already exercising their authority over French territories or who symbolize the highest intellectual and moral values of the nation, represents the country and the empire fighting for their existence.

I call to war, that is to say to combat or to sacrifice, all the men and all the women of the French territories which have rallied to me. In close union with our Allies, who proclaim their determination to contribute towards restoring the independence and greatness of France, our task is to defend against the enemy or against his auxiliaries a part of the national patrimony which is in our hands, to attack the enemy wherever it shall be possible, to mobilize all our military, economic and moral resources, to maintain public order and to make justice reign.

We shall accomplish this great task for France's sake, in the consciousness of serving her well and in the certainty of winning.

negotiate an agreement allowing the USA to utilize air and naval bases in the French colonial possessions of the American hemisphere.[29]

Upon learning of this initiative, taken without prior reference to British authorities, the honourable members of the Foreign Office literally went through the ceiling. Of course, de Gaulle had deliberately avoided any consultation with the British so as to show that the Empire Defence Council was entirely independent, and intended to negotiate on its own with other great powers. But the Under-Secretary of State, Sir Alexander Cadogan, was growing increasingly impatient with the state of French affairs, and he wrote in his diary:

> Tuesday, 5 November. Talk with H. Strang, R. Campbell and Mack about our general attitude and future policy towards Vichy. I hope we may play down de Gaulle, who I think is a loser, and there are signs that PM's faith in Spears may be waning! . . . Friday, 8 November. A ridiculous telegram from Brazzaville, showing that that ass de Gaulle is contemplating 'summoning Weygand to declare himself'. Just exactly what de Gaulle should not do at this moment. Drafted a reply to that effect and sent it to PM (whose faith in de Gaulle – and Spears – is, at last, I think, shaken).[29]

Sir Alexander Cadogan finally persuaded the Prime Minister to write a letter to de Gaulle asking him to come back to London. But he was mistaken in thinking that Churchill's faith in de Gaulle was shaken. Unlike Cadogan, the Prime Minister perfectly understood the Free French leader's motivations at the time; 'De Gaulle,' Churchill was to write, 'naturally resented any kind of truck on our part with Vichy, and thought we ought to be exclusively loyal to him. He also felt it to be essential to his position before the French people that he should maintain a proud and haughty demeanour towards "perfidious Albion", although an exile, dependent upon our protection and dwelling in our midst. He had to be rude to the British to prove to French eyes that he was not a British puppet.' And Churchill added: 'He certainly carried out this policy with perseverance.'[30]

At any rate, the Prime Minister wrote the following letter to de Gaulle on 10 November:

> I feel most anxious for consultation with you. Situation between France and Britain has changed remarkably since you left. A very strong feeling

has grown throughout France in our favour, as it is seen that we cannot be conquered and that war will go on. We know Vichy government is deeply alarmed by the very stern pressure administered to them by United States. On the other hand, Laval and revengeful Darlan are trying to force French declaration of war against us and rejoice in provoking minor naval incidents. We have hopes of Weygand in Africa, and no one must underrate advantage that would follow if he were rallied. We are trying to arrive at some *modus vivendi* with Vichy which will minimize the risk of incidents and will enable favourable forces in France to develop. . . . You will see how important it is that you should be here. I therefore hope you will be able to tidy up Libreville and come home as soon as possible. Let me know your plans.[13]

The 'tidying up' was completed on 12 November, and de Gaulle was able to visit Libreville three days later. He left Africa for England on 17 November.

De Gaulle returned to Britain at a time when the country emerged victorious from the great air battle with Germany. Yet he found the British 'strained and depressed'. He also found the Free French movement in disarray; there had been a series of bitter personal conflicts between the men de Gaulle had left in charge at Carlton Gardens, and a reorganization was evidently called for. Resuming his contacts in London with British officials and with the Prime Minister, de Gaulle took great pains to explain the uselessness of dealing with Vichy. To Hugh Dalton, he confided that Pétain 'suffered from senility, pessimism and ambition – a fatal combination'.[32] Sir Alexander Cadogan was present at a conversation between de Gaulle and Lord Halifax, and he noted in his diary: 'We drew him on Weygand, but he would have none of him – nor of Nogues. He thinks there is nothing to be done with Vichy. We can only make them small concessions – that will only defer their "grandes decisions", and meanwhile playing with Vichy may offend the mass of French people.'[33]

Lord Halifax naturally thought otherwise, and so did the Prime Minister. In spite of his preoccupation with the war in the Libyan desert and the situation in Greece – which the Italians had just invaded – Churchill maintained contacts with France by all available channels, with the purpose of bolstering Vichy resistance to German demands and dissuading the most rabid collaborationists from taking any rash initiatives. Thus Vichy had been informed through Madrid that 'the activities of de Gaulle in Central Africa in no way mitigated against the eventual integrity of the French Empire, and therefore the British government hoped that the French government would not support any opposition to de Gaulle in those regions since that must necessarily lead to British support of de Gaulle, and this would result in a clash between British and Vichy government forces, which the British were most anxious to avoid'.[34] The communication must have caused some perplexity in Vichy; nevertheless, the necessary assurances were received in London, and an uneasy *modus vivendi* was maintained along the lines defined during the Churchill-Rougier conversations – with the prospects of economic discussions and a relaxation of the blockade being used as a lever on the British side. On 5 December, in a letter to Churchill, Professor Rougier transmitted the following assurances from Marshal Pétain:

> 1. France would not sign a separate peace with the Axis before the end of hostilities between Great Britain and Germany.
> 2. France would not cede naval or air bases or the fleet to the Axis and would resist any attempt by Spain, Germany or Italy to seize the French colonies in North Africa.
> 3. France accepted the submission of French Equatorial Africa to General de Gaulle as a *fait accompli* till the end of the war on the understanding that the territories would then be restored to France and that meanwhile no attack would be directed against French West Africa, North Africa or Morocco.[35]

Churchill was actually kept informed of developments in Vichy by M. Dupuy, the Canadian Chargé d'Affaires, whom the Prime Minister called 'his little window on Vichy'. The information he brought back from France broadly confirmed the assurances relayed by Professor Rougier.[36] Besides, the arrest of Laval in Vichy on 13 December was in itself an encouraging sign. Yet Dupuy also reported many bizarre, contradictory and even distinctly alarming statements by the old Marshal. He reported for instance:

> I was enquiring about French bases in the Mediterranean. He (Pétain) said textually: 'If they are attacked, my orders are to defend them against anyone.' I concluded: 'Therefore you will never cede them to the Germans.' 'It depends,' he said, 'if in the course of the negotiation I am offered a satisfactory compensation I may be obliged to do it.' 'It would mean intervening on the German side against England,' I objected. His reply was: 'Not in an active but in a passive way only.' He went on saying that a British victory was to be desired and that he would never do

anything against our cause. I pointed out that this was in contradiction with what he had just said. He merely repeated his distinction between active and passive collaboration. I was unable to obtain anything more on the subject. He added however that up to this date the Germans had made no definite proposals.[37]

This was far from reassuring; and yet Dupuy's reports encouraged Churchill in the hope that someone in France – or in North Africa – would genuinely undertake to resist the Germans and actively help the British. In fact, the Prime Minister persisted in thinking that this man might well be General Weygand himself. Despite the latter's discouraging replies, Churchill still had delectable visions of a heroic Weygand brandishing the standard of revolt and opening the gates of North Africa to British troops. Indeed, Dupuy's compatriot, J. L. Ralston, was present when the Canadian chargé d'affaires gave Churchill a more detailed account of his trip to Vichy, and he noted on 21 December:

Churchill seemed to accept the impressions which Dupuy had gained. He wanted to be ready to help and to have it known that he was ready to help. It was important, however, that he must have word well in advance, because it would take weeks to get going after it was known that it was wanted. He was not going to fight his way in to a North African port. He must know that he would be received.

And some time later, Churchill added: 'We must help Weygand to keep the Germans out of Africa.'[38] 'Regarding de Gaulle,' Ralston continued, 'Dupuy thought he should be told that he should not take up activities against the French but that his energy should be devoted to fighting Italians.' This was not well received: 'Churchill said that he wasn't going to "card" his friends and make them enemies in the hope of making his enemies his friends.'[39]

This comment was typical of Churchill's attitude and mentality. For all his efforts to secure Vichy's passive and active co-operation, he had forgotten neither his obligations towards the Free French, nor the friendship that bound him to their leader. During this period, de Gaulle was a frequent visitor to Chequers. On these occasions, he and the Prime Minister would often discuss the lessons of history, the evolution of the war, the future of Germany, and even their own political problems; 'You know,' Churchill thus told de Gaulle, 'what a coalition is. Well! The British Cabinet is one.'[40] De Gaulle would come back from these week-ends much impressed by the Prime Minister's broadness of vision, powerful imagination and boundless energy. '*Quel grand artiste!*' the General often repeated. Churchill was no less impressed by the confidence, imperturbability and vast culture of his most uncommon guest. Ever a bad conspirator, he had eventually told the General all about the Rougier conversations. . . .[41]

As the year 1940 drew to a close, the two leaders could look back on their common action since the dark days of June with some pride and few regrets. France had been submerged by the Nazi onslaught, but England was fighting on – and in the person of General de Gaulle, the soul of France was fighting by her side. Churchill and de Gaulle understood this, and more than anything else, this understanding bound them together. But the year 1941 was only a few hours old when a grave event occurred that was to put their friendship to the test: the chief of the Free French naval forces, Vice-Admiral Muselier, was arrested and jailed by the British authorities. . . .

It all happened very quickly – a bit too quickly perhaps. The Intelligence Service had acquired four documents, allegedly eman-ating from the Vichy French Consulate in London, which proved that Vice-Admiral Muselier was in fact a traitor. According to these documents, it was Muselier who had betrayed the plans of the Dakar expedition and sent them to Vichy through the intermediary of the Brazilian Embassy. Another document showed that Muselier was plotting to hand over the submarine *Surcouf* to Vichy, and yet another showed that he had received £2000 for sabotaging the recruiting of sailors for the Free French naval forces.[41bis] On 1 January, the evidence against Muselier was brought before the Prime Minister, who reacted in characteristic fashion. Sir Alexander Cadogan noted in his diary: 'PM of course wants to hang him at once. I pointed out possible effect on de G. movement and suggested we must consult de G. first, who is away in the country. A. Eden agreed . . . H. H(opkinson) rang up to say Morton instructed by PM to proceed at once against Muselier and Co. I said PM ought to talk to A. first. A. rang up later. PM insists. I said all right provided he realizes what is at stake.'[42] Vice-Admiral Muselier was accordingly pulled out of his bed in the small hours and packed off to jail. Several of his men were likewise arrested. For good measure, Churchill wanted to declare war on Brazil. . . .[43]

To Anthony Eden, who had just replaced Lord Halifax as Foreign

Secretary,* fell the unpleasant task of informing General de Gaulle on the morning of 2 January. The latter was highly suspicious, and rather indignant at the way the whole matter had been handled. Two days later, he demanded the immediate release of the vice-admiral. Three days later, he handed a memorandum to General Spears showing that the incriminating documents were counterfeits. In the meantime, the unfortunate Muselier was still in prison, treated as a convicted criminal and pursued by the Prime Minister's ire. On 4 January, Cadogan wrote in his diary:

> Alexander rang me up this morning to say that M(uselier)'s lot should be alleviated. I agreed: I wanted to hand him over to Admiralty. But when Alexander realized that PM had had a hand in the affair, he went all wankly and said we should be very careful! I said I was quite prepared to take responsibility of making M. more comfortable. But I discovered later that Alexander had rung up PM and asked whether Admiralty could take over M. and PM said 'No!' How frightened of the PM all these people are. (So am I, because he's impulsive and undependable.) So when Admirable Dickens came to see me later I said I could do no more. M. had been moved from Pentonville to Brixton, which is better, and I rang up A. Maxwell and told him to do the best that Brixton allowed.[44]

On 8 January, just as de Gaulle was giving the British an ultimatum to set the vice-admiral free – failing which all relations between Free France and Britain would be immediately severed – he was informed that the whole affair was a deplorable mistake: the documents were fakes, the culprits had confessed – they were two men introduced into the Free French security services on British recommendation. These men, Howard and Collin, had a personal grudge against the vice-admiral, and had contrived to compromise him by forging Vichy documents. There was nothing left to do but to release the vice-admiral with suitable excuses – and the Prime Minister would apologize in person to General de Gaulle the very next day. . . .

It promised to be a stormy session: de Gaulle was the offended party, and Churchill himself had said to Eden: 'When I'm in the

---

*After resigning from his post as Foreign Secretary in February 1938, Anthony Eden often collaborated with Churchill in Parliament. He was appointed Secretary of State for War in May 1940, but at this post he was very much subordinate to Churchill, who considered military matters as his own preserve. The two men had frequent quarrels over strategic matters during the autumn of 1940, and Eden now welcomed his appointment to the post of Foreign Secretary as a chance to deal with the Prime Minister on a more equal footing.

wrong, I'm always very angry!'⁴⁵ But the threat was more apparent than real: de Gaulle was not a man to pick quarrels with the British when the honour of France was no longer at stake; '*L'homme c'est rien, la France, c'est tout. . . .*' Besides, he privately considered Vice-Admiral Muselier as 'an insufferable busybody'.⁴⁶ Churchill, on the other hand, was probably incapable of being angry with de Gaulle at this stage; later on, he would find it utterly impossible *not* to be angry at him – but let us not anticipate: the meeting of 9 January, at least, was to be a model of restraint and good manners:

> The Prime Minister began by saying how very deeply he regretted that this unfortunate matter should ever have arisen. Commandant Howard and Adjutant Collin had confessed that the documents had been forged by them.
>
> General de Gaulle said that he knew the burden which the Prime Minister and His Majesty's government were bearing and would only say that he wished that he had been consulted before the arrests had been made. He had always suspected Howard and Collin. In view, however, of the great importance of the interests at stake, he had no desire to press the matter.
>
> The Prime Minister . . . had wished to consult General de Gaulle before proceeding to the arrests; but de Gaulle was absent from London, and there was the possibility that the admiral and his companions might escape . . . The Prime Minister asked whether the General had any suggestions to make as regards the action that should be taken against Howard and Collin.
>
> General de Gaulle said that he was completely indifferent to their fate . . . (he) hoped . . . that in the future there would be complete confidence and prior consultations between His Majesty's government and himself on such matters.
>
> The Prime Minister agreed. He only wished that General de Gaulle had informed him earlier of his feelings about Howard and Collin.
>
> In conclusion, Mr Churchill said that General de Gaulle's attitude in this particular matter, as in all other matters, gave him a feeling of friendship and comradeship on which he set a high value. Nothing remained now but for him to ask the General to regard this regrettable incident as closed.
>
> General de Gaulle said that he was quite willing to do so.⁴⁷

The General probably forgave; he certainly did not forget. 'I will not conceal,' he later wrote, 'that this lamentable incident, which revealed how precarious our situation still was vis-à-vis our allies, did not fail to influence my conceptions of what our relations with the British state really ought to be.'[48] In other words, General de Gaulle was by now increasingly impatient with British bureaucracy and highly mistrustful of British Intelligence. He remained persuaded that the Intelligence Service had planted Howard and Collin in Carlton Gardens – which was quite untrue[48bis] – and he even ordered every British subject working for the Free French, including the charwomen, to be dismissed forthwith. It took much Franco-British diplomacy to get this order rescinded.

Yet the attention of the Free French leader and that of the Prime Minister were soon to be monopolized by much more momentous events; in the early months of 1941, the lifeline of Britain was being threatened by German submarine attacks all along the west coast of the British Isles: the Battle of the Atlantic had begun. In addition, ceaseless enemy air attacks in the Mediterranean were now forcing the British to divert their convoys to the long route around the Cape. In the desert of Tripolitania, the British troops were now confronted with General Rommel's Afrika Korps. Finally, the situation in the Balkans was distinctly worrying, and the British were now compelled to send troops from the Middle East to help in the defence of Greece. In all these matters, and many more, the Prime Minister ceaselessly advised, supervised, inspected, prodded and interfered.

Meanwhile, on a more modest scale, the Free French were fighting alongside their allies in Sudan, Egypt, Ethiopia and Erythrea. On 1 March, a Free French column under Leclerc, coming from Chad, had even occupied the oasis of Kufra in Southern Libya. As for General de Gaulle, he was trying to organize the takeover of Jibuti and French Somaliland; but a peaceful rallying of the colony had proved impossible, and for lack of transport, de Gaulle was compelled to postpone 'Operation Marie', the takeover of Jibuti by three Free French battalions under General Legentilhomme. There remained the possibility of a blockade that would force the colony to surrender. But here, British co-operation was indispensable – and it was not forthcoming. The British military authorities in the Middle East were against a blockade, the Foreign Office was not in favour of it either, and supplies were allowed to reach the colony without interference.

The General suspected that this refusal to co-operate was motivated by some dark British plot to take over the colony from France after the war – which was probably far-fetched. But it was quite obvious that London was still bent on appeasing Vichy as far as possible, and de Gaulle was to have more evidence of this when he turned his attention to another prospective theatre of operations: the Levant.

Here again, the Free French had hoped for a peaceful rallying of both Syria and Lebanon. In November 1940, General Catroux had approached Ambassador Puaux, High Commissioner in the Levant, and the Commander-in-Chief, General Fougère; this, however, had produced no results, and by the end of December, M. Puaux had in fact been replaced by General Dentz, a dedicated Vichyite, while the command of the troops passed to General de Verdilhac. A crackdown on Gaullist elements in Syria ensued, and the Free French lost all hope of a peaceful rallying of the Levant. But to General de Gaulle's amazement and consternation, the British maintained excellent relations with the new administration; at the beginning of February, the French ship *La Providence*, containing about 200 officers and men who had attempted to join the Allies and were being sent to France for punishment, was allowed to sail directly from Beirut to Marseilles without calling at Haifa. When de Gaulle protested to the Foreign Office, he received a disarmingly candid reply: 'General Dentz had guaranteed that no Free French sympathizers would be on board.'[49]

There was worse to come: General de Gaulle found out that the British were not even enforcing a blockade on the Levant. Wool, cotton, and even silk – very useful for making parachutes – were accordingly sent to Vichy, and thence to Germany. The British military authorities in Cairo and the civil administration in Palestine told General de Gaulle that 'a blockade would not only cause suffering in the Levant, but would adversely affect Arab opinion towards us and Free France in the neighbouring states'.[50] De Gaulle protested, and so did General Spears, head of the British Mission to the Free French. 'To de Gaulle and myself,' General Spears wrote, 'this attitude assumed the proportions of a tragedy.'[51]

The tragedy was far from over. At the beginning of February, it was reported that two German agents, Von Hintig and Roser, had arrived at Damascus, ostensibly on a commercial visit, and had contacted several Syrian personalities who appeared to have no commercial interests whatsoever. In Vichy, that same month, Admiral Darlan, well known for his violently anti-British views, became Vice-Premier, Foreign Minister and Minister of the Interior.

This, however, did not bring the slightest modification in British attitude towards the Levant. To be sure, the British Consul-General in Beirut had a French wife, and was very well treated by General Dentz;[52] besides, General Wavell, who already had his hands full with the Libyan and Abyssinian campaigns and was now to send forces to Greece, preferred to maintain a comfortable *modus vivendi* in the Levant. But General de Gaulle was beginning to wonder whether the British in the Middle East were at all interested in co-operating with Free France against Vichy.

By mid-April, with unrest threatening in Iraq, British troops retreating before the German armies in Greece, and the Luftwaffe already attacking the Suez Canal from bases in Rhodes, it seemed highly probable that the Germans would seek to use the Syrian airfields as their next stepping-stone. This was now becoming clear to some British officers, including Air Marshal Sir Arthur Longmore. Yet at a conference in Cairo on 15 April, when de Gaulle pressed General Wavell to agree to a Free French plan for entering Syria from northern Palestine, and asked for British assistance in the form of tanks, transport and air cover, he was met with a flat refusal. General Wavell needed all his forces on other theatres. De Gaulle and General Spears appealed to Anthony Eden, who was rather fearful of the consequences of such an operation on British relations with Vichy, but passed the buck to the Chiefs-of-Staff by stating that 'if we could put together a sufficent force to ensure success', he 'was prepared to risk the strain on our relations with Vichy'.[53] The Chiefs-of-Staff replied that 'any Free French coup against the Syrian administration must be ruled out absolutely, because at present General Wavell had neither the tanks nor the aircraft required and if he had, he would use them for even more imperative tasks elsewhere'.[54] After which they shoved back all initiative to the Foreign Office by suggesting that a solution be found by diplomatic means. The British Consul-General at Beirut was accordingly instructed to warn General Dentz against a possible German airborne attack on Syria – to which the latter replied on 29 April that his orders were to resist all aggression.[55] The Free French learned of his other statement that he would obey whatever orders he received from Vichy, but the British probably thought that he was talking in jest. . . . To crown the edifice, the British themselves signed a commercial treaty with General Dentz, thus ensuring that the Levant under Vichy rule would be well supplied. Negotiations were also under way in Aden for the supplying of Jibuti, the blockade of which de Gaulle had been demanding for several months. . . .

By the beginning of May, the British civil and military authorities in the Levant were as determined as ever to treat the Vichy officials as honourable gentlemen. They were therefore to receive a very rude shock when an anti-British revolt broke out in Iraq. Indeed, the leader of the revolt, Rashid Ali, appealed to Hitler for armed support . . . and the Germans immediately negotiated an agreement with Admiral Darlan providing for the bulk of the war material assembled in Syria to be transported to Iraq. Moreover, the German air force was to be given landing facilities in Syria. General Dentz received the necessary instructions, and to the surprise and consternation of the British, he obeyed them. By 12 May, German planes were therefore landing on Syrian airfields.

In Brazzaville, de Gaulle was enraged at all the blundering that had allowed this situation to develop. Yet he was left speechless when General Catroux and General Spears informed him from Cairo that his plan for an attack on Syria had again been rejected by the British Commander-in-Chief. 'An intervention in Syria,' Wavell had said, 'meant a dispersion of effort, and therefore defeat . . . the loss of Syria would be better than the risk of being beaten in detail owing to our intervening with inadequate forces.'[56] De Gaulle also received the following telegram from General Spears on 9 May:

> In view of fresh commitments it will be impossible to provide transport for the Free French troops for a month at the very earliest. This means that no operations by them can be contemplated for the moment. . . . The Commander-in-Chief asks me to tell you that, although personally always glad to see you, he sees no necessity for your coming to Cairo now or in the near future. There would in fact be some slight disadvantage in your doing so. The ambassador shares this view. . . .[57]

To be sure, Wavell now had to divert troops to Iraq, and he therefore had very few means left for an offensive in Syria. But General de Gaulle only saw the folly of abandoning Syria to the Germans; besides, he was already rather ill-disposed towards the British. During the weeks following the Muselier affair, he had come up with frequent outbursts against 'les Anglais' in general and the Intelligence Service in particular.[58] During the next two months, the British policy towards Vichy, Jibuti and Syria had added considerably to his exasperation and to his suspicions.* In April, when on a visit to Chad, he had asked Governor Lapie: 'Vous avez des Anglais, ici?'

Lapie: 'Oui, mon General.'
De Gaulle: 'Combien?'
Lapie: 'Dix-sept.'
De Gaulle: 'C'est trop!'

Shortly thereafter, Governor Lapie received a telegram instructing him to get rid of them.[59]

That same month, Sir Miles Lampson, His Majesty's Ambassador

*It should be remarked that during this whole period, General Spears tirelessly defended de Gaulle's cause – and loudly condemned Britain's policy with regard to Vichy. In a memorandum entitled *The Free French, Vichy and Ourselves*, Spears wrote:

Our painstaking attempts to propitiate the Vichy government might, conceivably, make a dispassionate observer conjure up the picture of a well-meaning person bent on feeding a lettuce to a rabbit while it is being chased around its cage by a stoat. A waste of lettuce, at best, since, if the rabbit were grateful, which would be unlikely, it will remain at the mercy of the stoat, bent on its ultimate destruction. Vichy is completely at the mercy of the Germans. Who can doubt it? Our pandering can no more alter the fact than can its own efforts at conciliation. . . . Meanwhile, thanks to Vichy, the French Empire is a powerful help to the Germans. Supplies to capacity pour into Marseilles from the French colonies, to be collected and distributed by the Armistice Commission at their own pleasure, while we look on, tirelessly offering lettuce to the Vichy rabbit which the German stoat occasionally allows it to nibble at, reckoning no doubt that in the end it will make for a more toothsome dinner.[60]

In another memorandum, Spears also wrote:

To give any support to General Weygand, who in an ever-growing degree is bound to bear part at least of the odium for France's defeat, is to undermine the position of General de Gaulle. We must, I submit, choose between these two men, but if we choose General de Gaulle, we should give him constant and unfailing support. If he feels that we remain faithful to the ideal of a Free France his loyalty can be relied upon. Should he at times run counter to our policy it will, in these circumstances, only be due to lack of knowledge or information. He will always be a loyal ally if we are ourselves loyal to the ideals we professed when he threw in his lot with us.[61]

In April 1941, Spears's admiration and sympathy for General de Gaulle was greater than ever, as evidenced by the following letter sent to S. Somerville Smith in London:

Constant drive . . . is certainly provided by de Gaulle whom I have really greatly admired on this trip. He never stops working, always remains perfectly balanced, never loses sight of his objective and has proved himself to be astonishingly shrewd in military matters.[62]

This admiration Spears certainly did not extend to General Catroux:

As far as Catroux is concerned, he can give quite sensible advice to which weight is added by a pontifical manner. His views, which never clash with those of the British authorities, civil or military, make him very welcome amongst our countrymen. He is, however, incapable of organizing anything and entirely devoid of 'drive'. His staff is farcical, comprising jejune officials who have found a haven of refuge in sleepy offices where nothing is ever planned much less carried out. I am quite satisfied that de Gaulle is right in having decided that, whilst anxious to take full advantage of Catroux's name, he cannot trust him with anything really difficult or important.[63]

in Cairo, had several talks with the General. He noted in his diary that de Gaulle, whom he found 'most impressive and rather attractive . . . shows a somewhat critical mood in regard to what he seems to consider lack of fixed policy in regard to Syria etc. . . . ' And on 15 April: 'De Gaulle somewhat aggressively claimed that we had had two chances of winning Syria to us but had taken neither. . . . As for Vichy he should have thought by now the British government had become disillusioned of any false hopes.'[64]

Yet General Spears's telegram, coming at a time when swift action was so obviously necessary, was for de Gaulle the last straw, and he decided to retaliate. On 12 May, he wrote to General Catroux:

> Given the negative policy which our British allies have thought it right to adopt in the Middle East as far as we are concerned, I consider that the presence in Cairo of a personality as considerable as yours and of a High Commissioner to represent Free France there is no longer justified. I am reserving the possibility of your return there later, in case events should make it necessary thanks to a recovery by the British. But for the moment I beg you to leave Cairo as soon as possible. . . . Please advise the British in Cairo of this decision. There is no reason for you to conceal from them the reason for your departure. On the contrary I ask you to make it plain to them. I am personally advising the London government. You will naturally not be replaced in your present functions.[65]

The day before, General de Gaulle had sent for the British Consul-General at Brazzaville, and given him a piece of his mind. The Consul-General then sent the following report to the Foreign Office:

> De Gaulle is, I think, extremely tired. Certainly exceedingly depressed. He recalled how his advice had been flouted in France until, just before the Armistice, he was called on when it was already too late. He feels that a similar fate has dogged all his attempts to make Great Britain understand what the Free French movement is. In so many quarters it is considered merely in terms of the number of units it can throw into the battle. Materially that counts for very little and, if Great Britain attaches so little value to the moral side of the movement that, instead of fostering it by all possible means, she weakens it by complaisance towards Vichy, then he must decide what is his fundamental duty towards France for whom he is trustee. He said he was the one man alone on whom this responsibility fell and that the burden was near to becoming more than he could bear. The General went on to express his complete inability to understand the attitude of His Majesty's government towards Pétain and Weygand, whose self-seeking, treason, mental decay and moral

untrustworthiness are for him so notorious as to be beyond discussion. He then went on to speak of his feelings of respect and friendship for the Prime Minister who, he said, was indeed one of the men who did realize the moral importance of his movement.[66]

Not only did the Prime Minister realize the moral importance of the Free French movement; he had also begun to realize the utter uselessness of dealing with Vichy. Admittedly, his direct and indirect approaches to Pétain and Weygand had been rebuffed one after the other, and he was finally growing impatient. On 12 February, he wrote to the Foreign Office:

> We have made Weygand great offers, to which we have had no reply. It is clear that he will be actuated only by forces set in motion by pressure of Nazis on Vichy. Our attitude at the present time should not be one of appeal to him. Until he has answered through some channel or other the telegram I sent him he ought not to be given supplies. Not one scrap of nobility or courage has been shown by these people so far, and they had better go on short commons till they come to their senses.[67]*

There was undoubtedly a childish side to Winston Churchill's temperament. The more he became disappointed with Vichy, the more he felt attracted to de Gaulle – and everyone was naturally expected to follow suit. Four days later, he wrote to the Minister of Economic Warfare:

> I agree about co-ordinated leaflets (for propaganda in France and Belgium), but all depends upon an intimate liaison between you and the Ministry of Information on the one hand and de Gaulle on the other. We must not tie de Gaulle up too tightly. We have never received the slightest good treatment or even courtesy from Vichy, and the Free French movement remains our dominant policy. I am sure if you consult with de Gaulle or his people all will be satisfactory. I think he is much the best Frenchman now in the arena, and I want him taken care of as much as possible.[68]

And the next day, upon hearing of Admiral Darlan's appointment as Vice-President and Foreign Minister, he wrote to the Foreign Office:

> I regard these developments with misgiving and mistrust. We have received nothing but ill-treatment from Vichy. It would have been better

---

*In fact, the torch was passed to the Americans, who continued to woo Vichy with commendable if unrewarded zeal.

to have had Laval, from our point of view, than Darlan, who is a dangerous, bitter, ambitious man, without the odium which attaches to Laval. I think it is important at the moment to be stiff with these people, and to assert the blockade whenever our ships are available. In the meantime an end should be put to the cold-shouldering of General de Gaulle and the Free French movement, who are the only people who have done anything for us, and to whom we have made very solemn engagements. The emphasis should be somewhat shifted.[69]

And six days later, on the same subject, Churchill again wrote to Sir Alexander Cadogan:

All this goes to show that we should continue to give increasing support to General de Gaulle. I cannot believe that the French nation will give their loyalty to anyone who reaches the Head of the State because he is thought well of by the Germans. We should reason patiently with Washington against giving any food to unoccupied France or North Africa. For this purpose all the unsatisfactory feeling about the Vichy-Weygand scene should be in the hands of our ambassador in Washington. I am sure Darlan is an ambitious crook. His exposure and Weygand's weakness will both, as they become apparent, inure to the credit of de Gaulle.[70]

The honeymoon continued through February and the beginning of March. Before leaving for Africa and the Middle East, de Gaulle was once again invited to Chequers for the week-end; he later wrote in his memoirs:

On 9 March, at dawn, Mr Churchill came and woke me up to tell me, literally dancing with joy, that the American Congress had voted the 'Lend-Lease Bill', which had been under discussion for several weeks. This was indeed good news, not only because the belligerents were from now on assured of receiving from the United States all the necessary fighting equipment, but also because America, by becoming, in Roosevelt's words, 'the arsenal of democracies', was taking a giant step towards the war. Then, wishing no doubt to profit by my good humour, Mr Churchill made his second communication. 'I know,' he said, 'that you have some complaints against Spears as head of our liaison with you. However, I must ask you expressly to keep him on and to take him with you to the Middle East. It is a personal favour you will be doing me.' I could not refuse, and on that we parted.*[71]

*The above account is probably unfair. During the spring of 1941, de Gaulle and Spears were still on fairly good terms, and General Spears had done more for Free France than any other foreigner, the Prime Minister excepted. Later initiatives taken by General Spears as well as de Gaulle's unforgiving nature have probably prompted this anachronism.

During his stay in Brazzaville and Cairo, de Gaulle was also to receive repeated marks of encouragement and support from the Prime Minister. Thus on 4 April, he was given the following telegram:

> We are very grateful for the help which the Free French forces have given us in the victorious African campaign. But for the disaster of Bordeaux the whole Mediterranean would now be an Anglo-French lake and the whole African shore would be free and embattled in the cause of freedom. You, who have never faltered or failed in serving the common cause, possess the fullest confidence of His Majesty's government and you embody the hope of millions of Frenchmen and Frenchwomen who do not despair of the future of France or the French Empire.[72]

In fact, the telegram had been amended by the Foreign Office. The original version would have caused de Gaulle even greater pleasure, for instead of: 'But for the disaster of Bordeaux . . .' Churchill had written: 'But for the treachery of Bordeaux. . . .'[73]

One may of course wonder why de Gaulle, having the full support of the Prime Minister, remained unable to secure British co-operation for his policy on Jibuti and Syria – all the more so as Churchill wrote him on 22 April: 'I always pay the greatest attention to your telegrams and do my utmost to aid you in every way.'[74] The answer is that Churchill did not exercise absolute authority at home or abroad, and often failed to secure compliance with his wishes on particular questions. Thus, the Foreign Office remained bent at that stage on keeping good relations with Vichy, and the War Office wanted to have as few relations as possible with General de Gaulle. On top of that, the British High Command in the Middle East pursued a strategy in which political considerations had very little place – and the Free French movement even less. As a result, Churchill's repeated injunctions to the Foreign Office to shift emphasis from Vichy to de Gaulle, just like his numerous instructions to the War Office for closer co-operation with the Free French movement, remained largely unheeded. The same applies to his many telegrams to General Wavell ordering him to co-operate with de Gaulle in Syria – and elsewhere. Thus on 1 April, Wavell received the following telegram from the Prime Minister: 'We consider that you should follow policy laid down in Chiefs-of-Staff telegram of 25 March as closely as possible, subject to any modification which may seem desirable after your discussions with

General de Gaulle. In particular, the initial approach to French Somaliland should be made by Free French authorities, and there should be no hesitation in using the blockade weapon to the full.'[75] As we know, all this was disregarded, and as Churchill's attention was then being monopolized by the retreat in Greece and the German threat in Crete, nothing more was done in the matter – until events in Iraq introduced an entirely new factor at the beginning of May.

The troubles that erupted in Iraq put the Syrian problem in a completely different light. For Churchill, as for de Gaulle, it was obvious that Syria would be the next stepping stone in the German effort to help the Iraqi rebellion. A major crisis was therefore impending, and no one could really stand up to the Prime Minister in times of crisis; for he then gave the matter his undivided attention, interfered at every level of decision, brushed aside all objections, mobilized the War Cabinet, intimidated the diplomats, browbeat the generals and bullied the Chiefs-of-Staff. On 8 May, he wrote to General Ismay:

> I must have the advice of the Staffs upon the Syrian business available for Cabinet this morning. A supreme effort must be made to prevent the Germans getting a footing in Syria with small forces and then using Syria as a jumping-off ground for the air domination of Iraq and Persia. It is no use General Wavell being vexed at this disturbance on his eastern flanks. . . . We ought to help in every way without minding what happens at Vichy. I shall be most grateful if the Staffs will see what is the most that can be done.[76]

And the very next day, having obtained the approval of the Defence Committee, he telegraphed to General Wavell:

> You will no doubt realize the grievous danger of Syria being captured by a few thousand Germans transported by air. Our information leads us to believe that Admiral Darlan has probably made some bargain to help the Germans to get in there. In face of your evident feeling of lack of resources we can see no other course open than to furnish General Catroux with the necessary transport and let him and his Free French do their best at the moment they deem suitable, the RAF acting against German landings. Any improvement you can make on this would be welcome.[77]

As we know, General Wavell was still reluctant to act. But he was now up against formidable odds. General de Gaulle's communication of 12 May announcing the withdrawal of Catroux from the Middle East and Churchill's impatience at the continuing delays resulted in precise instructions being given by the War Cabinet and the Chiefs-of-Staff: Wavell was now ordered to 'improvise the largest force that he could provide without prejudice to the security of the Western desert', and to 'prepare himself to move into Syria at the earliest possible date'.[78] At the same time, he was ordered to 'transport the Free French forces to positions near the frontiers and to give them all the assistance possible, especially as regards the air, as soon as General Catroux and General Legentilhomme should decide that the time to act had come'.[79] The same day, de Gaulle received a telegram from London, informing him of the orders sent to Wavell, simultaneously with another telegram from the PM:

> The question of Jibuti was discussed at a meeting of the Defence Committee which we held this afternoon, when it was decided:
> 1. That a strict blockade of Jibuti should be maintained.
> 2. That you should be requested not to remove General Catroux from Palestine. He may already be taking action.
> 3. That a cordial invitation should be sent to you to go to Cairo if you feel that guardianship of the Free French territories can be safely left.[80]

General de Gaulle was amazed and much gratified at this sudden about-face. Being well aware that only one person could have engineered it, he wrote to Churchill: '1) Thank you. 2) Catroux remains in Palestine. 3) I shall go to Cairo soon. 4) You will win the war.'[81] No doubt as a supreme mark of favour and approval, he wrote this in English. He had never done it before; he was never to do it again.

From then on, things went very quickly. General Wavell still ranted, protested, and even telegraphed to the CIGS threatening to resign in protest against the influence exercised by the Free French leaders on the Chiefs-of-Staff. That was probably a mistake: on 21 May, Wavell told the British Ambassador Sir Miles Lampson that 'he had had a rather bad night last night as he had been pulled out of bed in the small hours to receive two telegrams, the first from our Prime Minister ordering him regardless of anything else to back the Free French advance into Syria; and the second from General de Gaulle "ordering him" to do the same!'[82] The Prime Minister's telegram was unambiguous:

As you have clearly shown, you have not the means to mount a regular military operation, and, as you were instructed yesterday, all that can be done at present is to give the best possible chance to the kind of armed political inroad described in Chiefs-of-Staff message of twentieth. You are wrong in supposing that policy described in this message arose out of any representations made by the Free French leaders. It arises entirely from the view taken here by those who have the supreme direction of war and policy in all theatres. Our view is that if the Germans can pick up Syria and Iraq with petty air forces, tourists, and local revolts, we must not shrink from running equal small-scale military risks and facing the possible aggravation of political dangers from failure. For this decision we, of course, take full responsibility, and should you find yourself unwilling to give effect to it, arrangements will be made to meet any wish you may express to be relieved of your command.[83]

Wavell thereupon decided that it was safer to comply, and in spite of pressing commitments in Iraq, Crete and the Western desert, he set about finding the necessary means to support the Free French and cross into Syria at the earliest date. General Maitland Wilson was put in command of the British units. Wavell was of course distinctly unenthusiastic about the whole affair, and told General Spears that he 'refused to be rushed'.[84] Churchill, however, kept on bombarding him with explanatory, encouraging and inquisitive telegrams. Thus on 3 January: 'Please telegraph exactly what ground and air forces you are using for Syria. What are you doing with the Poles? It seems important to use and demonstrate as much air power as possible at the very outset, and even the older machines may play their part, as they did so well in Iraq.'[85]

Meanwhile, in Palestine, the Free French were preparing feverishly for the great operation. Catroux and de Gaulle were hoping that the French army in Syria would oppose the arrival of German air units, and therefore welcome the Free French forces. But on 21 May, a French defector, Colonel Collet, informed them that the Vichy French in Syria were not opposing the Germans . . . and would fight the Allies. Indeed, they had already assumed defensive positions on the border. With heavy hearts, the Free French therefore prepared for a fratricidal struggle.

The long-awaited Syrian campaign finally opened on 8 June. The day before, de Gaulle had received a warm and encouraging telegram from the Prime Minister: 'I wish to send you my best wishes for the success of our joint enterprise in the Levant. I hope that you are satisfied that everything possible is being done to provide support to the arms of Free France. . . . All our thoughts are with you and the soldiers of Free France. At this hour when Vichy touches fresh depths of ignominy, the loyalty and courage of the Free French save the glory of France.'[86] To which de Gaulle answered: 'I thank you from the depths of my heart. . . . Whatever happens the Free French are decided to fight and conquer at your side as faithful and resolute allies.'[87] At this moment, neither Churchill nor de Gaulle could foresee that Syria and Lebanon would effectively poison their mutual relations until the end of the war – and even some time after that. . . .*

---

*There were nevertheless a few tell-tale signs: in order to ensure that the Free French would be well received by the Arab populations, de Gaulle, on British advice, had promised independence to Syria and Lebanon (then under French mandate). The British had insisted on giving their guarantee to this promise, but de Gaulle considered that such a guarantee was incompatible with the sovereignty of France. Besides, the British assumed that total independence would be granted immediately, whereas de Gaulle did not contemplate granting it before the end of the war. To all this must be added Britain's pursuance of a pro-Arab policy in the whole region, and de Gaulle's eternal suspicion of British designs.

CHAPTER 6

The First Great Confrontation

The Syrian campaign began inauspiciously enough. The Free French forces, commanded by General Legentilhomme, numbered only 6000 infantrymen, with 8 guns and 10 tanks supported by 24 aircraft; as for the British, all General Maitland 'Jumbo' Wilson could muster was one Australian division, a cavalry and two infantry brigades, and the support of about 60 aircraft. They were to attack Vichy forces under General Dentz comprising 18 regular battalions with 120 guns, 90 tanks and as many aircraft; in all more than 30,000 men. The first week of the offensive was marked by a series of violent clashes, with numerous casualties on both sides. The Free French were stopped in front of Damascus, the Australians were held up on the coastal road, and British troops were severely mauled by a superior force near Kuneitra. It was only by the end of the second week, after reinforcements had been dispatched, that the scales began to tip in favour of the Allies. Damascus was captured on the 21st after fierce fighting at Kiswa, and three British and Indian brigades opened a new front by entering Syria from Iraq to the south and east. By the first week of July, when Aleppo, Homs and Damur were directly threatened and the collapse of the Vichy troops appeared imminent, General Dentz decided to ask for a cease-fire.

The least that can be said is that de Gaulle was not impressed by the performance of his British allies; they had been unable to provide him with tanks and trucks,[1] had no heavy or medium tanks themselves,[2] their advance had been extremely slow, their numerical weakness had greatly encouraged Vichy resistance, and they had been out-manoeuvred on several occasions by the Vichy Forces. Last but not least, de Gaulle was utterly disgusted with the British High Command and with General Wilson, whom he considered as worse than incapable.[3] However, it was not the fighting, but the armistice that precipitated a venomous quarrel between de Gaulle and His Majesty's government – a quarrel that was to have far-reaching consequences.

Already on 18 June, Vichy had asked the American Consul-General in Beirut to enquire of the British and the Gaullists what their conditions would be for a cessation of hostilities. In Cairo the next day, at a meeting with the British Ambassador Sir Miles Lampson, in the presence of Wavell and Catroux, de Gaulle laid down his conditions for an agreement, and after some discussion, all present agreed on the following terms, which were immediately dispatched to London:

> 1. An honourable treatment will be granted to all members of the armed forces and all civil servants.
> 2. The representation of France in the Levant will be assured by the Free French authorities within the framework of the independence which they have promised to Syria and the Lebanon and which Great Britain has guaranteed.
> 3. As regards the French troops and civil servants who want to join the Allies, they will be given full opportunity of remaining in the country, together with their families. All those who are not prepared to do so will be repatriated with their families when circumstances permit.
> 4. All war material is to be handed over to the Allies.
> 5. General de Gaulle considers it necessary that his representatives should take part in the negotiations and the answer to Beirut should be given in his name as well as in the name of the British authorities.[4]

But the next day, when de Gaulle was given a copy of the text that had been sent to Washington for transmission to Beirut, he found that the Foreign Office had disregarded his own terms on some essential points; indeed the text stated among others that 'negotiations for cessation of hostilities are to be carried out between General Wilson representing the Commanders-in-Chief, and the Vichy authorities in Syria'.[5] There was no word of Free French participation in the negotiations, no word either of the Free French authorities representing France in the Levant, and worse still, nothing indicated that Vichy forces would be really given a free choice between joining the Free French forces and returning to France. De Gaulle was later to write: 'no mention was made . . . of the precautions which I deemed necessary to prevent armed forces and civil servants in the Levant from being repatriated wholesale and compulsorily; and yet, I had to keep as many as possible. I therefore sent Mr Eden a formal protest, and warned him that for my part I was adhering to the conditions accepted on 19 June and would recognize no others.'[6]*

General Spears noted that on that occasion, de Gaulle was 'beside himself with rage'; he recalled the following dialogue:

> *De Gaulle:* 'I do not think I shall ever get on with "les Anglais". You are all the same, exclusively concentrated upon your own interests and business, quite insensitive to the requirements of others . . . you think I am interested in England winning the war? I am not. I am only interested in France's victory.'
> *General Spears:* 'They are the same.'
> *De Gaulle:* 'Not at all. Not at all in my view.'[7]

Early in July, with the end of the campaign now in sight, de Gaulle was to receive an even ruder shock. To be sure, he had secured an agreement that General Catroux should be present at the negotiations; he had also written to Churchill on 28 June that 'French opinion and international opinion will be very attentive to the way in which Great Britain will behave with regard to the position of France in this region', and he warned British authorities against giving 'the impression that the occupation of Syria by troops that are in part British and under British command is leading either to a displacement of authority to the detriment of France or to a sort of control over the authority of France'.[8]

But it was all in vain; General Dentz finally asked for a cease-fire on 10 July, and the plenipotentiaries gathered at Saint Jean d'Acre three days later. The newly-appointed British Minister of State, Captain Oliver Lyttelton, telegraphed instructions from Cairo to his representative at Saint Jean D'Acre, General Wilson, while the Vichy delegation was led by General Dentz's second-in-command, General de Verdilhac, and Free France was represented by General Catroux, who appears to have been very inconspicuous on that occasion. . . .

When the armistice terms were announced on 14 July, it was at

---

*It seems that back in London, de Gaulle and the Free French had been purely and simply forgotten . . . as Somerville-Smith, of the Spears mission, wrote to General Spears on 5 July: 'I told Morton that a mere messenger in the Spears mission would have introduced something to show that we were offering the conditions in full agreement with de Gaulle. Morton thought the idea so good that he mentioned it at his committee! The committee recommended that, in future, Departments should not forget de Gaulle!' (MEC, SPRS II/5, Somerville-Smith to Spears, 5/7/41)

once plain that only the immediate interests of British diplomacy
and of the British High Command had been safeguarded, while the
Vichy troops were being treated more than generously; they were to
be granted 'full honours of war', and even allowed to retain their
personal arms; they would be concentrated under the orders of their
leaders, and those who did not wish to join the Allied corps would be
repatriated by units – thus rendering any free choice almost
impossible; their equipment would be handed over to the British
only; moreover, the Special Troops of the Levant, made up of Syrian
and Lebanese volunteers, would purely and simply be placed under
British command; there was no reference at all to Free France,
except one that made matters even worse: General Wilson, without
even informing the Minister of State, had signed a secret protocol
with General de Verdilhac, under which it was agreed that no
contact should be permitted between the Free French and the Vichy
French.[9]

These terms represented a major setback to the Free French
cause. General Spears himself later agreed that they were 'quite
preposterous',[10] and the Minister of State, Oliver Lyttelton, was to
write in his memoirs: 'I freely admit, looking back on the wording of
the armistice, that we should have brought the Free French into its
terms in a way which we did not.'[11] In Brazzaville, General de
Gaulle's immediate reaction upon learning of these terms can only
be surmised; the agreement seemed to justify his worst fears and his
long-held suspicion of British policy: utter disregard of Free French
interests, criminal leniency towards Vichy, and an obvious desire to
supplant France in the Middle East. 'The text of the agreement,' he
later wrote, 'amounted to a pure and simple transference of Syria
and the Lebanon to the British.' To begin with, de Gaulle made a
rather offensive reference to the agreement in a statement to the
press on 16 July; he noted himself in his memoirs:

I let it be known that I repudiated the Saint Jean D'Acre convention.
After which, I left for Cairo, explaining to the British governors and
military leaders at each stage of my journey how serious the matter was.
I did so at Khartoum to General Sir Arthur Huddleston, Governor-
General of the Sudan, at Kampala to the Governor, at Wadi Halfa to
the manager of the Club, so as to have myself preceded by alarming
telegrams. On 21 July I made contact with Mr Oliver Lyttelton, Minister
of State in the British government.[12]

Indeed, de Gaulle's reaction to this unfortunate episode of War Office diplomacy took a form which will become increasingly familiar to the reader as events unfold: a sort of psychological warfare, in which British infringements of Free French interests met each time with fierce statements and stern threats calculated to embarrass and intimidate the British authorities responsible for these infringements. One of his first victims was the Minister of State in Cairo, Oliver Lyttelton.

The Minister of State was himself distinctly uneasy at the results achieved by General Wilson, especially after he had learned of the secret protocol. As General Spears later wrote: 'He was extremely worried, and also perturbed at the prospect of having to face de Gaulle on so bad a wicket.'[13] The General arrived at Lyttelton's office at about ten o'clock. He noticed that the Minister of State 'welcomed him with some embarrassment'. De Gaulle was later to state that he 'tried to avoid explosions' and 'cased himself in ice'.[14] Indeed, Lyttelton noted that the General 'was white with suppressed passion' and added: 'He . . . greeted me frigidly and launched into the most violent complaint about the British attitude.'[15] De Gaulle's argument cannot have come as a surprise to the Minister of State: 'The terms of the armistice and of the additional protocol were unacceptable and did not bind Free France; the British were trying to establish their authority over Syria and Lebanon, an authority which belonged to Free France alone; the rapid and wholesale repatriation of the Vichy troops was a terrible blow to Free France, and the conduct of the British in the whole affair was "incompatible with the honour and interests of France".' To this, Lyttelton retorted that Catroux, who had been present at the negotiations, had agreed to the terms of armistice; as for the protocol, he, Lyttelton, in collaboration with General Spears, had already taken steps to nullify it. But Lyttelton was not prepared for what followed: de Gaulle handed him a memorandum ending with these words: 'Free France, that is to say France, is no longer willing to entrust to the British military command the duty of exercising command over the French troops in the Middle East. General de Gaulle and the French Empire Defence Council are resuming the full and entire disposal of all the French forces of the Levant as from 24 July, 1941, at midday.'[16] The Minister of State later wrote: 'I was somewhat taken aback, but from some remote recess of my memory the diplomatic phrase "Non Avenu" came to the surface. I said

"General, I must regard this document as not received, and I cannot accept it".'[17]

In a report written to Churchill the next day, Lyttelton gave a more detailed account of what happened:

On receiving this document I asked General de Gaulle to withdraw it as it was in fact an ultimatum which would only be read as terminating an alliance between Free France and Great Britain. He then replied very rudely that if I intended to regard it as an ultimatum I could do so. He had merely stated facts and I could take them in any way I liked. I pointed out that the military fact remained that we could not divest ourselves of responsibility for a Syrian front upon which we might be attacked and that as a soldier he knew perfectly well that we could not rest upon the document as it was now presented. As a single document I must personally refuse to accept it; that if it was to have any possibility of acceptance, clearly a document setting out whole basis of military collaboration must accompany it. He replied in an airy way that there was no question about his willingness to collaborate with the British command. At this part of the discussion he said in a very rude and offensive way that he had no confidence in British High Command who had conducted the campaign in an unskilful and dilatory way. He was quite prepared at a later date to make suggestions as to how our military collaboration could be worked in with the complete sovereignty of France and Syria. I again pointed out that as long as this document was the only one before me I could not accept it.[18]

As Lyttelton later recalled: 'There was nothing for it but what women call "a scene", and a scene we certainly had.'[19] This continued until about half-past twelve, when the Minister of State suggested that further discussion be postponed until 6 p.m. that evening.

In the evening de Gaulle returned, somewhat better disposed, and Oliver Lyttelton, probably much relieved at this change in mood, proceeded to make several concessions. He agreed that General Dentz and several Vichy French officers should be segregated, if necessary in Palestine, that the British government should not intervene in political and administrative affairs in Syria, and that it would 'protect the historical interests of the French in Syria'.[20] De Gaulle ended by proposing a new agreement on the 'application' of the armistice convention, 'correcting in practice what was vicious in the text'. He also suggested that the Minister of State should limit the competence of the British command in Syria and Lebanon 'to the military operations against the common enemy'. And Oliver Lyttelton promised to 'think it over'.[21]

On the 22nd, the Minister of State announced that he agreed, and an 'interpretative agreement' was worked out the next day between the British and Free French delegations. That day, Sir Miles Lampson wrote in his diary:

> Back to the embassy where O. Lyttelton, de Gaulle and the rest of them were still closeted in my room. . . . They were wrangling about some stupid little phraseology in a document they had drawn up, it being apparently an 'interpretation' of the convention signed with Vichy.[21bis]

In fact, it was much more a correction than an interpretation: the Free French authorities would be permitted to contact the Vichy troops and 'explain their point of view to the personnel concerned'; it was now recognized that the war material was French property, and that the special troops of the Levant would be integrated into the Free French, not in the British forces.[22] De Gaulle's obstinacy and fits of temper had thus paid a handsome dividend, although the Free French leader had also made a mortal enemy in the process: General Spears, who had been scandalized by de Gaulle's treatment of Oliver Lyttelton during the interview of 21 July; for Spears, this had been a sort of revelation, and from then on, as Ambassador Miles Lampson noted with surprise, Spears devoted as much energy to combat de Gaulle as he had hitherto expended to defend him. De Gaulle was not immediately informed of this complete about-face – and there is no reason to think that he would have cared anyway – but he was quite satisfied with the result of his exertions. That evening, he wrote to the Free French delegation in London: 'In all, the British change of orientation is now favourable. The crisis has been hot, and is not entirely over.'[23]

Indeed it was not. For during the following weeks, in spite of the obvious good will of Captain Lyttelton, both the interpretative agreement and the repeated undertakings to recognize the historical interests of France in the Levant were completely disregarded by British military authorities on the spot. General Dentz remained in command of his troops, which were concentrated in the region of Tripoli and entirely isolated from the Free French pending re-embarkation – an isolation which was enforced by British military authorities, under the excuse that they 'feared disorders'. In Jezireh, at Palmyra, at Aleppo, in the Hauran, Free French officials also found their action constantly thwarted by British encroachments, some of which were the unfortunate results of an intricate policy conducted by the War Office and the Colonial Office – with grudging support from the Foreign Office – while the great majority were the result of carelessness or ill-inspired initiatives on the part of subordinate military commanders; thus, a British brigade, after having moved into the Jebel Druz, took the Druz squadrons under its authority, while the British command itself moved into the 'Maison de France', residence of the Free French delegate at the Soueida, hauled down the French flag on it and hoisted the Union Jack.[24] On another occasion, General Catroux, the Free French Delegate-General and Commander-in-Chief in the Levant, arrived at his headquarters to find an Australian guard outside who refused to allow him in; here again, the French flag had been replaced by the Union Jack.[25] The example of clumsy military diplomacy seemed to come from the top, with General Wilson even threatening at one point to proclaim martial law and take over all powers himself; but it certainly permeated to the bottom, as evidenced by the case of a British officer who refused an invitation to a dinner party which de Gaulle was giving, on the grounds that his presence would damage his relations with the Vichy authorities.[26]

Indeed, the curious fact remained that the British officers appeared to be much more in sympathy with the Vichy French they had just fought than with the Free French who had fought alongside them; the Vichy French officers, including General Dentz, were treated with every courtesy, and allowed to 'live it up' in Beirut; the Vichy troops sabotaged their weapons and equipment before surrendering them to the British; they embarked for France with little or no British control; the armistice commission simply ignored the Free French, and up to 7 August, the British military authorities even professed to have no knowledge of the de Gaulle/Lyttelton interpretative agreements.

The extraordinary blindness and folly of this policy only began to appear when it was learned that 52 British officers captured during the campaign had been shipped to France by General Dentz just before he asked for an armistice. Lyttelton at last reacted violently, and gave orders that General Dentz be arrested and kept in custody until the British officers were returned. Having realized that the armistice conditions were perhaps not being respected after all, he told as much to de Gaulle during a meeting in Beirut on 7 August, and promised that the Free French would henceforth be given the possibility of winning over the Vichy French. But it was already late in the day; only 127 officers and 6000 NCOs and men in all were won over to Free France. The great majority, 25,000 men, including officers, diplomats and civil servants, sailed back to France, many of them compulsorily.[27]

Needless to say, de Gaulle was enraged at all these blunderings. With the possible exception of Captain Lyttelton, he deeply mistrusted the British in the Levant *en bloc*, with General Wilson, the War Office, 'a fanatical group of British Arabophiles supported by the Colonial Office', and of course *l'Intelligence* very high on his priority list. He suspected, rightly or wrongly – and more often wrongly than rightly – that they were all in league to humiliate France and supplant her in the Levant; during July and August, he therefore used every weapon in his arsenal of psychological warfare to browbeat the British into respecting the sovereign rights of France. In so doing, he terrified his followers in Beirut, Cairo and London, for whom co-operation with Great Britain was vital to the continued existence of the movement. Nevertheless, de Gaulle insisted on returning blow for blow, and in the process showed himself to be a master gambler.

Thus, as we have seen, the Saint Jean D'Acre armistice agreement was met with an ultimatum that by 24 July at midday, the French forces in the Levant would cease to be at the disposal of the British command; this in turn enabled de Gaulle to secure the 'interpretative agreement' with Lyttelton. Later, when General Wilson threatened to proclaim British martial law and take over all power, General de Gaulle made it known far and wide that if such a usurpation of the sovereign rights of France were carried out, he, de Gaulle, would immediately break with England. The General even showed that he would not balk at military confrontation in upholding the rights of France; by the end of July, a strong Free French force under Colonel Monclar was sent to Soueida to reclaim the 'Maison de France', and recover the Druz squadrons. When the commander of the British brigade threatened to oppose them by force of arms, the Free French made it known that they would fight – and the British force commander predictably received orders to withdraw.[28]

But General de Gaulle could also use the more conventional means of diplomacy, though not always in a conventional way. During the summer, he sent Churchill several telegrams which were as firm as they were deferential: on 21 July, for instance, on the matter of the Saint Jean D'Acre armistice, he wrote to the Prime Minister: 'I am obliged to tell you that I myself and all the Free French consider this convention as fundamentally opposed to the military and political interests of Free France, that is to say of France, and as extremely painful, in its form, to our dignity. . . . I hope you personally may feel that such a British attitude, in a matter vital for us, considerably aggravates my difficulties and will have consequences which I deem deplorable from the point of view of the task I have undertaken.'[29] Towards Eden, he was no less firm, but slightly less courteous; thus, on 1 August, he sent a telegram to Professor Cassin instructing him to see Mr Eden and tell him that 'meddling by England was leading us to the gravest complications, and that the doubtful advantages that British policy could derive in the Levant from this neglect of the rights of France would be mediocre indeed compared with the major disadvantages which would result from an open quarrel between Free France and England.'[30] To other British ministers, he was harsh and even sarcastic at times; on 17 August, he handed the following note to General Spears for transmission to the ministries concerned:

I have decided that the company of Free French parachutists now in England shall come to the Levant. If British authorities do not agree to provide this company with special equipment, I regret this, but will not alter my decision. The company will come without equipment. As far as transport is concerned it will be difficult for the British to raise objection on this account in view of the French tonnage in use of which the British authorities profit directly and principally. My opinion is that it would be a good thing if the British Air Ministry and War Office renounced their belief that they are more qualified than myself to deal with questions concerning the Free French forces.[31]

But because then as later, de Gaulle considered that his staunchest ally was public opinion in France, Britain and the USA, he made the press and radio his most powerful weapons in countering the pro-Vichy or anti-Gaullist excesses of British policy in the Levant. Having started at Brazzaville on 16 July with a statement to the press which denounced the British armistice with Vichy, de Gaulle returned to Brazzaville at the end of August, and there he gave an interview to George Weller, Foreign Correspondent of the *Chicago Daily News*. This interview was to have the effect of a bombshell in Britain, which is hardly astonishing in view of some of the opinions expressed; the General was obviously letting off the pent-up rage that had accumulated for several months, while at the same time pursuing a calculated policy of rapprochment with the USA, inaugurated in May; this was the result, as noted by George Weller:

I am not keeping facts secret any longer. I have offered the United States the use of the principal ports in Free French Africa as naval bases against Hitler. I have offered them upon the basis of a long-term lease, analogous to the plan under which Britain offered her Atlantic bases to the United States. But I have not asked for any destroyers in return. I have asked only that the United States make use of these bases to counteract Dakar and make it more difficult for Hitler to thrust deeper into Africa, as he undoubtably will do as soon as he is able to release some forces from Russia.

Upon being asked why London did not finally close the door upon Vichy and recognize his government, de Gaulle answered:

England is afraid of the French fleet. What, in effect, England is carrying on is a wartime deal with Hitler in which Vichy serves as a go-between. Vichy serves Hitler by keeping the French people in subjection and selling the French Empire piecemeal to Germany. But do not forget that Vichy also serves England by keeping the French fleet from Hitler's hands. Britain is exploiting Vichy in the same way as Germany; the only difference is in purpose. What happens, in effect, is an exchange of advantages between hostile powers which keeps the Vichy government alive as long as both Britain and Germany are agreed that it should exist.[32]

Since the beginning of the Syrian campaign, the British government had followed developments in the Levant with a rather distant interest; after all, this was only a secondary theatre of war. Captain Lyttelton had been dispatched to Cairo, and would take care of all political problems as and when they arose; and everyone in the government agreed with the Prime Minister on the policy to be pursued: Britain's main goal in the Levant was to secure the independence of Syria and Lebanon. As Mr Eden later wrote: 'the Prime Minister and I were insistent that the Arab population should not be made to feel that they had merely exchanged one set of French masters for another.'[33] Why not? Because, for many British policy-makers, the Arabs were still much more important than the Free French; as someone said in the British Cabinet at the time, 'We might be able to reach a general settlement with the Arab countries, including a settlement of the Palestine question, which would bring us increased support throughout the world.'[34]

In spite of the strategic and political significance of events in Syria, it is a fact that Churchill did not follow them any more closely than his colleagues; the main reason for this is that he was by now almost entirely absorbed by operation 'Battleaxe', an all-out effort to beat Rommel in Libya. As Churchill himself later wrote: 'The tragedy of the evacuation of Greece, the distractions in Iraq and Syria, the dire struggle in Crete, all paled before the gleam of hope which we attached, and rightly, to victory in the Western desert.'[35] But victory eluded him that time, and Churchill's attention shifted to an even more momentous event: the German attack on the Soviet Union. All this explains why there was no personal intervention by Churchill after the start of the Syrian campaign, and why the telegrams he received from de Gaulle in late June produced no reaction on his part. It also explains why Churchill, like his colleagues, was somewhat taken aback by the Syrian armistice crisis after 14 July.

The armistice negotiations themselves had not been followed very closely by the British government. They had of course sent general instructions to Oliver Lyttelton, who had relayed them to General Wilson by telephone; but after that, General Wilson was left to negotiate on his own, and the results he came up with on 14 July certainly caused some surprise in London – though probably not as much as the secret protocol forbidding contact between Vichy and the Free French. Thus, Dejean, after an interview with Anthony Eden and Major Morton, wrote to de Gaulle; 'Our interlocutors did not conceal that they had received very scant information on the progress of negotiations, and that they were embarrassed at the results achieved.'[36] This was not only diplomatic talk, as evidenced by an internal Cabinet memorandum which stated, 'Our military authorities had in fact shown excessive generosity in their conduct of the armistice negotiations and made many concessions which His Majesty's government might not have approved had they been consulted.' But His Majesty's government were even more surprised – and shocked – by de Gaulle's reaction to these armistice terms; there was de Gaulle's statement to the press at Brazzaville on 16 July, in which he publicly advertised for the first time his disagreement with the British government; there was the ultimatum presented on 21 July during the interview with Oliver Lyttelton in Cairo; and worse still, there was de Gaulle's attitude towards the

Minister of State himself during that interview, an attitude described in detail in the latter's report to the Prime Minister the next day: 'He (de Gaulle) had worked himself into a state of bitter hostility to everything English; he had the appearance of not having slept; and it was impossible to make him see reason on any points.'

And the report ended with these words:

> I have telegraphed at such length because we are by no means out of the wood and there are clearly very many points upon which controversy may again break out, and if General de Gaulle spends another sleepless night the most unexpected demands may be presented tomorrow. After our first conversation yesterday both Spears and I felt that a complete breach was inevitable and that our minimum military requirements could not be safeguarded as long as General de Gaulle remained leader of Free French. Our fears may still be well founded . . . if this is a specimen of how diplomacy has to be conducted I feel glad I did not embrace it as a career.[38]

This report caused an immediate reaction in London; Professor Cassin later wrote: 'The very next day, Churchill and all other circles in London, including the Chamber of Commons, expressed their disapproval and genuine concern. The Prime Minister sent me one of his close friends . . . with instructions to ask me among others the following general question: "Is de Gaulle still a general, or has he become a politician?"'[39]

Churchill was in fact deeply affected by de Gaulle's reaction; the latter had advertised his disagreement with the British, had spoken slightingly of the British military authorities, shown a fair measure of Anglophobia and worse still, he had seriously quarrelled with the Minister of State, who was Churchill's close friend. Though Churchill completely omitted the whole episode from his memoirs, his feelings were best expressed by the following passage in a Foreign Office memorandum: 'There was some excuse for de Gaulle's indignation . . . but he largely destroyed his case by his intemperate and Anglophobe language with Mr Lyttelton and on private occasions.'[40] In the eyes of the Prime Minister, this intemperate reaction completely effaced the British mistakes which had given rise to de Gaulle's anger in the first place; this, added to General de Gaulle's methods of 'psychological warfare' against the British, contributed more than anything else to the violent quarrels that were to erupt in the future – and the first one was now very close at hand.

De Gaulle, as we have seen, considered that he was merely

reacting to provocation, and forcing the British to respect the rights of Free France, 'that is to say of France'. But Churchill did not see – or chose not to see – the reason for de Gaulle's hostile behaviour. As for de Gaulle, he seems never to have wondered whether frank and direct communication with the Prime Minister would not have afforded a better solution to his problems than the constant ultimata and incendiary statements thrown at lesser British officers or administrators; the reason for this probably being that he was well satisfied with the results of his exertions in defending the dignity of France. But as the summer progressed, and reports of de Gaulle's 'Anglophobe' moods, actions and statements piled up on Churchill's desk with monotonous regularity, the General's immense capital of sympathy with the British Prime Minister began to dwindle very fast indeed.

After the agreements with Lyttelton, de Gaulle went to Syria, and the Prime Minister received reports stating that 'While there he conducted himself with extreme arrogance, ignoring the spirit and sometimes even the letter of the agreement that he had just signed.'[41] At the beginning of August, there was a report from the British Head of Mission at Brazzaville, indicating that 'General de Gaulle, during his recent stay, expressed stronger anti-British feelings than usual'; and the report went on to state:

> The following remarks were made quite openly:
> 1. To a French naval officer: 'beware of British . . .'
> 2. Bulk of English soldiers and officials take no interest in Free French movement of which they are incapable of appreciating the importance.
> 3. Other English officials and statesmen are merely making use of Free French who must therefore look jealously after their own interests.
> 4. Very disparaging remarks concerning conduct of campaign in Syria, 'If he (de Gaulle) had been in command, the whole business would have been polished off inside a fortnight.'
> 5. There is one ray of hope. His (de Gaulle's) influence is growing stronger. His attitude was probably the determining factor in obtaining removal of General Wavell.
> 6. The Americans would shortly come into the war and it is principally to them that Free French must look for salvation.[42]

On 20 August, the Foreign Office also received an official letter from a British naval officer who wrote, 'The high-ups in the Free French here appear to be almost anti-British, [including] General de Gaulle himself, who when he is here does not hesitate to express his feelings and is very critical of many of the British efforts and almost all of their policy.'[43]

Countless other reports were coming in, including de Gaulle's statement to General Spears on parachutists,[44] and information that de Gaulle 're-appointed numerous Vichy officials who were avowedly anti-British and who were mistrusted and disliked by the local inhabitants, because he preferred to use doubtful Frenchmen rather than reliable Englishmen'.[45] There was also a statement by de Gaulle in private that many problems were solved because of his firmness towards the Minister of State, 'who enabled him to obtain 90 per cent of his demands', and to crown the edifice, it was learned at the end of the month that de Gaulle had forbidden General Catroux to communicate with Oliver Lyttelton in his absence.[46]

Colonel Passy, head of the Free French Secret Service, immediately felt the effects of the crisis: British Intelligence and the SOE almost suspended their relations with his organization; on 6 August, Lord Leathers told Jacques Bingen, Director of the French Merchant Marine, that His Majesty's government were becoming more and more impatient with General de Gaulle, and even added that 'they were looking for someone to replace him'.[47] Canada's Prime Minister, Mackenzie King, on a visit to England, noted in his diary: 'I found that he (Churchill) was getting impatient of de Gaulle. Lord Bessborough referred to him as a "male Joan of Arc". Someone said he had better be careful not to be burned by the English. It was quite clear that the Prime Minister feels he is trying to take too much into his hands.'[48]

Indeed, de Gaulle's fierce declarations appear to have affected the Prime Minister considerably; ever since June 1940, de Gaulle had been his friend, and Churchill's friends could do no wrong. Unlike de Gaulle, Churchill could never entirely divorce policy from sentiment; but he had to admit that this was 'very ungrateful talk', and what was worse, it seemed to betray a degree of Anglophobia. The 'ungrateful talk' Churchill probably would have forgotten quickly; the Anglophobia he could not forgive, and it remained at the back of his mind until the end of the war. To be fair, it must be admitted that de Gaulle never did much to dispel the Prime Minister's prejudice – which by then was not entirely unfounded either. At any rate, Churchill, increasingly alarmed, asked Dejean and other members of the Free French movement to persuade the General to return to England – no doubt hoping that this would put an end to de Gaulle's anti-English crusade. Dejean and Cassin did their best, and the Prime Minister was probably much relieved when the General announced that he would return. The relief was premature, however, for on his return trip, de Gaulle stopped in Brazzaville – and gave his famous interview to George Weller of the *Chicago Daily News*.

On 27 August, Churchill received extracts from the interview; they told of de Gaulle's offer of bases to the United States and of England's 'wartime deal with Hitler'.[49] This, for the Prime Minister, was the last straw: he immediately wrote to Eden, 'If de Gaulle's interview with the American press at Brazzaville is authentic he has clearly gone off his head. This would be a very good riddance and will simplify our further course.'[50]

The next day, Churchill was still smarting under the insult; in Cabinet, he stated that de Gaulle's behaviour in recent weeks had been 'very disturbing' and that he 'had made some extraordinary statements in an interview at Brazzaville'.[51] Clearly feeling that some retaliation was needed, he also asked Desmond Morton to 'inform him of any action in support of General de Gaulle which might usefully be delayed in view of the present situation'. But Churchill's Francophilia and respect for the French army never being far away, he added 'without repercussion on pay and comfort of de Gaulle's men'.[52] Major Morton made some suggestions, but Winston Churchill clearly had a few ideas of his own: on 30 August, he gave Morton the following directions:

1. No one is to see General de Gaulle.
2. No English authority is to have any contact with him when he arrives.
3. If he asks to see Sir A. Cadogan, Sir A. Cadogan should not see him.
4. If the occasion demands, it may be conveyed to him that a most serious situation has arisen with which the Prime Minister is dealing in person.
5. No one should see any of General de Gaulle's subordinates either.

These instructions were given to Major Morton by telephone, and when the latter objected that he had already seen Mr Cassin, the Prime Minister replied that he should not have done so; he added that General de Gaulle was to 'stew in his own juice for a week if necessary'.[54]

It was by now quite obvious that a first-class row was brewing, which would inevitably break out on de Gaulle's return. On both sides, however, some devoted men sought to wither the force of the explosion. Thus, on the French side, Dejean went to see Major Morton, and made some commendable exertions; he deplored the General's statement to the American press and added that

> General de Gaulle had no political experience whatever and was quite a child in politics; he would have to be educated and it would have to be impressed on him that he could not make statements of the kind reported . . . it would be a great pity if de Gaulle ceased to be head of the movement. He was thinking especially of the situation in France itself where resistance had been crystallized around his name . . . it would be a mistake to regard General de Gaulle as Anglophobe. Any Frenchman that was Anglophobe at the present moment would be a traitor to his country and General de Gaulle was an intelligent man. . . . Besides, General de Gaulle was in control of French Equatorial Africa, which was of great importance from the point of view of communications.[55]

Anthony Eden was just as active on the British side; that same day, he wrote to Churchill:

> It may well be we shall find that de Gaulle is crazy; if so, he will have to be dealt with accordingly. If, however, he shows indications of repentance, I hope that you will not underestimate your power to complete the cure. He has a real and deep respect for you which he does not extend to any of our military commanders. If we cannot come to terms with de Gaulle, the chief loss to ourselves will be in increased confusion in the minds of the French people. De Gaulle is of little importance outside France; he is of considerable importance inside it today as a rallying point against Vichy. If we are compelled to have overt differences with him, this will confuse French opinion at a time when it is rallying against Vichy. The other complication will also be much on your mind, i.e. French Equatorial Africa. . . .[56]

Apparently unaware of all the agitation, de Gaulle was flying peacefully towards England. In fact, he still considered himself to be the aggrieved party, and during the flight from Freetown to Bathurst on 29 August, he had confided to a fellow passenger that he was resolved to 'put his foot in it' as soon as he arrived in London.[57] As for the interview with George Weller, one may perhaps wonder how it was allowed to pass French censorship in Brazzaville before being dispatched to the USA; de Gaulle's ADC and Cabinet Chief, François Coulet, was to provide the answer:

The American journalist's article . . . submitted to Bréal, director of information at Brazzaville, had caused him some anxiety, so that he went to consult the Chief of Cabinet (F. Coulet). The latter, having lived for several days in an atmosphere of great tension, having heard de Gaulle's outburst on the subject, being in complete agreement with the views of his chief, and not thinking that it was his responsibility to moderate their expression, had not dared to enter the neighbouring office and submit the interview to the irate General a few hours before the return journey to London. So the text was sent uncensored to the American News Agency.[58]

On the last leg of his journey, de Gaulle finally received an urgent telegram, which was decoded in the plane; it was from Cassin and Pleven, who described with much alarm the effect produced in London by the news of the interview. Upon reading it, the General turned to his ADC and said simply, '*Vous êtes un sot.*' But upon landing in Britain, de Gaulle, seeing the tragic faces of the members of his movement, recovered all his equanimity and forgave his ADC.[59]

As soon as he arrived in London, de Gaulle was made to feel the full weight of the British government's displeasure – and as usual, the stage was well set; that same day, Churchill informed the Cabinet that, 'In view of General de Gaulle's disturbing behaviour in recent weeks, departments should for the time being adopt a cautious and dilatory attitude towards all requests made by the Free French.' For a start, steps were to be taken to prevent de Gaulle from delivering a broadcast that evening.[60]

The next day, the Prime Minister sent de Gaulle a chilling letter which ended with these words: 'Until I am in possession of any explanation you may do me the honour to offer, I am unable to judge whether any interview between us would serve a useful purpose.'[61] As for Churchill's instructions, they were obviously followed to the letter; in London, the journalist A. J. Liebling noted that de Gaulle 'was walking about in the streets contiguous to Carlton Gardens, his HQ, but he was by official decree out of town . . . neither the French nor British press was allowed to allude to his return to London'.[62] Hervé Alphand, just arrived in London from New York, also noted in his diary: 'All the English I have met during the last five days are criticizing the General and his collaborators violently and openly. . . . Frederick Leith-Ross, the blockade chief, told me that the General was not "behaving".'[63] Liebling's British friends said much the same: 'As soon as he (de Gaulle) makes it up with the PM it will be all right, but he has been a very naughty boy.'[64]

De Gaulle was remarkably unaffected by this enforced ostracism; he had of course gone through it before, and knew that it could not be maintained indefinitely. Besides, he could take a few counter-measures himself; thus, having been refused access to the BBC, he suspended all participation by the Free French in broadcasting from London. In addition, de Gaulle did have some officious contacts with the Prime Minister's entourage; as early as 2 September, he received Major Morton, to whom he confided that 'whereas the treatment accorded to him by the Prime Minister, the ministers and elsewhere on a high level was most generous', he had met with most serious obstruction from British officials in Syria.[65] De Gaulle went on to detail his complaints against these officials in general, and against Generals Wilson and Spears in particular.[66] As for the now famous note on Free French parachutists, de Gaulle, according to Morton, 'made the somewhat disarming statement that he regretted sending it but he was in a violent temper at the time'.[67] The next day, de Gaulle also sent a private letter to Churchill, airing his grievances but adding that he had 'a very good impression of his personal relations with the British Minister of State in Cairo'.[68] Always a bad hater, Churchill finally relented, and de Gaulle was told that the Prime Minister would see him on 12 September. Hervé Alphand, who had lunch with de Gaulle at the time, noted that the General was 'quite calm and sure of himself, peacefully awaiting the meeting which Churchill had promised him for the week after'.[69]

In preparing for this interview, Churchill was neither calm nor peaceful; he made enquiries on the status of the Free French movement, on how far de Gaulle represented the French people, and how he could be better 'controlled' by his own movement, through the setting up of a council for example. He also had the French department of the Foreign Office work out a list of complaints against General de Gaulle (it was not short),[70] and finally he declared in the Commons, after having recognized the 'special privileged position of France in Syria': 'I must make it quite clear that our policy . . . is that Syria shall be handed back to the Syrians, who will assume at the earliest possible moment their independent sovereign rights. We do not propose that this process . . . shall wait until the end of the war . . . there must be no question, even in war-time, of a mere substitution of Free French interests for Vichy

French interests.'[71] Finally came 12 September, the day of the long-awaited explanation.*

De Gaulle was expected at 10 Downing Street at 3 p.m. Sir John Colville, then Churchill's secretary, recalls in his memoirs:

> At five to three the bell from the Cabinet room rang and I went in. Mr Churchill informed me that when de Gaulle arrived he would rise and bow slightly but would not shake hands with him. He would indicate by a gesture that the General was to sit opposite him, on the other side of the Cabinet table. No doubt as a supreme mark of disapproval, he announced that he would not speak to him in French, but would converse through an interpreter. 'And you,' he said, 'will be the interpreter.'
>
> Punctually at 3 p.m. the General arrived. Churchill rose from his chair in the middle of the long Cabinet table, inclined his head slightly and gestured to the selected seat opposite him. De Gaulle seemed quite unabashed. He walked to his chair, sat down, gazed at the Prime Minister and said nothing.
>
> 'General de Gaulle, I have asked you to come here this afternoon.' Churchill stopped and looked fiercely at me. 'Mon Général,' I said, 'je vous ai invité de venir cet après-midi.'
>
> 'I didn't say Mon Général,' interrupted the Prime Minister 'and I did not say I had invited him.' Somehow I stumbled, with frequent interruptions, through the next few sentences.
>
> Then it was de Gaulle's turn. After the first sentence he turned to me and I interpreted. 'Non, non,' he interjected, 'ce n'est pas du tout le sens de ce que je disais.' But it was.
>
> Churchill said it was clear to both of them that if I could not do better than that I had better find somebody who could. So I escaped from the room with shame and telephoned to Nicholas Lawford at the Foreign Office. His French was immaculate. He arrived at the double and I showed him into the Cabinet room where no word had been spoken in the intervening minutes. It seemed no time at all before he emerged, red in the face and protesting that they must be mad: they had said he could not speak French properly and they would have to manage without an interpreter.[72]

It would have been awkward to have a proper row through an interpreter anyway. The official transcript of the discussion is of course somewhat sterilized, but it nevertheless gives a fair idea of how violent the initial exchanges must have been.

*In his memoirs, de Gaulle mistakenly gives 15 September as the date of the interview.

The Prime Minister said that he had witnessed with very great sorrow the deterioration in General de Gaulle's attitude towards His Majesty's government. He now felt that he was no longer dealing with a friend. He had received a letter from General de Gaulle on the subject of a recent press interview. Clearly an important person whose utterances carried weight was often in danger of being taken advantage of by newspaper correspondents. But quite apart from this matter, the Prime Minister had received evidence from many sources that General de Gaulle had throughout his recent travels left a trail of Anglophobia behind him. This was a most serious matter in all the circumstances, and the Prime Minister had been greatly pained by the accumulation of evidence he had received.

General de Gaulle said that it could not be seriously maintained that he was an enemy of Great Britain. His position and previous record made it inconceivable. He would, however, say frankly that recent events, especially in Syria, had profoundly disturbed him and cast doubts in his mind as to the attitude of many British authorities towards him and the Free French movement. These events, added to the great difficulties of his personal position, to his isolation, and no doubt to the factor of his personal temperament, had led him to utterances which must clearly have been disagreeable to British ears. He wished to express his frank regret for these utterances.

The Prime Minister said that he had been at great pains before General de Gaulle's arrival in Egypt to make it clear to all concerned that the General was the man he trusted and the man with whom he proposed to work. Everything had been done to smooth the path before General de Gaulle. No doubt there had been faults on the British side in handling relations, and he could well believe that General de Gaulle had suffered some annoyances. To some extent hitches of this nature were unavoidable, but General de Gaulle had become increasingly antagonistic, and had made no communication to the Prime Minister.

General de Gaulle reminded the Prime Minister of his message of 28 June, in which he had stated that any breach over Syria would have the most serious consequences on the Free French movement. On his arrival in Syria he soon realized that many of the British authorities had no conception of the status of the Free French movement. He found himself surrounded with political and military authorities who to all appearances had it as their aim to diminish the role of the Free French in Syria. His representatives had endured countless humiliations, and the agreements he had entered into with the Minister of State, apparently to their mutual satisfaction, had remained a dead letter for a whole fortnight. In normal circumstances difficulties of this sort between two countries would be smoothed out in a moment by their ambassadors.

At a time when France was broken and humiliated, his own efforts to vindicate her must fail if he met with such treatment.

The Prime Minister explained Britain's attitude with regard to Syria. Britain had no ambitions of any sort in that country, and no desire whatever to supplant France. Her one object was the defeat of Hitler, there and everywhere, and nothing must stand in the way of that purpose. Syria was an important unit in the Arab world, as well as one of the military factors in the defence of Egypt. We could not allow a repetition of events in Syria, the repercussions of which in adjacent territories endangered our military position. It followed that we had to be in control in Syria for all purposes connected with the winning of the war. That, he repeated, was the sole purpose that had brought us there. Clearly the securing of our position in the Arab world involved a transfer of many of the functions previously exercised by France in Syria to the Syrians themselves. . . . That was essential. The Arabs saw no sense in driving out the Vichy French only to be placed under the control of the Free French. They desired their independence, and had been promised it. Once again Britain sought no selfish advantage, pursued no imperial ambitions, in Syria. . . .

General de Gaulle denied that he entertained any suspicions of selfish British motives in Syria. Although British and French policies towards the Arab world were not the same, in Syria or elsewhere, there could be no disagreement on the principles laid down by the Prime Minister, and it was he himself who had promised the Syrians their independence. Similarly he had always recognized the fact that the ultimate military control must rest in British hands. The question was not one of principle – on which there was no disagreement – but one of method, regarding which he maintained that the Free French in Syria had been subjected to constant and unnecessary humiliations.

The Prime Minister said that he would be ashamed to use the British power, which in Syria was overwhelming, for any purpose not essential to the defeat of Hitler. For any such purpose, however, as to assure the necessary degree of security, he would not hesitate to use the full power at our disposal against anyone, in the knowledge that he would thus be serving the common cause. ·

General de Gaulle said that it was natural and good that British forces – whose overwhelming preponderance over the Free French in Syria he did not contest – should be used in all cases where their use would contribute to the defeat of the common foe.

The Prime Minister said that matters now seemed to be going more smoothly in Syria and that the relations between General Catroux and the British military authorities were now satisfactory.

The Prime Minister assured General de Gaulle that he was not unmindful of the importance to the common cause of so treating the Free French movement in Syria as to make the French nation realize that General de Gaulle was the guardian of its interests in Syria, and that those interests were pre-eminent as compared with those of other European countries. To strengthen General de Gaulle's position in France, he would particularly bear in mind the General's position as defender of the historic connection between France and Syria.

General de Gaulle said that he had much evidence to show that the necessity for the Syrian campaign had been understood in France, and that it had led to no stirring of anti-British or anti-Free French feeling.

The Prime Minister said that he had been anxious that developments in Syria should not damage General de Gaulle's standing in French eyes. It was no part of British policy to belittle the Free French contribution to the Syrian campaign.

General de Gaulle said that he hoped the Prime Minister had received, together with less welcome reports, echoes of the very deep and sincere admiration for the British imperial forces which he had repeatedly expressed in the past few weeks.

The Prime Minister then turned to the question of the leadership of the Free French movement. He had come to the conclusion that it would be in the Free French interest if a formal council were created, which would have an effective voice in shaping the policy of the movement of which General de Gaulle was the head as the recognized leader of all Free Frenchmen.

General de Gaulle agreed that there would be some advantage in his having about him some body analogous to a government. He had given the matter a good deal of thought, but there were some difficulties. . . . The creation of a representative council would inevitably bring political factors into play, and the unanimity of the movement might thereby be endangered. He would, however, give the whole question very careful thought. . . .

The Prime Minister said that he had a double object in view: to encourage General de Gaulle's supporters in France, and therefore to do nothing which would diminish General de Gaulle's stature as the champion of continued resistance to the enemy; and at the same time to improve relations between His Majesty's government and the Free French movement by giving the latter a broader basis. He believed that the latter purpose would be served by the creation of a council, with whom His Majesty's government would then deal. He was glad to hear that General de Gaulle proposed to give this matter his earnest attention.

In conclusion, the Prime Minister asked General de Gaulle to realize how important it was to give no ground to the suspicion that he (the General) entertained hostile thoughts towards Great Britain, or even

Churchill on a visit to the BEF in January 1940.
Left to right: General Ironside, Mr Churchill, General
Gamelin, Lord Gort.

A year later in England. Churchill between General
Sikorski and General de Gaulle, 15 February 1941.

The French National Committee. Devoted men, lengthy
deliberations, and '*Le Roi, c'est moi!*'
Left to right: Diethelm, Muselier, de Gaulle, Cassin,
Pleven, Valin.

The Queen visiting the Free French in the summer of 1940.
Her Majesty Queen Elizabeth between General de Gaulle and
Admiral Muselier.

Mr Churchill inspects Free French naval officers in Portsmouth dockyard,
January 1941.

De Gaulle inspecting Free
French unit, summer 1941.
'*Vous avez des Anglais ici?*'
'*Oui, mon General*'
'*Combien?*'
'*17*'
'*C'est trop!*'

The liberation of St Pierre et Miquelon, 24 December 1941.

'The action taken by the so-called Free French ships at St Pierre et Miquelon was an arbitrary action contrary to the agreement of all parties concerned.'

US Secretary of State, Cordell Hull.

Roosevelt and de Gaulle on speaking terms at last.

thoughts that might subsequently take on a hostile character. He wished to press this advice upon the General, because already some British figures entertained a suspicion that General de Gaulle had become hostile and had moved towards certain fascist views which would not be helpful to collaboration in the common cause.

General de Gaulle said that he would give the utmost weight to the Prime Minister's advice. He did not think that the accusation of authoritarian views could be maintained in the light of his most recent statements and of certain further statements he proposed to make. He begged the Prime Minister to understand that the leaders and members of the Free French movement were necessarily somewhat difficult people: else they would not be where they were. If this difficult character sometimes coloured their attitude towards their great ally . . . he could rest assured that their entire loyalty to Great Britain remained unimpaired.

Unaware of the turn taken by the conversation, Churchill's secretary was by then feeling some anxiety:

An hour slipped away and I began to fear violence. I tried to eavesdrop, but . . . double doors had recently been installed. I could hear nothing. I walked out into the hall and tried on General de Gaulle's cap, registering surprise at the remarkable smallness of his head. I did my best to concentrate on the papers on my desk. I had decided it was my duty to burst in, perhaps with a bogus message, in case some dire act had been committed. Perhaps they had strangled each other? Just then the bell rang and I went in to find the two of them sitting side by side with amiable expressions on their faces. De Gaulle, no doubt for tactical purposes, was smoking one of the Prime Minister's cigars. They were talking French, an exercise Churchill could never resist and one which his audience invariably found fascinating.[74]

Indeed, Churchill's last words were nothing if not amiable: the Prime Minister said that 'he would be glad to see General de Gaulle again at some future time if the latter wished. If the Minister of State came home, a meeting à trois might be convenient.'[75]

Having parted with some warmth after a very inauspicious start, the two mercurial leaders both felt that they had cause for satisfaction. Churchill, after all, had indicated that the British government would continue to respect the Cairo agreements on Syria, and would do its best to support de Gaulle's position; and de Gaulle had promised to consider the possibility of setting up a representative and democratic council – no very great concessions on the face of it, but the most important result was elsewhere: some of the misunderstandings caused by time, distance, suspicions, prejudices and intermediaries had been dispelled, and a measure of confidence and understanding had been restored between the two leaders. Deep down under, Churchill had boundless admiration for this solitary and unbending man who was the very incarnation of defiance in defeat – and de Gaulle knew that Churchill was one of the very few who really understood the sense of his mission. But anyone who assumed that the two men would from then on maintain normal and friendly relations would of course be grievously mistaken.

CHAPTER 7

The 'So-Called Free French'

During the latter part of the interview on 12 September, Churchill had insisted on giving de Gaulle some disinterested advice: 'It would be in the Free French interest if a formal council were created, which would have an effective voice in shaping the policy of the movement of which General de Gaulle was the head as the recognized leader of all Free Frenchmen.' Beneath the flowery diplomatic prose, there was a less disinterested motivation: during the weeks preceding the interview, Winston Churchill had been casting about for some way of curbing de Gaulle's anti-British excesses, and the creation of a council that would effectively control the General's policies and impulses seemed to offer the best guarantees in this respect. To be sure, de Gaulle's conception of leadership appeared to be *'le roi, c'est moi'*, but that didn't matter: Churchill only wanted to make him a constitutional monarch.

Naturally, the delicate task of 'putting the General in commission'* would have to be discharged by the French themselves; but then, there was no shortage of Frenchmen in London who disagreed with de Gaulle's recent anti-British outbursts and resented his autocratic style of leadership. Indeed, on 9 September, Desmond Morton had written to Churchill: 'I hear Free French HQ is getting nearly as tired as we are of their chief's ungovernable temper and lack of balanced judgement. . . . A number of Free French and several other Frenchmen of goodwill outside the movement are earnestly wondering how they can create a council to control the General's political actions. I fear they will not get far beyond wondering.'[1]

The last sentence was hardly encouraging, but Churchill had heard recently of one of these valiant Frenchmen; on 1 September,

---

*This expression was actually used by Churchill, and meant that de Gaulle's powers would be divided among a committee instead of being concentrated in one man.

he had received the following report: 'According to Admiral Dickens, Muselier . . . thinks de Gaulle is suffering from megalomania. . . . He feels that either they must change their leader or the leader must change his ways.'[2] Admiral Muselier was not unknown to Churchill; this was the same Muselier he had thrown in jail nine months earlier.[3] But then, that had been a dreadful mistake, and the past was the past. If Muselier intended to take de Gaulle's place, that of course would not do: politically, the admiral was known in British circles as a 'lightweight', and besides, Churchill had obligations towards de Gaulle, written and otherwise. But if Muselier only aimed at a democratization of the Free French movement, surely that was all to the good. The ubiquitous Desmond Morton was therefore instructed to mingle with Muselier's group and keep the Prime Minister informed[4] – perhaps also to offer a bit of moderating counsel in case the movement got out of hand.

Major Morton quickly learned that Muselier had some backing in the Free French movement. Two members of the admiral's staff, Moret and Schaeffer, told him that

> The naval and air staffs, the civilian staffs and a good number of the military bureau had been forming the conclusion that de Gaulle, while remaining useful as a symbolic figurehead and doubtless being valuable as a military commander, though this still required proving, could not be allowed to develop in the way he was going. Though honest, he was a fanatic approaching the unstable. He was no administrator, no diplomat, and if a politician, tending towards fascism. . . . The members of the Free French headquarters, apart from a few 'yes men', chiefly in the military bureau, were determined to force the General to set up a council.[5]

The news that the British Prime Minister had advised de Gaulle to set up just such a council and that the General had agreed to consider the idea came as a great encouragement to these champions of democracy; not surprisingly, they considered that democracy could only be guaranteed in the new set-up if power was exercised – well, yes – by themselves. De Gaulle? He would make a very good figurehead. On 19 September, the 'key men' in the conspiracy gathered for lunch in a private room at the Savoy. There was Admiral Muselier, Moret, Schaeffer and Labarthe, editor of the newspaper *France Libre*. Major Morton was also there as an observer, and so was Maurice Dejean, probably in the same capacity; finally, there was the host, Lord Bessborough, who was later heard to remark that 'he never knew that a revolution required so much brandy'.[6]

A revolution it was: Muselier told his friends that 'he had handed General de Gaulle a note on the previous evening with a request for an early answer. In the note, he asked de Gaulle to form immediately an executive council whose approval must be given in advance to all declarations and decisions involving policy. General de Gaulle himself would be the non-acting president, and Muselier the effective vice-president.'[7] The actual content of the letter was somewhat different, but the intention was the same: Muselier would be president of the executive council with all effective powers, and some of the most important functions on the council would go to his own men: Labarthe would be in charge of political direction and propaganda, and Moret would take the Secret Service and the navy. For good measure, Muselier would take care of national defence as well.[8] The admiral also told his friends during the lunch – whether before or after brandy is not known – that 'if de Gaulle would not accept the scheme, he (Muselier) would inform the British government that he and his fleet were at their complete disposal for the war, but not as adherents of General de Gaulle'.[9] That was probably as close to a threat of secession as one could get. At any rate, the party, minus Lord Bessborough and Desmond Morton, then left for Muselier's flat to draft a decree setting down the scheme in detail, which would then be submitted to de Gaulle's signature. It was clear that they expected full British backing for this scheme, which was in fact to be 'submitted to His Majesty's government for approval'.[10]

That evening, Desmond Morton gave Churchill a detailed account of what had taken place at the 'Savoy Summit'. The Prime Minister was quite satisfied: the council would surely have 'some permanent control over de Gaulle's political acts and utterances', he told Morton; the General 'would remain as a War Lord in control of the military aspect of the movement, and in this capacity we could easily control him'. Naturally, 'if the dissidents pressed General de Gaulle too far, he (the Prime Minister) might have to intervene (for example, send for General de Gaulle and Admiral Muselier and knock their heads together) in order to prevent a serious bust-up. However, he did not want to have to take action and hoped that the dissidents would be reasonable and that the row would be composed without his intervention.' And Desmond Morton also reported the

following, which is quite typical of Churchill's character as we know
it:

> The second stage would be that if the present difficulties were resolved
> and the council formed, the Prime Minister would after some time,
> perhaps a couple of months, do something to show a special mark of
> favour to General de Gaulle, which would be of benefit to our war effort
> and improve personal relations between General de Gaulle and the
> Prime Minister. In other words if General de Gaulle shows that he has
> learned sense, the Prime Minister would make him a great man.[11]

Meanwhile, at Carlton Gardens, the object of all these attentions
was carefully planning his next move: he had in fact decided to form
a 'National Committee', but it was quite different from what
Admiral Muselier had in mind. The latter's note of 18 September, as
well as the 'draft decree' of 19 September, had not been gratified
with an answer; when Muselier and Labarthe finally went to see de
Gaulle on the evening of the 21st, they were informed that there was
no question of the new committee being presided over by anyone
other than de Gaulle himself; the General was quite willing to
include Muselier and Labarthe in the committee, but as for Moret
replacing Passy as Intelligence chief, the answer was a flat *non*.
Muselier and Labarthe thereupon declared that they could not
accept a scheme which would leave de Gaulle in complete control of
policy and Passy as sole chief of Intelligence . . . and refused to join
the committee.[12]

Muselier probably thought that this would force de Gaulle to give
in. The next morning, he called Dejean, who was in charge of de
Gaulle's political Cabinet, and enquired whether the General had
changed his mind. Dejean answered that de Gaulle was in fact
preparing to announce the constitution of a National Committee
comprising neither Moret, Labarthe, nor Muselier; the admiral then
flew into a rage, and said that in this case, the fleet 'would become
independent and continue the war'.[13] Dejean naturally reported this
statement to de Gaulle; Muselier later claimed to have said: 'In this
case, I will have nothing to do with the committee and the navy will .
. . keep out of politics altogether and concentrate on the war, in close
liaison with the British Admiralty.'[14] The admiral therefore claimed
that Dejean had misrepresented his words in reporting to the
General. Unfortunately, this was less than the truth, and Dejean had
misrepresented nothing at all: in fact, a few hours later,
Muselier even informed the Admiralty that he was prepared to

put 'his' fleet at their disposal – which naturally caused some embarrassment in Whitehall.[15]

Upon being informed of Muselier's telephonic utterances, de Gaulle exploded, and the very next day, he sent Muselier an ultimatum:

> You have informed me of your decision to separate yourself and the navy from Free France . . . your action constitutes an intolerable misuse of the military command entrusted to you. . . . I give you 24 hours to come back to common sense and duty. Failing this, I will take all the necessary measures to ensure that you will be rendered harmless and that your conduct will be publicly known, that is to say stigmatized. I must add that . . . I have assured myself of the support of our British allies . . . who have recognized me as leader of the Free French.[16]

Muselier later wrote that de Gaulle was bluffing, and that he had not consulted the British.[17] De Gaulle was not bluffing; at 1 p.m. that day, he had seen Churchill and informed him that he proposed announcing to the press that very afternoon the creation of a National Committee composed of eight or nine members. Muselier would not be included, as it was the General's intention to relieve him of his command 'on the ground that, for reasons of personal ambition, the admiral had been disloyal to him'. Churchill was much alarmed: the whole scheme was evidently backfiring, and here was the 'serious bust-up' he had feared. The Prime Minister would have none of it: 'We could not permit an open rift to develop in the Free French movement at the present moment,' he told de Gaulle, and he pressed the General to postpone any final action for at least another 24 hours – in other words, not to announce the composition of his Committee until the mediators had had a chance to intervene. The General, who evidently felt that he was in a position of strength, agreed to the postponement.[18]

The mediators then set to work, and they worked fast; at 11 p.m., Churchill discussed the problem with Major Morton, the Foreign Secretary and the First Lord. The main conclusion was that Muselier would have to put his case in writing to de Gaulle 'in such a way that the latter would be unable to sustain his charge of disloyalty based on personal ambition'.[19] The next day, 24 September, Muselier, who had placed himself under the protection of the Admiralty, was prevailed upon to write a conciliatory letter to de Gaulle: 'His position had been misinterpreted,' he wrote, and the

General was asked to consider his telephone communication to M. Dejean as 'null and void'.[20] That afternoon, de Gaulle summoned Muselier, and they had an interview which de Gaulle then described to the Foreign Secretary as 'eminently satisfactory'. Eden therefore thought that everything had been patched up. But the interview had only been 'eminently satisfactory' for General de Gaulle; later in the afternoon, Somerville-Smith, of the Spears mission, met Muselier, who informed him categorically that 'far from settling matters, de Gaulle had taken the line that Muselier had been disloyal to him and they could no longer work together'.[21]

So the mediation had failed after all. Somerville-Smith immediately reported this to Morton, who at once advised Strang, the latter alerting Eden without delay. The heavy machine of mediation was then rolled out once again: de Gaulle and Muselier were summoned to the Foreign Office, where the General sat in one room for hours with the Foreign Secretary, while the admiral sat in another with the First Lord, and Cadogan plied between the two. In the end, the First Lord told Muselier that, in the interests of the general war effort, he should 'knuckle down to de Gaulle'. Eden, on the other hand, proceeded to persuade de Gaulle to withdraw his charges, and appoint Muselier as commissioner for the navy. After much hesitation and recrimination, the admiral and the General allowed themselves to be persuaded. The next day, 25 September, de Gaulle announced the composition of his committee,* and Muselier was included.** As for the rest, of course, de Gaulle had very much his own way: Moret and Labarthe were totally excluded from the set-up, and the president of the new committee was none other than de Gaulle himself; the commissioners were responsible to him only, and he had full powers to issue decrees and promulgate ordinances. It required a great deal of imagination to see the creation of the committee as weakening de Gaulle's power. For the Foreign Office and the Admiralty, the only consolation was that a major row and a cleavage within the Free French movement had been averted. Eden and Alexander did not ask for more.

*It included Pleven (Economy, Finance and Colonies), Cassin (Justice and Public Education), Dejean (Foreign Affairs), Legentilhomme (War), Valin (Air), Diethelm (Labour, Information, Action in France). Catroux and d'Argenlieu, on missions abroad, were members without portfolio.
**It is interesting to note that in his memoirs, de Gaulle did not mention the British mediation. He probably considered it as incompatible with the sovereignty of Free France, and therefore unworthy of being recorded by history.

Churchill did – and he was bitterly disappointed; the very next day, he wrote to Eden:

> This is very unpleasant. Our intention was to compel de Gaulle to accept a suitable council. All we have done is to compel Muselier and Co. to submit themselves to de Gaulle. I understood you were going to make sure that the resulting government represented what we want. It is evident that this business will require the closest watching, and that our weight in the immediate future must be thrown more heavily against de Gaulle than I had hoped would be necessary.[22]

At this juncture, Churchill probably thought that he had been outfoxed; if so, he was perfectly right.

De Gaulle was quite satisfied with the outcome of the affair: he had created a government without the name, and this could only reinforce the prestige of Free France; as for Muselier, he was undeniably competent as a navy man, and it was obvious that he could still render great services to Free France in this capacity. For the General, this was all that counted. De Gaulle certainly suspected the British Admiralty of having 'encouraged Muselier in his act of indiscipline',[23] but curiously enough, although he was later to accuse Churchill of the gravest misdeeds (wrongly, as it were), he never found out that the Prime Minister had played a role in the Muselier conspiracy – admittedly only as an 'interested observer', but then in every sense of the term.

After this second *Affaire Muselier*, Anglo-French relations returned to normal. To be sure, Churchill, fearing another anti-British campaign, gave directions that de Gaulle was on no account to leave the country – but as the General had no intention of doing so, he never learned of the ban . . . which was just as well. On the other hand, de Gaulle learned that the British Intelligence service and the SOE persisted in trying to recruit people who had left France to join the Gaullist movement. In retaliation, the General ordered Passy to 'cease all relations of any kind with the British services until the Frenchmen in question are handed back to us'.[24] Of course, this was not the first order of the kind, and as Free French Intelligence could only operate with British technical assistance, de Gaulle's instructions were very imperfectly carried out. After a few other minor explosions in Downing Street and Carlton Gardens, the year 1941 could well have ended peacefully for Franco-British relations –

had it not been for two tiny French islands off the coast of Newfoundland: St Pierre et Miquelon.

L'Affaire de St Pierre et Miquelon is a typical instance of a very unimportant event that accidentally inflated beyond all bounds – with somewhat surprising consequences. Ever since September 1940, when he was sailing for Dakar, de Gaulle had been planning a 'spontaneous change of administration' in St Pierre et Miquelon and French Guiana.[25] Indeed, the great majority of the 5000 inhabitants of St Pierre et Miquelon had not the slightest sympathy for the Vichy administration, and in February 1941, de Gaulle wrote to a French official that the liberation of the islands would be 'very easy', although it would be necessary to 'ascertain the co-operation of the British fleet and the tacit approval of Washington'.[26] The British had no objections at all: Vichy had a powerful radio transmitter on St Pierre, which was used to broadcast propaganda to America, and could be used to inform German submarines of the positions of Allied convoys crossing the Atlantic. The sooner the islands passed into Allied control the better. However, the geographical position of the islands certainly rendered Canadian permission necessary, and the political realities of the war made American agreement indispensable. Anthony Eden told de Gaulle as much when the latter informed him of his plan to rally the islands in the autumn of 1941.[27] There were few difficulties involved in securing Canadian assent, but American agreement was another matter altogether.

Ever since the outbreak of war, General de Gaulle had placed great faith in the United States. Like Churchill, he was certain that the Americans would eventually enter the war, and that their intervention would prove decisive. Unlike Churchill, he believed that the USA could be used as a counterweight to British influence. De Gaulle had therefore sent several missions to Washington,[28] had made repeated offers of co-operation to the State Department,[29] and even offered to grant the USA full use of Free French naval bases in Africa;[30] but these advances had met with no response.

For President Roosevelt, de Gaulle was 'just another French general', and since June 1940, Roosevelt had little respect for Frenchmen in general, and French generals in particular. Besides, seen from Washington, this particular French general appeared to be a puppet of the British, he was the man who had failed at Dakar, and anyway he was rumoured to have Fascist tendencies. That was more than enough to disqualify him as an interlocutor of the United States. But the real reason for this enforced ostracism was of course America's policy towards Vichy. Since the autumn of 1940, President Roosevelt, Secretary of State Cordell Hull and Under-Secretary of State Sumner Welles had done everything in their power to remain on close terms with the government of Marshal Pétain in Vichy. In doing so, they expected several results: the old Marshal might be encouraged to 'stand up in his boots', as Adolph Berle so elegantly put it,[31] the French fleet could be kept out of German hands, and North Africa might even be persuaded to take up arms against the Germans one day.

For all these reasons, Roosevelt had sent Admiral Leahy as his representative in Vichy, while Robert Murphy was sent to Algiers to look after American interests there. Long after Churchill had given up his dreams of seeing Pétain actively resist the Germans or Weygand 'raise the standard of revolt' in North Africa, the Americans had continued to woo Vichy with commendable if unrewarded determination; every type of inducement had been used in the process, including a partial lifting of the blockade which allowed North Africa to receive vast amounts of American supplies; but the results had been most discouraging: Pétain's senile moods were decidedly more collaborationist than resistant, Admiral Darlan had come to the fore in April 1941 with a definitely pro-German programme, and by November 1941, it was announced that Weygand, on whom the Americans pinned so much hope, was being recalled from North Africa. Meanwhile, in Algeria, Morocco and Tunisia, German agents arrived in increasing numbers and without the slightest hindrance; yet for all that, the American Secretary of State, undaunted, pursued his pro-Vichy policy with flat-footed determination.

Then came 7 December 1941, and the world war came knocking at America's door; a rude knock, but America had a strong door. For Churchill, the lonely struggle was over: at long last, there would be an Anglo-American coalition. As for de Gaulle, he immediately understood the direct implications of this momentous event: 'Well then,' he said to Billotte, 'this war is over. Of course, there are more operations, battles and struggles ahead; but in fact the war is over, as its outcome is no longer in doubt. In this industrial war, nothing can resist the power of American industry.' The General added these prophetic words: 'From now on, the British will do nothing without

Roosevelt's agreement.'*[32] For the time being, however, de Gaulle was reinforced in his resolve to rally all French possessions in the American hemisphere. At the beginning of December, Admiral Muselier was sailing for Canada to inspect the Free French naval units stationed there; but he was also entrusted with a highly secret mission: the rallying of St Pierre et Miquelon.

As Muselier was reluctant to undertake the operation without British agreement, de Gaulle sent a message to Churchill asking him if His Majesty's government had any objection to 'this little *coup de main*'.[34] Churchill consulted the Foreign Office, and the answer was: 'We would see no objection to the operation proposed by Admiral Muselier: indeed, we should prefer it.' The Chiefs-of-Staff were also consulted, and replied 'that they were strongly in favour of Admiral Muselier being authorized to rally St Pierre et Miquelon to Free France without his saying anything about it until it had been done'.[35] On 15 December, Churchill therefore agreed to 'unmuzzle Muselier', but he asked General de Gaulle to postpone the issue of executive orders for 36 hours while it was ascertained whether this action 'would be considered in any way embarrassing by the United States government'.[36]

America was now at war with Japan – and with Hitler. But as curious as it may seem, not even Pearl Harbor had changed American policy towards Vichy. In fact, a few days after 7 December, the American government had concluded with Admiral Robert, Vichy's High Commissioner for the Antilles, Guiana and St Pierre, an agreement involving the maintenance of the status quo in all French possessions of the Western hemisphere. In addition, Roosevelt had assured Pétain on 13 December that the USA intended to stand by the Havana Convention of 1940.** As in the past, therefore, everything would be done on the American side to propitiate Vichy. As for this troublesome wireless station in St Pierre, the USA had been negotiating with Canada for the last few weeks and it was agreed that the Canadians should send operators to supervise the messages transmitted by the station. In case of a refusal by the local governor, the two countries would apply economic pressure on the island. Everything was therefore being taken care of

*De Gaulle's statements to Passy that same day were even more prophetic: 'Now the war is definitely won! And after that will come two phases: the first will be the rescue of Germany by the Allies; as for the second, I fear that it will be a war between the Russians and the Americans.'[33]
**The Havana Convention of 1940 also guaranteed the status quo in the Western hemisphere.

in the most satisfactory way (for American interests) when on 16 December, President Roosevelt was told by the State Department that a message had been received from the Foreign Office. The message informed the State Department of the projected Free French operation, stated that the British had no objections to it, and enquired whether this action 'did not embarrass the United States government'.[37]

It certainly did. The President said that he was 'strongly opposed to the suggested action',[38] and this categorical answer was relayed to the Foreign Office. On the other hand, Roosevelt told Sumner Welles that he 'favoured Canadian action' in the island, and the Canadian authorities were informed accordingly.[39] For inner political reasons – the French Canadians were unreservedly pro-de Gaulle and anti-Vichy – as well as because the dispatch of Canadian personnel 'might arouse hostility among the islanders',[40] the authorities in Ottawa were reluctant to intervene. Besides, they would certainly do nothing without consulting the British. Three days later, in fact, Ottawa decided to shelve the whole scheme.

In London, meanwhile, the Foreign Office had received Roosevelt's negative reply and on the morning of the 17th, Mr Strang informed M. Dejean of the President's views, adding that as a result 'it was vital that any order that might have been given for the operations should be cancelled'. The Free French commissioner, after having referred to General de Gaulle, thereupon informed the Foreign Office that 'no orders would be issued for this operation'.[41] The Foreign Office therefore considered the matter as settled.

That was a mistake. When speaking to M. Dejean at the Foreign Office, Mr Strang had mentioned en passant that he 'had also heard from Washington that the United States and Canadian governments had discussed a plan by which the latter would send personnel to take charge of the wireless station, and that the US government had approved the proposal'.[42] After having instructed Dejean to give assurances to the Foreign Office that the Free French plan was called off, de Gaulle seems to have brooded over this passage of Mr Strang's communication.* Did de Gaulle genuinely believe that the Canadians would undertake the action? Were any enquiries made? Was the General merely looking for a suitable

---

*At Dejean's request, a written summary of Mr Strang's communication was sent to General de Gaulle a few hours later. The General seems to have based himself on this document rather than on Dejean's report.

pretext to proceed with the rallying operation? At any rate, as he later wrote: 'It being now a question of a foreign intervention on French territory, there could no longer be any hesitation. I gave Admiral Muselier the order to rally St Pierre et Miquelon at once.'*[43] It was thought inexpedient to inform the British or the American government of this sudden about-face, and on Christmas Eve, 1941, Admiral Muselier landed at St Pierre with a detachment of Free French Marines. They were received enthusiastically by the local population, and a plebiscite organized immediately afterwards gave a 90% majority in favour of Free France.

Churchill had arrived in Washington on 22 December to confer with the President on many momentous subjects and projects; the organization of the Grand Alliance, the Declaration of the United Nations, a common plan for future operations in North Africa, and of course the situation in the Pacific, which was grave in the extreme. The talks with the President and with Secretary of State Hull proceeded in the most friendly atmosphere, and Christmas Eve at the White House was a cheerful occasion, with the Canadian Prime Minister joining in as well. The next day, however, the President and the Prime Minister were somewhat taken aback when they read the following telegram sent by Muselier to the British Admiralty: 'I have the honour to inform you that in compliance with the order quite recently received from General de Gaulle and request of inhabitants I have proceeded this morning to island St Pierre and rallied people to Free France and Allied cause with enthusiastic reception.'[45]

The President and the Prime Minister were at first inclined to pooh-pooh the whole affair; not so the Secretary of State: 'Comparatively unimportant though the islands were,' he later

---

*The order to Muselier, dated 18 December, was couched in the following terms:

We have, as you asked, consulted the British and American governments. We know, from a source beyond doubt, that the Canadians intend to carry out the destruction of the St Pierre radio station themselves. In these conditions, I order you to proceed to the rallying of St Pierre et Miquelon by your own means and without saying anything to the foreigners. I take full responsibility for this operation, which has become indispensable in order to keep these French possessions for France.

It is not known where de Gaulle had heard of the Canadian government's intention of carrying out 'the destruction of the radio station'. The next day, in a telegram to the Free French delegation in Washington, he produced another version: 'The Canadian government is apparently planning to obtain, either by persuasion or by force, control of the St Pierre et Miquelon radio station.' By 27 December, de Gaulle had gone one step further: 'We had proof that Canada was preparing to occupy St Pierre et Miquelon.'[44] All this was wildly exaggerated.

wrote, 'their forcible occupation by the Free French was greatly embarrassing to us. . . . It might seriously interfere with our relations with Marshal Pétain's government.'[46] That, at least, was a frank admission. At any rate, Secretary of State Hull expressed his indignation by issuing the following communiqué:

> Our preliminary report shows that the action taken by the so-called* Free French ships at St Pierre et Miquelon was an arbitrary action contrary to the agreement of all parties concerned, and certainly without the prior knowledge or consent in any sense of the United States. This government has inquired of the Canadian government as to the steps that government is prepared to take to restore the status quo of the island.[47]

The answer to the latter enquiry was not long in coming: Prime Minister Mackenzie King was not prepared to restore Vichy authority in St Pierre, as 'Canadian feeling was relieved and pleased at the de Gaulle accomplishment'.[48] American public opinion was no less pleased with the action – which after all had been taken by an ally of the United States. The American public and press were therefore outraged at Hull's statement about the 'so-called Free French', and in the days that followed, the unfortunate Cordell Hull received huge piles of sarcastic and abusive letters addressed to 'the so-called Secretary of State', 'so-called State Department', etc. . . . This greatly distressed him, and he spent many a sleepless night as a result. Yet Hull persisted in his policy, and pressed Churchill to back him up in forcing de Gaulle to evacuate the island. In his memoirs, he recalled: 'I pointedly accused de Gaulle of being a marplot acting directly contrary to the expressed wishes of Britain, Canada, and the United States, and I asked the Prime Minister to induce him to withdraw his troops from St Pierre et Miquelon islands, with Canadians and Americans assuming supervision over the radio station at St Pierre.'[49]

Churchill was not forthcoming. He replied that 'if he insisted on such a request, his relations with the Free French movement would be impaired'.[50] In fact, the Prime Minister could not bring himself to take the whole affair seriously. 'Mr Hull,' he noted, 'pushed what was little more than a departmental point far beyond its pro- portions.'[51] Besides, President Roosevelt, while giving Hull token support in his anti-Gaullist crusade, remained very much on the

*Author's italics

sidelines. This was also Churchill's impression: 'The President in our daily talks seemed to me to shrug his shoulders over the whole affair. After all, quite a lot of other annoyances were on us or coming upon us.'[52] In case Churchill was still tempted to do anything in the matter, the telegram he received from the Foreign Office on 29 December would have been more than enough to discourage him: it said in substance that de Gaulle refused to recall his men from St Pierre et Miquelon, and that if action were taken to force him out, 'the whole business would kick up an unbelievable row, for which we could give no good public explanation'.[53] This was the first intimation by the Foreign Office that any action taken against de Gaulle would be unacceptable to British public opinion; there were to be many more later on. Finally, de Gaulle himself had sent a private letter to the Prime Minister:

> I have every reason to fear that the present attitude of the State Department at Washington towards, respectively, the Free French and Vichy may be doing a great deal of harm to fighting spirit in France and elsewhere.
>
> I am afraid of the unfortunate impression that will be produced on opinion in the Free French forces and territories, as also in not-yet-liberated France, by the sort of preference publicly accorded by the United States government to those responsible for capitulation and to those guilty of collaboration.
>
> It does not seem to me a good thing that, in war, the prize should be handed to the apostles of dishonour.
>
> I am saying this to you because I know that you feel it and that you are the only man capable of saying it as it should be said.[54]

Churchill was indeed that man; on 30 December at a joint session of the Canadian Parliament in Ottawa, he mentioned the men of Bordeaux and the men of Vichy, who 'lay prostrate at the foot of the conqueror', and he added, 'There is no room now for the dilettante, the weakling, for the shirker or the sluggard.' But then, evoking France and the Free French, the old Francophile became simply lyrical:

> Some Frenchmen there were who would not bow their knees and who under General de Gaulle have continued to fight on the side of the Allies. They have been condemned to death by the men of Vichy, but their names will be held and are being held in increasing respect by nine Frenchmen out of every ten throughout the once happy, smiling land of France. And everywhere in France, occupied and unoccupied, for their

fate is identical, these honest folk, this great people, the French nation, are rising again. Hope is springing again in the hearts of a warrior race ... and everywhere dawn is breaking and light spreading – reddish yet, but clear. We shall never lose confidence that France will play the role of free men again and, by hard paths, will once again attain her place in the great company of freedom-bringing and victorious nations.[55]

De Gaulle himself would have done no better; the General was naturally delighted, and the very next day, he echoed Churchill's words in a broadcast to France: 'We entirely concur,' he said, 'with this statement made yesterday by the great Churchill: "There is no room in this war for the dilettante, the weakling, for the shirker or the sluggard." '[56] That day, he also sent Churchill the following telegram: 'What you said yesterday about France at the Canadian Parliament has touched the whole French nation,' and he added, *'Du fond de son malheur, la vieille France espère d'abord en la vieille Angleterre.'*[57] To this, he received the following answer from the Prime Minister:

I have received your telegram and you may be sure I pleaded your case strongly to our friends in the United States. Your having broken away from agreement about St Pierre and Miquelon raised a storm which might have been serious had I not been on the spot to speak to the President. Undoubtedly, the result of your activities there has been to make things more difficult with the United States and has in fact prevented some favourable development from occurring. I am always doing my best in all our interests.[58]

Of this there was little doubt. On 1 January, Churchill, back in Washington, lunched with the President *en famille*, and J. P. Lash, who was also there, noted the following exchange: Hitler had sounded awfully anxious in his New Year's Day message!' Churchill observed, 'even invoking Almighty God'. 'But we have a pre-emption on the Deity,' he added. Perhaps it was the Prime Minister's reference to the Almighty that turned his thoughts to General de Gaulle: 'You're being nice to Vichy,' he jollied the President, 'we're being nice to de Gaulle.' He suggested that that was a fair division of labour. . . . The matter should be left to Hull and Halifax, the President indicated. 'Hell, Hull and Halifax,' the Prime Minister muttered.[59]

But the irascible Cordell Hull would not leave it at that. The 'mud batteries' had been turned against him by the American press and public, the British Prime Minister had made a speech in Ottawa that ridiculed his efforts to appease Vichy, and the President had given him very little support in the whole affair. The Secretary of State therefore proceeded to draft a face-saving declaration that could be agreed upon by Roosevelt and Churchill. But Churchill refused to sign it, and Roosevelt refused to press him.* Undaunted, Hull came up on 8 January with another draft agreement.

> . . . which would make withdrawal of the Free French forces from the islands agreeable to de Gaulle. This provided that the United States, Britain, and Canada would exercise joint supervision over the islands, which would be neutralized and demilitarized. Canada and the United States would provide personnel to control the wireless station. The Governor would be withdrawn for the duration of the war, to be succeeded by a consultative council. All armed forces would be recalled, and the United States and Canada would provide economic assistance.[60]

The President accepted this solution; so did Vichy. Churchill accepted it on condition that de Gaulle agreed. But by then, Cordell Hull had worked on the President, and even threatened to resign if he were not supported more firmly in the matter. For inner political reasons, Roosevelt could not afford to see his Secretary of State resign, and he therefore began to work on Churchill, going so far as to tell him that 'he might send the battleship *Arkansas* to drive the Free French by force out of the tiny islands, or he might establish a blockade to starve them into submission'.[62] Besides, Hull implied that the British government had secretly supported the Free French operation, thus in effect double-crossing the Americans. All this put Churchill in an embarrassing situation, and he began to press de Gaulle to accept the plan in order to avoid the complications that were beginning to threaten his privileged relationship with the Americans. Once again, Eden served as go-between, with strong prodding from the Prime Minister, who wrote to him on 13 January:

> You should tell de Gaulle that this is our settled policy and that he must bow to it. He has put himself entirely in the wrong by his breach of faith. If he is to retain any measure of our recognition he must send orders to Muselier which latter will obey. . . . However you dish it up he has got to

*In a memorandum written on 1 January, Roosevelt noted: 'I told the Secretary of State I thought it inadvisable to resuscitate this question. That the French admiral had already declined to leave St Pierre. That we cannot afford to send an expedition to bomb him out.[61]

take it. . . . They are in a mood to use force. . . . It is intolerable that the great movement of events should be obstructed, and I shall certainly not intervene to save de Gaulle or other Free French from the consequences.[63]

De Gaulle, however, was unmoved by arguments of this kind, and he made it plain when the scheme was presented to him:

Mr Eden saw me twice on 14 January, and put up a show of insisting that we should agree to the islands being neutralized, to the administration being independent of the National Committee and to a control by Allied officials established on the spot. As I refused such a solution, Mr Eden announced to me that the United States was thinking of sending a cruiser and two destroyers to St Pierre. 'What will you do then?' he asked me. 'The Allied ships,' I answered, 'will stop at the limit of territorial waters, and the American admiral will come to lunch with Muselier, who will be delighted.' 'But if the cruiser crosses the limit?' 'Our people will summon her to stop in the usual way.' 'If she holds her course?' 'That would be most unfortunate, for then our people would have to open fire.' Mr Eden threw up his arms. 'I can understand your alarm,' I concluded with a smile, 'but I have confidence in the democracies.'[64]

In fact, de Gaulle made a counter-proposal: Admiral Muselier would be recalled, and the fleet withdrawn; but to these official clauses would be appended three secret ones: the admiral would in fact remain, but would be 'merged' in the consultative council; the consultative council itself would be under the authority of the French National Committee; and the Free French Marines would remain in the islands.[65]

Later in the day, Eden noted Churchill's reaction to de Gaulle's counter-proposal:

The PM was very angry. He thought his original proposal eminently fair and reasonable. . . . He did not think the USA would accept the new draft. He could take no responsibility for it himself, but he would put it to the President if I so advised. . . . He feared that there would be an explosion. The secret clauses took away what was in the draft for publication. He thought that I had failed lamentably with General de Gaulle.

But the next day: 'Spoke to PM again at 1 a.m. . . . he had not yet seen the President, but was just going to see him. On reflection he seemed to think that the new proposals were not too bad. Hopkins considered them ludicrous.'[66] By the time he had seen the President, Churchill had changed his mind once again: the counter proposals were wholly unacceptable. It was agreed that on his return to

England, Churchill would try to get the General to drop his reservations. There was no doubt that Roosevelt could exert considerable influence upon Churchill whenever he chose.* In the meantime, however, the British Prime Minister had been repeatedly advised by his Cabinet that public opinion at home was delighted at the overthrow of Vichy rule in St Pierre, and that coercion of de Gaulle would be extremely unpopular. The whole matter therefore called for the greatest diplomacy.

Upon returning to London, Churchill sent for the General, who later described the interview in a letter to Admiral Muselier:**

Churchill was very tense, evidently weighed down by many pre-occupations. He insisted, with the greatest force, that we should accept, as far as we are concerned, the publication at Washington, in the name of the American, English and Canadian governments, of a communiqué whose text is as follows:

1. The islands are French and will remain French.
2. The Vichy administrator will be withdrawn. The administration will be carried out by the consultative council.
3. The consultative council will accept the appointment of Canadian and American officials to assist it in the exploitation of the wireless station in the common interest of the Allies.
4. The French National Committee has informed His Majesty's government in the United Kingdom that it has no intention of keeping its ships at St Pierre et Miquelon and that these ships would shortly resume their normal function, which is to attack the enemy wherever he is to be found.
5. The Canadian and American governments have agreed to undertake to continue giving economic assistance to the islands.

In the course of the discussion, Churchill, who was assisted by Eden,

*Except on a few questions which Churchill considered vital: the integrity of the British Empire was one of them.

**De Gaulle's description of the interview is far from exhaustive; there were several stormy passages, with Churchill pointing out that 'General de Gaulle had no right to take action in these unimportant territories without consideration for the Great Alliance without which France could not be restored,' and in fact accusing de Gaulle of a breach of faith in the matter. The following exchange is also of interest: 'De Gaulle asked the Prime Minister whether the proposed status meant that the islands would still belong to France. The Prime Minister said he did not know what de Gaulle meant by "France". There was the France represented by de Gaulle's comparatively small movement, there was Vichy France, and the France of the unfortunate inhabitants of the occupied territory. De Gaulle then said that the proposed arrangement was contrary to the agreement of 7 August 1940. The Prime Minister replied that the agreement had been based on a hope, which had since proved false, that de Gaulle would be able to rally an impressive number of Frenchmen. As the agreement stood, it was entirely in de Gaulle's favour without corresponding benefit to His Majesty's government.'[68]

made the point that, once the communiqué was published, nobody would bother any more about what was happening in the islands, that in consequence Savary would be able to keep the effective direction and that the local Marines would be maintained for the defence. The men who have enlisted will naturally be authorized to join the Free French forces. In a word – it is the expression used by Eden – our concessions would be concerned with appearances, but the realities would remain to us. . . .

It is a question, in short, of saving the face of Cordell Hull and the State Department.[67]

Churchill's and Eden's diplomacy finally paid off: de Gaulle agreed to stoop and conquer. In the meantime, the emotion having died down in the United States, the communiqué was not even published. St Pierre et Miquelon remained under Free French authority, and no one bothered about it any more.

During the next few weeks, relations between the Free French and the Americans slowly returned to normal – with no love lost on either side; but there was no improvement at all in Franco-British relations, and the man principally responsible for that was none other than the fearless head of the Free French navy, the impetuous champion of democratic Gaullism and the hero of St Pierre et Miquelon: Admiral Muselier *en personne*.

The admiral had returned to England on 28 February; the Free French and their leader gave him a hero's welcome, and de Gaulle immediately asked him to lead a new operation, this time for the rallying of Madagascar. But Admiral Muselier had other plans: he was dissatisfied with the way things had been managed during his absence, he blamed de Gaulle for having compromised his relations with the Americans during the St Pierre et Miquelon affair, he raved and ranted at the General's 'dictatorial tendencies'; in short, he was seized once again with the familiar demon of intrigue. On 3 March, to the amazement of all his colleagues, Admiral Muselier announced that he was resigning from the committee. De Gaulle accepted his resignation and proceeded to find him a successor, but the admiral announced that, having resigned from the committee, he intended to carry on as Commander-in-Chief of the Free French naval forces; in other words, the admiral intended to secede and take *his* fleet with him. At this juncture, the reader may well wonder whether he has not read all this before; actually, we are now in the midst of the third and last *Affaire Muselier*.

Once again, Admiral Muselier had the support of many anti-

Gaullist Frenchmen: Moret, Labarthe, Comert, etc. . . , but more important still, he had the full backing of the First Lord of the Admiralty, A. V. Alexander, who professed himself dissatisfied with 'de Gaulle's arbitrary methods and in particular with the dictatorial manner in which he treats the Free French naval staff'.[69] This time, the whole War Cabinet followed suit, and just three days after Muselier's resignation, they all agreed on the following resolution: 'We must insist upon Admiral Muselier retaining his post as Commander-in-Chief of the Free French navy. If General de Gaulle would not agree to this course himself, we should have to take the necessary action ourselves to make it effective.'[70] Once again, the matter was escalating from a purely internal strife to a Franco-British dispute. Anthony Eden, already a veteran of the first and second *Affaires Muselier*, was asked to convey the position of the War Cabinet to de Gaulle.

It was an unpleasant task, and an unsuccessful one. De Gaulle answered that 'he wondered whether the Secretary of State realized the gravity of the position' adding that 'as head of the Free French movement he could not allow his position to be shaken by Muselier's intrigues'. What followed was recorded in the following terms:

> The Secretary of State asked what the General intended to do with him (Muselier).
> General de Gaulle said that the admiral was no longer young, and was a tired man who indulged in drugs. He was morally unbalanced. He proposed, therefore, in the first place, to give him a rest, and Admiral Auboyneau would take over the national commissionership. Later on the admiral might be given command of certain operations or sent on a tour of inspection. He begged the Secretary of State not to press him to do something which it was impossible for him to do.
> The Secretary of State said that the fact that the War Cabinet, in the middle of the war, had spent three-quarters of an hour discussing the question showed that they regarded it as serious.
> General de Gaulle doubted whether the Admiralty looked at the position broadly enough. They liked the admiral because they were accustomed to dealing with him.
> The Secretary of State said that, as he had already repeatedly said, there was a good deal more in the question than that. He proposed not to accept the General's reply at once. His colleagues had it in their minds that, if the General refused, the Secretary of State should inform him that the consequences would be serious and that His Majesty's government might have to take certain measures. He would take the

responsibility of delaying such further communication to the General for 48 hours in order to give him time for reflection.

General de Gaulle replied that he had already reflected and that he doubted whether it would be necessary for him to see the Secretary of State again. The matter had, so far as he was concerned, been settled.[71]

According to Pleven, the General returned from this interview 'in a very excited state', and called an immediate meeting of the National Committee.[72] The British intervention had certainly added fuel to the flames and strengthened de Gaulle's resolve; Muselier's behaviour did the rest: having been ordered to take a thirty days' rest and not to reappear at navy headquarters in the interval, the admiral refused to comply . . . and was given thirty days' house arrest instead. In conformity with the jurisdiction agreement signed with the British in January 1941, de Gaulle then asked His Majesty's government on 11 March to ensure that the sentence was executed. As there was at first no response on the British side, de Gaulle suspended all dealings with them and retired to the country on 18 March. Fearing that the War Cabinet might carry out its threat and take action against him, the General left behind a secret testament; it was to be broadcast to the French people in case he 'was compelled to give up his undertaking and prevented from explaining the motives'.*[73]

This proved unnecessary. At the War Cabinet on 16 March, although the First Lord of the Admiralty continued to insist that 'the matter should be firmly handled', the Foreign Secretary flatly disagreed: 'The admiral had put himself in the wrong, and we were unlikely to secure this (the retention of his position) except at the cost of General de Gaulle throwing in his hand.'[74]

*This was the text of the secret testament:

If I am led to give up the work I have undertaken, the French nation will have to know why. My wish has been to keep France in the war against the invader. That is only possible at present side by side with, and with the support of, the British. But that is only conceivable in independence and dignity. Now, the intervention of the British government in the miserable crisis provoked by Muselier is as intolerable as it is absurd. It is also a flagrant violation of the undertakings made to me by the British government. To yield would be to destroy by my own act what sovereignty and honour is left to France. I will not do that.

The English intervention in the Muselier affair follows, moreover, a series of other pressures and abuses of the same sort – (example: what has happened in Syria) – which I have been able to repel only with great difficulty and which harass my confidence in the genuineness of the British as allies. France has already understood along what path and in what way I have done everything I could to serve her. She will understand that, if I stop, it is because my duty towards her forbids me to go farther. She will choose her road accordingly.

Men pass. France continues.

This was clearly undesirable for political reasons, and wiser counsel prevailed; the First Lord of the Admiralty was compelled to climb down, a compromise solution was worked out, and on 23 March, de Gaulle was informed that the British government no longer insisted that Muselier should remain Commander-in-Chief of the navy, and would ensure that the admiral was prevented from having any contact with elements of the French naval forces during a period of thirty days. The British government nevertheless expressed the hope that Admiral Muselier might thereafter be given 'suitable employment' . . . and the matter was dropped. De Gaulle had won; the British Admiralty had lost; the Foreign Secretary had once again averted a disaster; Muselier disappeared from the stage*; and Churchill, surveying the scene from the sidelines, was left to wonder how the intractable General could ever be 'put in commission'.

---

*A month later, de Gaulle asked Muselier to carry out a mission of inspection in Africa and the Levant. The admiral declined, and announced shortly afterwards that he was ceasing all collaboration with Free France.

CHAPTER 8

Perfidious Albion

It was the third spring of the war, and the Axis was still on the offensive; in Libya and in Russia, powerful German forces were preparing for yet another onslaught, while in the East, the victorious Japanese armies had submerged South-East Asia and were now threatening India and Australia. The mighty American war machine had not yet gathered momentum, the Soviet armies were still on the defensive, and Britain was suffering some cruel setbacks, of which the fall of Singapore was perhaps the most humiliating. Meanwhile, the darkness of tyranny still engulfed all German-occupied Europe, briefly dispelled at intervals by the fragile but sturdy flame of patriotic resistance. In France, this resistance had a symbol, the Cross of Lorraine, and an expression, the slow, dispassionate and resolute voice of Charles de Gaulle.

The solitary leader of Free France was as determined as ever to fuel the flames of French resistance. At the beginning of the year, a secret emissary, Jean Moulin, had been parachuted into France; his mission was to unify the various resistance movements under a single authority: that of General de Gaulle. But outside France, de Gaulle was obstinately pursuing an even more difficult and thankless task: to bring every single French colony and possession back into the struggle, while disproving Vichy accusations that he was merely a mercenary of the British; to send Free French troops to every theatre of war, and thus compel the Allies to recognize Fighting France as a partner and co-belligerent. He failed at Dakar and Djibuti, but succeeded in rallying Equatorial Africa, Syria and St Pierre. Each time, however, he met with the reluctance, the incomprehension, the passive and active opposition of his Anglo-Saxon allies, who had once and for all written off France as a factor to be reckoned with in this war; indeed, they insisted in treating the Free French movement as a subordinate body and an anonymous pawn on the vast chessboard of the world conflict.

As a result of all this, de Gaulle seemed to be perpetually waging a public war against Vichy and the Germans, and a private war against the British Admiralty, the Air Ministry, the War Office, the Intelligence Service, the Foreign Office, the Prime Minister, the State Department and the President of the United States. These periodical clashes with almost every echelon of the Allied hierarchy gave some rude jolts to the Franco-British alliance in the field,* and made de Gaulle an increasingly difficult man to deal with. In such cases, he could be less than generous in appreciating the Allied war effort, unreasonably suspicious in judging British motivations, and at times needlessly intransigent in defending the honour and dignity of France. As Pierre Brossolette said to Edmond Michelet at the time: 'The General must be constantly reminded that our enemy number one is Germany. For if he followed his natural inclination it would rather be Britain.'[2] Indeed, the General frequently accused Churchill of blindly following President Roosevelt's lead, of betraying the Free French movement[3], and of trying to make use of it for his own ends. Yet in between these fits of temper, de Gaulle continued to express the greatest respect and admiration for the British Prime Minister.

The respect and admiration were fully reciprocated, and so were the grievances – legitimate or not. During the spring of 1942, Churchill was still blaming de Gaulle for his 'breach of faith' in the St Pierre et Miquelon affair, for his 'autocratic methods' in ruling the Free French movement, for seeking to further his own interests at the expense of the general war effort,** for endangering the all-

*Colonel Passy later described the repercussions of the frequent clashes between de Gaulle and Churchill on his intelligence service: 'Each time, the (British) technical services went on strike, the planes broke down, the ships were docked for repair . . . and for weeks, we could determine with unerring accuracy the exact state of political relations between the French National Committee and His Majesty's government. . . . In the end, however, we always succeeded in drawing, the minimum necessary to keep the organization working at half-speed.'[1]

**The American Chargé d'Affaires Freeman Matthews reported on 9 April 1942 to the State Department:

Churchill . . . talked to me at some length . . . of his friends Reynaud and Mandel . . . and with much bitterness of Marshal Pétain. I found him likewise quite disappointed in General de Gaulle and almost equally bitter about him. He too used the phrase . . . that de Gaulle considers himself 'a modern Joan of Arc' but he feels that his name 'has become the symbol for resistance in France.' . . . He agreed that the emphasis should be on the military aspects of the 'dissident movement' rather than the political, but added that de Gaulle himself was the real problem.[4]

important relationship between Britain and the United States, and of course for his Anglophobic speeches and utterances – the Anglophile ones he conveniently chose to forget. All this explains why the Prime Minister maintained his order that de Gaulle should not be allowed to leave Britain. However, it does not entirely explain why the Free French were completely excluded from the Madagascar operation that started on 5 May 1942.

Free France was condemned to expand or die; for strategic and psychological reasons, it was highly desirable to rally the French colony of Madagascar to the Cross of Lorraine, and in the latter half of December 1941, General de Gaulle had raised this question with the Prime Minister and the Chief of the Imperial General Staff. In February and April 1942, he had repeatedly submitted plans for operations against the island, to be carried out by Free French troops with British air and naval support. But the General had only received polite acknowledgements from Downing Street and the War Office. In fact, both the Prime Minister and the Chiefs-of-Staff were well aware of the strategic importance of Madagascar, especially after the fall of Singapore. But previous experience in Dakar and Syria had shown that mixed Franco-British expeditions were less than successful. According to the British military chiefs, they had also shown that Free French participation was more likely to provoke a stubborn Vichy resistance – and Churchill had accepted this view. 'With memories of Dakar in our mind,' he wrote, 'we could not complicate the operation by admitting the Free French.'[5] The operation was therefore planned along purely British lines, and Churchill expected little or no resistance from the Vichy Governor-General of Madagascar, Annet, possibly because Mrs Churchill had once met him in a train and found him 'a charming man'.

In the event, 'Operation Ironclad', which was set in motion at dawn on 5 May, ran into heavy resistance. The immediate objective, Diego Suarez, was in British hands by the morning of the 7th, but no attempt was made to occupy the rest of the island, particularly Majunga and Tamatave, and the commander of the expedition, Admiral Syfret, was eventually instructed to seek a *modus vivendi* with the Vichy French authorities in Tananarive.*

*Admiral Syfret had originally been instructed to seek a *casus belli* with the local French authorities. A repeat of the telegram was prudently requested, and the new version called for a *modus vivendi* instead. When the staff officer in London responsible for the initial version was asked for an explanation, he exclaimed: 'Why the hell should I be expected to know French?'[6]

At three in the morning on 5 May, General de Gaulle was informed of the British landing by a phone call from a press agency. His immediate reaction was extremely violent; Churchill was gratified *in absentia* with all the accusations described above, and a few others as well. A more formal protest was sent to the Foreign Office the next day, and for several days after that, de Gaulle declined to see the Foreign Secretary. When he finally did see him on 11 May, the interview was an extremely frosty one:

> *Mr Eden:* 'Well then?'
> *De Gaulle:* 'But I have nothing to tell you!'
> *Mr Eden:* 'In that case, I will begin; we must deal with the question of Madagascar; you are dissatisfied? I must admit that I ought to have informed you, but we were afraid that you would insist in joining the operation, and we did not want to take responsibility for sending Frenchmen to fight against Frenchmen.'
> *De Gaulle:* 'I take those reasons for what they are worth. . . . Do you know what you are now going to do in Madagascar? Do you intend to take the whole island?'
>
> Mr Eden replied that no decision had yet been taken on this point, and regretted that the committee had not seen fit to express their agreement with the operation undertaken by the British.
>
> *De Gaulle:* 'How could we express our agreement when we do not know your intentions, and you don't know yourself what you are going to do? . . . Could we really be expected to approve a procedure by which Allied forces disposed of French territory without reference to us?'[7]

Above all, de Gaulle strenuously objected to the terms offered to Governor Annet: if he collaborated with the British, he would be left in office and the island would not be required to take part in the war. This was very similar to American dealings with Admiral Robert in Martinique – and de Gaulle did not hide that he considered it as a betrayal of his movement. For the next few weeks, the General, seething with rage, contemplated innumerable counter-measures: withdrawing to Equatorial Africa, publicly denouncing the British and the Americans in a vengeful broadcast, suspending all co-operation with the British government, etc. . . . His collaborators succeeded with great pains in dissuading him from taking such extreme measures.[8]*

*A British communiqué of 13 May had announced that the French National Committee would 'play its proper role' in the administration of the island. It was clear, however, that de Gaulle did not have much faith in such promises.

Churchill was by then seriously preoccupied with the evolution of the situation in Madagascar, where negotiations with the local Vichy authorities were proving entirely fruitless. He was even more preoccupied with the Japanese threat to India and the impending German offensive in Libya. Yet in the middle of all that, he found time to pursue a personal vendetta against General de Gaulle, and resisted all pleas by Eden and Charles Peake to allow the General to visit Africa. Eden had written on 27 May to the Prime Minister: 'I induced him (de Gaulle) to postpone his proposed trip to Africa. I fear, however, that a further attempt on my part would merely increase his suspicions of us which are seldom far below the surface. . . . I hope you will agree that for the sake of our future relations with him it would be best to let him go. He has been rather better lately.'[9] But Churchill replied three days later: 'I cannot agree. There is nothing hostile to England this man may not do once he got off the chain.'[10]

Eden translated this rude negative into a diplomatic hint to de Gaulle that His Majesty's government might want to consult him 'in this critical phase of the war', and that his absence from London would therefore be inadvisable. The General appeared to be flattered, and agreed to postpone his departure for six weeks. After which Eden set to work on Churchill, and finally persuaded him to receive General de Gaulle – no mean feat in itself. The interview was to take place five days later. It promised to be a stormy one, especially as de Gaulle had learned in the meantime that Britain and the United States were secretly planning an operation against Dakar and Niger, from which the Free French would be excluded once again. For good measure, he also suspected that the British were planning to return Madagascar to Vichy.[11] In retaliation, he was now contemplating a withdrawal to the Soviet Union with all of his forces.*

· The interview took place at Downing Street at 5.30 p.m. on 10 June, and as usual, nothing went as expected:

The Prime Minister congratulated General de Gaulle for the magnificent conduct of the French troops at Bir Hakeim.** 'It is,' he said, 'one of the finest feats of arms in this war.' Speaking of the battle, Mr Churchill

*Ambassador Bogomolov was indeed asked on 6 June to ascertain whether his government would agree to receive de Gaulle and his movement in the Soviet Union.
**At Bir Hakeim, in Eastern Libya, a Free French light division commanded by General Koenig repulsed all attacks by German and Italian troops from 27 May to 11 June, thereby delaying Rommel's offensive against the retreating British formations.

indicated that it would no doubt last for a long time. 'That is a very good thing,' he said, 'particularly for the Russians who are getting that much more relief' . . . Mr Churchill then broached the question of Madagascar. 'I know,' he said, 'that you have been offended because we undertook the expedition without you. We thought, rightly or wrongly, that we would meet with less resistance if we appeared there alone. We had also to take account of America's views. We were anxious to avoid complications as far as possible. What we wanted first and foremost was to get hold of Diego Suarez, to prevent the Japanese from getting a foothold there. But we have absolutely no ulterior motive and no political design on Madagascar. I don't want Madagascar! Indeed, we don't know exactly what we shall do there. It is a "very large" island; we should be glad not to be obliged to go too far.'

General de Gaulle pointed out that it would be dangerous not to assume control of the whole island. He renewed his proposal to use Free French troops there. He added: 'The method pursued by the British in this affair places the National Committee in an unacceptable situation vis-à-vis France and the French Empire. What we want is that Madagascar should rally to Free France and come back into the war.'

'I understand that,' said Mr Churchill, 'but in that case a fresh operation would perhaps be necessary. We have not yet come to any decision on the subject. Our present policy seems to cause you some anxiety, nonetheless we have no bad intention.'

'You must admit,' replied the General, 'that appearances are not always clear. You are keeping us outside the business and, at the same time, you are making arrangements on the spot with the Vichy people. Perhaps you have plans of the same kind – you, or the Americans, or the two together – as regards Dakar or the bend of the Niger. It would be dangerous to use or abuse the French people in this way. At present, it is true, the French people have other worries; Madagascar perhaps does not interest them very much. But later on all this will come up to the surface again. If we want to maintain Franco-British friendship for the future, we must, as from now, take care to avoid what might trouble it in a lasting way. The present war is not a colonial war, it is a moral war and a world war that we are waging together. For Britain, no colony, however fine, is worth the friendship of France.'

'We have no design on the French Empire,' repeated Mr Churchill. . . . 'He protested his good intentions,' de Gaulle noted, 'then suddenly, with a start: "I am the friend of France!" he cried. "I have always wanted, and I want, a great France with a great army. It is necessary for the peace, order and security of Europe. I have never had any other policy!" 'That's true,' I replied. 'You even had the merit, after Vichy's armistice, of continuing to play the card of France. That card is called de Gaulle: don't lose it now! It would be all the more absurd since you have reached the moment when your policy is succeeding and when Free France has become the soul and frame of French resistance. On these bases I too am faithful to you. But I have very few resources with which to bear the responsibility for the interests of France. This involves great difficulties for me. I ask you to help me to overcome them. I agree that, on the whole, you are not ill-disposed towards us. But there are grave exceptions. Also American policy towards us is atrocious; it aims at our destruction. Do you know that, for Memorial Day, the American government invited the Vichy military attachés and did not invite our officers? For the Americans, the Frenchmen of Bir Hakeim are not belligerents.'

"Yes," said Mr Churchill, "the Americans do not wish to give up their policy with Vichy. They imagine that Vichy will one day be so tormented by the Germans that it will resume the war at the side of the Allies. They think it is they who have prevented Laval and Darlan from giving the fleet to the Germans. After all, this policy is perhaps useful. For example, in the case of Madagascar, the American government had Laval told by Mr Tuck that, if France made war on Great Britain, she would be obliged to make it on America at the same time."[12]

> The General said that, whatever happened, Vichy would not give up the fleet and would not make war on behalf of Germany. The reason was simple and the Americans had nothing to do with it: it was that the French people were opposed to it. . . . The whole problem was to keep up the French people's will to resist, and to revive their will to fight. It was not by flouting the French who are fighting that this aim would be attained. From this point of view the Weygand episode was particularly significant. The whole policy carried on by America and Weygand had had the result, not of bringing back Weygand and North Africa into the war, but, on the contrary, of lulling to sleep the fighting spirit of the French in those territories.
>
> Mr Churchill did not dispute this.
>
> The British Prime Minister realized, indeed, with pleasure that France was recovering and was regrouping around General de Gaulle.
>
> The General pointed out that the organization of resistance in the interior would make better progress if the British services gave us better

help. 'I thought,' said Mr Churchill, 'that they were collaborating with you in a satisfactory way.'

'Yes, and no,' answered the General. 'They could act more quickly and more frankly than they are doing and place more resources at our disposal.'

The Muselier affair was then mentioned.

'You too,' declared the General, 'sometimes have to replace one admiral by another, and give him another command. . . .'

Mr Churchill smiled and did not insist.*

'All these affairs,' he said, 'are not very important. What is big and important is the war. We shall be in France perhaps next year. In any case, we shall be there together. We still have great obstacles to over-come, but I am sure that we will win. We are getting stronger. In 1943 and 1944 we will be stronger still. We will build so many aircraft, ships and tanks that we will gain the upper hand. If you have difficulties, remember that I too have them. For example, I recently had difficulties with the Australians. They were afraid of being invaded. They got excessively alarmed. They wanted me to send them ships. I hadn't got any. . . .'

Towards the end of the interview, Mr Churchill said that he had intentionally spoken in the Commons of the 'Fighting French'. 'Fighting France,' he added, 'sounds much better than Free France. The question ought to be studied with the Foreign Office.'

As he saw the General out, Mr Churchill said: 'We must see each other again.' He advised the General to broaden the basis of his committee – 'I shall not desert you,' he said in conclusion, 'you can rely on me.'

Mr Churchill saw the General out as far as the Downing Street door and signified that he would publish a communiqué on their conversation.'[13]

The interview with Churchill had an anaesthetic effect on the indomitable Free French leader. During the weeks that followed, he sent reassuring telegrams to General Catroux and seemed satisfied that the British had no designs on the bend of the Niger after all, that the Americans were not preparing to pounce on Dakar, that a Free French representative was not really being prevented from reaching Madagascar, that the British officers on the island were not blindly hostile to his movement and in sympathy with the local Vichy authorities, and that General Spears, now His Majesty's Minister in the Levant, was not working against Free French interests there – at

*At one point in the conversation, Churchill had told de Gaulle: 'I know that you embody the hopes and aspirations of a large number of Frenchmen. But do you think you can say that you are France?' To which the General answered: 'In present circumstances, no person or organization can really claim to represent the whole of France.'

least de Gaulle went so far as to give the impression that he no longer believed all this, which was slightly different. But Eden was quite content with that, and in fact he reinforced the treatment himself by receiving the General on several occasions, making several concessions, and requesting the Chiefs-of-Staff to show de Gaulle more of the British war effort while seeking his advice on military matters.* All this was applied with excellent effect, and both British and Frenchmen were amazed with the results: the Anglophobic talk ceased abruptly, de Gaulle went out of his way to praise the British and their Prime Minister in his public speeches, and he was even heard to express sympathy and understanding for British difficulties in Libya.[14]

All this was used by Anthony Eden to convince Churchill that a new attitude ought to be adopted towards General de Gaulle. It was by no means easy, and in fact took the better part of two months; in the end, however, Churchill gave in and lifted his ban on travel abroad by the General. On 28 July, de Gaulle was informed that there was no longer any objection to his proposed visit to Africa, and before leaving, he had a last interview with the Prime Minister:

'Well,' said Mr Churchill, 'you're off to Africa and the Levant.'

'I am pleased to be going to the Levant,' replied the General. 'Spears is active there. He is causing us trouble.'

'Spears,' continued Mr Churchill, 'has a lot of enemies. But he has one friend – the Prime Minister. When you get there, go and see him. I will cable him and tell him to listen to what you say.

'They say,' added Mr Churchill, 'that the independence of the Levant States is not a reality, and that the people are dissatisfied.'

'They are,' retorted the General, 'at least as satisfied in Syria and the Lebanon as in Iraq, Palestine or Egypt.'

The conversation then turned to Madagascar.

'If we did not undertake the operation with you,' said Mr Churchill, 'it

---

*On 24 June, the Minister of State in Cairo had reported that General Catroux had told him the following:

He was convinced that General de Gaulle would be far more reasonable and easy to handle if he could be seen by Cabinet ministers in London at frequent intervals and given as much information as possible. He also suggested that whenever it could be done, his advice should be sought. General de Gaulle's character should always be borne in mind. He was a very vain man and as such could be relied upon to respond to the above treatment.[15]

On 17 June, Charles Peake, the British representative to the French National Committee, had reported very much in the same sense: '(De Gaulle) has often expressed the wish to help and advise in any way possible, and he has sat up, night after night, assembling data and making notes in case his advice should be needed.'[16]

was because we did not wish to mix two things: conciliation and force. This had failed at Dakar.'

'We would have taken Dakar,' the General pointed out, 'if the British had not let Darlan's cruisers through the Straits of Gibraltar.'

Mr Churchill did not deny this.

'As for Madagascar,' the General continued, 'if you had let us land at Majunga while you operated at Diego Suarez, the affair would have been over long ago. We would have marched on Tananarive and everything would have been settled. Instead, you wasted your time negotiating with the representative of Vichy.'

'Yes, he's a bad man, that governor!' said Mr Churchill.

'Are you surprised?' the General retorted. 'When you deal with Vichy, you are dealing with Hitler – and Hitler is a bad man.'[17]

The conversation then turned to the possibility of a second front, and to the greatly increased armament production both in England and the USA. After which Churchill said:

'Your situation has been a difficult one lately. Our relations have not always been very good. Doubtless, there were wrongs on both sides. In the future, we must work together. Once you have completed your trip, come back quickly. If you meet with any difficulty, please communicate directly with me.'[18]

After a few more digressions on the past, the Prime Minister and the General parted on the best of terms. Shortly thereafter, de Gaulle left for Africa and the Levant. Syria and Lebanon were foremost among his preoccupations: 'Spears is active there, he is causing us trouble,' the French leader had told Churchill. This, however, was a gross oversimplification, for France's problems in the Levant were by no means limited to the deeds and misdeeds of the energetic British major-general who had risen so swiftly to the top of de Gaulle's rather crowded private demonology.

It will be recalled that when the Free French and British troops entered the Levant on 8 June 1941, General Catroux, as Delegate General and Plenipotentiary, had made the following proclamation: 'Syrians and Lebanese! In the name of France . . . and in the name of her chief, General de Gaulle, I come to put an end to the regime of the mandate and to proclaim you free and independent. . . .' But just like General Gouraud twenty years earlier, Catroux was giving the word 'independent' a somewhat restricted sense – as it immediately appeared when he formally declared the independence of Syria on 27 September 1941, and that of Lebanon two months later. On de

Gaulle's instructions, Catroux immediately confirmed that the mandate was not yet abolished: above the local governments, the French Delegate General would continue to rule by decree, the local troops and police would remain under French control, and so would economic affairs, public services and communications. For de Gaulle, effective independence could only come after the war, when the mandate would be formally surrendered to the League of Nations, and then only after both Syria and Lebanon had signed a treaty guaranteeing France's privileged position in the Levant; a position so privileged that it would once again limit the independence of the two states. Regimes pass, France remains. . . .

From the standpoint of international law, General de Gaulle was undoubtedly right: the Free French Committee having no international status, it had no power to negotiate the termination of the mandate; from a French political point of view, he was also right: Vichy would have made the most of de Gaulle's renunciation to France's traditional position in the Levant. However, the local populations in Syria and Lebanon did not appreciate these diplomatic and political niceties: for the last two decades, they had seen successive French governments pursue an intricate policy of divide and rule among the extraordinarily complex mosaic of races and religions* which make up the Levant. By the beginning of 1942, it was evident to all that Free French policy was evolving very much along the same lines, and this was much resented. The heads of government of the two states, Sheik Taj-Ad-Din and M. Naccache, had been appointed by Catroux himself, and the great majority of local politicians were clamouring for a democratically elected government and assembly, something the French Delegate General refused categorically; indeed, given the feelings of the local populations, elections would inevitably bring in a parliament and a government completely opposed to French rule, which would immediately demand the abolition of the mandate, and of course refuse to sign any treaty with the French.

This growing unpopularity of the French in the Levant made matters very difficult indeed: the French often had to rely on dubious

*Among the main races living in the Levant: Arabs, Turks, Greeks, Assyrians, Circassians, Chaldeans, Kurds, Jews, Persians, Armenians and Europeans. As for the religions: Sunnis, Shiites, Druzes, Alaouites, Ismaelis, Maronites, Greek Orthodox, Greek Catholics, Syrian Orthodox, Syrian Catholics, Nestorians, Protestants, Chaldean Catholics, Jews, Armenian Catholics, Armenian Gregorians, Roman Catholics, Russian Orthodox, etc. . . .

local personalities to run local administrations, mainly for want of better ones who would agree to co-operate; there was also an acute shortage of Free French civil servants, so that Vichy personnel was used extensively. This in turn did nothing to reinforce Free France's prestige with the local population. Last but not least, there was of course the British presence in the Levant: a whole army in fact, conspicuous, ubiquitous, cumbersome and highly embarrassing to the French administration. General Catroux and his subordinates accused the British officers of wanting to expel the French from the Levant, and they were not always wrong: for many officers of His Majesty's army, from the second lieutenant to the staff officer, F. F. did not necessarily mean Free French – or Fighting French, for that matter. Some of the unfortunate initiatives of the Syrian campaign were accordingly repeated at times, with predictable results.

The Free French and their leader, however, were less critical of the British soldiers than of the 'pan-Arabs', a very uncomplimentary phrase in Gaullian terminology; it included Sir John Glubb's Arab Legion, the Intelligence Service, the Colonial Office, the War Office, the Palestine High Commissioner, and a motley collection of political officers, special advisers, Iraqi and Egyptian agents, together with other shadowy figures of various descriptions; strange bedfellows they were in some cases, but the French in Damascus, Beirut and London genuinely believed that they were all in league to supplant the French in Syria and Lebanon. This was a hasty conclusion: although none of them had much sympathy for the Free French, and some of them indirectly worked against the interests of the French administration, there was certainly no concerted action to turn the French out of the Levant. This would have been entirely contrary to the policy of His Majesty's government as expressed by the Foreign Office and applied by the British Ambassador in Cairo, the Minister of State, and of course the newly appointed Minister to the Levant, Sir Edward Spears.

By now a familiar figure, the head of the Spears mission had certainly travelled a long way since his initial arrival in the Middle East. Ever since a certain very hot day in July 1941,[19] General Spears had begun to use his vast energy and influence against the very man he had hitherto helped to the best of his ability; by the end of 1941, the French even suspected him of urging the various ministries in London to resist General de Gaulle's demands – and their suspicions were perfectly well-founded.[20] General Spears was also accused of intervening ceaselessly in Syrian, Lebanese and French affairs, of inciting the natives to resist French rule, and of demanding elections and real independence for the Levant.

In calling for elections and effective independence for the Syrians and Lebanese, General Spears was acting well in accordance with Churchill's instructions. Indeed, just as in the summer of 1941, and for the same reasons, Churchill could not accept a pure and simple continuance of the mandate, coupled with a mere semblance of independence for the Levant; Britain had to 'do everything possible to meet Arab aspirations and susceptibilities',[21] as the discontent of the local populations could 'affect the safe conduct of military operations'.[22] Besides, Britain had given her guarantee to the French promise of independence in June 1941, she had recognized the two 'sovereign' states at the beginning of 1942, and her prestige in the Middle East was therefore at stake. As a result, the Minister of State, the British Ambassador in Cairo, General Spears, and the Prime Minister himself all applied considerable pressure on de Gaulle and Catroux to make Syrian and Lebanese independence a reality – by delegating powers to the local governments and of course by holding elections. It goes without saying that this pressure was much resented by the Free French in general, and by one general in particular.

But General Spears was not only instructed to foster the independence of the Levant states; he was also to 'maintain the Free French shop front',[23] and even to 'back the Free French wholeheartedly'. Wholeheartedly or not, this instruction too was carried out to the letter. Hence we find Spears refusing to back a Syrian nationalist and anti-French movement at the beginning of 1942,[24] and even a few months earlier demanding the withdrawal from Syria of three 'would-be Lawrences', Glubb, de Goury, and Buss, on grounds that 'their action serves to incite the natives to play Britain against Free France'.[25] The Free French would probably have rubbed their eyes had they seen telgrams such as these. To them, the name of Spears was the very synonym of anti-French agitation in the Levant.[26]

There was, however, a third aspect to the problem. The Levant states were under over-all British military authority as long as the war lasted; the British therefore considered that they should have a say in all administrative matters connected with security, public order, communications, etc. . . . In addition, they alone had the means to supply the states with food and raw materials. As on the other hand the French administration was rather inefficient and almost entirely devoid of means, though always extremely touchy on questions of sovereignty, most French, British and Franco-British ventures in the Levant usually foundered on endless bickerings, with the British being accused of meddling and plotting, and the French of being incompetent and anti-British. The wheat scheme* and the Haifa-Tripoli railway** were cases in point, and by no means the only ones.

Naturally, the British and Free French were not operating in a void, and relations with the Syrians and Lebanese of various races and religions provided a fertile ground for Franco-British clashes; tribal uprisings in the Hauran or the Euphrates – and there were quite a few – were immediately denounced as the work of British agents; the formation of local auxiliary units under British command was first authorized by General Catroux, but later opposed by General de Gaulle, and finally denounced as a British plot to take over Syria. There were also rumours that the British intended to annex part of southern Lebanon to Palestine, and favoured Arab expansion at the expense of Christian interests – rumours that were welcomed and amplified by the French for local propaganda purposes. The British were also accused by the French of actively supporting nationalist anti-French movements such as the *Bloc National*, while the French were accused by the British of supporting notorious local gangsters on grounds that they were pro-French.*** The French in turn recruited dubious local agents on grounds that they were anti-British, but denounced them as British spies as soon as they became anti-French as well. There were also brutal repressions in outlying villages by the local *Troupes Spéciales* under French command, causing much ill-feeling and new uprisings,

---

*The wheat scheme had been started on British initiative and with British funds, in order to make the Levant self-sufficient in cereal production. The French repeatedly denounced this scheme as a British bid to control the Levant by economic means.
**The Haifa-Tripoli railway had been built by the British, but the French claimed sovereignty over the portion running through the Levant, and often refused to let the British use it – which gave rise to numerous incidents.
***The Mokaddem scandal was a case in point. Mokaddem, a gangster who was accused of several murders, had been caught by the British army in possession of vast quantities of drugs. In fact, he had bribed British soldiers to get the drugs into Egypt. The French insisted on trying him by a French court-martial, then announced that they would release him – possibly because he was pro-French. The British thereupon made it known that they would rearrest him, and endless bitter palavers ensued.

which were again attributed to English agitation. On the other hand, the French were exasperated by the overwhelming display of British military power in the Levant, and the assertiveness of political officers attached to the Spears mission. They therefore sought to thwart them at every turn, and invariably denounced them as agents of the Intelligence Service; in addition, Vichy elements were often kept in the administration on grounds that they were anti-British, but many of them were anti-Free French as well. The British in turn made long lists of these individuals* and demanded their exclusion, but as this was done with a minimum of tact, it was not at all well received by the Free French, who considered it as yet another infringement of French sovereignty. In addition, individual members of the local governments, being often bypassed or superseded by the French Delegate General, took their complaints to the British, who, whether they responded sympathetically or remained non-committal, were immediately accused of plotting against the French. On the other hand, the British Minister's attitude towards the pro-French Lebanese President Alfred Naccache was usually less than deferential, and this naturally enraged the pro-French minority in Lebanon, to say nothing of the Free French authorities. Countless other minor matters, ranging from the destruction of the hashish crop to the victimization of pro-Free French Jesuits by pro-Vichy Jesuits, were as many occasions for Franco-British confrontations.[28]

None of this would have gone very far if the French Delegate General and the British Minister in the Levant had maintained satisfactory relations. This, however, was far from being the case; behind a thin veil of courtesy, Spears and Catroux were on very bad terms, the former having nothing of a diplomat except the name, and the latter, in spite of his title of Governor-General, being more of a diplomat than an administrator. Spears accordingly accused Catroux of incompetence and deviousness, while Catroux accused Spears of aggressively interfering with French administration. The situation was further complicated by the fact that Mrs Spears and Madame Catroux were at daggers drawn,[29] and that Madame Catroux was fairly hostile to General de Gaulle, probably because

*A typical list, set up by the Spears mission in January 1942, gave the name of fifty of these people, their posts in French administration, and an individual grading that ranged from 'anti-British' to 'pro-Vichy', 'doubtful', 'highly unsatisfactory', 'unreliable', 'most unreliable or even worse', 'anti-Free French', 'inefficient', and 'neurotic'. The French delegate to the Lebanese government, David, was described as 'avowedly pro-Vichy'.[27]

General de Gaulle was not above bullying her husband for being too weak in dealing with the British. As a result of all this, the most trivial incident in Franco-British relations was seized upon with alacrity by one side or the other, and was allowed to escalate until it reached a dimension completely out of proportion to its original importance – after which it landed on de Gaulle's or Churchill's desk, and became either 'a flagrant violation of French sovereignty, an insult to France and a new Fashoda', or 'yet another detestable instance of Anglophobia by this most hostile man'.

It may appear quite irrelevant. It is not; for the intricate combinations and repercussions of developments in the Levant were for evermerging in a sort of hideous witches' brew that simmered constantly and occasionally bubbled over. From this infernal cauldron sprang forth 90 per cent of the quarrels between de Gaulle and Churchill until the end of the war.

This lengthy digression has also given General de Gaulle ample time to reach Cairo, where his plane landed on 7 August. On arrival, he found that Churchill was also there, and they lunched together the same day. De Gaulle later recalled the gist of the conversation:

'I am here,' Churchill told me, 'to reorganize the command. At the same time, I shall look into our quarrels over Syria. Then I shall go to Moscow. All of which means that my trip is of very great importance and causes me some concern.'

'It is a fact,' I replied, 'that these are three serious questions. The first is entirely your affair. As for the second, which concerns me, and the third, which mostly concerns Stalin – whom you will doubtless inform that the second front will not be opened this year – I can understand your apprehensions. But you will easily overcome them if your conscience is clear.'

'My conscience,' Mr Churchill growled, 'is a good girl. I can always come to terms with her.'[30]

The next day, de Gaulle went to see the Minister of State, who was now Mr Casey, and discussions began in earnest. Casey not unexpectedly began by saying that there ought to be elections in the Levant. De Gaulle, 'uncompromising and intransigent',[31] answered that this was out of the question for the time being, and added:

It is true that you are much stronger than us in this part of the world. Because of our weakness and because of the successive crises in Madagascar, in North Africa, and ultimately in metropolitan France that will be added to those we are now grappling with, you are in a position to force us to leave the Levant. But you will achieve this goal only by arousing the xenophobia of the Arabs and by abusing your power in relation to your allies. As a result, your position in the Middle East will grow more unstable every day, and the French people will have an ineffaceable grievance against you.[32]

Casey recalled that 'the General . . . accused us of trying to oust the French from their position in Syria and Lebanon and a lot more. The discussion degenerated into a shouting match, he in French and I in English.'[33]

In other words, it all ended in a frightful row. This was most unfortunate, as Casey, in an effort to bring about a relaxation of the tension in Syria and Lebanon, had persuaded Churchill shortly before that General Spears ought to be recalled from the Levant. When Churchill was informed of the stormy interview between de Gaulle and Casey, he immediately changed his mind about the recall of Spears, as Catroux found out that same evening when dining with Churchill at the British Embassy. The Prime Minister growled:

De Gaulle is insufferable. He has treated the Minister of State very badly.
Catroux: 'You have complaints against de Gaulle. We have complaints against Spears. I know that what I'm going to tell you will be painful because Spears is your friend. . . .'
Churchill: 'Yes, he's my friend' (grumble).
Catroux: '. . . He's your friend, well then! Promote him, send him elsewhere, put him in the House of Lords, this will improve our relations. You know that I am a loyal ally and that I am naturally inclined towards conciliation. . . .'
Churchill: 'He's my friend.'[34]

That was that. Spears remained in the Levant, de Gaulle continued to browbeat and bully lesser British officials in an effort to uphold France's sovereign rights in the Levant, and Churchill received alarming reports on de Gaulle's threats and utterances. He even received a telegram from the General on 14 August, and it was devoid of amenity: 'It seems to me that the constant interventions of British representatives in the international and administrative policy of the Levant states and even in the relations between the local governments and the representatives of the French mandatory power are incompatible with British disinterestedness in Syria and Lebanon, with the respect of French policy and with the regime of the mandate.'[35]

On 23 August, having stopped in Cairo on his return trip from the Soviet Union, the Prime Minister had lunch with Alanbrooke, Cadogan and Spears. The latter noted that Churchill was 'in bubbling good humour', and evidently reluctant to have a showdown with de Gaulle on the matter of elections in the Levant. After all, Churchill said, the Levant was but 'a tiny part in the great story of the war' and he accordingly reminded Spears of Talleyrand's words: '*Pas trop de zèle.*'[36] But apart from a few recurrent bouts of sentimentalism when he evoked the unbending and solitary leader of Free France, the Prime Minister was once again beginning to feel the first pangs of acute Gaullophobia, and this condition worsened with every new report reaching him of the General's threatening behaviour. That day, he told Spears: 'De Gaulle is completely subservient with me, but what is odious is his insufferable rudeness to anyone on a lower level.' Speaking of the Lyttelton-de Gaulle agreements, the Prime Minister added that 'De Gaulle's attitude was such that we should consider whether, if he persisted in it, we should not tear up every single agreement come to with him up to the present.'[37]

De Gaulle naturally persisted, as he remained convinced that all his difficulties in the Levant came exclusively from British encroachments and interferences. Besides, there was still the unsettled question of Madagascar, and he had for some time been under the impression that the British and the Americans were preparing a large operation in North or West Africa, from which Fighting France would once again be left out; as a result, he saw no reason to spare the British, and a situation ensued that bore a striking resemblance to that of August 1941: Churchill was once again informed that de Gaulle was making anti-British statements, that he had been 'appallingly rude' to the British representative in Aleppo, and had told him 'not to meddle in French affairs'.[38] This time, there was no American journalist on hand to report de Gaulle's bombastic statements, but the American Chargé d'Affairs in Beirut, Mr Gwynn, served exactly the same purpose: he reported that during a private talk with him, de Gaulle had violently denounced the British, and even threatened to go to war with them.*[39]

*For good measure, de Gaulle informed the Minister of State and the Commander-in-Chief shortly thereafter that as French troops now outnumbered British troops in the Levant, he would take over military command in Syria and Lebanon as from 10 September. This caused some panic in the War Office and in Middle-East Headquarters, not least because no one there seemed to know exactly how many British troops there were in the Levant.

The State Department immediately relayed the report to London, and it was circulated to the War Cabinet. Spears and Casey supplied whatever additional material was required, and just like the previous year at the same time, de Gaulle was asked to return to London. He once again considered that there was no hurry, and replied politely to the Prime Minister that he 'was too busy'.[40]

There was, of course, another analogy with the situation in September 1941: Having read the latest reports on de Gaulle's utterances, Churchill was beside himself with rage, and de Gaulle's refusal to return to England made matters even worse. But this time, the situation was rendered even more delicate and more embarrassing by two important external factors. After nearly four months of fruitless negotiations with Vichy authorities in Madagascar, His Majesty's government had decided to proceed with the military occupation of the whole island; yet it was essential to associate the Fighting French with the subsequent administration of the island, first because Britain would inevitably be accused of colonialist designs on the French Empire if this were not done, and second because solemn promises to this effect had been made on 13 May, and it was impossible not to honour them.

Eden had forcefully represented this to Churchill, but even the Foreign Secretary had to admit that it was not possible to transfer the control of Madagascar to de Gaulle with the dispute over Syria at its present acute stage. This was conveyed to the General, together with a diplomatic hint that his return to London might end the deadlock over the Levant and thus permit the introduction of the Fighting French in Madagascar.

There was another reason why it was far preferable to have de Gaulle return to England as soon as possible. This was related to an operation so secret that it cannot even be revealed at this stage – though it was already clear at the time that the plan involved a part of the French Empire, that the Americans were heavily involved, and that the Fighting French were entirely excluded. The implications were also clear: if de Gaulle were abroad when the operation started, he might very well denounce His Majesty's government in a vengeful broadcast; and if the Fighting French had not been installed in Madagascar in the meantime, British policy with regard to the French Empire as a whole would be extremely difficult to justify. This brought the British back to their initial dilemma: There could be no concessions on Madagascar if the dispute over the Levant was not resolved, and it could not be resolved if de Gaulle did not return to England for discussions with His Majesty's government.

De Gaulle, with his extremely suspicious character, saw things in a different light. He deduced that the British had agreed to instal the French in Madagascar only at the expense of turning them out of the Levant – in other words, perfidious Albion at her very worst. As for the most secret operation mentioned above, de Gaulle had already received some information about it from his Intelligence network and his Commissioner for Foreign Affairs.[41] Although he was still uncertain as to the precise target and date of the expedition, he understood perfectly well that his presence abroad at the time of the operation would be most distasteful to the British. As a result, de Gaulle showed no unnecessary haste in responding to the 'invitation' of the British government. After completing a lengthy tour of French Equatorial Africa, he only returned to England on 25 September, with the firm intention, as he put it, of 'settling the matter once and for all'.[42]

De Gaulle was quite confident that, after an initial outburst, he and the Prime Minister would again reach at least a temporary understanding that would be satisfactory to French interests. He had no doubt at all that justice was on his side, as he had just written to Pleven: 'The manoeuvre of the British aims at putting the blame on us by stressing my personal behaviour. But the blame lies with those whose intolerable encroachments force me to adopt this attitude. I am quite sure that I will bring them to revise their stand in the interest of the common cause.'[43] As on the other hand, Churchill was scandalized by de Gaulle's behaviour and firmly resolved to bring him to heel, the coming interview between the two men promised to be less than amiable. But as Oliver Harvey noted at the time: 'We hope that after the usual explosion there will be the usual reconciliation.'[44] Finally, on the afternoon of 30 September, de Gaulle came to Downing Street; he was accompanied by Pleven. On the British side, Eden and Major Morton were also present, and the discussion began at 5.30 p.m.

Churchill began by thanking de Gaulle for having come back to England at his invitation, and the General later commented: 'I received this compliment in the same humorous vein.' But the humour soon disappeared, as the British transcript of the conversation clearly shows:

The Prime Minister said that he and the Foreign Secretary had both asked the General before his departure to avoid causing a lot of trouble in Syria, but General de Gaulle had certainly not been able to succeed in this. It was really essential to reach a perfectly clear understanding about the situation.

General de Gaulle said that he had expected to find certain difficulties in Syria over Franco-British relations, but these difficulties had been even greater than he had expected. . . . The sources of dispute could, however, have been avoided. They had created a feeling, which he hoped was not justified, of unhappy rivalry between us.

The Prime Minister said there was no question of rivalry. We had no aspirations in Syria. We had no special interest in Syria apart from winning the war and maintaining our pre-war commercial interests, which were very small. But we had given pledges to the Syrian people with the assent of General Catroux. We were determined to fulfil these pledges in the spirit and in the letter. We could not agree that our military position in the Near East should be endangered by any failure to fulfil these pledges.

De Gaulle answered that the Fighting French had special responsibilities towards the Syrians and Lebanese, as well as military responsibilities in the Levant. These could not be shared; de Gaulle quoted two instances when General Spears had bullied and threatened the President of Lebanon, Alfred Naccache, and he pointed out that it was the British who sought to compromise the independence of the two countries. Churchill naturally jumped at the opportunity:

The Prime Minister suggested that there was one very good step which could be taken towards making the independence of Syria and the Lebanon more of a reality. This was to hold elections. There ought to be elections. . . . The people must have an opportunity of expressing their opinion. We must be freed from any anxiety arising out of the possibility of insurrections which would endanger our military security.

General de Gaulle said there was no question of any insurrections. Syria and the Lebanon were calmer than any other part of the Near East, calmer, for example, than Iraq. He agreed that elections should be held, but they must be genuine elections. . . . The local populations, with whom he had been in close contact, were not asking for elections. The moment was not favourable, and they should be postponed until the situation allowed elections to be held.

The Foreign Secretary said that elections had recently been held in Egypt.

General de Gaulle said the situation there was quite different. It was a country with a relatively long democratic tradition, where there was only one strong political party. It was a united country and there was therefore little fear of political difficulties. Syria was a country of many different races and religions. The Alouites and the inhabitants of Deir-ez-Zhor had nothing in common with those of Damascus. Neither the Fighting French nor the governments at Damascus and Beirut could take the responsibility of holding elections, and the two governments would resign if they were forced to hold them.

The Prime Minister said that our idea was that there should be an immediate announcement that elections would be held before the end of the year. He could not understand why there should be difficulties over the elections if the local population were as favourable to the Fighting French as had been suggested.

General de Gaulle maintained that the difficulties would arise between the different sections of the local population, and not between them and the Fighting French.

The Prime Minister referred to the question of local military command. He understood that General de Gaulle had maintained that there were now more French soldiers than British in the Levant states, and that the local command should therefore pass to the Fighting French.

General de Gaulle said he could not understand why the French should not hold the command in Syria if they had the majority of the troops there. General Catroux or General de Larminat were surely capable officers.

The Prime Minister said that General de Gaulle did not realize the true proportion or balance of the forces in the Near East. We did not accept his figures. Nor could we agree to transfer the command to the French. We should, on the contrary, take steps to maintain it, and to avoid any troubles arising out of local difficulties with the Syrian populations.

General de Gaulle said there were no such troubles between the local populations and the Free French. The Prime Minister had raised two points. Firstly, concerning the elections, the mandate was held by the Fighting French, and yet it was the British who were insisting on elections. Secondly, as regards the command, the Prime Minister had issued what amounted to an ultimatum that the British would maintain it in all circumstances.

The Prime Minister said that it seemed they must now pass from the question of Syria without having reached any agreement whatever.

The Foreign Secretary said that we were continuously receiving complaints from the Fighting French of interference in the internal affairs of Syria. But we were bound to play our part in such affairs because we were the central authority for co-ordinating all questions in the Middle East concerning supply, finance and manpower. . . . But we had met with much French obstruction which had in many cases brought business to a complete standstill.

The Prime Minister said that General de Gaulle seemed to have no idea of the true position. Our burdens were being made much more difficult to bear. Firstly, the local populations were being irritated against the French. Secondly, General de Gaulle was making a continuous attempt to assert his local position in a way which had no connection with the common cause for which we were fighting. The General maintained that everything was going perfectly smoothly. Unfortunately, this was not so.

General de Gaulle maintained that they did not wish to create any difficulties for Great Britain or to increase her burden in the Near East. . . . The difficulty in his view was the behaviour of the local British representatives, which spoiled everything. He thought it would be better to take measures to improve local contacts rather than to discuss formulae.

The Prime Minister said that it was evident that they did not agree in any way about the Syrian position. He was sorry about that. We should certainly endeavour to secure what we regarded as necessary for our conduct of the war in that part of the world. The General would understand that with this extremely unhappy situation in Syria, which had grown so much worse during the General's visit, we were not very eager to open the way to similar difficulties in other important theatres of the war, as, for example, Madagascar.

General de Gaulle said that last year he had offered to bring Madagascar into the Allied front. He could have done it then and only required some British air support. He had received no reply to his suggestion. He had seen Mr Eden and General Brooke, but still had had no reply. Then he had learned from the papers that British troops were at Diego Suarez. He had seen Mr Eden. A communiqué had been arranged between them,· according to which the French National Committee would play its proper role in the administration of the island. The next step, however, had been British negotiations with Vichy through the Governor-General, Annet, in spite of the communiqué of 13 May. He could not make out whether we preferred to make arrangements with Vichy or with the Fighting French. Now we had entered Antananarivo, as he had always maintained we should have done long ago (the Prime Minister pointed out that we had other tasks for our troops at that time). General de Gaulle said that now we were at Antananarivo, the time had come to carry out our promises. But we maintained that we could not do so because of difficulties in Syria. This was a very serious situation and called in question the collaboration between France and England.

The Prime Minister corrected General de Gaulle and said 'between General de Gaulle and England'.[45]

At this juncture, the tone of the conversation sharpened noticeably. In fact, Churchill exclaimed in a furious voice: 'You claim to be France! You are not France! I do not recognize you as France!'[46]

General de Gaulle asked why we were discussing matters with him if he was not France.

The Prime Minister explained that all this was written down. General de Gaulle was not France, but Fighting France.

General de Gaulle asked why then were we discussing French questions with him.

The Prime Minister explained that we were now talking about the role of Fighting France in present circumstances and in different theatres of the war.

General de Gaulle maintained that he was acting in the name of France. He was fighting with, but not for, England. He spoke for France, to whom he was responsible. His attitude was borne out by that of the French people, who believed that he spoke for France and would only support him as long as they believed this.

The Prime Minister said that our difficulty was to decide what was France. He was always trying to derive a just impression of what was France. He recognized General de Gaulle as a very honourable part of France, but not as France. There were other parts and aspects of France which might become more prominent. In so far as General de Gaulle represented the combatant sentiments and the main body of opinion of Frenchmen, we were very glad to work with him. But at Madagascar our difficulties would have been much greater if the invasion had been one by de Gaulle troops. We had now succeeded in bringing the greater part of the island under our control. In the present state of the war we could not risk introducing confusion into Madagascar by forcing the representatives of de Gaulle on the local population. . . . The Prime Minister continued that he would, however, be quite agreeable to see the representatives of Fighting France in Madagascar, if they went there animated by friendly sentiments. But it would be wrong to create serious military difficulties at such a time. Apart from that, we could not help feeling that we should be used as roughly in Madagascar as we had been in Syria.

General de Gaulle said that if we attacked the French both at Madagascar and Syria, he certainly could not agree to that.

The Prime Minister said that this was a pity. He had hoped we would be able to conduct our campaigns together. This hope had been spoiled because General de Gaulle was so combatant that, not content with fighting Germany, Italy and Japan, he also wanted to fight England and America.

General de Gaulle said that he took this as a joke, but did not regard it as a very good joke. If there was one man that the British need not reproach, it was himself. But now things must take their course.

The Prime Minister said that they seemed still to be very far apart. There seemed little use to proceed further with the conversation. The General had been unsuccessful in winning the confidence of the Americans, who had also had hopes of working with him. He could not understand why the General did not try to make things go well. (The Foreign Secretary interjected that other allies did not find us so difficult to deal with.) General de Gaulle was his own worst enemy. The Prime Minister had hoped to work with him. Gradually, bit by bit, that hope had been destroyed. We carried a pretty heavy load on account of France. Things could not go on as they were.

General de Gaulle said that he asked for nothing. He had done what he had done, and he was ready to continue. But he could not accept any diminution of the position of France anywhere, or the neutralization of France by the French or their allies. . . . He must be intransigent or he would count for nothing in France. This was not only his duty, but a political necessity. If he represented the France of yesterday or tomorrow, he might act differently, but his responsibilities were greater than the means at his disposal. The Prime Minister attacked him for this or that, instead of allowing him to co-operate. He did not make difficulties in Syria, but he had sent men there who had made difficulties.

M. Pleven said that every Frenchman had the same feeling about Madagascar.

The Foreign Secretary asked what the Fighting French expected us to do. The position was that we had much greater difficulties with them than with all our other allies. The files in the Foreign Office concerning them were much larger than all the Allied files put together. The Fighting French liked to treat us and the Americans roughly, and thought that they would get their way by such tactics. These methods were the very worst methods to employ with us or with the Americans.

General de Gaulle maintained that he had not treated the Americans roughly. The State Department, which was in touch with certain émigrés, had a certain line of policy. He could do nothing about this.

The Prime Minister told the General that he had lost a great deal.

Perhaps he had not irredeemably compromised his position. But he had made great mistakes.

General de Gaulle said of course he had made mistakes. Everybody made mistakes. But his object was to bring France back into the war with the British. Unfortunately, we had isolated him and kept him on one side. We did not collaborate. When Diego Suarez was occupied the French had been irritated and humiliated. We must put ourselves in their place.

The Prime Minister said that the position was that the French hit us and we received the blows with great but not unlimited patience.

The Foreign Secretary asked again what the Fighting French expected us to do in Madagascar after our experience in Syria.

General de Gaulle said that the first question he had been asked by Frenchmen everywhere on his journey was what would happen to Madagascar. They wanted the island to be brought back into the war by the Fighting French.

The Foreign Secretary said that this was not surprising. We had been prepared to discuss and examine this question. But we did not wish to open another Syrian chapter in Madagascar.

The Prime Minister said he must say quite plainly that the great difficulty lay in working with General de Gaulle. General de Gaulle had shown marked hostility to us. Wherever he went there was trouble. The situation was now critical. It made him sad, since he admired the General's personality and record. But he could not regard him as a comrade or a friend. He seemed to wish to strengthen his position with the French by adopting brusque methods with us. He tried the same tactics with the Americans. This was a serious situation.

General de Gaulle said that this was very sad. He was told that he had given the impression that he wished to create a position for himself in France by hostility to England. He thought that the French in France would be very surprised if they were told such a story. His position in France depended simply on the fact that he had wanted to go on fighting with us. He still wanted to do so, or rather that France should do so. . . . But just because of this, and because of the importance of maintaining the alliance after the war, the French people must receive the impression that the Fighting French were regarded as real allies and not as creatures of the British.

The Prime Minister asked whether the General had anything to suggest. They were not advancing very much.

General de Gaulle said that he had no suggestions to make. A certain situation had arisen in Syria which he thought could easily be arranged. There was a certain situation in Madagascar, and certain promises which in his opinion could easily be carried out.

The Prime Minister said he thought the General had made a great mistake in repulsing the friendship we offered and breaking collaboration between us which would have been very helpful to the General. Matters must now take their course. Much could have been done. The General stood in the way of closer association.

The Foreign Secretary said that we had no desire to look after Madagascar. We had hoped that the Fighting French would endeavour to meet us over Syria, but they had refused to do so.

The Prime Minister said matters could not rest where they were. We could not go on carrying all the burden and allowing ourselves to be used as a convenient background against which General de Gaulle stood out. He had not helped us at all. Instead of waging war with Germany, he had waged war with England. This was a great mistake. He had not shown the slightest desire to assist us, and he himself had been the main obstacle to effective collaboration with Britain and America.

General de Gaulle said that he would accept the consequences ('je tiendrai les conséquences').[47]

It was clear that the dispute over the Levant had effectively poisoned the whole meeting, which ended in something perilously close to a rupture. Churchill was naturally beside himself with rage, though he merely told Eden that 'he was sorry for the man, he was such a fool'.[48] Eden was also scandalized, and said afterwards that 'he had never seen anything like it in the way of rudeness since Ribbentrop'.[49] Once again, Fighting France was made to feel the full weight of the Prime Minister's ire, and the ponderous machinery of systematic obstruction closed in on General de Gaulle and his movement. The flow of cypher telegrams from Carlton Gardens to French authorities in Africa, the Levant and the Pacific was cut off without explanation, and all co-operation between the French secret service and British Intelligence ceased abruptly as from 1 October.

The very next day, at a special meeting of the National Committee, the General told the French commissioners what had passed between him and Churchill, after which he added: 'If you consider that my presence at the head of the committee is detrimental to the interests of France, your duty is to tell me so, and I will resign.'[50] This was predictably turned down unanimously, and a vigorous counter-offensive was launched immediately afterwards; on 2 October, the Foreign Office was handed a note which expressed the committee's complete and unanimous solidarity with General de Gaulle.[51] That very same day, Admiral Auboyneau came to see

Admiral Dickens and told him that 'as the British government had apparently broken off relations with de Gaulle, he must warn him that the Free French navy was on the side of de Gaulle and would follow him'. He added that 'the Fighting French had not joined the British to see Britain seize and rule French territory'.[52] De Gaulle's personal assistant, Gaston Palewski, also came to tell Harvey and Morton that 'the General felt himself insulted (*outragé*) at the conversation between himself, the Prime Minister and Mr Eden on 30 September'.[53]

Once again, de Gaulle was contemplating a withdrawal of the Fighting French to Equatorial Africa, and Churchill was wondering whether His Majesty's government should not finally break with General de Gaulle. On 8 October, Gladwyn Jebb told Harold Nicolson that the row between Winston and de Gaulle was 'very serious', that 'relations have practically been sundered', and that things were 'likely to get worse'.[54] Never in fact had a complete rupture between the two men and their respective countries been so close as in the autumn of 1942.

For de Gaulle, of course, it was all Churchill's fault: '*Pauvre Churchill!* He's betraying us, and he's angry at us because he's forced to betray us.'[55] Churchill's feelings towards de Gaulle, on the other hand, remained as irrational and emotional as ever; some time earlier, after one of the Prime Minister's vengeful tirades against de Gaulle, Harold Nicolson had remarked: – 'You may be right, Mr Prime Minister, but surely all that is irrelevant, since General de Gaulle is a great man.'

'A great man?' Churchill exploded. 'Why, he's selfish, he's arrogant, he thinks he's the centre of the universe . . . he . . . You're right, he's a great man!'[56]

CHAPTER 9

Temporary Expedient

As the reader is probably aware by now, nothing could ever be taken for granted in the relationship between the British Prime Minister and the leader of Fighting France. On both sides, however, some dedicated men sought to renew the dialogue that had been so abruptly discontinued on the afternoon of 30 September. The indefatigable Anthony Eden, the conscientious Alexander Cadogan, the ubiquitous Desmond Morton, the devoted Charles Peake, the discreet Gaston Palewski, the highly excitable André Philip and the resolutely Anglophile Maurice Dejean all tried their hand at bringing about a reconciliation. They were not helped by de Gaulle's highly suspicious character, nor by Churchill's pugnacious temperament. Besides, as we know, this was much more than a personal quarrel: it was in the highest degree a political and diplomatic confrontation between two countries, two empires, two mentalities and two national interests.

Maurice Dejean, for one, saw no reason why the quarrel should not be resolved by diplomatic means. In the interest of the Franco-British alliance, he therefore undertook to negotiate with the Foreign Office on the vexed question of Syria, and took considerable personal risks in the process. Unfortunately, as this was not only a diplomatic affair, but also a highly emotional issue, Dejean's undertaking foundered just when it was on the point of succeeding; at the last moment, he was disavowed by General de Gaulle, and he resigned his post as Commissioner for Foreign Affairs on 20 October.*

*By the second week of October, Dejean and the Foreign Office had worked out a draft agreement on Syria; it provided for bilateral consultations on all Middle East affairs, the setting up of a mixed committee and mixed local commissions in the Levant. The French also promised to hold elections in Syria and Lebanon in early 1943. De Gaulle was held informed of the progress of negotiations, and did not disagree. However, Catroux, who was consulted in mid-October, flatly disagreed with the whole draft, which he effectively

It was clear that no diplomatic solution was in sight, and that a reconciliation between the two men was as remote and problematical as ever – unless of course the whole question of Franco-British relations was lifted from the level of hard realities to the sentimental and emotional plane which had never failed to work wonders in the past. Not surprisingly, it was the Prime Minister, ever a bad hater, who took the initiative; on 30 October, the olive branch was accordingly rolled out of Downing Street, and took the form of a visit to Carlton Gardens by Churchill's private secretary and right-hand man, Major Desmond Morton. As the minutes show, no effort was spared to reach a meeting of minds, and the interview was nothing if not successful:

> Major Morton called on General de Gaulle to convey the Prime Minister's congratulations on the recent exploits of the submarine *Juno* in the North Sea and of our troops on the Egyptian front . . . 'The Prime Minister,' added Major Morton, 'was just recently talking about you, and he again mentioned the immense admiration he had for you and the work you have accomplished in the last two-and-a-half years.'

> General de Gaulle in turn asked Major Morton to convey to Mr Churchill his congratulations on the great successes now being won by the British troops in Egypt, and he assured him that his admiration for the Prime Minister and the things he had accomplished since taking office was at least as great.

> Major Morton told General de Gaulle that . . . while glancing through the reports of the British War Office for the last two-and-a-half years, he had noticed that the advice of General de Gaulle in respect of the policy to be followed with regard to France had been faithfully adhered to by the British government up to the time of the Dakar affair. From that time on, he had noticed that things had changed, and he asked the General to what he attributed this.

> General de Gaulle agreed that, up to the Dakar expedition, his opinions had been taken into account, except (he stressed) in the case of Mers-el-Kebir – an exception which Major Morton readily

demolished in a long telegram to de Gaulle. The General thereupon declared that the draft agreement was unacceptable and when Dejean objected that he was morally committed in his negotiations with the British, de Gaulle asked him to submit his resignation.[1] On 27 October, Eden minuted: 'I for one shall continue to resent Dejean's removal and I don't care if the Free French know it.'[2] Shortly thereafter, Dejean became Ambassador to the Allied governments in exile. Pleven temporarily replaced him as Commissioner for Foreign Affairs.

readily admitted. As for ulterior developments, the General found two reasons for the change: one was deep-rooted, the other more immediate. After Dakar, the British government had changed its policy. It had drawn closer to Vichy, and had since then never ceased to try and come to terms with them. The other reason was Syria. Since June 1941, France and Great Britain had found themselves once more at loggerheads on a theatre in which they had always been in conflict. These, according to General de Gaulle, were the two reasons that had gravely compromised the good relations between the French National Committee and the British government.

Major Morton deplored the fact that relations were not closer and expressed the hope that every effort would be made, on both sides, to bring about a more favourable evolution.[3]*

When the next day, Charles Peake saw the new Commissioner for Foreign Affairs *ad interim* in order to 'admonish him about Syria', he was amazed to hear that de Gaulle 'had been very *ému* by what Major Morton had said to him', and that the General 'was delighted at the Prime Minister having made this gesture and felt that the situation had improved remarkably'.[4] This in turn was very much appreciated at Downing Street and at the Foreign Office, and negotiations over Madagascar took a new turn. Finally, on 6 November, the day after an armistice had finally been concluded at Madagascar, Mr Eden, 'all sugar and honey', as de Gaulle recalled, proposed that a joint communiqué be issued, announcing that de Gaulle's appointee as High Commissioner for the Indian Ocean, General Legentilhomme, would leave forthwith to take over the administration of Madagascar. De Gaulle also received a gracious invitation to visit the Prime Minister on 8 November. But as can be imagined, there was much more than sentiment behind Churchill's sudden about-face.

At the end of July, 1942, after long Anglo-American discussions at the level of the Chiefs-of-Staff, Churchill had finally persuaded President Roosevelt to give up 'Operation Sledgehammer', an attempt to land in France and form a bridgehead around Cherbourg that very autumn. Instead, Roosevelt had been persuaded to accept 'Torch', which called for an Anglo-American landing in North Africa by the end of October. Here, then, was the ultra-secret operation on which de Gaulle had gradually received information during the summer and early autumn. This information came from

*In his memoirs, de Gaulle mistakenly gave 23 October as the day of the interview.

Free French sources in Gibraltar, Tangier . . . and Vichy.[5] Churchill had given strict instructions from the start that the 'leaky' Fighting French were not to be informed.[6] Besides, even if he had wanted to inform them, he would have been overruled by President Roosevelt. Indeed, it had been agreed that the whole operation would proceed under American command, while Churchill had explicitly agreed to be Roosevelt's 'lieutenant' for the occasion[7] – and the American President had several very good reasons for keeping the Fighting French out of 'Torch'.

The first reason was purely visceral: Roosevelt had disliked de Gaulle from the start, he distrusted him since Dakar, and hated him since St Pierre et Miquelon. The President was encouraged in this attitude by some of his closest advisers, including Admiral Leahy, recently returned from Vichy, Under-Secretary of State Sumner Welles, and of course Secretary of State Cordell Hull, who had a deep personal grudge against de Gaulle ever since a certain Christmas eve of 1941. Besides, the most influential expert on French affairs in Washington was none other than Alexis Léger, Secretary-General of the Quai d'Orsay before the war, and a fierce opponent of de Gaulle ever since. All these men had conjured the picture of a Fighting French General who was nothing but a Fascist, an adventurer and a would-be dictator, and Roosevelt was all too eager to accept this as the unqualified truth.[8]

The second reason was naturally related to American policy towards Vichy. The return to power of the pro-German Pierre Laval in France had certainly rendered President Roosevelt more cautious in his dealings with Vichy, though less for moral than for electoral reasons. However, numerous contacts were still being maintained in Vichy and in North Africa, and Roosevelt was confident that 'Torch' would vindicate the French policy he had pursued ever since 1940. After all, this policy had allowed him to send to North Africa vast numbers of highly active and rather inexperienced consuls, vice-consuls and various other agents, who were now preparing the ground for 'Torch' under the direction of the no less active but somewhat more experienced Robert Murphy. In fact, Roosevelt was convinced that the Americans were so popular with Vichy that there would be little or no resistance to the landings, provided that no Fighting Frenchmen or Englishmen were in sight. Just to make sure, Roosevelt planned to send a warm personal appeal to Marshal

Pétain which began with 'My dear old friend'. The appeal was so warm, in fact, that it made Churchill uneasy, and he begged the President to 'tone it down a bit'.[9]

The third reason for the exclusion of General de Gaulle from 'Torch' was that Roosevelt relied on a very different sort of Frenchmen to help him into North Africa. The first one to be approached was General Weygand, about whom the Americans still entertained many illusions even after his recall from North Africa. But to Robert Murphy, who contacted him in Cannes on 17 July, Weygand answered in a broken voice that 'at my age, one does not become a rebel'.[10] Admiral Darlan, the Vichy Commander-in-Chief and Vice-President of the Council, whose position had been much weakened after Laval's return to power, hinted that he might cooperate if he were given supreme command of the expedition, but the admiral was judged too dangerous, too compromised and too compromising to be made party to the operation. In the end, there remained only one man, on whom President Roosevelt pinned great hopes. His name was General Giraud.

General Henri Honoré Giraud was 63 years old, tall, forceful, energetic, and with no claim to being an intellectual. He had been captured by the Germans in 1940, but escaped from a prison fortress in April 1942, and later made his way to Vichy. There, he was contacted by the Americans, and after long parleys with Robert Murphy, he agreed to co-operate, provided that the Gaullists and the British were excluded from the operation.[11] In addition, he asked to be given command of the expedition, and mistakenly understood that the Americans agreed to that also. By the end of October, President Roosevelt was accordingly convinced that Giraud (code-name: 'King Pin') would give him the political key to North Africa and bring all Frenchmen there to co-operate with the Allies.

So much for the political side of the operation. The military side was planned with the usual American thoroughness, while the British Chiefs-of-Staff and Intelligence Service injected some precious local knowledge and strategic wisdom. Finally, the command of the expedition was entrusted to a little-known but highly competent Major-General, Dwight D. Eisenhower. The landing was originally scheduled for the end of October, and Roosevelt characteristically told General Marshall: 'Please make it before election day.'[12] But the Congressional elections were to take place on 3 November, and D-

Day for North Africa was finally postponed to 8 November. Undaunted, Roosevelt said that it would show how politically disinterested he was . . .

By the end of October, Churchill was delighted with the progress of preparations, and highly excited at the prospect of the impending attack. General Clark recalled that he was 'happy as a detective story fan', and the Prime Minister even told him: 'Keep in mind that we'll back you up in whatever you do.'[13] Still, it was *French* North Africa, and Churchill wanted to inform de Gaulle in the greatest secrecy on the eve of the landing. Roosevelt, on the other hand, would not hear of it, so the idea was abandoned. But Churchill was still somewhat sentimental in these French affairs, and besides, he did not have an entirely clear conscience in the matter. 'I was conscious of our British relationships with de Gaulle,' he later wrote, 'and of the gravity of the affront which he would have to suffer by being deliberately excluded from all share in the design. . . . As some means of softening this slight to him and his movement, I arranged to confide the trusteeship of Madagascar to his hands.'[14]

To Eden, Churchill said at the time that this would be 'de Gaulle's consolation prize for the shock and disappointment to come from 'Torch' and the appearance of Giraud in the ring'.[15] But as usual with Churchill, sentiment was intimately mixed with expediency. The truth was that de Gaulle's possible reactions upon learning of the Anglo-American landing were greatly feared in Downing Street, and in the frightful row that would probably ensue, it was a good thing to be able to point to the British government's good record on Madagascar. This was the real reason why Eden, 'all sugar and honey', had come to see de Gaulle on 6 November, and had told him the good news about the transfer of Madagascar to Gaullist authority, while conveying to him an invitation to lunch at Chequers on 8 November – a day that was expected to be rather agitated.

In the early hours of 8 November, a mighty amphibious army, supported by overwhelming air and naval forces, landed at seven points along the coast of Morocco and Algeria. From then on, nothing really went as planned: the French were not at all impressed by the American uniform, and fierce resistance was encountered at Algiers, Oran and Casablanca. Worse still, the Americans discovered in the early hours of the operation that

Admiral Darlan was in Algiers to visit his son who was sick in hospital, and the admiral, who held undisputed control over all French forces in the area, was not at all co-operative.* There was even worse: General Giraud had been secretly taken out of France and brought to Gibraltar by submarine on the eve of the landing, but upon learning that he was not to be given command of the operation, the general refused to co-operate.[16] Endless palavers ensued, and it emerged that Giraud had come with a plan of his own . . . for the immediate liberation of France.** The plan, code-named 'Plan L', was a remarkable exercise in wishful thinking, and could only be described as '*C'est magnifique, mais ce n'est pas la guerre*'. But the fact remained that Giraud was conspicuously absent from Algiers on 8 November, that Vichy French resistance to the expedition was continuing, and that the Americans were left to deal with Admiral Darlan.[17]

At six o'clock that morning, de Gaulle was awakened and informed by his Chief-of-Staff, Colonel Billotte, that the landing was being carried out. Thus, after Mers-el-Kebir and Madagascar, Fighting France was once again being presented with a *fait accompli*. De Gaulle, in his pyjamas, thundered: 'Well, I hope the people of Vichy throw them into the sea. You can't break into France and get away with it.'[18] By eleven a.m., however, he had already regained his composure, and Charles Peake, who had come to Carlton Gardens to assess the force of the impending gale just before de Gaulle met the Prime Minister, made an encouraging report: The atmosphere was 'not so bad as he had feared', and 'if a genial note can be struck at the beginning of the meeting the General may be put into the right mood at once and the luncheon may pass off fairly successfully'.[19]

At twelve o'clock, the General arrived at Downing Street, and the discussions began at once: 'During the conversation,' de Gaulle recalled,

---

*Darlan had been briefly arrested by a group of young Gaullists who had taken to arms upon learning of the landing, but the Americans took too much time to reach Algiers, and Darlan was freed before daybreak by the French police. After that, the police arrested the Gaullists, as well as General Juin, who had secretly joined the Allies.
**Morgenthau later noted in his diary: 'The President told me that they had the most terrible time with General Giraud at Gibraltar because he wanted to have everything to say over English, American and Free French, and it finally got to the point when they had to tell him that they would send him back to France.'[17]

The Prime Minister was to lavish upon me every sign of friendship, but he could not conceal that he felt some embarrassment. He told me that, although the British fleet and air force were playing an essential role in the operation now under way, British troops were serving in a purely accessory capacity. For the moment, Great Britain had had to leave all the responsibilities in the hands of the United States; Eisenhower was in command – The Americans had demanded that the Free French be left out. 'We have been obliged to go along with this,' Mr Churchill declared. 'Rest assured, however, that we are not revoking any of our agreements with you. Ever since 1940, we have promised you our support. Despite the incidents that have occurred since then, we intend to keep that promise. Besides, as the North African engagement increases in scope, we, the British, will have to come on to the scene; we will then have our word to say. And that word will be on your behalf.' And Mr Churchill, showing signs of emotion, added, 'You have been with us during the worst moments of the war. We shall not abandon you now that the horizon is brightening.'

The British ministers then informed me that the Americans were in the process of landing at several points in Morocco, as well as at Oran and Algiers. The operation was not going smoothly, especially at Casablanca, where French forces were putting up a vigorous resistance. General Giraud had been taken on to a British submarine off the Côte d'Azur and brought to Gibraltar. The Americans were counting on him to take command of the French troops in North Africa and to reverse the situation. But already his success seemed dubious. 'Did you know,' Churchill also asked me, 'that Darlan is in Algiers?'

To all these explanations, I replied in substance: 'The fact that the Americans have landed in Africa, where both English and Free French forces have been struggling for over two years, is in itself a highly satisfactory development. I can also see in it, for France, the possibility of recovering an army and perhaps a fleet which would fight for her liberation. General Giraud is a great soldier, and I wish him well in his undertaking. It is too bad that the Allies have prevented him from coming to an agreement with me, for I would have been able to procure other help for him besides wishes. But sooner or later, we shall come to an agreement, especially if the Allies abstain from intervening. As for the operation now in progress, I am not surprised that it is a difficult one. In both Algeria and Morocco, there are military elements that fought us in Syria last year and which you allowed to re-embark despite my warnings. Furthermore, the Americans intended to play off Vichy against de Gaulle in North Africa. I have never ceased to think that, should the occasion arise, they would have to pay for it. Now they are paying, and of course we French must pay as well. However, given the feelings in our soldiers' hearts, I believe that the battle will not be long. But whatever its duration, the Germans will certainly rush in.'

I then expressed to Churchill and Eden my astonishment at discovering that the Allied plan did not first of all aim at occupying Bizerta, for the Germans and the Italians were obviously going to land there in order to enter Tunisia. If the Americans did not want to risk a direct landing there, I could, if requested, have contributed the Koenig Division. The British ministers admitted this, while repeating that the operation was under American control. 'I cannot understand,' I told them, 'how you British can stand aside so completely in an undertaking that is of such primary concern to Europe.'

Mr Churchill asked me how I envisioned future relations between Fighting France and the North African authorities. I replied that the most important was to achieve unity, and that contacts ought therefore to be established as soon as possible. This implied that in Algiers, the regime and the key men of Vichy were removed from the scene, for the whole French resistance could not tolerate their remaining in function. If, for example, Darlan were to rule North Africa, no agreement would be possible. 'At any rate,' I added, 'nothing is more important for the time being than to bring the battle to a halt.'[20]

Churchill, clearly delighted with what he heard, answered that:

At the present moment, General Giraud's role was purely military. The British government hoped that all differences would be avoided between the French wishing to continue the struggle with the Allies. He had no wish to interfere in questions of persons, which were to be settled between Frenchmen, but there was one point on which the British government was extremely firm: General de Gaulle and the French National Committee were the only authorities recognized by them to rally all the French who wished to help the cause of the United Nations. The British government therefore intended to carry on giving all possible help to Fighting France, and the Prime Minister stressed this with particular warmth, while expressing his great attachment to General de Gaulle.

General de Gaulle replied that:

His aim had always been to continue the struggle by the side of the Allies with as many French people and French territories as possible; that Fighting France was eager to welcome all those who wished to fight; that names and personalities were unimportant and that he had only his country's interests at heart. Knowing that the Allies had no designs on the French territories in North Africa, he hoped that the French population would warmly welcome the Allied troops that had come to liberate them. The General added that he would broadcast a speech along these lines that very evening.[21]

Churchill had not dared hope for such understanding and spirit of co-operation. In an animated voice, he presently began to speak of Rommel's defeat, which was a certainty ever since El Alamein: '*Les bons jours commencent,*' he exclaimed in French, with tears in his eyes: 'I shall never forget those who did not desert me in June 1940, when I was all alone. You'll see: One day, we'll go down the Champs Elysees together.'[22]

By the time the interview ended, Churchill was immensely relieved and pleased at de Gaulle's unexpected attitude. The very next day, he cabled to General Spears that 'support of Fighting France and collaboration with her remained the cornerstone of the British government's policy towards France'.[23] Less than six weeks before, he had been contemplating a complete break with General de Gaulle.

As for the General, he reportedly emerged from Downing Street 'wreathed in smiles'.[24] After all, the Prime Minister had assured him that in spite of Roosevelt's unfortunate initiative, he, Churchill, would continue to support Fighting France to the very end. Besides, it now seemed clear that Roosevelt's attempt to split the French camp by introducing Giraud into North Africa was doomed to failure. Giraud himself was a good general, and he could certainly be brought to collaborate with Fighting France; soon, therefore, French North Africa would re-enter the war under the Cross of Lorraine. That evening, at the BBC, de Gaulle broadcast the following message to his compatriots:

France's allies have undertaken to associate French North Africa with the war of liberation. They are beginning to land enormous numbers of troops there. . . . Our Algeria, our Morocco, our Tunisia are to serve as a starting point for the liberation of France. This undertaking is led by our American allies. . . . French leaders, soldiers, sailors, airmen, civil servants, French settlers in North Africa, arise! Help our Allies! Join them without reservations. Fighting France adjures you to do so. Don't worry about names or formulas. Only one thing counts: The salvation of the Motherland! All those who have the courage to rise in spite of the enemy and the betrayal are in advance approved, welcomed and acclaimed by all the Fighting French. Ignore the traitors who try to persuade you that the Allies want to take our empire for themselves. The great moment has come. This is a time for common sense and courage. Everywhere, the enemy is faltering and giving way. Frenchmen of North Africa, if through your efforts we re-enter the battle from one end of the Mediterranean to the other, then, thanks to France, the war will be won.[25]

By that time, however, events in North Africa were taking an unexpected turn: The Americans now had Darlan in their power and fighting had ceased in Algiers, but the Vichy French were still fighting everywhere else, and only Darlan had the power to order a cease-fire. Indeed, General Mark Clark, who represented General Eisenhower in Algiers, found out that no one in North Africa was prepared to accept the authority of General Giraud, who had finally arrived on 9 November. On the other hand, the fighting had to cease at all costs in Algeria and Morocco, especially as the Germans were now funnelling troops into Tunisia with the complicity of the local Vichy authorities. It was an impossible situation, but General Clark was a man of decision, and by his own admission, he was 'not too familiar with politics'.[26] As a result, he finally struck a bargain with Darlan on the morning of the 10th: the admiral would 'take responsibility for North Africa in the name of the Marshal', and in exchange, he would issue a general cease-fire order. Eisenhower arrived in Algiers the same day, and endorsed the bargain. After all, the Giraud solution had failed, and dealing with Darlan would save many American lives: 'I am only a soldier,' Eisenhower had said, 'I do not understand anything about diplomacy.'[28]

The State Department did, but it had absolutely no part in the negotiations. President Roosevelt did not, and his grasp of the issues involved was imperfect to say the least. For him, Darlan, Giraud and de Gaulle were just 'three prima donnas', and his solution to the problem was disarmingly simple: 'Put all three of them in one room alone, and then give the government of the occupied territory to the man who comes out.'[29] Failing that, the solution advocated by Eisenhower was quite acceptable. Had Darlan collaborated with Hitler for more than a year? Had he praised the Germans as being 'far more generous than the British'? Had he abandoned French Indochina to the Japanese? Had he allowed the Germans to use French airports in Syria? Had he allowed Rommel's Africa Korps to be supplied through Tunisia? Had he not said only six months earlier that 'England will have to pay one day'? Was he not the second most hated man in France after Laval? Had he not ordered the French to fire on the Americans only two days earlier? Was he not a

collaborator, a declared enemy and a traitor? Seen from Washing-
ton, it probably didn't look that bad, and Eisenhower received the
go-ahead: three days later, Darlan became 'High Commissioner for
North Africa' with American support, but still 'in the name of the
Marshal'.* He was immediately recognized as such by Noguès,
Chatel, Bergeret, Boisson . . . and Giraud, who was named military
Commander-in-Chief as a sort of consolation prize.

The news of the negotiated cease-fire and of Darlan's assumption
of power in North Africa under American auspices was greeted in
London with amazement and consternation: the Fighting French
were dumbstruck, de Gaulle was incredulous, Churchill was
disgusted: 'Darlan ought to be shot,' the Prime Minister
exclaimed.[30] But before 'Torch', Churchill had promised President
Roosevelt to back him in whatever he did, and he was now in a most
embarrassing situation. On 16 November, de Gaulle was received
for lunch at Downing Street, and he noted that 'Mr Churchill
appeared to be in quite a good mood, though he seemed
preoccupied', and that 'Mr Eden showed some embarrassment'. A
lively discussion ensued:

> The Prime Minister told the General that he understood his feelings
> perfectly and shared them. But he remarked that we were at present in
> the thick of the fight, and that what counted was to chase the enemy out
> of Tunisia. The Allied military authorities had to take practical
> measures in North Africa to secure this objective while at the same time
> securing the co-operation of the French troops. 'As to the attitude of the
> British government,' Mr Churchill added, 'it remains the same, and all
> engagements entered into with you remain valid. The arrangements
> made by General Eisenhower are essentially temporary and not binding
> on the future . . .'

> General de Gaulle told the Prime Minister that he took note of the
> British attitude, but that he wished to make known his own; 'We are no
> longer in the eighteenth century,' he declared, 'when Frederic paid
> people at the Court of Vienna to seize Silesia, nor at the time of the
> Renaissance, when one made use of the stalwarts of Milan or the
> Spadassins of Florence. And even in those days, such men were not
> chosen to lead liberated peoples. We are making war with the blood and
> soul of the peoples. Here are the telegrams I have received from France.
> They show that France is plunged in amazement. Imagine the

*This was of course a fiction: by that time, the Marshal had publicly disavowed Darlan,
who was denounced by Vichy as a traitor . . . and the Germans had invaded the unoccupied
zone of France.

incalculable consequences if France came to the conclusion that for her Allies, liberation meant Darlan. You might perhaps win the war militarily; but you would lose it morally, and there would be only one victor in the end: Stalin.'

Mr Churchill repeated that present events would in no way prejudice the future . . .

General de Gaulle observed that in any case, it was his duty to let France know that he opposed the present dealings, and he asked for permission to broadcast this through the BBC. The Prime Minister readily assented.

Before the General and Mr Churchill went into luncheon, Mr Eden, who now had to leave, took the General aside and told him how worried and anxious he was over this whole business. 'It is not a clean one,' said General de Gaulle, 'and I am sorry that you should dirty your hands with it.'

During luncheon, the anxiety of the guests, particularly the ladies, spoke strongly for the feelings of all. Even Mrs Churchill was unable to lighten the atmosphere. After lunch, Mr Churchill drew General de Gaulle into his study, where they had a private conversation: Mr Churchill told the General that his position was magnificent. Darlan had no future. Giraud was finished politically. 'You stand for honour,' he told the General. 'Yours is the true path, you alone will remain. Do not collide head-on with the Americans. It is useless and you will gain nothing. Have patience and they will come to you, for there is no alternative.' Then Mr Churchill denounced Darlan. He could find no words, he said, to describe him or to express his disgust.

General de Gaulle said he was surprised that the British government . . . allowed itself to follow the American lead. 'I don't understand you,' he said to Mr Churchill. 'You have fought since the first day. One could even say that you personally symbolize this war. Your armies are victorious in Libya. Yet you allow yourself to be towed along by the United States whose soldiers have never even seen a German. It is up to you to take over the moral direction of this war. Public opinion in Europe will be behind you.'[31]

At this stage, de Gaulle noted: 'These words made a profound impression on Mr Churchill, and he wavered perceptibly . . .'[32]

Mr Churchill reminded General de Gaulle that he had followed this course when, in his speech the other day at the Guildhall, he had praised the General and the patriots who in France followed him in legions, while he let it be understood that Giraud was famous only for his escapes.

De Gaulle answered that he was grateful to the Prime Minister for having made this subtle distinction, but nevertheless he believed that the

Prime Minister now had the opportunity of assuming a position of great importance, and that he should assume it without delay. He added that: 'The Americans were now dealing directly and fully with the people of Vichy, who had changed their stripes for the occasion. But Vichy represented many things and all of them were directed against England. The more the latter tolerated the American game, the more she was in danger of allowing forces to develop which would one day turn against her.'

The conversation ended on a cordial note: 'Mr Churchill asked the General to remain in close contact with him, and to come and see him as often as he wished: every day if he liked.'[33] And the very next day, Churchill cabled to Roosevelt:

I ought to let you know that very deep currents of feeling are stirred by the arrangement with Darlan. The more I reflect upon it the more convinced I become that it can only be a temporary expedient, justifiable solely by the stress of battle. We must not overlook the serious political injury which may be done to our cause, not only in France but throughout Europe, by the feeling that we are ready to make terms with the local Quislings. Darlan has an odious record. It is he who has inculcated in the French navy its malignant disposition by promoting his creatures to command. It is but yesterday that French sailors were sent to their death against your line of battle off Casablanca, and now, for the sake of power and office, Darlan plays the turncoat. A permanent arrangement with Darlan or the formation of a Darlan government in French North Africa would not be understood by the great masses of ordinary people, whose simple loyalties are our strength.[34]

The great masses of ordinary people certainly did not understand, as President Roosevelt himself had already found out: A deluge of protests was reaching the White House every day, and the President, being an astute politician, was already taking steps to allay the criticism. In fact, he had just declared at a press conference:

I have accepted General Eisenhower's political arrangements made for the time being in Northern and Western Africa.

I thoroughly understand and approve the feeling in the United States and Great Britain and among all the other United Nations that in view by the American uniform, and fierce resistance was encountered at Algiers, Oran and Casablanca. Worse still, the Americans discovered in the early hours of the operation that Admiral Darlan was of the history of the past two years no permanent arrangement should be made with Admiral Darlan . . . The present temporary arrangements in North and West Africa is only a temporary expedient, justified solely by the stress of battle.

The present temporary arrangement has accomplished two military objectives. The first was to save American and British lives, and French lives on the other hand.

The second was the vital factor of time. The temporary arrangement has made it possible to avoid a 'mopping-up' period in Algiers and Morocco which might have taken a month or two to consummate. Such a period would have delayed the concentration for the attack from the west on Tunis, and we hope on Tripoli . . .

Admiral Darlan's proclamation assisted in making a 'mopping-up' period unnecessary. Temporary arrangements made with Admiral Darlan apply, without exception, to the current local situation only.[35]

That was five 'temporary' and two 'for the time being' in a rather short statement, but then the President did not fear to labour the point. In his private talks, he also made it clear that he would use Darlan as long as he needed him, and to justify his policy, he quoted 'an old Bulgarian proverb', which soon became 'an old Rumanian proverb', then 'a Serbian proverb,' and finally 'an old Orthodox proverb used in the Balkans'. This proverb, according to the President, said: 'You can walk with the devil until you get to the other side of the bridge', though it soon became: 'To cross the bridge you can walk with the devil', then: 'Crossing a stream it is permissible to ride on the back of the devil until you get to safety,' and by the time he told it to Morgenthau: 'You must walk with the devil as far as the bridge, but then you must leave him behind.'[36]

Whatever the tenor of the proverb or the devil's exact position on the bridge, it was clear that Roosevelt intended to pursue his policy of collaboration with the men of Vichy in North Africa as long as this was not too costly for his political image at home. A formal agreement to this effect was signed on 22 November between General Clark and Admiral Darlan; the Temporary Expedient threatened to last for some time to come.

By that time, however, the prolongation of co-operation with Darlan was giving rise to an ever increasing wave of indignation in Britain. The press protested loudly, Parliament was restive, the exile governments in London were complaining bitterly, the SOE reported that the deal with Darlan 'has produced violent reactions on all our subterranean organizations in enemy-occupied countries, particularly in France, where it has had a blasting and withering effect'[37]. The staff dealing with France in PWE and the BBC had resigned almost to a man,[38] and within the British government itself, several ministers were outspokenly hostile to President Roosevelt's North African policy; Anthony Eden was one of them, as he never failed to remind the Prime Minister.

Churchill, however, remained faithful to his policy of supporting the President. This he had promised to do, and besides, now as ever, how could the war be won without a close Anglo-American partnership? Churchill, by his own admission, was still the President's 'ardent and active lieutenant'.[39] As such, he rejected and resented the wave of criticism aimed at Roosevelt's policy, and this produced in him a state of mind which he himself later sought to define:

> 'I was conscious of the rising tide of opinion around me. I was grieved to find the success of our immense operation, and the victory of Alamein, overshadowed in the minds of many of my best friends by what seemed to them a base and squalid deal with one of our most bitter enemies. I considered their attitude unreasonable and not sufficiently considerate of the severities of the struggle and the lives of the troops. As their criticisms became sharper I grew resentful, and also somewhat contemptuous of their sense of proportion. . . .'[40]

Although Churchill did not admit it, his reaction to the criticism levelled at Anglo-American policy took an unexpected form: not only did it prompt him to close ranks with President Roosevelt; it also increasingly estranged him from de Gaulle . . . and even brought him closer to Admiral Darlan! By 26 November, he was actually telling Eden that 'Darlan has done more for us than de Gaulle'.[41] Two days later, after the scuttling of the French fleet at Toulon, Oliver Harvey noted in his diary: 'P.M. is getting more and more enthusiastic over Darlan.'[42] Considering that the Prime Minister had previously called Darlan 'a rogue', 'a scoundrel', 'a traitor', 'a turncoat', and had stated only a fortnight earlier that 'he ought to be shot', this was indeed a startling about-face, and it certainly seems to show the occasional fragility of Churchill's mercurial temperament. But the most surprising was probably the speech he delivered at a secret session of Parliament less than two weeks later. It was considered a masterful speech then and later, and rightly so. There was a brilliant exposition of the problems that had beset the Allies during the first days of 'Torch', a striking description of Marshal Pétain (which he pronounced 'Petaigne') as an antique defeatist, and even a defence of Darlan's usefulness, together with an expression of understanding for the admiral's present plight. But for reasons that will soon become obvious, no one has ever cared to publish what Churchill said about General de Gaulle during that secret session. In view of the Prime Minister's warm and friendly attitude towards the General less than a month earlier, it certainly makes surprising reading:

I must now say a word about General de Gaulle. On behalf of HMG I exchanged letters with him in 1940 recognizing him as the leader of all Free Frenchmen wherever they might be who should rally to him, in support of the Allied cause. We have most scrupulously kept our engagements with him and have done everything in our power to help him. We finance his movement. We have helped his operations. But we have never recognized him as representing France. We have never agreed that he and those associated with him, because they were right and brave at the moment of French surrender, have a monopoly on the future of France. I have lived myself for the last 35 years or more in a mental relationship and to a large extent in sympathy with an abstraction called France. I still do not think it is an illusion. I cannot feel that de Gaulle is France, still less that Darlan and Vichy are France. France is something greater, more complex, more formidable than any of these sectional manifestations.

I have tried to work as far as possible with General de Gaulle, making allowances for his many difficulties, for his temperament and for the limitations of his outlook. In order to sustain his movement at the moment of the American occupation of French North Africa and to console him and his friends for their exclusion from the enterprise we agreed to his nominee, General Legentilhomme, being proclaimed as High Commissioner for Madagascar, although this adds somewhat to our difficulties in pacifying that large island, which oddly as it seems to us would much prefer Darlan. We are at the present time endeavouring to rally Jibuti to the Free French Movement. Therefore I consider that we have been in every respect faithful in the discharge of our obligations to de Gaulle, and we shall so continue to the end.

However you must not be led to believe that General de Gaulle is an unfaltering friend of Britain. On the contrary, I think he is one of those good Frenchmen who have a traditional antagonism ingrained in French hearts by centuries of war against the English. On his way back from Syria in the summer of 1941 through the French Central and West African Colonies, he left a trail of Anglophobia behind him. On 25 August 1941, he gave an interview to the correspondent of the *Chicago*

Daily News at Brazzaville in which he suggested that England coveted the African colonies of France and said: 'England is afraid of the French fleet. What in effect England is carrying out is a wartime deal with Hitler in which Vichy serves as a go-between.' He explained that Vichy served Germany by keeping the French people in subjection and England by keeping the fleet out of German hands. All this and much more was very ungrateful talk, but we have allowed no complaint of ours to appear in public.

Again this year in July, General de Gaulle wished to visit Syria. He promised me before I agreed to facilitate his journey, which I was very well able to stop, that he would behave in a helpful and friendly manner, but no sooner did he get to Cairo than he adopted a most hectoring attitude and in Syria his whole object seemed to be to foment ill-will between the British military and Free French civil administrations and state the French claims to rule Syria . . . although it had been agreed that after the war and as much as possible even during the war, the Syrians are to enjoy their independence.

I continue to maintain friendly personal relations with General de Gaulle and I help him as much as I possibly can. I feel bound to do this because he stood up against the men of Bordeaux and their base surrender at a time when all resisting will-power had quitted France. All the same, I could not recommend you to base all your hopes and confidence upon him, and still less to assume at this stage that it is our duty to place, so far as we have the power, the destiny of France in his hands. Like the President in the telegram I have read, we seek to base ourselves on the will of the entire French nation rather than any sectional manifestations, even the most worthy.[43]

De Gaulle never heard of this vengeful broadside, and it was just as well. But the General had not failed to note a marked change in Churchill's attitude during the past few weeks, as he confided to Mr Trygve Lie, the Norwegian Foreign Minister. The latter noted in his report to the Norwegian government: 'De Gaulle was also dissatisfied with Mr Churchill; he mentioned that he had seen him four times since the Darlan agreement, and each time (Churchill) had shown himself more submissive in his attitude towards the Americans.'[44]

De Gaulle was of course extremely bitter at the Americans for having reinstated Vichy in North Africa. In several broadcasts, he stressed that the Fighting French, who meant to stand for the honour of France, could have nothing to do with a notorious collaborator and traitor. Although in this affair the Americans were opposing him actively and Churchill backed him less and less, de

Gaulle had many other allies in his crusade against the Darlan deal: he had received innumerable telegrams of support from resistance organizations in France, for whom Darlan was a sworn enemy; he had the wholehearted backing of all the exile governments in London, who feared that the Americans would likewise co-operate with the Mussert, Degrelle, Nedić and other Quislings after the liberation of their own countries. In addition, de Gaulle, as we know, could count on the discreet but active sympathy of Anthony Eden, who understood much better than the Prime Minister how disastrous the American initiative had been from a moral and psychological point of view. This sympathy and understanding was in fact to prove an invaluable asset for the Free French cause until the very end of the war. Finally, there was another support for de Gaulle that was less discreet but just as efficient: that of the British press, which continued to denounce the Darlan deal with un-diminished ferocity. By the middle of December, even *The Times* had joined the fray, and it stressed the 'grave misgivings aroused . . . by Darlan's own past record and recent pretensions'.[45]

By that time, the press campaign against the 'temporary expedient' was also gathering momentum on the other side of the Atlantic. Reports were now coming in that Gaullists, Jews, and officers who had helped the Allies during 'Torch' were once again being persecuted in North Africa. The men of Vichy, the German sympathizers, the anti-British and anti-American officers had been reinstated, while Axis agents were crossing the Algerian and Moroccan borders entirely unhindered. In the United States, this was splendid material for the press and for the President's opponents. Roosevelt knew it perfectly well, and he was highly embarrassed. His statements on the 'temporary expedient' had evidently failed to disarm the criticism, especially as Admiral Darlan now seemed more powerful than ever in Algeria and Morocco. To be sure, the President said privately that he would soon get rid of him, while stating publicly that he 'would certainly receive General de Gaulle if he came to Washington', but that was not enough to calm the political storm that was threatening his administration during the last month of 1942.

By that time, however, Admiral Darlan's position in North Africa was not as strong as it appeared from the outside: Marshal Pétain had disavowed him, the Gaullists were denouncing him, the Giraudists hated him, the British despised him, the Americans publicly described him as a 'Temporary Expedient', and in Algiers, numerous factions were plotting against him. Among these were the Monarchists assembled around the Comte de Paris, who thought he could regain his throne if Darlan disappeared, and had many contacts with several other factions in Algiers, including the clergy and the Gaullists. In fact, a Fighting French emissary, General d'Astier de la Vigerie, reached Algiers on 20 December. There, he had a stormy meeting with Admiral Darlan. But he also had prolonged contacts with several other circles, first and foremost with some Monarchist members of the clergy.

General d'Astier left Algiers four days later and returned to London, where de Gaulle was becoming increasingly impatient with the turn of events in North Africa and the disunity among Frenchmen. He was also submerged by discouragement at times, and he had even confided to Charles Peake six days earlier that he was thinking of disbanding his organization.[46] Whether he really meant it is difficult to say, but by 24 December, this was already irrelevant; for on that day, it was learned that Admiral Darlan had been assassinated in Algiers by a young Monarchist named Fernand Bonnier de la Chapelle.

CHAPTER 10

Shotgun Wedding

Rarely in recent history can a political assassination have been so unanimously condemned and so universally welcomed as the abrupt dispatch of Admiral Darlan on Christmas Eve, 1942. For President Roosevelt – who denounced the murder – it afforded a very acceptable solution to the thorny problem of the 'temporary Expedient', which had caused so much agitation in the American press. Of course, the attempt by the Comte de Paris to replace Darlan was immediately brushed aside; what would the American elector say if the President of the United States helped to restore monarchy in France? But when it was announced shortly thereafter that General Giraud had been appointed High Commissioner and Commander-in-Chief in French Africa by a Vichyite imperial council composed of Boisson, Chatel, Noguès, and Bergeret, Roosevelt had every cause for satisfaction; Giraud, unlike Darlan, was not compromised with the Germans, he had an impeccable record as a soldier, little interest in politics and no ties with de Gaulle. Neither, in fact, was Giraud's nomination a pure coincidence; Churchill later wrote that 'indirect though decisive pressure was exerted by the American authorities to achieve the appointment of Giraud to supreme . . . political power in North Africa'[1] – and that was almost an understatement. Should any other competent French administrators be needed in North Africa, Roosevelt felt that he could provide them himself, and in fact, Marcel Peyrouton, Vichy Ambassador in Argentina, was asked by the State Department to serve as Governor-General of Algeria. To be sure, he had been Vichy Minister of the Interior, but that did not trouble the President. Besides, Roosevelt would supervise the whole setting himself when he came to Casablanca in mid-January for the 'Symbol' conference with Churchill.

Winston Churchill, behind an equally virtuous indignation at the

Christmas Eve assassination, was in fact as relieved as the President. Having sided with him after the agreement with Darlan, Churchill had had to share the barrage of criticism aimed at American policy in North Africa, and had found it distinctly uncomfortable. Now, as he writes in his memoirs, 'Darlan's murder, however criminal, relieved the Allies of their embarrassment at working with him, and at the same time left them with all the advantages he had been able to bestow during the vital hours of the Allied landings.'[2] Churchill was also quite satisfied with the appointment of Giraud, though not for the same reasons; here at last was a chance to bring unity between Frenchmen in London and in North Africa, and to form a 'French nucleus, solid and united',[3] which would also be easier to deal with than the London committee and its irascible leader. To Churchill's added satisfaction, General de Gaulle had no objections to conferring with Giraud, thus making a North African settlement possible at last.

After having called Darlan's assassination a 'detestable crime'[4], de Gaulle had no reason either to be dissatisfied with the turn of events: the main obstacle to unity had been removed, and a strong national French authority could now be set up. Besides, de Gaulle was quite prepared to give General Giraud the command of all French troops fighting for the liberation of France. On 25 December, he sent Giraud a telegram calling for the establishment of a national authority; it ended with these words: 'I propose, mon Général, that you should meet me as soon as possible on French soil, either in Algeria or in Chad, in order to study the means of grouping together under a provisional central authority all French forces inside and outside the country and all French territories which are in a position to fight for the liberation and the salvation of France.'[5] General de Gaulle was aware that Giraud was backed by President Roosevelt, who had no sympathy for the Free French; but de Gaulle was to leave on 26 December for a long-delayed meeting in Washington with the American President, and he was confident that he would succeed in altering Roosevelt's point of view.

Nothing, however, was to go according to plan. De Gaulle was unable to leave at the appointed date on account of 'bad weather', and the next day, he received a note from the American government announcing that the trip was indefinitely postponed by decision of the President. There was no reply from Giraud either, and on 27 December, de Gaulle had an interview with Churchill which 'painfully impressed him', as he later confided to Soustelle. Churchill had told him bluntly that he would do nothing to oppose American policy, even if Washington handed over all of French Africa to General Giraud alone.[6] Finally, when General Giraud's answer arrived on 29 December, it proved to be most unsatisfactory: 'Owing to the deep emotion aroused . . . in North Africa by the recent assassination, the atmosphere is at present unfavourable to a meeting between us.'[7] De Gaulle answered him on 1 January that 'the unification of the empire as a whole and of all French forces in contact with the resistance must not be postponed' and offered to meet Giraud elsewhere than in Algiers, for example in Fort-Lamy, Brazzaville or Beirut.

De Gaulle, however, had few illusions: Roosevelt's attitude, Churchill's statements, Giraud's reply, the latest events in North Africa where several prominent Gaullists had just been arrested, all seemed to indicate that Giraud, with American backing and British connivance, intended to exclude the Free French from North Africa; De Gaulle therefore reacted in a characteristic and by now familiar way: through the British and American press, he appealed to public opinion; after a first broadcast on 28 December and numerous private communiqués, de Gaulle issued the following declaration on 2 January 1943:

> Internal confusion continues to grow in North Africa and in French Equatorial Africa. The reason for this confusion is that French authority has no solid base there since the collapse of Vichy, as Fighting France is kept away from these French possessions. . . . The way to remedy this confusion is to establish in North Africa and in French Equatorial Africa, as in all other French overseas territories, an enlarged provisional central authority . . . on 25 December, in agreement with the National Committee and with the Empire Defence Council, I suggested to General Giraud that we met at once and in French territory, to discuss means of achieving this end. I believe, in fact, that France's position and the course of the war in general, will brook no delay.[8]

The declaration, revealing de Gaulle's efforts towards unity and Giraud's dilatory attitude, was extremely embarrassing to the British government; Winston Churchill tried vainly to delay its publication; Sir Alexander Cadogan was more successful in obtaining a slight, but not unimportant, modification: the passage 'Fighting French is kept away from those French possessions', was replaced by the more innocuous 'Fighting France is not officially represented in those French possessions'. Even in its amended form, the declaration had the effect of a bombshell; in fact, it was to set off an impressive series of chain reactions in Britain and the United States.

President Roosevelt and the State Department had hoped that Admiral Darlan's disappearance would put an end to the violent press campaign which, ever since mid-November 1942, had denounced the Machiavellism and immorality of American policy. But de Gaulle's public and private statements after 25 December were taken up by the British press, and soon relayed to the American press, thus giving rise to yet another wave of indignation on both sides of the Atlantic; in early January 1943, there was a tremendous current of sympathy for the solitary plight of General de Gaulle and his 'gallant Fighting French'; while the State Department was swamped with a deluge of abusive mail which soon dwarfed the huge pile accumulated after the St Pierre et Miquelon affair.

The first to react to this new barrage of criticism was predictably Secretary of State Cordell Hull, a favourite target of press criticism and public indignation since his unfortunate anti-Gaullist utterances of December 1941. This time, the Secretary of State laid the blame for the press attacks squarely on the British; on 5 January, he sent the following message to the Foreign Office:

> In the absence of Lord Halifax, I called in Sir Ronald Campbell on 31 December and told him that many of us in the government were becoming concerned seriously about the development of what apparently was British policy regarding such questions as the case of Darlan, particularly concerning the way it is exploited by the British radio and press and persons in the British government who are associated with de Gaulle publicity. I made the statement that this kind of propaganda was directly aimed at arousing bitterness against the United States government, was distinctly harmful, and resentment was felt by many people in the United States who were interested much more in driving the Axis out of Africa than in hair-pulling about personal political rivalries among the French.[9]

There was another message on 7 January, from which it appeared clearly that anger was getting the better of the Secretary of State's sound judgement:

> I told Lord Halifax . . . that this fanfare in support of de Gaulle's political aspirations was carried on while the battle for a great part of Africa and the western Mediterranean area had become increasingly

serious, and was forcing the American and French generals in command to take out time from their essential military duties to go to the rear to calm a confused situation and discuss the political aspirations of de Gaulle. I said in conclusion that continuing British support for de Gaulle's endeavours for political preferment at the expense of the prosecution of the African battle would give rise soon to differences between our two countries.[10]

Roosevelt was also stung by the press campaigns, but being first and foremost a politician, he was mostly concerned with the damage it could do to his democratic image in the country. Although Roosevelt had not the slightest interest in promoting French unity, it began to dawn on him that de Gaulle could not be entirely excluded from the Algiers set-up and he accordingly instructed Robert Murphy in Algiers to devise a merger scheme associating the General with the North African administration – in a subordinate position of course. Meanwhile, Cordell Hull continued to express his indignation to the unfortunate British diplomats in London: 'I insist,' he said on 7 January to Sir Ronald Campbell, 'that where there is a plain and palpable interference with the prosecution of the North African campaign by pure brazen politics it is high time, in my opinion, that this should receive the serious attention of the British government.'[11]

Churchill was by then faced with an uncomfortable situation: on the one hand, he valued his relations with the United States above everything else, and he would have liked nothing better than to see the cumbersome General sink into oblivion. But the old problem remained; Churchill had solemnly pledged to support de Gaulle in 1940, and he could not go back on his word. A few new problems had also emerged in the meantime, which further complicated the situation: the Darlan episode in North Africa had enormously increased de Gaulle's prestige, the General now had very substantial backing in France, and British public opinion, not to speak of parliamentary opinion, was now overwhelmingly in his favour; any measure taken against him would hence be detrimental not only to France, but to the Prime Minister's own position as well. There was no question of muzzling the press either, although the Foreign Office did all in its power to discourage pro-de Gaulle outbursts in Parliament.[12] Last but not least, the situation in North Africa was highly disturbing by the beginning of January: all Vichy administrators were being reinstated, the pro-German collaborationists reappeared, the Gaullists were thrown in jail, the dreaded Service d'Ordre Legionnaire still held sway over the population, communications with Vichy were maintained, and Vichy legislation remained in force. In England, press criticism of the British government for tolerating this state of affairs and backing American policy in North Africa mounted correspondingly.

Faced with this situation, Churchill, advised by Anthony Eden, could only do one thing: continue to press for the establishment of a single authority in North Africa, which would replace the French National Committee and Giraud's administration; after all, as he wrote to Eden, 'The French cannot be wholly denied some form of national expression in their present phase.'[13] Thus Churchill and the Foreign Office continued to encourage a meeting between de Gaulle and Giraud, and the Right Honourable Harold Macmillan, who had just been appointed Minister Resident at Allied Headquarters in Algiers, was instructed to work towards the same goal. Apart from that, His Majesty's government could only assure the British press, public and Parliament that no effort was being spared to bring about a merger in North Africa, and also try to attenuate the State Department's obsessive Gaullophobia and suspicion of British policy. Anthony Eden had to bear all this in mind when he received the American Chargé d'Affaires on 8 January to give him the British government's reply to the two telegrams sent by Secretary of State Hull. Eden later wrote:

> I said that there were several things in these two telegrams which I must call in question. I fear that Mr Hull did not understand the state of British opinion on these difficult French questions. I had no idea what Mr Hull meant when he spoke of persons in the British government who were associated with de Gaulle publicity. No such person existed. Indeed most of our time was spent in trying to damp down de Gaulle's activities and his publicity. Still less would we be associated, as Mr Hull suggested, with any kind of propaganda which was aimed at arousing bitterness against the United States government. . . . As regards the second telegram . . . I said that my impression was that General Eisenhower had had to return from the front because Darlan had been assassinated, and not to discuss the political aspirations of de Gaulle. In any event . . . we had only one object in this French business, and that was to do all we could to bring Frenchmen together to fight in the war against the Axis. We had no particular brief for de Gaulle, nor did we say necessarily that he should be the leader if the various French factions were to join forces. We were not likely to put obstacles in the way of the acceptance of any

leader that the Free French movement or the French in North Africa could agree to accept. For the rest, we had done everything we could to keep the press quiet on this issue . . . but the task had not always been easy. The British people did not like either Darlan or Vichy, and nothing that any government here could say would alter that point of view. The only way to put matters right between us was to agree firmly upon a policy in this French quagmire.[14]

There was only one place where such an agreement could be reached: Casablanca, where both Churchill and Roosevelt were to proceed with their staffs in the greatest secrecy to discuss their next strategic move in the war.

Winston Churchill arrived at Casablanca on 13 January. President Roosevelt arrived the next day. The conference was to be held on the near-by hill of Anfa, entirely requisitioned by the US Army. The military staffs were to meet in a modern hotel and some elegant villas set in tropical gardens nearby were at the disposal of the Prime Minister and the President. Roosevelt had not really come to Casablanca to discuss French politics; Robert Murphy had been instructed to collaborate with the British representative, Harold Macmillan, in reaching a satisfactory agreement on that matter before the opening of the conference, and the President would concern himself with more worthy and momentous subjects. General Eisenhower, who conferred with him on the first day, was to write in his memoirs:

His optimism and buoyancy, amounting almost to lightheartedness, I attributed to the atmosphere of adventure attached to the Casablanca expedition. Successful in shaking loose for a few days many of the burdens of state, he seemed to experience a tremendous uplift from the fact that he had secretly slipped away from Washington and was engaged in a historic meeting on territory that only two months before had been a battleground. While he recognized the seriousness of the war problems still facing the Allies, much of his comments dealt with the distant future, the post-hostilities tasks, including disposition of colonies and territories. He speculated at length on the possibility of France's regaining her ancient position of prestige and power in Europe and on this point was very pessimistic. As a consequence, his mind was wrestling with the question of methods for controlling certain strategic points in the French Empire which he felt that the country might no longer be able to hold.[15]

Robert Murphy's narrative confirms Eisenhower's impressions on many points:

The tone of the conference was set by President Roosevelt, who repeatedly expressed his delight over this brief escapade from Washington's around-the-clock politics. His mood was that of a schoolboy on vacation, which accounted for his almost frivolous approach to some of the difficult problems with which he dealt. Inside Casablanca's toy suburbia, with its languid climate and exotic atmosphere, two world problems were discussed simultaneously. In one large banquet room at the Anfa Hotel, American and British military chiefs debated global war strategy.[16]

The other subject being discussed was hardly a world problem, though it certainly threatened to become one: during his first conversations with Churchill, Murphy and Macmillan, President Roosevelt learned that public opinion, the press and Parliament in England were expressing increasing indignation over the aftermath of the Darlan deal and the continued exclusion of the Free French from North African affairs. But there was more: Roosevelt was also given the latest American newspaper clippings and magazine articles, most of which acidly and sarcastically denounced his handling of French affairs in North Africa; worse still, some of the columnists and commentators who were the most violent in this respect had always been staunch supporters of his liberal policies at home. Roosevelt immediately sensed the danger of this, and however unwillingly, he settled down to discuss and reorganize French politics with the British Prime Minister in his sumptuous requisitioned villa; to Cordell Hull, he sent the following cable: 'It had been my hope that we could avoid political discussions at this time, but I found on arrival that American and British newspapers had made such a mountain out of rather a small hill that I should not return to Washington without having achieved settlement of this matter.'[17]

Roosevelt had no doubt at all that he could find a solution to the thorny problem of French unity – a solution that would be satisfactory to the French, or, failing that, to American public opinion. But as we have seen, his mood was 'that of a schoolboy on vacation', and he certainly approached this difficult problem in a lighthearted and frivolous way. Hence the solution he proposed to Churchill: 'We'll call Giraud the bridegroom, and I'll produce him from Algiers, and you get the bride, de Gaulle, down from London, and we'll have a shotgun wedding.'[18] It was all disarmingly simple; get the two Frenchmen together, persuade them to unite, and both

Roosevelt and Churchill, posing as benevolent sponsors, would silence their critics at home.

The British Prime Minister was somewhat taken aback; he may have felt that the problem was a bit more complicated than that, or remembered that de Gaulle always loudly denounced Anglo-Saxon intrusions in French affairs. The idea of sponsoring the 'bride' probably did not appeal to him either: the Americans had always over-estimated his influence over de Gaulle. But Roosevelt probably would not understand a refusal to summon the General, and after all, de Gaulle had expressed a desire to meet Giraud. At any rate, Roosevelt could be quite persuasive and Winston Churchill, coming back well after midnight from his second day of discussion with the President, muttered to his private detective W. H. Thompson: 'We have to marry these two somehow!'[19] The very next day, 16 January, Churchill sent the following telegram to General de Gaulle:

> I should be glad if you would come to join me here by first available plane which we shall provide, as it is in my power to bring about a meeting between you and General Giraud under conditions of complete secrecy and with the best prospects. It would be advisable for you to bring Catroux with you as Giraud will want to have somebody, probably Bergeret. The conversations would however proceed between the two French principals unless found otherwise convenient. Giraud will be here on Sunday and I hope weather permitting you will arrive Monday.'[20]

The 'bridegroom', General Giraud, arrived from Algiers on 17 January. His first visit for with President Roosevelt, with whom he had a cordial interview.* Roosevelt said he hoped to see him head the military set-up, 'with General de Gaulle as second in command and some third person as political head of French North Africa'.[21] An hour later, Giraud also visited Churchill in the neighbouring villa; their conversation gives a good idea of Churchill's pre-occupations at the time.

> *Churchill*: I am so glad to see you again! So much has happened since Metz.** But you haven't changed a bit.
> *Giraud*: Neither have you, Mr Prime Minister.

*Giraud asked the President for equipment and arms for three hundred thousand men and Roosevelt agreed. The President was not impressed by Giraud: 'I am afraid we're leaning on a very slender reed. He's a dud as an administrator, he'll be a dud as a leader.' (E. Roosevelt: *A Rendezvous with Destiny*, p.330.)
**Churchill had met Giraud in Metz before the war.

Churchill: That's true. I'm strong. And yet it's hard. But whisky is the water of life. Will you have a whisky?

(Churchill went on to talk about the French fleet in Alexandria, then about Mers-el-Kebir.)

Churchill: But that is the past, let bygones be bygones. Let's talk about the future. Have you heard from de Gaulle?

Giraud: No.

Churchill: Neither have I. It's astonishing. He ought to be here. I gave him all the means to come. He's being pig-headed, naturally. A tough customer, your friend de Gaulle. Do you know him?

Giraud: He served under my orders in Metz.

Churchill: Are you on good terms?

Giraud: Not bad.

Churchill: He's quite a character. I shall never forget that he was the first foreigner, not to say the only one, who didn't despair of England in June 1940. In the interests of France, and in our common interests, I would very much like to see you both reach an agreement. He would then leave London, and settle in Algiers with you. That would be ideal.

Giraud: Of course.

Churchill: But he has to come first. I am going to cable him that you are already here; he ought to arrive any time now. You'll settle your military problems with the General Staff in the meantime. Come and see my maps.[22]

Churchill's uneasiness proved more justified than his optimism; back in London, on 16 January, de Gaulle was unaware that the Prime Minister had left for Africa. He was expecting a new invitation to Washington from President Roosevelt. Giraud's reply to his second telegram had been as unsatisfactory as the first: invoking 'previous commitments', Giraud had written that no meeting was possible before the end of January. De Gaulle, however, felt that he was in a strong position: the illusion of Vichy's independence had been completely dispelled by the events of November 1942, the Foreign Office was giving him a larger measure of support, close contact was now established with the resistance inside France, public opinion in French North Africa was becoming increasingly pro-Gaullist, and General Giraud was known to be incompetent in political matters; only de Gaulle could represent the Republic, and the spirit of French resistance. The only possible solution was therefore to set up an enlarged National Committee in Algiers with de Gaulle as President, while Giraud became Commander-in-Chief of the army; there was no getting away from that. 'The Americans,' he said confidently to Alphand, 'will realize this within a fortnight.'[23] But there was still no letter from President Roosevelt. Instead, on 16 January, there was a call from Anthony Eden, asking de Gaulle to come to the Foreign Office the next morning.

De Gaulle met the Foreign Secretary at noon the next day. Sir Alexander Cadogan was also present at the interview. Eden started by telling the General that he had a highly confidential communication to make to him from the Prime Minister, who was now in North Africa. De Gaulle was then given the text of Churchill's telegram of 16 January, inviting him to Casablanca. Eden later reported:

He read it quietly until he read the name of General Bergeret, when he exclaimed: 'Oh, they are even going to bring that man along,' or something to that effect. When he had finished his reading the General expressed no pleasure at the message. He said that he had wished to meet General Giraud immediately after the assassination of Admiral Darlan, but General Giraud had not then been willing. The time was not now so opportune. Nor did he feel happy at the idea of meeting General Giraud under the auspices of the other two great Allies. He would be too much in the position of a man under pressure to compromise when he knew that he should not compromise.

Eden pointed out the advantages of such a meeting, adding that 'the Prime Minister had gone to considerable pains to arrange this'. 'General de Gaulle,' Eden continues,

said that he understood that the initiative might well be the Prime Minister's, but on the other hand our interests and his might not be precisely the same. We had never been willing to understand that the Fighting French movement was the real force in France today. There was really nothing else except Vichy and Fighting France. General Giraud, who balanced at some place midway between them, held no position at all. . . . Sir A. Cadogan and I contested these statements and asked General de Gaulle whether he now wished to come to terms with General Giraud. He replied that he was prepared to meet General Giraud at Fort Lamy, the two of them alone together. . . . The right course now in General de Gaulle's view was for General Giraud to rally to the Fighting French. . . . I told General de Gaulle that I thought it inconceivable that after the Prime Minister and the President of the United States had agreed to promote this meeting he should be unwilling to go to play his part. I had no doubt myself that the Prime Minister had explained to the President the position of General de Gaulle, and here was an opportunity for himself to do so in person, which was precisely what he had been intending to do by a visit to the United States.

General de Gaulle said that that was a different proposition. If the President wished to see him, he could always call upon him in America, nor could there be any invitation to him to meet anybody on French soil ... General de Gaulle argued that if the victory was to be won for Vichy elements, France would not have won much from the war. He maintained that General Giraud represented very little and repeated his sense of embarrassment which he would feel at being expected to come to terms with him in the presence of two foreign states ... in the end the General undertook to think the matter over and either to come to see me this afternoon or to send me his reply at 3.30 p.m.[24]

De Gaulle did not need long to make up his mind. He later recalled his reflections:

My reaction was unfavourable. Mr Eden no doubt implied that Mr Roosevelt was also in Morocco, where the Allied leaders were holding a conference in order to determine their joint plans. But why, then, had Churchill neglected to tell me so? Why did he not assign any other goal to the invitation than a meeting with Giraud? Why was this invitation sent to me in his name alone? If I had to go to the Anfa conference to enter a race wearing the British colours while the Americans backed their own entry against me, the resulting comedy would be indecent, not to say dangerous.[25]

Without having consulted any member of the committee, the General came back to the Foreign Office at 5 p.m. and handed Eden a note for Mr Churchill – it was a polite but firm refusal:

The message from you which was delivered to me today by Mr Eden was somewhat unexpected. As you know, I have telegraphed several times to General Giraud since Christmas, urging him to meet me. Although the situation has moved since Christmas in the direction which now renders an understanding less easy, I would gladly meet General Giraud in French territory anywhere he likes as soon as he wishes, with all necessary secrecy. I am now sending him an offer to maintain direct liaison between us. I value most highly the sentiments which inspire your message and thank you very heartily for them. Allow me to say, however, that the atmosphere of an exalted Allied forum around the Giraud–de Gaulle conversations as well as the suddenness with which those conversations have been proposed to me, do not seem to me to be the best for an effective agreement. Simple and direct talks between the

French leaders would, in my opinion, be the best design to bring about a useful arrangement. I should like to assure you once again that the French National Committee in no way disassociates the higher interests of France from that of the world and of the United Nations. . . . I am telegraphing again to General Giraud to repeat once more my proposal for an immediate meeting – a proposal to which I have so far received no precise reply.[26]

This telegram was received at Anfa early on 18 January; Churchill was mortified. The refusal of the invitation was already embarrassing by itself, but received in Roosevelt's presence, it was a direct affront. The fact that the President was treating the matter as a trivial competition between them to set up 'a shotgun wedding' did nothing to improve matters. The day before, Roosevelt had sent the following message to Eden: 'I have got the bridegroom, where is the bride?'[27] Now, upon hearing of de Gaulle's refusal, Roosevelt merely laughed, and Robert Murphy writes that he 'rather enjoyed Churchill's discomfiture'.[28] In fact, he implied that Churchill was an irresponsible father unable to discipline an unruly child, and he tremendously enjoyed the image – Churchill much less so. In the process, no one really bothered to examine the reasons for de Gaulle's refusal.

> *Roosevelt:* You've got to get your problem child down here.
> *Churchill:* De Gaulle is on his high horse. I can't move him from London. Jeanne d'Arc complex . . .[29]
>   And again:
> *Roosevelt:* Who pays for de Gaulle's food?
> *Churchill:* Well, the British do.
> *Roosevelt:* Why don't you stop his food and maybe he will come?[30]

Churchill then left the scene to brood in his own villa, and Roosevelt, not fearing to labour the point, dispatched the following telegram to Cordell Hull:

We delivered our bridegroom, General Giraud, who was most co-operative on the impending marriage, and I am sure was ready to go through with it on our terms. However, our friends could not produce the bride, the temperamental lady de Gaulle. She has got quite snooty about the whole idea and does not want to see either of us, and is showing no intention of getting into bed with Giraud. We are going to do the best we can under these circumstances and I think I can bring something out of this that will be pretty good. Giraud gives me the impression of a man who wants to fight and has no great interest in civil affairs.[31]

In fact, Giraud visited Roosevelt at 6 p.m. that evening, and Churchill joined them shortly afterwards; Giraud recalls in his memoirs:

> Mr Churchill presently made his entry . . . he threw his hat on the sofa and grumbled that de Gaulle was making a fuss about coming, under some pretext or other. He would therefore cable London that such an attitude was unacceptable, and that either General de Gaulle came here, or the subsidies paid by the English Treasury to the National Committee would be withheld. If he refused to come to Casablanca, the initial agreement concluded in 1940 between him and His Majesty's government would be cancelled. . . . Mr Roosevelt approved this attitude.[32]

Churchill again went back to his villa and set to work drafting a note to Eden. It read:

> If you think well you should give the following message to de Gaulle from me:
>
> (Begins) I am authorized to say that the invitation to you to come here was from the President of the United States of America as well as from me. I have not yet told General Giraud . . . of your refusal. The consequences of it, if persisted in, will in my opinion be unfavourable for you and your movement. First we are about to make arrangements for North Africa, on which we should have been glad to consult you, but which must otherwise be made in your absence. The arrangements when concluded will have the support of Great Britain and the United States. The fact that you have refused to come to the meeting proposed will in my opinion be almost universally censured by public opinion and serve as a complete answer to any complaints. There can of course be no question of your being invited to visit the United States in the near future if you reject the President's invitation now. My attempts to bridge the difficulties which have existed between your movement and the United States will have definitely failed. I should certainly not be able to renew my exertions in this direction while you remain the leader of the above movement. The position of His Majesty's government towards your movement while you remain at its head will also require to be reviewed. If with your eyes open you reject this unique opportunity we shall endeavour to get on as well as we can without you. The door is still open. [end]
>
> I leave you latitude to make any alterations in the message which you

may think desirable, so long as its seriousness is not impaired. . . . Here I have been all these days fighting de Gaulle's battles and making every arrangement for a good reconciliation between the different sections of Frenchmen. If he rejects the chance now offered I shall feel that his removal from the headship of the Free French movement is essential to the further support of this movement by His Majesty's government. I hope you will put as much of this as you think fit to him. For his own sake you ought to knock him about pretty hard.[33]

In London, Anthony Eden received this message on the morning of 19 January; the Cabinet was summoned for 5 p.m. and informed of its content. By and large, the whole Cabinet agreed that 'de Gaulle had a strong position with the British press and public, and that any suggestion of "Muniching" him would be strongly resented in the country'. It was also found that any repudiation of de Gaulle would shatter French resistance.[34] The Cabinet therefore decided to 'soften down' the message, and this was accordingly done: the somewhat high-handed 'We are about to make arrangements for North Africa, on which we should have been glad to consult you' was replaced by the more democratic 'We should have been glad for you to have participated in these consultations'; the warning that: 'The position of His Majesty's government towards your movement while you remain at its head will also require to be reviewed' was dropped, and the somewhat insignificant conclusion that in case of a new refusal 'we shall endeavour to get on as well as we can without you' was replaced by the more diplomatic 'the consequences of the future of the Free French movement cannot but be grave in the extreme'.[35]

Thereupon, Anthony Eden asked de Gaulle to come to the Foreign Office, but the General answered that he was otherwise engaged. Shortly after 6 p.m., René Pleven came to see Lord Strang: he told him that de Gaulle anticipated that the Prime Minister's message would be sharp, and he couldn't trust himself not to burst out with remarks that he would afterwards regret.[36] Eden therefore had the Prime Minister's 'softened' telegram delivered to de Gaulle instead.

The General, 'without paying much attention to the threats contained in the message – which after many experiences no longer impressed me much'[37], nevertheless decided that the message was serious enough to be brought before the National Committee. At the committee meeting the next day, de Gaulle showed no enthusiasm for the trip to Anfa, where he 'would be submitted to all sorts of pressures', and 'may even find it impossible to confer alone with Giraud'.[38] However, there was great pressure in favour of the trip from several members of the committee, particularly Catroux and Pleven, and the committee as a whole finally recommended that de Gaulle accept the invitation, if only 'to hear the suggestions that would be made'.[39] On the afternoon of 20 January, de Gaulle finally decided, somewhat reluctantly, in favour of acceptance: 'I will go to Morocco, because of Roosevelt's invitation. I wouldn't have gone for Churchill alone.'[40]

At 5 p.m., de Gaulle went to see Eden, told him that he now agreed to go and gave him the following message for the Prime Minister:

> It appears from your second message that you and President Roosevelt are there with the object of coming to some agreement with General Giraud over the future of French North Africa. You are kind enough to propose my taking part in the discussions, adding however that the agreements will be concluded without my participation if need be . . . the decisions that have been taken without the knowledge of Fighting France concerning North and West Africa as well as the upholding in these regions of an authority stemming from Vichy, have led to an internal situation which does not seem to satisfy the Allies completely, and which, I can assure you, does not satisfy France at all. President Roosevelt and you are asking me presently to take part, without warning, in discussions of which I know neither the programme nor the conditions, and during which I will be led to discuss matters concerning the whole future of the French Empire and of France itself. I recognize, however, despite these questions of form, grave though they may be, that the general situation of the war and the position in which France is temporarily placed cannot allow me to refuse to meet the President of the United States and his Britannic Majesty's Prime Minister. I therefore agree to join in your meeting. I shall be accompanied by General Catroux and Admiral d'Argenlieu.[41]

At Anfa on 21 January, the conference was drawing to an end, and the Chiefs-of-Staff had finally reached an agreement on future strategy: immediately after the liberation of Tunisia, the next target would be Sicily; the British planners had finally persuaded the Americans, who had wanted a landing in France for 1943 instead. But Churchill had another reason to be satisfied: that evening, in the President's villa, Elliott Roosevelt was talking with his father when . . . 'Winston bounced in: "wanted to tell you" – he beamed – "de Gaulle. It begins to look as though we'll be successful in persuading him to come down and join our talks." FDR said nothing for a moment, then moved on towards his bedroom door: "Congratulations, Winston. I always knew you'd be able to swing it.'"[42]

De Gaulle's plane landed at Fedala, near Casablanca, at 11 a.m. on 22 January. With the General were Catroux, d'Argenlieu, Palewski, and Hettier de Boislambert. They were received at the airport in great secrecy by Colonel de Linarès, Mr Codrington, and the American General Wilbur, whom de Gaulle had known previously at the *Ecole supérieure de Guerre*. De Gaulle's impressions were decidedly negative: no troops presented arms, but there were American sentries everywhere; he was driven to Anfa in an American car, lodged in a villa requisitioned by the Americans, with American soldiers assigned to household tasks, in a conference area encircled by a barbed wire fence and guarded by American sentries – all this on a territory under French sovereignty. 'In short,' de Gaulle later wrote, 'it was captivity;' it was even more: 'a sort of insult'.[43]

De Gaulle was therefore in an ugly mood when he arrived at the luncheon given in his honour by General Giraud. He began with a sarcastic – 'Bonjour, mon Général. I see that the Americans are treating you well!'[44] – And then he exploded, 'What is this? I offered to meet you four times, and we must now meet among foreigners in this barbed wire compound? Don't you realize how distasteful this is from a national point of view?'[45]

De Gaulle recalls however that the ensuing meal was 'cordial'; yet it began inauspiciously enough: upon being informed that the house was guarded by American sentries, de Gaulle refused to sit down until they had been replaced by French soldiers.[46] After the meal, whatever cordiality there was quickly disappeared. Giraud stated that he 'was not interested in political matters', that he supported the Vichy 'proconsuls' Noguès, Boisson, Peyrouton and Bergeret, and indicated that although he was determined to fight the Germans, he had nothing against the Vichy regime.[47] As for de Gaulle, he said that he had come most unwillingly, and refused to discuss under Anglo-American supervision. He also had some harsh words for Churchill and Roosevelt.[48] No further meeting was agreed upon, and de Gaulle returned to his villa.

Later in the afternoon, de Gaulle, who had remained indoors 'with calculated reserve', received a visit from Mr Macmillan; the latter finally persuaded him to go and see Churchill at his nearby villa.

'A very stony interview,' Churchill later commented.[49] But de Gaulle gives us a rather more detailed account: 'Upon meeting the Prime Minister, I told him that I would never have come had I known that I would be surrounded, on French soil, by American bayonets. "This is an occupied country!" he cried.'[50]

Churchill countered with an explosion of his own, 'making it clear', as he later wrote, 'that if he (de Gaulle) continued to be an obstacle, we should not hesitate to break with him finally'.[51] In fact, Churchill growled in his approximate French: *'Si vous m'obstaclerez, je vous liquiderai!'*

After which, de Gaulle remembers,

> both of us having calmed down, we came to the heart of the matter. The Prime Minister informed me that he and the President had agreed on a solution to the problem of the French Empire. General Giraud and General de Gaulle would be set up as joint chairmen of a governing committee on which they and all the other members would enjoy equal status in every respect. But Giraud would exercise supreme military command, since the United States, who would supply the reunified French army, were unwilling to deal with anyone else. 'Undoubtedly,' Mr Churchill remarked, 'my friend General Georges could be added to your group as third president.' As for Noguès, Boisson, Peyrouton and Bergeret, they would retain their positions and join the committee. 'The Americans had now accepted them and wanted them to be trusted.'
>
> I replied to Mr Churchill that the solution might seem adequate at the quite respectable level of American sergeant majors, but that I did not believe that he himself could take it seriously. As for me, I was obliged to take into account what remained of French sovereignty. I had, as he well knew, the highest consideration for him and for Roosevelt, but could by no means recognize their authority to deal with the question of power in the French Empire. The Allies had, without me, and indeed against me, set up the system now functioning in Algiers. Apparently finding it only half satisfactory, they now proposed to submerge Fighting France in it. But Fighting France would have none of it; if it must disappear it preferred to do so with honour.
>
> Mr Churchill did not seem to grasp the ethical aspect of the problem. 'Look at my own government,' he said. 'When I originally formed it, appointed as I was for having long fought the spirit of Munich, I included all our most notorious Municheers in it. Well, they played the game so well that today you can't tell them from the rest.'
>
> To speak in that way, I replied, you must have lost sight of what has happened to France. As for me, I am not a politician trying to set up a cabinet and find a majority in Parliament.

The Prime Minister urged me nevertheless to consider the project he had just explained to me. 'Tonight,' he added, 'you will confer with the President of the United States, and you will see that he and I are at one on this matter.'[52]

In his diaries, Churchill's doctor, Lord Moran, describes what followed:

When at last they emerged from the little sitting-room in our villa, the Prime Minister stood in the hall watching the Frenchman stalk down the garden path with his head in the air. Winston turned to us with a whimsical smile: 'His country has given up fighting, he himself is a refugee, and if we turn him down he is finished. Well, just look at him! Look at him!' he repeated. 'He might be Stalin, with two hundred divisions behind his words. I was pretty rough with him. I made it quite plain that if he could not be more helpful we were done with him.'
    'How,' I asked, 'did he like that?'
    'Oh,' the Prime Minister replied, 'he hardly seemed interested. My advances and my threats met with no response.'[53]

That evening, President Roosevelt was giving a dinner for the Sultan of Morocco. Churchill, according to Hopkins, 'was glum and seemed to be real bored' – possibly because no alcohol could be consumed. After dinner, Churchill told Roosevelt that he had 'handled de Gaulle pretty roughly'.[54] He suggested that Roosevelt should postpone his meeting with the General until the next morning, but on Hopkins's advice, the President decided to receive him that same evening.

Late in the evening, de Gaulle met President Roosevelt for the first time. Harry Hopkins wrote that the General 'arrived cold and austere'.[55] Elliott Roosevelt, who was also there, added, 'He stalked in . . . giving us the impression that thunder clouds were billowing around his narrow skull.'[56] The President, dressed in white and sitting on a large sofa, was all smiles and bade the General sit next to him.[57] De Gaulle was later to write: 'That evening we vied in good manners, but by mutual agreement we maintained a certain vagueness on the question of France. He sketched lightly the same figure that Churchill had outlined so heavily and gently gave me to understand that such a solution would prevail in the end because he himself had decided upon it.'[58] And again: 'Roosevelt showed himself eager to reach a meeting of minds, using charm rather than reason to convince me. . . .'[59] Elliott Roosevelt's narrative confirms this impression: '"I am sure that we will be able to assist your great country in re-establishing her destiny," said father, all charm. His visitor merely grunted. "And I assure you it will be an honour for my country to participate in the undertaking." "It is nice of you to say so," said the Frenchman icily.'[60]

But Elliott Roosevelt was not present when the discussion began in earnest, as the President had insisted on speaking to de Gaulle privately. One of Roosevelt's aides, Captain McCrea, nevertheless took a few notes, 'from a relatively poor point of vantage – a crack in a door slightly ajar'.[60bis] The President began by saying that 'the whole purpose of his meeting with Mr Churchill was "to get on with the war", and supply an answer to the question, "Where do we go on from here?"' He proceeded to discuss the political situation in North Africa, and remarked with considerable understatement that 'he supposed that the collaboration on the part of General Eisenhower with Admiral Darlan had been the source of some wonderment to General de Gaulle'. Nevertheless, 'he thoroughly approved of General Eisenhower's decision in this matter and real progress was being made when the admiral met his untimely death'. As for the exercise of sovereignty in North Africa, 'none of the contenders for power in North Africa had the right to say that he, and only he, represented the sovereignty of France. . . . the Allied nations fighting in French territory at the moment were fighting for the liberation of France and they should hold the political situation in "trusteeship" for the French people.' In other words, the President stated that France was in the position of a little child unable to look out and fend for itself and that in such a case, a court would appoint a trustee to do the necessary. 'The only course of action that would save France,' the President concluded, 'was for all of her loyal sons to unite to defeat the enemy, and when the war was ended, victorious France could once again assert the political sovereignty which was hers over her homeland and the empire.'[60ter]

From his uncomfortable vantage point behind the crack in the door, Captain McCrea was having some trouble overhearing the conversation: 'In view of the fact that General de Gaulle talked in so low a tone of voice as to be inaudible to me, I cannot supply any comments made by him.' In fact, de Gaulle 'pointed out delicately that the national will had already made its choice and that, sooner or later, the authority established in the empire and ultimately in metropolitan France would be chosen by France alone'.[61]

There were in fact several other witnesses to this 'private conversation', as Harry Hopkins noted that day:

In the middle of the conference I noticed that the whole of the Secret Service detail was behind the curtain and above the gallery in the living-room and at all doors leading into the room and I glimpsed a tommy-gun in the hands of one. I left the conference and went out to talk to the Secret Service to find out what it was all about and found them all armed to the teeth with, perhaps, a dozen tommy-guns among the group. I asked them what it was all about. They told me they could not take any chances on anything happening to the President. None of this hocus-pocus had gone on when Giraud saw the President and it was simply an indication of the atmosphere in which de Gaulle found himself at Casablanca. To me the armed Secret Service was unbelievably funny and nothing in Gilbert and Sullivan could have beaten it. Poor General de Gaulle, who probably did not know it, was covered by guns throughout his whole visit. . . . *

But Roosevelt and de Gaulle took the greatest care to avoid a clash, and after half an hour, both having made their point, they parted 'satisfied and relaxed'.[62] On the way back to his villa, de Gaulle confided to Hettier de Boislambert: 'You see, I have met a great statesman today. I think we got along and understood each other well.'[63]

Nothing of the sort happened the next day during de Gaulle's second meeting with Giraud. The latter, not surprisingly, was in favour of Roosevelt's and Churchill's plan, and reaffirmed that he was not interested in politics. De Gaulle sought to convince him that he had compromised his political position by pledging allegiance to Marshal Pétain and that he should join Fighting France in the capacity of Commander-in-Chief. Giraud, however, insisted on having the dominant role, with Fighting France joining him instead of the reverse. Finally, the two generals agreed only to establish a liaison between them and parted frigidly.

It was by now obvious that Churchill and Roosevelt had not succeeded in bringing the two French factions together. But it must also be remembered that the President's main goal was quite different: he wanted to *show* the world – more precisely American public opinion – that he had brought the two generals together, thus silencing his most vocal critics at home and abroad; a well-worded communiqué would do just that, and the President spent part of the

*Sherwood: *Roosevelt and Hopkins*, p. 685.

night drafting it with Robert Murphy and Winston Churchill. The latter would certainly have preferred a real reconciliation between the two generals; but this now seemed impossible and besides, he, Churchill, also had a public opinion to satisfy; he thus followed the President's lead. According to the draft communiqué, the two generals were to proclaim themselves in agreement with 'the principles of the United Nations' and announce their intention of forming a joint committee to administer the French Empire during the war.[64] Both generals would act as joint chairmen. De Gaulle and Giraud were invited to authorize the communiqué. Giraud readily accepted. There remained to convince de Gaulle.

General de Gaulle had learned the day before that Roosevelt had completely neglected French interests in his talk with the Sultan of Morocco, that, during a conversation with Giraud, Churchill had arbitrarily estimated the value of a pound sterling in North Africa at 250 French francs – instead of the 176 Francs agreed upon in London – and that Churchill and Roosevelt had allegedly agreed to bestow upon General Giraud 'the right and duty of acting as a trustee for French interests, military, economic and financial, which are or which hereafter become associated with the movement of liberation in French North and West Africa'.* To crown it all, de Gaulle had just been informed that the conference would end the next day – and not once had he been consulted by the Allies on military matters. The General was still smarting under these 'insults' the next morning when Robert Murphy and Harold Macmillan submitted to him the draft communiqué; de Gaulle wrote in his memoirs:

> the formula was no doubt too vague to commit us to much, but it had the triple disadvantage of being dictated by the Allies, of implying that I renounced whatever was not merely the administration of the empire, and lastly of pretending that we had reached an agreement, when in fact we had not. After finding out the opinion – unanimously negative – of my four companions, I informed the messengers that an enlargement of French national authority could not be brought about by the intervention of a foreign power, no matter how high and how friendly. Nevertheless, I agreed to see the President and the Prime Minister before the conference was concluded that afternoon.[65]

Churchill was by then most unfavourably disposed towards

---

*In fact, Churchill had not approved the text; he had not even seen it. When he was informed at the beginning of February, he had it substantially altered.

General de Gaulle: the General had refused to come to Anfa, when he finally came he refused to get along with Giraud, then he refused the Anglo-American plan for French unity, and now he was even refusing a face-saving communiqué designed to attenuate the effects of his refusal. There were no doubt occasions when the Prime Minister understood de Gaulle's lonely effort to uphold France's honour and sovereignty against foreign encroachments; this, however, was no such occasion: he, the British Prime Minister, was being ridiculed in front of the President of the United States by a man who was widely considered as his 'creature'. There was not the slightest excuse for de Gaulle's behaviour. The fact that he may have been right was in fact an aggravating circumstance in the Prime Minister's eyes. To say that Churchill was unfavourably disposed is an understatement: he was beside himself with rage.

General de Gaulle's farewell visit to the Prime Minister was therefore uncommonly animated, even by Churchillian standards; the latter chose to omit any reference to it in his memoirs. Not so General de Gaulle:

'Owing to Mr Churchill's dispositions, we had an extremely bitter interview. It was to be the roughest of all our wartime encounters. The Prime Minister showered me with bitter reproaches in which I could see nothing but an alibi for his own embarrassment. He declared that on his return to London he would publicly accuse me of having blocked the agreement, would rouse public opinion in his country against me and would appeal to that of France.'[66] The Prime Minister added that if de Gaulle did not sign the communiqué, he would 'denounce him in the Commons and on the radio'. De Gaulle was unimpressed and answered that the Prime Minister was 'free to dishonour himself'.[67] 'I merely replied,' de Gaulle later wrote, 'that my friendship for him and my attachment to the British alliance led me to deplore his attitude. In order to satisfy America at any cost, he was espousing a cause unacceptable to France, disquieting to Europe and regrettable for England.'[68] Whereupon de Gaulle walked off to see the President.

In the meantime, Harry Hopkins, after having seen Macmillan, told the President that de Gaulle objected to the communiqué. 'He was none too happy about it,' Hopkins wrote,

> but I urged him not to disavow de Gaulle even though he was acting badly. Believing as I did and still do that Giraud and de Gaulle want to work together I urged the President to be conciliatory and not to beat de

Gaulle too hard. If there is any beating to be done let Churchill do it because the whole Free French movement is financed by them. I told the President I thought we would get an agreement on a joint statement issued by de Gaulle and Giraud – and a picture of the two of them . . . Giraud arrived at 11.30 – de Gaulle was with Churchill by this time. Giraud wanted a confirmation on supplying his army but the President referred him to Eisenhower. The conference went well. Giraud will play ball with de Gaulle. Giraud goes out, de Gaulle and his staff come in, de Gaulle calm and confident – I liked him – but no joint communiqué and Giraud must be under him. The President expressed his point of view in pretty powerful terms and made an urgent plea to de Gaulle to come to terms with Giraud to win the war and liberate France.[69]

The President, de Gaulle later recalled,

told me how sorry he was that agreement between Frenchmen should remain uncertain and that he himself had not been able to prevail upon me to accept even the text of a communiqué. 'In human affairs,' he said, 'the public must be offered some drama. The news of your meeting with General Giraud in the midst of a conference in which both Churchill and I are taking part, if it were to be accompanied by a joint declaration of the French leaders – even only a theoretical agreement – would produce the dramatic effect required.'

'Let me handle it,' I replied. 'There will be a communiqué, even though it cannot be yours.' Thereupon I presented my colleagues to the President and he introduced me to his.[70]

'At this moment,' Hopkins notes, 'the Secret Service called me up to tell me Churchill was outside. He was talking to Giraud, saying good-bye to him. Churchill walked in and I went after Giraud believing that if the four of them could get into a room together we could get an agreement. This was nearly 12 o'clock and the press conference was to be at that hour. The President was surprised at seeing Giraud but took it in his stride.'[71]

And de Gaulle recalls: 'Mr Churchill, General Giraud and their suites came in, followed by a crowd of military leaders and Allied officials. While everyone was gathering round the President, Churchill loudly reiterated his diatribe and his threats against me, with the obvious intention of flattering Roosevelt's disappointed vanity.'[72]

Robert Murphy, who was also present, remembers the Prime Minister's diatribe: 'Churchill, in a white fury over de Gaulle's stubbornness, shook his finger in the General's face. In his inimitable French, with his dentures clicking, Churchill exclaimed: "Mon Général, il ne faut pas obstacler (sic) la guerre!"[73]

The General paid no attention, and neither did Roosevelt. The latter, de Gaulle wrote,

> adopted by contrast the kindest manner in order to make me a last request on which he had set his heart.
>
> 'Would you at least agree,' he said, 'to being photographed beside me and the British Prime Minister, along with General Giraud?'
>
> 'By all means,' I answered, 'for I have the highest regard for this great soldier.'
>
> 'Would you go so far as to shake General Giraud's hand in our presence and in front of the camera?' the President cried.
>
> My answer, in English, was, 'I shall do that for you.' Whereupon Mr Roosevelt, delighted, had himself carried into the garden where four chairs had been prepared beforehand, with innumerable cameras trained on them and several rows of reporters lined up with their pens poised.[74]

And Hopkins noted in his diaries:

> I don't know who was the most surprised – the photographers or de Gaulle – when the four of them walked out – or rather the three of them because the President was carried to his chair. I confess they were a pretty solemn group – the cameras ground out the pictures. The President suggested de Gaulle and Giraud shake hands. They stood up and obliged – some of the cameramen missed it and they did it again. Then the Frenchmen and their staffs left and Churchill and the President were left sitting together in the warm African sun – thousands of miles from home – to talk to the correspondents of war and the waging of war.[75]

What followed was the famous 'Unconditional Surrender' statement. But de Gaulle had already left the scene. Before flying back to London, he wrote a draft communiqué which Giraud accepted; it began thus: 'We have met, we have talked', and went on to affirm the faith of both generals 'in the victory of France and the triumph of human liberties'. There was also a concrete element: a permanent liaison was to be established between them.[76] In spite of the unfortunate 'Joan of Arc' episode,* de Gaulle flew back to

*During their first talk on 22 January, the President had told de Gaulle that he could not recognize him as sole political leader of France, because he, de Gaulle, had not been elected by the French people. De Gaulle replied that Joan of Arc had drawn her legitimacy from her

London convinced that he had made some impression on the
American President. In a letter to General Leclerc shortly after his
return to Britain, de Gaulle wrote: 'My conversations with
Roosevelt were satisfactory. I have the impression that he has found
out what Fighting France is.'[77] There may have been a large amount
of wishful thinking in this appreciation, but there was at least as
much on the President's part when he believed after Anfa that he had
decisively helped to solve the 'French problem'. Roosevelt seems to
have been taken in by the artificial reconciliation he had staged at
Anfa, and believed for several weeks thereafter that he could
successfully 'manage' General de Gaulle.[78]

Winston no longer entertained any such illusions. The conference
at Casablanca had been a great success for British strategy; it had
also been a personal defeat for Churchill's diplomacy in French
affairs. Immediately after the conference, Churchill and Roosevelt
went to Marrakesh. At dinner that same evening, the American
Vice-Consul Kenneth Pendar asked Churchill about de Gaulle. 'He
looked annoyed,' Pendar writes, 'and replied with a typical
Churchillian phrase: "Oh, don't let's speak of him. We call him
Jeanne d'Arc and we're looking for some bishops to burn him."'[79] It
is typical of Churchill that his indignation at de Gaulle's attitude in
no way diminished his concern for France – indeed, having thus

---

action when she took up arms against the invaders. On the morning of the 24th, when
Macmillan reported that de Gaulle's proposal to Giraud was that 'he, de Gaulle, was to be
Clemenceau, and Giraud Foch', FDR exclaimed: 'Yesterday he wanted to be Joan of Arc –
and now he wants to be . . . Clemenceau.' Roosevelt then made up the following story, which
progressively inflated beyond all bounds: to Hull, he said that de Gaulle 'walking up to him
rather stiffly, had remarked: "I am Joan of Arc, I am Clemenceau!"' (Hull, *Memoirs*, Vol. 2,
p.1208.) Roosevelt then told Ambassador Bullit that he had said to de Gaulle: 'General, you
told me the other day you were Jeanne d'Arc and now you say you are Clemenceau. Who are
you?' And de Gaulle had replied: 'I am both.' (Bullitt: *For the President, secret and personal*, p.
568.) Later, FDR confided to others that he had replied to de Gaulle that 'he should make up
his mind which one of these he was really like because he surely could not be like both of them'.
(Sherwood, *Roosevelt and Hopkins*, p. 686.) By the time Kenneth Pendar, the American Vice-
Consul, heard the story 'from high authority', it ran like this: 'President Roosevelt told de
Gaulle that France was in such dire military straits that she needed a General of Napoleonic
calibre. 'Mais je suis cet homme,' said de Gaulle. She was, went on the President, in such a bad
financial state that she also needed a Colbert. 'Mais,' said de Gaulle, simply, 'je suis cet
homme.' Finally, said the President, controlling his amazement, she was so devitalized
politically that she needed a Clemenceau. De Gaulle drew himself up with dignity and said,
'Mais je suis cet homme.' (K. Pendar: *Adventures in Diplomacy*, p. 141.) The story seems to
have been readily accepted because it was told by the President himself. By the time it reached
the press, de Gaulle had also become Louis XIV, Foch, Bayard etc. Before leaving Anfa,
General de Gaulle heard some of the early versions; he was not amused . . .

spoken to Pendar, he turned to Hopkins and said, 'Now, Harry, when you get back, urge on everyone the importance of getting arms over here as quickly as possible. It's the only way to build up the French.'[80] Churchill often said, with tears in his eyes, 'There will always be a France,' and as he had told his doctor two days before: 'France without an army is not France.' At the time he had added: 'De Gaulle is the spirit of that army. Perhaps the last survivor of a warrior race.'[81]

Underneath it all, there is no doubt that Churchill still admired de Gaulle – but he also learned to hate him; although Churchill was a notoriously bad hater, he was to make an exception in this case. As for de Gaulle, he returned to London 'deeply indignant at the treatment he had received from the British Prime Minister'.[82] Hence the relations between Fighting France and her British ally during the next few months promised to be very uncomfortable indeed.

CHAPTER 11

The Winding Road to Unity

By February 1943, the tide of war was beginning to turn against the Axis: in the Pacific, the Japanese had lost the initiative to the Americans after Midway and Guadalcanal; in North Africa, the British had taken Tripoli, and in Russia, the Soviet army had just forced von Paulus to capitulate at Stalingrad. De Gaulle, as we know, had never doubted that the Allies would win the war in the end; he had proclaimed it as early as June 1940. But the General's goal was slightly different: to make sure that France won the war as well; and by February 1943, this goal seemed more remote than ever. In France, under German rule, the Milice and the STO* had just been instituted; Fighting France was reluctantly supported by the British and actively opposed by the United States; French North Africa was under military occupation by the Americans, officiously governed by Vichy administrators and politically represented by a military figurehead, General Giraud, who depended for his support on the Americans and the Vichy administrators; finally, all three combined to keep the Gaullists out of North Africa.

De Gaulle was not overawed by these formidable odds. For him, the important thing in French affairs was the mass of public opinion in France, and he was now convinced that this mass was with him. French resistance movements, ranging from Right-wing to Communist, had indicated their support for de Gaulle, their repudiation of Vichy and their mistrust of Giraud. When French ships from Morocco or Algeria reached English or American ports, hundreds of sailors defected to Fighting France; even in North Africa, de Gaulle perceived a marked evolution of public opinion in favour of his movement. By mid-February, he was planning to send Jean Moulin back to France, with the mission of creating a unified resistance council for the whole country; the council was to be

*Service du Travail Obligatoire: Compulsory Labour Service.

presided over by Jean Moulin himself, acting as de Gaulle's representative, and would form the nucleus of a political body representing resistant France, and one day liberated France. With such a power base, de Gaulle felt confident that Fighting France would triumph in the end – and he acted accordingly.

The General gave a press conference at his London headquarters on 9 February. On the subject of North Africa, he declared: 'What we want, and what France wants, is not an agreement between two generals. That is meaningless. The grave question of North Africa has often been presented as the crystallization of a personal rivalry between two generals. That, I believe, is a bad joke; the stakes are infinitely higher: a union of France's empire for the liberation of France and the realization of the goals set by France herself.' Replying to all those who accused Fighting France of being a political organization, de Gaulle exclaimed: 'No politics? Is there a single state in the world today that wages war for something else than for politics?'

Speaking of Anfa, de Gaulle went out of his way to express his admiration for President Roosevelt as 'the man who has the highest aims in this war'.[1] The United States could give invaluable help to Fighting France, and de Gaulle remained convinced that, in spite of the State Department's hostility, he could remove the misunderstandings that separated him from the President. On 14 February, he wrote to Secretary of State Hull: 'Please convey to the President of the United States the expression of my great pleasure in having established a first contact with him. A Frenchman could not but be deeply touched by his feelings of ardent sympathy for France.'[2]

De Gaulle's unusual cordiality was not extended to the British Prime Minister. In his press conference of 9 February, after having spoken at length of his conversations with the American President, he added: 'As for Mr Churchill, well, we have been waging a difficult war side by side for two years now, and I don't think it would have served any useful purpose to tell him things he ought to know by now.' Not a word had been exchanged between the French leader and the British Prime Minister since their encounter at Anfa, and it seems safe to assume that de Gaulle had not yet forgiven Churchill for his behaviour on that occasion. The General was making plans to visit Free French troops in the Levant, Tripolitaine and Equatorial Africa at the beginning of March. It was also agreed that he would meet General Eisenhower, probably in Tripoli. De Gaulle, as a matter of course, therefore asked the British government for facilities to travel by air to Cairo.

The General had not been informed of Churchill's persistent hostility to his person, and he probably wouldn't have cared even if he had. But the fact remains that Churchill had neither forgotten nor forgiven the affront received at Anfa in Roosevelt's presence. On 9 February, Oliver Harvey wrote in his diary: 'PM has come back even more anti-de Gaulle than when he left – outraged at de Gaulle's slowness in accepting the invitation to Casablanca when he had done everything he could to make him acceptable to the Americans. He now talks of breaking him. Anthony Eden reasoned with him as usual, receiving, again as usual, no help from Attlee who could only nod his head in approval of whatever nonsense PM said.'⁴ But Anthony Eden had an unexpected ally in high places; on 9 February, King George VI wrote in his own diary: 'Prime Minister to lunch. He is furious with de Gaulle over his refusal to accept FDR's invitation to meet him and Giraud. . . . I warned Winston not to be too hasty with de Gaulle and the Free French National Committee. . . . I told Winston I could well understand de Gaulle's attitude, and that of our own people here, who do not like the idea of making friends of those Frenchmen who have collaborated with the Germans.'⁵

Churchill, whose respect for the King knew no limits, must therefore have been in a slightly mellower mood when he met Massigli that same afternoon. Even then, he spoke his whole mind to the French Commissioner for Foreign Affairs, stating that:

> He continued to recognize an obligation to General de Gaulle and would fulfil it as long as General de Gaulle fulfilled his part. He realized that de Gaulle had considerable support in France, though he observed that this was in great part due to the facilities we had afforded him. He was, however, no longer prepared to deal with de Gaulle personally so long as he claimed or acted as though he possessed supreme authority over the Free French movement. He would only deal with him as the mouthpiece of the National Committee. It was, therefore, up to Mr Massigli to see that the National Committee exercised control over the General and that the General spoke only in its name – he would not have de Gaulle setting up as a dictator here.⁶

As one imagines, Churchill's efforts in this direction were no more successful than in the autumn of 1941. He also tried some diplomacy of his own in North Africa, and wrote a telegram to Harold Macmillan, Minister Resident in Algiers, urging that 'every opportunity should be taken to press for the admission of Mr P. E. Flandin into French North African administration'. Flandin was a personal friend of the Prime Minister, but he had also been Minister of Foreign Affairs in the Vichy government; Eden, anticipating the effect of such a measure on the Fighting French in general, and on General de Gaulle in particular, held up the telegram. Churchill growled and shouted, then told Eden the next morning: 'Perhaps we had better not send it.'[7]

In the meantime, however, there was a fresh development in French affairs: on 22 January, the British government received de Gaulle's request for facilities to travel to Cairo. Churchill's reaction was immediate and violent: if the General went to the Middle East and Africa, he would make some new anti-British statements and stir up trouble in North Africa. To the King, Churchill wrote that day: 'The eruption of de Gaulle or his agents into this field, especially if forcibly introduced by us, would cause nothing but trouble. It is entirely his fault that a good arrangement was not made between the two French factions. The roughness with which he refused the President's invitation (and mine) to come and make a friendly settlement at Casablanca has put him and his French National Committee practically out of court with the Americans.'[8] Churchill seems to have thought that de Gaulle intended to go to Algiers and challenge Giraud – which was not the case – but judging from the latter part of the letter, it is obvious that the Anfa humiliation was still rankling with him. Churchill's reply to de Gaulle's request was therefore a flat refusal, which the Foreign Office translated into a discreet hint to Massigli that the General would be well advised to postpone his trip. This was successful for a time, but Churchill, by now familiar with de Gaulle's reactions, anticipated that the General might reply to this refusal by publicly denouncing the British government. To counter the effect this might have on British, French and American public opinion, the Prime Minister therefore instructed the Foreign Office to prepare a document entitled 'Guidance for the press and the BBC in the event of a break with General de Gaulle',[9] which was to be a round denunciation of the General, complete with all his past anti-British statements and activities.

In anticipation of de Gaulle's next move, Churchill was distinctly uneasy. On 28 February, Oliver Harvey wrote in his diary about the

Prime Minister: 'The old boy is in a rage again with de Gaulle. He wishes force used if necessary to prevent his leaving the country to visit Syria and Africa, declares that he is our "foe". . . . In 1940, he couldn't do enough for de Gaulle, too much. Now because de Gaulle has grown up and has ways of his own, he is furious and wants to break with him. The Prime Minister behaves like a foolish father to a wayward son.'[10]

In spite of Massigli's diplomacy, de Gaulle finally became impatient – and probably suspicious. On 2 March, he sent for Charles Peake, the British representative accredited to the French movement, and asked him bluntly to let him know in 24 hours when he could start or whether he was a prisoner – adding that in the latter case, the consequences would be most grave.[11] This was a sort of ultimatum, and the Cabinet, which met on the morning of 3 March, considered it as such: its members concluded that it was 'highly undesirable that the General should go from England at this moment'. That evening, Charles Peake wrote the following letter to Massigli: 'I am instructed to represent that, in the view of His Majesty's government, the present moment is not well chosen for an extended visit of the kind now contemplated. . . . They regret, therefore, that they cannot at present accord the facilities for which General de Gaulle has asked.'[12]

Having read this, de Gaulle said *'Alors, je suis prisonnier!'* He left London and retired to Hampstead. Whereupon Churchill phoned Charles Peake and told him: 'I hold you responsible that the Monster of Hampstead does not escape.'[13]

This, however, wasn't the end of Churchill's troubles. Irritated by Gaullist propaganda, annoyed by the continuing defection of sailors who left French ships in American ports to join the Fighting French, enraged by continuing press criticism of the State Department's French policy, Cordell Hull and Franklin Roosevelt again made their displeasure known in London. At the beginning of February, Anthony Eden had received 'rather a stiff request' from Cordell Hull: 'Some annoyance has been shown by the President at the continued propaganda emanating from the de Gaulle headquarters in London. The President labels their attitude as a continuing irritant. He knows that the PM would agree with him, and hopes that you can take further steps to allay the irritation.' Eden replied to the American Chargé d'Affaires Freeman Matthews, 'We have no means of closing down Carlton Gardens and indeed, I feel sure that it would be unwise to do anything of the kind.'[14] De Gaulle's press conference of 9 February produced a fresh outburst in Washington, and Roosevelt even sent a personal message to Churchill. The President chose to ignore de Gaulle's flattering reference to his person, and took exception to his harsh criticism of Allied policy in North Africa; but above all, he again implied that Churchill was not restraining de Gaulle as he ought to.

This was most embarrassing to the Prime Minister. He had, as we have seen, very little control over de Gaulle's activities, and any attempt at censoring his speeches usually produced major rows which everyone was anxious to avoid. In spite of his anger at the Fighting French leader, Churchill once again had to keep in mind the support de Gaulle enjoyed in France and in British public opinion, as well as the binding agreements signed with him in the summer of 1940 – agreements which he probably bitterly regretted by now. Once again, Churchill, who earnestly wanted to help France, found himself trapped between public opinion at home which accused him of not supporting de Gaulle, and the President of the United States who accused him of supporting de Gaulle against the American government. To the President, Churchill answered, 'We too did not like what de Gaulle said at his press conference on 9 February,' and added: 'I am pressing very strongly that there should be substituted for de Gaulle, de Gaulle in council, i.e. put him in commission.'[15]

Churchill, as we know, had no success at all in putting de Gaulle in commission. But American pressure continued to be applied, and Eden felt its full weight when he travelled to Washington in March and met Secretary of State Hull, who was still suffering from an acute case of Gaullophobia. After the interview, Eden wrote:

Mr Hull unburdened himself of his grievances which were in the main that, while he had been pursuing a policy of maintaining relations with Vichy in which His Majesty's government agreed, he had been subject to much criticism in the British press and by the Fighting French; the mud batteries had been turned on against him. I explained along the usual lines that while there had been agreement as to the desirability of American representation at Vichy, the British people felt neither sympathy nor admiration for Pétain and Vichy dominion. Nothing either you, or I, or anybody else, could say would alter this.[16]

Cordell Hull recorded that 'Eden made a mild effort to justify Great Britain's cause by mentioning the aid that de Gaulle had given

Britain in the war. I contended that the tremendous aid the United States had given Britain and the whole Allied cause through its Vichy policy more than counter-balanced this assistance.'[17]

On 22 March, Hull returned to the subject: 'I again took up with Eden . . . the question of North Africa and the position of the de Gaulle organization. . . . I remarked that our own policy towards the French situation had always been that no supreme political power should be set up now to exercise control over the French people. No provisional government should be created or recognized, and any political activities should be kept to the minimum dictated by necessity.'[18]

This is where the British and the American policies diverged. The British government would have much preferred to deal with a single French authority, and the Foreign Office, with Churchill's full backing, was working feverishly towards that goal. The American government, on the other hand, was still in favour of 'keeping the situation fluid' and dealing with weak local authorities – including Vichy. It was also much easier to deal separately with the French authorities in the Pacific Islands and in Martinique. The State Department even intended that Allied forces landing in France in the future should administer liberated French territory; this, for the British, was not politically feasible, and Eden expressed his disagreement. He found even more to disagree with during his talks with President Roosevelt:

'On the night of my talk with Hull,' Eden recalls,

I dined alone with the President and Harry Hopkins. Mr Roosevelt expatiated happily to me about his views on European problems. He thought that after the war armaments in Europe should be concentrated in the hands of Britain, the United States and Russia. The smaller powers should have nothing more dangerous than rifles. He seemed to be ignoring the obvious difficulty of disarming neutral countries, but I did not take the idea as a serious proposal and it passed with little comment. . . . On the future of Germany the President appeared to favour dismemberment as the only wholly satisfactory solution. He agreed that, when the time came, we should work to encourage separate tendencies within Germany and foresaw a long 'policing' of that country. More surprisingly, he thought that the three powers should police Europe in general. I pointed out that the occupied countries, as they then were, would want to put their own house in order and I thought we should encourage them to do so. We should have our hands quite full enough with Germany. Roosevelt next showed anxiety about the future of Belgium and described the project which he had mentioned to Mr Oliver Lyttelton a few months before, for a new state called 'Wallonia'. This would include the Walloon parts of Belgium with Luxembourg, Alsace-Lorraine and part of northern France. I recorded on this point that I poured water, I hope politely, and the President did not revert to the subject.[19]

Eden left Washington on 30 March, and at a press conference that day, the President summed up the results of their talks: 'If you want to be didactic and put it in terms of figures, I would say that so far . . . we are about 95 per cent together.'[20] The remaining 5 per cent consisted mostly of France.

Whatever Churchill's feelings towards de Gaulle, he still had an official commitment towards the Fighting French movement, and a personal commitment towards France. On 30 March, he wrote to Eden: 'A proposal to rank France lower than China even in matters affecting Europe, and to subjugate all Europe after disarmament to the four powers, would certainly cause lively discussion. I feel sure that while listening politely you have given no countenance to such ideas. You were quite right to protest about France.'[21]

De Gaulle, mercifully unaware of Roosevelt's plans for the future of France, still expected an invitation to Washington which did not materialize. He was also anxious to fly to North Africa, where General Catroux was negotiating with Giraud – the latter had now taken some steps towards democratization of his regime, and even abolished part of the Vichy legislation in North Africa. After that, the Fighting French movement and de Gaulle himself had been submitted to enormous pressure from the press, from Mr Macmillan, and even from Cardinal Spellman to submit to General Giraud and accept the plan devised at Anfa. But de Gaulle had sent a memorandum to Giraud on 26 February, with the conditions he considered necessary for unity between them, namely: armistice of 1940 to be considered null and void; certain Vichy administrators to be expelled from their posts; Republican legality to be reinstated in French North Africa; then the setting up of a central power having all the attributes of a government, as well as a consultative assembly representing French resistance. By the end of March, de Gaulle still had received no answer to that memorandum, and the negotiations between Catroux and Giraud seemed to be getting nowhere either. De Gaulle had again requested a plane from the British, and this time a Liberator had been put at his disposal. But on 30 March, he was informed that one of the plane's engines required repairs and that this would delay his departure for several days; His Majesty's government were still having second thoughts about letting de Gaulle leave England for North Africa. But there was also a new development; the Prime Minister now agreed to see General de Gaulle.

Churchill's abrupt change in mood was due largely to the persistent efforts of de Gaulle's Commissioner for Foreign Affairs. On 23 March, Mr Massigli had seen Charles Peake and, in order to convince him, had deployed all his diplomatic talents, which were not small. Charles Peake later reported:

> He (Massigli) thought that . . . General de Gaulle would himself want to leave for Algiers about the 31st March. Mr Massigli then asked me whether the Prime Minister would receive the General before the latter left. I said that if Mr Massigli was making a request for this, I would certainly put it forward, but that I did not think it likely that the Prime Minister would feel able to accede . . . the reason lay in the record of General de Gaulle's own behaviour.
>
> Mr Massigli said he did not contest that General de Gaulle was an unusually difficult and unsatisfactory man with whom to do business, but, speaking to me as a friend, he begged me to use my best endeavours to persuade the Prime Minister to see the General before he left. It was of course true that General de Gaulle had been built up by the British government, but the fact remained that he *had* been built up, and he thought that, on any objective consideration, it would now be agreed that his position in metropolitan France was paramount, and that the tendency was for it to become so elsewhere. He felt it right, speaking personally and very confidentially, to warn me of the dangers which must inevitably lie ahead if General de Gaulle should go to North Africa feeling that the Prime Minister's face was turned against him . . . and it was surely therefore of real advantage, purely as a matter of policy, that the Prime Minister should say a kind word to him before he left. One of General de Gaulle's limitations, as I would know well, was that he was apt to nurse a grievance and to brood over fancied wrongs. Would it not be wise, in the interests of Anglo-French relations, to remove any pretext for his doing so? The Prime Minister was so great a figure and so magnanimous that he believed that if this appeal were conveyed to him, he would not be deaf to it. Moreover, General de Gaulle cherished a deep-seated admiration for the Prime Minister and, he was sure, would respond to a kind word from him.[22]

The Prime Minister could rarely resist such arguments, and he agreed to receive General de Gaulle on 30 March. But that day he found out that de Gaulle had not requested an interview, and refused to make any appointment until requested. De Gaulle of course refused to request, but Charles Peake and Massigli intervened again, blurred the issue, rounded the edges, and de Gaulle was finally received by the Prime Minister on 2 April, in the presence of Massigli and Cadogan.

This was the first time de Gaulle and Churchill met since the Anfa conference – and once again, the first exchanges were devoid of amenity; '*Enfin*,' said de Gaulle, '*Je suis prisonnier, bientôt vous m'enverrez à l'Île de Man.*' To which Churchill answered in his best French: '*Non, mon Général, pour vous, très distingué, toujours la Tower of London.*'[23] The Prime Minister went on to state that the plane requested by de Gaulle would be made ready, but would it not be preferable to await Eden's return from the USA before leaving? And would not General Catroux come to London to report? Churchill then reminded de Gaulle that the situation had turned to his disadvantage owing to his refusal to come to Casablanca. If there were no preliminary agreement between Giraud and de Gaulle, or if there were disorders, the United States would back General Giraud and there was not much the British government could then do to support the Fighting French . . . it would be a grave and deplorable thing if severe incidents were to occur during the General's visit. A solution must therefore be sought in a friendly atmosphere.

De Gaulle 'wished to assure Mr Winston Churchill that his purpose in leaving for Algiers was not to start a battle. On the contrary, he intended to achieve a union, if that was really possible. . . .'

After a few more exchanges of a general nature, Churchill became somewhat sentimental: 'He was convinced,' he said, 'that a strong France was in the interests of Europe and especially of England. . . . The Prime Minister was a European, a good European – at least he hoped so – and a strong France was an indispensable element in his conception of Europe. The General could rely on these assurances, whatever unpleasant incidents might occur. It was a principle of English policy . . . which corresponded to the interests of France, of Great Britain, and also of the United States. The Prime Minister again asked the General to rely on this declaration, and to remember it in times of difficulty.'

Not to be outdone, de Gaulle replied that,

'It was precisely because he saw England's and the Prime Minister's position the way the latter had just exposed it that he had continued the war at England's side ever since the French armistice was signed.'

Churchill was quick to exploit this perceptible warming in the atmosphere; he once again introduced the matter of the 'pro-consuls'. 'There is the case of Peyrouton, that of Noguès . . . and of Boisson. Boisson appears to me to be quite a capable man; he has helped the Allies a great deal.' To which de Gaulle replied: 'The only question is whether or not Governor Boisson has served France.'

Winston Churchill did not insist. To sum up, he stressed that he was convinced of the necessity of an agreement with General Giraud . . . he remained favourable to the idea of a dual leadership. He would cable General Eisenhower, and also Mr Macmillan, who would certainly extend all possible help to General de Gaulle. Churchill's last words were to reaffirm that he 'had never ceased to be, and he remained, a friend of France'.[24]

Although the interview ended amiably enough, de Gaulle was not satisfied with its results; immediately after leaving Downing Street, 'wanting Churchill to show his hand',[25] he announced that he still proposed to go to Algiers, and without accepting any prior conditions. But two days later, the Foreign Office gave General de Gaulle a message from Eisenhower, in which the latter wrote that he 'would be most grateful if General de Gaulle would postpone his departure until he feels that groundwork for an agreement has been laid sufficiently firmly to ensure its rapid consummation. His reason for this request is that in view of the rapidly approaching crisis of battle in Tunisia it would be very undesirable to have at the same time a protracted political crisis.' The message concluded by saying that Eisenhower 'certainly does not wish to embarrass General de Gaulle, and he feels confident that the latter will not wish to embarrass him'.

The note was accompanied by a message from Churchill: 'The reason given seems decisive for the moment. I believe that General de Gaulle, as a soldier, will appreciate the force of this. A very great battle is impending. Eisenhower and Giraud must be able to devote their whole attention to the operation.'[26]

On 7 April, the Prime Minister let it be known officially that 'He had been throughout in the fullest agreement with General Eisenhower in deprecating a visit by General de Gaulle during the battle crisis in Tunisia, which required the undivided attention of the Allied High Command.'²⁷ This seemed decisive; it was not. De Gaulle, after having flown into a rage and made some very bitter comments on American policy in front of Ambassador Winant, was informed by Admiral Stark that the message had not really come from Eisenhower, but from 'Allied Command'. Two days later, this was confirmed by Tixier in Washington: 'I learn from well-informed sources that General Eisenhower's cable was in fact due to a British initiative.'²⁸*

De Gaulle therefore concluded that Churchill had engineered the whole affair to prevent him from leaving England, and their mutual relations sank to new depths. Meanwhile, on 6 April, Hugh Dalton was present when the Prime Minister stated that de Gaulle, 'though he has undeniable qualities, is a great fool and very anti-British'. There followed yet another tirade on Casablanca, then: 'If ever de Gaulle comes to power in France, he will try to build up his popularity by being anti-British. If he were to come out now to Algiers, he might fly off to Brazzaville or Syria and do much harm in either.'²⁹ A month earlier, Churchill had refused de Gaulle permission to go to Brazzaville and Syria on grounds that he might fly off to Algiers and stir up trouble there.

In the meantime, negotiations were proceeding between Generals Giraud and Catroux in Algiers, with some pressure being brought to bear on de Gaulle from several of his collaborators, including Catroux, to accept Giraud's political and military predominance. But on 9 April, Catroux brought back to London Giraud's answer to the memorandum of 23 February: the latter proposed to establish a 'council of overseas territories' with no political power; as for the Commander-in-Chief, General Giraud, he would not be subordinate to this council, but to the Allied High Command. This was wholly unsatisfactory, and on 15 April, the National Committee unanimously approved de Gaulle's reply to Giraud demanding once again the formation of an executive committee with real powers, the subordination of the Commander-in-Chief to the committee, and

*Churchill had requested Macmillan in Algiers to ask General Eisenhower whether it would be expedient for de Gaulle to come to North Africa at that final stage of the Tunisian campaign. But Eisenhower was absent, and the Allied headquarters answered non-committally that 'A crisis . . . might endanger communications', which Macmillan dispatched to London in the form of a plea – allegedly from Eisenhower – 'not to complicate the situation until the military operations . . . had been concluded'. On the basis of this, the Foreign Office made the message which was passed on to de Gaulle as coming from General Eisenhower.

the resignation of Vichy elements who had collaborated with the Axis.

Giraud's power was now waning. In North Africa, more and more soldiers were defecting to the Fighting French troops, and mass demonstrations in Algiers clamoured for de Gaulle's arrival. On 26 April, M. Peyrouton, Governor-General of Algeria, told General Catroux that on de Gaulle's arrival, he would resign and ask to join the army. Besides, de Gaulle's support in France was increasing daily and some key men like General Beynet, Couve de Murville, and 'Blanc', chief of the powerful OCM (*Organization Civile et Militaire*) in the occupied zone, had publicly rallied to de Gaulle. The Free French leader was aware of all this, and it was reflected in his conversations with Giraud's representative, General Bouscat, on 20 April: 'If there is no agreement, that will be too bad! All France is with me . . . my resistance and combat groups are everywhere and growing stronger each day . . . France is Gaullist, fiercely Gaullist. She cannot change . . . we must not forget that we are alone among foreigners; for the Allies are foreigners. They may become our enemies tomorrow. Giraud is subordinating himself to the United States. He is preparing France's servitude and will be gravely disappointed.'[30]

Giraud had not yet accepted his defeat. On 27 April, he wrote to de Gaulle that he renounced the predominant position he had asked for, but maintained his proposal of a powerless council. He also asked for a meeting well away from Algiers, at Biskra or 'in a building of the American airport' at Marrakesh – which was of course entirely unacceptable. To Bouscat, de Gaulle said the next day: 'Giraud refuses to understand. He wants to be Chief of Government and Commander-in-Chief. Out of the question!'[32] Four days later, de Gaulle again told Bouscat that he 'wanted to go to Algiers, only to Algiers', and added:

Why doesn't he want me to go to Algiers? Because he is afraid of demonstrations? Because he is afraid that the crowd will shout 'Vive de Gaulle!' So what? If there is further delay it will be worse . . . you see, I maintain my three demands: my going to Algiers, first, also the exclusion of Peyrouton, Noguès and Boisson. I cannot work with these three men who collaborated with Vichy. But I don't want them shot. Let them just resign . . . then we'll see. Peyrouton is the least dangerous. He wants to enter the army; that is very good. Later on, we'll be able to employ him. For the time being it's impossible.[32]

De Gaulle went on to say that he agreed to share executive power with Giraud: 'And that is a lot!' he added, 'For who is Giraud? What does he represent? Nothing. He has no one behind him . . . It could be very simple: I land at Maison Blanche airport – from there I go to the Palais d'Été – Am I acclaimed by the crowd on the way? You can't help that . . . I then appear at a balcony with Giraud. The union is concluded. It's all over.'[33]

This delectable vision was still a bit optimistic in view of Giraud's attitude by the end of April. But if Giraud still refused to understand, Churchill, informed by Macmillan of what was happening in French North Africa and repeatedly briefed by Anthony Eden, finally recognized that de Gaulle had won the first round. He said as much to the General, whom he received on 30 April after having promised Eden 'to be nice to him'.[34] Finally, he encouraged the General to go to Algiers without delay and added that he would back any agreement giving de Gaulle and Giraud equal power in North Africa. He again intervened in favour of Peyrouton, Noguès and Boisson – and again in vain. 'A satisfactory conversation,' de Gaulle recalled.[35] But Churchill was highly vulnerable to influence from other quarters, and he was now going to the United States for talks with President Roosevelt, who had never been a Gaullophile, and Secretary of State Hull, who was more Gaullophobe than ever. On 4 May, the British Prime Minister sailed for the United States.

Churchill was not alone in thinking that de Gaulle had won the first round in his struggle for power in North Africa; President Roosevelt had anxiously followed developments there, and had come to the same conclusion. On 8 May, he handed Hull a memorandum which he intended to give to Churchill. It said among other things that: 'The issue presented in the French situation has come to a head and we must take a definite position that will determine the future of the controversy.'[36]

In other words, Churchill was going to be submitted to the same anti-Gaullist pressures as Anthony Eden had been in March – with two important differences: the pressures would be far heavier, and Churchill was much more vulnerable to American pressure than his Foreign Secretary.

Upon arrival in Washington, Churchill told the British Ambassador Lord Halifax that 'he would bet that he, Winston, would slang de Gaulle more than Hull would'.[37] In fact, Churchill had just received a memorandum from Roosevelt full of fresh grievances against the General:

> I am sorry, but it seems to me the conduct of the Bride continues to be more and more aggravated. His course and attitude is well nigh intolerable. . . . De Gaulle is without question taking his vicious propaganda staff down to Algiers to stir up strife between the various elements, including the Arabs and Jews. . . . De Gaulle may be an honest fellow but he has the Messianic complex. Further he has the idea that the people of France itself are strongly behind him personally. This I doubt. . . . That is why I become more and more disturbed by the continued machinations of de Gaulle.
>
> In my judgement there should be a reorganization of the French National Committee removing some of the people we know to be impossible, such as Philip, and include in it some of the strong men like Monnet and others from Giraud's North African administration and possibly one or two others from Madagascar, etc. Furthermore, I am inclined to think that when we get into France itself we will (?) have to regard it as a military occupation run by British and American generals. . . . All in all, I think you and I should thrash out this disagreeable problem and establish a common policy. I think we might talk over the formation of an entirely new French committee subject in its membership to the approval of you and me. I do not think it should act in any way as a provisional government, but could be called advisory in its functions.
>
> Giraud should be made the Commander-in-Chief of the French army and navy and would of course sit on the advisory national committee. I think he has shown fine qualities since we saw him at Casablanca.
>
> I do not know what to do with de Gaulle. Possibly you would like to make him Governor of Madagascar![38]

But in spite of the Prime Minister's 'favourable' dispositions, Roosevelt made little headway during his first conversations with him on the subject, and he finally asked Churchill to talk to Hull about it, hoping no doubt that the latter would be more convincing. Hull accordingly called on Churchill at the White House on 13 May, and noted in his memoirs that:

> Mr Churchill said the President had suggested he might talk to me about de Gaulle. He was not pushing forward de Gaulle, he pointed out, although he had heard it reported that we felt that de Gaulle was receiving British financial support with which to do the things that were most objectionable to us. He and Eden found de Gaulle terrible to get on with, and he wanted it understood that they were not undertaking to

build him up. He added that we on the other hand should not get behind Giraud and pit him against de Gaulle, one reason being that de Gaulle was considered a symbol of French resistance and the British just could not throw him overboard, notwithstanding his many very objectionable and difficult ways.

The one big point in the situation, I said, that should appeal to both our governments alike is that if this de Gaulle matter is allowed to go forward as it has been, it will undoubtedly bring about serious friction between our two governments. . . .

Mr Churchill replied, first, that he personally was utterly disgusted with de Gaulle and, second, that the British were not aiding him as much as I seemed to think.

I suggested that there were numerous ways for the British to get away from their build-up of de Gaulle, rapidly or gradually, if the latter course should prove necessary.

I made no special impression on the Prime Minister concerning this point, since he continued to urge that this government should not support Giraud to the point of engaging in a quarrel with de Gaulle and the British. I replied that this would be the inevitable outcome of the British policy in regard to de Gaulle.

Our conversation ended without any particular accord.[39]

However, the Prime Minister continued to be submitted to daily pressure, and by 22 May, the Washington atmosphere had obviously begun to leave its mark. On that day, during a lunch at the British Embassy for President Roosevelt and the Canadian Prime Minister, Churchill stated that 'He had raised de Gaulle as a pup', but that the latter 'now bit the hand that fed him.' He also complained of de Gaulle's immense vanity.[40] Henry Wallace, who was present at the lunch, also wrote in his diary: 'Churchill spoke very contemptuously of the vanity, pettiness and discourtesy of de Gaulle, saying he had raised him from a pup but that he still barked and bit.' The rest of the conversation is no less interesting – and typical: 'He (Churchill) said he thought there ought to be three regional organizations and one supreme. He visioned the USA, British Empire and Russia really running the show. The USA would have membership in the American and Pacific region. Britain in all three. The USA might or might not have membership in the European.' As for Churchill's vision of post-war Europe: 'A Danubian Confederation with Bavaria as a part of it. Prussia would stand by herself with 40 million people. France would be made strong even though she did not deserve it. The Scandinavian countries would be a block. He had no ideas about handling Switzerland or the Low Countries.'[41]

But Roosevelt had some ideas about handling General de Gaulle, and he passed on to Churchill more and more of the documents which he regularly received from Secretary of State Hull. There was a report from Ambassador Winant in London indicating that General Cochet, who had recently come from France, had told two Frenchmen, Roger Cambon and Pierre Comert, that 'to his amazement, General de Gaulle had said privately to him that he no longer had confidence in the Anglo-Saxons and that in the future he would base his policy solely on Russia . . . and perhaps on Germany'.[42] There also came a dispatch from Robert Murphy in Algiers – General Catroux had apparently shown him a telegram from de Gaulle expressing his distrust of American policy, which he asserted was opposed to French unity and a strong France.[43] This was no less offensive for being true, and Roosevelt did not conceal his indignation.

Churchill finally gave in and wrote the following telegram to Eden and Attlee:

> I must now warn you solemnly of a very stern situation developing here about de Gaulle. Hardly a day passes that the President does not mention it to me. Although this is done in a most friendly and often jocular manner, I am sure that he feels very strongly indeed upon it and I see real danger developing if matters are not gripped.
>
> I send you in my immediately following a memorandum which he had himself prepared for me before I arrived, marked A. Also a memorandum with which the State Department furnished him, marked B. I also send you a paper, marked C, and a Secret Service Report, D, which the President handed me a day or two later, together with other telegrams marked E,F,G,H, respectively. In fact there is not a day that he does not hand me one or more of these accusing documents. There are others which I could send but I forbear.
>
> In addition I am sending you by air mail an American Secret Service Report by Mr Hoover [not the ex-President] about inducements alleged to have been offered to the *Richelieu* sailors to desert de Gaulle, which caused much embarrassment to the United States. The gravamen of this is that the President feels this is done with our British money given to de Gaulle, and only politeness prevents the suggestion that our financial relations with the United States make it in a certain sense almost American money.
>
> Now I am sure all this has got to stop. De Gaulle has hopelessly

missed his market in North Africa. He is in my opinion absorbed in his own personal career which depends on a vain endeavour to make himself the arbiter of the conduct of every Frenchman following the military defeat. I ask my colleagues to consider urgently whether we should not now eliminate de Gaulle as a political force and face Parliament and France upon the issues. The French National Committee would in this case be told that we will have no further relations with them or give them any money whatever so long as de Gaulle is connected with their body. We should of course pay the soldiers and sailors who are now serving. I should be quite ready myself to defend this policy in Parliament and will show them and the world that the 'No Surrender' movement in France, around which the de Gaullist legend has been built up, on the one hand, and this vain and even malignant man on the other, have no longer any common identity. . . .

Other points against de Gaulle are as follows. He hates England and has left a trail of Anglophobia behind him everywhere. He has never himself fought since he left France and took pains to have his wife brought out safely beforehand.* He is now banding on the Communist movement in France, although telling us he is the sole obstacle to it. The President has even suggested to me that Giraud may be in danger of assassination at the hands of de Gaullists. He has not, however, supplied me with his evidence of this.

I beg that you will bring this before the Cabinet at the earliest moment. Meanwhile and pending my return the strictest control of de Gaulle's movements and of Free French propaganda by radio and in the press should be maintained. . . . When we consider the absolutely vital interest which we have in preserving good relations with the United States, it seems to me most questionable that we should allow this marplot and mischief-maker to continue the harm he is doing. I shall be glad to hear from you before I leave.

Please see also my immediately following documents X and Y just sent me by the President.[44]

A few hours later, Churchill sent another telegram to Eden:

I have just had a talk with Léger. He was in the best of health and mental vigour. He informed me he could never work with de Gaulle and did not wish to come to England while de Gaulle was our man. On the other hand, he agrees entirely with the de Gaullist movement and considers that if it were freed from de Gaulle it would spell a good hope for France. He did not wish to go to Africa because that again was sectional, but he would gladly go if any arrangement could be made between Giraud and

*This was remarkably unfair and quite untrue. Madame de Gaulle arrived in Britain on 19 June 1940, two days after her husband – and Churchill knew it.

the French National Committee minus de Gaulle. His views are in fact identical with my own. . . .

I am increasingly convinced that I ought to write to de Gaulle a letter telling him that in consequence of his behaviour we cannot any longer recognize the validity of the letters exchanged between us, but that we will of course continue with the fullest co-operation with the French National Committee and we will endeavour to bring about the largest possible union of Frenchmen ready to advance against the Germans.

If we could get Herriot and Léger on to the London committee minus de Gaulle, it would be possible to make with Giraud a thoroughly strong representative circle of France during the war period. I am quite sure we cannot go on as we are now. . . .[45]

Finally, in a third telegram, Winston Churchill enclosed the 'incriminating' documents he had received from Roosevelt.

In London, meanwhile, de Gaulle, unaware of all the agitation, was impatiently awaiting the outcome of Catroux's negotiations in Algiers. On 4 May, he had declared somewhat abruptly in a public speech at Grosvenor House that 'There must be an end to delays'.[46] But by mid-May, the General had every reason to be optimistic: in North Africa, whole regiments of French troops were leaving Giraud's army to join the Fighting French forces. More important still, he had just received a telegram from Jean Moulin in Paris, announcing the creation of the CNR, *Conseil National de la Resistance*. In the name of the CNR, Jean Moulin addressed the following message to the leader of Fighting France:

On the eve of the departure of General de Gaulle for Algiers, all the movements and parties of the Resistance, in the northern and in the southern zones, wish to renew, to him and the National Committee, the assurance of their absolute attachment to the principles which they both embody and must integrally uphold. All the Resistance movements and parties declare that the meeting must take place at the HQ of the Algerian Government General, in the open and among Frenchmen. They also declare:

1. That political problems must not be excluded from the conversations.
2. That the people of France will never agree to General de Gaulle being subordinate to General Giraud, and demand the immediate installation of a provisional government in Algiers under the presidency of General de Gaulle, with General Giraud as military chief.

3. That General de Gaulle will remain the sole leader of French Resistance whatever the outcome of negotiations.[47]*

The General's hand was of course immensely strengthened by this telegram. Giraud himself realized it at once, and on 17 May, he asked de Gaulle to come to Algiers at once, so that a central executive committee could be formed. This committee would have supreme power, de Gaulle and Giraud would each preside over it in turn, and it would originally be composed of six members, including two proposed by de Gaulle and two by Giraud. This was satisfactory as a basis for discussions, and there was now no doubt that de Gaulle would go to Algiers.

The British government was impressed by this unequivocal declaration of support for de Gaulle emanating from the French Resistance movements, and much relieved at Giraud's change of mind. After seven months of discussions and conflict, a union between the two rival factions was at last within reach. Anthony Eden and Clement Attlee must therefore have been dumbfounded when they received Churchill's telegrams from Washington calling for a break with de Gaulle. The War Cabinet was summoned, and met on the evening of 23 May. The minutes of the meeting are dry but instructive:

The War Cabinet met to consider three telegrams from the Prime Minister (Pencil Nos. 166, 167 and 181) about relations between General de Gaulle and General Giraud. . . .

The War Cabinet were informed of the present position as to the negotiations between General de Gaulle and General Giraud. General de Gaulle had been invited by General Giraud to visit Algiers, subject to two conditions which it seemed probable that he would accept. . . .

The War Cabinet took the view that it was extremely difficult to see how we could break with General de Gaulle at the moment when he was on the point of reaching agreement with General Giraud. If General de Gaulle made trouble after an agreement had been reached we should be in a stronger position to insist upon his withdrawal, should this later prove necessary.

The War Cabinet were given information as to a number of specific matters which would have to be taken into consideration before a decision could be reached to break with General de Gaulle; e.g.

1. There were 80,000 Fighting French troops in different parts of the

*Jean Moulin was arrested by the Gestapo on 27 May and tortured to death shortly thereafter.

world. We should experience particular trouble in French Equatorial Africa (where the troops were virulently de Gaullist), and also in Syria and North Palestine, if we were now to break with the General.

2. The First Lord of the Admiralty said that there were 47 French officers and 6000 other ranks of the Fighting French navy, which manned 4 efficient submarines, 15 destroyers, corvettes and sloops; in all, 57 ships. The view of the Admiralty was that a break with General de Gaulle would certainly cause some temporary difficulties and inconvenience. . . .

5. The Deputy Prime Minister said that if we were to take action against General de Gaulle, many Frenchmen who were now opposed to him would rally to him. The name of 'de Gaulle' was regarded as a symbol of the Republic, and the de Gaullist movement stood for the Entente.

6. It was also pointed out that if we broke with General de Gaulle during or immediately after the Prime Minister's visit to the United States, the inference would be drawn that we had done so under pressure from the United States.

·8. . . . The effect on political opinion in this country should also be borne in mind.

The War Cabinet then considered three draft telegrams to the Prime Minister which had been prepared in the Foreign Office. Various amendments were agreed upon, to incorporate points made during the discussion.
The War Cabinet approved the three draft telegrams to the Prime Minister, as amended, and authorized their dispatch.'[48]

In his diary, Anthony Eden wrote that evening: 'Cabinet at 9 p.m. re de Gaulle and Winston's proposal to break with him now. — Everyone against and very brave about it in his absence.'[49] In the late hours of 23 May, the British Prime Minister accordingly received three telegrams from London. The first, Alcove no. 370, read:

Your telegrams . . . have been considered by the Cabinet and the following represents our unanimous view.

1. It is disturbing that such a stream of American reports should have gone to Washington without the ambassador having spoken to the Foreign Secretary about them. We had no idea that de Gaulle situation was rankling so much just now. We are fully conscious of the difficulties which de Gaulle has created for us, and of your position under heavy

pressure from the Americans. We do not however consider that the policy which you so strongly recommend is practicable for the following reasons.

2. The latest phase of the Giraud-de Gaulle negotiations indicates that union is nearer than it has been at any time. De Gaulle has been invited by Giraud to Algiers subject to the acceptance of two conditions and it seems probable that he will accept. . . . We anticipate an early application from de Gaulle for transport facilities. It has been the policy of HMG and the USG for the past four months to bring the two generals together and this policy was blessed by the President and yourself at Anfa. If, as we believe, it was the right policy then, it is in our view even more the right policy now when both generals appear to be on the point of achieving the union which they were then pressed to bring about.

3. We are advised that there is no likelihood of any of the present members of the French National Committee continuing to function if General de Gaulle were removed by us. The same is probably true of the Free French fighting forces. . . .

4. Is there not also a real danger that if we now drove de Gaulle out of public life at this moment when a union between the two French movements seems on the point of being achieved we would not only make him a national martyr but we would find ourselves accused by both Gaullists and Giraudists of interfering improperly in French internal affairs with a view to treating France as an Anglo-American protectorate? If so, our relations with France would be more dangerously affected than by a continuance of the present unsatisfactory situation.

5. On the other hand we are equally with the President and Mr Hull alive to the unsatisfactory character of the present arrangement but having regard to the developments mentioned at the beginning of paragraph 2, surely this is not the moment to try and tackle it by the drastic measures proposed by the President. . . .

6. We are sending you in a separate telegram comments on the various memoranda. They contain little that is not known to us and they can hardly be said to have been written by unbiased and objective observers.[50]

In the second telegram, the venomous memoranda passed on by President Roosevelt were unfavourably commented upon. Some were corrected, others were disagreed with, the greater part were not taken seriously.[51] The third telegram, Alcove 372, concluded:

We think it well to bear all this in mind. It shows that apart from the political objections to the course which the President advocates, a precipitate break with de Gaulle would have far-reaching consequences in a number of spheres which the Americans have probably never thought about. . . .

We are sorry not to be more helpful, but we are convinced that the Americans are wrong in this and advocate a line which would not be understood here, with possible evil consequences to Anglo-American relations. We do hope that a decision on this question can await your return.[52]

This energetic reply, and some of the information it included, had the desired effect on the Prime Minister. He replied the next morning:

It is a new fact to me that de Gaulle is about to meet Giraud, and I agree that we should await the results of their meeting. I have given you my warning of the dangers to the Anglo-American unity inherent in your championship of de Gaulle. We have been met here in a spirit of generous consideration . . . and an agreement most satisfactory to the Chiefs-of-Staff is being reached over the whole strategic field . . . In many other ways we are receiving indispensable help, and I should be very sorry to become responsible for breaking up this harmony for the sake of a Frenchman who is a bitter foe of Britain and may well bring civil war upon France.[53]

The matter was thus dropped, for the time being. But Churchill's account of this agitated episode in his memoirs is something of an understatement: 'It hung in the balance whether we should not break finally at this juncture with this most difficult man. However, time and patience afforded tolerable solutions.'[54]

In London, General de Gaulle was preparing to leave for North Africa. On 25 May, he had written to Giraud: 'I intend to arrive in Algiers before the end of this week, and I will be happy to work with you in the service of France.'[55] The rest was described by de Gaulle himself:

Before leaving England, I wrote to King George VI to tell him how grateful I was to him, to his government and to his people for the reception they had given me during the tragic days of 1940 and for the hospitality they had granted ever since to Free France and to its leader. Intending to pay a visit to Mr Churchill, I learned that he had just 'left for an unknown destination'. I therefore took leave of Eden instead. The meeting was a friendly one. 'What do you think of us?' the British minister asked me. 'No people can be more likeable than yours,' I observed. 'Of your policies, I cannot always say the same.' As we re-called the many dealings I had had with the British government, Mr Eden good-humouredly said: 'Do you know that you have caused us more difficulties than all our other European allies put together?' 'I don't doubt it,' I replied, smiling also, 'France is a great power.'[56]

These difficulties were far from over, and no one was more aware of it than Winston Churchill; for upon leaving the US, he did not return to London. Instead, he secretly flew to Algiers in order to supervise the preparations for 'Husky', the landing in Sicily, and also to convince Generals Eisenhower and Marshall that the next move ought to be an attack on the Italian mainland. He also had another reason for being there: the union between de Gaulle and Giraud would be a momentous event, and Churchill was irresistibly attracted by momentous events; besides, he wished to set the stage and to bolster and encourage his old friend General Georges,* whom he hoped to include in the future French council. Finally, he wanted to stand by to intervene personally – or order an armed intervention – in case things turned sour between the two French factions. But Churchill remembered his experience at Anfa, and did not entirely trust his own qualities as a diplomat; on 28 May, he therefore sent the following telegram to Clement Attlee: 'It seems to me important that Eden should come here for a few days. He is much better fitted than I am to be best man at the Giraud-de Gaulle wedding. He ought to be conscious of the atmosphere and in touch with the actors in what may easily be a serious drama.'[57]

That same evening, Churchill had a long talk with Admiral Cunningham, Harold Macmillan and Robert Murphy, who sent a long report to Washington on the conversation. This report was later published in the 'Foreign Relations of the United States' series, but a large part of it was too sensitive to be included. What follows is the uncensored version:

We discussed various ramifications of the French problem. Eden will arrive tomorrow at noon. The Prime Minister said he was here to visit the troops and British navy and to contribute what he could to a favourable adjustment of the French situation which will and must, he said, demonstrate Anglo-American solidarity.

He arraigned de Gaulle more vehemently and vituperatively than at Anfa, saying that de Gaulle is anti-British and anti-American and that we could count on de Gaulle to play the fool. The Prime Minister voiced much misgiving. He referred to the President's invitation to Giraud to

*General Georges had been secretly spirited out of France ten days before on Churchill's orders.

visit the USA and said that he would like you to know that he believes that it would be most unwise for Giraud to absent himself in the first part of June as planned because . . . and he repeated this several times . . . in his opinion de Gaulle is fully capable of a putsch. He said he had no illusions about de Gaulle's thirst for personal power.

He plans that the British government will cancel its present arrangements with the FNC which will be transferred to Algiers, lock, stock and barrel. . . . We would then deal jointly with the central organization established in North Africa, making whatever financial, lend-lease and political arrangements we may see fit. The PM says that the facilities of the BBC in London will no longer be available to de Gaulle.

We discussed at great length the constitution of the new French Executive Council. . . . The PM said that he had persuaded and aided General Georges to leave France and that he believed that Georges could make a real contribution. At any rate he has known him for many years and says that he represents a certain continuity in Anglo-French relations which is most desirable. The PM also urged that if possible Alexis Léger be induced to proceed to Algiers and I agreed that we should support him if necessary as a possible member of the Executive Committee. I believe that after several days General de Gaulle and his partisans will become aggressive. The PM said he is convinced that this is so. I asked him for his opinion regarding the Clark-Darlan accord of 22 November which is the formal basis for our operations in this area. He said that in his opinion nothing should be done about it and no concessions made for several weeks at least until we know whether 'de Gaulle would play the fool or not'. He again stressed the necessity for a united front in this connection.[58]

To his old friend General Georges, Churchill had also said that day: 'I gave him (de Gaulle) £25 million and he said the worst things about the British and the United States. If he returns to London without having reached an agreement with the people here, his position will change.'[59]

On 30 May, de Gaulle landed at Boufarik airport near Algiers. . . .

CHAPTER 12

Grudging Recognition

General de Gaulle's arrival in Algiers on 30 May was very different from his landing at Anfa four months earlier. This time, General Giraud was at the airport, a French guard of honour was on hand, a band played the *Marseillaise*, the American and British representatives were *behind* the French officials, and de Gaulle was driven to Algiers in a *French* car. The banquet that followed and the popular demonstrations in Algiers that afternoon also made a very favourable impression on the General, but the following day, at the Lycée Fromentin, discussions began in earnest, and there the atmosphere changed completely.

That morning, the two delegations sat face to face. Giraud was assisted by Jean Monnet and General Georges, and de Gaulle by Catroux, Philip and Massigli. It was quickly agreed that these seven men would make up a government committee, which would be enlarged later on. Then, however, General de Gaulle proceeded to say that no useful work could be done unless two basic conditions were met: the military command ought to be subordinate to the government committee, and certain Vichy officials in North Africa, namely General Noguès, Governor-General Boisson and the recently arrived Marcel Peyrouton should resign their functions at once. Giraud indignantly refused both conditions, and no agreement at all was reached that day.

During the next two days, General de Gaulle's position seemed precarious indeed: alone with only a handful of men, he was surrounded by an atmosphere of conspiracy, and accused by Giraud of trying to set up 'a totalitarian regime'. Furthermore, he was soon informed that armoured forces were being concentrated around Algiers, that Giraud had ordered the arrest of all Fighting French soldiers on leave in North Africa, that all key points in Algiers were occupied by troops and police forces, and that the man who had just

been appointed as Chief of the Police in Algiers was none other than
. . . Admiral Muselier in person!

But de Gaulle was unimpressed by all this sabre-rattling, and in
the end, it was Giraud who had to give in. On 3 June there was a
second meeting of the two delegations, and it was agreed that
Boisson, Peyrouton and Noguès would fade out of the picture; after
that, everyone agreed on the setting up of a French Committee of
National Liberation initially comprising seven members, with de
Gaulle and Giraud as co-presidents. The committee was to 'exercise
French sovereignty' and 'direct the French war effort in all forms
and in all places'.[1] After seven months of negotiations, horse-
trading, intrigues and manoeuvres, French unity had been re-
established at last.

Immediately upon landing in Algiers, General de Gaulle was
informed that Churchill had arrived there a few days earlier in the
greatest secrecy, and had been joined by Anthony Eden. This
naturally aroused the General's suspicions, all the more so as
Churchill was being kept informed of the progress of the de Gaulle-
Giraud negotiations by General Georges. As the latter had sided
with Giraud during the negotiations, de Gaulle was not slow in
suspecting some British plot against him, orchestrated by Churchill
of course. But there was no such thing, and now that unity had been
agreed upon at last, de Gaulle, Giraud and the five Commissioners
received an invitation to lunch with the Prime Minister on 6 June. De
Gaulle accepted without the slightest show of enthusiasm, but he
accepted nevertheless, and the conversation between him and
Churchill on that occasion was an interesting one, as de Gaulle later
recalled:

> When I remarked how strange his presence at such a time and under
> such conditions had appeared to us, he protested that he was in no way
> attempting to meddle in French affairs. 'All the same,' he added, 'the
> military situation compels His Majesty's government to keep track of
> what is happening within North Africa, which is an essential zone of
> communications. We should have had to take steps if too brutal a shock
> had occurred – if, for instance, you had devoured Giraud all at once.'[2]

De Gaulle protested that nothing was further from his mind, and
they parted on the best of terms.

Upon leaving North Africa, Churchill wrote to President
Roosevelt:

We had the whole French committee to lunch on Friday and everybody seemed most friendly. General Georges, whom I got out of France a month ago and who is a personal friend of mine, is a great support to Giraud. If de Gaulle should prove violent or unreasonable, he will be in a minority of five to two and possibly completely isolated. The committee is therefore a body with collective authority with which in my opinion we can safely work. I consider that the formation of this committee brings to an end my official connection with de Gaulle as leader of the Fighting French which was set out in the letters exchanged with him in 1940 and certain other documents of later date, and I propose insofar as is necessary to transfer these relationships, financial or otherwise, to the committee as a whole.[3]

For almost a week, Anthony Eden had been working on the Prime Minister, which goes far towards explaining the latter's benign and almost Gaullophile mood; in fact, after his discreet presence behind the scenes in Algiers and the luncheon given to the members of the new committee, Churchill felt a bit like the godfather of a re-emerging France.[4] Besides, the new committee would certainly be much easier to deal with than de Gaulle himself, especially with Giraud, Georges and Catroux as members. Upon returning to England, Churchill was therefore beaming with pride and satisfaction, and by no means unwilling to consider the next step advocated by his Foreign Secretary: an official recognition of the French National Committee.

In reality, the union that had been achieved between the two French factions was an extremely precarious one, for the thorny problem of the relations between the newly-elected committee and the High Command had not yet been settled in practice, and a new crisis soon arose. General de Gaulle wanted the High Command and the Commissariat for National Defence to be separate, with the former being subordinate to the latter. General Giraud not only opposed this separation: he claimed to exercise the functions of Commander-in-Chief and Commissioner for National Defence, while at the same time retaining his position as co-President of the Committee of National Liberation. But for de Gaulle, this would have been contrary to French traditions, to plain common sense, and to the agreement just signed by General Giraud himself. As a result, the quarrel continued for the better part of two weeks, with de Gaulle threatening to resign from the committee, Giraud invoking American support, Churchill and Roosevelt meddling through their representatives on the spot and siding with Giraud, and the press on both sides of the Atlantic clamouring for an end to rivalries among Frenchmen, while generally backing General de Gaulle.

Churchill was somewhat alarmed at the pro-de Gaulle sympathies displayed by the British press. By 12 June, the Prime Minister's latent Gaullophobia had already returned, and it was considerably reinforced by the news of the fresh quarrel that had erupted between Giraud and de Gaulle, by the announcement that 'his' original committee of seven men had already been broadened to fourteen (with a majority of de Gaulle followers), and of course by the constant pressure applied on him by President Roosevelt. Once again, all the old grudges which Churchill had been nursing since the summer of 1941 returned *en bloc*, and once again the Prime Minister embarked on an energetic anti-de Gaulle crusade.

The first effects of this new storm were immediately felt by Harold Macmillan in Algiers, who received dozens of strongly-worded telegrams direct from the Prime Minister – something which naturally exasperated Anthony Eden. But this was not all: on 12 June, the British press received the following secret circular:

The Prime Minister is somewhat concerned at the apparent bias in favour of de Gaulle in the press messages from Algiers and in their presentation at this end. De Gaulle owes everything to British assistance and support but he cannot be considered as a trustworthy friend of our country. Wherever he has been, he has left a trail of Anglophobia behind him. . . . It is part of his policy to gain prestige in France by showing how rough he can be with the British and now with the Americans. He has undoubtedly Fascist and dictatorial tendencies. At one time he represents himself as the sole barrier against Communism; at another, as enjoying Communist support.

Nevertheless, in spite of these just grounds for complaint we have always treated him with scrupulous fairness on account of the legend which has been raised about his name in France through the publicity facilities we have given him. We still hope that he will settle down to loyal teamwork with the new committee. Up to the present he is struggling for complete mastery. Should he succeed in this, very serious differences will immediately open between him and the United States. We have to be very careful that these differences do not spread to the relations between Britain and America. The President, who is the best and truest friend that Britain and Europe ever had, has strong views on the subject. . . .

It is hoped therefore that the British newspapers will preserve an attitude of coolness and impartiality in these French quarrels, and do their best to prevent them becoming an impediment to the vigorous conduct of the war.[5]

This imperative piece of advice was signed by the Prime Minister himself.

In the days that followed, the British press showed few signs of heeding the Prime Minister's counsel. There was, however, a noteworthy article in the *Observer* of 13 June:

> Last night's reports from Algiers suggested that General de Gaulle was still on his high horse and insisting that if General Giraud is Commander of the Army, he should be Minister of Defence and Giraud's superior. De Gaulle, if these reports are true, is behaving unwisely. The feeling in London is against him. He has been lavishly helped and generously befriended. But now those who have shown greatest sympathy and tolerance find their patience strained. If General de Gaulle continues his displays of intransigence and if he fails to behave co-operatively and responsibly, he will very soon find himself without friends. He should realize that this is his last chance to retain them. American patience has already reached the point of exhaustion. And nobody is going to allow Anglo-American relations to be disturbed for the sake of a man whose friendliness towards both countries has been no more cordial than he considered strictly necessary. We can do our duty to the people of France in other ways.[6]

The style and the ideas expressed here may seem familiar to the reader. The article was not signed, and there was a very good reason for that: it had been written by Winston Churchill![7] On 15 June, Sir Alexander Cadogan noted in his diary: 'Deadlock seems to persist between de Gaulle and Giraud. PM becoming again temperamentally anti-de Gaulle.'[8]

Once again, however, there was a clear limit to the Prime Minister's recurrent anti-de Gaulle outbursts: after the Darlan episode had mobilized public opinion, the press, the Labour Party and the majority of the government in favour of de Gaulle, it was obviously impossible to get rid of him. Besides, there was absolutely no one to put in the General's place. The French Resistance knew it, the Foreign Office knew it, de Gaulle himself knew it, Churchill knew it, and de Gaulle knew that Churchill knew it. . . .

President Roosevelt did not know it. He had backed Pétain, Weygand, Giraud, Darlan, Giraud again, and he was as determined as ever to have his way in French affairs. In this respect, the latest news was most depressing for the American President: the formation of the Algiers committee, which he had done his best to prevent during the preceding months; the dismissal of the Vichyites, including Peyrouton, whom the Americans themselves had sent to Algiers; the latest quarrel between de Gaulle and Giraud, with every prospect that the former would soon control the French army, and that the latter would be outmanoeuvred, outfoxed and reduced to impotence; the news that the committee was now planning to replace Boisson as Governor-General of West Africa; and finally, the enlargement of the committee from seven to fourteen members, which had been announced on 8 June, but which was only noticed in Washington on 16 June.

The last three items were probably the most distasteful to the President, who decided to act without delay – and he contemplated no half measures; on 17 June, he wrote to Churchill:

> I am fed up with de Gaulle, and the secret personal and political machinations of that committee in the last few days indicate that there is no possibility of our working with de Gaulle. If these were peace times it wouldn't make so much difference but I am absolutely convinced that he has been and is now injuring our war effort and that he is a very dangerous threat to us. I agree with you that he likes neither the British nor the Americans and that he would double-cross both of us at the first opportunity. . . . We must divorce ourselves from de Gaulle because, first, he has proven to be unreliable, unco-operative, and disloyal to both our governments. Second, he has more recently been interested far more in political machinations than he has in the prosecution of the war and these machinations have been carried on without our knowledge and to the detriment of our military interests. One result of this scheming on the part of de Gaulle has been that Eisenhower has had to give half his time to a purely local political situation which de Gaulle has accentuated. The war is so urgent and our military operations so serious and fraught with danger that we cannot have them menaced any longer by de Gaulle. . . .
>
> All of the above can be put by us in language which will be mutually agreeable. Above all I am anxious that the break be made on a basis and for reasons which are identical with both our governments. . . .
>
> The first step in any event should be the deferment of any meeting of the French committee in North Africa until later. . . . Will you communicate with Macmillan to co-operate with Eisenhower in postponing any further meeting of the French committee in North Africa? I am anxious to have your thoughts on this as soon as possible.[9]

The same day, Roosevelt also sent a steady stream of telegrams to General Eisenhower in Algiers: 'For your exclusive information,' he wrote in the first one, 'I want to state that we will not permit, at this time, de Gaulle to control through his partisans on any committee, or direct himself, the French army in Africa, either in the field of operations, or training or supplies.'[10] And in the second one: 'I want it distinctly understood that under no circumstances will we approve the removal of Boisson from Dakar. . . . Dakar is of such vital importance to protection of South Atlantic and South America that I should be compelled to send American troops there if any problematical changes were sought by de Gaulle. . . . You may inform Giraud and de Gaulle of my decision.'[11] And in yet another: 'It is important that you should know for your very secret information that we may possibly break with de Gaulle in the next few days.'[12]

To make the offensive complete and prepare American opinion for the impending break, a gigantic press campaign was started throughout the United States, presenting General de Gaulle in the most unfavourable light. It was scarcely credible, as de Gaulle was described both as a Fascist and a Communist (financed by Stalin), but that was not considered important.

In the event, the whole undertaking misfired badly, and even backfired to some extent: The President's insistence that Giraud should be Commander-in-Chief was conveyed to de Gaulle by Eisenhower on 19 June, and it provoked an outburst of indignation within the committee; the majority of its members considered it as a flagrant violation of French sovereignty, and thereupon informed Giraud that he had to submit himself to the committee or resign. Simultaneously, a 'military committee' was set up, and it was presided over by none other than de Gaulle himself.* Roosevelt's demand that Governor-General Boisson be maintained in his post also fell through when it was announced that Boisson himself had decided to resign. As for the press campaign, it soon provoked a violent backlash in the American and British press in the form of a vigorous denunciation of the President's handling of North African affairs. Finally, for reasons we already know, Churchill refused to break with de Gaulle and his committee, and Roosevelt, for electoral reasons, was unwilling to take sole responsibility for a unilateral rupture.

*The French High Command remained divided, however, with Giraud as Commander-in-Chief in North and West Africa, and de Gaulle as Commander-in-Chief for all other empire forces. However, it was clear that this was only a temporary solution.

It was not without regrets that Churchill had refused to follow the President's lead. That he persisted in his refusal was entirely due to the constant and tireless efforts of his Foreign Secretary, who received some valuable assistance from Harvey and Cadogan in London and Macmillan in Algiers. It goes without saying that these French affairs provoked numerous crises, heated controversies and late-night wrangles between the Prime Minister and his Foreign Secretary during June and the better part of July. Every time, Churchill grunted, scowled, growled and snarled, but Anthony Eden always emerged victorious in the end.

By the beginning of July, however, the Foreign Secretary had taken on an even more formidable task: to get the Prime Minister to recognize the committee, and persuade President Roosevelt to follow suit; for Anthony Eden remained convinced that Britain's relations with France would be all-important in the post-war era, and that the absence of formal ties during the war would heavily prejudice these relations. But Churchill refused to see beyond the present war, he was still furious with de Gaulle, and a few excerpts from Eden's diary will give an idea of the extraordinary difficulties involved in the Foreign Secretary's undertaking:

> 8 July: Defence committee began with a fierce argument about the French. A reply from FDR had encouraged W. to say that nothing would induce him to recognize committee, coupled with a tirade against de Gaulle. I retaliated that Americans had mishandled French problem from beginning, their treatment of de Gaulle would soon make him national hero. Alec C. [Cadogan] backed me and was told he had been 'frequently wrong'. A turbulent and rather ludicrous interlude.
> 12 July: Dined with him [Prime Minister]. Stimson and the Winants also there. Stimson left soon after dinner and we had a fierce but friendly argument about French in Cabinet room until 2 a.m. I told W. again all I felt. He maintained that de Gaulle could not be allowed to dominate committee and he must see how things worked out before recognition was accorded. Admitted that if we broke on this I should have much popular support, but warned that he would fight vigorously to the death. I told him I wasn't contemplating resignation. We agreed each to put our ideas down on paper.
> 13 July: Sent Winston my memorandum at lunchtime as agreed. Surprised to get further letter from him, rather formal. Went over to see him at 7 p.m. and asked him why. He said he didn't like my paper and thought we might be coming to a break.[13]

Naturally, there was no break, and Eden stood his ground. He had solid backing in the Cabinet and in Parliament, and he was further helped by the news that Halifax in Washington and Eisenhower in Algiers had both advocated immediate recognition of the French National Committee.[14] Finally, on 19 June, to Eden's great surprise, Churchill offered to telegraph to Roosevelt urging recognition; and the next day, the Foreign Secretary noted:

> 20 July: After dinner went across to No. 10 at Winston's request. He showed me his message to President about recognition, which is admirable. He remarked that he seemed now to have swallowed my thesis whole, to which I said that it would be truer to say that he was asking Americans to face up to realities of our situation.[15]

The telegram for the President was couched in the following terms:

> I am under considerable pressure from the Foreign Office, from my Cabinet colleagues, and also from the force of circumstances, to recognize the Committee of National Liberation in Algiers. What does recognition mean? One can recognize a man as an emperor or as a grocer. Recognition is meaningless without a defining formula. Until de Gaulle went to North-West Africa and the new committee was formed all our relations were with him and his committee. I stated to Parliament on 8 June that 'The formation of this committee with its collective responsibility supersedes the situation created by the correspondence between General de Gaulle and myself in 1940. Our dealings, financial and otherwise, will henceforward be with the committee as a whole.' I was glad to do this because I would rather deal with the committee collectively than with de Gaulle alone. I had in fact for many months been working to induce or compel de Gaulle to 'put himself in commission'. This seemed to be largely achieved by the new arrangements. Macmillan tells us repeatedly that the committee is acquiring a collective authority and that de Gaulle is by no means its master. . . . He strongly recommends a measure of recognition. He reports that Eisenhower and Murphy both agree with this. . . .
>
> I am therefore reaching the point where it may be necessary for me to take this step so far as Great Britain and the Anglo-French interests set out above are concerned. If I do, Russia will certainly recognize [them], and I fear lest this might be embarrassing to you.
>
> I do hope therefore that you will let me know (a) whether you could subscribe to our formula or something like it, or (b) whether you would mind if His Majesty's government took that step separately themselves. There is no doubt whatever in my mind that the former would be far

better. There are a lot of good men on the committee – Catroux, Massigli, Monnet, Georges, and of course Giraud, who arrived here yesterday. He will certainly raise all this and bring it to a head.[16]

Churchill was to quote this telegram in his memoirs, but he naturally left out the last paragraph, which said:

As you know I have always taken the view that de Gaulle should be made to settle down to honest team work. I am no more enamoured of him than you are, but I would rather have him on the committee than strutting about as a combination of Joan of Arc and Clemenceau. Pray therefore let me know your wishes, for I try above all things to walk in step with you and the advantages of our joint action in this affair are especially obvious.[17]

Roosevelt saw the advantages of a joint action, but he saw no advantage at all in recognizing the committee, as his answer made perfectly plain:

I do not think we should at any time use the word 'recognition', because this would be distorted to imply the we recognize the committee as the government of France as soon as we land on French soil. Perhaps the word 'acceptance' of the committee's local civil authority in various colonies on a temporary basis comes nearer to expressing my thought. We must however retain the right and continue the present practice of dealing directly with local French officials in the colonies whenever military advantages to the Allied cause so dictates. Martinique is an illustrative example.[18]

This was clearly disappointing to the Foreign Secretary. It also came at a time when the British government was assailed by many grave preoccupations, with the fighting raging in Sicily, the military situation in South-East Asia highly uncertain and the development of the German secret weapon daily becoming more threatening. But Anthony Eden refused to be deflected from his course, and he kept up his pressure in favour of recognition, arguing that this was the best possible way of strengthening the committee and encouraging it to stand up to de Gaulle. Churchill, whose dispositions towards the General had not changed,* was always accessible to such arguments. Besides, he could hardly resist the enormous pressure

*On 15 July 1943, Churchill wrote to Lord Halifax: 'I have had a long experience of the character and conduct of de Gaulle and it will be an ill day for France, and afterwards detrimental to England, if he gained the mastery.'[19] As usual, of course, the dislike was mixed with sentimentalism and admiration; thus, on 23 July, he wrote to Macmillan: 'Why can he (de Gaulle) not be a patriot, and sink his personal vanity and ambition? Then he might find friends who would recognize the good that is in him.'[20]

being brought to bear on him by public opinion, the press and Parliament in favour of a prompt recognition. There was also considerable pressure from Canada, Australia, South Africa and all the London-based exile governments. But the strongest and most embarrassing pressure certainly came from Parliament. The session of 14 July, for instance, was an animated one:

> Mr Martin asked the Secretary of State for Foreign Affairs whether recognition of the FCNL* has now taken place.

This drew a somewhat embarrassed reply from Anthony Eden, followed by a new request from Mr Martin:

> Will they (His Majesty's government) speed up recognition as fast as they can?[21]

There was no reply, but the pressure was kept up the following week:

> Mr Boothby asked the Secretary of State for Foreign Affairs whether it is the intention of His Majesty's government to give *de facto* recognition to the French Committee of Liberation?

Eden replied that the government was 'in discussion with other Allied governments' on the subject of recognition.

> Mr Boothby: 'Is it not desirable to give that status as soon as possible?[22]

And on 21 July:

> Mr Ivor Thomas asked the Secretary of State for Foreign Affairs whether he is now able to announce recognition of the FCNL as trustee of all French interests? . . . Is the Right Honourable Gentleman aware that recognition has now been given by all the governments of the occupied territories, and can he explain this delay in recognition by the United Kingdom?
> Anthony Eden: We are in consultation with other Allied governments on the subject.[23]

And by 4 August:

> Mr Boothby asked the Secretary of State for Foreign Affairs whether, in view of the agreements which had been reached between Generals de Gaulle and Giraud . . . His Majesty's government will now accord *de facto* recognition to the FCNL?
> Mr Hammersley asked the Secretary of State for Foreign Affairs

* French Committee of National Liberation

whether in view of the recent arrangements, His Majesty's government will now recognize the FCNL?

Mr Eden: HM's government are in consultation with the major Allied governments on the question of recognition. I cannot say any more at present.

Mr Boothby: Is my Right Honourable friend aware that many people would be very glad to see recognition accorded to the French National Committee at the earliest possible time? . . .

Mr Hammersley: Is it not desirable to get that authority recognized as soon as possible?

Mr Astor: Can my Right Honourable friend give any indication when he will be able to make a statement?

Mr Eden: I cannot.[24]

All this may explain why the question of recognition was very much on the minds of both Eden and Churchill when they arrived at Quebec in the middle of August for the 'Quadrant' conference with their American counterparts and the Allied Chiefs-of-Staff. At the conference, the whole course of the war was reviewed, and many weighty decisions were taken concerning further operations in Italy, the setting up of a supreme command for South-East Asia, strategic plans for the offensive in Burma, an outline plan for 'Overlord', and the ultra secret 'Tube Alloys'* project. But much time and energy was also devoted to the vexed question of recognition of the FCNL, with Churchill and Eden in the front line as champions of French interests.

Upon arrival in Quebec, Churchill had had a long talk with the Canadian Prime Minister, who noted in his diary: 'Churchill emphasising how very warmly the President felt against de Gaulle. Said that he, himself, thoroughly disliked de Gaulle, though he had many manly qualities. He went so far as to say that he was one of these Frenchmen who hated Britain and might even be prepared to join with the Germans in attacking Britain some time. . . . (Churchill) enlarged repeatedly on de Gaulle's mischief-making and the concern he had caused in different countries. . . .' After this ferocious diatribe, Churchill told MacKenzie King that he hoped to get the President to recognize the French committee, and he asked the Canadian Prime Minister to help him in the undertaking![25]

The first conversations with Hull and Roosevelt convinced Churchill that the going would be rough: neither the President nor his Secretary of State would contemplate using the word

*The atomic bomb.

recognition'. But by 18 August, Eden had also arrived, and two days later, he joined the campaign in favour of recognition. His first visit was to Secretary of State Hull, and he noted that day:

> 20 August: More work after luncheon and then talk for more than two hours with old Hull. Most of it was about recognition of French committee. I failed to make any impression and we both got quite heated at one time when I told him we had to live twenty miles from France and I wanted to rebuild her so far as I could. This was a first, though small, step. He retorted by accusing us of financing de Gaulle, with implication that our money had been used to attack him, Hull, for a long time past.[26]

In fact, Hull had gone over all the old stories, including St Pierre et Miquelon. He also said that 'the committee in Algiers would be ephemeral, and would destroy itself'. 'This,' he added, 'would justify the policy hitherto pursued [by the United States], which was not without importance for electoral reasons.'[27] And Eden finally noted: 'I like the old man but he has an obsession against Free French which nothing can cure. I eventually suggested we each take our own course.'[28]

The discussion between the two Foreign Secretaries was resumed on the 22nd:

> Mr Eden brought up the subject of relationship with the French Committee of National Liberation. . . .
>
> The discussion ran along the lines of the British taking the position that de Gaulle was their only friend in 1940, the Secretary raising as against this attitude the objectives and actions of the United States government, including the prevention of the French fleet and the French North African bases from falling into German hands, Admiral Leahy's work in keeping up the spirit and courage of the French population in France, the US naval support long before we were in the war, and the lease-lend aid. Hull finally showed Eden a draft formula, but the latter said he felt that the Prime Minister could not accept a formula which did not contain the word, 'recognition'. . . .
>
> Mr Eden made the suggestion at the end of this discussion that it might be necessary for the two governments to adopt their own formulas and make their own announcements in their own separate ways.
>
> The Secretary followed this by a remark that such a procedure even if done at identically the same moment, would mean an obvious divergence of views.

Mr Eden said that he realized any such policy would be so considered and regretted any such possibility.

The Secretary replied that he very much regretted the consideration of such a divergence of views but that if the British could stand it, we could.[29]

That same day, the question was also debated between Churchill and Roosevelt, and the discussion covered much the same ground:

Mr Churchill said that all the liberal elements in the world, including the governments-in-exile and the Soviet government, were demanding an immediate decision granting full recognition to the committee.

The President took the view that we had to think of the future of France herself. He said this would be in no way advanced by turning over the whole control of the French liberation movement to the present group comprising the French committee.[30]

The two statesmen reached the same conclusion as their Foreign Secretaries, as Churchill wrote to Attlee that evening: 'We have . . . agreed that they should publish their document, and we ours and the Canadians theirs . . . I have pointed out in the plainest terms to the President that they will certainly have a bad press, but he says he would rather have a sheet anchor out against the machinations of de Gaulle.'[31]

By the last day of the conference, 24 August, the participants were nowhere nearer an agreement on the matter, and Hull recalled:

The President said he did not want to give de Gaulle a white horse on which he could ride into France and make himself the master of a government there. I was willing to deal with the French committee on all French territories over which the committee exercised control, but no further, and the President backed me up completely. The President offered to wager Eden a dinner that before many months had run he would have quite a different view of the French committee from that he had now. Eden said he did not want to take the bet. After the conference was over the President said he thought he could have made much further headway with Churchill on the matter if it had not been for Eden.[32]

Of this there was not the slightest doubt, but there was nothing to be done, and the two governments accordingly issued separate statements. The British one, which was published on 27 August, began thus:

His Majesty's government in the United Kingdom recognize forthwith the French Committee of National Liberation as administering those French overseas territories which acknowledge its authority and as having assumed the functions of the former French National Committee in respect of territories in the Levant. His Majesty's government in the United Kingdom also recognize the committee as the body qualified to ensure the conduct of the French effort in the war within the framework of inter-allied co-operation.[33]

The American formula was naturally more limited,* but the very fact that there was one, and that it even bore the word 'recognize', could be considered as a victory for British diplomacy. However, as later events were to show, this did not bring the slightest change in the President's feelings towards the committee in general, and towards the General in particular.

In Algiers, the British statement was taken for what it was: a limited *de facto* recognition that was not essentially different from the recognition granted to General de Gaulle personally in June 1940. The American formula was even more restrictive,** which did not surprise General de Gaulle. During the summer he had seen Roosevelt redouble his efforts to build up Giraud against him and the committee; thus, Giraud had been invited to the United States at the beginning of July and was received by the President at the White House. Unfortunately, the scheme backfired once again, because Roosevelt's insistence during the whole of Giraud's visit that France had temporarily ceased to exist, coupled with the lack of any reference to the French committee, had angered the American press and public opinion, while damaging Giraud's stature in

*Main extracts from the American statement, also released on 27 August:

In view of the paramount importance of the common war effort, the relationship with the French Committee of National Liberation must continue to be subject to the military requirements of the Allied commanders.

The government of the United States takes note, with sympathy, of the desire of the committee to be regarded as the body qualified to ensure the administration and defence of French interests. The extent to which it may be possible to give effect to this desire must however be reserved for consideration in each case as it arises.

On these understandings the government of the United States recognizes the French Committee of National Liberation as administering those French overseas territories which acknowledge its authority.

This statement does not constitute recognition of a government of France or of the French Empire by the government of the United States.

**The Soviet formula, on the other hand, was much more generous than the two others: The Kremlin recognized the French Committee as 'representing the state interests of the French Republic', and as 'the sole representative of all French patriots in the struggle against Hitlerism'. Hence de Gaulle's repeated statements in September and October that France 'must be with Russia in the future',[34] which caused much alarm in London, Washington and Algiers. On 20 October, de Gaulle confided to the Dutch envoy in Algiers that: 'He did not believe there was anything to fear from the Soviet Union. That country would be too busy with its own reconstruction and internal affairs to start revolutions in other countries. Indeed, the Russian red wine had already become 'très rosé'.[34bis]

Algiers. Having recognized this, Roosevelt tried to find yet another French personality who could be more successful in opposing de Gaulle. The General thus learned during the autumn that the old radical leader Edouard Herriot had been contacted, as well as the unfortunate President Lebrun. In the event, however, both men refused to leave France, and Roosevelt was forced to fall back on Giraud – whose position was by now extremely precarious. In fact, he was to be the hapless victim of Roosevelt's continued hostility towards General de Gaulle – and also, admittedly, of his own lack of political judgement.

By the beginning of September, de Gaulle was still dissatisfied with the dual leadership of the committee, and with the independent role exercised by the Commander-in-Chief; this he considered as a source of weakness which could not fail to be exploited by the Allies. It was the Italian situation that finally brought matters to a head: after the campaign in Sicily and the fall of Mussolini, Marshal Badoglio had secretly contacted the Allied Command, and on 4 September an armistice was signed between him and General Eisenhower. But only a week earlier, General de Gaulle had been given to understand by a memorandum from the Allied Command that he would be invited to send a representative to attend the signing of the armistice. In the event, de Gaulle was only informed four days *after* the signature, and the excuse given by the Allied representatives was that General Giraud had been kept informed all along, and had made no special request. . . . De Gaulle and the rest of the Committee were naturally shocked that Giraud had not seen fit to inform his colleagues of what he knew, but Giraud denied vigorously that he had been informed, and the matter was dropped; until it was learned just after the insurrection in Corsica that for several months, General Giraud's agents had been arming the Corsican patriots with British help, but without informing the Committee.* This was not forgotten. A month later, after a victorious campaign under General Giraud's leadership, Corsica was liberated; but yet another month later, Giraud had ceased to be co-president of the French committee.** Theoretically, the change was made with his agreement, as evidenced by the fact that he personally signed the ordinance abolishing the co-presidency. But

*The matter was rendered even more delicate by the fact that the weapons had been supplied to the *Communist* resistance.
**General Giraud remained Commander-in-Chief, though not for long.

then, Giraud frequently signed documents without having read them. By 8 November, at any rate, de Gaulle was left in sole command of the FCNL, and he was almost immediately confronted with an extremely grave Franco-British crisis – which, like most grave Franco-British crises in those days, originated in the Levant.

As a result of strong British pressures, General Catroux had finally agreed to hold elections in the Levant, which was accordingly done in July 1943 and with predictable results: the French did their very best to influence the elections in a pro-French way, not fearing to make use of dubious personalities in the process.[35]* The British also intervened, allegedly in an attempt to 'shame the French into reducing to a minimum the degree of direct interference in the elections which they could get away with'[36] – which in turn gave rise to French accusations that the British were rigging the elections and bribing the electors.[37] Be that as it may, the elections in both Syria and Lebanon resulted in a resounding victory for the Nationalist and anti-French parties, and as a result, Bechara el Khoury became President of the Lebanese Republic, with Riadh es Solh as his Prime Minister.

At a special session of Parliament on 7 October, Riadh es Solh indicated the intention of his government to implement the complete independence of Lebanon by a series of constitutional amendments. The proposed amendments amounted to nothing less than a unilateral abrogation of the mandate, and drew an immediate protest from the French Delegate General in the Levant, Ambassador Helleu. The protest was in fact accompanied by dark threats that implementation of these amendments would have 'grave consequences'. On 8 November, however, while the Delegate General was in Algiers to receive instructions, the Lebanese Chamber met and voted the amendments to the constitution by 48 votes to 0.

It is not known what precise instructions were given to Ambassador Helleu in Algiers, though it can be safely surmised that de Gaulle ordered him to be firm, while Catroux and Massigli were much more moderate, and the rest of the committee was kept very much in the dark.[38] Upon returning to Beirut, at any rate, Helleu seems to have added a personal touch to his instructions: in the early morning of 11 November, the Sûreté Générale, supported by

*The notorious Mokkadem was released from jail to participate in the elections as a pro-French candidate. He was rearrested after the elections.

Senegalese, Lebanese and French troops, arrested the Lebanese President, the Prime Minister and the Ministers of the Interior, Foreign Affairs and Supply. The same morning, Ambassador Helleu issued a series of decrees dissolving the Chamber, declaring the constitution suspended and appointing Emile Eddé as Head of State and of the government.

By locking up the members of the only constitutionally-elected government that Lebanon had seen for the last twenty-five years, the French triggered a formidable storm: riots erupted in Beirut, Tripoli and Saida, and they were ruthlessly suppressed with some loss of life. Lebanese public opinion was unanimous in denouncing the French action, and Emile Eddé was unable to form a government. General Spears lodged a protest couched in none too diplomatic terms, the United States and the Soviet governments followed suit, and the neighbouring Arab countries were unanimous in demanding the restoration of the *status quo ante*.

General de Gaulle reacted in a surprising way: he not only refused to disavow Ambassador Helleu, but he also denounced the whole affair as a *British* provocation to oust the French from the Levant. The committee, however, found some difficulty in following his reasoning, and wiser counsel finally prevailed: on the 13th it was decided that General Catroux would go to Beirut with full powers to settle the matter in a peaceful way. But on 19 November, the British delivered a note to Catroux demanding the release of all the Lebanese personalities by 22 November, failing which they would be set free by British troops and martial law would be proclaimed. This was considered by de Gaulle as an ignominious violation of French sovereignty, Catroux called it 'another Fashoda', and both agreed that perfidious Albion was once again seeking to humiliate France. De Gaulle naturally thundered against all his 'traditional' enemies – General Spears, the War Office, the Colonial Office, '*l'Intelligence*', and of course Winston Churchill, who was certainly behind it all.*

In the event, Catroux himself found out that the best way of restoring calm in Lebanon was to free all the imprisoned ministers

---

*During the past three months, de Gaulle had received many echoes of Churchill's persistent Gaullophobia. Thus, on 10 October, Massigli had reported the following views expressed by Anthony Eden: 'The Prime Minister still hasn't overcome his prejudices against General de Gaulle: he loves France; he will do everything for her; he will do nothing for the General.'[39] However, de Gaulle's accusations during the Lebanese crisis were groundless, though everyone in the British Cabinet had been shocked by the French action, and even the Francophile Anthony Eden agreed that Britain could not stand by without intervening.

and reinstate the President. In fact, he eventually had to reinstate all the other ministers as well. But in the meantime, he had also discovered that Ambassador Helleu 'ceased to be lucid at certain hours of the day',[40]* which was something of a drawback for someone exercising the functions of Delegate General. Helleu was accordingly recalled to Algiers, and everything slowly returned to normal in the Levant – at least on the surface, for both the Syrian and Lebanese governments, with the support of the great majority of their public opinion, henceforth categorically refused to recognize the French mandate or to sign a treaty with the French.

This, however, was not sufficiently appreciated in Algiers, because General de Gaulle persisted in considering the whole matter from the restricted standpoint of French sovereignty and British perfidy. In the midst of the great torment of war, this peculiar and ineradicable prejudice certainly boded ill for the future of Franco-British relations.

---

*The allusion is a bit vague. A report sent to Mr Van Kleffens by the Dutch Chargé d'Affaires Mr Bentinck on 19 November throws a little more light on the matter: 'Ambassador Helleu constantly imbibes vast amounts of alcohol.'[41] The theory that he had done just that before ordering the arrest of the Lebanese President and ministers cannot be dismissed lightly.

CHAPTER 13

AMGOT or GPRF?

By the end of 1943, it was obvious to all that de Gaulle's position had remarkably improved: only a year earlier, he had to rely almost entirely on British help and hospitality, he had less than 100,000 men under his command, and he had seen North Africa liberated by the Anglo-Americans without Free French participation, then taken over by a pro-Vichy and pro-Allied French faction that was clearly hostile to his own movement. But by December 1943, the forces of Fighting France numbered 400,000 men who were being armed and equipped by the United States, and had fought on every theatre from Africa to Italy. More important still, there was now in France a unified Resistance movement, which had recognized de Gaulle as its leader; this had considerably strengthened the General's position among the United Nations, and would strengthen it even further during the coming invasion of France. Furthermore, de Gaulle was now at the head of an empire that was significantly enlarged by the addition of North Africa and strategically reinforced by the rallying of Senegal, with its great naval base at Dakar. Finally, by the end of 1943, the French Committee also had its independent seat in Algiers; and de Gaulle was its sole leader, for Giraud had just been eased out of his post as co-president of the FCNL.

To the British Prime Minister, ever a friend of France, these developments were most heartening – except for the last one, of course, which was profoundly distasteful; '*Ce n'est pas ce que nous avons voulu, Roosevelt et moi*,' he told his old friend General Georges during a short stop in Algiers harbour on his way to Tehran.[1] The fact that General Georges himself had seen fit to resign from the committee naturally made things even worse; to Roosevelt, Churchill telegraphed that he was not at all content with the changes. But Eden succeeded in persuading the Prime Minister that the committee was now more democratic and more representative of France, and that it would have more control over General de Gaulle.[2] Churchill finally accepted this, but there was much worse to come: the arrest in Beirut on 11 November of the Lebanese President, the Prime Minister, and several of his ministers, together with the suspension of the Lebanese constitution. The very next day, Churchill wrote to Roosevelt:

> You have, no doubt, been informed of the lamentable outrages committed by the French in Syria. These completely stultify the agreements we have made with the French and also with the Syrians and Lebanese. There is no doubt in my mind that this is a foretaste of what de Gaulle's leadership of France means. It is certainly entirely contrary to the Atlantic Charter and much else that we have declared. . . . Already we have seen the character of the body we recognized at Quadrant totally altered by de Gaulle's complete assumption of power. The outrages in the Levant are of a different character, and afford full justification, with the support of world public opinion, of bringing the issue with de Gaulle to a head. . . . Meanwhile, I am inquiring carefully into the state of our forces in the Levant. At the same time, should action be taken, it would be necessary to take precautions in North Africa, for I assure you there is nothing this man will not do if he has armed forces at his disposal.[3]

The commotion created by Ambassador Helleu's high-handed action in Beirut had hardly died down when Churchill received yet another blow. The Prime Minister was in Carthage, recovering from an attack of pneumonia, when the French committee announced the arrest of Governor Boisson, Marcel Peyrouton and P. E. Flandin. Churchill, as we know, was partial to these men and he reacted violently. He wrote to Anthony Eden on 21 December:

> I am shocked by the imprisonment of Boisson, Peyrouton and Flandin. The first two placed themselves in what afterwards through our victories came to be de Gaulle's jurisdiction as a result of definite action for which the United States and to a large extent we bear responsibility. To Boisson we owe the delivery of Dakar. Peyrouton was invited in by Giraud and his journey was approved by the State Department. I met both these men at General Eisenhower's invitation when at Algiers in February. . . . I certainly did say to both of them, 'March against the Hun and count on me'. It will be necessary for me to make this public if de Gaulle proceeds to extremities against them. As to Flandin no specific obligation exists. But having acquainted myself in detail with his actions over the last ten years, I am of opinion that for the French committee to proceed against him would be proof that they are unfit to be considered in any way the

trustees of France, but rather that they are small, ambitious intriguers, endeavouring to improve their position by maltreating unpopular figures . . .[4]

Churchill was once again allowing his generosity and imagination to obscure his sound judgement; for Governor-General Boisson had not 'delivered Dakar' until a fortnight after Darlan surrendered to the Anglo-Americans in North Africa. Thereafter, he submitted to Admiral Darlan only, and did absolutely nothing to help the Allied cause. Besides, it was the very same Governor Boisson who had given the order to fire on British and French forces during the Dakar expedition in 1940, and had cruelly mistreated Gaullists – as well as English subjects – interned in French West Africa during the next two years. To Roosevelt, Churchill also wrote that he had certain obligations to Peyrouton and Boisson, and he added: 'It seems to me that the American obligation is even stronger, because we were admittedly following your general lines. I trust, therefore, you will take what steps you can to impress upon the French committee the unwisdom of their present proceedings.'[5]

In Washington, President Roosevelt was more than ready to oblige. After having said that 'he thought the time had come to eliminate de Gaulle and to give the committee a sense of the realities of the situation,'[6] Roosevelt telegraphed General Eisenhower instructing him to inform the committee that 'in view of the assistance given to the Allied armies during the campaign in Africa by Boisson, Peyrouton and Flandin', they (the committee) were 'directed to take no action against these individuals at the present time'. This was nothing if not an ultimatum, but on receiving a copy of it, Churchill telegraphed to Eden on 23 December that he 'felt it essential for us to support the President'.[7]

The Foreign Office, however, could not agree. Macmillan was instructed to persuade General Bedell Smith, Eisenhower's Chief-of-Staff, to take no action in the sense indicated by the President: 'The committee would certainly refuse to obey the instruction. Our bluff would be called, and we cannot allow the bluff to be called. We should therefore have to take military action to enforce our demands, and this would almost certainly lead to the fall of the committee.'[8] Eden himself telegraphed to Churchill that he disagreed with the Prime Minister's view of the accused men's previous record, and that he regarded the instructions sent to Eisenhower as extraordinarily dangerous, since they might well result in the collective resignation of the committee. There followed a barrage of weighty arguments: there would then have to be an administration headed by Generals Giraud and Georges and based on such support as they could get from the army. This in turn would have a disastrous effect on French morale and probably make further co-operation with French resistance groups impossible. It would also greatly increase the danger of civil war after liberation and might well bring about a situation in which British and American troops would have to be diverted from their proper tasks to the maintenance of order in North Africa. Worse still: 'British public opinion would be shocked, and we should find it hard to justify the President's action before Parliament.' Finally, Eden pointed out that the Resistance leaders were primarily responsible for the purges, and must be acting on the orders of the CNR, which represented most of the militant elements in France, 'with whom we could not afford to quarrel'. 'We ought to act through the moderates in the committee,' he wrote, 'and not to drive them into line with the extremists.'[9]

This had the desired effect: Churchill growled, reproached Macmillan for not having 'conveyed the gravity of the issue' to the French committee, but he began to give way. On 25 December, General Bedell Smith wrote to President Roosevelt:

> For your personal information, the Prime Minister was at first very angry at the arrest of Boisson, and he is still urging us to take a very positive stance, while at the same time he is communicating with the Foreign Office in the direction of milder action; his inclination is pugnacious, but he will back down in the face of FO opposition as he has always done in the past if it came to an issue. Consequently, in the event of an abrupt break with the committee which might upset our military plans, the onus would be borne by the US.[10]

This argument, coupled with a report by Ambassador Edwin Wilson that the committee had acted under pressure from the French Resistance, and that a trial would take place only after the liberation of France, persuaded the President to back down and cancel his previous instructions to Eisenhower. Though he very much wished to eliminate de Gaulle as a political force, he had no intention of bearing sole responsibility for the act. He estimated – correctly, as it happened – that American public opinion was not ready for that.

Churchill, to the great relief of Eden and Macmillan, was

gradually coming round to a more sober view of things; on Christmas day he wrote to Eden:

> I agree with you that the literal execution of his instructions would not have been the best way to handle matters, but I was sure that Bedell Smith and Wilson together would do all the softening that was necessary. I am certainly not going to leave the President in the lurch, having myself opened the matter to him. . . . My constant purpose is the restoration of the greatness of France, which will not be achieved by the persecution mania of the committee, nor by their violent self-assertion of French dignity, nor will France be helped by de Gaulle's hatred of Britain and the United States. In order to bring home to the committee the unwisdom of their present attitude and the harm which it will do their country and themselves, a stern pressure should now be maintained. This is more likely to bring them to reason than smooth diplomatic conversations. As I shall be forced to remain in these parts for the best part of a month, I propose myself to see various members of the committee and of the Resistance groups and possibly de Gaulle himself, but I want a harder atmosphere established.[11]

Of the harder atmosphere, there was to be very little. But Churchill had sufficiently mellowed to contemplate the possibility of seeing de Gaulle. In a few more days, he would go one step further, and invite the General to dine and sleep at his villa on 3 January. As Macmillan wrote in his diary, 'Churchill feels about de Gaulle like a man who has quarrelled with his son. He will cut him off with a shilling. But (in his heart) he would kill the fatted calf if only the prodigal would confess his faults.'[12]

But the prodigal showed not the slightest inclination to confess his faults. Worse still, unlike the British Prime Minister, de Gaulle could bear a grudge for a long time, and by the end of December 1943, in spite of de Gaulle's great respect for the man, his feelings towards the Prime Minister were less than friendly; in mid-November, Churchill had stopped in Algiers on his way to Tehran without even asking to see the committee or its president,* and after that neither Churchill nor Roosevelt had bothered to inform him of what had been said at Tehran; on his return journey, the Prime Minister had treated North Africa as his own country and ignored the Governor-General of Tunisia and Morocco; and of course, there was the British ultimatum in the Lebanese affair, not to mention Anglo-

---

*This, in turn, was intended by Churchill as a mark of disapproval for the elimination of General Giraud from the Committee.

American policy one month earlier in Italy; on 17 December, de Gaulle had said to François Coulet: 'Roosevelt and Churchill have corrupted this war. Yes, that is the problem: they have chosen the easiest way and that should never be done in war. You've seen the result: Pétain, Badoglio, Von Papen . . . and it isn't yet over.'[13] There were a few other assorted grudges that were even older.

On New Year's Day, de Gaulle received Churchill's gracious invitation for 3 January; it ended with these words: 'This would give us an opportunity of long-needed talks. My wife is with me here, and if Madame de Gaulle would care to accompany you, it would give us both much pleasure.'[14] A man may have friends, a state, never; besides, was such short notice really compatible with the dignity of France? De Gaulle declined the invitation, pleading the pressure of his other engagements.

Churchill must have been mortified, but he was not discouraged. Having learned that de Gaulle would arrive in Marrakesh on 12 January, he instructed Macmillan to convey another invitation to the irascible General. Thus, on 3 January, Macmillan went to see General de Gaulle.'* That evening, he wrote the following report to Anthony Eden:

> I called on de Gaulle this morning after two telephone conversations with Colonel Warden** to convey an invitation from Colonel Warden to come to Marrakesh as soon as possible to spend an afternoon and evening for long-needed conversations. De Gaulle, as I rather expected, did not show any great alacrity to accept. Indeed, he reminded me of the many indignities that the Prime Minister had heaped upon him, including circulation to English and American press of a bitter attack upon him. I said that this was all quite beside the point. The Prime Minister had intended to visit Algiers on his way back from Cairo and de Gaulle had already accepted this proposal. He was only prevented from doing so by reasons of health. It was clearly impossible for him now to return from Marrakesh to Algiers and it would be missing a golden opportunity, both for France and England, if General de Gaulle refused to go. . . .
> De Gaulle was in rather a sulky mood but I think was really more anxious not to seem to accept too promptly in order to save face. I have had a private talk with Massigli who of course agreed it is essential that he should go. What the outcome of the meeting will be no one can tell, but I am sure that you will agree that now the invitation has been given I

*De Gaulle in his memoirs mistakenly ascribes the visit to Duff Cooper.
**Winston Churchill.

must see that it is accepted. I have not made any report to Colonel Warden as I do not wish to report anything except de Gaulle's acceptance and the date chosen. For this I am still hoping.[15]

What happened later in the day can be read in Macmillan's diary:

Winston has been ringing me up all day in a great state of anxiety and emotion. He told me to cancel the invitation to de Gaulle, since he could not be kept waiting – it was monstrously undignified, I was weakly pandering to the French, etc. . . .

I told Winston that I would see de Gaulle and cancel the invitation. . . . Naturally, the Prime Minister did not really wish to cancel the visit. He only wanted to preserve his dignity and give vent to his feelings on the telephone. (To which, of course, the French listen intently all day.) He showed his disappointment when I agreed to cancel the invitation, and at the end of each of his calls (three today before dinner) ended by saying he would leave it to me.

But later on that evening, de Gaulle informed Macmillan that he 'accepted Churchill's invitation with pleasure'. 'I rang up Winston,' Macmillan continues, 'and gave him de Gaulle's message. He received it with a gasp of surprise, relief, and some disgust into the bargain. But I rang off before he could say much.'[16]

De Gaulle had not accepted the invitation without hesitation: 'On French territory,' he remarked, 'the British Prime Minister's visit was naturally due to the President of the French government; nevertheless, in consideration of the person and the circumstances involved. . . .'[17] De Gaulle obviously thought that Churchill was very ill indeed; on 11 January, the General said to his colleagues on the committee: 'He's on the wane. I don't think he'll be able to regain complete control. He's in Morocco to get set up again. I will leave tomorrow and meet him in Marrakesh.'[18]

On 10 January, Duff Cooper, the new British diplomatic representative with the French Committee of National Liberation, arrived at Marrakesh with his wife and was taken to Churchill's villa.

'There,' Diana Cooper wrote, 'was our old baby in his rompers, ten-gallon hat and very ragged oriental dressing-gown, health, vigour and excellent spirits.' And Duff Cooper noted:

I had a long talk with him before dinner . . . he is still very sticky about de Gaulle and I'm afraid their interview on Wednesday is not likely to be successful. He keeps harping on General Georges and wants to get him back into the committee. He also feels personally responsible for the future of Boisson, Peyrouton, and favourably inclined towards Flandin. He admits that Giraud is no use, but wants him to remain as a kind of figurehead, 'a sort of Duke of Cambridge', as he puts it, 'with a Wolseley in the shape of de Lattre'.[19]

The next day, 11 January, Churchill wrote to Harry Hopkins: 'De Gaulle is coming to see me here on the 12th, and I shall do my utmost to make him realize the disservice he does to France by his known hostility to our two countries, by whose arms alone France can be liberated and restored.'[20] Duff Cooper wrote:

I sat between Winston and Colville at dinner, and all went well until just as we were leaving, when a message came from Algiers to say that General de Lattre de Tassigny, whom Winston had invited for later in the week, had reported that de Gaulle, whose permission to come he had asked, had answered that it would be most inopportune for him to do so at the present time. This produced an explosion. Winston wanted to send a message at once to tell de Gaulle not to come. I did my best to calm him, and he decided to do nothing.

12 January was to be the big day, and Duff Cooper recalls:

I was woken by the telephone ringing at 8.15 a.m. Colonel Warden (the code name under which the Prime Minister was travelling) wished to speak to me. He said he had been thinking things over. The matter was not so simple, would I go over to see him? I got over to him in half an hour. He was in bed, and had apparently worked himself up again about de Gaulle. He suggested sending him a note to the airfield to say he was sorry he had been troubled to come so far, but that he would not be able to see him after all. I strongly dissuaded him from this course, pointing out we knew nothing of the reasons which had caused de Gaulle to prevent de Lattre from coming here. He might have perfectly good reasons for having done so. . . . This worked, but Winston then said he would receive de Gaulle on a purely social basis, would talk about the weather and the beauty of the place and then say goodbye. This was better, but I suggested that Palewski (de Gaulle's private secretary) would probably ask me whether there were going to be serious conversations after lunch – what was I to say? He said he didn't mind having a talk if de Gaulle asked for it, but that he would not take the initiative. Nor would he see him alone. If he did, de Gaulle would misrepresent what he had said. I must be present and Max (Beaverbrook) too, and de Gaulle could bring whom he liked.[21]

Lady Diana Cooper also recalls that morning:

A lot of rehearsing is gone through of the way the General will be brought in, who will stand where and who will interpret. The morning's last resolution is that pleasantries shall be talked at lunch and that no 'conference' should take place. But Clemmie has given him a Caudle curtain lecture on the importance of not quarrelling with Wormwood.* She thinks it will bear fruit. As Wormwood is sure to take offence, it's hardly worth all the planning. Anyway Flags bungled the arrival completely.**[22]

'The General,' Churchill remembered, 'arrived in the best of humour, greeted Mrs Churchill in English, and spoke it throughout the meal. To make things equal, I spoke French.'[23] Duff Cooper adds:

> All passed off well, Winston was in a bad mood when de Gaulle arrived and was not very welcoming. He had just read of the shooting of Ciano, Bono, etc., which had rather shocked him. As lunch proceeded, however, Winston thawed. He had Diana on one side and Palewski on the other. I sat on the other side of Palewski and was able to inform him quietly of the delicacy of the situation and of the PM's irritation over the de Lattre episode. De Gaulle sat opposite, next to Clemmie. When the ladies left, Winston invited de Gaulle to sit next to him, but things were still sticky.[24]

'After lunch the ladies went off to visit the bazaars,' Churchill wrote, 'and de Gaulle and I and the other men settled down in the garden for a long talk. I had a lot of awkward subjects to deal with, and I thought my speaking French would add a lighter touch to them.' Mr Nairn, who made a few notes immediately afterwards, recalled: 'I heard Mr Churchill say to Mr Duff Cooper in English in a very audible whisper, "I'm doing rather well, aren't I? Now that the General speaks English so well, he understands my French perfectly." Then everyone, General de Gaulle setting the example, burst out laughing. The Prime Minister continued in French, but the super-sensitive General was completely disarmed and ready to accept Mr Churchill's comments in a friendly and helpful spirit.'[25] The General's helpful spirit somehow escaped Duff Cooper: 'The conversation lasted about two hours. Winston was admirable, I thought, and de Gaulle very difficult and unhelpful. He talked as though he were Stalin and Roosevelt combined.'[26] As for Churchill's conversation, it consisted mainly, according to the Prime

*De Gaulle.
**'Flags' was an officer on Churchill's staff. He showed the guests in through the wrong entrance. (Lady Diana Cooper to the author, 17 May 1979.)

Minister himself, 'of a prolonged complaint and lecture in good manners and bad French upon the General's many follies.'[27]

The first issue raised by Churchill will surprise no one:

The Prime Minister pointed out to de Gaulle the unwisdom of alientating his own goodwill and that of the President of the United States by the prosecution of those who, whatever their previous misdeeds might have been, had rendered services to the Allied cause and who had therefore reason to believe that they could rely on the Prime Minister's and the President's protection. There could be no doubt that had M. Boisson not handed over Dakar to the Allies, invaluable time would have been lost and much British and American blood would have been spilled. M. Peyrouton had been definitely encouraged by the British and American governments to leave his safe retreat and to return to North Africa, where so long as he continued in office he had rendered useful services. The Prime Minister had attended a luncheon party where both these gentlemen were present and on leaving them had said, 'Comptez sur moi'.

In the case of M. Flandin there was no similar commitment on the part of the British or American governments, but of the three who had been arrested he was certainly the least guilty. . . . The Prime Minister felt that if the line dividing the guilty from the innocent were to be drawn at the level which would include M. Flandin among the guilty, the future of France would prove very tragic and civil war would be almost inevitable.[28]

There happened to be lying on the table a copy of the local newspaper which announced in large headlines the debate which had taken place in the French Assembly on the previous day – when all the members had demanded more severe penalties for those who had been guilty of collaboration with the enemy. General de Gaulle pointed to it and said that that was his answer. He had caused the assembly to be set up in pursuance of his democratic policy, and having set it up he was bound to be influenced by its opinion and to listen to its demands. . . .

'France had suffered for a long time, and was still suffering,' he said. 'The people wanted those responsible for capitulation to be punished, and if revolutionary convulsions were to be avoided, public opinion should not be given the impression that the guilty people may escape without punishment.'[29] At the same time he could assure the Prime Minister that the men under arrest would come to no harm until they were tried after the liberation of France and that meanwhile they were not being ill-treated.[30]

The Prime Minister agreed that France was suffering, that her young people were being deported or had taken to the woods, and stated that he had the issue of their liberation very much in mind. And as de Gaulle stressed that they were no longer receiving weapons and supplies, the PM pointed out that the necessary orders could be given to insure that they were effectively supplied. The details of this could be worked out with Mr Duff Cooper. . . . De Gaulle then expressed his satisfaction that such an old friend of France as Mr Duff Cooper had been appointed as British Ambassador to the committee.

'Yes,' said the PM, 'I sent Mr Duff Cooper in order to smooth things down and dispel misunderstandings between us; but you must be tolerant . . . we are going to put many lives at risk, and there must be as little loss as possible.' De Gaulle agreed, provided that the policy adopted did not give rise to a revolutionary agitation.

The Prime Minister evoked the past. He deplored the conflict that had arisen between himself and the man whom he had recognized at Tours as the 'man of destiny' . . . and yet, friendship between the two people had to survive this war and extend into the post-war period.

General de Gaulle agreed that it was necessary for England and France to end this war together, as genuine comrades in arms.

Mr Churchill asked if, according to General de Gaulle, Franco-British friendship should not only last until the end of the war, but also extend to the post-war period.

De Gaulle: 'France will be exhausted after this terrible ordeal, and to recover, she will need help from all quarters, especially from the United States and Great Britain.'

'If this is so,' the PM declared, 'we should deal gently with each other. Lord Beaverbrook can be a witness that during the whole war, I have always endeavoured to deal gently with Mr Roosevelt and Mr Stalin, and yet I am at the head of a mighty army and a vast empire.'

General de Gaulle replied that although he had brought over French co-operation at a time when England was isolated and threatened with defeat, he had not been 'dealt with gently' the way the PM indicated. He reminded him that the North African operation had been undertaken without him and even without his prior knowledge.

(Here the Prime Minister interposed that the invasion had been primarily an American operation, that his own part in it, as he had always said, had been that of lieutenant to the President, and that, as such, he could not take anybody into consultation without the President's consent.) 'Besides,' Churchill added, 'Darlan brought us a dividend . . . and another difficulty that arose between us was the Lebanese affair. You acted there with dangerous brutality. We only put Gandhi in jail when it appeared clearly that his action could serve

Japanese designs. You must reckon with public opinion in the democracies. . . .'

General de Gaulle observed that this was the reason why he had immediately sent General Catroux to smooth things over. 'That is why,' he added, 'I found your ultimatum incomprehensible. You should know that if I send Catroux, this rules out the use of force. . . .'

The Prime Minister mentioned the case of General Georges, an officer for whom he had the highest regard, whom he had himself encouraged to come out of France and who had now been dropped from the committee. General de Gaulle replied that he also respected General Georges but that it was not possible always to find a place in the government for everyone whom one respected. He had offered General Georges the post of Grand Chancellor of the Legion of Honour and had not even received a reply to his offer.

The Prime Minister then referred to General de Lattre de Tassigny whom he did not know personally and of whom he had never heard until he was informed by his advisers that the general was a very distinguished soldier whom it would be desirable for him to meet. He had therefore sent him an invitation only to be informed that de Gaulle had forbidden him to accept it.

General de Gaulle protested that he had intended nothing of the kind. He had known that General de Lattre had duties to perform elsewhere at the time suggested for the visit and had therefore said it would be inopportune.

Finally, the Prime Minister reminded General de Gaulle of his prediction that the General would finally win the day, he said that he was glad to see his prediction become a reality, and he had no doubt that the same thing would happen again in France.

De Gaulle was prompt to seize the opportunity: 'That is an added reason to recognize here and now that the civil administration of liberated French territory should be the committee's responsibility.'

Duff Cooper intervened here to say that this 'was a technical and complicated matter better dealt with either in London or in Washington where legal and other experts could be consulted.'

The interview was now coming to an end, and Duff Cooper noted: 'Although the Prime Minister spoke with great frankness, the tone of the interview throughout was friendly and there was no danger at any time of its degenerating into a quarrel.'[31] Better still, the latter part of the interview, according to the French minutes, 'was most cordial, with Mr Churchill showing all exterior signs of emotion'.[32]

This could hardly be expected of General de Gaulle; but he did the

next best thing, and asked Churchill '*Aimeriez-vous passer les troupes françaises en revue?*'
Churchill: '*J'aimerais. Je ne l'ai pas fait depuis 1939.*'
De Gaulle: '*Eh bien! Nous passerons ensemble les troupes en revue.*'*[33]

The interview ended at 5.00 p.m., and both men parted on the friendliest terms. Diana Cooper recalls that 'by five it was over and was declared first to have done no harm, and later to have been really quite a success. Duff and his master did a quick change of coat, Duff praising the other's patience and deploring Wormwood's vile temperament, manners etc., and the other talking most indulgently about him.'[34] De Gaulle was also in an indulgent mood after the meeting; as the British Consul later reported:

> In the course of a conversation which I had today with Monsieur Aveillé, the president of the local branch of *Front National de la Libération* he told me that he had had two interviews with General de Gaulle, one of which took place on Wednesday evening shortly after the General had taken leave of the Prime Minister. The General had asked him if he knew why he had come to Marrakesh and Monsieur Aveillé replied that he supposed that he had come to meet Mr Churchill. 'Yes,' had said General de Gaulle, 'but my reason for coming to see him was to try to effect a reconciliation – and I think I have succeeded.' Monsieur Aveillé said that the General had gone on to remind him of the situation in which the British had found themselves in summer 1940 and to stress how, in spite of their own great peril, they had continued to give so much help to the French. 'We must not forget,' said the General 'that the British were in a *sale trou*; and I wonder whether we would have done as much for them had our positions been reversed.' Monsieur Aveillé said that he had been greatly impressed by the General's look of pleasure and satisfaction; he had met him on previous occasions, but never had he seen him so happy.[35]

Thus the familiar pattern was repeated, and once again the meeting between the two leaders had yielded very few concrete results: Churchill had only given vague assurances about arming the French Resistance, and entirely eluded the all-important question of civil administration in liberated French territories. As for de Gaulle, he had made no concessions in the matter of Boisson, Peyrouton and Flandin, and had not even contemplated Generals

De Gaulle: Would you like to review the French troops?
Churchill: I would. I haven't done it since 1939.
De Gaulle: Well, then, we will review the troops together.

Giraud and Georges' return to the committee. It appears once again that the respect and admiration which both men felt for each other every time they met blinded them temporarily to the fact that neither one of them was making the slightest concession. They may also have felt that they were bound by a common love for France – though it was probably not the same love, and certainly not the same France.

The review of French troops the next morning proved a success, as Duff Cooper reported to the Foreign Office: 'The Prime Minister and the General stood side by side at the saluting base and took the salute. The troops – French, Moroccan, Algerian and Senegalese – presented a smart appearance, and the obvious endeavour of these small contingents worthily to represent the great tradition of the French army presented a moving spectacle. There was much shouting of "Vive Churchill" and "Vive de Gaulle".[36] 'The ceremony took place amid the liveliest popular enthusiasm,' de Gaulle recalled, 'for the crowd of Marrakesh, as for the crowds everywhere else which would see the newsreels without knowing what went on behind the scenes, the appearance of Churchill and de Gaulle side by side meant that the Allied armies would soon march together to victory, and that was all that mattered. I said this to the Prime Minister, and we agreed that it was the crowd which was right after all.'[37] 'When the Prime Minister left,' Duff Cooper continued, 'the General said a few words through the microphone. He spoke of the rebirth of the French army and the renewal of the Anglo-French alliance and referred to the privilege they had enjoyed of having the British Prime Minister present on such an historic occasion.'[38]

The next day, of course, the magic of Marrakesh had already receded. The French Commissioner of the Interior, D'Astier, saw de Gaulle that day, and the French leader mentioned Churchill in the following terms: 'He is very tired . . . he is on the wane . . . yes, I told him about the armament question. He agrees, but we shouldn't count on it; what would they get out of it?'[39] D'Astier then went to visit Churchill in Marrakesh to persuade him to arm the Resistance. The Prime Minister (whom D'Astier described as 'an old new-born baby') told him: 'He's a great man, your de Gaulle, "*c'est l'homme de la France.*" I have always backed him, but how can we get along? He hates England.'[40]

The Prime Minister probably did not believe this himself, nor did

he really believe that he could secure the French committee's
political compliance in exchange for an increased supply of arms to
the Resistance – though he evidently saw no harm in trying: 'Yes, I
agree, *il faut faire la guerre*, we will help you; but you must
behave.'[41] And the best way to behave, according to Churchill, was
of course . . . to free Boisson, Peyrouton and Flandin. This was
quickly becoming an obsession with the man. . . . However, there
was no doubting Churchill's willingness to help France and bolster
French Resistance. He gave the necessary instructions at the end of
the month, and by the first full moon of February, armament for
16,000 men was parachuted to the Resistance; the quantity was to be
doubled the next month.[42] Likewise, Churchill was anxious to
accede to French demands that they should participate in the
coming battle of France; he therefore lifted one after the other the
numerous administrative and material obstacles that prevented the
Leclerc armoured division from being included in the Allied
expeditionary force.

In Algiers, by the end of January 1944, General de Gaulle was
confronted with several preoccupying problems: on the one hand, he
was in precarious health, suffering from a bout of malaria and
kidney trouble. In France, on the other hand, the Germans and their
French collaborators had stepped up their campaign against French
Resistance, and many groups were being eliminated. Within the
Resistance itself, Communist elements were rapidly increasing their
influence, and secretly pursuing a policy which had little in common
with that of the National Committee; this, in turn, was not entirely
unrelated to de Gaulle's insistence that French forces – notably the
Leclerc division – should participate in the coming invasion of
northern France. For although de Gaulle had not been informed of
the target date for 'Overlord', he knew it to be imminent. He also
knew that the success or failure of the mission he had assumed in
June 1940 would depend on the way France was liberated; and there
precisely lay the greatest threat to the authority of the FCNL and its
unbending leader.

On 9 September, 1943, the Committee had sent to Washington
and London a draft memorandum determining the conditions under
which the French administration would co-operate with Allied
forces during the future battle of France. The French administration
would naturally be subordinated to the FCNL and its representatives. According to the draft project, each major Allied unit would

also be accompanied by French officers in charge of 'administrative liaison' with local authorities; these officers had already been trained and sent to England under the command of Hettier de Boislambert. But by the spring of 1944, there was still no reply from London or Washington to the French proposal. And yet the only alternative to the proposed agreement was negotiation with the Vichy authorities in France, or a direct administration by the Allies on the model of the Italian AMGOT (Allied Military Government in Occupied Territories).

To the British authorities, the French proposal was profoundly embarrassing, because it raised a fundamental issue which no one was prepared to face: that of the recognition of the FCNL, and its right to take over the administration of liberated France. The Foreign Office, as ever the most favourable to Fighting France, was in favour of giving the Allied Commander-in-Chief temporary responsibility for civil administration in war zones. But this civil administration would be French in character and personnel, and would in due course come under a provisional French authority – which would necessarily be the FCNL, as the Foreign Office knew of no other which had the support of French Resistance and public opinion. The War Office, on the other hand, had different plans; they contemplated the setting up of a 'military administration, staffed by American and British civil affairs officers, and continuing during the first six months after the liberation of French territory'.

As usual, however, the position of the Prime Minister was the most important and – again as usual – it was strongly influenced by Churchill's peculiar prejudices: his distrust of de Gaulle and his constant urge to intervene in French affairs. On 26 January, 1944, he wrote to his Foreign Secretary:

> I am not in favour at the present time of making arrangements for the French committee to take over the civil administration in any parts of France we may liberate. We have no guarantee at present that de Gaulle will not hoist the Cross of Lorraine over every town hall, and that he and his vindictive crowd will not try to peg out their claims to be the sole judge for the time being of the conduct of all Frenchmen and the sole monopolists of official power. That is what the President dreads, and so do I. It may well be that in two or three months a different atmosphere will prevail on the French committee. Already there are improvements. Meanwhile it would be most foolish for us to give ourselves over to them and thus throw away one of the very few means of guiding them and making them 'work their passage' which we still possess.[43]

Clearly, the Prime Minister did not consider that there was any urgency in the matter of civil administration. As curious as it may seem, he was still more interested in the fate of Boisson, Peyrouton and Flandin. There was also something else: Churchill asked D'Astier, who had come to warn him of the danger of an Allied military government in France, 'Would you do me a favour? . . . No, no, that would be embarrassing for you. You couldn't do it. . . . Still, if you meet General Georges, give him my regards.'[44] A few days later, Churchill wrote to Duff Cooper what he had in mind: 'You may now sound de Gaulle about sending Georges to London as personal military liaison with me as Minister of Defence – do not, on the other hand, make the démarche in such a way as to encounter a refusal.'[45] But Churchill was also anxious to remain on friendly personal terms with the man he distrusted and admired at the same time. On 2 February he wrote him the following message: 'Accept my compliments on the magnificent way in which your troops are fighting in the present battle. It is a comfort to have strong French army formations alongside British and Americans in the line. It reminds us of old times and it is the herald of new times.'[46]

In view of Churchill's constant admiration for the French army and his sentimental attachment to France, it may appear curious that he remained blind to the pressing necessities of an agreement on civil administration in liberated territories. His distrust for de Gaulle, his idea that civil administration could be used to 'guide' the French committee in France after landing, do not entirely explain the Prime Minister's reluctance to deal with the matter; the truth is that Churchill was as determined as ever to avoid a quarrel with the American government over de Gaulle and to support any initiative taken by President Roosevelt in French affairs. But the President's past initiatives in French affairs had often been most unfortunate, and there were very few signs of an improvement for the future.

President Roosevelt's policy towards France continued to be guided by the same principles as before: an unqualified opposition to General de Gaulle and his FCNL, a certain appetite for some parts of the French Empire,[47] a total disregard for French sovereignty, and a persistent sympathy for the old Marshal, all this hidden under a virtuous cloak of respect for the 'real wishes' of the French people, considered as unable to express themselves during the war – and probably for a certain time after that. All these elements were still very much present when the matter of civil administration was examined in Washington at the end of 1943.

There was very little ambiguity about President Roosevelt's position on that matter; he made it quite plain in a letter sent to Secretary of State Hull from Cairo on 27 November, 1943: 'I am convinced that no final decisions or plans concerning civil affairs for France should be made at this time. . . . The thought that the occupation when it occurs should be wholly military is one to which I am increasingly inclined.'[48] By the spring of 1944, the President's policy had not changed – and some preparations were being made to implement it: the structures of an AMGOT for France were devised, and administrators were being trained in Charlottesville; within the short span of two months these men were to learn the French language – and the art of being French Prefects; they were accordingly dubbed the 'Sixty Day Marvels'. Finally, as there was no question of the French committee issuing currency in liberated France – this would imply Allied recognition of the committee's sovereignty – the American government set out to print its own military francs, to be issued in France by the Allied military commander; these notes were to be inscribed with the motto, 'Liberté, Égalité, Fraternité' and a French flag on one side, and the words 'La République Française' on the other. But President Roosevelt even objected to that; he only wanted the inscription, 'La France'. Morgenthau and John MacCloy tried to change his mind, but FDR replied, 'How do you know what kind of a government you will have when the war is over? Maybe it will be an empire.'— 'That is just what we don't want to imply. . .' Morgenthau pointed out. 'It seems to me if you put on the words "La République Française", it isn't going to tie your hands at all.'

'Henry,' Roosevelt said, 'you talk just like the British Foreign Office.'

'Mr President,' Morgenthau replied, 'I have never been so insulted in ten years.'

But as the discussion continued, Morgenthau noted,

The answer always came back that he (FDR) didn't want anything on the money which would indicate which kind of a government it was going to be. I argued and MacCloy argued and while the President was in a grand humour, he had all his 'Dutch up' and you couldn't budge him at all. He said, 'I have heard all these arguments. De Gaulle is on the wane.' . . . We got off the 'Liberté, Égalité, Fraternité'; he said we

couldn't have that. He also asked for 'La France' . . . off. So it got back to
the flag and nothing else.[49]

Finally, on 15 March, Roosevelt issued a draft directive to the
Allied Commander-in-Chief, specifying that General Eisenhower,
once in France, 'may consult the FCNL' – but he could also deal
with any other *de facto* French authority if he deemed it desirable,
though 'not the Vichy government as such' – which still left the door
open for dealings with individual members of that government. The
President, it is true, was not very well informed of the situation in
France. A month earlier, Admiral Leahy had advised him that
'when Allied troops enter France, the most reliable person to whom
we could look for help in rallying the French was Pétain.'[50]

Roosevelt's March 15th directive to Eisenhower did not remain
secret for very long; less than a week later, the French committee was
informed of it, and M. Viénot went to see Anthony Eden to tell him
that 'he was a good deal troubled by the reports which he had
received of the most recent proposal for the administration of
France when the Allied armies entered that country,' and he added,

> If, in fact, the whole situation was left vague and the responsibility was
> placed on the Commander-in-Chief, what other outcome could result
> but something very like anarchy or AMGOT? In practice what would
> happen? In one city the Commander-in-Chief would appoint some
> official who might share the view of the French Committee of National
> Liberation. In another district he might appoint an official who was
> sympathetic to Vichy and in a third a Communist. Who was to co-
> ordinate these various authorities if not the French committee? Surely it
> would be a terrible burden to place upon the Commander-in-Chief, and
> if it were placed on him it could only result in his administering France.[51]

The Foreign Secretary entirely agreed and said that the formula
'the Commander-in-Chief may consult' should be replaced in the
directive with 'will consult' the French committee.[52] 'My own
conviction,' Eden later wrote, 'was that the Resistance movement in France, and indeed the majority of French opinion was
overwhelmingly behind de Gaulle and that, if we were to treat the
National Committee of Liberation shabbily, or with apparent
mistrust, we should damage Anglo-French relations at the very
moment when they might soon play an influential role in the world
again.'[53]

There remained of course to convince Churchill that amendments
to the directive were necessary and that a telegram to this effect

should be dispatched to President Roosevelt. This of course was no easy task, especially as the French committee had just taken an initiative which was profoundly distasteful to the British Prime Minister: the former Vichy Minister of the Interior, Pucheu, had been shot in Algiers two days earlier. Eden's efforts were therefore unsuccessful. Ambassador Viénot decided to try his own hand and had an interview with Churchill on 4 April.

The Prime Minister, who was obviously tired, first told him that 'France would for a long time remain under the jurisdiction of the Allied Commander-in-Chief' and that 'there would be great battles in France,' but as this was beside the point, Churchill switched to more familiar ground:

> The French committee had failed to obtain the confidence of the President. He too [the PM] had been deeply wounded at this attitude. All his life he had been a friend of France. He was still looking for the France he used to know, '*Je cherche la France que j'aime*'; he did not recognize it in General de Gaulle. He was always thinking what he could do to help Britain's allies, but at Marrakesh General de Gaulle had not betrayed a similar spirit of reciprocity. Far from having any personal bias against General de Gaulle, he admired him in many ways, but he felt he was not a friend of England.

Viénot again tried to bring back the conversation to the President's directive; after agreeing that 'there had been grave misunderstandings,' he remarked that in France, 'apart from Vichy, no possible authority other than the committee presented itself'. But Churchill replied that President Roosevelt's formula 'was not devised hastily. It was worked out after very careful consideration. It would be difficult to persuade him to alter it, especially after Pucheu's murder.'

Viénot then assured him that 'Pucheu would not be a precedent,' which gave the Prime Minister a chance to take up his favourite theme:

'I hope not. When I was in Algiers I was invited to luncheon by Giraud to meet Flandin and Peyrouton. It would be distressing if they were killed.' After which, Churchill returned to his diatribe:

> At Quebec he and Mr Eden had brought great pressure upon the President in French interest. Their efforts had been stultified by General de Gaulle's attitude . . . nevertheless matters had been patched up. General Georges, who was an old and trusted friend, had been included in the subsequent French committee. He had been dismissed without

warning.* Even so, he, the Prime Minister, had taken the initiative in impressing on Soviet authorities and the President that France should be represented on the Mediterranean Commission. France must seek to understand the President and to avoid rubbing him the wrong way.

Returning at last to the directive, Churchill told Viénot that he would 'think about it'.

This was not encouraging; in fact, after having read a record of the conversation, Massigli decided it was wiser not to show it to General de Gaulle.[55] And yet, these were but moderate words compared to Churchill's outburst when he learned shortly thereafter that General Giraud's appointment as Commander-in-Chief had just been cancelled by decree of the committee.

For all his invectives against the French committee and its intractable leader, Churchill was not entirely blind to the fact that the President's directive was ill-conceived and could not be accepted in its present form. On the other hand, as he said to Under-Secretary of State Stettinius, he 'did not want to bother the President about it at this time'.[56] However, it was just as impossible to take no action at all, for D-Day was approaching fast, and the British press was becoming increasingly preoccupied by the lack of any dispositions for civil administration in France after the Allied landing. By the end of March, the *Manchester Guardian*, the *Observer*, the *Daily Herald* were clamouring for increased Allied co-operation with the committee, and the *Daily Herald* even revealed that de Gaulle had made proposals for civil administration six months earlier, and received no reply. Why are the French notes left unanswered for six months?, the *Daily Herald* asked; and what about this directive to General Eisenhower, empowering him to deal with the local authority of his choice? Obviously, political co-operation between the Allies was not functioning properly, the paper concluded.[57] By the beginning of April, *The Times* and the *Economist* were going one step further: they asked that the FCNL be officially recognized as the provisional government of France.[58] Even the *Daily Mirror*, usually indifferent to international politics, joined the fray and asked for frank co-operation with General de Gaulle and the committee.[59] It was obvious that Parliament and public opinion would soon follow suit.

This was clearly embarrassing. Churchill was once again caught

*As we know, this was not so; General Georges had resigned from the committee on his own initiative.

between his allegiance to the President and his public opinion at home. Besides, France, for all her mistakes, was still France; the Prime Minister finally decided to ask Roosevelt for a modification of the directive in the sense indicated by Eden. In addition, as he recognized that the lack of understanding between Roosevelt and de Gaulle was at the root of all evil, he endeavoured to bring about a meeting between the two men. The attempt to obtain a modification of the directive was a complete failure; on 17 April, Churchill was informed that the President had refused any amendment and disapproved of the substitution of 'should' for 'may', as 'General Eisenhower should have complete discretion in the matter of civil government.'[60] Churchill of course did not insist: 'It would be a great mistake for him,' he wrote to Lord Cranborne, 'to have a row with the President on these small points for the sake of the Free French. . . . He obtained a large number of very favourable and friendly decisions from the President every week and did not want to spoil their relationship.'[61]

The attempt to arrange a meeting between Roosevelt and de Gaulle looked more promising; FDR answered on 13 April: 'I have no objection to a visit from de Gaulle.'[62] Having then informed General de Gaulle through Duff Cooper that 'he thought he could persuade the President to ask General de Gaulle to visit him, if the latter agreed', Churchill received an unexpectedly gracious answer from the General, who was himself most anxious to talk to the President. Duff Cooper reported that 'de Gaulle . . . said he would be most happy to accept such an invitation at any time'. 'The General,' Duff Cooper added, 'asked me also to convey to you an expression of his personal gratitude for the suggestion in which he saw convincing proof of your sympathy, and which he would remember even if the proposal should not prove successful.'[63]

It did not prove successful. That same day, President Roosevelt, ever mindful of his domestic political image at the approach of elections, cabled to Churchill: 'I will extend no formal or informal invitation.'[64] Churchill, however, was not discouraged. On 16 April, he wrote to Duff Cooper: 'If de Gaulle can stoop so far as to inquire through his ambassador in Washington whether a visit from him would be agreeable . . . and if he lets me know that he will do this beforehand, I will make sure that a favourable answer will be given before the démarche is made.'[65]

De Gaulle was not a man to stoop – except for the good of

France. Churchill was thus allowed to proceed with his complicated diplomacy, which he did with unflagging zeal; on 20 April, he wrote to Roosevelt: 'General de Gaulle would like to enquire, through his representative in Washington, whether a visit from him to you would be agreeable . . . you might do him a great deal of good by paternal treatment and indeed I think it would be a help from every point of view.'[66] Roosevelt replied dryly that the question should be 'raised about one month from now by French representatives in Washington'.[67] But Churchill was nothing if not tenacious; the next day, he wrote to the President: 'I had hoped you would go a little further than this. After all, this man, whom I trust as little as you do, commands considerable forces including naval forces and the *Richelieu*, which are placed most freely at our disposal, and are in action or eager for action. He presides over a vast empire, all the strategic points in which are at our disposal.'[68]

Roosevelt refused to budge, no doubt encouraged in this by Cordell Hull, who had written to him that 'the PM's intervention is rather clearly designed to get us definitely and irrevocably tied to de Gaulle prior to the landing, so that we will be committed to him even if events do not turn out as anticipated'.[69] The President, therefore, sent another negative reply to Churchill, who finally gave up: 'I press it no more,' he replied on 24 April.[70]

No prospect of a reconciliation between de Gaulle and Roosevelt, very little hope that an acceptable directive would finally be issued to the Commander-in-Chief, and all this only five weeks before the planned date for the great landing in France; it was all most embarrassing – but there was much worse to come.

For reasons that went back to the Dakar expedition in 1940, both Roosevelt and Churchill had decided that the French committee should not be kept informed of the preparations for the landing in France. The date of the landing was also to remain secret – it would be Madagascar and North Africa all over again – and on 12 April, Churchill wrote to FDR: 'I agree that FCNL should not be made a party in any way to the details of 'Overlord'. I have tried to further their own wish to have the Leclerc armoured division included in the forthcoming battle. But the presence of this single division will not give them any right to be informed of our secrets . . . and they should be told so without delay. . . .'[71] This, however, was not as easy as it looked, for the French committee had in London a 'Military Delegate for the Northern Theatre of Operation', who was to co-operate with General Eisenhower after landing. This delegate was none other than General Koenig, the hero of Bir Hakeim, and he had another title, which to the Allied HQ was more important than all the others: Commander-in-Chief of all French Forces of the Interior; these Resistance forces had an extremely important role to play before, during and after D-Day. Hence it was impossible not to co-operate with General Koenig – and it was most difficult to co-operate with him without co-operating with General de Gaulle, to whom General Koenig had the duty to report. Finally, it was decided not to inform Koenig in advance.

An added complication arose at about the same time; starting at midnight on 17 April, the British government imposed a ban on all Allied cipher communications with the outside world until the day of invasion. This included diplomatic communications, and was rigorously enforced. Apart from drawing the enemy's attention to impending operations, the ban had other unfortunate effects: it drew a storm of protests from Allied nations, and especially from exile governments in London; the French committee, of course, was not excepted, and all French cipher communications between Algiers and London were cut off. De Gaulle, predictably, was outraged: 'This precaution, taken unilaterally by the Anglo-Americans in regard to the French, whose forces, like their own, were to play an essential role in the operations, and whose territory would be the theatre of battle, struck us as an insult.'[72] De Gaulle, of course, was not a man to take an insult without retaliating.

By the beginning of May, less than four weeks before 'Overlord', there was still no agreement over civil affairs, and the Foreign Office was becoming increasingly alarmed. On 8 May, Eden sent another minute to the Prime Minister:

> We have to make up our minds whether we are prepared to work out plans with the French committee on the basis that we would deal with them as the authority in France when sufficient areas had been liberated to make civil administration possible . . . there is no other authority with whom we could deal. We must therefore try to obtain the agreement of the Combined Chiefs-of-Staff on the necessary instructions for General Eisenhower. It is clear that the attitude of the United States Chief-of-Staff is determined by the strong feelings of the President. The Chiefs-of-Staff seem to have been about to give the 'all clear' when they were pulled up by the President . . .

In a second minute on 9 May, Mr Eden repeated his view that 'if the President continues to refuse an agreement, there would be a real estrangement between us and the French committee. No one – except the Russians – would gain from this state of things and the position of our friends among the French in relation to General de Gaulle would be weakened.'[73]

The situation was rapidly becoming impossible, and all elements combined to build up an inextricable vicious circle: no one knew who would be responsible for civil administration in liberated areas after landing; an agreement on this could be negotiated between General Koenig and General Eisenhower – but Eisenhower did not have the necessary permission from President Roosevelt, who refused to deal with the French committee; as for General Koenig, he could not negotiate without communicating with the French committee, which he was prevented from doing by the ban on cipher communications. This ban, in turn, had caused General de Gaulle to retaliate by forbidding General Koenig or Ambassador Viénot to settle any question with the Allies until further notice. . . . For good measure, the General also refused to receive the British diplomatic representative in Algiers and made a fiery speech in Tunis denouncing the delays in Allied conversations, while expressing the 'hope that France would in the future be a centre of direct and practical co-operation with the West, and a permanent ally of Russia'.[74] This in turn infuriated the Prime Minister, who alone could have appealed to the President in favour of negotiations with the committee on civil administration; Churchill accordingly replied to Eden on 10 May that he refused to quarrel with the President over this matter and added that 'De Gaulle, for all his magnitude, is the sole obstacle to harmonious relations between Great Britain and America on the one hand, and the skeleton and ghost of France on the other.' The Prime Minister thought that the General's speech in Tunis showed what use he would make of power. 'He will be the bitterest foe we and the United States have ever had in France.'[75]

This was interesting, but afforded no solution to the pressing problems of the hour. To make things worse, the British press was continuing its attacks on the government's French policy, and Parliament was now following suit with some embarrassing questions already being raised in Commons; thus, on 19 April:

Mr Mander asked the Secretary of State for Foreign Affairs whether recognition will be given to the authority of the French Committee of National Liberation as the territory of France becomes liberated; and whether that subject had been discussed by the European Advisory Commission.

Sir Richard Acland asked the Secretary of State for Foreign Affairs whether he can make any statement about the relative powers and duties of the French Committee of National Liberation and the Commander-in-Chief Allied Forces in relation to the civil administration of such French territories as will be liberated from the enemy. . . .

Mr Graham White: May I ask if, in any subsequent discussion that takes place, the Right Honourable Gentleman will not lose sight of the fact that the recognition of different authorities in different parts of France will be one certain way of ensuring civil war in France?

Mr Law: I hope we shall not lose sight of anything.

Mr Granville: Does the Right Honourable Gentleman mean that none of these subjects, even when they are really important, is to be discussed by the European Advisory Commission? Is that what his answer really means?[76]

And on 3 May:

Mr Martin asked the Secretary of State for Foreign Affairs whether an agreement has yet been concluded with the FCNL for the administration of territory in Metropolitan France as it may be liberated from the Germans.

Mr Antony Eden: Conversations are being held between the Supreme Allied Commander and the French military mission in this country under Koenig.

Mr Martin: Does this mean that the authority with which we deal in liberated France will be the FCNL?

Mr Antony Eden: Yes, Sir.[77]

This was a half truth at best, and Eden knew it. The conversations being held between the French and the American representatives were pointless, as neither of them had any mandate to conclude an agreement. As for the answer to the second question, it was the expression of a hope rather than a reality. But the pressure being exerted from all sides was considerable, and no one felt it more acutely than the Foreign Secretary. Duff Cooper had proposed on 8 May that a way out of the deadlock could be found if de Gaulle himself were invited to London to take part in the talks. Finally, after a gruelling session that ended at 3.15 a.m. on 11 May, Eden succeeded in convincing Churchill that this could well be the solution, and the Prime Minister agreed to try and enlist Roosevelt's support for the proposal. The next day, Churchill accordingly wrote to the President:

> As the hour approaches we feel it indispensable to have some kind of understanding with the French National Committee. . . . We must presently be faced with a public complaint that no kind of arrangement has been made with the French National Committee for the employment of French forces outside or inside France. We could quite well dispense with French aid from outside in the operation, ... However General Eisenhower says that he attaches great importance to the action to be taken by the French Resistance groups on and after D-Day, and undoubtedly we must take care that our joint troops do not suffer heavier losses owing to the fact that no agreement has been made for the employment of the French Resistance groups. . . . I therefore propose to you that General de Gaulle, together with one or two of his committee, should be invited to come here on say 18 May in the utmost secrecy: That you should either entrust your case to General Eisenhower or send over someone specially to meet them. The Foreign Secretary or I would conduct the discussion with de Gaulle and any of your representatives you may choose. We will make the best proposals we can to you without agreeing to anything until we have heard from you. It may be that no agreement will be reached because they are unreasonable, in which case we have done our best, and he will have put himself hopelessly in the wrong. In any case we shall have done our duty by the soldiers and you will have the fullest opportunity of seeing the best lay-out we can get for you to consider.[78]

The President replied the next day that he had no objection to an invitation to de Gaulle to discuss 'your associations in military or political matters', though the Prime Minister should consider keeping the General in the UK until after D-Day.[79] This of course was not helpful. The Canadian Prime Minister, then in London, noted in his diary: 'Churchill is really very worried, most anxious to do the right thing.'[80] As Churchill pointed out to Eden,

> It is clear to me that de Gaulle would not accept to come here on the basis that he could not leave again till after D-Day and could not correspond again except through our British and American cyphers. All this would involve persistent disputes and I do not see how, even if he got here, he could be prevented from full correspondence with his government which, after all, rules the French Empire. He could certainly only stay a few days or perhaps a week from the centre of government, and would make himself intolerable if kept here under duress until the flag had fallen. I regard it as out of the question for him to come and return back

before D 1. He would not come alone and would certainly have colleagues and some sort of staff with him, an ADC and a servant – but anything he picked up here from any members of the Free French movement would have many opportunities of going about the country, would certainly leak out at Algiers, and would be swiftly transferred from there via Oran to Spain, and via Spain to Germany.[81]

Therefore, there was only one alternative left: wait for D-Day, and then 'send a cordial invitation to de Gaulle to come here as soon as he likes'. For the Prime Minister this was obviously the solution; 'I am sure,' Churchill wrote to Eden on 16 May, 'that within one week, while the battle is going forward and before any portion of ground which could be handed over to civil power has been gained, we could reach a working arrangement about the civil administration. We might even get him into a friendly mood.'[82]

That was probably asking too much, but from then on, everything was done to make the plan a success and to ensure that de Gaulle accepted the invitation – which was by no means a foregone conclusion. The invitation would have to be a cordial one, the Prime Minister would send his own York aeroplane to fetch the General in Algiers, Eden suggested that 'It would be well to state that His Majesty's government hope that he and his party will be the guest of His Majesty's government during their stay in this country,'[83] and in the meantime Churchill would send de Gaulle his warmest congratulations on the conduct of the French troops in Italy. Finally, Duff Cooper cautiously informed the General that the British government was inviting him to London 'to settle the question of recognition and that of administrative co-operation in France'.[84]

To everyone's relief, the General was 'in a most reasonable mood'[85] and accepted the invitation – not without conditions, however: he must have the assurance that he would be able to communicate in code with his government in Algiers – and then, there was something else:

As for signing an agreement with political implications, I would have many reservations to make. . . . we were not interested in a formal recognition. . . . Besides, the Committee of Liberation will assume the title of government of the Republic forthwith, whatever the opinion of the Allies might be. As for the conditions of our co-operation in the military command, we have long since specified them in the memorandum to which we have received no answer. The British government was perhaps ready to agree to it now, but the American government was not. What good would it do for the French and the English to agree on measures which could not be applied without Roosevelt's consent? We were, of course, prepared to negotiate the practical methods of co-operation, but providing there were three parties present, not two.[86]

Churchill, of course, knew very well that an agreement was impossible without the presence of an American representative. The assumption by the committee of the title 'Provisional government of the Republic' came as a disagreeable shock to him; but there was no more time for recriminations. 'Overlord' was now less than two weeks away, and France could not be liberated without French participation – besides, the Free French had shown their valour during the Italian campaign, and the British, with their Prime Minister in the lead, had been most impressed. Churchill had tried as long as possible to follow the President's line, but the position was fast becoming untenable. The great majority of the British press was now clamouring for a change in policy: *The Times* called for a complete agreement with de Gaulle's administration,[87] the *Manchester Guardian* demanded full recognition of the Committee,[88] and the *Daily Mail* fumed against His Majesty's government's dilatory policy in French affairs.[89]

On 24 May, Churchill made a long speech in Commons; having explained the state of British relations with each of the European countries in turn – and spoken very generously of General Franco in the process – the Prime Minister came to the subject of France:

There is no doubt that . . . the French Committee of National Liberation presides over, and directs, forces at the present time which, in the struggle against Hitler in Europe, give it the fourth place in the Grand Alliance. The reason why the United States and Great Britain have not been able to recognize it yet as the government of France, or even as the provisional government of France, is because we are not sure that it represents the French nation in the same way as the governments of Britain, the United States and Soviet Russia represent the whole body of their people. The committee will, of course, exercise the leadership to establish law and order in the liberated areas of France under the supervision, while the military exigency lasts, of the supreme Allied Commander, but we do not wish to commit ourselves at this stage to imposing the government of the French committee upon all of France which might fall under our control without more knowledge than we now possess of the situation in the interior of France. At the same time I must make it clear that we shall have no dealings with the Vichy government, or anyone tainted with that association, because they have decided to follow the path of collaboration with our enemies. Many of them have definitely desired, and worked for, a German victory. . . . With the full approval of the President of the United States I have invited General de Gaulle to pay us a visit over here in the near future and my Right Honourable friend the Foreign Secretary has just shown me a telegram from Mr Duff Cooper, in Algiers, saying that General de Gaulle will be very glad to come. There is nothing like talking things over, and seeing where we can get to. I hope he will bring some members of his government with him so that the whole matter can be reviewed.[90]

This was undoubtedly a masterly speech, but for once, to Churchill's dismay, the Honourable Members of Parliament considered that it was not good enough. The first to speak after the PM was the Honourable Member for West Leicester, Mr Harold Nicolson:

I cannot fully explain either to myself or to others the true nature of the policy adopted by His Majesty's government towards France. . . .

It seems to me and to many Frenchmen that the United States government, with His Majesty's government in their train, instead of helping the French and welcoming them, lose no opportunity of administering any snub which ingenuity can devise and ill-manners perpetrate. . . . It is most unwise, most weak and most ill-informed of the United States government to refuse to accord any special recognition to the National Committee or provisional government. I am convinced that this is a grave error of policy. It is not only inexpedient, it is not only unfair but it may expose us to an absurd situation. . . .

I expect every moment to open my paper and read that the Soviet government have recognized the de Gaulle committee as the provisional government of France. We will come in late, ungracious, ungenerous, and unthanked, creeping in at the last moment and giving no recognition of the deep feeling of respect and admiration that we have for what the National Committee has been able to do. We refuse to recognize them. There may be reasons for this which are not within our control. But we go much further than that. We refuse to let them communicate at a moment of immense urgency with their government in Algiers. We refuse to allow them to attend the European Council; this appears to be grotesque. Here is an Allied body discussing the future of Europe and France is not to be there. This is grotesque. It is a discourtesy such as one would hardly adopt towards a neutral and certainly not towards an ally which has recovered herself and regained her repute among the nations of the world. . . . I only trust that when my Right Honourable friend has heard what other Members have to say – and I am sure that Members of all parties feel as deeply as I do upon it – that he will realize that there is wide perturbation on this subject.[91]

There was indeed wide perturbation. Shortly thereafter, the Honourable Captain Grey declared: 'I want to ask again that the National Committee of Liberation be recognized by us, if necessary unilaterally, as the provisional government of France.'[92] And the Honourable John Dugdale:

> I would ask the Prime Minister and Foreign Secretary if they cannot be a little more definite in requesting that the American government agree with us in recognizing the de Gaulle government as soon as possible. There are many things that can be said against de Gaulle, but he did stand out in 1940 as, indeed, the PM stood out, and we must never forget that. . . . I cannot see why we should question the *bona fides* of General de Gaulle and his provisional government.[93]

And the Honourable Vernon Bartlett:

> I was very sorry to hear today that the Prime Minister could not go further than he did in that matter. I think, as the Honourable Member for West Leicester (Mr H. Nicolson) said in his admirable speech, that the time has very definitely come when General de Gaulle represents France as much as any other leader in any other Allied country. I know he is a difficult man. I met him first in February 1940, behind the Maginot Line and had to stand for two hours in the snow watching his beastly tanks going up and down a hill. I was clad only in an ordinary London suit and overcoat. He had a leather overcoat and high boots, and I have had a certain resentment against him ever since. He is a difficult man, but every time we postpone the full recognition of the Committee of National Liberation in Algiers, we are playing definitely into the hands of the worst elements in the French Liberation movement. I take the case of France as an illustration of our foreign policy generally . . .[94]

After that, during the next three days, *The Times*, the *Manchester Guardian*, the *Daily Mail*, the *Economist* echoed the words of the Honourable Members of Parliament.[95] The number of private letters the Prime Minister received on this subject is not known, but it must likewise have been considerable. It was quite clear at any rate that by following the President's line, Churchill was in great danger of losing the support of Parliament and of public opinion at home. On 27 May, he finally overcame his reluctance and wrote to the President:

You will see what has passed about de Gaulle coming here and what I have said in Parliament on the subject. There is very strong feeling here after the recent fighting in Italy in favour of the French. We are going to liberate France at the cost of much British and American blood. The feeling is that he should be with us. But who is 'he'? When this works out in the person of de Gaulle, all these difficulties which you and I know so well, emerge. I feel, however, that we should be in a difficulty if it were thought that more British and American blood were being spilled because we have not got the French national spirit working with us. There is a strong French movement here and of course they do not know, nor can we tell them, all the faults and follies of de Gaulle. This is only another reason why you and I should consult together in the near future. Of course I shall keep you informed every day about any talk that may occur with de Gaulle. He has lately shown some signs of wishing to work with us and after all it is very difficult to cut the French out of the liberation of France. I should be grateful for a full expression of your views.[96]

In a supreme effort to persuade President Roosevelt, Churchill sent another telegram immediately after:

I would earnestly ask you to send over someone of the rank of Stettinius to express your point of view. I see the growth of opinion very powerful here and the feeling that the French should be with us when we liberate France. Naturally there is a great wave of sentiment for France on account of bravery and success of French troops . . . in our Italian battle. There is also the sense that they should share in the work which we have in hand. No one will understand them being cold-shouldered.[97]

At Churchill's request, Ambassador Harriman also sent the President a telegram: 'The Prime Minister promises he will faithfully follow your line regarding de Gaulle but warns that the Foreign Office and some members of his Cabinet are insistent on going further, in fact so is House and British public. He really feels the need of help in coping with him* and his own associates and hopes you will send Stettinius over or someone else of equal position in Washington.'[98]

These were pathetic appeals from the Prime Minister, who obviously felt he could no longer master the situation; but Roosevelt was unimpressed: on 27 May, he wrote 'I am hopeful that your conversation with General de Gaulle will result in inducing him to actually assist in the liberation of France without being imposed by

*'Him' probably means de Gaulle.

us on the French people as their government. Self-determination really means absence of coercion.'⁹⁹

Four days later he sent another refusal, short and cutting: 'I think I can only repeat the simple fact that I cannot send anyone to represent me at the de Gaulle conversation with you.'¹⁰⁰

Churchill was now caught between two uncompromising positions: the President's determination to ignore de Gaulle, and de Gaulle's determination to take control of liberated France. British public opinion was clearly on de Gaulle's side, and Churchill was clearly committed to following the President's line – but he was not at all convinced that it was the right one. The Prime Minister was more than ever 'anxious to do the right thing', but no one could deny that this was an impossible situation.

In Algiers, General de Gaulle had no such preoccupations; he felt that his position was unassailable, and wrote as much to Ambassador Viénot:

> I agreed to the principle of the visit to London, for I see no reason why we should avoid the discussions proposed to us on the eve of the decisive battle . . . As to future talks, this is what I told Mr Duff Cooper: We have nothing to ask. The forms of recognition of the French government by London and Washington now interest us very little. The moment has passed when agreeable formulas might have been useful. . . . The essential point is our recognition by the French people and that is now a *fait accompli*. . . . As to the functions and the exercise of French administration in the liberated territory of France, there is no question either. We are the French administration. . . . There is us, or chaos. If the Western Allies bring about chaos in France, it will be their responsibility, and we believe that they will be the losers in the end. . . .
>
> You may be right in thinking that the invitation from the British government is due, in part, to a desire for a real *rapprochement* with France. But I am not as convinced of this as you are. I have often seen marks of apparent good will suddenly lavished by the English which resulted – by design or by chance – either in a concrete advantage sought at our expense, or in some support given to a manoeuvre by Mr Roosevelt to influence public opinion against us. . . . The government will study the whole affair calmly at its session of 26 May, and define the positions we will take up in the London negotiations.¹⁰¹

On 26 May, the Committee of Liberation, which became that very day the 'Provisional Government of the French Republic', officially approved de Gaulle's position. It was agreed that no minister would accompany him on his trip, so as to make it clear that he was coming to observe the beginning of operations, and maybe even visit the combat zones in France, but not to negotiate a partial agreement.[102] This de Gaulle repeated to Duff Cooper the following day.

That day, 27 May, Duff Cooper had just received a telegram from London instructing him to inform de Gaulle that he was being invited as a guest of His Majesty's government and that he would have full liberty of communications. There was, however, no indication of a date for the visit. Duff Cooper wrote in his diary: 'I went to see de Gaulle this afternoon to convey to him the invitation and assurances I had received in the morning. I had hoped he would be pleased but he gave no indication of being so, and was as grumpy and sulky as usual, complaining bitterly about the intention of the American government to issue their own francs when they entered France.'[102]

Back in London, there was renewed discussion on the date for de Gaulle's arrival; and the Foreign Secretary later wrote:

> During a Cabinet meeting on the evening of 30 May the Prime Minister told us that he was preparing to issue this invitation on D-Day. I said I was unhappy about this, because I expected that once we and the Americans landed in France, General de Gaulle would feel it essential to make some statement. If he did so in Algiers without having consulted us, it might well be unhappily phrased, and we had to consider the consequences of this possibility upon our future relation with France. De Gaulle should therefore arrive before D-Day. The Prime Minister decided that the Chiefs-of-Staff should consider the military implications of my proposal.[103]

In fact the opinion of the Chiefs-of-Staff on the matter was decidedly negative, as H. B. Mack informed Sir Alexander Cadogan the next morning:

> I learn that the Chiefs-of-Staff at their meeting this morning were more than usually stubborn and short-sighted. Their general attitude was that they didn't want de Gaulle here at all (they all three dislike him intensely), and that he should certainly not come here before D-Day, in spite of the JIC's recommendation. I do not think that they produced any valid reason for this view except their personal dislike for that unsympathetic individual to all except his compatriots. General Ismay spoke up in favour of General de Gaulle being allowed here on D-2 but was squashed by the three Chiefs-of-Staff. The matter will now presumably come before the War Cabinet.[104]

This was to prove unnecessary: Anthony Eden had more influence on Churchill than the Chiefs-of-Staff, and the final decision was taken that afternoon: 'I discussed this point with the Prime Minister,' Eden wrote, 'and he accepted that General de Gaulle must be told about "Overlord" before it was launched. This being so, it was evidently safer to tell him in England than in Algiers. The invitation was finally sent off.'[105] It was brief and most gracious: 'Come please now with your colleagues at the earliest possible moment and in the deepest secrecy. I give you my personal assurance that it is in the interests of France. I am sending my own York and another York for you.'[106]

During the next three days, Ambassador Duff Cooper had a fairly difficult time in persuading de Gaulle to accept the invitation. The latter started by saying that there was no point in going if the negotiations were not tripartite, that it was all 'a ploy to get him to make a speech which would give the French people the false impression that he was in agreement with the British and the Americans, when in fact he was not', and many other things of like sort.[107] But the British Ambassador had the support of Massigli and of several other French commissioners. After two animated sessions of the National Committee, de Gaulle finally made up his mind, and Duff Cooper noted in his diary on 3 June: 'I felt extremely anxious this morning and was most relieved when Palewski turned up with a letter from de Gaulle agreeing to go. . . . We then had to make the necessary arrangements as soon as possible. . . . We arrived at the airfield about three o'clock. The two Yorks were there and most of the party had assembled. De Gaulle himself was the last to arrive and I was relieved when I saw him inside the plane.'[108]

With an uncompromising de Gaulle on his way to England and Churchill nervously awaiting the day of decision, there were not a few people in London and Algiers who feared that things in England would not go smoothly during the next 72 hours. But not even the most pessimistic among them could suspect the extraordinary drama that was to unfold in London on the very eve of the greatest landing operation in history. At dawn on 6 June, the fighting would not be limited to the beaches of Normandy: the battle raging in London at the same time, if less deadly, would be every bit as ruthless; neither could there be any doubt as to the identity of the two protagonists.

CHAPTER 14

The Longest Night

In London, everything was now planned and ready. De Gaulle was
to arrive on 4 June, D-Day minus one. He would then be taken to
Eisenhower's headquarters and 'brought into the show', as
Churchill wrote to Roosevelt. At the beginning of the operation, he
would broadcast to France, immediately after Eisenhower, and
Churchill was confident that all would go well: 'I have very little
doubt,' he wrote to the President,

> that de Gaulle can be persuaded to say the right thing. Therefore, on D
> plus 3 or 4, we will have discussions with him and his people in London,
> and I must explain to him that there will be no French territory worth
> speaking of for a good many days, only the bombed and shell-torn
> beaches. I will do the best I can with him during the week D-2 to 8 or 9. I
> will tell him what you say, namely, that if he sent you a message asking if
> you would see him, you will answer an immediate and cordial
> affirmative. Meanwhile, I shall have explored the ground as far as
> possible with him beforehand.[1]

All the problems of the hour, the absence of an agreement on civil
administration, the dispute over Allied military currency in France,
de Gaulle's intransigence, the British press and Parliament's
Francophilia, President Roosevelt's Gaullophobia, all this would be
pushed into the background by the great operation now impending.
Formez vos bataillons, and *Marchons!*

It was all quite well organized and thought-out. Almost as well, in
fact, as the preparations for the greatest landing operation of all
time. For all southern England was by then a vast military camp;
eight divisions, 150,000 men, 11,000 first-line aircraft and 4000 ships
of all types were poised and ready for the initial cross-Channel
attack. They were backed by a gigantic army of two million men,
guided by an intricate plan with split-second timing, and preceded
on their target by a highly efficient network of sabotage and

deception. One element, however, totally escaped planning: the weather conditions on 4 June were unfavourable, and they were expected to reach storm proportions the next day. This was to cause the greatest anxiety among military and political chiefs during the next 48 hours. But undetected by meteorologists, another storm of a different kind was about to break out in London on the very eve of D-Day.

De Gaulle landed near London on the morning of 4 June. At the airport, a band played the '*Marseillaise*', and in London, the General was given the following letter from Winston Churchill:

> My dear General de Gaulle,
>
> Welcome to these shores! Very great military events are about to take place. I should be glad if you could come to see me down here in my train, which is close to General Eisenhower's headquarters, bringing with you one or two of your party. General Eisenhower is looking forward to seeing you again and will explain to you the military position which is momentous and imminent. If you could be here by 1.30 p.m., I should be glad to give you *déjeuner* and we will then repair to General Eisenhower's headquarters.
>
> Let me have a telephone message early to know whether this is agreeable to you or not.[2]

In order to be nearer the scene of battle, the Prime Minister had established his headquarters in a special station near Portsmouth. 'This,' Eden commented, 'was an imaginative but uncomfortable exercise on Mr Churchill's part. The accommodation was limited and there was only one bath, adjoining his own compartment, and one telephone. Mr Churchill seemed to be always in the bath and General Ismay always on the telephone. So that, though we were physically nearer to the battle, it was almost impossible to conduct any business.'[3] And Duff Cooper added: 'His staff were all complaining bitterly of the discomfort and inconvenience. One of them said to me that he intended to lead a reformed life in the future because he now knew what hell was like.'[4] But Churchill, well-satisfied with the installation, was now prepared to greet General de Gaulle and 'bring him into the show'. With him were Bevin, General Ismay and Field-Marshal Smuts. They were soon joined by the Foreign Secretary.

'I arrived in time,' Eden recalls, 'to walk down the railway line with de Gaulle. The Prime Minister, moved by his sense of history, was on the track to greet the General with arms outstretched.

Unfortunately de Gaulle did not respond easily to such a mood.'⁵ This was not necessarily due to the presence of Field-Marshal Smuts. General de Gaulle was here to represent a state, and a state does not engage in effusions; besides, he had not come for his recreation, but to uphold the interests of France – and these interests were gravely threatened at the very moment of liberation. For all that, the conference in the Prime Minister's train began pleasantly enough.'

Churchill was seated at the centre of a large green table, between Eden and Duff Cooper. De Gaulle was facing him, with Viénot on one side and General Béthouart on the other. 'Churchill appears tired,' the latter noted, 'he is clearly moved, his hands are shaking.'⁶ The Prime Minister presently began to speak:

He had wished to see General de Gaulle in order to tell him – as he had been unable to do by telegraph – of the forthcoming operation. He felt that it would have been a very bad thing in the history of our two countries if an operation designed to liberate France had been undertaken by British and American forces without the French being informed. His intention had been to invite the General a little before D-Day.... He then explained the exact objectives of the operation. A very considerable force would be sent to seize bases, ports and bridgeheads. Many would sail from this country, but also, later on, many direct from the United States. There was now not much hope of beginning before D plus 3, but the situation would be reviewed every 24 hours. He had taken upon himself the responsibility of entrusting General de Gaulle with our secret. By doing so, he had enabled General Eisenhower to deal more freely with the technical aspects of the operation.

General de Gaulle thanked the Prime Minister. He said that the operation was clearly an affair of momentous importance. He had himself thought that now was the moment to carry it out. He had not of course known anything about the date before; but he felt that he should tell the Prime Minister that people in Algiers who listened to the messages transmitted in French by the BBC had inferred from the recent increase in such messages that it was about to begin.

The Prime Minister said that such messages seemed to him unwise. We ourselves had done much in the way of deception and rumours, and when the armada actually sailed it was proposed that a series of declarations should be issued by General Eisenhower and by the rulers of such countries as the enemy might expect us to be about to attack. For example, there would be messages from Queen Wilhelmina and King

Haakon. He hoped that General de Gaulle would be ready to send such a message to France. Originally, the declarations would have been made this evening; but now the General would have one or two days to prepare his. It need not be long, but it should be encouraging and designed to create uncertainty in the enemy camp.

General de Gaulle said he would be very glad to do this, for two reasons. First, he considered that the operation was very important and well prepared. Second, he was glad to know the reason why the Prime Minister had invited him to come to this country was to inform him about the operation. The question of the message would be easy to arrange. He assumed that after the battle was launched he would be able to return to Algiers.

The Foreign Secretary said that it was true that the great operation now impending had taken all our thoughts, but after it had been launched (or in the interval while it was retarded) we thought it would be useful to discuss certain political questions.

General de Gaulle said that he felt that it was quite right that he should be in this country at this moment and he thanked the Prime Minister for having thought of inviting him now. It was important for the future of both our countries that we should be together when the operation began. That was why he had expressed his thanks. . . .[7]

'In all sincerity,' de Gaulle recalled in his memoirs,

I expressed my admiration to the Prime Minister for this outcome of his efforts. That Great Britain, after so many ordeals so valiantly endured and thanks to which she had saved Europe, should today be the base for the attack on the Continent and should engage such tremendous forces in it, was a striking justification of the courageous policy which he himself had personified since the darkest days. Whatever coming events were still to cost France, she was proud, in spite of everything, to be in line at the side of the Allies for the liberation of Europe. . . . At this historic moment the same current of esteem and friendship swept over everyone present, Frenchmen and Englishmen alike.[8]

At quarter past two, everyone sat down to lunch, and all went well until dessert, when Churchill suggested that they might talk about 'political matters'. De Gaulle looked sternly at the Prime Minister and answered without amenity: 'Political matters? Why?' Churchill was somewhat taken aback, but he continued:

He had been in correspondence with the President for some time. The President had begun with the idea of wanting General de Gaulle to come to the United States, but he did not want to invite him formally. In his recent telegrams he had seemed less desirous of receiving a visit, partly because of the treatment accorded to General Giraud. It should be remembered that the President had made the arrangement about equipment for the French forces with General Giraud; and General Giraud had gone.

General de Gaulle answered that there was no hurry, and that 'he thought that at this moment it was better that he should be here than in Washington.'[9]

The Prime Minister replied that 'he thought that this was true, so far as the beginning of the battle was concerned. But in the interval we might discuss the question of the administration of liberated France. He must warn the General that the part of France at first liberated might not be big, and might contain only a few French people, under heavy fire. The President said that General Marshall would be able to speak with General de Gaulle on all *military* affairs, but he had twice refused to give his consent to conversations between representatives of the three countries on political matters. The Prime Minister was free to talk *à deux*. But he felt sure that, if General de Gaulle were to express the wish to visit the President he would be made most welcome. . . .

General de Gaulle reaffirmed that there was no hurry, and added coldly, '*C'est la guerre, faites-la, on verra après.*'[10]

Churchill was clearly disappointed, but he went on: 'After the battle, General de Gaulle might go to America for discussions with the President, or alternatively he might return to Algiers and have no conversations either with Britain or with the USA, the two powers who were losing their men to liberate France, and without whose help France could not be liberated. It was for General de Gaulle to decide which course he would follow. . . . but he would strongly advise him to go to the USA and if in the interval we could have discussions here, so much the better. For example, we might discuss the question of currency notes. As regards America, the President was capable of being persuaded. He had not been hostile to the General at Casablanca. He had told the Prime Minister that he thought the General was a mystic, and that he was much interested in him. The Prime Minister believed that General de Gaulle could live agreeably with the President. It was true that the President might lose power in 1945, but until then he was all-powerful, and all our information was that he would then be re-elected for 4 years. France would need his friendship, and it was the General's duty to gain it, just as it was the duty of a soldier to charge an enemy battery. . . .'[11]

De Gaulle, unmoved, repeated simply: '*C'est la guerre, faites la guerre.*'

Anthony Eden then decided to intervene: He had 'reason to believe that, if General de Gaulle were to say that he was willing to go to America, it was not impossible that we might be able to have preliminary discussions on political matters here, at which the American Ambassador could be present[12]. . . . it must not be forgotten that Great Britain was also concerned in this. We had made a definite offer to General de Gaulle to begin discussions. If the offer were not accepted, we could not help it; but we should regret it.'[13] Bevin thought well to add that 'the Labour Party would resent it.'

This finally caused the explosion; de Gaulle turned around, glared at him, and thundered:

It is all very well to talk like that. On more than on one occasion I have tried to initiate discussions. I have made proposals as long ago as last September but have received no reply. It therefore does not mean anything to say that the British Labour Party would be offended. The battle is about to begin and I will speak on the wireless. That is all right. But as regards discussing the question of administration, it is clear that the President has never wanted to see me, and yet now suddenly I am being told, I must go and talk to the President, etc. . . .[14] Why do you seem to think that I need to submit my candidacy for the authority in France to Roosevelt? The French government exists. I have nothing to ask, in this respect, of the United States of America nor of Great Britain. This being said, it is important for all the Allies that the relations between the French administration and the military command should be organized. Nine months ago we proposed as much. Since the armies are about to land in France, I understand your haste to see the question settled. We ourselves are ready to do so. But where is the American representative? Without him, as you well know, we can decide nothing in this respect. Furthermore, I notice that the Washington and London governments have made arrangements to do without an agreement with us. I have just learned, for example, that despite our warnings, the troops and services about to land are provided with so-called French currency, issued by foreign powers, which the government of the republic refuses to recognize and which, according to the orders of the inter-Allied command, will have compulsory circulation on French territory. I expect that tomorrow General Eisenhower, acting on the instructions of the President of the United States and in agreement with you, will proclaim that he is taking France under his authority. How do you expect us to come to terms on this basis?[15] *Allez, faites la guerre, avec votre fausse monnaie!*[16]

There was a very heavy silence, then Churchill replied with increased exasperation that 'whether or not General de Gaulle visited the President was a matter for the General himself to decide. But he strongly advised him to do so. . . .' And then, in an even angrier voice:

> He must tell him bluntly that, if after every effort had been exhausted the President was on one side and the French National Committee of Liberation on the other he, Mr Churchill, would almost certainly side with the President, and that anyhow no quarrel would ever arise between Britain and the United States on account of France. As regards the civil affairs agreement, he would sum up the view of His Majesty's government as follows: If General de Gaulle wanted us to ask the President to agree to give him the title deeds of France, the answer was 'No'. If he wanted to ask the President to agree that the Committee of National Liberation was the principal factor with whom we should deal in France, the answer was, 'Yes'. To which de Gaulle replied icily that 'He quite understood that in case of a disagreement between the United States and France, Great Britain would side with the United States.'[17]

The debate had by now degenerated into a shouting match, with Churchill growling that 'he had expressed his own personal opinion which he had little doubt would be endorsed by the House of Commons in view of the relations subsisting throughout the Anglo-American society and brotherhood-in-arms which nothing could break.'[18] This, however, was far from certain. Eden shook his head, and Bevin unexpectedly joined the fray. He said to de Gaulle in a booming voice: 'The Prime Minister has told you that in every case he would side with the President of the United States. I want you to know that he has spoken in his own name, and not in the name of the British Cabinet.'[19] With that, the "conference" was over and so was the luncheon. Before it ended, however, Churchill melancholically raised his glass 'to de Gaulle, who never accepted defeat.' De Gaulle replied, 'To England, to Victory, to Europe.'[20] Clearly, this had been no ordinary meeting. But then, these were no ordinary men.

That afternoon, Churchill and Eden drove de Gaulle to General Eisenhower's headquarters in a wood nearby. 'He was most ceremoniously received,' Churchill recalled. 'Ike and Bedell-Smith vied with one another in their courtesy. Presently Ike took him to the map tent, and for twenty minutes imparted to him the whole story of what was about to happen.'[21] 'Eisenhower', de Gaulle wrote, explained to us with great clarity and self-command his plan for the landing and the state of preparations . . . I could see that, in this extremely complex and hazardous operation, the Anglo-American gift for 'planning' had been exercised to the maximum degree. However, the Commander-in-Chief still had to fix the day and the hour and, in this matter, was subject to the severest perplexity. Indeed everything had been calculated for the landing to take place between June 3rd and 7th. Once this date had passed, the tide and moon would require the operation to be postponed for about a month. Yet the weather was extremely bad. For the barges, the landing stages and the landing craft, the state of the sea made navigation and boarding problematical. Nevertheless, the order for launching or postponement had to be given by the following day at the latest.[22]

General Eisenhower, unlike his British counterparts, had learned to appreciate de Gaulle's military judgement. Besides, the Allied Commander-in-Chief was a born diplomat; he therefore asked de Gaulle for his opinion in the matter, and the French leader, no doubt flattered by this attention, was glad to advise: 'I will only tell you that if I were you, I should not delay.'[22] Alas! This was not only a military problem. As de Gaulle was preparing to leave, Eisenhower told him, with evident embarrassment: 'General, on the day of the landing, I will broadcast a proclamation to the French population, and I would like you to do the same.'

De Gaulle: 'You, broadcast a proclamation to the French people? By what right? And what will you tell them?'[23] The Commander-in-Chief handed him the typewritten document, which de Gaulle read . . . . and found unsatisfactory. 'Eisenhower,' de Gaulle recalled,

urged the French nation to 'carry out his orders'. He declared that 'In the administration, everyone will continue to fulfil his functions unless contrary instructions are received.' Once France was liberated, 'The French themselves would choose their representatives and their government.' To sum up, he appeared to be taking charge of our country even though he was merely an Allied general entitled to command troops, but not in the least qualified to intervene in the country's government.[24]

But for de Gaulle, the proclamation had another grave defect: General Eisenhower, carrying out President Roosevelt's instructions, had not once mentioned the Free French leader or his movement. This was unacceptable, and de Gaulle said as much. Eisenhower, it seems, replied diplomatically that this was only a draft, and that he was ready to alter it on de Gaulle's suggestion.* It was agreed that de Gaulle would inform Eisenhower the next morning of the changes he deemed necessary.²⁵ De Gaulle, in a sombre mood, drove back to the train with Churchill, to whom he expressed his misgivings in no uncertain terms. After that, Churchill recalled, 'I had expected that de Gaulle would dine with us and come back to London by this, the most convenient route, but he drew himself up and stated that he preferred to motor with his French officers separately.'²⁶

'I feel chilled,' Churchill said to Eden.

The next morning, 5 June, de Gaulle sent Eisenhower a corrected version. 'As I expected,' de Gaulle later wrote, 'I was informed that it was too late, for the proclamation was already printed (it had, in fact, been printed eight days earlier) and was now to be rained down on France at any moment. Indeed, the landing was to begin the following night.'²⁷ So the landing in France would be carried out without an agreement on French civil administration or French currency, and even without an acceptable proclamation to the French people. France would not really be liberated, but occupied, like Italy. De Gaulle was furious. To be sure, Eisenhower had repeatedly assured him that in practice, he would always deal with the committee once in France. But this, to the French leader, was not good enough. Fighting France – that is to say, France – was evidently being bypassed and insulted. General de Gaulle, as we know by now, was not a man to accept insults without retaliating.

That same morning, at 4 a.m., General Eisenhower had finally taken the fateful decision: the great attack would be launched in the first hours of 6 June. A gigantic machine was now set in motion, and that afternoon, Mr Charles Peake, Foreign Office political adviser to SHAEF, came to inform General de Gaulle of the part he would have to play the following morning; first, the Heads of State of Western Europe would broadcast to their peoples: the King of Norway, the Queen of the Netherlands, the Grand Duchess of Luxemburg, the Prime Minister of Belgium. Then, Eisenhower would read his proclamation and finally, de Gaulle would speak to the French people. This was counting without the personality of

*De Gaulle well remembers that Eisenhower offered to alter the proclamation. Duff Cooper (*Old Men Forget*, p. 330) confirms this. Eden speaks of a 'misunderstanding' and General Béthouart (*Cinq années*, p. 244) remembers Eisenhower as having said that the document 'had been approved by his government and he could make no alterations'.

General de Gaulle – and his mood at that time. He refused flatly. 'By speaking after the Commander-in-Chief,' the General answered in substance, 'I would appear to sanction what he said – of which I disapprove – and assume an unsuitable rank in the series of speeches. If I were to broadcast, it could only be at a different hour and outside the series.'[28]

In the last 24 hours, Churchill had been in a state of high nervous tension. He knew perhaps better than anyone else the risks involved in an amphibious attack against a strongly fortified coast; he believed that the casualties among the Anglo-American force would be considerable, and the uncertainties of the weather had of course added to his anxieties. At this point, in the afternoon of 5 June, he was informed that General de Gaulle refused to broadcast to the French people. This information – which was not entirely accurate* – had a devastating effect on the Prime Minister; the conference of the preceding day still rankled with him, but this confirmed his worst suspicions: de Gaulle was indeed an 'obstructionist saboteur'. Churchill gave vent to his rage at the ensuing Cabinet meeting, and Sir Alexander Cadogan noted on that occasion: 'Cabinet 6.30. We endured the usual passionate anti-de Gaulle harangue from PM. On this subject, we get away from politics and diplomacy and even common sense. It's a girls' school. Roosevelt, PM, and – it must be admitted de Gaulle – all behave like girls approaching the age of puberty. Nothing to be done.'[29]

Half-way through the Cabinet meeting, news came that General de Gaulle was also refusing to let the 200 French liaison officers embark for France, since there was no agreement as to their duties. This left the Prime Minister speechless with rage.

Several dramatic hours were to follow. At 9 p.m., Churchill was informed that there had been a misunderstanding: General de Gaulle had not refused to broadcast, but had only refused to do so immediately after Eisenhower. But the Prime Minister – who had been drinking a large number of whiskies – was beside himself with rage: 'De Gaulle was to speak at the hour and place assigned to him, he had to give in, etc. . . .'[30]

At 10.30, as the invasion fleet was sailing towards France, the French Ambassador, Pierre Viénot, was called to the Foreign Office. He confirmed to Eden that there had been a misunderstanding about the broadcast, but he also reaffirmed that the liaison officers would

*Charles Peake had obviously misunderstood the General's meaning.

not be sent. Eden asked him to try and persuade de Gaulle to reverse his decision, and Viénot undertook to see the General.

At 11.30, Ambassador Viénot saw de Gaulle at the Connaught Hotel. The General denied having ever refused to broadcast and launched into a violent diatribe against Churchill, Eden, Britain and the British. He worked himself up into a towering rage, and copiously insulted Viénot in the process. 'I've never had such a dressing-down in my whole life,' the ambassador later confided.[31]

At 1 a.m., as the first Allied paratroopers were already jumping over France, Viénot returned to the Foreign Office. There, he found Mr Eden with the Prime Minister, and repeated that de Gaulle had not refused to broadcast, though he maintained his decision concerning the liaison officers, in the absence of an agreement on civil administration. Churchill exploded, roared, bellowed, was incoherent with rage.[32] 'The Prime Minister,' Eden reported in a very attenuated description of the outburst, 'made plain his entire lack of confidence in General de Gaulle and his conviction that as long as he was at the head of French affairs there would be no good relations between France, Great Britain and the United States. He said that the General was an enemy and many other things of like sort.'[33] Viénot was again copiously insulted, and left in protest. Churchill then sent for Desmond Morton, and gave him the following instructions: 'Go and tell Bedell-Smith to put de Gaulle in a plane and send him back to Algiers – in chains if necessary. He must not be allowed to re-enter France.'[34]

At 3 p.m., the unfortunate Viénot returned to the Connaught Hotel, and found de Gaulle in a somewhat calmer mood. In the meantime, Desmond Morton, before carrying out his instructions, alerted Eden, who endeavoured to reason with the Prime Minister in the early morning hours. The latter had already dictated a letter to de Gaulle ordering him to leave England at once.[35]

'Well,' Eden confided to Bruce Lockhart the next day, 'we've had a crazy night.'[36] This was a typical understatement on Eden's part. But France – and England – owed much to the Foreign Secretary; for at dawn on 6 June, the order to expel the General had been cancelled,[37] and the Prime Minister's letter to de Gaulle had been burnt. The longest night was over; the longest day had just begun.

As the morning progressed, it became apparent that the landing in Normandy was going fairly well. There were already three divisions ashore, and the casualties were light. In London, everyone was immensely relieved, but at the Foreign Office there was no time for jubilation, as all were engaged in frantic diplomatic activity: Eisenhower had spoken alone to France that morning, and the people of France would soon wonder why de Gaulle remained silent. Eden had therefore asked Charles Peake to convince the General to broadcast as soon as possible. When the General finally agreed to record his speech at noon, there remained the thorny problem of checking de Gaulle's speech in advance – de Gaulle would of course refuse to submit his script in advance, and in fact Viénot did not dare ask him.[38] But there was always the risk that de Gaulle, in his present mood, might denounce Britain and the United States on the very day of the landing. Sir Alexander Cadogan noted in his diary: 'Got Duff round about 11.15 and told him he must see de Gaulle and try to get his script and tell him not to be silly about his liaison officers. But Duff couldn't get an audience till afternoon, so it was agreed we should have to check de Gaulle from the disc and stop it if it was too bad.'[39]The recording at Bush House went without a hitch, and de Gaulle delivered one his most magnificent speeches on that occasion:

La bataille suprême est engagée . . . Bien entendu, c'est la bataille de France, et c'est la bataille de la France! . . . Pour les fils de France, où qu'ils soient, quels qu'ils soient, le devoir simple et sacré est de combattre l'ennemi par tous les moyens dont ils disposent . . . Les consignes données par le gouvernement français et par les chefs français qu'il a qualifiés pour le faire doivent être exactement suivies . . . Derrière le nuage si lourd de notre sang et de nos larmes, voici que reparait le soleil de notre grandeur![40]*

'*Les consignes données par le gouvernement français*' – not even '*le gouvernement provisoire*' – and Bruce Lockhart, who was waiting for the script, recalled: 'I rushed down to the Foreign Office to seek Mr Eden's approval. He was engaged when I arrived, and Mr Duff Cooper was waiting in the Private Secretaries' room. But today I had priority, and Mr Eden saw me almost at once. I gave him the text and drew his attention to the omission of "Provisional". He read it through. He pointed to the omission: "I'll have trouble with the

*'The decisive battle has begun. . . . Of course, it is the battle of France, and it is France's battle! . . . For the sons of France, whoever they may be, wherever they may be, the simple and sacred duty is to fight the enemy with all available means. . . . The directives issued by the French government and by the French leaders who have been delegated to issue them must be followed to the letter. . . . Behind the heavy clouds of our blood and our tears, the sunshine of our greatness is presently reappearing!'

Prime Minister about this," he said, "but we'll let it go." He was smiling.'[41]

After a busy night patching up Franco-British relations, the Foreign Secretary had worked all morning without interruption. He also kept up his pressure on the Prime Minister, and wrote him the following note: 'What I suggest is that you should authorize me to repeat to Viénot that we are prepared to discuss these civil affairs matters with the French committee. . . . At the same time I hope that you will also feel able to send a message to the President urging him to authorize Winant to sit in with us. The result of our work would of course be *ad referendum* to you and to the President. . . . The present position is unfair to His Majesty's government and dangerous to Anglo-American relations.'[42]

But Eden's troubles with the Prime Minister were far from over, as his diary shows:

6 June: . . . Brief rest in afternoon. W. rang up about seven and long argument ensued about de Gaulle and French. Again soon after midnight W. rang up in a rage because Bevin and Attlee had taken my view. Argument continued for forty-five minutes, perhaps longer. I was accused of trying to break up the government, of stirring up the press on the issue. He said that nothing would induce him to give way, that de Gaulle must go. There would be a Cabinet tomorrow. House of Commons would back him against de Gaulle and me and any of the Cabinet who sided with me, etc. FDR and he would fight the world. I told him that I heard that [Admiral Raymond] Fenard [French naval representative in United States] had arrived with a personal message from FDR to de Gaulle. He did not like that. I didn't lose my temper and I think that I gave as good as I got. Anyway I didn't budge an inch. Two hours later Brendan [Bracken] rang me up to say that he had been called lackey of Foreign Office, etc., but that, in the middle, message from FDR came inviting de Gaulle to United States.[43]

The Foreign Secretary was to be kept awake that night also. . . . For several hours, he told Churchill in substance: 'We must either break with de Gaulle – which means breaking with France – or conclude an agreement with him. There is no middle course. We must point this out to the President, and tell him that de Gaulle must be supported.'[44]

On Eden's instructions, Duff Cooper had also been working on General de Gaulle during the afternoon of 6 June. The task was no easier, as evidenced by Duff Cooper's report:

I saw General de Gaulle this afternoon. He was calm but depressed. He felt that he had been brought over here solely with the object of impressing upon the French people the idea that he and the committee were completely at one with the United States and Great Britain and that if he consented to assist in giving that impression he would be deceiving the French people. . . . I then raised with him the question of the liaison officers whom he had refused to send abroad with our troops. I pointed out to him that his refusal would be interpreted as a reluctance to assist us in battle and that it would only do him and his cause great harm. . . . After some argument he consented to reconsider his decision and said that he would consult with General Koenig to see how many of these officers could be sent. . . . He felt that he was making a concession and a 'gesture'. He said that he was always making concessions but that nobody ever made them to him.[45]

On the evening of the next day, Eden took over from Duff Cooper. The Foreign Secretary was 'fresh' from another night of argument with Churchill, a renewed argument on the telephone with the Prime Minister on the same subject from 8.30 to 10 in the morning, then from 11.20 to 11.40, then after 6 p.m. in the Cabinet. All the same, he took on General de Gaulle at dinner that same evening.

Duff Cooper, Charles Peake, Pierre Viénot, Gaston Palewski and de Gaulle's ADC, Leon Teyssot, were also present at the dinner. Teyssot described the dinner in the following terms: 'Stormy. De Gaulle shouts at Eden. Says it's a scandal that the British should follow the American lead and accept their counterfeit money.'[46] The General was rarely helpful, even to his allies in the British Cabinet. Eden, however, was unimpressed:

I told the General that we wished to discuss with the French committee the problem of civil affairs in France. We would keep the United States government informed and would do what we could to encourage them to participate. . . .

General de Gaulle then made a long lament. He said that he had never been so unhappy about our relations as now. He had been grateful for the Prime Minister's action in receiving him on his arrival and telling him of the battle. But still nothing had been arranged about civil administration in France.

I told the General that our intention was to discuss just this problem. It would be days, perhaps weeks, before we commanded any territory except the beaches. In the meantime let us work together to agree a plan. The General asked what would be the value of such a plan unless the Americans would also agree and made further complaints. . . I

The conference at Anfa, January 1943.
Left to right: Giraud, Roosevelt, de Gaulle and Churchill.

Smiles before the cameras, tommy-guns behind the curtains, and
a Churchillian *'Si vous m'obstaclerez, je vous liquiderai!'*

Anthony Eden with Friend.
Boundless patience, treasures of diplomacy . . . and many
sleepless nights.

'You have insulted France and betrayed the West. This cannot be forgotten!'

'I ask my colleagues to consider urgently whether we should not now eliminate de Gaulle as a political force . . . It seems to me most questionable that we should allow this marplot and mischief-maker to continue the harm he is doing.'

The conference at Anfa, January 1943.
Left to right: Giraud, Roosevelt, de Gaulle and Churchill.

Smiles before the cameras, tommy-guns behind the curtains, and
a Churchillian '*Si vous m'obstaclerez, je vous liquiderai!*'

Anthony Eden with Friend.
Boundless patience, treasures of diplomacy . . . and many
sleepless nights.

'You have insulted France and betrayed the West. This cannot be forgotten!'

'I ask my colleagues to consider urgently whether we should not now eliminate de Gaulle as a political force . . . It seems to me most questionable that we should allow this marplot and mischief-maker to continue the harm he is doing.'

The return to France. Normandy 14 June 1944. De Gaulle in a
British jeep. Although not visible in this photograph, it was flying
the Tricolour pennant and bearing the Cross of Lorraine.

A hero's welcome.

Anglo-French relations. In the
top picture Churchill visits
Paris for the first time after the
Liberation.

At the Arc de Triomphe,
11 November 1944.

'I shall never forget those who
did not desert me in June 1940,
when I was all alone. You'll
see: one day, we'll go down the
Champs-Elysées together!'
(Winston Churchill to Charles
de Gaulle, 8 November 1942)

'One is always right to trust
France!'

continued that what we were asking him to do was to work with us so that the civil administration of France could be set up. . .

The General said that he understood, but continued to complain about our dependence on American policy. I retorted that it was a fatal mistake in national policy to have too much pride. 'She stoops to conquer' was an action which we could each of us find useful to observe at times.

[There was a longish pause there, as all the British present tried to find some way of translating 'She stoops to conquer' into French.]

Having pondered over this de Gaulle repeated the difficulty he felt in entering into conversations which might lead nowhere. They would give a false impression of an agreement which did not exist, while the Supreme Commander issued a series of edicts which affected the future of France.

M. Viénot, who was present, at this stage put in a plea that the conversations on civil affairs should go forward. General de Gaulle replied that M. Viénot could certainly conduct them himself.[47]

This was in fact no great concession on General de Gaulle's part. Viénot could always talk with the British. He, de Gaulle, rejected in advance any agreement that would have to be submitted to the United States for approval. In fact, those qualified on the French side to negotiate and sign such an agreement were still in Algiers, and de Gaulle had not the slightest intention of calling them to London. But the General had other preoccupations: the internal situation in France, the attitude of the Communists within the Resistance movement, and of course the circulation in France of Allied military currency – 'les faux billets'. Besides, how would he and his movement be received once they landed in France? Among all these uncertainties, there were a few bright spots: the Resistance was fighting extremely well, and General Eisenhower himself had acknowledged it in no uncertain terms; moreover, all communications between London and Algiers had now been re-established; finally, de Gaulle had noticed that there were serious divergences within the British Cabinet. It was obvious that Mr Bevin and Mr Eden were opposed to Churchill's policy of systematically following Washington's lead in French affairs. It was no less obvious that they had the great majority of Parliament and public opinion behind them in this matter. But as General de Gaulle wrote to his commissioners in Algiers: 'While the fighting lasts, Churchill will remain very much in charge; and the British personalities favourable to Free France cannot get Mr Churchill to change his policy, as the latter has become blind and deaf.'[48]

Churchill had perhaps become blind, but he was certainly not deaf. On 7 June he yielded to Eden's arguments, and wrote to President Roosevelt asking him once again whether Ambassador Winant might not be authorized to participate in the talks on civil administration. There was also a renewed plea for a meeting between de Gaulle and the President: 'I think it would be a great pity if you and he did not meet. I do not see why I should have all the luck.'[49]

Needless to say, Churchill's anger at de Gaulle's behaviour had not yet subsided; it resurged in each of his quarrels with Eden, in each of his letters to President Roosevelt. 'The Prime Minister,' Oliver Harvey noted on 9 June, 'is almost insane at times in his hatred of General de Gaulle.'[50] Had de Gaulle consented to negotiations on civil affairs with Ambassador Viénot? 'Out of the question!' Churchill exploded. Did de Gaulle want to go to Normandy? 'Wait and see how he behaves!' Churchill replied.[51] 'Remember,' he wrote to Eden, 'that there is not a scrap of generosity about this man, who only wishes to pose as a saviour of France in this operation without a single French soldier at his back.'[52] Churchill himself went to visit the beaches of Normandy with Field-Marshal Smuts on 12 June.

As usual, Churchill was unable to maintain a negative attitude for very long. After a few more early-morning shouting matches with Anthony Eden, he authorized negotiations with Ambassador Viénot. He also reluctantly allowed de Gaulle to visit Bayeux in Normandy, though he tried to limit the General's movements there as much as possible.[53]* However, the concessions came too late to prevent a deluge of protests from the British press, Parliament and public opinion. The *Daily Mail*, *The Times*, the *Economist*, the *Manchester Guardian* called for immediate recognition of de Gaulle's movement, protested loudly against the use of Allied military currency, denounced Washington's policy in French affairs as well

---

*'It would not be possible for de Gaulle to hold a public meeting there, or gather crowds in the streets. He would no doubt like to have a demonstration to show that he is the future President of the French Republic. I suggest that he should drive slowly through the town, shake hands with a few people, and then return, leaving any subsequent statement to be made here. On the other hand, everything in the way of courtesy should be done to him.' (Churchill to Eden, 13/6/44). The Prime Minister was to raise objections to de Gaulle's trip until the very last minute, but the majority of the Cabinet brushed them aside.

as the British government's subservience in the matter, and voiced indignation at Churchill's visit to France without General de Gaulle. A cartoon showed Churchill and Field-Marshal Smuts on their way to France, with General de Gaulle stranded on the English coast; the caption read: 'One of our liberators is missing.'

However, all this was nothing compared to the storm that was raised in Parliament on French affairs. On 14 June, Question Time in Commons was unusually animated:

Mr Boothby asked the Secretary of State for Foreign Affairs:
1. Whether it is proposed to recognize the National Committee as the provisional government of France;
2. Whether he can make any statement about the negotiations with General de Gaulle; and whether any agreement has been reached with regard to the administration of occupied territory of France;
3. Whether any issue of French currency has been made to the Allied troops now fighting in France; and, if so, by whom it is backed.
4. Mr Martin asked the Secretary of State for Foreign Affairs whether conversations on the relations of the French Committee of National Liberation with the British government, especially on matters concerning civil administration in France before elections can be held there, have taken place; and whether he can make a statement on the matter.

Mr G. Strauss asked the Secretary of State for Foreign Affairs whether he can make any statement about the large issue of French banknotes printed in the United States for the use of Allied soldiers in France; whether this was done in agreement with the French authorities; and whether any arrangement has been made as to the responsibility for redeeming these notes.

Mr Cocks: 'Will the government send a firm request to America to appoint a political representative over here to discuss with the Right Honourable Gentleman and General de Gaulle this question of civil administration?'

Churchill: 'In addition to our relations with the French Committee of National Liberation, headed by General de Gaulle, we have also to consider our very close relations with the United States and their relations with the body I have just mentioned . . . I therefore appeal to the House not to disregard my counsel.'

Mr Edgar Granville: 'Will the Right Honourable Gentleman bear in mind that, in recent debates, the House of Commons has expressed a very strong view on this question, which did reflect a fairly general opinion in this country; and will he also bear in mind that, while there may be complete silence in the House, the press of the United States and of this country is openly debating the matter? Will the Right Honourable

Gentleman also bear in mind that many of us are being pressed by our constituents – (Interruption) – many of us are being asked if the Right Honourable Gentleman cannot give an assurance that there is nothing to prevent General de Gaulle from landing in France if he so wishes?'
Churchill: 'That last question is one which I hope may be found capable of solution.'
Earl Winterton: 'May I ask the Prime Minister if he will have regard to the fact that some of us who are not pressing for a debate, are yet disturbed by the most searching and painful anxiety about the position of General de Gaulle. . . .'[54]

The press and Parliament were merely reflecting the current trend of public opinion – and there was no doubt that the sympathies of the British public lay more than ever with General de Gaulle and his 'gallant Free French'. For Churchill, who had done so much for France and for General de Gaulle, it must have been particularly galling to be accused of neglecting the interests of France at the very hour of liberation. He had not even the consolation of seeing President Roosevelt vindicated; for the American and British Intelligence officers in liberated France had all reported the same attitude among the French population: 'There is one name and one name only on every lip – de Gaulle. About this there could be no doubt and no two opinions. The testimony was overwhelming and indeed seemingly unanimous.'[55]

Unaware of these developments, de Gaulle had embarked for France on the morning of 14 June. Not knowing how he would be received in Normandy, the General was in a sombre mood. A few days earlier, he had seen a film of Marshal Pétain's visit to Paris; the Marshal had been received in triumph and acclaimed by a delirious crowd of 200,000.[56] De Gaulle was also preoccupied by the prospects of a struggle with the Allies over the administration of the small part of liberated French territory, and at this moment, his feelings towards Roosevelt and Churchill were less than amiable. On the previous evening, Anthony Eden had given a dinner at the Foreign Office in the General's honour. On that occasion, the Foreign Secretary, ever a diplomat, had said to General Béthouart:

'I know the Prime Minister, he is a sensitive man. I am sure that if General de Gaulle were to send him a telegram of greetings and thanks during the visit to your country tomorrow, this would immediately dispel the present misunderstanding. Would you do me the favour of trying to get him to do this?'

General Béthouart answered that he was quite willing, but that 'this was more than a misunderstanding, it was a political question of capital importance.' The Foreign Secretary should therefore consult Ambassador Viénot; this Eden proceeded to do, and General Béthouart recalled the rest in his memoirs: 'De Gaulle observed the scene, and perhaps heard part of the conversation. He motioned to Viénot, left the table, and led him to a corner of the room. At the table, everyone was silently looking on, intrigued if not amazed. They heard a harsh 'non' and they all looked at their plates, as de Gaulle and Viénot joined the table again.'[57]

Churchill's absence at the dinner had not passed unnoticed, of course. But that was not all, as de Gaulle noted in his memoirs: 'While I was dining at the Foreign Office with the British ministers, except Mr Churchill, and as I was being congratulated on being able to set foot on the soil of metropolitan France, a letter from Mr Churchill, delivered to Mr Eden at the meal, raised last-minute objections to my plan. But Eden, having consulted his colleagues around the table, particularly Clement Attlee, informed me that the whole Cabinet was standing by the original arrangements.'[58]

Now, on the deck of the French destroyer *La Combattante*, de Gaulle was silent and concentrated. With him were Admiral d'Argenlieu, Palewski and Viénot. The latter, finding the heavy silence difficult to bear, remarked: 'Do you realize, mon Général, that four years ago today, the Germans were entering Paris?' Back came the answer, brief and harsh: '*Eh bien, ils ont eu tort!*'[59]

The party landed shortly after 2 p.m. on the beach near Courseulles. De Gaulle first went to visit Montgomery at his headquarters, but needless to say, he had not come to France just to visit Montgomery. He then proceeded to Bayeux, with two important objectives in mind: to supervise the installation of François Coulet as Commissioner of the Republic for the liberated territory of Normandy, thus effectively undermining American attempts to instal an administration of their own. This went on without a hitch. The second purpose, which to de Gaulle was just as important, was to establish a personal contact with the French people. It was to be a resounding success, as de Gaulle later recalled with some emotion: 'We proceeded on foot, from street to street. At the sight of General de Gaulle, the inhabitants stood in amazement, then burst into cheers, or into tears. Coming out of their houses, they escorted me amidst an extraordinary display of emotion. The children surrounding me, the women smiling and sobbing. The men with hands outstretched. We thus walked on together, fraternally, overwhelmed, and we felt the joy, pride, and faith in the nation surging again from the abyss.'[60]

Having addressed the population of Bayeux gathered on the Place du Château, and then visited the town of Isigny, de Gaulle re-embarked that evening with his party. He was satisfied with the results of his visit; in France, the people had responded the way he had hoped they would: they had put their trust and their faith in de Gaulle. Tomorrow, no doubt, all France would do the same. De Gaulle was also well satisfied with his exertions to stave off the AMGOT in France. To Béthouart, he said on the return trip, 'You see, we just had to present the Allies with an accomplished fact. Our administration is now in place. You'll see that they will say nothing.'[61]

Indeed, the Allies said nothing; they did not immediately grasp the significance of François Coulet's installation in Bayeux. On the other hand, they were much impressed by the reception the French population had given General de Gaulle; indeed, the reports were unanimous: 'It was evident that General de Gaulle's name was well-known to the population and that they were delighted to see him. They turned out in hundreds and threw flowers into the jeeps.'[62] Another report to the Foreign Office described the 'generally unhelpful attitude of the British military authorities towards General de Gaulle's party; the party seemed to have been regarded as tiresome visitors on an unnecessary sightseeing tour. The historical significance of the occasion was apparently quite overlooked and no attempt seems to have been made to adopt plans to meet General de Gaulle's convenience.' And the following comment was added to the report: 'In the light of all this muddle and lack of consideration it is surprising that General de Gaulle should have returned from Normandy in such a benign mood.'[63]

It was not at all surprising; in fact, de Gaulle had not noticed the coolness of the British reception; he had only felt the warmth of the French reception. Upon returning to England, he had found that the news of this reception had travelled far and wide. He had seen in the British press the accounts of the debate in Parliament the day before; furthermore, between 8 June and 20 June, the exiled governments of Czechoslovakia, Poland, Belgium, Luxemburg, Yugoslavia and Norway, ignoring British and American objections, officially recognized the provisional government of the French republic; last but not least, the dangers of a takeover by AMGOT in France now seemed to have markedly receded. Insufferable in adversity, de Gaulle was magnanimous in victory, as Eden found out to his surprise when he made a farewell visit to the General on the afternoon of 16 June:* 'I went to see the General in Carlton Gardens. This was the first time I had done so. I was received with some ceremony, a guard of honour being drawn up outside, with officers posted at intervals up the stairs. De Gaulle talked easily for twenty minutes. As I commented at the time, "He is at his best as host."[64]

'The General,' Eden reported, 'said that he was very grateful for the hospitality and courtesy extended to him during his visit here, and that he had written a letter to the Prime Minister to express his thanks. Although he admitted that there had been difficulties in our discussions he was glad that he had come and he thought we had made progress. As he now saw matters there were really only two important points outstanding. The first was the administration of France. . .'[65] 'Mr Eden,' de Gaulle recalled, 'now proposed to establish a plan with Viénot which he himself would communicate to Washington and which, he was quite sure, would be signed simultaneously by France, England and America. This procedure seemed acceptable to me, and I said so to Mr Eden.'[66] 'As regards recognition', Eden noted,

> The General said that he attached little importance to this. Forms were of no account. I said that I had observed that the committee had abstained from asking for any recognition as a provisional government, and I had therefore always assumed this was not a main issue between us. The General confirmed this. He went on to say that the second point was that of currency, about which he much hoped that some arrangement would be arrived at. . . . He then spoke of the Resistance movement. . . . He thought that good work was being done and he understood that some German divisions had been diverted to deal with the activities of the Resistance movement. . . . The General was in a more reasonable mood than I have ever known him, and emphasized that despite the difficulties there had been, his desire was above all to work closely with ourselves and the Americans.[67]

'Then,' de Gaulle recalled, 'I wrote to Mr Churchill to salve the wounds he had inflicted on himself.'[68] It was indeed a soothing letter; the General had the greatest esteem and admiration for

*In his memoirs, de Gaulle mistakenly gives the date as 15 June.

Britain's indomitable Prime Minister and after all, at this time of rising fortunes, France could well afford to be generous:

> Upon leaving Great Britain, to which you kindly invited me at a moment of decisive importance to the successful conclusion of this war, I would like to extend my sincerest thanks for the welcome extended to me by His Majesty's government.
>
> After the lapse of a year since my last stay in your noble and valiant country, I have been able to see and feel that the courage and power of the people of Great Britain were of the highest order and that their feelings of friendship for France were stronger then ever. I can assure you, in return, of the deep confidence and unbreakable attachment which France feels towards Great Britain.
>
> During my visit, I was also able to measure the magnificent effort being made by the British navy, army and air force in the battle now being waged on French soil by the Allies and by France, and which, I am certain, will end in a common victory. For your country, which has been in this war the last and impregnable bastion of Europe, and is now one of its foremost liberators, as for yourself, who have never ceased nor will cease to direct and inspire this immense effort, this is, allow me to tell you, an immortal honour.[69]

If de Gaulle was a magnanimous victor, Churchill was a bad loser. His reply was much colder:

> Dear General de Gaulle,
>
> I thank you for your letter of 16 June, and for the complimentary expressions which it contains. I had high hopes when you arrived that we might have reached some basis of collaboration, and that I might have been of assistance to the French Committee of National Liberation in coming to more friendly terms with the government of the United States. I am grieved that these hopes have not been realized except that there is a possibility that the discussions on an expert level may arrive at some modification of the present deadlock.
>
> Ever since 1907, I have in good times and bad times been a sincere friend of France, as my words and actions show, and it is to me an intense pain that barriers have been raised to an association which to me was very dear. Here in this visit of yours, which I personally arranged, I had the hope that there was a chance of putting things right. Now I have only the hope that it may not be the last chance.
>
> If nevertheless I may presume to offer advice, it would be that you should carry out the visit which has been planned to President Roosevelt and try to establish for France those good relations with the United States which are a most valuable part of her inheritance. You may count

on any assistance I can give in this matter, which is one of great consequence to the future of France.[70]

'I sat with him while he dictated it,' Duff Cooper recalled. 'When he had finished he said, "I'm sorry but that's the best I can do." '[71] In a letter to Eden, Duff Cooper gave further indications as to Churchill's state of mind concerning de Gaulle: 'The Prime Minister says he will denounce him as the mortal foe of England.'[72]

That evening, General de Gaulle left the United Kingdom. In Algiers, and later in Paris, many more battles still awaited him – and not all of them against the Germans.

CHAPTER 15

Liberation

In June 1944, President Roosevelt was still pursuing a cautious and highly complex policy in French affairs – a policy that was influenced more than ever by domestic and electoral considerations. Indeed, in the cut-throat competition of American electoral politics, failing to back a winner could be just as disastrous as backing a loser. In French affairs, President Roosevelt had already backed several losers, and he still could not bring himself to consider General de Gaulle as a winner. Yet he could take no chances, and at the end of May, he entrusted the head of the French naval mission in Washington, Admiral Fenard, with a message for General de Gaulle. The message was as complicated as the policy it reflected: 'If he (de Gaulle) asked me if I would see him if he came over, I would reply in the affirmative most cordially.'[1] There was of course no question of an official invitation: in American politics, acknowledging a mistake could be even more disastrous than not backing a winner.

In Algiers, de Gaulle received the message with little surprise and much suspicion. He had been led several times before to expect an invitation to Washington, and nothing had ever come of it. Besides, de Gaulle was not unaware of the political game that was being played, and wanted above all to avoid giving the impression that he had anything to ask from the American President. He had therefore answered non-committally that he took note of the invitation and that the matter should be re-examined at a later date, as he was now leaving for London.

On 6 June, however, another message from Roosevelt was received in London. This time, the President also proposed a definite date for de Gaulle's visit, and there was no doubt that he now attached some importance to it. De Gaulle was correspondingly reserved and unenthusiastic; he replied cautiously on 14 June that he 'sincerely hoped that circumstances would allow him to undertake the trip'.[2] In fact, after hesitating for some time, he finally decided it was in France's interest that he should go. During the next few months, there would be huge Allied offensives on French territory, and it might still be possible to reach a *de facto* agreement on civil administration with the American government. De Gaulle, of course, had no intention of negotiating in Washington himself, but his visit might improve relations at the top and pave the way for negotiations through ordinary diplomatic channels. On 26 June, the General therefore informed President Roosevelt that he accepted the invitation.[3]

Roosevelt answered politely and with some hypocrisy that he 'was very pleased that General de Gaulle expressed a desire to visit America with the purpose of having conversations with the President. . .'[4]— Underneath it all, Roosevelt's opinion of General de Gaulle was in fact, as negative as ever: 'A narrow-minded French zealot with too much ambition for his own good and some rather dubious views on democracy.'[5] On 14 June, Stimson also noted in his diaries: 'FDR . . . believes that de Gaulle will crumble and that the British supporters of de Gaulle will be confounded by the progress of events . . . he thinks that other parties will spring up as the liberation goes on and that de Gaulle will become a very little figure. Said that he already knew of some such parties. . . .'[6] Five days before de Gaulle's arrival in Washington, Roosevelt gave his considered opinion of General de Gaulle: 'He's a nut.'[7]

For all this, de Gaulle's visit to the United States was quite successful. He arrived on 6 July, accompanied by General Béthouart, Gaston Palewski and Colonel de Rancourt, and was most cordially received at the White House. The discussions with the President were quite friendly; Roosevelt explained how the United States would henceforth intervene in world affairs, politically through the United Nations, and militarily through a string of bases set up all around the world – including on French territories. De Gaulle was somewhat taken aback, but merely pointed to the danger for the post-war world of a weakened Europe in general, and a weakened France in particular. General de Gaulle also had talks with numerous American personalities, including General Marshall, Admiral King, Henry Morgenthau, Henry Wallace and of course Cordell Hull, whom he actually liked.[8] The mayor of New York, Fiorello La Guardia, gave the indomitable French leader a triumphal reception, and Canada received him with moving demonstrations of support and affection. De Gaulle returned to Algiers on 13 July; on arrival, he learned that the American government had recognized the French Committee of National Liberation as the *de facto* authority in the civil administration of France.

Back in London, where a civil affairs agreement had been quietly negotiated between Ambassador Viénot and the Foreign Office, the President's abrupt decision took everyone by surprise. Oliver Harvey noted in his diary:

> Both Prime Minister and Anthony Eden rather bitter at this sudden volte-face without warning. As PM said to A.E.: 'The President has treated you badly,' making it appear that it has been himself and nobody else who has got us all out of the jam, when it was he alone who had created the jam in order to acquire for himself credit by removing it. What a slippery politician he is. Viénot, our good friend, in a great stew when he heard what the President had done. He came round to see me at once and urged the great need to put things in their right perspective through radio and press as otherwise French opinion in France which had been kept deliberately in the dark during the long Anglo-American wrangle would really suppose it was the Americans and not us who had done all the work. 'J'ai peur que vous ne soyez cocu!' We laughed and thanked him but told him we thought the French and everybody else would see through these electoral manoeuvres in America. A.E., however, was seriously annoyed.[9]

Anthony Eden had some reason to be annoyed: British diplomacy was once again trailing behind the State Department. 'Can't we really have a foreign policy of our own?' the Foreign Secretary asked.[10] Actually Eden had been applying pressure on the Prime Minister to obtain something more than a *de facto* recognition of the FCNL: a formal recognition of the French provisional government as such, to be announced if possible on 14 July. The Prime Minister, however, would have none of it. 'The President,' he wrote to Eden, 'had already come a long way, and he, Churchill, was not prepared to dissociate himself at this stage "from his nomenclature".'[11]

In fact, Churchill hoped that by following the President's lead in diplomacy, he might get him to adopt British strategic conceptions. After all, the Americans had given in to British pressure before; they had accepted 'Torch' and 'Husky', they had agreed to abandon 'Sledgehammer'. This time, the Prime Minister wanted nothing less than a complete change in the strategy agreed upon at Tehran.

Operation 'Anvil', the landing in southern France that was being prepared for mid-August, seemed to him quite useless. Another operation offered much brighter prospects. In Italy, Rome had fallen on 4 June, and Kesselring's army was in full retreat; should not General Alexander be allowed to pursue the Germans further north, down the Po Valley, through the Ljubljana Gap and on to Vienna, Budapest and beyond? The British, American and French armies would thus draw many German divisions away from the west, and also reach the Balkans before the Soviet troops. It was an attractive prospect, but impossible to realize if the Americans persisted in their plans for operation 'Anvil', as three American and four French divisions would then have to be withdrawn from General Alexander's command to participate in the operation. Yet Eisenhower insisted that 'Anvil' should be allowed to proceed in direct support of 'Overlord'. Only Roosevelt could reverse that decision, and the President was unwilling to go back on a promise made to Stalin at Tehran.

Churchill finally gave in and the landing in southern France, rechristened 'Dragoon', was planned for 15 August. But the Prime Minister continued to have great doubts as to the wisdom of this strategy; he had other preoccupations also. In the Levant, General Spears had intervened in the Franco-Syrian dispute over control of the *Troupes Speciales*, and had offered to supply arms to the Syrian Gendarmerie. Eden was incensed, though not as much as General de Gaulle, who told Duff Cooper that he feared Anglo-French relations would never improve so long as the British pursued their present policy in the Levant.[12]

In spite of all these difficulties, indeed because of them, Churchill, much encouraged by his Foreign Secretary, would have liked to improve his relations with the French committee and its intransigent leader. On 2 August, he spoke in Commons on the war situation, and noted

> The great improvement in the relations of the French National Committee headed by General de Gaulle with the government of the United States. This arose in part from the careful spadework done over here by my Right Honourable friend the Foreign Secretary and by the great success which attended General de Gaulle's visit to the President of the United States. In these last four years I had many difficulties with General de Gaulle, but I have never forgotten, and can never forget, that he stood forth as the first eminent Frenchman to face the common foe in what

seemed to be the hour of ruin of his country and, possibly, of ours, and it is only fair and becoming that he should stand first and foremost in the days when France shall again be raised, and raise herself, to her rightful place among the great powers of Europe and of the world. . . . Our landing in Normandy, the course of the war, the whole tide of events show quite clearly that we shall presently once again have to deal with the problem of France and Germany along the Rhine, and from that discussion France can by no means be excluded. It is evident from what I have said that I look forward to the closest association of the British Empire, the United States and the Russian and French representatives in the settlement of these important European problems.[13]

A week later, Churchill informed Ambassador Duff Cooper that he would stop in Algiers on his way to Rome, and would welcome the opportunity of a talk with General de Gaulle. Duff Cooper was to write in his memoirs:

It seemed to me. . . . that no more suitable moment could have been chosen for the Prime Minister's arrival, which would provide an excellent opportunity for him and the General to make up their quarrel. . . . I went to see de Gaulle at six o'clock and gave him the information. He said that he thought nothing would be gained by an interview with the Prime Minister at the present time. I did my best to persuade him to change his mind, reminding him of the extremely warm terms in which the Prime Minister had referred to him in the House of Commons, and saying that it was only common civility to pay a call on so distinguished a traveller passing through French territory. I spent three-quarters of an hour with him, but did not succeed in convincing him, though I persuaded him to send a polite letter to the PM saying that he did not wish to disturb the short period he was to have at Algiers between his two flights. . . . It occurred to me during dinner that it was worth while making one more appeal to General de Gaulle, so I wrote him a letter, pointing out that he had promised to write a letter . . . and that, as he was prepared to make such a gesture, why not go a little further and pay a call, which would have a much more useful effect? He replied that he had already written the letter which Palewski would deliver the next morning. I could do no more. . . .[14]

'*Je n'ai rien à lui dire*', de Gaulle had told Duff Cooper.[15] It is unclear whether the General was still nursing an old grudge, or whether he wished to express his displeasure at recent events in the Levant. At any rate the Prime Minister, landing incognito at Maison Blanche airport near Algiers on the morning of 11 August, was given the following message: '. . . All things considered I think it preferable that I should not see you this time, so that you may take some rest between two flights. . . .'[16]

'I thought this needlessly haughty,' Churchill wrote in his memoirs.[17] In fact, he had been stung by the affront, and wrote to Eden the next day: 'This . . . is certainly a good indication of the relations we shall have with this man as he, through our exertions, gains supreme power in France . . . certainly it was a great mistake to give de Gaulle the opportunity of putting this marked affront on the head of a government which has three-quarters of a million soldiers fighting, with heavy losses, to liberate France. I trust to you to raise this point formally with Massigli and see that it is brought home to de Gaulle. I ask you to act in this matter.'[18]

Naturally, Churchill changed his mind a few days later, and wrote to Eden: 'Unless you have already acted, I am of the opinion that it is better not to mention the de Gaulle incident to Massigli either formally or informally.'[19] But the treatment meted out to him at Algiers continued to rankle, as evidenced by Diana Cooper's recollections of an embassy dinner in Rome on 20 August: 'I didn't do at all well with Duckling* because my face reminds him instantly of de Gaulle. This gives him apoplexy, so I turn from him to Ambassador Kirk. . . . I turn with a new subject to Duckling, but again my face transports him back immediately to de Gaulle, and apoplexy envelops him. It's made our meeting impossible.'[20]

The climate had not improved in Algiers either. On 15 August, de Gaulle learned that Churchill had gone to Corsica without warning French authorities of his coming. The General flew into a rage, and told Massigli to raise the matter with Duff Cooper. This was probably a bit childish on the General's part, but then there was now much nervousness in Algiers: Operation 'Dragoon' was underway, with advanced elements of the First French Army and of the Fourth American Corps already landing on the Mediterranean coast of France. In Normandy, the German front was crumbling, and the road to Paris opened before the American columns and General Leclerc's 2nd Armoured division. In Paris, the insurrection was about to begin, with massive strikes already paralysing the capital. And yet, at a time when victory was in sight, de Gaulle was beset with anxiety; for he had learned that two different factions were striving to take power in the capital before the arrival of the Allied columns. Laval was behind the first plot: he was trying to get Herriot to summon the long defunct National Assembly of 1940, which would legalize the formation of a government of national

*Winston Churchill.

unity. There was also a second plot by Communist elements of the Resistance aiming at a takeover in Paris, under the guise of an anti-German insurrection.

To de Gaulle, the latter plot seemed by far the more dangerous, though the former, if successful, would surely receive American backing. The American plan to bypass Paris seemed to de Gaulle a confirmation of his suspicions. The General left Algiers on 18 August, and after stopovers in Casablanca and Gibraltar, he landed in France, at Maupertuis, on the morning of 20 August. There he learned that the insurrection had begun in Paris; there was no time to lose. De Gaulle put the utmost pressure on General Eisenhower and told him that if there was further delay in launching the final attack on Paris, he would himself order Leclerc to undertake the operation. Finally, on 22 August, Eisenhower gave the go-ahead, and the Second Free French Armoured division, supported by the Fourth American division, began its race towards Paris. The rapid succession of events, Herriot's refusal to co-operate – and Hitler's explicit orders – had finally foiled Laval's plans to set up a 'national' authority in Paris. Likewise, de Gaulle's triumphal entry into the capital on 25 August foiled the plan conceived by 'progressist' elements of the Resistance to set up a 'popular' government in Paris. De Gaulle had proved his point: *La France libre* was indeed *la France*. There remained for the General to consolidate his authority over the country, and to mobilize its resources for the complete liberation of the territory and the final assault on Germany.

In Britain, the liberation of Paris was greeted with extraordinary demonstrations of enthusiasm. Already in the evening of 23 August, the BBC had announced somewhat prematurely that Paris was in the hands of the French forces of the interior. The very next day, as the fighting was still progressing, King George VI sent a warm and touching telegram of congratulations to General de Gaulle. There was no doubting the immense relief and satisfaction of the English people, their King and Prime Minister on that occasion. As usual, however, the Prime Minister had mixed feelings about the new master of France. Two weeks later, at the Quebec conference, where Churchill and Roosevelt examined many serious world problems – not always in a serious way* – the conversation repeatedly centred

---

*The two men had thus put their signature under a 'programme . . . looking forward to converting Germany into a country primarily agricultural and pastoral in its character'.[21] Eden intervened in time to quash the project.

on de Gaulle. The Canadian Prime Minister, who was also present, heard many of these exchanges and wrote in his diary:

Quebec 11 September 1944: It was clear that Churchill feels as strong as ever against de Gaulle. The President mentioned that he and de Gaulle were now friends. Princess Alice* and I also stood up for de Gaulle and spoke of favourable impression he made here. Finally Mrs Churchill – I think it was – said 'We are all against you.' It was mentioned that de Gaulle had two strains in him and he was quite a different man at times . . . The President felt he would either be President or in the Bastille a year from now.[22]

12 September: Churchill . . . greatly feared, and the President agreed, there would be civil war in France, and that of a terrible kind. Churchill . . . seemed more reconciled to de Gaulle's position in conversation today than yesterday.[23]

17 September, at dinner: Churchill sat and talked like one who was father of a family . . . he spoke about the war and a good deal about de Gaulle toward whom he still entertains feelings of great distrust. Spoke of difficulties of getting de Gaulle to allow some of his people to cross over into France at the time of the invasion, of his being at heart an enemy of Britain, of his being ungrateful and that at any moment he might show a different side of his nature. Admitted quite frankly that he was much abler in every way than Giraud. . . . Also said that de Gaulle had a popular appeal. He did not think he would escape very serious situations in France in the course of a year.[24]

It was quite obvious that Churchill remained caught between his admiration for the man, his distrust for the politician, his anxieties for the future of France, and his subordination to Roosevelt's diplomacy in French affairs – as Foreign Secretary Eden found out when he tried once again to get both men to recognize the French provisional government: 'A pretty hopeless discussion,' he noted on 15 September, 'each going off in turn on a tirade against de Gaulle. Winston did however go so far as to say that he would rather have a de Gaulle France than a Communist France, a distinct advance!'[25] Four days later, Roosevelt wrote to Secretary of State Hull: 'I have had lengthy talks with PM in regard to recognition of provisional government in France. He and I are both very much opposed to it at this time. The provisional government has no direct authority from the people. . .'[26]

That seemed final; it was not. In Great Britain, enormous pressure was building up in favour of recognition of the French provisional government. On 28 September, Churchill announced in Commons

*Aunt of King George VI and wife of the Count of Athlone, Governor-General of Canada.

that recognition was being extended to the Italian government. On the subject of France, he said:

> Naturally, we, and, I believe, the United States and the Soviet Union, are most anxious to see emerge an entity which can truly be said to speak in the name of the people of France – the whole people of France. . . . As an interim stage, the Legislative Assembly would be transformed into an elected body, reinforced by the addition of new elements drawn from inside France. To this body, the French Committee of National Liberation would be responsible. Such a step, once taken, when seen to have the approval of the French people, would greatly strengthen the position of France and would render possible that recognition of the provisional government of France, and those consequences thereof, which we all desire to bring about at the earliest moment.[27]

The Members of Parliament were not impressed. Sir Edward Grigg replied: 'I think . . . that we are entitled to take our own line whatever our great Allies may think. I hope we shall . . . not hesitate at once to recognize the French provisional government.' And Sir Percy Harris: 'It would be a fine gesture for this country to recognize the provisional government. It is humiliating to the French that we should have recognized the Italian government.'[28] The British press naturally echoed these words – and so did the French press.* From Paris, Duff Cooper, who had reopened the British Embassy a month earlier, wrote to Harold Nicolson:

> My difficulties have been increased by the PM's references to France in his last speech, and Anthony's answer to your question, although it cleared up the ambiguity, did not make matters much better from the French point of view, for they cannot see what on earth it has to do with us whether they have a large Consultative Assembly or a small one; and they ask bitterly what we should say if de Gaulle, in a public speech, were to express the view that it was about time we had a General Election. I am afraid that the quarrel between Winston and 'Le Grand Charles' will never be made up, and the President, who although being more disingenuous can conceal his feelings in public, will continue to nurse a grudge against de Gaulle for having succeeded in spite of him. These personal misunderstandings are really very unhappy, because they may

---

* One of the most virulent in this respect was *Le Franc Tireur*, which wrote in its editorial of 5 October: 'The US and Britain have recognized the Italian government. That is good news for the latest country to join the United Nations. It is probable that the Rumanian government which succeeded Antonescu's will also be recognized. Then it will be the turn of Bulgaria, and one day, let us hope, of Hungary. It goes without saying that after the final victory the governments that are set up in Berlin and Tokyo will also be recognized. It will then only remain for our Anglo-American allies to establish normal relations with the Papuans, the Hottentots and the Lapps. After which, who knows, we French may at last get a look in.'[29]

spoil the wonderful opportunity that exists of forming a firm and lasting friendship between the two countries. Never have the English been so popular in France as they are today, and the most popular of all of them is the Prime Minister, who would get a delirious welcome if he came here. But he could only come here as a friend of de Gaulle, and they would have to be seen together. One drive down the Champs-Elysées would be quite enough. The general public have not the slightest idea that they are anything but the firmest of friends. But he cannot come until we have recognized their government, and the longer we put off doing so now, the more foolish we appear, and the less thanks we shall get, when we eventually do so.[30]

It was the anomalous position of Duff Cooper as ambassador to an unrecognized government that triggered a fresh spate of attacks on the foreign policy of His Majesty's government. On 18 October, Mr Boothby put the following question to Foreign Secretary Eden in the Commons: 'Does not my Right Honourable Friend think it rather ridiculous to give a man the personal status and rank of ambassador and to refuse to recognize the government to which he is in fact accredited?'[31]

The Right Honourable Foreign Secretary needed no prompting. Only a week before he had been in Moscow with Churchill, and in the midst of much haggling with Stalin over zones of influence in Eastern Europe, he had again raised the question of France with the Prime Minister: 'More argument about France (W.C.) which didn't advance matters much; the drip-drip of water on a stone,' Eden wrote in his diary on 12 October.[32] But a constant drip of water can pierce the hardest stone: Two days later, Churchill wrote to President Roosevelt: 'I have been reflecting about the question of the recognition of the French provisional government. I think events have now moved to a point where we could take a decision on the matter consistently with your own policy and my latest statement in the House of Commons . . . There is no doubt that the French have been co-operating with Supreme Headquarters and that their provisonal government has the support of the majority of French people. I suggest therefore that we can now safely recognize General de Gaulle's administration as the provisional government of France.'[33]

The President was still more than reluctant. He would not hear of recognition until the French had set up a 'real' zone of the interior, and he so informed Churchill on 20 October.[34] But the Prime Minister, now in Cairo, was kept informed of the state of opinion at home, and the reports received left no room for doubt. Sir Alexander Cadogan had written to the Foreign Secretary on 20 October:

> As you know, of course, continued withholding of recognition causes increasing bewilderment and criticism, not only in French circles. As cordial relationship with a restored and liberated France is a vital British interest, I should have hoped the President might have allowed our right to a preponderant voice in this matter. Further delay merely embitters the situation and cannot be explained or justified by any arguments that I have seen. Is there any chance of the Prime Minister telling the President that he can see no virtue in further delay which merely postpones and makes more difficult the resumption of fully cordial relations, that our future security is in some degree at stake and that he feels therefore that there is everything to be gained, and little to be risked, by taking the plunge at an early date? I personally should like to see a date set not much later than a week from now, and I should like the President to be so informed and to see his reaction. But I suppose this might be inadvisable on the eve of the election, though it may possibly be that the imminence of that event might make the President hesitate to be isolated on this question.[35]

The last argument was not without force. The President was certainly not willing to lose votes at the approaching elections by appearing to lag behind on recognition of de Gaulle's government. And this would inevitably happen if the British decided to go ahead with recognition on their own. Churchill's latest telegrams seemed to indicate that they would do just that; Roosevelt therefore decided it was time to act – and the State Department was not overly scrupulous in its choice of methods. On 21 October, Sir Alexander Cadogan wrote in his diary: 'Woken up by resident clerk this morning to say that Cafferey, in Paris, has been instructed by State Department to say US government are "prepared" to recognize, God help us! Is this simple inefficiency and crossing of wires or are the US trying to do us down? Anyhow, I thought Massigli had better know the truth. . . .'

And the next day, 22 October:

> Message this morning from US Embassy that their embassy in Paris has been instructed to 'recognize' tomorrow afternoon. So at once telegraphed to Duff to do the same! The ways of these Americans are too odd! I don't know whether this is only the State Department – not what the President thinks. But I don't care: we're not going to be left out on a limb in this show. Telegram from A. saying I ought to explain to

Massigli what had happened. I have replied that I had already done that yesterday morning! Lunch at home. Back at F.O. at 3.30 and sent minute down to meet PM at aerodrome telling him what had happened about recognition and what I had done. Home about 6.30. PM rang up from Chequers. He seemed quite happy about it, but said that Russians would be annoyed. I said very likely but we had kept them informed of the whole comedy, and they would have seen it was not our fault![36]

Churchill was in fact amazed by the American initiative – it was evidently not his idea of a loyal collaboration; but he wrote to Roosevelt diplomatically: 'I was naturally surprised at the very sharp turn taken by the State Department and on arrival here I find the announcement is to be made tomorrow. We shall, of course, take similar and simultaneous action. I think it likely that the Russians will be offended. Molotov in conversation said that he expected they would be made to appear the ones who were obstructing, whereas they would have recognized long ago but had deferred to American and British wishes. I hope therefore it has been possible to bring them in.'[37]

That same day, 23 October, Sir Alexander Cadogan noted:

PM on phone again at 9.30. He had just received a message from President saying 'I will communicate with you again (about recognition of French provisional government) when Eisenhower announces establishment of interior zone, probably in two or three days' time. But it's been done!! The man is out of touch. PM said it would be a good thing to put off for a day or two. I said might be, but present situation was that US Embassy in Paris had their instructions, which they would carry out. Obviously we could only clear it up at the other end, so I rang Winant, who promised to telephone. Unfortunately, it was then 5 a.m. in Washington. We plainly can't stop Duff and let the Americans get in ahead of us. No further word from Winant by lunch time, so I sent minute over to PM, to catch him on his arrival, explaining situation. I'd arranged to flash a message to Paris after lunch if that was necessary. 3.30 Winant rang up to say, in American, 'Cleared everything: Schedule holding.' Passed this on to No. 10 and things took their course and we have all, thank God, Americans British and Russians, recognized de Gaulle.[38]

Sir Alexander Cadogan's relief was shared by a great many people in Britain and France. But de Gaulle was not one of them – or if he was, he took the greatest pains not to show it: on 25 October, he told the representatives of the Allied press: 'The French government is satisfied to be called by its name.' It was obvious that the General had other preoccupations – and the first of these was the armament of his troops. Indeed, de Gaulle was planning to set up ten additional divisions before the spring of 1945. This would enable the French army to play a major role in the liberation of the territory and the final attack against Germany, with all the military and political consequences it implied. But de Gaulle strongly suspected that the Americans were working against this plan, and this was reflected in his answers to the Allied journalists:

> I can tell you that our Allies have not supplied us with enough arms for a single large French unit since the beginning of the battle of France. We must of course, take into account the considerable difficulties which the Allied command has had to face until now. The battle itself demands enormous work in repairing the destroyed ports and means of communication, and in supplying the forces in the lines, and that explains, to a certain extent, why the amount of armament necessary for the arming of large new French units has not arrived until now.
> Question – You said, General: 'to a certain extent'?
> Answer – Yes, I did say 'to a certain extent'.[39]

By the end of October 1944, another question of some importance was being studied in the Chanceries of London and Paris: The prospect of a visit to Paris by Prime Minister Churchill on Armistice Day, 11 November 1944. The diplomats on either side of the Channel had little reason to believe that such a visit would improve the relations between Churchill and de Gaulle; they had many reasons to think that it would not. To begin with, there were the events of the last five months: the bitter conflicts over Syria and Lebanon, the political quarrels of June, the snub administered to Churchill in August, the Quebec conference in September, from which France had been excluded, Churchill and Eden's visit to Moscow in October, with the French kept outside and left in ignorance of the results, France's continued exclusion from the European Advisory Commission and from the Dumbarton Oaks conference, the prolonged delays in recognizing the provisional government, and finally the obvious lack of goodwill in supplying the French army – one could hardly conceive of a worse background for a state visit. Besides, there were the difficult dispositions of the two statesmen. De Gaulle had not wanted to invite Churchill on that date at all; but Duff Cooper had persuaded Massigli, and the latter had convinced Georges Bidault, the new French Foreign Minister, who had worked on de Gaulle. 'De Gaulle would have preferred

another date,' Bidault recalled, 'but I managed to arrange it for that
particular day. It is a good thing to honour warriors in their old age.
But it is also a good thing to show them your gratitude right away.
There is nothing falsely sentimental in the idea: good politics has no
place for anger or ingratitude.'[40]

Churchill, on the other hand, had told Duff Cooper that he would
go to France anyway, even uninvited, 'to see General Eisenhower'.
Duff Cooper had told him that this 'would be the last nail in the
coffin of his relations with de Gaulle,'[41] after which he proceeded to
persuade Massigli that an invitation was required, with the results
described above. This was of course an extremely fragile basis for a
reconciliation.

After the invitation had been issued on 30 October, and accepted
three days later, some of the preliminary arrangements gave ground
to fear that it would indeed be a frosty meeting: the Prime Minister
initially indicated that his wife would not be accompanying him;
besides, Churchill had been invited to stay at the Quai d'Orsay
during his visit to Paris, but the British thought that the comfort of
the British Embassy was to be preferred.[42] And then, there was the
agenda of the visit, which was irreproachable except for the fact that
the French wanted to discuss political matters at some point during
the visit. Knowing what these matters were, and the climate of some
of the past political discussions between the two men, one could
perhaps be pardoned for feeling some apprehension. Still, there was
no getting out of it, as Bidault had warned that 'unless conversations
took place towards a better understanding, the relations between the
Prime Minister and General de Gaulle might get worse'.[43] That
hardly seemed possible, but no one was prepared to take the risk.

To top it all, the British security authorities had asked that the
visit to Paris should be postponed, because of the danger of an
attempt on the Prime Minister's life by German agents still at large
in the city; as a result, there was still some uncertainty as to
Churchill's visit by 9 November. On that date, however, there was
not the slightest uncertainty as to Churchill's feelings towards de
Gaulle: 'PM still violently anti-de Gaulle,' Oliver Harvey noted in
his diary, and he added: 'De Gaulle . . . believed to be in a nasty and
clamorous mood. . . . We all tremble for the result.'[44]

On 10 November, Churchill and Eden flew to Paris; the Prime
Minister was naturally accompanied by Mrs Churchill, and even by
their daughter Mary. 'We gave them the best possible reception,' de

Gaulle recalled, 'with Bidault and several other ministers, I went to meet them at Orly and drove the Prime Minister to the Quai d'Orsay where he was to stay.'[45] Indeed, the whole of the first floor of the Quai d'Orsay had been put at the visitors' disposal, and Churchill was evidently well satisfied with the arrangement; 'Everything was mounted and serviced magnificently,' he wrote, 'and inside the palace it was difficult to believe that my last meeting there . . . with Reynaud's government and General Gamelin in May 1940 was anything but a bad dream.'[46] 'The Prime Minister,' Duff Cooper wrote, 'was delighted to find that he had a golden bath, which had been prepared by Goering for his own use, and still more delighted that the Foreign Secretary's bath was only silver. Diana and I dined with him and his party, making twelve in all, and we passed a happy evening.'[47]

The following day, Armistice Day, was to be a memorable occasion: 'At eleven o'clock,' Churchill recalled, 'de Gaulle conducted me in an open car across the Seine and through the Place de la Concorde, with a splendid escort of *Gardes Municipales* in full uniform with all their breastplates. They were several hundred strong, and provided a brilliant spectacle, on which the sun shone brightly. The whole of the famous avenue of the Champs-Elysées was crowded with Parisians and lined with troops. Every window was filled with spectators and decorated with flags.'[48] 'The reception had to be seen to be believed,' Duff Cooper noted. 'It was greater than anything I have ever known. There were crowds in every window, even in the top floors of the highest houses and on the roofs, and the cheering was the loudest, most spontaneous and most genuine.'[49] 'Never have I heard such a sustained roar of cheering as heralded their approach,' General Ismay also wrote.[50] Churchill, in RAF uniform, wearing a cap with gold oak leaves, stood in the open car, waved and gave his famous v sign; the crowds yelled '*Vive de Gaulle! Vive Churchill!*' And the Prime Minister recalled: 'We proceeded through wildly cheering multitudes to the Arc de Triomphe, where we both laid wreaths upon the tomb of the Unknown Warrior. After this ceremony was over the General and I walked together, followed by a concourse of the leading figures of French public life, for half a mile down the highway I knew so well.'[51]

It was indeed an impressive procession down the Champs-Elysées. De Gaulle, Churchill, Bidault and Eden walked in front, followed by

Cadogan, Duff Cooper, and General Ismay, who noted, 'We all proceeded on foot . . . to a dais about half a mile distant. Again the pent-up emotion of perhaps half a million Parisians broke loose like a flood. Some were cheering; some were laughing; some were sobbing; all were delirious. "Vive Churchill! Vive de Gaulle! Vive l'Angleterre! Vive la France!" '[52] From the tribune, the British guests then watched a march-past of French and British troops, which lasted a whole hour. 'Whenever there was a pause in the procession,' Duff Cooper noted, 'there were loud cries of "Churchill" from all the crowd.'[53]

'When this was over,' the Prime Minister recalled, 'I laid a wreath beneath the statue of Clemenceau, who was much in my thoughts on this moving occasion.'[54] 'On my orders,' de Gaulle wrote, 'the band played "Le Père la Victoire". – "For you!" I said to him in English. And it was only his due. Besides, I remembered that at Chequers, on the evening of a black day, he had sung me our old song by Paulus word perfect.'[55] De Gaulle was indeed a perfect host that day.

After having visited the Invalides, where they bowed before Foch's grave and bent for a long moment over Napoleon's tomb, the party proceeded to the Ministry of War, which was the temporary seat of the Presidency. An official luncheon was given there, and at dessert, de Gaulle made a short speech:

Monsieur le Premier Ministre de Grande-Bretagne, Monsieur le Secrétaire d'Etat, Messieurs,

Once again Mr Winston Churchill and Mr Anthony Eden are in Paris. If the French government, Paris and all France are profoundly happy, I can assure our visitors that they are not surprised. To tell you the truth, since the last visit which the Prime Minister of Great Britain paid us, France, Paris and the government have had to get through some quite difficult moments. But they never doubted that those cruel days would pass, and that an eleventh of November would come when we would see what we saw today.

It is true that we would not have seen it if our old and gallant ally England, and all the British dominions under precisely the impulsion and inspiration of those we are honouring today, had not deployed the extraordinary determination to win and that magnificent courage which saved the freedom of the world. There is no French man or woman who is not touched to the depths of their hearts and souls by this.

Hitler used to say in the old days that he was building for a thousand years. I cannot say what will remain of his system in a thousand years. But I do know that France, which has some experience of blood, sweat and tears, will not have forgotten in a thousand years what was accomplished in this war through blood, sweat and tears by the noble people the Right Honourable Mr Winston Churchill is leading with him to the heights of one of the greatest glories in this world. . . .

Gentlemen, we raise our glasses in honour of Mr Winston Churchill, Prime Minister of Great Britain, and to Mr Anthony Eden, Secretary of State for Foreign Affairs, and to those important figures accompanying them, and also in honour of the government of His Britannic Majesty, and in honour of England, our ally in the past, the present and the future.[56]

Churchill had tears in his eyes when he replied:

It is difficult for me to speak on a day such as this, which fills us with emotion. For more than thirty years I have defended the cause of friendship, of comradeship, and of alliance between France and Great Britain. I have never deviated from that policy throughout the whole of my life. For so many years past have these two nations shared the glories of western Europe that they have become indispensable to each other. It is a fundamental principle of British policy that the alliance with France should be unshakeable, constant, and effective. This morning I was able to see that the French people wanted to march hand in hand with the British people.

It gave me so much pleasure to see Paris again, this Paris which is a brilliant star shining above the world. I saw the French army march along the Champs-Elysées just before the war. What a lot of sacrifices have had to be made since then! What a lot of suffering has had to be endured! How many good friends have been lost; what memories remain with us today! It is a privilege for me to be at the side of General de Gaulle. In spite of all the critics, we still believe in the defeat of the enemy.

One night in October, 1940, during the worst of the raids on London, I did not fear to address the French people in French to tell them that a day would come when France would take her place among the great nations and play her part as the champion of liberty and independence. In thanking General de Gaulle for the words he has just spoken, I should be lacking in truth and gratitude if I did not pay tribute to the capital part he has played in this transformation which has brought us to a moment in history when all we have to do is be worthy of our destiny in order to start a new era of vision and greatness.[57]

'After the meal,' de Gaulle recalled,

Winston Churchill told me he had been deeply touched by what he had just seen and heard. 'Could you tell me,' I asked 'What struck you most?' 'Ah!,' he answered, 'it's the unanimity! After so many events during which you and I have been so fiercely attacked and reviled in France by so many speeches and writings, I found that only enthusiasm met us as we passed. This means that deep in its heart the French people was with you, who served it, and with me, who helped you to do so.' Churchill added that he was impressed by the orderliness of the ceremonies. He admitted that the British Cabinet had deliberated a long time before approving his trip, so great had been its apprehension of upheaval in Paris. Instead of that, everything he had seen was quite orderly, the crowds respecting the barriers and quite capable of bursting into cheers or keeping silent according to the demands of the situation, and the splendid troops – yesterday's French forces of the interior – parading in good marching order. 'I felt,' he declared, 'as if I were watching a resurrection.'[58]

Duff Cooper noted:

After lunch we went upstairs – de Gaulle, Coulet, Massigli, Chauvel and Palewski on one side of the table. Winston, Anthony, Alec Cadogan and I on the other. We talked for about two hours – Winston talking most of the time in his uninhibited and fairly intelligible French. He speaks remarkably well but understands very little. Both he and de Gaulle were in the happiest of humours. It was all very different from the interview at Marrakesh. There was not an unpleasant word said, although nearly every subject, including Syria, was covered.[59]

The transcripts of the meeting amply confirm Duff Cooper's judgement:

General de Gaulle opened the conversation by evoking the question of French rearmament. 'Was Great Britain interested in the presence of a strong French army on the Continent?' he asked Mr Churchill.

Churchill: The reconstruction of the French army is the basis of our own policy. Without the French army there can be no lasting settlement in Europe. Great Britain alone does not have the elements of a large army. She therefore has a primary interest in the rebirth of a large French army. On this policy my opinion has never varied.

Therefore only the stages of French rearmament are at issue, not the principle itself. In this respect, the problem depends essentially on the duration of hostilities. . . . If we admit that the war will last another six months, it will not be possible to put many more new divisions equipped for modern forms of warfare into the field in so short a time.

De Gaulle: A beginning must be made nevertheless. Up to now, we have received no arms or equipment since the fighting on French soil began. A few weeks ago, some people believed that the war was practically over. I must say that neither you nor I shared this belief. Today things look different. What do our Allies think? We need to know.

Churchill: I will examine what we have and let you have a report. Perhaps we will be able to give you some second class equipment which is already somewhat out of date, but useful for training purposes.

De Gaulle: That would be something anyhow. We do not intend to create large units conforming to the most recent British or American tables of equipment straight away.

Churchill: How many divisions will you have by the spring?

De Gaulle: In addition to our eight front-line divisions we shall have eight new ones. We have the men and the officers we need. We lack transport material, heavy weapons and radio equipment. We have rifles, sub-machine and machine guns; we are wanting in tanks, guns, trucks and transmissions equipment.

Churchill: The Americans believe they can end the war before any new division has been set up. They intend, therefore, to retain all available tonnage for the units already formed.

De Gaulle: The United States may be mistaken. Besides, Great Britain, much more than the United States, must consider events in Europe beyond the immediate future. A victory over Germany gained without the French army would be difficult to exploit politically. The French army must have a share in the fighting, so that the French people may feel, like their Allies, that they have defeated Germany.

Churchill: We will examine the question with the Americans. I shall stress the importance of letting France have a part of the victory.

De Gaulle: . . . In any case, I will bear in mind what you have told us about your possible contribution to our rearmament.

M. Bidault: There are two things to be borne in mind. If France does not participate in the victory operations, the French occupation troops will have no fighting spirit. The Germans will not consider them as victors. And yet, the French do not wish to appear in Germany only as the heirs of the victors. . .

De Gaulle: M. Bidault is right. All this is very important from a psychological point of view.

Churchill: What is equally essential is the role which the French army will have to play later, in a few years' time.

De Gaulle: That is yet another problem. We have been given to understand that you have reached an agreement with the Russians and the Americans over the division of Germany into zones of occupation.

Churchill: That is correct; at least provisionally.

De Gaulle: May I enquire what has been decided?

Churchill: There will be two zones of occupation: a Russian zone, and a Western zone, the north of which will be occupied by the British and the south by the Americans.

Mr Eden: We intend to give you a part of our own zone.

De Gaulle: Which one?

Churchill: This remains to be discussed. It should be easily arranged amongst friends.

De Gaulle: The occupation of Germany offers no attractive prospect, but we consider it necessary that the country should be occupied for a certain time. If this view prevails, we insist on having our own zone, first for reasons of propriety and second because we can never again leave our eastern borders uncovered. . . . We cannot afford another invasion.
Churchill: At six o'clock this evening an official announcement of your participation in the consultative commission in London will be made. Your point of view must be discussed within this organization.
De Gaulle: What common stand could we both take on the treatment of Germany, in agreement with the Russians and Americans?
Churchill: It is true that we must have a common position. You are the principally interested party.
De Gaulle: What does Stalin think?
Churchill: In Moscow we spoke chiefly of the conduct of the war, Poland and the Balkans. It was agreed that Greece was in the English sphere of influence, Rumania and Hungary in that of Russia and Yugoslavia and Bulgaria were zones of common interest . . .'

There was some further discussion on how Germany should be treated after the war, and Churchill stated that, although the matter had been discussed at Tehran, Quebec and Moscow, nothing had yet been decided. The Polish question was also discussed, with Churchill explaining that he was determined to give Poland a territory equivalent in size to what she possessed before the war, to which de Gaulle answered: 'I am pleased to see that your position with regard to Poland is the same as my own.' As for Italy:

De Gaulle: Well then? You have accepted Bonomi?
Churchill: I wanted to keep Badoglio.
De Gaulle: I know; that is why I'm asking.
Churchill: The new régime is a weak one. Nevertheless the Italians agree to fight. There will be troubles in Italy. There are already troubles in Greece. In Yugoslavia, Tito's behaviour is not irreproachable; but he is fighting our enemies. That is the criterion which guides our policy everywhere.

As for us, we have no territorial ambitions. We shall emerge from this war weakened economically for some time, but we desire to make no claims on anyone, least of all on France, our sister nation. In no part of the world do we wish to undermine your position, not even in Syria.
De Gaulle: Did the President tell you in Quebec about his projects concerning bases?

Churchill: Dakar?

De Gaulle: Yes, and Singapore. In Washington the President explained his conception to me, namely that he regards himself as the 'trustee' of the American continent, whose security rests on the eventual support of French, English and Dutch strong points, especially in the Pacific. He also mentioned Dakar. I replied: 'If you are speaking of the cession of bases, the answer is No! If, on the other hand, you are suggesting an international system whereby bases would be submitted to an identical statute and the sovereignty of each would be respected, then we can discuss it.'

Churchill: In your opinion, should these bases be placed under the authority of the United Nations?

De Gaulle: No. It can only be a question of the right to utilize them.

Churchill: There must, however, be an international security organiz- ation that will be granted the prerogatives in certain parts of the world. . . We have no intention either of abandoning our sovereign rights.

De Gaulle: Yes. You alone are qualified to administer your own bases. We alone have the right to administer ours.

Churchill: There will perhaps be regional councils. . . .

The General then mentioned the problem of Indo-China, but Churchill merely replied that this should be discussed with the Americans. Then:

De Gaulle: We Frenchmen have no intentions other than to rebuild our country and retain alliances with you and with Russia, and of course to keep the friendship of America. There is, besides, a service to be rendered to the latter by warning them against the temptation of upsetting the status quo. England and France have been settled for a long time in India and Indo-China and in various places in the Far East. We know these countries well. We know that we must not proceed there with any hasty changes.

As to Syria and Lebanon, we want their real independence. We are acting as you have acted in Iraq and Egypt. . . . We do not feel that our dominant influence in the Levant can do you any harm. . . .

Churchill: The great colonial empires obviously have many common conceptions. It is easier for the Russians and the Americans to call for disinterestedness.

De Gaulle: Certainly, and that is why we must avoid disputes over secondary issues.

Churchill: Events in the world have progressed so swiftly in the way you hoped for that you must now have patience and confidence in the future. Let us not dramatize. Let us continue our talks. . . . I assure you. . . that we have no desire to take your place in Syria or in the Lebanon.

De Gaulle: Why do you insist so much on our renouncing the command of the special troops? We need them to maintain order, for which we are responsible until our mandate expires.

Mr Eden: I thought that you were pledged to transfer the special troops to the States without awaiting the end of hostilities?

De Gaulle: No! We wish to do so when the war is over. Until then, we are responsible for maintaining order in the States, and you know it.

Mr Eden: I thought you were committed to this transfer without awaiting the end of the war.

M. Massigli: No!

M. Bidault: No deadline has been set.

De Gaulle: We shall have to discuss the problem of the Near East as a whole one day.

Churchill: When you promised independence to the States, the situation in the Mediterranean was extremely critical. We guaranteed this commitment of yours.

De Gaulle: We still adhere to it.

Churchill: We do not contest the position that France will have in the Levant through her treaties. We shall not quarrel with you over a position analogous to our own in Iraq. The position is not perfect, but it is tolerable. So put out of your minds any idea that we have ambitions in Syria and Lebanon.

M. Bidault: We do not suspect that the English have the dark design of supplanting us in the Levant. But our local representatives sometimes feel that yours would be only too pleased to see them purely and simply eliminated, and are expecting us to depart. What we wish is to remain present in the States with such advantages as the treaties may grant us.

Churchill: The States want their independence. You run the risk of causing trouble.

Mr Eden: We have told the Syrians and the Lebanese that we were in favour of negotiations. I would not be surprised if the Russians and the Americans had used a different language.

M. Bidault: Our presence in Syria and the Lebanon, where Frenchmen have fallen in battle against each other, is a sacred patrimony for us. Our quarrel on this subject is like a thorn which must be extracted in the interests of our relations.

Churchill: I will support your demands about Syria and the Lebanon at the Peace Conference, but not to the extent of starting the war again.

De Gaulle: In any case, it is in your interests to inform us as far as possible of the progress of problems in which the interests of both of us are engaged. We shall thus avoid misunderstandings. We will do the same for you.

Churchill: Colonies today are no longer a pledge of happiness, or a sign of power. India is a very heavy burden to us. Modern squadrons are worth more than overseas territories.

De Gaulle: You are right. And yet you wouldn't exchange Singapore for squadrons.

Churchill: We have had an extremely friendly exchange of views, which we must soon take up again. The essential thing is to rebuild a strong France. But it will be difficult for us to help you at this moment, for lack of tonnage. Yet it is your essential task. Allow me to congratulate you on the stability that you have already managed to bring to your country. The demonstration of the strength of France this morning was impressive. Before I left England, the people were afraid.

De Gaulle: . . . Of the FFI?

Churchill: Yes. But everything worked out well.

De Gaulle: One is always right to trust France.[60]

Upon these solemn words the discussion ended, and everyone declared it a success. It had indeed been, as Churchill put it, 'a friendly exchange of views' – and judging by past experiences, this in itself was no mean achievement – but then, the presence of Massigli, Bidault and Eden had clearly had a moderating influence. Besides, the discussions proceeded on fairly general lines precisely to avoid a clash, and the thorny question of the Levant was dropped just as the exchange of views was becoming less friendly. On other matters, such as the reconstruction of the French army, there was evidently a great measure of understanding and identity of purpose. Moreover, it was clear that both men had been much impressed and mellowed by the extraordinary demonstrations of sympathy they had witnessed that morning. Finally, this was no longer a meeting between the Prime Minister of Great Britain and the exiled leader of an unrecognized movement, but a formal meeting between two acknowledged statesmen. That could not fail to influence the atmosphere of the talks and the attitudes of the two interlocutors.

That evening, de Gaulle gave a dinner in Neuilly for his guests, and all passed off quite pleasantly. By the end of the evening, one could see no trace of the old antagonism: 'As an unforgettable day drew to its close, Churchill said to an associate of de Gaulle's; "Your friend de Gaulle is really quite nice. I'm beginning to like him," to which the Frenchman replied, "It's about time you did, sir." And to this same man, an hour or two later, de Gaulle said, "He was nice, your friend Churchill." '[61]

The following day was just as successful. There was a meeting of foreign ministers in the morning, where the thorny problem of the Levant was again tackled – again without much success, but this was not unexpected. Churchill stayed away from it all, and visited the Allied Expeditionary Forces Club; but in the afternoon, he was received at the Hotel de Ville by the mayor, the municipal council, the Paris Committee of Liberation and many of the fighters of the August battles. The Prime Minister had himself expressed the wish to meet 'the men behind the insurrection'. For him, this was to be another very moving occasion, and Georges Bidault recalled that 'a young Communist called Tollet, who was head of a temporary municipality, gave the English Prime Minister a swastika emblem which had been captured during the Liberation. Churchill thanked him for it in that moving French of his, full of invented words and expressions, yet understood by all.'[62] 'Not for one moment did Winston stop crying,' Eden later confided, 'and he could have filled buckets by the time he received the Freedom of Paris.'[63]

Indeed, Churchill then addressed the Paris Liberation Committee with deep emotion and bad French:

It is with the most vivid sensations that I find myself here this afternoon. I am going to give you a warning: be on your guard, because I am going to speak, or try to speak, in French, a formidable undertaking and one which will put great demands on your friendship for Great Britain. . . .

When I spoke to you in French from London four years ago, four years almost to a week, I said I had always known for certain that France would again take her place with the greatest nations and exercise her power and her influence on the whole development, cultural, political and military, of the future world. . . . Now most of France is free. Great battles are being joined. I well understand that you wish to take as great a part as possible in the line of battle, and it is essential that you should be helped as far as possible by the Allies. . . . Well, we will do our best to enable everything possible to be done so that the forces of France may be actively engaged against the enemy in the months that remain to us in this frightful war.

But there are other battles to win. There are other works to accomplish, and if in your courtesy you will allow me, at this moment when you have arranged in my honour a demonstration which I shall remember to the last moment of my life, I will say these words to you: unity, unity, stability and solidarity!

This is the moment when the whole might of the nation should be directed to the foundation, on an unshakeable basis, of the grandeur and authority of the great French people. Happily, you have at your head an unconquerable leader, General de Gaulle. From time to time I have had arguments with him about matters relating to this difficult war, but I am absolutely sure that you ought to rally round your leader and do your utmost to make France united and indivisible. This is the moment to forget many things, to remember great things, and it is the moment when France should take her place with the other great powers and march with them . . .[64]

Before he left the Hotel de Ville, Churchill whispered to Emmanuel d'Astier: '*Allons tout de même . . . il faut suivre de Gaulle, c'est la seule voie. . . .*'[65]

That evening, Churchill told de Gaulle: 'I expected to find myself surrounded by noisy and reckless insurgents. I was received by a procession of Members of Parliament, or men who looked like them, saluted by the *Garde Républicaine* in full dress uniforms, taken into a hall filled with an ardent but reasonable crowd, addressed by orators who are certainly preparing their candidacy for the elections. Your revolutionaries look like our Labour Members! This is fine for law and order, but not very picturesque.'[66]

After a dinner at the British Embassy, the two men left Paris: de Gaulle took Churchill on a visit to General de Lattre's First Army; and the former recalled: 'During the whole of 13 November, under ceaselessly falling snow, Mr Churchill saw the renascent French army, its major units in position, its services functioning, its general staffs at work, its generals quite confident, everything ready for the offensive which was to be launched the next day. He seemed to be deeply impressed by it all; and stated that he felt more justified than ever in placing his confidence in France.'[67] Churchill was indeed quite pleased with the excursion:

All the arrangements for the journey in a luxurious special train were most carefully made and we arrived in plenty of time for the battle. We were to go to an observation point in the mountains, but owing to bitter cold and deep snow the roads were impassable and the whole operation had to be delayed. I passed the day driving with de Gaulle and we found plenty to talk about in a long and severe excursion inspecting troops at intervals. The programme continued long after dark. The French soldiers seemed in the highest spirits. They marched past in great style and sang famous songs with moving enthusiasm. . . . All went well and in the train the dinner was pleasant and interesting. I was struck by the awe and even apprehension which half a dozen high generals showed to de Gaulle in spite of the fact that he had only one star on his uniform and they had lots. During the night our train divided. De Gaulle returned to Paris and our half went on to Rheims arriving next morning when I went to Ike's headquarters. In the afternoon I flew back to Northolt.[68]

For the French public, it was obvious that the visit had been a resounding success. For the diplomats accompanying the two statesmen, it appeared to have done no harm. For de Gaulle, it was clearly a failure; to be sure, he had been happy to show the Prime Minister that de Gaulle had the French people behind him; but beyond all the demonstrations of friendship, he had eyed Churchill suspiciously, and the account he later gave of the talks held on 11 November was remarkably unfair when compared to the actual minutes of the conversations. His suspicion that Churchill went to see 'the men behind the insurrection' at the Hotel de Ville in the hope of 'finding opponents of de Gaulle among them'[69] is equally typical and far-fetched.

De Gaulle, however, had more serious reasons to be dissatisfied with Churchill's visit. For on 12 and 13 November, the two men had also engaged in less spectacular private talks, where more fundamental issues were raised. Churchill had proposed the negotiation of a Franco-British treaty of alliance, and de Gaulle had replied:

Should England and France agree and act together on tomorrow's settlements, they will wield enough power to prevent anything being done which they themselves have not accepted or decided. It is this mutual resolve which should be the basis of the alliance you offer us. Otherwise, why sign a document that would be ambiguous? The equilibrium of Europe, a guarantee of peace along the Rhine, the independence of the Vistula, Danube and Balkan states, co-operation and association with the peoples all over the world to whom we have brought civilization, an organization of nations which will be something else than an arena for disputes between America and Russia, and lastly the recognition in politics of a certain conception of man despite the progressive mechanization of societies – are these not our great interests in tomorrow's world? Let us then agree to uphold these interests together. If you are willing to do so, I am ready. Our two countries will follow us. America and Russia, hampered by their rivalry, will be unable to counter it. Moreover, we shall have the support of many states and of world opinion, which have an instinctive fear of giants. Eventually England and France will create peace together, as twice in thirty years they have together confronted war.[70]

Such were de Gaulle's views on the post-war world. During the next quarter of a century, he would never appreciably depart from them. But this was the first time General de Gaulle offered a privileged partnership to a European power; it was also the last time he offered it to England. Churchill, however, had very different views:

Be assured, that I do not envisage a Franco-British schism. You are the witness and the proof of what I have done to prevent one in the most difficult circumstances. Even today, I offer you a formal alliance. But in politics as in strategy, it is better to persuade the stronger than to go against them. That is what I am trying to do. The Americans have immense resources. They do not always use them to the best advantage. I am trying to enlighten them, without forgetting, of course, to serve my country's interests. I have formed a close personal tie with Roosevelt. With him, I proceed by suggestions in order to channel things in the right direction. At present Russia is a great beast which has been starved for a long time. It is not possible to prevent her from eating, especially since she now is in the middle of the herd of her victims. But she must be kept from devouring everything. I am trying to restrain Stalin, who has a large appetite, but is not devoid of common sense. Besides, after a meal comes digestion, and then the dozing Russians will have their difficult moments. Meanwhile, I am present everywhere, yield nothing for nothing, and manage to secure a few dividends.[71]

It was a polite refusal, which de Gaulle, of course, interpreted without indulgence:

England was in favour of France's political reappearance, she would be increasingly so for reasons of equilibrium, tradition and security, she desired a formal alliance with us, but she would not consent to link her policy with ours, in the belief that she could play her own game between Moscow and Washington, limit their demands, but also take advantage of them. . . . In fact, they were pursuing certain precise goals in areas where the positions of states and the status quo were not yet firmly established and offered to British ambitions numerous opportunities of manipulation and expansion. This was especially true in the Mediterranean. According to London's plans, Athens, Belgrade, Beirut, Damascus and Tripoli under various forms of association would tomorrow supplement British influence previously dependent on Gibraltar, Malta, Cyprus, Cairo, Amman and Baghdad. Thus the concessions which Great Britain could not avoid making to Russian voracity and American capitalist ideology would find their counterpart. No ordeal changes the nature of man; no crisis that of states.[72]

Hence there was to be no genuine Franco-British rapprochement that autumn. For all that, the French people were quite right: the visit had been a magnificent display of Franco-British solidarity. The diplomats were also right: it had done no harm. De Gaulle was not wrong either: 'A state is the coldest of cold monsters.'

CHAPTER 16

A Mortal Foe of England

Churchill was much impressed by everything he had seen in Paris, and not surprisingly, he returned to England much better disposed towards de Gaulle. On 15 November, he wrote to Roosevelt:

> I certainly had a wonderful reception from about half a million French in the Champs-Elysées . . . I re-established friendly private relations with de Gaulle, who is better since he has lost a large part of his inferiority complex. . . . Generally I felt in the presence of an organized government, broadly based and of rapidly growing strength, and I am certain that we should be most unwise to do anything to weaken it in the eyes of France at this difficult, critical time. I had a considerable feeling of stability in spite of Communist threats, and that we could safely take them more into our confidence. I hope you will not consider that I am putting on French clothes when I say this.[1]

Early in December, the Prime Minister's new-found sympathy for General de Gaulle had not yet receded; indeed he went so far as to say in Commons on 8 December: 'De Gaulle is a man of honour, and has never broken his word'[2] – a statement he would not have made a month earlier – or a month later, for that matter. One victim of this sudden outbreak of Gaullophilia was General Spears, who received a telegram from Churchill 'suggesting' that he should resign as from 15 December.[3]*

By that time, Churchill was highly preoccupied with the latest developments in the military situation. In Italy, the Allies remained bogged down south of the Po Valley, and in northern France, though advancing on a very large front that stretched from Holland

---

*Eden, Duff Cooper and Cadogan had been pressing for General Spears's removal from the Levant for many months, and Massigli had told Duff Cooper on 22 June that 'No assurance, however solemn, will be considered by us as valid so long as General Spears remains in Beirut.'[4] But before his visit to France, Churchill had repeatedly refused to recall his Minister to the Levant.

to the Swiss border, they were still contained west of the Rhine. The precariousness of this position fully appeared when on 16 December, the Germans suddenly struck through the Ardennes with ten Panzer and fourteen infantry divisions. Yet Churchill had by then even graver preoccupations: In Greece, which the Germans had evacuated by mid-November, the Communist elements regrouped in EAM and ELAS were trying to seize power by force of arms. British troops under General Scobie confronted them in Athens, and Churchill, ignoring the outcries of public opinion at home and abroad, gave full and personal backing to his general on the spot. Sir John Colville recalled that in December, 'Greece preoccupied Churchill to the exclusion of almost everything else,' and that he 'dwelt endlessly on Greek affairs'.[5] By 25 December, in fact, the Prime Minister was in Athens to supervise and mediate. It was clear to him that Communism was threatening Europe even before Naziism had been completely defeated.

In France at that time, General de Gaulle was coming to the same conclusion. To be sure, he had succeeded in foiling the Communist threat at home by dissolving the *Milices Patriotiques* and including several Communists in his government; but his visit to Moscow at the beginning of December convinced him that he would receive no support from Stalin for his claims to the left bank of the Rhine – though Stalin himself would deal much as he pleased with the countries of Central Europe and the Balkans. Beneath the cordiality of the reception in Moscow and the façade of the Franco-Soviet pact signed on that occasion, de Gaulle saw the ruthless policy pursued by the Kremlin and the threat it would imply for Western Europe in the very near future; far from being able to count on Soviet support in dealing with the Anglo-Saxons, de Gaulle realized that he would soon need Anglo-Saxon help in opposing the Soviet Union.

For the time being, this help was required above all to liberate the territory of France. But by the end of December 1944, there was still little progress in that direction; worse still, the German counter-offensive in the Ardennes, backed by jet planes and Panzer tanks, was seriously threatening the Allied front; on 1 January General Eisenhower even ordered the American troops to withdraw from the Rhine to the Vosges, thus leaving Strasbourg at the mercy of an enemy attack. The city had been recently liberated, and its reoccupation by the Nazis would be for all Frenchmen a political disaster and a human tragedy. De Gaulle would have none of it, and after ordering the French troops to defend Strasbourg at all costs, he wrote to Eisenhower asking him to reverse his decision, at the same time telegraphing to Roosevelt and Churchill to ask them for support. Roosevelt predictably refused to intervene. No less predictably, Churchill left for France immediately; and when de Gaulle arrived at Eisenhower's Versailles headquarters on the afternoon of 3 January, he found that Churchill was already there.

In his memoirs, de Gaulle wrote that he then proceeded to persuade Eisenhower to alter his strategy, and that Churchill merely backed him up. That is certainly inaccurate: Alanbrooke's diaries show that Churchill had already persuaded Eisenhower to reverse his decision *before* de Gaulle's arrival.[6] The Prime Minister himself was to write modestly: 'I chanced to be at Eisenhower's head-quarters at this juncture, and he and Bedell-Smith listened attentively to my appeal.' And he added, 'Eisenhower cancelled his instructions, and the military necessity which might have made the evacuation of Strasbourg imperative never arose. De Gaulle expressed his gratitude.'[7] General Juin, who accompanied de Gaulle on that occasion, later confirmed this version – except as regards the expression of gratitude:

> As soon as we entered, he (Churchill) announced that everything was settled and that Strasbourg would not be abandoned after all – which Eisenhower confirmed. There was not even a debate . . . Before leaving, Churchill expressed the desire to have a talk with de Gaulle in a small room adjoining Eisenhower's office. The General having beckoned me to follow, I witnessed the following conversation:
>
> Churchill began by saying that Eisenhower was not always aware of the political consequences of his decisions, yet for all that, he was an excellent supreme commander, and he had a heart – as he had just shown. But de Gaulle remained obstinately silent, so that in the end Churchill did not know what to say. Finally, he decided to strike a pleasant note:
>
> 'Well then, *mon Général*, you finally got the scalp of General Spears, didn't you?'
>
> De Gaulle remained silent.
>
> 'Are you now awaiting his funeral?'
>
> De Gaulle merely shook his head and presently began to speak, asking Churchill about his trip to Greece. The latter was much relieved to hear his interlocutor speak at last. His face lit up and he exclaimed:
>
> 'Oh, yes, very interesting, it was good sport, indeed . . .'
>
> 'But they shot at you?' de Gaulle interrupted.

'Yes, and the most extraordinary thing is that they shot at me with the weapons I had given them.'

'It's the kind of thing that happens,' de Gaulle concluded; and thereupon we parted.

On the way back, I could not help telling (de Gaulle) that he should at the very least have expressed his thanks to Churchill. 'Bah!' he answered, and with a gloomy expression he went back to his thoughts.[8]

Gloomy thoughts they were: the Nazi threat had not yet disappeared, the Soviet threat was already emerging, and the Anglo-Saxon Allies were still reluctant to give military and economic help to the French army; yet de Gaulle was resolved to see that army cross the Rhine and claim its fair share in the defeat and occupation of Germany. In the diplomatic sphere, the Allies were likewise most unhelpful; while de Gaulle was in Moscow, Churchill had cabled to Stalin proposing the conclusion of a tripartite pact between France, Britain and the Soviet Union. This had made the General furious, for he considered it as an attempt to undermine his own efforts to conclude a Franco-Soviet pact.* But there was much worse: at the beginning of January, the American and British press had announced that Roosevelt, Churchill and Stalin would soon hold a conference to discuss the fate of Germany, the future of Central Europe, and the setting up of the United Nations; of course no one had thought of inviting de Gaulle. To be sure, the General had been informed privately that it was Roosevelt who opposed it; but he strongly suspected that neither Churchill nor Stalin were very anxious to see him take part in this exclusive gathering, and his suspicions were well founded. If General de Gaulle took the view that no lasting settlement in Europe could be concluded in the absence of France, the Big Three considered that no settlement at all could be concluded in the presence of General de Gaulle.

Duff Cooper was therefore to write with typical British understatement that 'The General was not in the sunniest of moods during these early months of 1945.'[9] The British Ambassador knew this better than anyone else; for weeks, he had tried to persuade de Gaulle of the necessity for a Franco-British treaty, which would indeed have been a suitable counterpart to the Franco-Soviet alliance. But for the General, there could be no such treaty until all outstanding problems between the two countries had been settled, including of course the Levant and France's claim to a secure

*Of course it was nothing of the kind.

frontier along the Rhine. Of course, Duff Cooper had found the Foreign Minister, Georges Bidault, most anxious to negotiate, but then the British Ambassador was well aware that de Gaulle's Foreign Minister played very little part in the formation of French foreign policy.

In pressing for a Franco-British alliance, Duff Cooper was acting well in accordance with Foreign Office policy. Anthony Eden, who had been warned that the Americans would withdraw their troops from Europe shortly after the defeat of Germany,[10] was anxious to secure French co-operation for the post-war era; after all, a renewal of German adventurism would have to be prevented, and besides, Eden was less anxious than ever to 'share the cage with the bear'. But Churchill, although aware of all these arguments, was in no hurry to sign a treaty; he believed that Britain had nothing to gain from it at that time, that Roosevelt would not approve of it, and that de Gaulle would set impossible conditions for signing it. Besides, the friendly atmosphere of November and December had now vanished, and Churchill had once again worked himself up into a towering rage against de Gaulle. On 19 January, he wrote to Eden: 'I cannot think of anything more unpleasant and impossible than having this menacing and hostile man in our midst, always trying to make himself a reputation in France by claiming a position far above what France occupies, and making faces at the Allies who are doing the work.'[11] A week earlier, he had also told his Foreign Secretary: 'As I have frequently pointed out, de Gaulle will be a great danger to peace and to Britain in the future.'[12]

Eden, however, continued to work on the Prime Minister, and by the time Churchill arrived at Yalta on 3 February, though his Gaullophobia was as lively as ever, his Francophilia had entirely reappeared – which was indeed fortunate for France, as both Stalin and Roosevelt had come to the conference with the firm intention of disregarding French interests. The first meeting between Roosevelt and Stalin at the Livadia Palace on 4 February is quite instructive in this respect:

> The President . . . inquired how Marshal Stalin had gotten along with General de Gaulle.
>
> Marshal Stalin replied that he had not found de Gaulle a very complicated person, but he felt he was unrealistic in the sense that France had not done very much fighting in this war and de Gaulle

demanded full rights with the Americans, British and Russians who had done the burden of the fighting.

The President then described his conversation with de Gaulle in Casablanca two years ago when de Gaulle compared himself with Joan of Arc as the spiritual leader of France and with Clemenceau as the political leader.

Marshal Stalin replied that de Gaulle did not seem to understand the situation in France and that in actual fact the French contribution at the present time to military operations on the Western Front was very small and that in 1940 they had not fought at all. . . .

The President said he would now tell the Marshal something indiscreet, since he would not wish to say it in front of Prime Minister Churchill, namely that the British for two years have had the idea of artificially building up France into a strong power which would have 200,000 troops on the eastern border of France to hold the line for the period required to assemble a strong British army. He said the British were a peculiar people and wished to have their cake and eat it too. The President then said that he understood the tripartite zones in regard to occupation of Germany were already agreed upon, to which Marshal Stalin appeared to agree, but he went on to say that one outstanding question was that of a French zone of occupation. The President said he had a good deal of trouble with the British in regard to zones of occupation. . . .

Marshal Stalin inquired whether the President thought France should have a zone for occupation, and for what reason.

The President said he thought it was not a bad idea, but he added that it was only out of kindness.

Both Marshal Stalin and Mr Molotov spoke up vigorously and said that would be the only reason to give France a zone. Marshal Stalin said that the question would have to be considered further here at Yalta.[13]

The discussions on the role to be allotted to France were therefore uncommonly animated during the next few days – and both Churchill and Eden were left alone to defend French interests, which they did with the utmost vigour:

Churchill: . . . The French want a zone and I am in favour of granting it to them. I would gladly give them part of the British zone. All we want is this. It does not affect the Soviet zone. Will our Russian allies agree that the British and Americans get together on a zone to allot to the French? The line of the Moselle seems a convenient place to let them in. They are not in a position to occupy a large zone.

Marshal Stalin: Would it not be a precedent for other states?

Would it not mean that the French become a fourth power in the control machinery for Germany which, so far, is only for the three of us?

Churchill: Our answer is that France should come in and as its army grows take a larger part in the occupation.

Marshal Stalin: I think there might be complications in our work if we have a fourth member. I suggest another method – for the British to get the help of France or Holland or Belgium in occupation but not give them rights in the control machinery. We might ask on our side to invite other states to help occupy our zone but not to sit in on the control machinery.

Churchill: The discussion is on the immediate question of France. They have had long experience in occupying Germany. They do it very well and they would not be lenient. We want to see their might grow to help keep Germany down. I do not know how long the United States will remain with us in occupation. (The President: 'Two years.') Therefore the French army should grow in strength and help us share the burden. If Russia wants some other power in her zone we should not object . . .

President Roosevelt: I should much rather have a small number on the control machinery. I should be just as satisfied if the French are not in on the control machinery.

Marshal Stalin: I should like to repeat that if we let the French in on the control machinery it would be difficult to refuse other states. I agree that the French should be great and strong but we cannot forget that in this war France opened the gates to the enemy. This is a fact. We would not have had so many losses and destruction in this war if the French had not opened the gates to the enemy. The control and administration of Germany must be only for those powers standing firmly against her from the beginning and *so far* France does not belong to this group.

Churchill: We were all in difficulties early in this war and France went down before the new tanks and I admit they were not much help in this war. But the fact remains they are the neighbour of the Germans and the most important neighbour. British public opinion would not understand if decisions vital to France are being made with regard to Germany over France's head. I hope, therefore, that we shall not decide for an indefinite exclusion of France for all time. I was very much against General de Gaulle's coming here and the President's view was very much the same. Apparently Marshal Stalin feels the same. But the fact remains that France must take her place. We will need her defence against Germany. We have suffered badly from German robot guns and should Germany again get near to the Channel coast we would suffer again. After the Americans have gone home I must think seriously of the future. I propose to offer the French a zone out of present British and American zones and that technical studies be made of the French position in the control machinery.

Marshal Stalin: I am still against France taking part in the control machinery. . .

President Roosevelt: (On the basis of a note from Mr Hopkins) I think we have lost sight of the French position on the European Advisory Commission. I suggest that the French have a zone of occupation but that we postpone discussion on control machinery. Others might want to come in, such as Holland or Austria.

Marshal Stalin: I agree. . .

Mr Eden: If the French are to have a zone, how can they be excluded from the control machinery? If they are, how can their operation of their zone be controlled?

Marshal Stalin: They could be controlled by the power from which they obtained the zone.

Churchill and Mr Eden: We cannot undertake to do that and the French would never submit to it.[14]

As usual when there was no agreement, the question was referred to the Foreign Secretaries 'for further study'. But when the Foreign Secretaries met two days later, Eden found Molotov and Stettinius still opposed to French participation in the control commission. Yet both Eden and Churchill kept up the pressure, with the latter declaring at the fourth formal meeting on 7 February: 'If the French were given a zone without participation they would cause endless trouble,' and he added heatedly: 'All this argument seems to me futile. I feel sure that the French will take no zone unless they are given participation in the control council. I must say I think they are right.'[15] At the eighth formal meeting four days later, Churchill's two partners finally gave in: 'The President then said he had changed his mind in regard to the question of the French participation in the control commission. He now agreed with the views of the Prime Minister that it would be impossible to give France an area to administer in Germany unless they were members of the control commission. He said he thought it would be easier to deal with the French if they were on the commission than if they were not.*

Marshal Stalin said he had no objections and that he agreed to this.[16]

This being settled, the Big Three went on to discuss weightier matters, such as the setting up of the United Nations, the Polish question and Russian participation in the war against Japan. The

*Harry Hopkins had supported Churchill and Eden from the beginning and he had finally persuaded Roosevelt to give in.

British also obtained that France should be one of the inviting powers to the San Francisco Conference.

If de Gaulle learned of the efforts that had been deployed on his behalf during this conference, he certainly did not go out of his way to thank his two champions. Besides, he considered that France's participation in the control commission was no more than her due, and de Gaulle's exclusion from Yalta was clearly an affront to French sovereignty. In addition, he considered that the public statements issued at the end of the conference did not pay sufficient attention to France. Finally, he suspected (rightly) that the Anglo-Americans had made excessive concessions to Stalin on Eastern Europe. For all these reasons, de Gaulle decided to turn down an invitation by President Roosevelt to meet him at Algiers after the conference. After all, the President was inviting him, de Gaulle, to a meeting on French territory! The fact that he had extended a similar invitation to the Negus of Ethiopia naturally made things even worse.

During the next two months, there was no perceptible improvement in Franco-British relations. Ambassador Duff Cooper continued to press for the conclusion of a treaty, Bidault and Eden supported him, Churchill and de Gaulle would not hear of it. Franco-American relations were not cordial either: when the Japanese attacked Indo-China at the beginning of March, President Roosevelt refused to provide transportation and air cover for the French expeditionary forces. In April, the French troops that had entered Germany occupied Stuttgart, which was not in their allotted zone – but as France had not been made a party to negotiations on the occupation of Germany, de Gaulle refused to evacuate the city, and this caused quite a stir in the United States. That month, President Roosevelt died, and was succeeded by Harry Truman. Yet there was no improvement in Franco-American relations: at the beginning of May, the French troops occupied several Italian enclaves on the French side of the Alps, as well as the cantons of Tende, La Brigue, and Vintimille. The Americans immediately demanded the evacuation of these territories, but General Doyen, obeying instructions from higher authority, informed them that any American move to set up an Allied military administration in that region 'would assume a clearly unfriendly character, even a hostile character, and could have grave consequences'.

Thus, as the American, British, Soviet and French troops were inexorably closing in on the capital of the German Reich, while in the east the Soviets imposed Communist rule from Poland to Rumania, tension was steadily mounting between the French and the Americans – with the British naturally supporting the latter. On 8 May, at long last, the Reich capitulated – but yet another crisis in relations between the Western Allies was now to break out, and this time, the British were directly involved. Not surprisingly, the theatre of confrontation was once again the Levant.

According to General de Gaulle, there was no reason why a crisis should break out in Syria: Free France had proclaimed the independence of the State in 1941; since then, the main levers of control, administration, finance, economy, diplomacy and security, had been gradually transferred to the Syrian government, and Free France had even secured the invitation of Syria to the San Francisco Conference. Of course, French troops remained in the Levant, and Free France retained the Syrian *Troupes Spéciales* under her command, but then France, as the mandatory power, was responsible for order and defence in the area. Finally, de Gaulle and Catroux had pledged to abolish the mandate and give total independence to both Syria and Lebanon once the United Nations had been set up – and once the two states had signed economic, cultural and military treaties giving France a privileged position in the Levant.[17]

For all that, things were not quite as idyllic as they appeared to be. Indeed, the French Delegate General in the Levant continued to wield considerable power, while his subordinates still had a tendency to treat Syria as a conquered country and the Syrians as unruly subjects. French officials still intervened actively in Syrian politics, and their troops even prevented the Syrian gendarmerie from taking action against the followers of Suleiman Murchid, a dangerous fanatic and bandit of the Mokaddem class. The Syrian government therefore continued to demand the complete evacuation of Syria by the French troops, and the transfer of the *Troupes Spéciales* to Syrian control.

For all these reasons and a few others, the French continued to be extraordinarily unpopular in Syria by the beginning of 1945. In January, violent anti-French demonstrations broke out in Damascus and various other cities around the country. The French replied by sending in tanks, which only aggravated the tension. Mr Terence Shone, the new British Minister, observed that in Damascus, 'personal contacts between local French authorities and members of the Syrian government had virtually ceased; they merely exchanged curt notes.'[18] All this led to a rapid deterioration in Franco-Syrian relations, and the Syrian ministers, like their Lebanese counterparts, now refused even to consider the proposals for cultural, economic and military conventions that would give France a privileged position in the Levant after the expiry of the mandate. The Syrian President had even told the British Minister that he 'would cut off his right hand rather than sign a treaty with the French'.[19] Even allowing for the traditional Mediterranean gift for overstatement, it was quite obvious that feelings towards the French throughout the Levant were more hostile than ever. They even worsened considerably at the beginning of April when it was learned that the Delegate General in the Levant, General Beynet, who was to open negotiations with the Syrian authorities, had not yet returned from Paris; worse still, there were now rumours that the French had decided to send troop reinforcements to the Levant.

It seems inconceivable that General de Gaulle had not grasped the depth of anti-French feeling among the Syrian population, as well as the resolute hostility of the Syrian government to the maintenance of French privileged positions in Syria. And yet, in his speeches, in his correspondence and in his memoirs, de Gaulle makes little or no mention of these obvious facts. On the contrary, he attributes all French difficulties in the Levant to the sinister hand of perfidious Albion. In this matter, the General never changed his mind, as his memoirs make abundantly clear:

> Among the national ambitions that were reflected in the world conflict, there was Britain's ambition to dominate the Middle East. With the end of the war in Europe, the opportunity had come. The invasion and its consequences had stripped an exhausted France of her former power. As for the Arabs, a political game as subtle as it was costly had rendered a number of their leaders accessible to British influence. Above all, the economic organization set up by Great Britain . . . had given her full power over the trade, that is to say the existence, of the Middle Eastern states, while 700,000 British soldiers and numerous air squadrons dominated land and sky alike. Finally, at the bargaining session of Yalta, Churchill had persuaded Roosevelt and Stalin to leave him a free hand in Damascus and Beirut.[20]

To General de Gaulle, it was quite obvious that the British were once again stirring up trouble in the Levant with the intention of ousting the French and taking their place. He had just learned that a British division from Palestine was to join the 9th Army in the Levant, and this added to his suspicions. At the end of April, de Gaulle therefore decided to send out three battalions of reinforcements in the cruisers *Montcalm* and *Jeanne d'Arc*. This would no doubt intimidate the Syrians – and the British.

It is true that certain archives in France and England remain obstinately closed to the historian; yet after a close examination of the documents now available – of which there are not a few – one cannot help thinking that the General was once again seriously deluded in his appreciation of British policy in Syria and Lebanon. Indeed, the British position on the Levant had remained very much as it was described by Churchill and Eden to General Spears in June and December 1943: 'All arguments and means of pressure used by the Levant people against the French might one day be turned against us; we should discourage the throwing of stones since we have greenhouses of our own – acres and acres of them; it should be our endeavour to damp down the whole issue in order not to raise very great difficulties for ourselves; there is no question of our trying to take the place of the French in the Levant,' and of course, once again: *'surtout pas trop de zèle!'*[21] On his way back from Yalta, Churchill had met the President of Syria, Shukri-al-Quwati, and urged him to make a peaceful settlement with France. But as usual, there was another side to the problem: if the French continued to refuse independence to the Levant States, the Arabs in Egypt, Iraq and elsewhere would inevitably blame the British for remaining passive. As Mr Terence Shone wrote at the time: 'We should meet with very great criticism both at home and in the Commonwealth and Empire if by failing to keep the French up to their promises we found our whole position in the Middle East threatened where we had fought so hard to maintain it. We were entitled to expect the French not to put us in this position.'[22] On 26 January, Eden had likewise written to Duff Cooper, 'The French must see that there were limits to the extent to which we were prepared to incur mistrust and hostility or, still more, endanger our position in the Middle East on their behalf.'[23]

The Prime Minister, the Foreign Secretary and the new British Minister to the Levant were therefore entirely in agreement as to the policy to be followed: they should put pressure on the French to grant full independence to the Levant States and to present them with moderate conditions for a treaty, while refraining from armed provocation; at the same time, Britain should press the Syrian and Lebanese governments to come to terms with the French and to calm down anti-French outbursts throughout the country. In the process, the British naturally got the worst of both worlds: the French accused them of interfering with their prerogatives as a mandatory power, with the sinister design of replacing them one day; the Arabs, on the other hand, accused them of collusion with the French . . . and yet the British pursued their policy with undiminished resolve, while Mr Churchill declared in Commons: 'I must make it clear that it is not for us alone to defend either Syrian or Lebanese independence or French privilege. We seek both, and we do not believe that they are incompatible.'[24] The trouble was that the French still opposed Syrian and Lebanese independence, while the Syrians and Lebanese categorically rejected French privilege.

The role of mediator in such circumstances was an ungrateful one, but by the beginning of May, Churchill was still prepared to assume it; in fact, he had temporarily forgotten his grudges against General de Gaulle, and was even prepared to go and discuss the situation with him: 'It may well be', he wrote to Duff Cooper on 8 May, 'that I could go and see him quietly one of these days on a trip to France, though I should like to know beforehand that he would not have the door banged, barred and bolted against me.'[25] And two days later: 'I should like an opportunity to discuss the Levant with de Gaulle. I should be quite ready to see him here though I cannot at the moment say how soon it would be possible to make arrangements to receive him in due style.'[26] De Gaulle was himself quite ready to discuss the question with the British Prime Minister, but the French initiative of sending reinforcements to the Levant put everything in jeopardy – and triggered a formidable chain reaction.

Mr Terence Shone was later to write;

It had been strongly represented to the French government, both by His Majesty's government and the United States government, that the dispatch of French troops and warships to the Levant at such a time would inevitably be regarded in the Levant States as provocative and as a threat to bring the States' government to heel in their negotiations with the French. It seemed, indeed, that if we failed to stop such developments, the States' governments would be likely to lose all confidence in us, quite apart from the harm which might result to our own position in the whole Arab world. . . . The French government, however, remained unmoved by our representations. In a conversation with His Majesty's Ambassador in Paris on 30 April, General de Gaulle had said he did not understand why the matter should concern the Commander-in-Chief, Middle East Forces. . . . He insisted that the maintenance of order in the Levant States was a French responsibility under the Lyttelton – de Gaulle agreement and that he could not hand over the *Troupes Spéciales* to the States without increasing the number of regular French troops. He went on to say there would be no disorder in the States unless it were stirred up by the British, a statement to which Mr Duff Cooper took strong exception, pointing out that we had never attempted to stir up disorder but had on the contrary done everything in our power, as we were still doing, to improve relations between France and the States. General de Gaulle remained incredulous and it was clear that, despite all our statements to the contrary, he firmly believed it was the policy of His Majesty's government to weaken the position of France in the Levant.[27]

On 4 May, Churchill sent de Gaulle a personal message regretting that the General appeared to view the situation in the Levant States in the light of the respective prestiges of France and Great Britain; the Prime Minister added that he was ready to withdraw all British troops from the Levant as soon as the French had concluded a treaty with Syria and Lebanon. And he concluded: 'If you reinforce your troops at this moment, the Levant States, who have been waiting for treaty proposals for some time past, may well suppose that you are preparing a settlement to be concluded under duress. This might injure both your and our relations with them and poison the atmosphere for the negotiations you are about to begin. I hope therefore that you will help me in avoiding this addition to our troubles. Good wishes.'[27] The British authorities then proposed that the troops be conveyed discreetly to Alexandria on British merchant ships. But all this would have been incompatible with French sovereignty, so the reinforcements duly arrived in Beirut, and General Beynet, the Delegate General, returned from Paris with new proposals for a Franco-Syrian and Franco-Lebanese treaty. The conditions were not particularly generous, the French demanded military bases in Syria, no reference was made to the transfer of the *Troupes Spéciales* to Syrian authority, and General Beynet's arrival coincided suspiciously with the landing of French reinforcements in Beirut. The Syrian and Lebanese governments refused to negotiate under such conditions, and gigantic strikes followed by mass demonstrations immediately broke out.

The violence was particularly serious in Syria. At Aleppo, on 20 May, demonstrators stoned French military outposts and murdered two French officers and one soldier. The French opened fire and sent in tanks to clear the streets. During the following days, gigantic demonstrations broke out in Damascus as well as in the Druze and Alawi districts, where individual Frenchmen were attacked in the streets. As for General Beynet, he mentioned in front of the British Commander-in-Chief the possibility of 'performing a surgical operation'.[28] On 25 May, in a last-ditch effort to avert an explosion, the British had appealed to the Syrian government to keep control of the situation. The next day, in Paris, Ambassador Duff Cooper brought de Gaulle a British proposal to open conversations on the Levant either in Paris or London. 'All was going well,' Duff Cooper reported, 'and he [de Gaulle] had almost agreed to conversations . . . and to making a statement that no more troops would be sent to the Levant meanwhile, when I mentioned that the Americans would take part in such conversations. Thereupon he flew into a rage, said that the Americans were in no way concerned, and that he would not allow France to be put into the dock before the British and the Americans. I argued vainly with him for some time and left him still sulky.'[29]

That afternoon, Duff Cooper went to see the Foreign Secretary, Georges Bidault, 'who spoke of resigning if he failed to make any impression on General de Gaulle. He remarked that General Beynet had not carried out the instructions which he, Monsieur Bidault, had given him; he had no doubt received different instructions later from General de Gaulle.'[30] What these different instructions were is not known, but they were probably interpreted too literally; the next day, 27 May, the Syrian government was apparently informed of a draft proclamation by General Oliva-Roget, the French delegate in Damascus, which referred to the imminence of 'la grande bagarre.'[31] It was no understatement; in his memoirs, General de Gaulle described what followed:

> On 27 May, the French forces and special troops had put an end to disorders in every region of the country except the Jebel Druze . . . It was then that the Syrian ministers and their British advisers, seeing that the situation was turning to their disadvantage, laid their trump cards on the table. On 28 May, in Damascus, all our posts were attacked by bands of rioters and units of the Syrian gendarmerie, all armed with machine guns, automatic rifles and British grenades. For twenty-four hours, the

sound of gunfire echoed through Damascus. But on the 29th, it appeared that our men had held fast and the rebels, hard pressed, had had to take refuge in such public buildings as the Houses of Parliament, the Town Hall, Police Headquarters, the Serail, the Bank of Syria, etc. . . . General Oliva-Roget, French delegate in Syria, ordered an assault on these centres of insurrection. This was accomplished in twenty-four hours by our Senegalese troops and a few Syrian companies, two cannons and one aeroplane being also used. By the evening of 30 May, the French authorities were in control of the situation.[32]

There are several bizarre elements in this version of events. None of the eyewitnesses in Damascus on 28 May could see or hear the all-out attack against French posts that was supposed to have lasted 24 hours. On the contrary, Damascus was described the next morning as 'unnaturally quiet'. In fact, General Oliva-Roget himself only claimed to have been attacked on the 29th at 7.15 p.m. – and his troops started shelling the city immediately thereafter. Even at that later date, there were apparently no eye-witnesses to these violent and concerted Syrian attacks, and the premises of the French delegation, which had allegedly borne the brunt of the attack, were found on later investigation to 'show scarcely a trace of bullet marks'.[33] Even more mysterious is the claim that 'the Syrian ministers and their British advisers' were behind the insurrection. The very personality of these ministers and of the Syrian President makes this contention highly unlikely; besides, no one seems to have seen these aggressive British advisers, whose advice would have been highly incompatible with Foreign Office policy as we know it. Finally, the statement that 'by the evening of May 30th, the French authorities were in control of the situation' is rather misleading. By that date, in fact, the French authorities did *not* control the situation; they did not even control their own troops, who continued to shell the city indiscriminately until 31 May, and after that continued to fire wildly at civilians, public buildings, ambulances, the Orient Palace Hotel, the American School, and even a British Red Cross train. The fact that there was also much looting by the French, Senegalese and Special Troops during those days and after is disputed by no one.[34] Finally, de Gaulle does not mention General Catroux's contention that General Oliva-Roget, in command of the French troops, suffered from a nervous imbalance[35] – yet this is hardly reassuring.

At any rate, de Gaulle goes on to state that:

During these three weeks of rioting, the British had not stirred . . .

Everything seemed to indicate that our 'allies' were only marking time while they thought that the Special Troops would refuse to obey us and that we would lose control of events. . . . But once they saw that the revolt was collapsing, their attitude changed abruptly . . . On the evening of 30 May, Massigli, our ambassador, was summoned by Mr Churchill, in the presence of Mr Eden, to receive a serious communication. The British government . . . asked the French government to order a cease-fire in Damascus and announced that, if the fighting continued, His Majesty's forces could not remain inactive.[36]

This may seem rather devious on the part of the British, yet it is only child's play compared to what followed. De Gaulle continues:

Upon being informed of this, I recognized that if our men were to be attacked by British troops and Syrian insurgents, they would find themselves in an untenable position. . . . Our military action had . . . achieved its purpose. Whatever my indignation, I decided to order a cease-fire. . . . Georges Bidault . . . cabled this information to Beynet at eleven p.m. on 30 May. . . . The British Embassy was informed and Massigli was instructed to notify Eden at once. If the British had only wanted to obtain a cease-fire, the affair would have ended there. But they had a very different aim; that is why London, learning that the French had decided on a cease-fire, quickly set in motion a carefully prepared scheme designed to inflict a public humiliation upon France. Mr Churchill, who had evidently been informed that fighting had ceased in Damascus, thereupon launched a threatening ultimatum; he was certain that we had no power to react, he welcomed the opportunity of posing as a protector of the Arabs, and hoped that in France the shock would weaken de Gaulle politically, and perhaps even drive him from power. At 4 p.m. on 31 May, Mr Eden read to the House of Commons a message which I had allegedly received from the Prime Minister. Yet the Secretary of State knew that at that hour I had received nothing at all.[37]

The message which was read in Commons and given to de Gaulle an hour later was couched in the following terms:

In view of the grave situation which has arisen between your troops and the Levant States, and the severe fighting which has broken out, we have with profound regret ordered the Commander-in-Chief Middle East to intervene to prevent the further effusion of blood in the interests of the security of the whole Middle East, which involves communications for the war against Japan. In order to avoid collision between British and French forces, we request you immediately to order the French troops to cease fire and to withdraw to their barracks. Once firing has ceased and order has been restored we shall be prepared to begin tripartite discussions in London.[38]

The message, and even more the delay involved in delivering it, roused the General's fury: 'This delay,' he wrote, 'adding a breach of all usages to the insolence of the text, could have no other purpose than to keep me from making known in time that the fighting had stopped in Damascus, which would have removed all pretext for the British ultimatum.'[39]

One cannot help admiring the extraordinary Machiavellism displayed by Churchill in the whole affair – that is, until one becomes aware of the many inaccuracies and half-truths contained in the General's narrative. Thus, there is nothing to support de Gaulle's contention that the British chose to intervene only because the Syrians were being defeated; after an indiscriminate shelling that claimed at least 1000 victims in Damascus alone – with British subjects among them – it is not too far-fetched to suppose that the British, who had a whole army in the Levant, were now finding it impossible to remain passive for political as well as humanitarian reasons. Besides, all existing accounts of Churchill's words and deeds at the end of May show that he was more reluctant than ever to become involved in the crisis: thus, he had stated at a Cabinet meeting on the evening of 30 May that 'We wanted to avoid the use of force against allies,' and that 'We must . . . avoid being manoeuvred into a position in which we had to carry alone the burden of setting matters right,' although on the other hand, 'We should not give the impression in the Arab world that the British government had done nothing to assist Syria and the Lebanon against French aggression.'[40] That same evening, Churchill drafted his telegram to de Gaulle, and reluctantly contemplated the sending of instructions to the Commander-in-Chief, Middle East, to enter Damascus and restore order; in fact, he had decided to do nothing before consulting President Truman. Churchill's extreme reluctance to act was quite obvious, and the design of humiliating France was evidently the very last thing on his mind.

The next passage of de Gaulle's indictment is another case in point: 'London, learning that the French had decided on a cease-fire, quickly set in motion a carefully prepared scheme . . .' There is not the slightest indication that the Foreign Office had been informed of the cease-fire order by the morning of the 31st – and there are some indications that it had not. In fact, the French command in Damascus may not have been informed of it either, as the city was still being heavily shelled that morning – which also throws a new light on de Gaulle's next sentence: 'Mr Churchill, who had evidently been informed that fighting had ceased in Damascus, thereupon launched a threatening ultimatum.' Mr Churchill could not possibly have been informed that fighting had ceased in Damascus before his message was read in Commons, quite simply because the fighting had not ceased at all by that time. Although the shelling itself had ceased around noon, heavy fighting continued to rage in the city throughout the day. The argument that Churchill merely conceived the ultimatum as a way of humiliating de Gaulle after the end of hostilities in Damascus is therefore difficult to take seriously.*

On the evening of the 31st, de Gaulle sent instructions to General Beynet: He was not to resume the fight unless forced to do so, but he should maintain his positions and refuse to comply with any order given by the British command. By noon of the next day, General Paget arrived in Beirut, and de Gaulle later wrote:

> General Paget had organized . . . a provoking military display. Several fighter squadrons escorted the plane that brought him to Beirut; on the way from the airport to the residence of the French Delegate General, he was preceded by a column of tanks and followed by a long line of armoured vehicles. . . . General Paget . . . delivered a detailed ultimatum to General Beynet. . . . The Englishman declared that 'he had received orders from his government to assume command in Syria and Lebanon'. He accordingly instructed the French authorities to 'execute without discussion all the orders he would give them', and for a start, he directed our troops to 'cease fighting and withdraw to their barracks'. General Beynet did not fail to inform General Paget that he only took orders from General de Gaulle and his government. He pointed out that the order to cease fire was now without object, as it had already been executed following the orders he had given himself in accordance with my instructions. Our troops would now remain where they were. As for the British forces, they could continue to come and go as they pleased; we had no objections to that . . . General Paget, his tanks, his armoured vehicles and his air squadrons thereupon quietly withdrew.[41]

The impression given here is that of a useless military parade by overwhelming British forces at a time when perfect order had been

*There remains the inexplicable delay in delivering the message to de Gaulle before it was read to the House of Commons. Yet this is a shaky basis to support the allegation of an intricate anti-French plot.

re-established everywhere. France, draped in all her pride and dignity, had then taught a lesson to the British, who retired in awe and shame. In Damascus, however, facts did not entirely measure up to this exalted image; for the British armoured columns arrived there at a time when the French troops had just stopped killing Syrian gendarmes and civilians, but were still looting indiscriminately, while the enraged Syrians had just begun to assassinate isolated Frenchmen and were in turn looting French property on a large scale. In the event, no one in Damascus and other Syrian towns was really sorry to see the British stepping in – not even the French civilians, who had to be protected by British armour from the wrath of the Syrian population. Moreover, when the Syrian Méhariste Squadrons of the *Troupes Spéciales* mutinied and turned against their French officers, many of the latter owed their lives to British intervention.[42] The British troops were in fact to form a screen between the Syrians and the French, who had to be escorted out of the main cities under armed protection.

But all this was irrelevant; from the point of view of France's prestige and sovereignty – and de Gaulle knew of no other – there could be no anti-French sentiment in the Levant: the disorders were only the work of a few agitators paid by London. As for the British intervention of 1 June, it was a new Fashoda, a grave affront to a weakened ally, the culmination of a long effort to expel France from the Levant; the General implied as much at a press conference on 2 June. Two days later, he summoned Ambassador Duff Cooper, and told him: 'I admit that we are not in a position to wage war against you at the present time. But you have insulted France and betrayed the West. This cannot be forgotten.'[43] And Duff Cooper noted: 'We had a stormy interview. He could not have been more stiff if he had been declaring war. He told me that French soldiers in the Levant had been ordered to stay where they were and to fire on Syrian or British troops if force were used against them. We got into heated argument. He is genuinely convinced that the whole incident has been arranged by the British so as to carry out their long-planned policy of driving the French out of the Levant in order to take their place.'[44]

De Gaulle's fury was exacerbated by the fact that he found little support among the French for his policy of 'firmness' in the Levant. The great war in Europe was over, and no one wanted to start a new conflict elsewhere for a matter of prestige – least of all against Great

Britain, which was immensely popular in France at the time. The Anglophilia of the press, of Parliament, and of his own ministers was observed with dismay by General de Gaulle,[45] who did not even have the whole-hearted support of his Minister of Foreign Affairs, Georges Bidault. The latter, who was kept very much in the dark as to General de Gaulle's real policy and intentions in the Levant, forcefully opposed any new military initiatives – such as the naval bombardment of Beirut[46] – and was more than ever in favour of a Franco-British rapprochement.*

Yet de Gaulle continued to vent his fury on the British, their ambassador and their Prime Minister. Behind his difficulties with the Americans on the occupation of the Italian cantons, he saw the hand of Churchill, who 'preparing a decisive manoeuvre in the Levant, found it expedient to begin by involving Washington in a quarrel with Paris.'[47] De Gaulle was often blinded by suspicion in his relations with the British; he could never take an objective view of happenings in the Levant; but when the British were involved in the Levant, the General seemed to lose all sense of proportion. Whether he ever forgave Churchill for his intervention in Beirut and Damascus that summer is not known, but it is far from certain.

General de Gaulle would have been much surprised if he had seen the instructions sent to General Paget by the Prime Minister. For on 3 June, Churchill had written to the Commander-in-Chief: 'As soon as you are master of the situation you should show full consideration to the French. We are very intimately linked with France in Europe, and your greatest triumph will be to produce a peace without rancour . . . In view of reports that French soldiers have been killed, pray take the utmost pains to protect them.'[48] Churchill's moderate dispositions were equally reflected in the speech he made in Commons on 5 June:

> When regrettable incidents like those in Syria occur between nations so firmly attached to one another as are the French and the British, and whose fortunes are so closely interwoven, it is nearly always a case of 'the less said the better'. . . . The sense of General de Gaulle's speech on 2 June was to suggest that the whole trouble in the Levant was due to British interference. I think . . . that far from stirring up agitation in the Levant States our whole influence has been used in precisely the other

*The Dutch Ambassador in Paris, De With, reported to Foreign Minister Van Kleffens: 'Bidault told me that he could easily settle matters in the Levant if he were given a free hand – in other words, if there were no interference from de Gaulle.'[46bis]

direction. . . . We have done our utmost to preserve calm, to prevent misunderstandings, and to bring the two sides together.[49]

While Churchill writes in his memoirs that he 'was most anxious not to vex the French more than was inevitable', he says nothing of his feelings towards General de Gaulle; it is perhaps as well. President Truman's special representative, Davies, who saw Churchill at the time, reported that he 'was completely fed up with de Gaulle'[50] – and this may well have been an understatement. There is little doubt that the General's admittedly unfair accusations had once again aroused the Prime Minister's latent Gaullophobia; besides, on 2 June, while the Franco-American dispute over the Italian cantons was still in full swing, General Doyen had sent yet another threatening letter to his American counterpart, indicating that he would oppose the setting up of Allied military government in the territories he occupied 'by all necessary means without exception'. Upon learning of this, Churchill immediately wrote to President Truman: 'Is it not rather disagreeable for us to be addressed in these terms by General de Gaulle, whom we have reinstated in France at some expense of American and British blood and treasure? Nonetheless, our policy with France is one of friendship.' Churchill quotes this telegram in his memoirs, but he omits the last sentence: 'It is de Gaulle who needs correction.'[51]

Churchill was evidently prepared to administer the correction himself. He therefore advised the President to make public his reply to de Gaulle, in which he stated that he was obliged to cease delivery of US equipment or ammunition to France in view of the threat to use them against American soldiers.[53] In the event, wiser counsel prevailed, and Truman decided not to publish the message. But Churchill wrote to him the next day: 'I believe that the publication of your previous message would have led to the overthrow of de Gaulle, who after five long years of experience I am convinced is the worst enemy of France in her troubles. I consider General de Gaulle one of the greatest dangers to European peace. No one has more need than Britain of France's friendship, but I am sure that in the long run no understanding will be reached with General de Gaulle.'[54] Three days later, he also wrote; 'Between us and France, there can be no bridge via de Gaulle, ever. . . . De Gaulle's present programme of defiance and scorn to Britain and the US . . . leads only to unimaginable misery and misfortune.'[55]

In the meantime, devoted diplomats at the Quai d'Orsay and the Foreign Office were still pressing for a Franco-British treaty, for tripartite talks on the Levant, or even a five-Power conference on the Near East. But de Gaulle would not hear of tripartite talks, Churchill would not hear of a five-Power conference, and neither Churchill nor de Gaulle would hear of a Franco-British treaty. By the middle of June, de Gaulle was still pursuing a personal vendetta against the British action in the Levant, and Churchill was still expressing his hostile feelings towards de Gaulle. To Sir Alexander Cadogan, who was once again advocating Anglo-French talks, Churchill wrote on 23 June: 'There can be no hurry about this. The French have no army yet nor have they even the foundations of a democratic government. The personality of de Gaulle stands as a shocking barrier. . . . I should not be in favour of making an alliance with France at the present time. I do not wish to see General de Gaulle over here or go to Paris to see him.'⁵⁶

As it happened, Churchill was the first to abandon his pugnacious mood – though not without considerable hesitation. On 28 June, less than a month before the Potsdam conference, Ambassador Duff Cooper received the following telegram from the Foreign Office: 'Before deciding finally whether he can go to France next week for his projected holiday, the Prime Minister feels that in the prevailing uncertainty of our relations with France you should receive a further assurance from the French government that his presence would not be unwelcome.'⁵⁷ By 12 July, we find Churchill enjoying a much-needed rest at Hendaye, in South-West France. There, the British Consul, Bryce Nairne, and a French friend, General Brutinel, tried to persuade him to resume contacts with de Gaulle. In his diary, Lord Moran recorded the Prime Minister's reaction:

De Gaulle would love to hand out a snub to him. Besides, the time could hardly be more unpropitious for any advance to him; just before the Potsdam conference, from which de Gaulle was excluded. General Brutinel waited patiently for a lull, then, when the PM had subsided, he explained that he only wanted to approach de Gaulle to suggest he should come to see the Prime Minister. Winston would have none of this; he complained that de Gaulle had sent a telegram to Roosevelt asking for assistance. He could trust America not to take France's colonies; he could not trust Britain. And this, said Winston scornfully, at a time when we were pouring men into France for her relief. No, he would not see him. General Brutinel was puzzled. After all, it was the

Prime Minister who had begun the whole business; it was he who had suggested breaking his journey to Berlin at Paris in order to see de Gaulle. Then, on second thoughts, it occurred to him that he might be snubbed. If, the PM ruminated, it had been the other way round, if, for instance, de Gaulle were in Scotland, he would have sent him a telegram to welcome him and to ask if he could do anything for him. No such telegram had come from de Gaulle when the PM came to France. So, after many hesitations and endless perambulations, he decided to do nothing till Duff Cooper arrived in the afternoon.[58]

Duff Cooper himself noted that day:

The PM wanted to consult me as to the desirability of my approaching de Gaulle with the suggestion that they might have a conversation in Paris on Sunday if the PM stopped there on his way to Berlin. I was very strongly in favour of the plan. The French have now handed over the Special Troops to the Syrians, and if we could now come to an agreement for the simultaneous Anglo-French evacuation of the Levant the whole question might be settled without any of the delays or difficulties of an international conference. We argued the subject at great length, before and after dinner, and the PM changed his view more than once, but when we eventually went to bed at 2 a.m. I had convinced him and had his authority to take up the matter in Paris.

And the next day, the ambassador added: 'I felt that we should leave early, as there was no time to lose if I was to succeed in my mission . . . left the Parme aerodrome at 10 a.m. and arrived in Paris at 12.30. I was greeted at the embassy by a message from the Prime Minister to say that I was to take no action whatever on the subject we had discussed last night.[59]

Hence there was to be no meeting between the two statesmen before the Potsdam conference; but no great harm was done thereby, as it would merely have resulted in a new confrontation on the Levant and related issues. And yet, at the Potsdam conference ten days later, although both Stalin and Truman stated that they 'had come to discuss world affairs', and although Truman insisted that he had not come 'to hear Tito, de Gaulle and Franco,'[60] it is a fact that France was defended, and well defended, by a remarkably vocal and eloquent champion; and when her position in the Levant was called in question by a Soviet memorandum submitted to the participants, no one spoke for France . . . except the Prime Minister of Great Britain, the very man who, according to de Gaulle, had tried ever since 1941 to expel France from the Levant!

Churchill: In consideration of France's long, historic connection with Syria and the Lebanon, we agreed not to object to France having a favoured position, if that could be satisfactorily arranged with the governments of Syria and the Lebanon. We have told General de Gaulle that as soon as he makes a satisfactory treaty with Syria and the Lebanon, we will withdraw our troops. The withdrawal of our troops now would lead to the massacre of French civilians and French troops there. We should not like to have that happen. It would lead to great excitement throughout the Arab world, and make the maintenance of peace more difficult in Palestine and Iraq. It might affect Egypt too. We could not have a worse moment for this disturbance. It would endanger lines of communication through the Suez Canal through which both British and American supplies are proceeding for the war against Japan. General de Gaulle has acted very unwisely in this region, against our advice and entreaty. The outbreak was caused by 500 troops being sent on the ship. They could do nothing but strike a spark. Lately, de Gaulle has agreed to hand over the *Troupes Spéciales* to the Syrian government, and I trust we shall be able to reach, if not an agreement then some sort of settlement with him which would guarantee the independence of Syria and the Lebanon, and secure some recognition for the French – their cultural and commercial interests, which they have built up over so many years.

Let me repeat, Britain will not remain there one day longer than necessary. We will be delighted to withdraw from a thankless task, assumed in the interest of our Allies, as well as ourselves. In view of the states interested, we do not welcome the proposal to have a conference in which the United States and the Soviet Union would enter with Great Britain and France. The whole burden has been borne by us with no help. . . .

Mr Eden: (interrupting) Except for the diplomatic approval of the United States.

Churchill: (continuing) If the United States desires to take our place, it might open a new question.

President Truman: No thank you, Mr Churchill. . . . We are in slight disagreement with the Prime Minister, however, in one regard. We are in favour of equal treatment for everybody in the area with no one having a privileged position.

Marshal Stalin: Including France?

President Truman: Yes.

Marshal Stalin: May I infer that my colleagues do not recognize any special privileges for France in the area?

President Truman: I certainly do not.

Churchill: We would like to see France have a privileged position there. We agreed to this when we were weak. We cannot change now. This agreement, however, was only as far as the United Kingdom is concerned. We would not make any serious effort to help France obtain privileges. If they do so, we shall smile benignly.

Marshal Stalin: From whom can France get these privileges?

Churchill: From Syria and Lebanon.

Marshal Stalin: Only Syria and Lebanon?

Churchill: Only. The French have large interests there. They even have a tune: 'Pars (Partant?) pour la Syrie.' (laughter). Their interests go back to the Crusades.

President Truman: The United States favours equal rights for everyone.

Churchill: Will you prevent Syria from giving privileges to France?

President Truman: No, but we are certain that the Syrians will not give France privileges.

Marshal Stalin: The Syrians are reluctant to do so. (Laughter). I welcome the full explanation given to us on this subject by Mr Churchill and am happy to withdraw my paper.[61]

There is no evidence that de Gaulle was ever informed of this intervention. If he was, he probably did not believe it – or he may have thought that it was another devious trick; at any rate, he makes no mention of it in his memoirs. In Potsdam, meanwhile, the Big Three continued their discussions on the future peace treaties, the shape of the Polish and German borders, the treatment of Germany and the war against Japan. In the process, many concessions were made to the Soviet Union; some were unavoidable, others were not, and all of them were bitterly regretted shortly afterwards. But Winston Churchill was not to see the end of the conference: On 25 July, the British electorate gave the Labour Party a crushing majority, and Churchill resigned the very next day.

De Gaulle was not astonished by this abrupt disavowal: 'To minds inclined towards sentimentality', he wrote, 'this disgrace suddenly inflicted by the British nation upon the great man who had so gloriously led her to salvation and victory might seem surprising. Yet there was nothing in it that was not in accordance with the order of human affairs. . . . [Winston Churchill's] nature, identified with a magnificent undertaking, his countenance, chiselled by the fires and frosts of great events, had become inadequate in this era of mediocrity.'[62]

But behind an impassive mask, de Gaulle greeted the event with mixed feelings:

In some respects, this departure facilitated the conduct of French affairs; in others, it did not. At any rate, I witnessed it with melancholy. It is true that within the alliance, Churchill had not dealt gently with me; and lately, in the Levant, his behaviour had even been that of an enemy. All in all, he had supported me as long as he took me for the head of a French faction which was favourable to him and could be used to good effect. Besides, this great political mind had remained convinced that France's role was a necessary one, and this exceptional artist was certainly aware of the dramatic character of my undertaking. But when he had seen me representing an ambitious France, apparently seeking to recover her power in Europe and abroad, Churchill had naturally felt something of Pitt's spirits in his soul. In spite of all that, the essential and ineffaceable fact remained that without him, my undertaking would have been vain from the start, and that by lending me a strong and willing hand in those days, Churchill had decisively helped the cause of France . . . To be sure, Churchill and de Gaulle had had to carry out their tasks under different conditions; indeed, fierce quarrels had divided them. But they had nonetheless sailed side by side for more than five years, guided by the same stars on the raging sea of history. The ship led by Churchill had now been moored fast. Mine was coming in sight of port. Upon learning that England had asked her captain to relinquish the command to which he had been called when the tempest rose, I foresaw the moment when I would also leave the helm of France, on my own initiative, just as I had taken it.[63]

The moment had not yet come. That summer, General de Gaulle visited the defeated Reich, inspected French troops and supervised the installation of a French occupation zone in Germany. By mid-August, Japan had stopped fighting, but in Europe, it soon appeared that the new-found peace was a precarious one, and that a fresh conflict between East and West would soon put an end to it. A month earlier, de Gaulle had accepted an invitation to visit President Truman in Washington; 'It was natural that President Truman should be anxious to consult France,'[64] the General wrote without undue modesty. The visit began on 22 August, and the two statesmen had several talks covering a wide range of topics: The internationalization of the Ruhr, the Soviet threat, the French position in Indo-China, the future of the colonies – and de Gaulle once again mentioned the 'deplorable British intervention in the Levant'.[65] Truman and de Gaulle parted on the best of terms; it had indeed been a frank explanation with very few concrete results, as

President Truman evidently had no intention of treating France as a great power.

De Gaulle then proceeded to Canada, where he was triumphantly received by the people and the authorities. On 28 August, he had a long private conversation with the Canadian Prime Minister, Mackenzie King, who noted in his diary: 'It was clear from what de Gaulle said . . . that he thought Churchill and the President had gone too far in what they had done for Russia at Potsdam. . . . When I spoke of Churchill, he used the expression 'poor Churchill', as much as to say that he felt sorry for him in his defeat though he was not saying anything about him one way or the other.'[66]

In Britain, meanwhile, a new team had taken the reins of power. At the Foreign Office, Ernest Bevin explained his policy with regard to France, and Oliver Harvey noted on 13 August: 'In reference to the personal antagonism of de Gaulle and Winston Churchill he said that he had no *amour propre* and had no feelings of that kind at all, but he wished to get better relations with France as well as with the other Western countries. He wished particularly to build up on trade with France and to develop a kind of vested interest in good relations with the different French ministers. He wished to strengthen them as against the personal policy of de Gaulle.'[67] This was hardly a new departure; Winston Churchill had tried to do just that for the last five years, and with conspicuously little success.

Churchill was now a private citizen – admittedly not an ordinary private citizen. As a Member of Parliament, he kept a watchful eye on foreign affairs; as an unrepentant Francophile, he kept many contacts on the other side of the Channel; on 25 October, Duff Cooper wrote to the new Prime Minister, Clement Attlee, to inform him that Churchill would go to Brussels on 15 November to receive the Freedom of the City; but on the way, he would like to stop in Paris to see 'some of his old friends' – in the event Herriot and Blum.* There was apparently no question of meeting another 'old friend', as Duff Cooper was quick to point out: 'My own view is that it would serve no useful purpose and may do harm. Nor do I think that either of the great men would be over-anxious to meet one another.'[68]

For once, Ambassador Duff Cooper was entirely wrong; the two great men *were* most anxious to meet one another, which they did on

*Churchill was also to take his seat in the Academy of Political and Moral Sciences to which he had just been elected.

13 November. That day, in Paris, the newly-elected Constituent Assembly was to vote for a President of the government. De Gaulle had studiously ignored the week-long debate that preceded. In fact, he had presented no programme, and even refused to appear as a candidate: '*On me prendrait comme j'étais, ou on me prendrait pas.*'[69] As a result, the General was not unduly worried by the outcome of the vote that afternoon – and Churchill found him in the most relaxed mood. Duff Cooper later noted:

> We lunched with General de Gaulle. He was wearing a dark blue suit, in which he looks so much better than in uniform. I never liked him or admired him so much. He was smiling and courteous and treated Winston with much more deference than he ever did when Winston was Prime Minister. And although this was the day and almost the hour at which his whole future was at stake . . . not only was he perfectly calm but one might have thought he was a country gentleman living far away from Paris. There were no interruptions, no telephone calls or messages, no secretaries hurrying in and out, no sign that anything was happening, although Winston insisted on staying till three-thirty talking about the past, and the Assembly was meeting at three. When he left, the General came to the front door with him and bowed as the car drove off.[70]

That afternoon, de Gaulle was elected President of the government by 550 votes to 0.

CHAPTER 17

Entente Cordiale

On the evening of 13 November 1945, Winston Churchill, learning of the election results, sent de Gaulle an enthusiastic letter; recalling Plutarch's remark: 'Ingratitude towards great men is the mark of a strong people,' Churchill wrote: 'Plutarch lied!' But de Gaulle was unconvinced: 'I knew that the vote was a tribute to my past actions, and in no way a commitment for the future.'[1] The General was entirely right: no sooner had he proceeded to form a government than he found himself thwarted at every turn by the hostility of the Socialists, the reluctance of the Radicals, the ambitions of the Communists, the passivity of the Right, the intrigues of the Assembly and the agitation of the trade unions. This return to the disastrous practices of the past was witnessed with increasing dismay by General de Gaulle; besides, having exercised unquestioned authority over Free France at a time of mortal danger, he was now finding it difficult to preside over the squabbles, petty problems and economic miseries of postwar France; '*Je n'ai pas sauvé la France pour m'occuper de la ration de macaronis,*' he said to Georges Bidault at the time.[2] And then there was something else: the Assembly had been elected to prepare a constitution for France, and the project it was elaborating was the opposite of what de Gaulle had in mind: an all-powerful Assembly, a subordinate executive, an insignificant President. The project was to be submitted to a referendum in April 1946; as President of the government, de Gaulle had no power to modify it, and no liberty to attack it. By resigning his function, on the other hand, he could recover his freedom of action, and explain the whole matter to the French people. A particularly distasteful debate at the Assembly on 1 January, when the Socialists insisted on slashing the military budget by 20 per cent only a few hours before the final vote, definitely convinced de Gaulle that he could not preside over a Fourth Republic that was fast becoming a replica of the Third: after having contemplated – and rejected – the idea of staging a coup d'état,* the General announced his resignation on 20 January 1946.**

Having resigned, de Gaulle expected to be called back by giant popular demonstrations; but no such thing occurred, and the General had to embark on an almost solitary crusade against the faulty institutions of the Fourth Republic – a crusade that was to last twelve years. He met with some success when the first draft constitution was rejected by the French people in May 1946, but had to concede defeat when the second draft, though not significantly different from the first, was accepted five months later. He expected to be recalled to power as soon as a new world conflict broke out, and the proclamation of the Truman doctrine, the unsuccessful Moscow conference of Foreign Ministers in April 1947, the failure of the London conference eight months later, the setting up of the Kominform and finally the beginning of the Berlin blockade in July 1948 seemed to indicate that this moment was not far away. In the meantime, de Gaulle had founded the RPF (*Rassemblement du Peuple Français*), which he conceived as a gigantic movement to oppose the existing institutions, the regime of the parties and the agitation of the Communists – a movement that would bring de Gaulle back to power. Yet in spite of the international tensions and their political repercussions in France, the RPF and its solitary leader failed to unite all Frenchmen under the Cross of Lorraine. De Gaulle was now distrusted by the Right because of his previous policy of nationalization, and by the Left because of his alleged fascist tendencies. He was also actively opposed by the reigning 'Third Force' coalition of Socialists, Radicals and MRP, whose position was now bolstered by the salutary economic effects of the Marshall Plan. Finally, the RPF itself was weakened by internal squabbles and the participation of a few rather dubious elements.

For all these reasons, de Gaulle found himself increasingly isolated in his crusade against the existing regime. Yet he continued

*Colonel Passy confided to an American diplomat in April 1946: 'If the General had been able to gather around him 10,000 trustworthy and resolved men – as the Communists had done – he would have taken power by a coup. But the hesitations and reluctance of the General had made this impossible.'[3]

**In December 1945 and early January 1946, de Gaulle had also found himself in disagreement with his Foreign Minister about the Levant. The French and British diplomats had concluded on 13 December a preliminary agreement for French and British evacuation of Syria. On 4 January, de Gaulle had denounced this 'so-called agreement' as 'a piece of trickery'.[4]

to denounce the omnipotence of the Assembly, the paralysis of the executive, the tragic ballet of revolving Cabinets and the inconsistent policies emerging from the general confusion. Not unexpectedly, de Gaulle was most vocal in denouncing the regime's foreign policy, which he considered as incompatible with the security and sovereignty of the French nation. He thus challenged the government's policy over Indo-China, Germany, the Council of Europe, NATO, the Schuman Plan, and the European Defence Community (EDC). Having loudly denounced the Allied policy of setting up a central administration in Germany, which might become 'the nucleus of a Reich', de Gaulle slowly evolved towards the idea of a new Europe led by France and Germany. As a result, when the newly-elected German chancellor, Konrad Adenauer, proposed a Franco-German Union at the beginning of 1950, his proposal was warmly welcomed by General de Gaulle. On 16 March, the General responded with enthusiasm to the idea of 'rebuilding the Empire of Charlemagne'.

The project of a European Defence Community was naturally attacked with particular vigour by de Gaulle, who considered that it would deprive France of one of the most important attributes of sovereignty: her armed forces, which would then be drowned in a multinational mass under no definite leadership – or worse, under American leadership. As both the Americans and the British were doing their utmost at the time to promote the scheme – though keeping out of it themselves – they gradually became privileged targets for de Gaulle's ire and sarcasm, coming second only to the men and institutions of the Fourth Republic. By November 1953, de Gaulle was unleashing his most violent attack on the EDC, and on 'les Anglo-Saxons':

Nothing is more curious than the public or private interventions of the United States to compel France to ratify a treaty that would condemn her to decay.... Yes, Britain too is demanding that we join EDC, though nothing in the world would induce her to join herself.... Sacrifice your sovereignty, abandon your soldiers to the discretion of others, lose your dominions, that is good for Paris, not for London! ... Britain wants no commitment on the Continent, except in the form of a few divisions and a few squadrons ... she will no doubt leave a few soldiers in Germany, and no doubt she will have some attentive observers attached to EDC. It's always a good thing to be informed, especially if it commits you to nothing. It's not at all unpleasant to be the guest of honour at the banquet of a society to which you pay no dues. . . After all, if France is so determined to separate herself from her overseas territories, well, why not? In the event of a world crisis, a situation might well result which would give certain opportunities to Lord Louis Mountbatten, Commander-in-Chief in the Western Mediterranean, or to Lord Alexander, *Vicomte de Tunis*, if you please.[5]

By this time, however, de Gaulle's movement had all but disintegrated. In March 1952, 27 members of the RPF had supported the investiture of M. Antoine Pinay; a year later, the municipal elections proved catastrophic for the RPF. Though the movement itself did not entirely disappear, the Gaullist deputies ceased thereafter to benefit from the General's leadership, and under the name URAS (*Union Républicaine d'Action Sociale*), they joined the political fray by participating in coalitions and even entering several governments of the Fourth Republic. De Gaulle was now alone, and his chances of ever coming back to power seemed more remote than ever.

In Britain, as we know, Winston Churchill had entered the opposition earlier than de Gaulle; he was to leave it much sooner too. But in opposition, Churchill, unlike de Gaulle, spoke more as a counsellor than as a challenger. By the spring of 1946, we find him denouncing the mortal perils of Soviet expansionism in his famous Fulton speech. Six months later, in Zurich, he was to declare: 'We must build a kind of United States of Europe', and he added:

> I am now going to say something that will astonish you. The first step in the re-creation of the European family must be a partnership between France and Germany. In this way only can France recover the moral leadership of Europe. There can be no revival of Europe without a spiritually great France and a spiritually great Germany. The structure of the United States of Europe, if well and truly built, will be such as to make the material strength of a single state less important. Small nations will count as much as large ones and gain their honour by their contribution to the common cause . . . If this is their wish, they have only to say so, and means can certainly be found, and machinery erected, to carry that wish into full fruition.[6]

Thus, almost twenty years after having stated that we 'must use of our influence to modify the age-long antagonisms . . . between Germany and France',[7] Churchill was once again advocating a Franco-German reconciliation. And once again, he was defending the idea with boundless drive and energy. On 14 May, 1947, he declared at the Albert Hall: 'Germany today lies prostrate, famishing among ruins. Obviously no initiative can be expected from her. It is for France and Britain to take the lead. Together they must, in a friendly manner, bring the German people back into the European circle.'[8] And the next year, on 28 October, 1948: 'It has been my hope that France, which we see in such political confusion and weakness, will find a way out of her own troubles and a path to true European leadership by stretching out her hand to her enemy of a thousand years, and in the moment of absolute German prostration, bring them back to the circle of Christendom and the family of Europe.'[9] On 28 March, 1950, the theme was once again broached in Commons with deep conviction and compelling eloquence:

> We are presently to have a meeting at Strasbourg of the Council of Europe and the Assembly where, we trust, in spite of all that has happened, French and German hands will be clasped in concord. I recommend to the House that we should do all in our power to encourage and promote Franco-German reconciliation as an approach to unity, or even perhaps some form, in some aspects, of union. . . . France and Britain, both sorely distressed, can combine together and, thus joined, have the superior power to raise Germany, even more shattered, to an equal rank and to lasting association with them.[10]

As we know, de Gaulle had welcomed Chancellor Adenauer's call for a Franco-German Union only twelve days earlier; this warm endorsement had not escaped Churchill, who added:

> Almost the same time that I spoke in the Defence debate, a statement was being made by General de Gaulle on Franco-German relations. As the House knows, I have not always seen eye to eye with that patriotic Frenchman, who represented in the war more than any other man the will to live of France. Certainly there is no one in France who could have opposed with more vigour and injurious effect the reconciliation between French and German people. He represents the most powerful forces which could have been arrayed on the wrong side. But what did he say? He spoke of the proposal which Dr Adenauer had just made for an economic union between France and Germany. I shall read his words. He said:
>
> 'I have followed for thirty years the ideas of the German Chancellor. In what this good German has said I have found the echo of the call of Europe. . . . Why should not the Rhine become a street where Europeans meet, rather than a ditch dividing hostile camps?'

Some will call Dr Adenauer's proposal for an economic union between Germany and France premature, unsure, only partly thought out. Surely, however, it lies near the root of the matter. What we want is far more than that, but these two speeches by General de Gaulle and Dr Adenauer together constitute a memorable event.[11]

Thus, although they disagreed on just about everything else: the EDC, the Council of Europe, NATO, the Schuman Plan* etc, de Gaulle and Churchill agreed at least on the necessity of bringing Germany into the nucleus of a new Europe. By the end of the next year, Churchill was in power for the second time, and sought to re-establish the close relationship with the United States that had been the foundation of his wartime policy. He was to remain in office for three and a half years. In the meantime, de Gaulle, disappointed by the failure of the RPF, annoyed by the defection of the Gaullist deputies, enraged at the inconsistent policies of the successive French governments, had decided to retire from public life and withdraw to Colombey-les-deux-Eglises. There he was to write his memoirs and await another chance to work for the greatness of France. By the end of 1955, that chance seemed remote at best, and de Gaulle was perfectly aware that he might never again intervene in French public affairs – except, as he put it, in the event of 'a rather unusual shock'.

During these years in the wilderness, there is no evidence that General de Gaulle corresponded with Winston Churchill, though it is not unlikely. At any rate, a sort of indirect dialogue continued between the two men, a dialogue in which the past occupied more place than the present; thus, someone having reported to the General that Churchill, driven into a conversational corner, had conceded that de Gaulle was a great man, the latter replied: 'Ah, he said that, did he, *le monstre de Downing Street*'.[12]** De Gaulle was also told of a statement by Churchill that 'the Cross of Lorraine was the heaviest cross he had had to bear during the war', whereupon the General commented: 'If we consider that the other crosses Churchill had to bear were the German army, submarine warfare, the bombing of Britain and the threat of annihilation, then when he says that the heaviest of all these was de Gaulle, it is quite a tribute to a

*As leader of the Opposition Churchill was in favour of British participation in negotiations both for the EDC and the Schuman Plan.
**This reply shows that de Gaulle had been informed of Churchill's comment in 1943 about 'the monster of Hampstead'[13] . . . and that he had an elephant's memory.

man alone, without an army, without a country, and with only a few followers.'[14]

Although the two men did not meet during that period, Churchill, while on a private visit to the South of France, was on hand to listen to one of de Gaulle's memorable RPF speeches. It was at Nice on 12 September, 1948, and Churchill had surveyed the event from a window overlooking the Place Masséna. With him was Alexander Korda, who asked Churchill on that occasion: 'Winston, did you really say that of all the crosses you ever had to bear, the heaviest was the Cross of Lorraine?' 'No,' Churchill grunted, 'I didn't say it; but I'm sorry I didn't, because it was quite witty . . . and so true!'[15]

In June 1955, someone mentioned Churchill in front of de Gaulle, whereupon the General said: 'Churchill is now too old. He is ill at ease in these times of mediocrity. Besides, he was a fighter rather than a real statesman.'[16] Whether Churchill would have subscribed to the latter part of this statement is doubtful, but he obviously agreed with the former: a few weeks earlier, the indomitable Prime Minister had finally stepped down and passed the torch to his *alter ego* Anthony Eden.

Three years passed. From his retreat at Colombey, de Gaulle surveyed the French political scene with a mixture of sarcastic amusement and deep melancholy. He had seen incapable men jockeying for office, mediocre men swept away by the fury of events, and capable men paralysed by shifting coalitions and inadequate institutions. He had witnessed the loss of Indo-China, the burial of the EDC, the granting of 'internal autonomy' to Tunisia, the independence of Morocco, the early stages of the Algerian revolt and the failure of the Suez operation. 'My chances of ever returning to power are very slim', de Gaulle confided to a friend, 'except if these imbeciles persist in their idiotic policies.'[17]

In the end, the Algerian crisis proved too much for the ephemeral governments of the Fourth Republic; supported by fragile coalitions, they were too weak to negotiate usefully and too indecisive to wage war successfully. A new Cabinet crisis and a conspiracy of the extreme Right, by triggering the 13 May *putsch* in Algeria, finally brought about the 'rather violent shock' envisioned by General de Gaulle. To be sure, the men behind the *putsch* had not the slightest intention of returning de Gaulle to power, but a few energetic Gaullists in Paris and Algiers made sure that they did. Faced with the alternative of a military coup or de Gaulle's return to power, the men of the Fourth Republic finally chose the lesser evil. By the beginning of June 1958, General de Gaulle had received the investiture of the National Assembly, together with full power to draft a new constitution.

The last Premier of the Fourth Republic was now faced with a formidable task; he was to supervise the drafting of the constitution, which would then be submitted to a referendum; in Algeria, he had to restore order, reassure the army, appease the *Ultras* and try to negotiate with the Algerian rebels; in France, he had to reorganize the machinery of government, and prepare the legislative elections. But among this flurry of activity, de Gaulle found time for a measure which seemed to him necessary and long overdue: in Paris, on 6 November, 1958, Sir Winston Churchill was solemnly presented with the *Croix de la Libération*.

It was a moving ceremony. In the presence of all the *Compagnons de la Libération*, de Gaulle himself decorated the old fighter, the illustrious statesman and the life-long friend of France.* 'I want Sir Winston Churchill to know this,' the General said in a short speech, 'Today's ceremony means that France remembers what she owes him. I want him to know this: the man who has just had the honour of bestowing this distinction upon him values and admires him more than ever. . . .'[18]

Churchill, evidently much moved, replied,

I am going to speak English today. I have often made speeches in French, but that was wartime, and I do not wish to subject you to the ordeals of darker days. I am particularly happy that it should be my old friend and comrade, General de Gaulle, who should be paying me this honour. He will always be remembered as the symbol of the soul of France and of the unbreakable integrity of her spirit in adversity. I remember, when I saw him in the sombre days of 1940, I said 'Here is the Constable of France.' How well he lived up to that title! Now he is back again in a position of the greatest and gravest responsibility for his country. The problems which confront us are no less important than our struggle for survival eighteen years ago. Indeed, in some ways they may be more complicated, for there is no clear-cut objective of victory in our sight. It is harder to summon, even among friends and allies, the vital unity of purpose amidst the perplexities of a world situation which is neither peace nor war. . . . I think that I can claim always to have been a friend of France. Certainly your great country and your valiant people

*Curiously enough, Anthony Eden, to whom Free France owed so much, was never decorated. However, he was often received at the Elysée in the years that followed.

have held a high place in my thoughts and affection in all the endeavours and great events with which we have been associated in the last half-century.... The future is uncertain, but we can be sure that if Britain and France, who for so long have been the vanguard of the Western civilization, stand together, with our empires, our American friends and our other allies and associates, then we have grounds for sober confidence and high hope.

I thank you all for the honour you have done me.

Vive la France![19]

Pierre Lefranc, who had organized the ceremony, recalls what followed:

The band played 'God Save the Queen' and the 'Marseillaise'. Churchill reviewed the troops – very slowly – and the General seemed to find the tour a bit lengthy.... At lunch, Churchill, sitting opposite the General, began to talk with some animation; he evoked one or two wartime episodes, in French.... Churchill spoke even slower than he walked, and we all suffered from the heavy silence following each word pronounced in an improvised French. The General tried to keep the conversation going, but Churchill launched into yet another narrative, and the anxious anticipation of the next word began anew. He talked of 1940. 'Pauvre grande France', he sighed; after which he evoked a rather unclear episode of the Great War. Foch was mentioned, and then Reynaud came back to the fore; 'Pétain! Un malheur!' then the landing in Normandy; 'Il y avait du vent, beaucoup. Soldats magnifiques. Le roi ne pouvait pas être là. Alors moi non plus. Je regrette encore.' We accompanied him to the Rolls-Royce of the ambassador, which was parked just under the balcony. In the garden he turned back towards de Gaulle and waved at length with his hat.

'How sad!,' de Gaulle told me in the lift.[20]

Before the year was over, the last Premier of the Fourth Republic had been elected first President of the Fifth. The most pressing task that lay ahead was evidently the solution of the Algerian problem, and by 1959, General de Gaulle was thinking in terms of an 'association with France', preceded by the 'self-determination' of the Algerian people. Yet he had to manoeuvre cautiously to disarm the partisans of 'Algérie Française', while pursuing the campaign against the Algerian insurgents – two most delicate undertakings, neither of which was entirely successful. In the midst of this tense political climate, another of de Gaulle's war-time companions came to Paris, and was received with great ceremony: he was General Eisenhower, the former Supreme Commander in Europe, now President of the United States. During the conversations that followed, many important issues were examined, including de Gaulle's idea of a three-power directorate to supervise world affairs – but the two men naturally recalled the past as well: 'According to Roosevelt,' de Gaulle said, 'I claimed to be Joan of Arc. He was mistaken; I only claimed to be General de Gaulle. . . . Churchill said during the war that the "heaviest cross he ever had to bear was . . . the Cross of Lorraine". But in spite of that, not only myself, but also France and the whole free world were greatly indebted to Churchill. . . . I knew how much he liked medals. When I returned to power, I bestowed the Order of the Liberation upon him, and I did it under the watchful eye of Napoléon! . . . How he cried, but what a great artist!'[21]

Six months passed. At the beginning of April 1960, de Gaulle, for the first time in more than fifteen years, returned to the country that had welcomed him during the dark days of defeat. A triumphal reception was given to the Free French Leader who had become the President of France; but one of the General's first visits was to his old wartime companion, who received him in his home: 'Winston, pink-cheeked and looking distinguished in a cutaway coat and floppy black velvet bow tie, stood in the doorway and greeted him in French: *"Vous êtes le bienvenu chez moi, Jusqu'à fin de ma vie vous serez le bienvenu."* '[22] There followed a short and moving conversation; upon leaving, de Gaulle said, in English: 'Goodbye, Sir Winston,' and Churchill added, '*Vive la France!*' 'These were the last words I heard him say,' de Gaulle later wrote.[23]*

The next day, 7 April, in Westminster Hall, General de Gaulle addressed both Houses of Parliament. Louis Kirby of the *Daily Mail* described this solemn moment:

> Surrounded by the dazzling pageantry of Yeomen of the Guard and Gentlemen-at-Arms, the eyes of President de Gaulle and Sir Winston Churchill suddenly met. It happened as bandsmen in scarlet tunics broke into the 'Marseillaise'. General de Gaulle, in black morning dress, was standing stiffly to attention in front of the Chair of State as he prepared to address members of both Houses of Parliament. But as he saw the hunched figure of Sir Winston in the front row, his clenched hands jerked. He swallowed, his face coloured and tears came to his

*This is not quite true. The two men met again six months later in southern France, where Churchill was spending his holidays. They had a long conversation at the Nice Préfecture, after which de Gaulle returned to his official tour, and Churchill to his holiday.

eyes. Sir Winston, too, faltered. Blinking hard, he began to study the pink and blue hydrangeas separating them.[24]

De Gaulle presently began to speak, recalling the past in dispassionate but moving tones: 'The liberation of Europe,' he said, 'invested Winston Churchill with the immortal glory of having been the leader and the inspiration not only of Britain in the sternest test she has ever known, but also of many others. . . .' And much was said in few words when the General added: 'If it came about in those days of June, 1944 that I found myself by no means always and entirely in agreement with my most illustrious friend on particular points, it is perhaps because success, henceforth assured, led us into some degree of intransigence. Four years earlier our discussions were less stubborn! But see how time undertakes to bring out in relief what matters and to wipe out what counts for little.'[25] De Gaulle went on to speak of France's friendship and admiration for the British people, and a witness noted: 'As General de Gaulle ended, none could be unaware of the surge of emotion that passed through Westminster Hall. . . . He came down the stone steps, at once an exalted and a rather mystical figure, paused to exchange a word with Mr Macmillan, and then walked – or rather marched – down the red carpet of honour . . . to the great doors that lead out from history into the troubled world of today.'[26]

The two great statesmen did not lose touch with each other. Pierre Galante wrote that

They kept contact by telegram or in letters, de Gaulle's usually handwritten, creating what Sir Winston's son Randolph called 'the correspondence of two giants of history, recognizing one another and speaking to each other from the summits of history.' This correspondence would continue almost as long as Churchill lived, and so would the feeling of deep regard and respect that they shared, despite all their wartime quarrels. Randolph Churchill had the explanation for that too: "My father had a delicate task, that of supporting de Gaulle against the Americans, particularly in the latter part of the war when Britain became, in respect to the American war effort, the junior partner.'[26]

Randolph might have added that the Foreign Office had an even more delicate task at times, that of supporting de Gaulle when Churchill sided with the Americans against him. But this had lost all importance; only friendship and mutual respect now remained between the two great leaders. During the next two years, de Gaulle's successful efforts to extricate France from the rut of the

Algerian war and restore the greatness of France were followed with interest and admiration by Winston Churchill, who was now a private citizen living his last years in retirement; and de Gaulle never failed to enquire after the health of his partner in war and his friend in peace.

For all these demonstrations of Franco-British friendship, General de Gaulle categorically opposed Britain's entry in to the Common Market at the beginning of 1963. Those who saw in this refusal a kind of revenge for the past misdeeds – real or imagined – of perfidious Albion were far off the mark; those who thought that de Gaulle had betrayed his English friends on that occasion understood nothing at all. The General simply believed that as matters stood at the time, British participation was probably not in the interest of Europe, and certainly not in the interest of France – which in the end was all that mattered. 'A man may have friends, a nation, never.'

General de Gaulle had given his friend Winston Churchill a large Gallic cock made of glass, which the old Prime Minister treasured until his dying day.[27] That day finally came on 24 January, 1965. Among the numerous tributes rendered to Churchill's memory, there was a short message from de Gaulle: 'I see in the passing away of this very great man the death of my war companion and friend.' He also wrote to the Queen: 'In the great drama he was the greatest of all.'[28] Every year after that, on 24 January, Winston Churchill's widow received a message written in the General's hand.[29] The last one was received in January 1970. By November of that year, General de Gaulle himself had passed away.

In France, de Gaulle's gigantic stature continues to inspire and guide the men in power – and even the men in opposition, who fought him for a quarter of a century. For the British, however, Charles de Gaulle remains the tall General who came to share Britain's ordeal in 1940, as much as the ill-tempered statesman who could say *non* – and often did. In Britain, of course, no one has forgotten Winston Churchill. He may at times be the object of witticism and criticism, but he still commands unanimous respect, affection and admiration. The French have not forgotten him either – perhaps because he was the symbol of liberty beckoning to them when they were enslaved, and the image of cheerfulness smiling at them when they were liberated; perhaps also because he often addressed them in a French that was as unreal as it was endearing; or perhaps after all because he loved France and they knew it.

The journey is at an end. Yet after all that, one may still wonder what General de Gaulle really thought of Winston Churchill.

'*Churchill? Un grand Artiste!*'

But then, there remains to know what Winston Churchill really thought of General de Gaulle.

'*De Gaulle? Ah! C'est l'Homme de la France!*'

Notes

INTRODUCTION

1. M. Gilbert, *W. S. Churchill*, vol. 3 (Heinemann, London, 1971), p. 535.
2. *Ibid*, p. 561.
3. Captain X, *With Winston Churchill at the Front* (Gowans, London, 1924) p. 69. Also O. Lyttelton, *Memoirs of Lord Chandos* (Bodley Head, London, 1962), p. 51.
4. Parl. Deb., House of Commons, 29 June 1931
5. *Ibid.*, 23 March 1933.
6. *Ibid.*, 7 November 1933.
7. W. Churchill, *Second World War*, vol. 1, bk. 1 (Cassell, London, 1948), p. 80.
8. House of Commons, 11 November 1936.
9. P. Guedalla, *Mr Churchill* (Hodder & Stoughton, London, 1945), p. 266.
10. R. W. Thompson, *Churchill and Morton* (Hodder & Stoughton, London, 1976), p. 148.
11. M. Gilbert, *op. cit.*, vol. 4, p. 609.
12. House of Commons, 23 November 1932.
13. R. W. Thompson, *op. cit.*, p. 21.
14. M. Gilbert, *op. cit.*, vol. 5, p. 735.
15. *Ibid.*, p. 654.
16. *Ibid.*, pp. 861, 943, 1075.
17. R. W. Thompson, *op. cit.*, p. 22.
18. M. Gilbert, *op. cit.*, vol. 5, p. 687.
19. *Ibid.*, p. 296.
20. K. Feiling, *N. Chamberlain* (Macmillan, London, 1946), p. 406.
21. M. Gilbert, *op. cit.*, vol. 5, p. 1065.
22. J. Lacouture, *De Gaulle* (Seuil, Paris, 1965), p.13.
23. C. de Gaulle, *L'Appel* (Plon, Paris, 1954), p. 2.
24. L. Nachin, *C. de Gaulle, Général de France* (Berger-Levrault, Paris, 1971), p. 33.
25. C. de Gaulle, *L'Appel, op. cit.*, p. 4.
26. C. de Gaulle, *Vers l'Armée de Métier* (Berger-Levrault, Paris, 1934).
27. *Ibid.*, p. 31.

28. R. Bouscat, *De Gaulle – Giraud* (Flammarion, Paris, 1967), p. 40.
29. J. Vendroux, *Cette chance que j'ai eue* (Plon, Paris, 1974), p. 58.
30. G. Bonheur, *Charles de Gaulle* (Gallimard, Paris, 1958), p. 80.
31. R. Tournoux, *Pétain et de Gaulle* (Paris, Plon, 1964), p. 98.
32. C. de Gaulle, *L'Appel, op. cit.*, p. 2.

CHAPTER 1

1. W. Churchill, *My Early Life* (Thornton and Butterworth, London, 1930), p. 13.
2. W. Churchill, *Complete Speeches*, R. R. James, edit. (Chelsea House, London, 1974), vol. 7, p. 7357.
3. *Ibid.*
4. C. de Gaulle, *Mémoires. L'unité*, p. 647.
5. W. Churchill, *Great Contemporaries* (Odhams, London, 1948), p. 146.
6. *Ibid.*, p. 237.
7. *Ibid.*, p. 236.
8. M. Gilbert, *W. Churchill*, vol. 4, p. 608.
9. W. Churchill, *Complete Speeches*, vol. 4, p. 3387.
10. *Ibid.*, pp. 3767–4.
11. *Ibid.*, vol. 5, p. 5059.
12. *Ibid.*, p. 5058.
13. House of Commons, vol. 276, 14 March 1933, col. 1819.
14. W. Churchill, *Complete Speeches*, vol. 5, p. 5238.
15. *Ibid.*, p. 5916.
16. R. S. Churchill, *Winston S. Churchill*, vol. 2 (Heinemann, London, 1978), p. 531.
17. W. Churchill, *Complete Speeches*, vol. 6, p. 5814.
18. House of Commons, vol. 333, 24 March 1938, p. 1443.
19. *Daily Telegraph*, 14 April 1938.
20. W. Churchill, *Complete Speeches*, vol. 6, p. 6069.
21. *Ibid.*, p. 6125.
22. M. Gilbert, *W. Churchill, op. cit.*, vol. 5, p. 786.
23. B. Liddell Hart, *The Liddell Hart Memoirs*, vol. 2 (Cassell, London, 1965), p. 303.
24. W. Churchill, *Complete Speeches*, vol. 6, p. 5916.
25. R. W. Thompson, *Churchill and Morton* (Hodder & Stoughton, London, 1976), p. 72.
26. *Chips, Diaries of Sir H. Channon* (Weidenfeld, London, 1967), p. 381.

27. M. Gilbert, *W. Churchill*, vol. 5, p. 929.
28. *Ibid.*, p. 928.
29. *Ibid.*, p. 978.
30. L. Blum, *Mémoires*, vol. 4, p. 390.
31. W. Churchill, *The Second World War* (Cassell, London, 1947), vol. 1, p. 220.
32. *Ibid.*
33. M. Gilbert, *op. cit.*, vol. 5, p. 862.
34. L. Spears, *Assignment to Catastrophe*, vol. 1 (Heinemann, London, 1954), pp. 6–7.
35. W. Churchill, *Speeches*, vol. 6, p. 6126.
36. M. Gilbert, *op. cit.*, vol. 5, p. 1075.
37. R. Tournoux, *Pétain et de Gaulle* (Plon, Paris, 1964), p. 19.
38. C. de Gaulle, *L'Appel*, p. 2.
39. Interview of General Billotte by the author, 5 April 1979.
40. *Ibid.*
41. C. de Gaulle, *Le Salut* (Plon, Paris, 1959), p. 45.
42. C. de Gaulle, *L'Appel*, p. 3.
43. C. de Gaulle, *Vers l'armeé de métier* (Berger-Levrault, Paris, 1934), p. 18.
44. C. de Gaulle, *L'Appel*, p. 3.
45. C. de Gaulle, *Vers l'armeé de métier*, p. 30.
46. J. Vendroux, *Cette chance que j'ai eue* (Plon, Paris, 1974), p. 58.

CHAPTER 2

1. J. Marin, *De Gaulle* (Paris, Hachette, 1973), p. 53.
2. W. Churchill, *Second World War*, vol. 1, p. 527.
3. W. H. Thompson, *Sixty Minutes with Churchill* (C. Johnson, London, 1953), p. 45.
4. P. Villelume, *Journal d'une défaite* (Fayard, Paris, 1976), p. 337.
5. W. Churchill, *Second World War*, *op. cit.*, vol. 2, pp. 38–9.
6. D. Dilks, *Cadogan Diaries* (Cassell, London, 1971), p. 286.
7. H. Ismay, *Memoirs* (Heinemann, London, 1960), p. 126; W. Churchill, *op. cit.*, vol. 2, p. 41.
8. W. Churchill, *op. cit.*, vol. 2, p. 42.
9. H. Ismay, *op. cit.*, p. 127.
10. *Ibid.*
11. W. Churchill, *op. cit.*, vol. 2, p. 42.
12. *Ibid.*, p. 43.

13. CAB 99/3, Supreme War Council, 11th meeting, 16/5/40.
14. Dilks, *op. cit.*, p. 285.
15. W. Churchill, *op. cit.*, vol. 2, pp. 45–6.
16. *The Private Diaries of Paul Baudouin* (Eyre and Spottiswoode, London, 1948), p. 33.
17. H. Guderian, *Erinnerungen eines Soldaten* (Vowinckel, Heidelberg, 1951), p. 99.
18. CAB 99/3, SWC, 12th meeting, 22/10/40.
19. CAB 99/3, SWC, 13th meeting, 31/10/40.

CHAPTER 3

1. House of Commons, 4 June 1940.
2. W. Churchill, *Second World War*, vol. 2, p. 46.
3. W. Churchill, *Complete Speeches*, vol. 6, p. 6221.
4. See p.
5. L. Spears, *Assignment. . .* , *op. cit.*, vol. 1, p. 165.
6. *Ibid.*, p. 167.
7. L. Spears, *op. cit.*, vol. 2, p. 70.
8. W. Churchill, *Second World War*, vol. 2, p. 128.
9. C. de Gaulle, *L'Appel*, pp. 43–4.
10. *Ibid.*
11. *Ibid.*, p. 44.
12. P. Reynaud, *Mémoires*, vol. 2 (Flammarion, Paris, 1963), p. 389.
13. See p.
14. *The Times*, 7 June 1940.
15. C. de Gaulle, *op. cit.*, pp. 47–8.
16. *Ibid.*, p. 46.
17. A. E. Dossier Dejean I. E2, 11/6/1940, Londres.
18. C. de Gaulle. *op. cit.*, p. 52.
19. W. Churchill, *Second World War*, vol. 2, p. 136.
20. CAB 99/3, SWC, 11/6/40, also: L. Spears, *op cit.*, vol. 2, pp.140–1, and P. Reynaud, *Au coeur de la mêlée* (Flammarion, Paris, 1951).
21. P. Villelume, *Journal d'une défaite* (Fayard, Paris, 1975), p. 407.
22. H. Ismay, *op. cit.*, p. 140; W. Churchill, *Second World War*, vol. 2, p. 137.
23. L. Spears, *op. cit.*, vol. 2, p. 146; CAB 99/3, SWC, 11/6/40.
24. *Ibid.* Also: Villelume, *op. cit.*, p. 410.
25. H. Ismay, *op. cit.*, p. 140; W. Churchill, *op. cit.*, vol. 2, p. 138.
26. L. Spears, *op. cit.*, vol. 2, p. 150.

27. A. Eden, *Memoirs, The Reckoning*, p. 116.
28. L. Spears, *op. cit.*, vol. 2, pp. 150–70; Villelume, p. 411; W. Churchill, vol. 2, p. 137.
29. *Ibid.*, p. 171.
30. C. de Gaulle, *L'Appel*, p. 54.
31. W. Churchill *Second World War*, vol. 2, p. 136.
32. L. Spears, *op. cit.*, vol. 2, p. 139.
33. A. Eden, *op. cit.*, p. 116.
34. W. Churchill, *Second World War*, vol. 2, p. 142.
35. C. de Gaulle, *L'Appel*, p. 54.
36. W. Churchill, *Second World War*, vol. 2, p. 142.
37. E. Loewenheim *et al., Roosevelt and Churchill* (Dutton, New York, 1975), p. 99.
38. L. Spears, *op. cit.*, vol. 2, p. 170.
39. P. Baudouin, *9 mois au Gouvernement* (Table Ronde, Paris, 1948), p. 150; Reynaud, *Mémoires, op. cit.*, vol. 2, p. 401; Spears, *op. cit.*, vol. 2, p. 224.
40. W. Churchill, *Second World War*, vol. 2, p. 158.
41. CAB 99/3, SWC, 13/6/40.
42. *Ibid.*
43. L. Spears, *op. cit.*, vol. 2, p. 203; CAB 99/3, SWC, 13/6/40.
44. P. Baudouin, *op. cit.*, p. 155.
45. H. Ismay, *op. cit.*, p. 144.
46. D. Dilks, *Cadogan Diaries, op. cit.*, p. 298.
47. W. Churchill, *Second World War*, vol. 2, p. 163.
48. L. Spears, *op. cit.*, vol. 2, pp. 205–7; P. Baudouin, p. 102; CAB 99/3, SWC
49. P. Baudouin, *op. cit.*, p. 155; P. Reynaud, *Au coeur de la mêlée*, p. 770.
50. L. Spears, *op. cit.*, vol. 2, p. 207. See also: W. Churchill, *Second World War*, vol. 2, p. 160; P. Reynaud, *Au coeur* . . . p. 771.
51. L. Spears, *op. cit.*, vol. 2, p. 210. The official minutes (CAB 99/3) agree almost word for word with this version, though they are much less precise at times.
52. P. Reynaud, *Mémoires, op. cit.*, vol. 2, p. 403.
53. L. Spears, *op. cit.*, vol. 2, p. 210. See also CAB 99/3, SWC; P. Reynaud; *Au coeur* . . . p. 771; W. Churchill, *Second World War*, vol. 2, p. 161; P. Baudouin (*op. cit.*, p. 156) naturally omits all reference at this point to Churchill's refusal to release France from her obligation. The accounts given by Spears (vol. 2) and de Margerie (in Reynaud, *Au coeur* . . .) agree word for word. J. Leasor's version in *War at the Top* (Michael Joseph, London, 1959), is unreliable.
54. C. de Gaulle, *L'Appel*, p. 57.
55. *Ibid.*, p. 57.

56. L. Spears, *op. cit.*, vol. 2, p. 216; Reynaud, *Au coeur* . . . p. 773.
57. CPA, MG.26 J.13. *Mackenzie King Diaries*, 1944. p. 653. 11 July 1944.
58. P. Reynaud, *Au coeur* . . . pp. 773–4.
59. L. Spears, *op. cit.*, vol. 2, p. 162.
60. W. Churchill, *Second World War*, vol. 2, p. 162.
61. Interview of M. Geoffroy de Courcel by the author, 24 April, 1979.
62. H. Amouroux, *Le 18 Juin 1940* (Fayard, Paris, 1964), p. 325.
63. L. Spears, *op. cit.*, vol. 2, pp. 218–19.
64. C. de Gaulle, *L'Appel*, p. 58.
65. *Ibid.*
66. *Ibid*, p. 59.
67. F. Benoist Méchin, *Soixante jours qui ébranlèrent L'Occident*, vol. 3 (Albin-Michel, Paris, 1956), p. 234.
68. C. de Gaulle, *L'Appel*, p. 59.
69. H. Ismay, *Memoirs*, *op. cit.*, p. 142.
70. W. Churchill, *Second World War*, vol. 2, p. 165.
71. *Ibid.*, p. 163.
72. J. Colville, *Footprints in Time*, p. 86.
73. W. Churchill, *Second World War*, vol. 2, p. 180.
74. J. Colville, *op. cit.*, pp. 86–7.
75. W. Churchill, *Second World War*, vol. 2, p. 181.
76. J. Colville, *op. cit.*, p. 88.
77. C. de Gaulle, *L'Appel*, pp. 63–4.
78. P. Reynaud in *Churchill by his Contemporaries* (Hutchinson, London, 1953), p. 321.
79. C. de Gaulle, *L'Appel*, p. 64.
80. W. Churchill, *Second World War*, vol. 2, p. 183.
81. J. Colville, *op. cit.*, p. 88.
82. W. Churchill, *op. cit.*, p. 183.
83. L. L. Woodward, *British Foreign Policy in the Second World War*, vol. 1 (HMSO, London, 1970), p. 280.
84. C. de Gaulle, *L'Appel*, p. 64.
85. W. Churchill, *op. cit.*, vol. 2, p. 189.
86. C. de Gaulle, *op. cit.*, p. 65.
87. J. Auburtin, *Le Colonel de Gaulle*, (Plon, Paris, 1965), p. 174.
88. C. de Gaulle, *op. cit.*, p. 63.
89. *Ibid.*, p. 65.
90. *Ibid.*
91. *Ibid.*
92. W. Churchill, *op. cit.*, pp. 191–2.
93. H. Amouroux, *op. cit.*, p. 353.
94. L. Spears, *op. cit.*, vol. 2, p. 193.
95. J. Leasor, (J) *War at the Top*, *op. cit.*, p. 92.

96. L. Spears, *op. cit.*, vol. 2, p. 323.
97. C. de Gaulle, *Le Salut*, p. 204.
98. C. de Gaulle, *L'Appel*, p. 70.
99. C. de Gaulle, *Le Salut*, p. 204.

CHAPTER 4

1. CAB 65/7, WM 171 (40) 11, 18/6/40.
2. *Ibid.*
3. C. de Gaulle, *L'Appel*, p. 71.
4. A. Gillois, *Histoire secrète des Français à Londres* (Hachette, Paris, 1973), p. 59.
5. *Cadogan Diaries*, pp. 304–6.
5bis. Lord Gladwyn, *De Gaulle*, in *The History Makers* (Sidgwick & Jackson, London, 1973), p. 364.
6. CCAC, SPRS, 1/136–2, Vansittart Committee.
7. *Ibid.*, SPRS 1/137–2b, also: C. de Gaulle, *L'Appel*, pp. 75–6; L. Spears (L): *Two Men who Saved France* (Eyre & Spottiswoode, London, 1966), p. 157; A. Weil-Curiel, *Le jour se lève à Londres*, (Myrte, Paris, 1945), p. 289; Passy, *Souvenirs*, vol. 1, *op. cit.*, p. 24.
8. CCAC, SPRS 1/137–2b, 2/7/40.
9. Passy, *Souvenirs*, vol. 1, *op. cit.*, p. 41.
10. C. de Gaulle, *L'Appel*, p. 275.
11. C. Fouchet, *Au Service du Général de Gaulle* (Plon, Paris, 1971), p. 21.
12. R. Cassin, *Les hommes partis de rien* (Plon, Paris, 1975), p.77.
13. C. de Gaulle, *L'Appel*, p. 270.
14. W. Churchill, *Second World War*, vol. 2, p. 172.
15. CAB 65/7. Winston Churchill 177 (40) 8, 23/6/40.
16. C. de Gaulle, *L'Appel*, p. 270.
17. CAB 65/7, *op. cit.*
18. *Ibid.*, WM 178 (40) 8, 24/6/40.
19. R. Cassin, *op. cit.*, p. 76.
20. CAB 65/8, 28/6/40.
21. W. Churchill, *Second World War*, vol. 2, p. 206.
22. R. Tournoux, *Pétain et de Gaulle, op. cit.*, p. 229.
23. L. Spears, *Two Men Who Saved France, op. cit.*, p. 164. See also CCAC, SPRS 1/136/1.
24. C. de Gaulle, *L'Appel*, pp. 275–6.
25. CCAC, SPRS 1/134/1 De Gaulle.
26. R. Tournoux, *Pétain et de Gaulle, op. cit.*, p. 230.

27. FO 371/24340, Richmond Temple Report, 24/9/40.
28. R. Mengin, *No laurels for de Gaulle, op. cit.*, p. 103.
29. C. de Gaulle, *L'Appel*, p. 87.
30. Parliamentary Debates, House of Commons, vol. 364, col. 1169, 20/8/40.
31. W. Churchill, *Second World War*, vol. 2, p. 566.
32. *Ibid.*, p. 569.
33. *Ibid.*, p. 579.
34. CAB 65/14, WM (40) 219th concl. conf. Annex. 5/8/40.
35. W. Churchill, *Second World War*, p. 577.
36. CCAC, SPRS 1/134/3, D. Morton to H. Dalton, 18/8/40.
37. W. Churchill, *op. cit.*, vol. 2, p. 588.
38. L. Spears, *Two men. . .* , p. 145.
39. C. de Gaulle, *The call to Honour*, Documents, pp. 24–6.
40. R. Cassin, *Les hommes . . .* , *op. cit.*, p. 105.
41. C. de Gaulle, *L'Appel*, p. 81.
42. *Ibid.*, p. 80.
43. *Ibid.*, pp. 282–3.
44. *Ibid.*, p. 88.
45. *Ibid.*, p. 90.
46. *Ibid.*, p. 97.
47. PREM 3/276, Consul General, Dakar to FO, 4/7/40.
48. CAB 80/15, COS (40) 585, 29/7/40.
49. A. Marder, *Operation Menace* (OUP London, 1976), pp. 16–17.
49bis. Gilbert, *W. Churchill*, vol. 5, p. 297.
50. C. de Gaulle, *L'Appel*, p. 97.
51. ADM 199/907 Winston Churchill to General Ismay for COSC, 8/8/40. A slightly altered version is to be found in W. Churchill, *Second World War*, vol. 2, p. 422.
52. A. Marder, *Operation Menace, op. cit.*, p. 25.
53. L. Spears, *Two Men. . .* , p. 183.
54. W. Churchill, *Second World War*, vol. 2, p. 424.
55. CCAC, SPRS 1/136/1 Dakar, 9/8/40.
56. L.E.H. Maund, *Assault from the Sea* (Methuen, London, 1949), p. 72.
57. J. R. M. Butler, *Grand Strategy*, vol. 2 (HMSO, London, 1957), p. 316.
58. *Ibid.* See also Passy, *Souvenirs*, vol. 1.
59. CCAC, SPRS 1/136/5 Hollis to Spears, 28/8/40.
60. ADM 199/1931, Lieutenant R. T. Paget to A. V. Alexander, FLA, 29/8/40.
61. L. Spears, *Two Men. . .* , p. 183; A. Marder, *Operation Menace*, pp. 47–8.
62. G. Catroux, *Dans la bataille de Mediterranée* (Julliard, Paris, 1949), p. 24.

63. W. Churchill, *Second World War*, vol. 2, p. 428.
64. CCAC, SPRS 2/6, Spears Diaries, 25/9/40.
65. R. Tournoux, *Pétain and de Gaulle, op. cit.*, p. 127.
66. CCAC, SPRS 2/6, *op. cit.*, no. 25, 26/9/40
67. *Ibid.*, 1/10/40.
68. *Daily Mirror*, 27/9/40.
69. House of Commons, Parl. Deb., vol. 365, col. 298–301, 8/10/40.
70. CPA, RG–25–D.I. vol. 779, file 378, High Commissioner for UK to Canadian Prime Minister, 25/9/40.
71. R. Murphy, *Diplomat among Warriors* (Doubleday, NY, 1964), p. 69.

CHAPTER 5

1. W. Churchill, *Second World War*, vol. 2, p. 450.
2. LSE, *Dalton Diaries*, vol. 23, 3/9/40.
3. G. Catroux, *Dans la bataille de Mediterrannée* (Julliard, Paris, 1949), p. 20.
4. *Ibid.*, p. 21.
5. C. de Gaulle, *L'Appel*, p. 113.
6. G. Catroux, *op. cit.*, p. 20.
7. L. Woodward, *British Foreign Policy*, vol. 1, p. 410.
8. CCAC, SPRS 1/136, W.C. to C. de G. no. 1256, 2/10/40.
9. *Ibid.*
10. *Ibid.* Tel. from Governor of Nigeria to Colonial Office no 1321, 3/10/40. Also: C. de G., *The Call to Honour*, Documents, p. 43.
11. C. de Gaulle, *The Call to Honour*, Documents, p. 45.
12. *Ibid.*
13. W. Churchill, *Second World War*, vol. 2, p. 454.
14. H. Ismay, *Memoirs, op. cit.*, p. 175.
15. W. Churchill, *Second World War*, vol. 2, p. 451.
16. W. Churchill, *Complete Speeches*, vol. 6, pp. 6296–8. Also W. Churchill, *Second World War*, vol. 2, p. 453.
17. FO 371/24361, Minutes of conversation between PM, S. of S. and Prof. Rougier, 25/10/40. See also: L. Rougier, *Mission secrète à Londres* (Beauchemin, Montréal, 1946), pp. 68–72.
18. CAB 65/9, WM (40) 277, 25/10/40.
19. CAB 84/21, JP (40) 577 (E), 24/10/40.
20. L. Rougier, *op. cit.*, p. 72.
21. *Ibid.*, p. 76.
22. *Ibid.*

23. *Ibid.*, pp. 81–2.
24. C. de Gaulle, *The Call to Honour*, Documents, p. 50.
25. *Ibid.*, pp. 52–3.
26. FO 371/24302, Note of informal meeting at Cabinet War Room, 31/10/40.
27. *Ibid.*
28. C. de Gaulle, *The Call to Honour*, p. 46.
29. CCAC, SPRS 2/7, Col. Williams to Gen. Spears, no. W. 33, 28/10/40.
29bis. *Cadogan Diaries*, p. 336.
30. W. Churchill, *Second World War*, vol. 2, p. 451.
31. *Ibid.*, p. 457.
32. LSE, *Dalton Diaries*, vol. 23, 14/12/40.
33. *Cadogan Diaries*, p. 337.
34. NA St. Dept. 851.01/203, Memo of conversation between Ray Atherton and N. M. Butler, British Chargé d'Affaires ad interim, 14/11/40.
35. FO 371/24361, Rougier to W.C. and Lord Halifax, 5/12/40.
36. CCAC, SPRS 1/136/8, FO Minute, 19/12/40.
37. NA St. Dept. 740.0011 EW 39/6923, from Dupuy, Canad. Chargé d'Affaires for Mr Strang, Foreign Office. Relayed to US Secretary of State by F. Matthews, US Chargé d'Affaires, tel. no. 1045, 27/11/40.
38. CPA, MG26 J4, Memo and Notes, vol. 327, file 3452, Ralston Diary, 21/12/40.
39. *Ibid.*
40. C. de Gaulle, *L'Appel*, p. 123.
41. R. Cassin, *Les hommes*, *op. cit.*, p. 236.
41bis. MEC Spears Box I/2, 'Muselier' (copies in author's possession).
42. *Cadogan Diaries*, p. 347.
43. BM, *Harvey Diary*/56397, 2/1/41.
44. *Cadogan Diaries*, p. 347.
45. *Ibid.*, p. 348.
46. Passy, *Souvenirs*, vol. 1, p. 121.
47. FO 954/8, Memo of conversation between General de Gaulle and Winston Churchill, 9/1/41.
48. C. de Gaulle, *L'Appel*, p. 126.
48bis. MEC Spears, Bx I/2, 'Muselier'
49. CCAC, SPRS 1/137/2C, Gen. Spears to Sir A. Cadogan, 17/2/41.
50. L. Spears, *Fulfilment of a Mission* (Leo Cooper, London, 1977), pp. 27–8.
51. *Ibid.*, p. 27.
52. *Ibid.*, p. 26.
53. A. Eden, *Reckoning*, p. 244.
54. *Ibid.*, p. 245.

55. *Ibid.*
56. L. Spears, *Fulfilment. . .*, p. 62.
57. C. de Gaulle, *Call to Honour*, Documents, p. 140.
58. Passy, *Souvenirs*, vol. 1, pp. 136 and 145.
59. Interview of P. O. Lapie by the author, 5/4/79.
60. CCAC, SPRS 1/137/2, *The Free French, Vichy and Ourselves*, undated memorandum.
61. *Ibid.*
62. SPRS 1/137/1, Spears to Somerville-Smith, 21/4/41, Brazzaville.
63. *Ibid.*
64. T. E. Evans, *Killearn Diaries* (Sidgwick and Jackson, London, 1972), pp. 154 and 162.
65. C. de Gaulle, *Call to Honour*, Documents, p. 142.
66. FO 954/8, Parr to FO, no. 182, 14/5/41, Brazzaville.
67. W. Churchill, *Second World War*, vol. 3, p. 650.
68. *Ibid.*, p. 651.
69. *Ibid.*, p. 653.
70. *Ibid.*, p. 657.
71. C. de Gaulle, *L'Appel*, p. 385.
72. PREM 3 120/10A, W. C. to C. de G., (Cairo) 3/4/41.
73. *Ibid.*
74. *Ibid.* W.C. to C. de G., (Brazzaville) 22/4/41.
75. W. Churchill, *Second World War*, vol. 3, p. 77.
76. *Ibid.*, p. 289.
77. *Ibid.*
78. *Ibid.*, p. 290.
79. C. de Gaulle, *Call to Honour*, p. 148.
80. *Ibid.*, p. 149.
81. *Ibid.*, p. 152.
82. *Killearn Diaries*, *op. cit.*, p. 174, 21/5/41.
83. W. Churchill, *Second World War*, vol. 3, p. 292.
84. L. Spears, *Fulfilment. . .*, p. 84.
85. W. Churchill, *Second World War*, vol. 3, p. 292.
86. MEC Spears IA, W.C. to C. de G., no. 1911, 6/6/41.
87. *Ibid.*, C. de G. to W.C., no. 1744, 7/6/41.

CHAPTER 6

1. E. Muselier, *De Gaulle contre le Gaullisme*, (Chêne, Paris, 1946), p. 218.
2. J. R. M. Butler, *Grand Strategy*, vol. 2, p. 520.

3. FO 371/28545, Minute by H. B. Mack, 4/9/41.
4. C. de Gaulle, *L'Appel*, p. 424.
5. *Ibid.*, p. 427.
6. *Ibid.*, p. 162.
7. L. Spears, *Fulfilment of a Mission*, p. 121.
8. C. de Gaulle, *L'Appel*, p. 121.
9. O. Lyttelton, *Memoirs of Lord Chandos*, p. 247; MEC, Spears Papers, Bx 1B/J, 25/7/41; L. Spears, *Fulfilment. . . , op. cit.*, p. 127.
10. *Ibid.*, p. 123.
11. O. Lyttelton, *Memoirs, op. cit.*, p. 246.
12. C. de Gaulle, *L'Appel*, p. 165.
13. L. Spears, *Fulfilment. . . , op.cit.*, p. 127.
14. C. de Gaulle, *L'Appel*, p. 165.
15. O. Lyttelton, *Memoirs*, p. 247.
16. C. de Gaulle, *L'Appel*, p. 446.
17. O. Lyttelton, *Memoirs*, p. 247.
18. L. Spears, *Fulfilment. . .* , p. 134.
19. O. Lyttelton, *Memoirs*, p. 248.
20. L. Spears, *Fulfilment. . .* , p. 136. C. de Gaulle, *L'Appel*, p. 168.
21. C. de Gaulle, *L'Appel*, p. 169.
22. L. Spears, *Fulfilment. . .* , pp. 143–5. C. de Gaulle, *L'Appel*, p. 169.
23. C. de Gaulle, *L'Appel*, p. 453.
24. C. de Gaulle, *L'Appel*, p. 172.
25. FO 371/28545, Minute by H. B. Mack, 4/9/41.
26. *Ibid.*
27. C. de Gaulle, *L'Appel*, p. 175.
28. *Ibid.*, p. 172.
29. *Ibid.*, p. 446.
30. *Ibid.*, p. 173.
31. PREM 3 120/2, Cairo to FO, no. 2661, 25/8/41 quoting tel. from Spears mission no. 70, 17/8/41, Beirut.
32. *Chicago Daily News*, 27/8/41.
33. A. Eden, *The Reckoning*, p. 249.
34. CAB 65/19, WM 87 (41) 2, 28/8/41.
35. W. Churchill, *Second World War*, vol. 2, p. 298.
36. AE/CNF37, Dejean to de Gaulle no. 472.
37. PREM 3 121/5, WP (43) 341, 7/8/43.
38. L. Spears, *Fulfilment. . .* , pp. 135–6.
39. R. Cassin, *Les hommes partis de rien*, p. 358.
40. PREM 3 121/5, WP (43) 341, 7/8/43.
41. *Ibid.*
42. FO 371/28545, from C. in C., Middle East to WO 88526, 4/8/41.
43. *Ibid.*, 20/8/41.

44. See p. 145.
45. PREM 3 120/2, 1/9/41. *C. de Gaulle's attitude to British authorities in Syria.*
46. *Ibid.*
47. Passy, *Souvenirs*, vol. 1, p. 216.
48. CPA, MG26 J.13. *King diaries*, 24/8/41.
49. PREM 3 120/5, 27/8/41.
50. *Ibid.*, P.M. to Sec. of State, 27/8/41.
51. CAB 65/19, WM 87 (41) 2, 28/8/41.
52. FO 371/28545, D. Morton, Minute 28/8/41.
53. *Ibid.*, Minute by H. B. Mack, 30/8/41.
54. *Ibid.*
55. *Ibid.*, Minute by D. Morton, 1/9/41.
56. *Ibid.*, Eden to W. Churchill, Note on C. de Gaulle, 1/9/41.
57. FO 371/28545, Conversation avec le General durant le trajet Freetown – Bathurst, 29/8/41.
58. F. Coulet, *Vertu des temps difficiles* (Plon, Paris, 1967), p. 160.
59. *Ibid.*
60. CAB 65/19, WM 88 (41) 7, 1/9/41.
61. PREM 3 120/5, W. Churchill to C. de Gaulle, 2/9/41.
62. A. J. Liebling, *The Road Back to Paris* (M. Joseph, London, 1944), p. 137.
63. H. Alphand, *L'étonnement d'être*, *op.cit.*, p. 88.
64. Liebling, *op.cit.*, p. 138.
65. PREM 3 120/5. Interview de Gaulle-Morton on 2/9/41.
66. FO 371/28545, Minute by H. B. Mack, 4/9/41.
67. PREM 3 120/5, *op. cit.*, 3/9/41.
68. *Ibid.*, C. de Gaulle to W. Churchill, 3/9/41.
69. H. Alphand, *L'étonnement. . .*, *op. cit.*, p. 89.
70. PREM 3 120/2, 'Complaints against C. de Gaulle', 2/9/41.
71. House of Commons, Parl. Deb., vol. 374, 9/9/41.
72. Colville, *Footprints. . .*, *op. cit.*, pp. 113–14.
73. PREM 3 120/2, Recording of meeting between the Prime Minister and C. de Gaulle at No. 10, 12/9/41.
74. J. Colville, *op. cit.*, pp. 114–15.
75. PREM 3 120/2, *op. cit.*

CHAPTER 7

1. PREM 3 120/5, D. Morton to W.C., 9/9/41.
2. *Ibid.*, D. Morton to W.C., 1/9/41.
3. See p. 120.
4. MEC, Spears II/5, note by Somerville-Smith, Spears Mission, 20/9/41.
5. FO 371/28545, D. Morton to H. B. Mack, 17/9/41.
6. MEC, Spears II/5.
7. *Ibid.*
8. E. Muselier, *De Gaulle contre le Gaullisme*, pp. 227–8.
9. MEC, Spears II/5, *op.cit.*, 20/9/41.
10. *Ibid.*
11. FO 371/28545, Note by H. B. Mack, 20/9/41.
12. E. Muselier, *De Gaulle, op. cit.*, p. 231. Also, MEC. Spears II/5, Note by Somerville-Smith, Spears Mission, 25/9/41.
13. C. de Gaulle, *L'Appel*, p. 221.
14. E. Muselier, *op. cit.*, p. 231.
15. MEC, *op. cit.*, 25/9/41.
16. FO 371/28545, See also Muselier, *op. cit.*, pp. 232–3.
17. E. Muselier, *op. cit.*, p. 233.
18. MEC, *op. cit.*, 25/9/41.
19. *Ibid.*
20. E. Muselier, *op. cit.*, p. 234.
21. MEC, *op. cit.*, 25/9/41.
22. PREM 3 120/4, W.C. to A. Eden, 26/9/41.
23. *Ibid.*, D. Morton to W.C., 24/9/41.
24. Passy, *Souvenirs*, vol. 1, p. 218.
25. CCAC, SPRS 2/6, C. de G. to Muselier and Fontaine, 18/9/41.
26. FO 371/28240, De Gaulle to Garreau-Dombasle, no. 107, 2/2/41.
27. C. de Gaulle, *Call to Honour*, Documents, p. 231.
28. *Ibid.*, p. 215.
29. FDR/PSF, Diplomatic, Biddle, Box 34, memorandum 26/5/41.
30. See p. 146.
31. A. Berle, *Navigating the Rapids*, p. 388.
32. P. Billotte, *Le temps des armes* (Plon, Paris, 1972), p. 187.
33. Passy, *Souvenirs*, vol. 1, p. 236.
34. C. de Gaulle, *Call to Honour*, Documents, p. 235.
35. FO 371/31873, Saint Pierre et Miquelon, diary of events.
36. *Ibid.*
37. FDR/PSF, Safe file. France, Cont. 4, St. Pierre-Miquelon.
38. *Ibid.*

39. CPA, RG–25–D.I., vol. 778, file 374, memo for Prime Minister on St. Pierre et Miquelon, 3/12/41.
40. *Ibid.*, Secr. of State for Ext. Affairs to Canadian Minister in Washington, no. 543, 19/12/41.
41. FO 371/31873, *op. cit.*, diary of events.
42. *Ibid.*
43. C. de Gaulle, *L'Appel*, p. 185.
44. *Ibid.*, p. 500.
45. PSF/Safe file, France, Cont. 4, St. Pierre-Miquelon.
46. C. Hull (C), *Memoirs*, vol. 2 (Hodder & Stoughton, London, 1948), p. 1130.
47. *Ibid.*
48. CPA, MG26,J.13, *Mackenzie King Diaries*, 1941, p. 1193, 25/12/41.
49. C. Hull, *Memoirs*, vol. 2, p. 1132.
50. *Ibid.*
51. W. Churchill, *Second World War*, vol. 3, p. 591.
52. *Ibid.*
53. Sherwood, *Roosevelt and Hopkins* (Harper, NY, 1948), p. 483.
54. C. de Gaulle, *L'Appel*, p. 503.
55. W.Churchill, *Complete Speeches*, vol. 6, p. 6543, 30/12/41.
56. BBC Speech by General de Gaulle, 31/12/41.
57. PREM 3 120/10A, C. de G. to W.C., 31/12/41.
58. C. de Gaulle, *The Call to Honour*, Documents, p. 250.
59. J. P. Lash, *Roosevelt and Churchill*, (Norton, NY, 1976), pp.15–16.
60. C. Hull, *Memoirs*, vol. 2, p. 1135.
61. E. Roosevelt (edit.), *FDR: His Personal Letters*, (Duell, NY, 1950), 1/1/42.
62. R. Sherwood, *Roosevelt and Hopkins, op. cit.*, p. 489.
63. CPA, RG–25–D.I., vol. 778, file 375, W.C. to A. Eden no. 25, 13/1/42.
64. C. de Gaulle, *L'Appel*, pp. 186–7.
65. FO 371/31873, note by A. Eden, 14/1/42.
66. *Ibid.*, 15/1/42.
67. C. de Gaulle, *Call to Honour*, Documents, p. 266.
68. MEC, SPRS 1/137/2. Somerville-Smith to Spears, 24/1/42. Also, F.O. 371/31873, note of a conversation between General de Gaulle and the Prime Minister, 22/1/42.
69. CCAC, SPRS 1/137/2, A. V. Alexander to Spears, 16/2/42.
70. CAB 65/25, WM 29 (42) 2, 5/3/42.
71. FO 954/8, record of conversation between the Secretary of State and General de Gaulle at FO, 6/3/42.
72. CCAC, SPRS 1/137/2, Peake to FO no. 16, 6/3/42.
73. C. de Gaulle, *L'Appel*, p. 223.
74. CAB 65/25, WM 34 (42) 4, 16/5/42.

CHAPTER 8

1. Passy, *Souvenirs*, vol. 2, p. 149.
2. J. R. Tournoux, *op. cit.*, p. 94.
3. Interviews of General Billotte (5/4/79), of M. Dejean (16/1/79), of M. G. Palewski (4/4/79).
4. NA St. Dept. 740.0011 EW 39/20906. F. Matthews to Secretary of State, no. 1731, 9/4/42.
5. W. Churchill, *Second World War*, vol. 4, p. 199.
6. L. Grafftey-Smith, *Hands to Play* (Routledge, London, 1975), p. 38.
7. AE CNF/93, Madagascar. Entretiens Eden-de Gaulle, 11/5/42. See also FO 954/8, Eden to Peake no. 183, 11/5/42.
8. G. Catroux, *Dans la bataille*, p. 276. Also H. Alphand, *L'étonnement d'être*, p. 114.
9. PREM 3 120/7, Eden to W.C., 27/5/42.
10. *Ibid.*, W.C. to Eden, 30/5/42.
11. PREM 3 120/10a, Minister of State, Cairo, to FO, no. 797, 10/6/42.
12. C. de Gaulle, *L'Appel*, p. 209.
13. FO 371/32097, Entretien entre M. Churchill et le General de Gaulle du 10 Juin 1942. (The record was made by the French and communicated to the Foreign Office.) See also, C. de Gaulle, *L'Appel*, p. 604, which is less complete, but more precise at times.
14. FO 371/31949, Eden to Peake 26/6/42, 29/6/42, etc. See also H. Alphand, *L'étonnement d'être*, p. 117.
15. FO 371/31949, Minister of State, Cairo, to FO no. 907, 24/6/42.
16. *Ibid.*, C. Peake to FO no. 92, 17/6/42.
17. C. de Gaulle, *L'Unité*, p. 346. See also PREM 3 120/7, Entretien du General de Gaulle avec M. Churchill, 29/7/42.
18. PREM 3 120/7, 29/7/42. (This whole passage is not reproduced in de Gaulle's memoirs).
19. See p. 142.
20. MEC, Spears Bx II/6, Spears to A. V. Alexander, 2/2/42. See also II/5, report by Somerville-Smith on Spears's mission, 29/7/42.
21. *Ibid.*, Bx IA/1, W.C. to C. de G., no. 1911, 6/6/41.
22. *Ibid.*, Bx II/4, note of a meeting between PM and General de Gaulle, 1/10/41.
23. *Ibid.*, Bx II/6, Spears to J. Hamilton, 29/1/42.
24. *Ibid.*, Spears to Minister of State, no. 696, 4/3/42.
25. *Ibid.*, Bx IA, Spears to WO, 8/7/41. See also Minister of State to FO, no. 42, 14/8/41.
26. Passy, *Souvenirs*, vol. 2, p. 214; J. Soustelle, *Envers et contre tout*, vol. 1, p. 340, etc . . . Both passages are very similar, as they are

both inspired by de Gaulle's speech of 19 June 1945. De Gaulle, however, was hardly a dispassionate observer of events in the Levant . . .

27. MEC, Spears II/5, Hamilton to Minister of State, Cairo, 25/12/41. Also *Organization of Administration in Syria and Lebanon*, Annex to War Cabinet Committee on Foreign (Allied) Resistance, CFR (CEP) (42) 2, 13/1/42.

28. On all these matters, see MEC, Spears IA; IB; I/1; II/4; II/5; II/6; also, G. Catroux, *Dans la bataille*; C. de Gaulle, *L'Appel* and *L'Unité*; S. Longrigg, *The French Mandate*; N. A. Ziadeh, *Syria and Lebanon* (E. Benn, London, 1957), etc . . .

29. Interview of M. Maurice Dejean by the author.

30. C. de Gaulle, *L'Unité*, p. 16.

31. Casey, *op. cit.*, p. 126.

32. *Ibid.*

33. *Ibid.*

34. G. Catroux, *Dans la bataille*, *op. cit.*, p. 282.

35. AE CNF 40, C. de Gaulle, to Pleven for W.C., 14/8/42.

36. MEC, Spears Diary I/1, 23/8/42.

37. *Ibid.*

38. *Ibid.*, 25/8/42.

39. *Ibid.*, 23/8/42. See also WP (43) 341, 7/8/43: 'Outline of relations between HM's Government and General de Gaulle between June 1940 and June 1943'.

40. *Ibid.*, 3/9/42.

41. AE CNF 93, Dejean to C. de G., 7/9/42. Also Passy, *Souvenirs*, vol. 2, p. 215.

42. G. Catroux, *Dans la bataille*, p. 287.

43. AE CNF 38, C. de G. to R. Pleven, no. 1170, 5/9/42.

44. BM, *Harvey Diaries*/56399, 22/9/42; J. Harvey, *War Diaries of Oliver Harvey*, 1941–45, (Collins, London, 1978), p. 159.

45. FO 371/31950, Record of a meeting between the PM, the SSFA and General de Gaulle on 30 September 1942, at 5.50 p.m.

46. C. de Gaulle, *L'Unité*, p. 33.

47. FO 371/31950, *op. cit.*

48. BM, *Harvey Diaries*/56399, 1/10/42, J. Harvey, *op. cit.*, p. 164.

49. *Ibid.*

50. J. Soustelle, *Envers et contre tout*, vol. 1, p. 365. See also Passy, *Souvenirs*, vol. 2, p. 249.

51. *Ibid.*

52. FO 371/31950, Admiral Dickens to First Lord, 2/10/42.

53. *Ibid.*, D. Morton to Lawford, 19/10/42. Also BM, *Harvey Diaries*/56399, 1/10/42.

54. H. Nicolson, *Diaries*, p. 249.

55. Interview of General Billotte by the author, 5/4/79.

56. Gillois (A), *Histoire secrète des Français à Londres* (Hachette, Paris, 1973), p. 251.

CHAPTER 9

1. For a detailed account of the affair, see: J. Soustelle, *Envers et contre tout*, vol. 1, pp. 365–7, but above all: UD U25–1/2, Conversation between Trygve Lie (Norwegian Foreign Minister) and Maurice Dejean, 3/11/42. Also: FO 371/31997, note of 20/10/42, and FO 371/31950, C. Peake to FO no. 148, 4/10/42.

2. FO 371/31997. Minute by A. Eden, 22/10/42.

3. C. de Gaulle, *L'Unité*, p. 380.

4. FO 371/31950, C. Peake to W. Strang, 31/10/42.

5. M. Clark, *Calculated Risk* (Harper, New York, 1950), p. 53.

6. *Ibid.*

7. E. Loewenheim, *Roosevelt and Churchill, op. cit.*, p. 251.

8. On all this, see: NA War Dept. ABC 336, ABC 384 and OPD 336, France, sect. I case 53. Also NA State Dept. 851.01/627A, Memo of conversation Leger-Welles, 13/8/42, and FO/954, Halifax to FO no. 573, 11/9/42. Other sources: Leahy, *I Was There*; R. Murphy, *Diplomat among Warriors*; and McGregor Burns, *Roosevelt, Soldier of Freedom*, p. 287.

9. W. Churchill, *Second World War*, vol. 4, p. 545.

10. R. Gosset, *Algiers 1941–43* (J. Cape, London, 1945), p. 52.

11. J. Soustelle, *Envers et contre tout*, vol. 1, p. 441.

12. McGregor Burns, *Roosevelt, Soldier of Freedom, op. cit.*, p. 290.

13. M. Clark, *op. cit.*, 17/10/42.

14. W. Churchill, *Second World War*, vol. 4, p. 542.

15. BM *Harvey Diaries*/56399, 5/11/42; J. Harvey, *op. cit.*, p. 177.

16. See H. Giraud, *Un seul but, la victoire* (Julliard, Paris, 1949), pp. 16–28. Also: Passy, *Souvenirs*, vol. 2, pp. 354–5.

17. FDR, *Morgenthau Diaries*, vol. 5, 12/11/42.

18. P. Billotte, *Le temps des armes*, p. 239.

19. FO 371/31950, note for Secretary of State, 8/11/42.

20. C. de Gaulle, *L'Unité*, p. 43.

21. *Ibid.*, p. 392.

22. J. Soustelle, *Envers et contre tout*, vol. 1, p. 452.

23. AE CNF 191 (Grand-Bretagne), Diplo. à Francom, Beyrouth, no. 815, 10/11/42.
24. H. Nicolson, *Diaries*, p. 256, 2/11/42.
25. C. de Gaulle, *L'Unité*, p. 393.
26. M. Clark, *Calculated Risk*, p. 107.
28. R. Gosset, *Algiers*, *op. cit.*, p. 223.
29. FDR, *Morgenthau Diaries*, vol. 5, 12/11/42. Also C. Hull, *Memoirs*, p. 1198.
30. J. Soustelle, *Envers et contre tout*, vol. 2, p. 12.
31. C. de Gaulle, *L'Unité*, pp. 403–5.
32. *Ibid.*, p. 52.
33. *Ibid.*, p. 405.
34. W. Churchill, *Second World War*, vol. 4, p. 568.
35. R. Sherwood, *Roosevelt and Hopkins*, pp. 653–4.
36. AE CFLN/1463, A. Philip & AE no. 964, 20/11/42; FO 954/8, Eden minute no. 374, 20/11/42; FDR, *Morgenthau Diaries*, vol. 5, 17/11/42.
37. M. R. D. Foote, *SOE in France* (HMSO, London, 1966), p. 221.
38. *Ibid.*
39. Prem 3 120/8, W.C. to F.D.R. no. 205, 22/11/42.
40. W. Churchill, *Second World War*, vol. 4, p. 567.
41. BM, *Harvey Diaries*/56399, 26/11/42; J. Harvey, *op. cit.*, pp. 192–3.
42. *Ibid.*, 28/11/42; J. Harvey, p. 193.
43. X.
44. UD U25–1/2, Notat av Utenriksminister Trygve Lie, 9/12/42.
45. *The Times*, 17/12/42.
46. A. Eden, *The Reckoning*, p. 359.

CHAPTER 10

1. W. Churchill, *Second World War*, vol. 4, p. 578.
2. *Ibid.*
3. *Ibid.*
4. A. Eden, *The Reckoning*, *op. cit.*, p. 359.
5. C. de Gaulle, *L'Unité*, p. 71; W. Churchill, vol. 4, p. 579.
6. J. Soustelle, *Envers et contre tout*, p. 87.
7. C. de Gaulle, *op. cit.*, p. 72.
8. J. Soustelle, *op. cit.*, p. 107; C. de Gaulle, *op. cit.*, p. 432.
9. FO 954/8, Enclosure 1 to tel. no. 42 from State Dept., 5/1/43.

10. *Ibid.*, Enclosure 2.
11. C. Hull, *Memoirs*, p. 1207.
12. FO 954/8, Eden to Vansittart, 8/1/43; Randolph Churchill to W.S.C., 28/12/42.
13. A. Eden, *The Reckoning*, p. 361.
14. FO 954/8, Eden to Halifax no. 42, 8/1/43.
15. D. D. Eisenhower, *Crusade in Europe* (Heinemann, London, 1948), p. 151.
16. R. Murphy, *Diplomat among Warriors*, p. 165.
17. R. Sherwood, *Roosevelt and Hopkins* (Harper, NY, 1948), p. 678.
18. S. Rosenmann, *Public Papers and Addresses of F. D. Roosevelt*, 1943, p. 83.
19. W. S. Thompson, *Sixty Minutes with Churchill* (C. Johnson, London, 1953), p. 71.
20. C. de Gaulle, *Unity*, Documents, p. 126.
21. M. Clark, *Calculated Risk*, p. 148.
22. H. Giraud, *Un seul but, la victoire* (Julliard, Paris, 1949), pp. 91–3.
23. H. Alphand, *L'étonnement d'être*, p. 133.
24. FO 954/8, *Minutes of Conversation Eden – de Gaulle*, 17/1/43.
25. C. de Gaulle, *L'Unité*, p. 75.
26. FRUS, Casablanca, 1943, p. 815.
27. A. Eden, *The Reckoning*, p. 363.
28. R. Murphy, *Diplomat. . .* , p. 172.
29. E. Roosevelt, *A Rendezvous with Destiny*, p. 327.
30. W. Leahy, *I Was There*, p. 173; C. Hull, *Memoirs*, vol. 2, p. 1208.
31. FRUS, Casablanca, 1943, p. 816.
32. H. Giraud, *Un seul but. . .* , pp. 98–9.
33. W. Churchill, *Second World War*, vol. 4, p. 610.
34. BM, *Harvey Diaries*/56399, 19/1/43; J. Harvey, *op. cit.*, p. 211.
35. W. Churchill, *Second World War*, vol. 4, p. 610.
36. BM, *Harvey Diaries*, *op. cit.*, 20/1/43. Also D. Dilks, *Cadogan Diaries*, p. 505 and J. Harvey, *op. cit.*, p. 211.
37. C. de Gaulle, *L'Unité*, p. 76.
38. J. Soustelle, *Envers. . .* , *op. cit.*, vol. 2, p. 119.
39. Passy, *Souvenirs*, *op. cit.*, vol. 2, p. 374.
40. J. Soustelle, *Envers. . .* , *op. cit.*, vol. 2, p. 119.
41. C. de Gaulle, *L'Unité*, p. 439.
42. E. Roosevelt, *A Rendezvous. . .* , *op. cit.*, p. 330.
43. C. de Gaulle, *L'Unité*, p. 77.
44. M. Peyrouton, *Du service public à la prison commune* (Plon, Paris, 1950), p. 224.
45. C. de Gaulle, *L'Unité*, p. 77.
46. C. H. de Boislambert, *Les Fers de l'Espoir* (Plon, Paris, 1973), p. 380.

47. C. de Gaulle, *L'Unité*, p. 77; AFF ETR CFLN 1517. Compte rendu de la conférence d'Anfa, 29/1/43.
48. H. Giraud, *Un Seul but*, *op. cit.*, p. 99.
49. W. Churchill, *Second World War*, vol. 4, p. 611.
50. C. de Gaulle, *L'Unité*, p. 78.
51. W. Churchill, *Second World War*, vol. 4, p. 611.
52. C. de Gaulle, *L'Unité*, p. 79.
53. Lord Moran, *Struggle for survival* (Constable, London, 1966), p. 81.
54. R. Sherwood, *Roosevelt and Hopkins*, *op. cit.*, p. 690.
55. *Ibid.*, p. 685.
56. E. Roosevelt, *A rendezvous*, *op. cit.*, p. 331.
57. C. H. de Boislambert, *Les Fers*, *op. cit.*, p. 381.
58. C. de Gaulle, *L'Unité*, p. 80.
59. *Ibid.*, p. 97.
60. E. Roosevelt, *op. cit.*, pp. 331–2.
60bis. FRUS, Casablanca Conference, 1943, p. 694.
60ter. *Ibid.*, pp. 695–6.
61. C. de Gaulle, *L'Unité*, p. 80.
62. Boislambert, *Les Fers*, *op. cit.*, p. 383.
63. *Ibid.*
64. C. de Gaulle, *L'Unité*, p. 84.
65. *Ibid.*, p.84. The formula can also be found in Hull, vol. 2, p. 1209.
66. C. de Gaulle, *L'Unité*, pp. 84–5.
67. J. Soustelle, *Envers*, *op. cit.*, p. 124.
68. C. de Gaulle, *L'Unité*, p. 85.
69. R. Sherwood, *Roosevelt and Hopkins*, *op. cit.*, p. 693.
70. C. de Gaulle, *L'Unité*, *op. cit.*, p. 104.
71. R. Sherwood, *Roosevelt and Hopkins*, *op. cit.*, p. 693.
72. C. de Gaulle, *L'Unité*, p. 85.
73. R. Murphy, *Diplomat*, *op. cit.*, p. 175.
74. C. de Gaulle, *L'Unité*, p. 85.
75. R. Sherwood, *Roosevelt and Hopkins*, p. 693.
76. C. de Gaulle, *L'Unité*, p. 86.
77. AE CNF 131. Pol ext/43, 28/1/43.
78. H. Macmillan, *Blast of War*, p. 265; Murphy, *op. cit.*, p. 176.
79. K. Pendar, *Adventures*, p. 148.
80. *Ibid.*
81. Moran, *Struggle for survival*, *op. cit.*, p. 81.
82. FO 954/8, Eden to Peake, 28/1/43.

CHAPTER 11

1. *France* 10/2/43.
2. FDR/PSF Dipl. France 43 Bx 42. Stark to Hull for Roosevelt, 14/2/43.
3. *France* 10/2/43.
4. BM, *Harvey Diaries*/56399, 9/2/43; J Harvey, p. 218.
5. J. W. Wheeler-Bennett, *King George VI* (Macmillan, London, 1958), p. 560.
6. FO 371/36047, Strong minute, 10/2/43.
7. A. Eden, *The Reckoning*, p. 367.
8. W. Churchill, *Second World War*, vol. 4, p. 657.
9. FO 371/36064, Guidance for the press, 5/3/43.
10. BM, *Harvey Diaries*/56399, 28/2/43; J. Harvey, p. 224.
11. *Ibid.*, 3/3/43.
12. C. de Gaulle, *Unity*, Documents, pp. 139–40.
13. H. Nicolson, *Diaries*, p. 284, 12/3/43.
14. FO 954/8, Telegram Eden to Halifax, no. 135, 4/2/43.
15. NA St. Dept. 741.51/2.1343. W.C. to F.D.R., 12/2/43.
16. A. Eden, *The Reckoning*, p. 372.
17. C. Hull, *Memoirs*, vol. 2, p. 1213.
18. *Ibid.*, p. 1215.
19. A. Eden, The Reckoning, pp. 372–3.
20. R. Sherwood, *Roosevelt and Hopkins, op. cit.*, p. 720.
21. FO 954/8, W.C. to Eden, Tel. no. 2077, 30/3/43.
22. FO 371/36047, C. Peake to H. B. Mack, 23/3/43.
23. Birkenhead, *Halifax* (H. Hamilton, London, 1965), p. 537.
24. AE CFLN/1463, dossier Massigli. Notes on conversation de Gaulle/Churchill, 2/4/43; Woodward, *BFP* II, p. 427; C. de G., *L'Unité*, p. 96.
25. C. de Gaulle, *L'Unité*, p. 96.
26. A. L. Funk, *The crucial years*, p. 115.
27. W. Churchill, *Complete Speeches*, vol. 7, p. 6767, 7/4/43.
28. AE CFLN/1463, Tixier,Washington, to Massigli, London, no. 1576, 9/4/43.
29. LSE, *Dalton Diaries*, vol. 28, 1943, p. 99, 6/4/43.
30. R. Bouscat, *Dossier d'une mission*, pp. 93–4.
31. *Ibid.*, p. 115.
32. *Ibid.*, pp. 127–8.

34. BM, *Harvey Diaries*/56399, 30/4/43; J. Harvey, p. 252.
35. C. de Gaulle, *L'Unité*, p. 99.
36. C. Hull, *Memoirs*, pp. 1217–18.
37. Birkenhead, *Halifax, op. cit.*, p. 537.
38. FO 371/36047, Memo for W.S.C., 8/5/43.
39. C. Hull, *Memoirs*, pp. 1218–19.
40. CPA MacKenzie King Diaries, 19/5/43.
41. J. M. Blum, *Diary of H. Wallace* (Houghton, Boston, 1973), p. 202.
42. FO 371/36047, Winant to S.S., Wash no. 3413, 17/5/43.
43. C. Hull, *Memoirs*, p. 1219.
44. FO 371/36047, PM to Dep.PM & FS. Pencil no. 166, 21/5/43.
45. *Ibid.*, PM to FS. Pencil no. 181, 21/5/43.
46. C. de Gaulle, *Discours*, vol. 1, pp. 284–90.
47. C. de Gaulle, *L'Unité*, p. 101.
48. CAB 65/38, WM (43) 75th Concl. Minute 1, Conf. Annex, 23/5/43.
49. A. Eden, *Reckoning*, p. 386.
50. CAB 65/38, Telegr. Alcove 370, For PM from Dep.PM & FS, 23/5/43.
51. *Ibid.*, Alcove 371, 23/5/43.
52. *Ibid.*, Alcove 372. 23/5/43.
53. FO 371/36047, PM to Dep.PM & FS. Pencil no. 227, 24/5/43.
54. W. Churchill, *Second World War*, vol. 4, p. 716.
55. C. de Gaulle, *L'Unité*, pp. 101–2.
56. *Ibid.*, p. 102.
57. W. Churchill, *Second World War*, vol. 4, p. 729.
58. FDR/MR Special File FNC/Sect. 1. For President from Murphy No. 996, 30/5/43. Also a censored version in FRUS 1943, vol. 2, p. 127.
59. C. Paillat, *L'échiquier d'Alger* (Laffont, Paris, 1967), p. 250.

CHAPTER 12

1. C. de Gaulle, *L'Unité*, p. 108.
2. *Ibid.*, p. 110.
3. Loewenheim, *Roosevelt and Churchill*, p. 338, W.C. to F.D.R. no. 300, 6/6/43.
4. AE CFLN/1464, Conversation Massigli–Eden, 17/7/43.
5. PREM 3 121/1, Circular signed W.S.C., 12/6/43.
6. *The Observer*, 13/6/43.
7. AE CFLN/1463, Rapport de M. Viénot du 20/6/43. The article was originally a memorandum for the information of Cabinet members,

but it was also communicated to the press, and *The Observer* published it almost *in extenso*.

8. *Cadogan Diaries*, p. 536, 15/6/43.
9. PREM 3 181/2, F.D.R. to W.C. no. 288, 17/6/43.
10. FDR/MR Secret File FNC 1 sect. I, F.D.R. to Eisenhower, no. 493, 17/6/43.
11. *Ibid.*, Special Files FNC Bx. 13, sect. I, F.D.R. to Eisenhower, 17/6/43.
12. *Ibid.*, Secret File *op. cit.*, F.D.R. to Eisenhower, no. 511, 17/6/43.
13. A. Eden, *The Reckoning*, pp. 397–8.
14. L. Woodward, *British Foreign Policy*, vol. 2, p. 452.
15. A. Eden, *The Reckoning*, p. 398.
16. W. Churchill, *Second World War*, vol. 5, pp. 159–60.
17. PREM 3 181/2, W.C. to F.D.R. no. 373, 21/7/43.
18. W. Churchill, *op. cit.*, vol. 5, pp. 160–1.
19. FO 954/8, W.C. to Halifax, no. 4665, 15/7/43.
20. *Ibid.*, W.C. to Macmillan, no. 20, 23/7/43.
21. Parl. Deb., House of Commons, vol. 391, col. 170, 14/7/43.
22. *Ibid.*, 21/7/43. col. 870.
23. *Ibid.*, col. 1553.
24. *Ibid.*, col. 2272, 4/8/43.
25. CPA, MG26 J.13, MacKenzie King Diaries, 10/8/43, p. 629.
26. A. Eden, *The Reckoning*, p. 402.
27. AE CFLN/1464, Viénot à Massigli, no. 963, 2/9/43.
28. A. Eden, *The Reckoning*, p. 402.
29. FRUS, Quebec, 1943, pp. 916–17.
30. C. Hull, *Memoirs*, vol. 2, p. 1241.
31. W. Churchill, *Second World War*, vol. 5, p. 80.
32. C. Hull, *Memoirs*, *op. cit.*
33. FRUS, Quebec, 1943, pp. 1170–1.
34. FO 954/8, Eden to Macmillan, 11/10/43.
34bis. MVBZ, Londens Archief, Politieke Rapporten/Algiers. Dutch Envoy, Algiers, to Minister Van Kleffens, no. 91/30, 21/10/43.
35. This was frankly admitted in confidential reports by the French themselves. See AE CNF/Londres, dossier 44, Helleu à CNF no. 986, 22/6/43, and no. 422, 26/6/43. See also MEC Spears II/4.
36. MEC, Spears III/3, Memorandum on elections, 25/10/43.
37. See for instance C. de Gaulle, *L'unité*, p. 194.
38. AE CNF/1480, Massigli a Viénot, 20/11/43.
39. AE CFLN/1464, Rapport de M. Massigli sur l'entrevue avec Eden, 10/10/43.
40. AE 1468, Syrie-Liban 43–4, Catroux à de Gaulle, no. 1614, 23/11/43.

41. MVBZ, Londens Archief, G II, Syrië en Libanon, Doos 47, Chargé d'Affaires Bentinck to Foreign Minister Van Kleffens, no. 3738, 19/11/43.

CHAPTER 13

1. C. Paillat, *L'échiquier d'Alger*, *op. cit.*, p. 355.
2. L. Woodward, *British Foreign Policy*, vol. 3, p. 2.
3. FDR/MR, Special File FNC, 1 sect. 3. W.C. to F.D.R., no. 504, 13/11/43.
4. PREM 3 182/3, W.C. to Foreign Secretary, Frozen no. 779, 21/12/43.
5. *Ibid.*, W.C. to F.D.R. no. 513, 21/12/43.
6. NA St. Dep. 851.01/12. 2243 Secret memorandum by H. F. Matthews, 22/12/43.
7. L. Woodward, *British Foreign Policy*, vol. 3, p. 6.
8. FO 954/8, Macmillan to A. Eden, no. 2784, 23/12/43.
9. L. Woodward, *British Foreign Policy*, vol. 3, pp. 6–7.
10. FDR/MR Special File, *op. cit.*, Memo by General Bedell-Smith to F.D.R., 25/12/43.
11. PREM 3 182/3, W.C. to FS, Frozen 875, 25/12/43.
12. H. Macmillan, *Blast of War*, p. 441.
13. F. Coulet, *Vertu*, p. 215.
14. W. Churchill, *Second World War*, vol. 5, p. 401.
15. FO 954/9, Resident Minister, Algiers to FS no. 24, 3/1/44.
16. H. Macmillan, *Blast of War*, pp. 447–8.
17. C. de Gaulle, *L'Unité*, p. 214.
18. E. d'astier, *Les dieux et les hommes* (Julliard, Paris, 1952), p. 28.
19. Diana Cooper, *Trumpets from the Steep* (R. H. Davis, London, 1960), p. 178. Duff Cooper, *Old Men Forget*, *op. cit.*, pp. 318–19.
20. FDR/MR Bx. 13, Hopkins 44, W.C. to H. Hopkins, 11/1/44.
21. Duff Cooper, *op. cit.*, p. 319.
22. Diana Cooper, *op. cit.*, p. 179.
23. W. Churchill, *Second World War*, vol. 5, p. 401.
24. Duff Cooper, *op. cit.*, p. 319.
25. W. Churchill, *op. cit.*, p. 401.
26. Duff Cooper, *op. cit.*, p. 319.
27. PREM 3 181/10, W.C. to F.D.R., no. 559, 30/1/44.
28. *Ibid.*, Duff Cooper to FS, no. 19, 16/1/44.
29. AE CFLN/1464, Compte-rendu de l'entretien entre le General de Gaulle et W. Churchill à Marrakech, 12/1/44.

30. PREM 3 181/10, Duff Cooper to FS, *op. cit.*
31. *Ibid.*, and AE CFLN/1464, *op. cit.*
32. *Ibid.*
33. E. d'Astier, *Sept fois sept jours* (Gallimard, Paris, 1961), p. 167.
34. Duff Cooper, *op. cit.*, p. 179.
35. PREM 3 181/10, HM's Consul to Mr A. N. W. Napier, no. 4, 15/1/44.
36. *Ibid.*, Duff Cooper to FS, 16/1/44.
37. C. de Gaulle, *L'Unité*, p. 216.
38. PREM 3 181/10, *op. cit.*
39. E. d'Astier, *Sept fois, op. cit.*, p. 167.
40. *Ibid.*, p. 171.
41. *Ibid.*, p. 172.
42. J. Soustelle, *Envers, op. cit.*, vol. 2, p. 356.
43. PREM 3 177/6, W.C. to FS, 26/1/44.
44. E. d'Astier, *Les dieux, op. cit.*, p. 94.
45. PREM 3 177/6, W.C. to FS, 26/1/44.
46. AE CFLN, 1483, W.C. to C. de G. and Gen. Giraud, 2/2/44.
47. NA St. Dep. 851.01/3–2444, Memo of conversation between the President and the Hon. Edwin C. Wilson.
48. *Ibid.*, Ref. subj. files, Memo for S. S. Hull from F.D.R., Cairo, 27/11/43.
49. Blum, *Morgenthau Diaries, op. cit.*, p. 168.
50. FO 954/9, Halifax to FS, no. 550, 3/2/44.
51. *Ibid.*, FS to Duff Cooper, no. 119, 30/3/44.
52. AE CFLN/1464, Viénot to C. de G., no. 1696 Diplo, 31/3/44.
53. A. Eden, *The Reckoning, op. cit.*, p. 447.
54. AE CFLN/1480, Record on interview between W.C. and Ambassador Viénot at 10, Downing Street, 4/4/44 and *Harold Nicolson's diaries*, p. 359.
55. AE CFLN/1464, Massigli to Duff Cooper, 19/4/44.
56. C. Hull, *Memoirs*, vol. 2, p. 1429.
57. *Daily Herald*, 29/3/44.
58. *Times*, 5–6/4/44.
59. *Daily Mirror*, 5/4/44.
60. C. Hull, *op. cit.*, vol. 2, p. 1430.
61. L. Woodward, *British Foreign Policy*, vol 3, pp. 33–4.
62. FDR/MR, Bx 31, Special Files, French Civil Affairs, F.D.R. to W.C. no. 521, 13/4/44.
63. FO 954/9, Duff Cooper to W.C., no. 438, 4/4/44.
64. *Ibid.*, W.C. to Duff Cooper, 14/4/44.
65. *Ibid.*, W.C. to Duff Cooper, no. 353, 16/4/44.
66. *Ibid.* W.C. to F.D.R., 20/4/44.

68. *Ibid.*, W.C. to F.D.R., no. 656, 22/4/44.
69. FDR/MR, *op. cit.*, French Civil Affairs, memo for F.D.R. from S. S. Hull, 24/4/44.
70. FO 954/9, W.C. to F.D.R., no. 67, 24/4/44.
71. FDR/MR, *op. cit.*, W.C. to F.D.R., no. 643, 12/4/44.
72. C. de Gaulle, *L'Unité*, p. 220.
73. L. Woodward, *British Foreign Policy*, *op. cit.*, vol. 3, pp. 40–1.
74. C. de Gaulle, *Discours et Messages*, vol. 1, p. 405.
75. L. Woodward, *British Foreign Policy*, *op. cit.*, vol. 3, p. 42.
76. *House of Commons*, Parl. Deb. vol. 399, col. 179, 19/4/44.
77. *Ibid.*, col. 1295, 3/5/44.
78. FDR/MR, Map Room SF Cont. 31.011. France, civil affairs, W.C. to F.D.R., no. 674, 12/5/44.
79. L. Woodward, *British Foreign Policy*, vol. 3, p. 43.
80. CPA, MG 26 J.13, *Mackenzie King Diaries*, 13/5/44.
81. FO 371/41992, W.C. to FS, 14/5/44.
82. *Ibid.*, W.C. to FS, Eisenhower, Ismay, 16/5/44.
83. *Ibid.*, FS to W.C.
84. C. de Gaulle, *L'Unité*, p. 221.
85. FO 371/41992, *op. cit.*, no. 615, 23/5/44.
86. C. de Gaulle, *L'Unité*, p. 221.
87. *Times*, 15/5/44.
88. *Manchester Guardian*, 16/5/44.
89. *Daily Mail*, 23/5/44.
90. *House of Commons*, Parl. Deb., vol. 400, col. 780–1, 24/5/44.
91. *Ibid.*, col. 790–1.
92. *Ibid.*, col. 830.
93. *Ibid.*, col. 860.
94. *Ibid.*, col. 885–6.
95. *Times, Manchester Guardian, Daily Mail,* 25/5/44; *Economist,* 27/5/44.
96. FDR/MR, Bx 31, *op. cit.*, W.C. to F.D.R., no. 682, 27/5/44.
97. FO 371/41992, W.C. to F.D.R., no. 684, 27/5/44.
98. FDR/MR, Bx 31, *op. cit.*, Ambassador Harriman to F.D.R., no. M.18773, 29/5/44.
99. *Ibid.*, F.D.R. to W.C., no. 544, 27/5/44.
100. *Ibid.*, and FRUS 1944. vol. III, pp. 693–4; F.D.R. to W.C., no. 546, 31/5/44.
101. C. de Gaulle, *L'Unité*, p. 637.
102. *Ibid.*
103. A. Eden, *Reckoning*, *op. cit.*, p. 452.
104. FO 371/41993, H. B. Mack to A. Cadogan, 31/5/44.

105. A. Eden, *Reckoning*, p. 452.
106. C. de Gaulle, *Unity*, Documents, p. 337.
107. Duff Cooper, *Old Men . . .* pp. 328–9.
108. Duff Cooper, *Old Men . . .* p. 329.

CHAPTER 14

1. FDR/MR, Bx 31, Special Files, French Civil Affairs, W.C. to F.D.R., no. 688, 1/6/44.
2. C. de Gaulle, *Unity*, Documents, p. 337.
3. A. Eden, *Reckoning*, p. 453.
4. Duff Cooper, *Old Men . . .* p. 330.
5. A. Eden, *Reckoning*, *op. cit.*, p. 452.
6. E. Béthouart, *Cinq années d'espérance* (Plon, Paris, 1968), p. 241.
7. CAB 66/50, Record of a conversation between the PM and C. de Gaulle, 4/6/44.
8. C. de Gaulle, *L'Unité*, p. 223.
9. CAB 66/50, *op. cit.*
10. E. Béthouart, *Cinq années*, *op. cit.*, p. 243.
11. FO 954/9, Notes of conversation between the PM and C. de G. at luncheon on 4/6/44.
12. CAB 66/50, *op. cit.*
13. FO 954/9, *op. cit.*
14. *Ibid.*
15. C. de Gaulle, *L'Unité*, p. 224.
16. E. Béthouart, *Cinq années*, *op. cit.*, p. 243.
17. CAB 66/50, *op. cit.*
18. *Ibid.*
19. C. de Gaulle, *op. cit.*, p. 224.
20. E. Bethouart, *Cinq années*, *op. cit.*, p. 243.
21. W. Churchill, *Second World War*, vol. 5, p. 556.
22. C. de Gaulle, *op. cit.*, p. 225.
23. E. Béthouart, *Cinq années*, *op. cit.*, p. 244.
24. C. de Gaulle, *op. cit.*, p. 225.
25. *Ibid.*
26. W. Churchill, *op. cit.*, vol. 5, p. 556.
27. C. de Gaulle. *op. cit.*, p. 226.
28. *Ibid.*
29. *Cadogan Diaries*, *op. cit.*, p. 634.

30. A Gillois, *Histoire secrète des Français à Londres*, 40–4 (Hachette, Paris, 1973), p. 23.
31. E. d'Astier, *Les dieux et les hommes*, p. 146; E. Béthouart, *Cinq années*, *op. cit.*, p. 245.
32. E. d'Astier, *op. cit.*, p. 146.
33. FO 954/9, Report of conversation by M. A. Eden, 6/6/44.
34. A. Gillois, *op. cit.*, p. 24.
35. Duff Cooper, *Old Men . . . op. cit.*, p. 331; d'Astier, *op. cit.*, p. 147.
36. B. Lockhart, *Comes the Reckoning* (Putnam's, London, 1947), p. 301.
37. FO 954/9, Note to Foreign Secretary, 6/6/44.
38. *Cadogan Diaries*, *op. cit.*, p. 635.
39. *Ibid.*
40. C. de Gaulle, *L'Unité*, p. 227.
41. B. Lockhart, *op. cit.*, p. 635.
42. A. Eden, *Reckoning*, *op. cit.*, p. 454.
43. *Ibid.*, p. 455.
44. BM, *Harvey Diaries*/56400, 7/6/44; J. Harvey, p. 343.
45. FO 371/41993, Record by Mr Duff Cooper of a conversation with General de Gaulle, 6/6/44.
46. A. Gillois, *Histoire secrète*, *op. cit.*, p. 30.
47. A. Eden, *Reckoning*, pp. 454–5.
48. AE CFLN/1465, General de Gaulle to Queuille, Massigli, Pleven, etc . . . no. 2932, 6/6/44.
49. F.D. Lowenheim, *op. cit.*, p. 523, doc. 372, W.C. to F.D.R., 7/6/42.
50. BM, *Harvey Diaries*/56400, 9/6/44; J. Harvey, p. 343.
51. *Ibid.*
52. FO 371/41994, W.C. to Eden, 1774/D, 13/6/44.
53. *Ibid.*
54. *House of Commons*, Parl. Deb. vol. 400, col. 1950 to 1957, 14/6/44.
55. FO 954/9, Summary of a report by an officer of the British Intelligence Corps, 14/6/44.
56. R. Tournoux, *Pétain et de Gaulle*, p. 316.
57. E. Béthouart, *Cinq années*, *op. cit.*, p. 247.
58. C. de Gaulle, *L'Unité*, p. 229.
59. R. Aron, *Histoire de la libération de la France*, (Fayard, Paris, 1959), p. 78.
60. C. de Gaulle, *L'Unité*, p. 231.
61. E. Béthouart, *Cinq années*, *op. cit.*, p. 251.
62. FO 371/41994, Report on General de Gaulle's visit to Normandy, by Commander Pinks, 14/6/44.
63. *Ibid.*
64. A. Eden, *Reckoning*, p. 457.
65. FO 371/41993, Mr Eden to Mr Holman, Algiers, no. 235, 16/6/44.

66. C. de Gaulle, *L'Unité*, p. 231.
67. FO 371/41993, *op. cit.*
68. C. de Gaulle, *L'Unité*, p. 231.
69. *Ibid.*, p. 646.
70. C. de Gaulle, *Unity*, Documents, p. 345.
71. Duff Cooper, *Old Men . . .* p. 334.
72. FO 954/9, Duff Cooper to Eden, 16/6/44.

CHAPTER 15

1. FDR/MR, Bx 31, Spec. files, French civ. aff., F.D.R. to W.C., no. 552, 4/6/44.
2. FDR/PSF, Dipl. France, 44–5, Bx 42, C. de G. to F.D.R., 14/6/44.
3. *Ibid,* – Cont. 34. France 44/45, C. de G. to F.D.R., 26/6/44.
4. *Ibid.,* – Box 42, Memo for C. de G. from F.D.R., 27/6/44.
5. H. L. Stimson, *On Active Service*, p. 546.
6. *Ibid.*, p. 551.
7. W. D. Hassett, *Off the Record*, p. 257.
8. CPA, MG26 J.13, *Mackenzie King Diaries*, 11/7/44.
9. BM, *Harvey Diaries*/56400, 15/7/44.
10. *Ibid.*
11. L. Woodward, *British Foreign Policy*, vol. 4, p. 76.
12. Duff Cooper, *Old Men . . .* pp. 334.
13. Parl. Deb. House of Commons, vol. 402, col. 1479 – 1480, 2/8/44.
14. Duff Cooper, *Old Men . . .* pp. 335–6.
15. E. d'Astier, *Les Dieux*, p. 160.
16. PREM 3 121/3, C. de G. to P.M. (Col. Kent), 11/8/44.
17. W. Churchill, *Second World War*, vol. 4, p. 79.
18. PREM 3 121/3, W.C. to Eden, 12/8/44.
19. *Ibid.*, W.C. to Eden, tel. no. 105, 18/8/44.
20. Diana Cooper, *Trumpets*, p. 212.
21. FDR/Morgenthau, vol. 6, p. 1453, Quebec, 15/9/44.
22. CPA, MG26 J.13, *Mackenzie King Diaries*, 11/9/44, p. 811.
23. *Ibid.*, p. 818.
24. *Ibid.*, p. 862.
25. A. Eden, *The Reckoning*, p. 477.
26. FDR/PSF Dipl. France 44–5, Box 42, Memo for SS from F.D.R., 19/9/44.
27. Parl. Deb., House of Commons, vol. 403, col. 495, 28/9/45.

28. *Ibid.*, col. 620 and 625, 29/9/44.
29. *Franc Tireur*, 5 October 1944, quoted in A. L. Funk, *Crucial Years*, p. 292.
30. *Harold Nicolson's Diaries*, p. 403.
31. Parl. Deb., House of Commons, vol. 403, col. 2350, 18/10/44.
32. A. Eden, *Reckoning*, p.483, 12/10/44.
33. W. Churchill, *Second World War*, vol. 6, p. 215; Loewenheim, *Roosevelt and Churchill*, p. 585.
34. PREM 3 177/7, F.D.R. to W.C., Drastic no. 180, 20/10/44.
35. FO 951/9, A. Cadogan to SSFA, no. 1589, 20/10/44.
36. *Cadogan Diaries*, p. 674.
37. Loewenheim, *op. cit.*, p. 593, tel. no. 803, 23/10/44.
38. *Cadogan Diaries*, pp. 674–5.
39. C. de Gaulle, *Le Salut*, p. 338.
40. G. Bidault, *D'une résistance à l'autre* (Presses du Siècle, Paris, 1965), p. 72.
41. Duff Cooper, *Old Men* . . . p. 340.
42. FO 951/9, Duff Cooper to W.C., no. 355, 2/11/44.
43. L. Woodward, *British Foreign Policy*, vol. 3, p. 86.
44. BM, *Harvey Diaries*/56400, 11/11/44; J. Harvey, p. 365.
45. C. de Gaulle, *Le Salut*, p. 51.
46. W. Churchill, *Second World War*, vol. 6, p. 218.
47. Duff Cooper, *Old Men* . . . p.340.
48. W. Churchill, *op. cit.*, vol. 6, p. 218.
49. Duff Cooper, *Old Men* . . . p. 341.
50. H. Ismay, *Memoirs, op. cit.*, p. 381.
51. W. Churchill, *op. cit.*, vol. 6, p. 218.
52. H. Ismay, *Memoirs, op. cit.*, p. 387.
53. Duff Cooper, *Old Men* . . . p. 341.
54. W. Churchill, *op. cit.*, vol. 6, p. 218.
55. C. de Gaulle, *Le Salut*, p. 49.
56. *Ibid.*, p. 359.
57. W. Churchill, *Speeches*, vol. 7, p. 7031.
58. C. de Gaulle, *Le Salut*, p. 49.
59. Duff Cooper, *Old Men* . . . p. 341.
60. C. de Gaulle, *Le Salut*, pp. 350–9.
61. P. Galante, *De Gaulle*, p. 119.
62. G. Bidault, *D'une résistance à l'autre*, p. 72.
63. H. Nicolson, *Diaries*, vol. 2, p. 412.
64. W. Churchill, *Speeches*, vol. 7, pp. 7031–3.
65. E. d'Astier, *Les dieux*, p. 164.
66. C. de Gaulle, *Le Salut*, pp. 51–2.
67. *Ibid.*

68. W. Churchill, *op. cit.*, vol. 6, p. 219.
69. C. de Gaulle, *op. cit.*, p. 52.
70. *Ibid.*
71. *Ibid.*, p. 53.
72. *Ibid.*, p. 54.

CHAPTER 16

1. FO 371/42117, W.C. to F.D.R., no. 822, 15/11/44.
2. Parl. Deb., House of Commons, 8/12/44.
3. MEC, Spears Papers, Box I/1, 15/12/44.
4. AE CFLN/1468, Syrie – Liban, Entretien Massigli – Duff Cooper, 22/6/44.
5. J. Colville in *Action This Day* (Macmillan, London, 1968), p. 51.
6. C. de Gaulle, *Le Salut*, p. 149; A. Bryant, *Triumph in the West*, (Collins, London, 1959), p. 374.
7. W. Churchill, *Second World War*, vol. 6, p. 245.
8. A. Juin, *Mémoires*, vol. 2 (Fayard, Paris, 1960), pp. 85–6.
9. Duff Cooper, *Old Men . . .* p. 348.
10. FRUS, Yalta and Malta, p. 286.
11. FO 951/9, Winston Churchill to A. Eden, 19/1/45.
12. *Ibid.*, 11/1/45.
13. FRUS, Yalta and Malta, 1945, p. 573.
14. *Ibid.*, p. 629.
15. *Ibid.*, pp. 710 and 718.
16. *Ibid.*, p. 899.
17. See C. de Gaulle, *Le Salut*, p. 184.
18. MEC, *Shone Papers*, British Legation, Beirut, to FO no. 69, 30/4/45.
19. *Ibid.*, Spears II/6, Spears to A.E. 28/8/44. Also Woodward, *British Foreign Policy*, vol. 4, p. 301.
20. C. de Gaulle, *Le Salut*, p. 185.
21. See p. 200.
22. MEC, *Shone Papers*, British Legat. to FO no. 69, 30/4/45.
23. *Ibid.*, p. 3.
24. Parl. Deb., House of Commons, 27/2/45.
25. FO 954/9, Winston Churchill to Duff Cooper, 8/5/45.
26. *Ibid.*, 10/5/45.
27. MEC, *Shone Papers*, T. Shone to A.E., 25/8/45.
27bis. L. Woodward, *British Foreign Policy*, vol. 4, p. 332.
28. MEC, *Shone Papers*, *op. cit.*

29. Duff Cooper, *Old Men* . . . p. 353.
30. MEC, *Shone Papers, op. cit.*, p. 10. This is confirmed by J. Chauvel, *Commentaire*, vol. 2 (Fayard, Paris, 1972), p. 103.
31. *Ibid.*
32. C. de Gaulle, *Le Salut*, p. 190.
33. MEC, *Shone Papers, op. cit.*, pp. 12–13. See also FRUS, 1945, vol. 8, (Near East), p. 1115.
34. *Shone Papers. Ibid.*
35. G. Catroux, *Dans la bataille*, p. 211, ('un état d'émotivité maladive.')
36. C. de Gaulle, *Le Salut*, p. 190.
37. *Ibid.*
38. W. Churchill, *Second World War*, vol. 6, p. 491.
39. C. de Gaulle, *Le Salut*, p. 192.
40. L. Woodward, *British Foreign Policy*, vol. 4, p. 335.
41. C. de Gaulle, *Le Salut*, pp. 193–4.
42. MEC, *Shone Papers, op. cit.*, pp. 17–19. Also FRUS, 1945. vol. 8, pp. 1131–3, Report by Minister Wadsworth to the US Secretary of State, 2/6/45.
43. C. de Gaulle, *Le Salut*, p. 194.
44. Duff Cooper, *Old Men* . . . p. 354.
45. J. Vendroux, *Cette chance que j'ai eue*, p. 124.
46. G. Bidault, *D'une résistance à l'autre*, p. 105.
46bis. MVBZ, Londens Archief G II, Syrië en Libanon, Doos 47, Ambassador de With to Foreign Minister van Kleffens, no. 3197, 30/6/45.
47. C. de Gaulle, *Le Salut*, p. 181.
48. W. Churchill, *Second World War*, vol. 6, p. 492.
49. Parl. Deb., House of Commons, 5/6/45.
50. W. Leahy, *I Was There*, (Gollancz, London, 1950), p. 441.
51. PREM 3 121/5, Winston Churchill to H. Truman, 3/6/45.
53. PREM 3 121/5, Truman to Winston Churchill, no. 60, 6/6/45.
54. *Ibid.*, Winston Churchill to Truman, no. 77, 7/6/45.
55. FO 954/9, Winston Churchill to Law, 10/6/45.
56. FO 954/9, Winston Churchill to Sir A. Cadogan, 23/6/45.
57. *Ibid.*, FO to Ambassador, Paris, no. 1182, 28/6/45.
58. Moran, *Struggle for Survival*, p. 263.
59. Duff Cooper, *Old Men* . . . p. 357.
60. FRUS, Potsdam, 1945, vol. 2, p. 136.
61. *Ibid.*, pp. 315–19.
62. C. de Gaulle, *Le Salut*, p. 203.
63. *Ibid.*, pp. 204–5.
64. *Ibid.*, p. 208.
65. *Ibid.* p. 554.

66. CPA, MG26 J.13, *Mackenzie King Diaries*, 1945, 28/8/45, p. 827.
67. BM *Harvey Diaries*/56400, 13/8/45.
68. BDL, Attlee Papers, Bx 4, (*Churchill*), D. Cooper to C. Attlee, 25/10/45.
69. C. de Gaulle, *Le Salut*, p. 273.
70. Duff Cooper, *Old Men . . .* p. 358.

CHAPTER 17

1. C. de Gaulle, *Le Salut*, p. 274.
2. G. Bidault, *D'une résistance à l'autre*, p. 80.
3. NA St. Dep. Office of European Affairs, Bx 13, Chipman, April 1946.
4. C. de Gaulle, *Le Salut*, p. 645.
5. C. de Gaulle, *Discours et Messages*, Dans l'Attente, pp. 594–5.
6. W. Churchill, *Complete Speeches*, vol. 7, p. 7381.
7. See p. 28.
8. W. Churchill, *Complete Speeches*, vol. 7, p. 7485.
9. *Ibid.*, p. 7726.
10. *Ibid.*, See vol. 8, p. 7981.
11. *Ibid.*, p. 7982.
12. P. Galante, *The General* (L. Frewin, London, 1968), p. 27.
13. See p. 262.
14. R. Gary, *LIFE*, December 1958.
15. Remy: *Dix ans avec de Gaulle* (Paris, France-Empire, 1971), p. 338.
16. J. R. Tournoux, *La tragédie du Général*, p. 191.
17. *Ibid.*, p. 218.
18. C. de Gaulle, *Discours et Messages*, Avec le Renouveau, p. 60.
19. W. Churchill, *Complete Speeches*, vol. 8, p. 8687.
20. P. Lefranc, *Avec qui vous savez* (Plon, Paris, 1979), pp. 50–1.
21. V. Walters, *Services discrets*, p. 254.
22. P. Galante, *The General, op. cit.*, p. 135.
23. C. de Gaulle, *Mémoires d'Espoir*, vol. 1, le Renouveau (Plon, Paris, 1970), p. 250.
24. P. Galante, *op. cit.*, p. 136.
25. *The Times*, 8/4/60.
26. P. Galante, *op. cit.*, p. 135.
27. Interview of Sir John Colville by the author, 8/3/79.
28. *The Times*, 25/1/65.
29. Interview of Sir John Colville, *loc. cit.*

Abbreviations

ADM	Admiralty
AE	Affaires Etrangères
AMGOT	Allied Military Government in Occupied Territories
BDL	Bodleian Library, Oxford
BM	British Museum
BUL	Birmingham University Library
CAB	Cabinet papers, PRO
CCAC	Churchill College Archive Centre
CIGS	Chief of the Imperial General Staff
CNR	Conseil National de la Résistance
CPA	Canadian Public Archives
EAM ELAS	Greek Communist revolutionary movements
EDC	European Defence Community
FCNL	French Committee of National Liberation
FDR	Franklin D. Roosevelt Library, Hyde Park, New York
FFI	Forces Françaises de l'Intérieur
FNC	French National Committee
FNSP	Fondation Nationale des Sciences Politiques, Paris.
FO	Foreign Office
FRUS	Foreign Relations of the United States
FS	Foreign Secretary
GPRF	Gouvernement Provisoire de la République Française
LHCMA	Liddell Hart Centre for Military Archives, London
LSE	London School of Economics
MEC	Middle East Centre, Oxford
MI	Military Intelligence
MR	Map Room (FDR archives)
MRP	Mouvement Républicain Populaire
MVBZ	Ministerie Van Buitenlandse Zaken (Netherlands Foreign Ministry, The Hague.)
NA	National Archives, Washington
NATO	North Atlantic Treaty Organization
OCM	Organization Civile et Militaire

PREM	Prime Minister's papers, PRO
PRO	Public Records Office, London
PSF	Private Secretary's File (FDR archives)
PWE	Political Warfare Executive
RPF	Rassemblement du Peuple Français
SHAEF	Supreme Headquarters, Allied Expeditionary Force
SHAT	Service Historique de l'Armée de Terre, Vincennes
SOE	Special Operations Executive
SSFA	Secretary of State for Foreign Affairs
STO	Service du Travail Obligatoire
UD	Utenriksdepartement (Norwegian Foreign Ministry, Oslo)
URAS	Union Républicaine d'Action Sociale
X	Private archives

Archive Sources

CANADA

CPA   (*Canadian Public Archives*), Ottawa.
       CPA/RG25 series A12 Canada House.
       CPA/MG26 ,,,, J13 Mackenzie King Diaries
       CPA/MG26 ,,,, J4 Vol. 327, Ralston Diaries

FRANCE

AE   (*Affaires Etrangéres*), Paris.
       AE, CNF (1941–1943)
       AE, CFLN (1943–1944)
       AE, Dossiers Dejean and Massigli.
FNSP   (*Fondation Nationale des Sciences Politiques*)
       Archive Daladier (1939–1940)
SHAT   (*Service Historique de L'Armée de Terre*)
       Etat major, Service des T.O.E., (1939–1940)
X   (*Private archives*)

GREAT BRITAIN

CAB   (*Cabinet Papers*), London.
       CAB 99/3 (Supreme War Council), CAB 65, CAB 66, CAB 84.
PREM   (*Prime Minister's Papers*)
       PREM 3
LHCMA   (*Liddell Hart Centre for Military Archives*)
       Alanbrooke and Ismay Papers.
FO   (*Foreign Office*)
       FO 371 Political/France
       FO 954 Eden Papers.

BDL (*Bodleian Library*, Oxford)
    Attlee Papers
ADM (*Admiralty*)
    ADM 199
BUL (*Birmingham University Library*)
    Chamberlain Papers
BM (*British Museum*)
    Harvey Diaries
LSE (*London School of Economics*)
    Dalton Diaries
CCAC (*Churchill College Archive Centre, Cambridge*)
    Spears Papers 1940
MEC (*Middle East Centre, Oxford*)
    Spears Papers 1941–1945
    Shone Papers

NETHERLANDS

MVBZ (*Ministerie van Buitenlandse Zaken*), The Hague.
    Londens Archief, Politieke Rapporten
        ,,   ,,   Geheim Archief G2
        ,,   ,,   Brandkastdossiers
        ,,   ,,   Ned. Gezantschap te Londen 1937–1945

NORWAY

UD (*Utenriksdepartementet*), Oslo.
    Utenriksminister Trygve Lies Arkiv, UD u-25, 1940–1945

UNITED STATES

NA (*National Archives*), Washington DC
    State Department, War, OSS
FDR (*Franklin D. Roosevelt Library*), Hyde Park, New York.
    PSF Diplomatic, France.
    Map Room/Special File.

Select Bibliography

The most important sources for the de Gaulle-Churchill relations naturally remain:

W. S. Churchill, *The Second World War*, vol. 1 to 6 (Cassell, London, 1948–54).

C. de Gaulle, *Mémoires de Guerre*, vol. 1 to 3 (Plon, Paris, 1954–59).

The diaries and memoirs of the main actors and eyewitnesses are of crucial importance. On the British side:

A. Eden, *The Reckoning* (Cassell, London, 1965).

H. Macmillan, *The Blast of War 1939–45* (Macmillan, London, 1967).

D. Dilks (Edit.), *Diaries of Sir Alexander Cadogan 1938–1945* (Cassell, London, 1971).

A. D. Cooper, *Old Men Forget* (R. H. Davis, London, 1953).

H. Ismay, *Memoirs* (Heinemann, London, 1960).

A. Bryant, *The Turn of the Tide* and *Triumph in the West* (Collins, London, 1957–59). (Based on the Alanbrooke diaries).

J. Harvey (Edit.), *War Diaries of Oliver Harvey, 1941–1945* (Collins, London, 1978).

H. L. Chandos, *Memoirs* (Bodley Head, London, 1962).

L. C. Moran, *The Struggle for Survival* (Constable, London, 1966).

E .L. Spears, *Assignment to Catastrophe*, vol. 1 and 2 (Heinemann, London, 1954).
Two Men Who Saved France (Eyre and Spottiswoode, London, 1966).
Fulfilment of a Mission (Leo Cooper, London, 1977).

As well as two extremely valuable testimonies:

J. Colville, *Footprints in Time* (Collins, London, 1976).

R. W. Thompson, *Churchill and Morton* (Hodder & Stoughton, London, 1976).

On the French side:

Passy, *Souvenirs*, vol. 1 and 2 (Solar, Monte Carlo, 1947).
vol. 3 (Plon, Paris, 1951).

J. Soustelle, *Envers et contre tout*, vol. 1 and 2 (R. Laffont, Paris, 1947–50).

P. Reynaud, *Mémoires*, vol. 2 (Flammarion, Paris, 1963).

G. Catroux, *Dans la bataille de Méditerranée* (Julliard, Paris, 1949).

T. D'Argenlieu, *Souvenirs de Guerre* (Plon, Paris, 1973).

R. Cassin, *Les hommes partis de rien* (Plon, Paris, 1975).

F. Coulet, *Vertu des temps difficiles* (Plon, Paris, 1967).

R. Bouscat, *De Gaulle-Giraud, dossier d'une mission* (Flammarion, Paris, 1967).

P. Lefranc, *Avec qui vous savez* (Plon, Paris, 1979).

E. Larminat, *Chroniques irrévérencieuses* (Plon, Paris, 1972).

P. Billotte, *Le temps des armes* (Plon, Paris, 1972).

H. Boislambert, *Les fers de l'espoir* (Plon, Paris, 1973).

E. d'Astier, *Sept fois sept jours* (Gallimard, Paris, 1961).

A. Gillois, *Histoire secrète des Français à Londres* (Hachette, Paris, 1973).

A. Bethouart, *Cinq années d'espérance* (Plon, Paris, 1968).

G. Bidault, *D'une résistance à l'autre* (Presses du Siècle, Paris, 1965).

A. Juin, *Mémoires*, vol. 2 (Fayard, Paris, 1960).

J. Vendroux, *Cette chance que j'ai eue* (Plon, Paris, 1974).

Remy, *Dix ans avec de Gaulle* (France Empire, Paris, 1971).

And an article by Geoffroy de Courcel: 'De Gaulle-Churchill' in *Revue de la France Libre*, no. 226, 1979.

H. Giraud, *Un seul but, la victoire* (Julliard, Paris, 1949), is interesting, though extremely naïve.

H. de Kerillis, *De Gaulle Dictateur* (Beauchemin, Montréal, 1945), is to be approached with the greatest caution.

E. Muselier, *De Gaulle contre le Gaullisme* (Chêne, Paris) 1946, is much too partial to be taken seriously.

On the American side:

C. Hull, *Memoirs* (Hodder & Stoughton, London, 1948).

M. Clark, *Calculated Risk* (Harper, New York, 1950).

W. Leahy, *I Was There* (Gollancz, London, 1950).

R. Sherwood, *Roosevelt and Hopkins* (Harper, New York, 1948).

R. Murphy, *Diplomats among Warriors* (Doubleday, New York, 1964).

D. Eisenhower, *Crusade in Europe* (Heinemann, London, 1948).

K. Pendar, *Adventures in Diplomacy* (Cassell, London, 1966), is rabidly anti-de Gaulle and misleading at times.

The books written by British, French or American historians and journalists on Churchill or de Gaulle before, during or after the war are much too numerous to be mentioned here.

Many official histories and document series have proved invaluable for this study, especially: E. L. Woodward, *British Foreign Policy in the Second World War*, HMSO, 1970–, *Foreign Relations of the United States*, 1942–45, State Dept., Washington, and House of Commons, *Parliamentary Debates*, 1930–50.

Index

François Kersaudy was born in Paris in 1948. After study in the United States, France, Vietnam and Austria, he graduated from the Institute of Political Science in Paris and received a doctorate in contemporary history from the Sorbonne. He was for three years a research Fellow at Oxford University, and now teaches at the Sorbonne. His first book, published in 1977, was on the origins of the Norwegian campaign. With a working knowledge of eight foreign languages, Dr. Kersaudy has conducted historical research at forty diplomatic and military archives in ten countries.